J-BOY

BY BIBLOS

Contents

Translation	Earl Gertwagen, Sachiko Sato, Issei Shimizu
Lettering	Will Allison, Amelia Cantlay, Pat Duke, Steve Kitzes, Elise Knowles, Erica Jeng, Wendy Lee, Jessica Liu, Rachel Livingston, Geoff Porter, Jennifer Skarupa
Editing	Daryl Kuxhouse, Wendy Lee
Graphic Design	Mr. Wasabi, Wendy Lee
Editor in Chief	Mr. Wasabi
Publisher	Hikaru Sasahara

English Edition Published by
DIGITAL MANGA PUBLISHING
A division of DIGITAL MANGA, Inc.
1487 W 178th Street, Suite 300
Gardena, CA 90248
www.dmpbooks.com
First Edition: November 2006
ISBN: 1-56970-875-4
1 3 5 7 9 10 8 6 4 2
Printed in Hong Kong

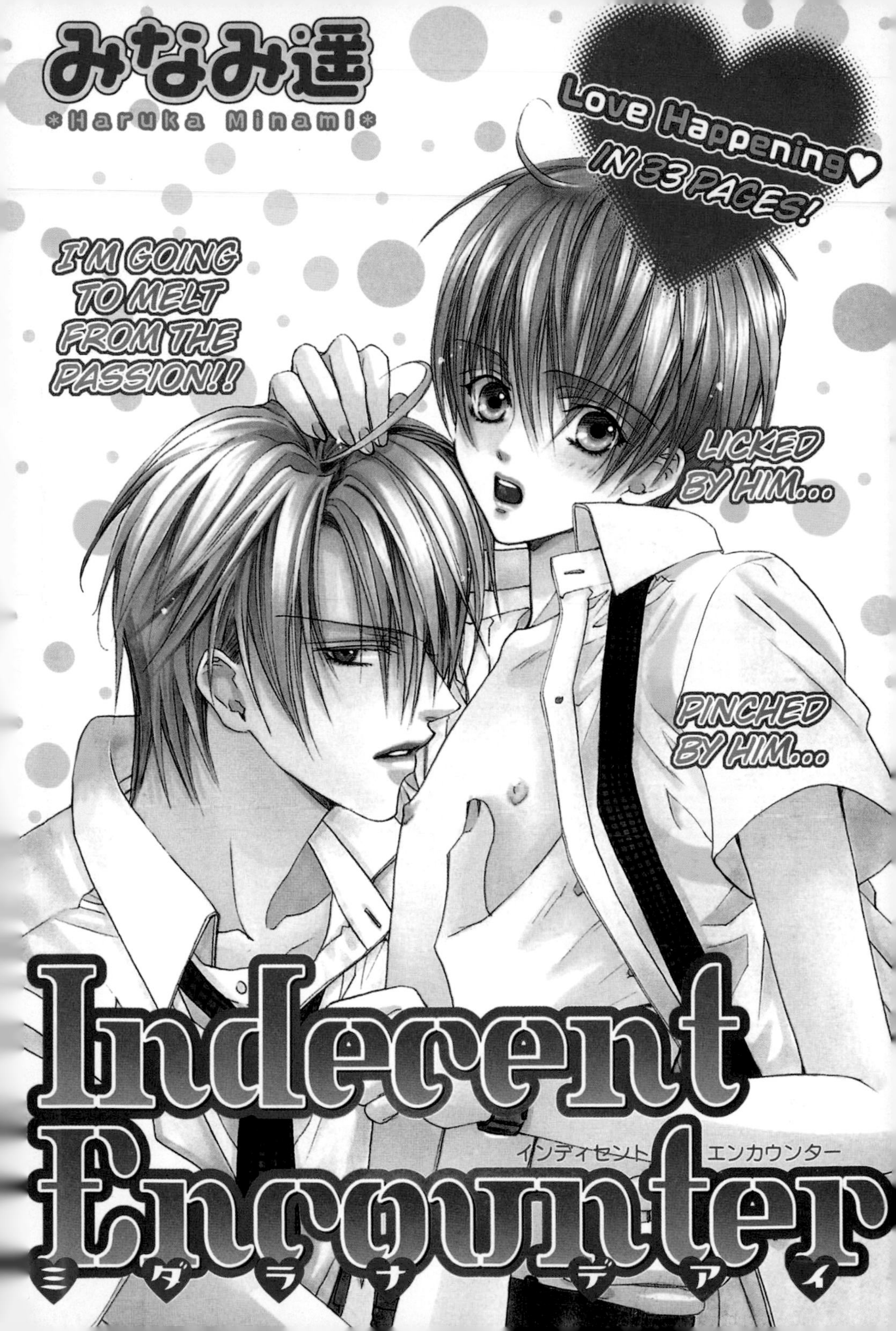
みなみ遥
Haruka Minami
Love Happening♥
IN 33 PAGES!
I'M GOING TO MELT FROM THE PASSION!!
LICKED BY HIM...
PINCHED BY HIM...
Indecent Encounter
インディセント エンカウンター
ミダラナデアイ

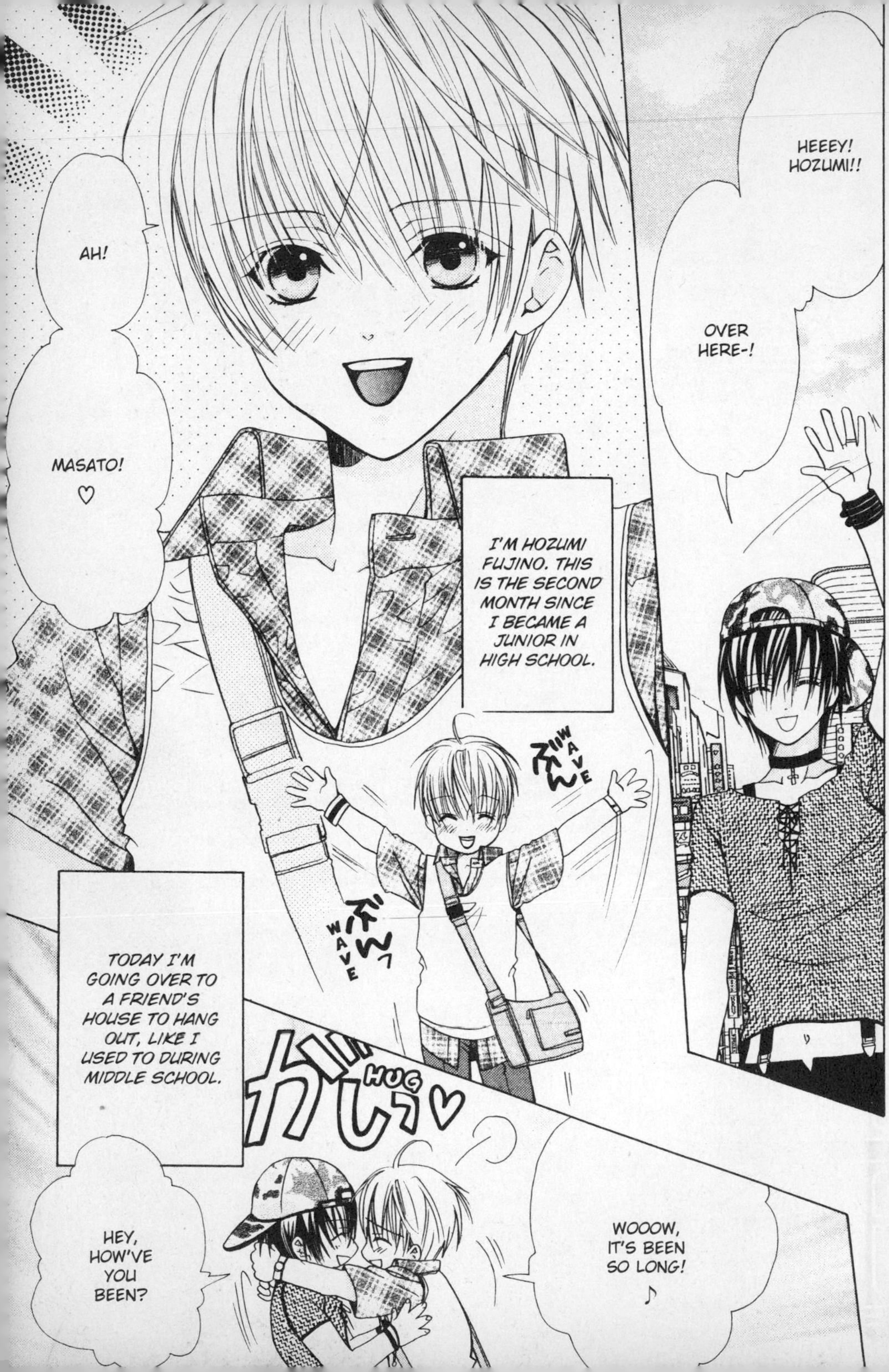
HEEEY! HOZUMI!!
OVER HERE-!
AH!
MASATO! ♡
I'M HOZUMI FUJINO. THIS IS THE SECOND MONTH SINCE I BECAME A JUNIOR IN HIGH SCHOOL.
WAVE
WAVE
TODAY I'M GOING OVER TO A FRIEND'S HOUSE TO HANG OUT, LIKE I USED TO DURING MIDDLE SCHOOL.
HUG
WOOOW, IT'S BEEN SO LONG! ♪
HEY, HOW'VE YOU BEEN?

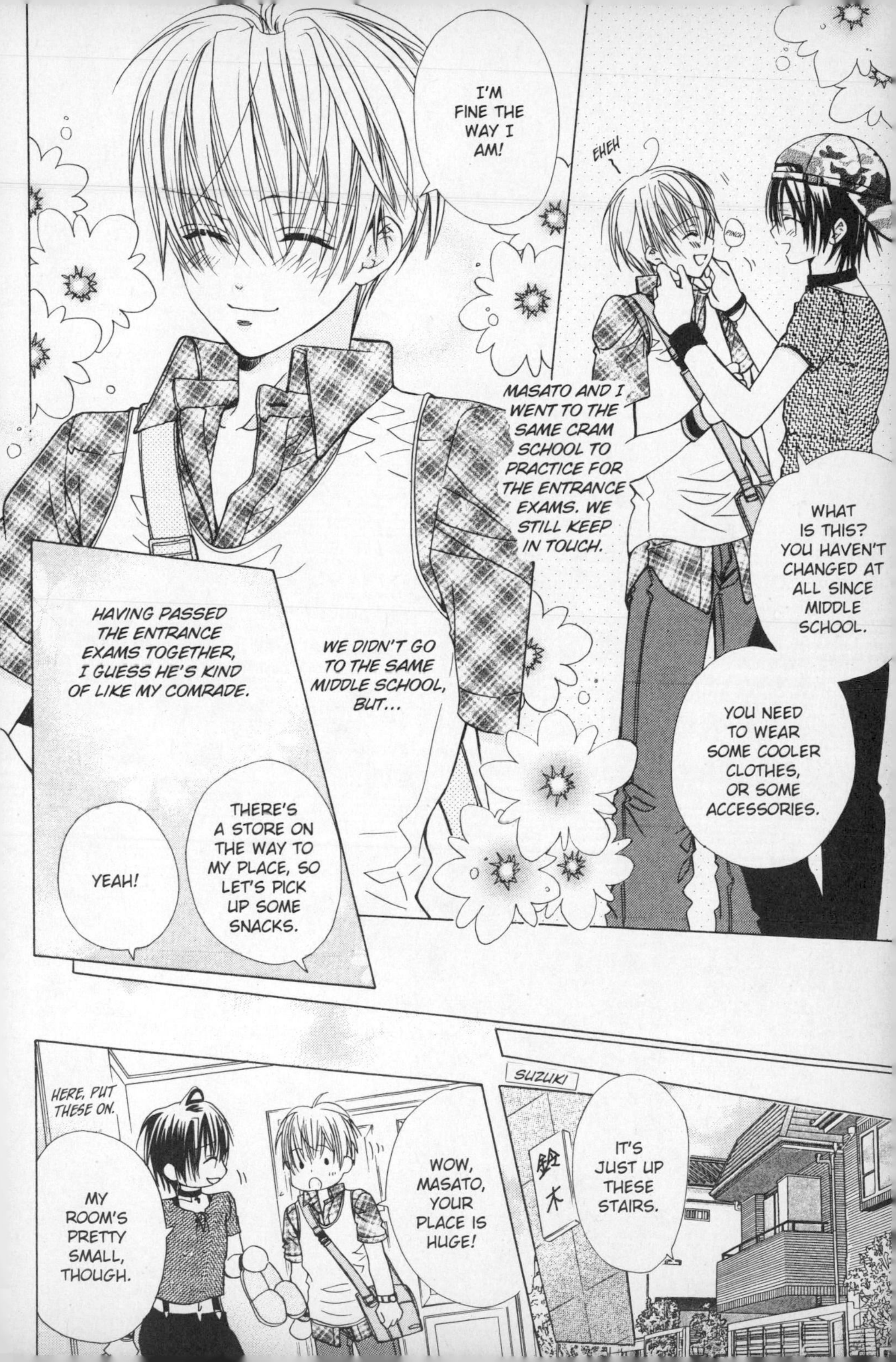
EHEH
PINCH
MASATO AND I WENT TO THE SAME CRAM SCHOOL TO PRACTICE FOR THE ENTRANCE EXAMS. WE STILL KEEP IN TOUCH.
WHAT IS THIS? YOU HAVEN'T CHANGED AT ALL SINCE MIDDLE SCHOOL.
YOU NEED TO WEAR SOME COOLER CLOTHES, OR SOME ACCESSORIES.
I'M FINE THE WAY I AM!
WE DIDN'T GO TO THE SAME MIDDLE SCHOOL, BUT...
HAVING PASSED THE ENTRANCE EXAMS TOGETHER, I GUESS HE'S KIND OF LIKE MY COMRADE.
THERE'S A STORE ON THE WAY TO MY PLACE, SO LET'S PICK UP SOME SNACKS.
YEAH!
SUZUKI
IT'S JUST UP THESE STAIRS.
WOW, MASATO, YOUR PLACE IS HUGE!
MY ROOM'S PRETTY SMALL, THOUGH.
HERE, PUT THESE ON.

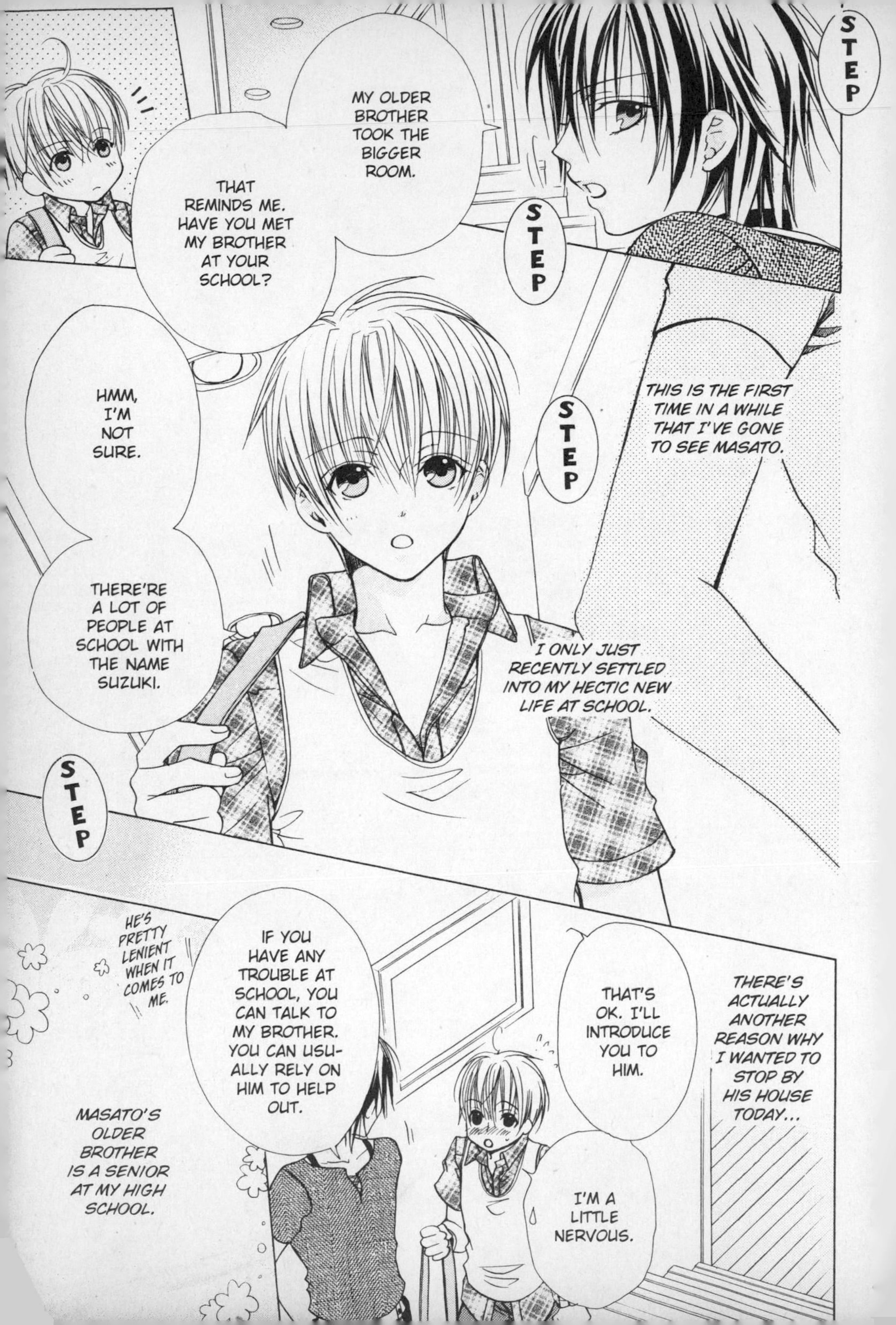
STEP
MY OLDER BROTHER TOOK THE BIGGER ROOM.
THAT REMINDS ME. HAVE YOU MET MY BROTHER AT YOUR SCHOOL?
STEP
THIS IS THE FIRST TIME IN A WHILE THAT I'VE GONE TO SEE MASATO.
STEP
HMM, I'M NOT SURE.
THERE'RE A LOT OF PEOPLE AT SCHOOL WITH THE NAME SUZUKI.
I ONLY JUST RECENTLY SETTLED INTO MY HECTIC NEW LIFE AT SCHOOL.
STEP
THERE'S ACTUALLY ANOTHER REASON WHY I WANTED TO STOP BY HIS HOUSE TODAY...
THAT'S OK. I'LL INTRODUCE YOU TO HIM.
IF YOU HAVE ANY TROUBLE AT SCHOOL, YOU CAN TALK TO MY BROTHER. YOU CAN USUALLY RELY ON HIM TO HELP OUT.
HE'S PRETTY LENIENT WHEN IT COMES TO ME.
I'M A LITTLE NERVOUS.
MASATO'S OLDER BROTHER IS A SENIOR AT MY HIGH SCHOOL.

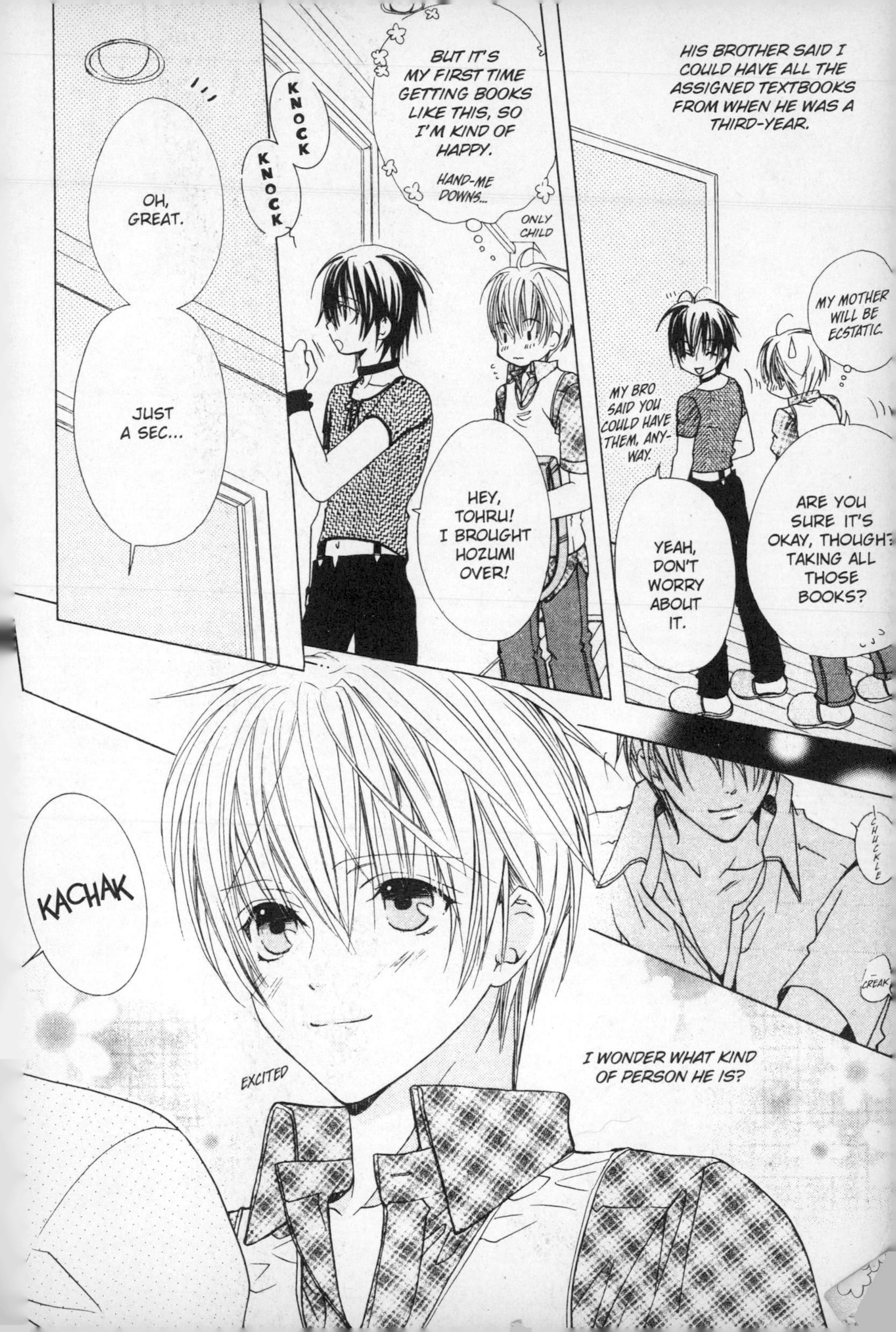
HIS BROTHER SAID I COULD HAVE ALL THE ASSIGNED TEXTBOOKS FROM WHEN HE WAS A THIRD-YEAR.
MY MOTHER WILL BE ECSTATIC.
ARE YOU SURE IT'S OKAY, THOUGH? TAKING ALL THOSE BOOKS?
MY BRO SAID YOU COULD HAVE THEM, ANYWAY.
YEAH, DON'T WORRY ABOUT IT.
BUT IT'S MY FIRST TIME GETTING BOOKS LIKE THIS, SO I'M KIND OF HAPPY.
HAND-ME DOWNS...
ONLY CHILD
KNOCK
KNOCK
HEY, TOHRU! I BROUGHT HOZUMI OVER!
OH, GREAT.
JUST A SEC...
CHUCKLE
CREAK
KACHAK
I WONDER WHAT KIND OF PERSON HE IS?
EXCITED

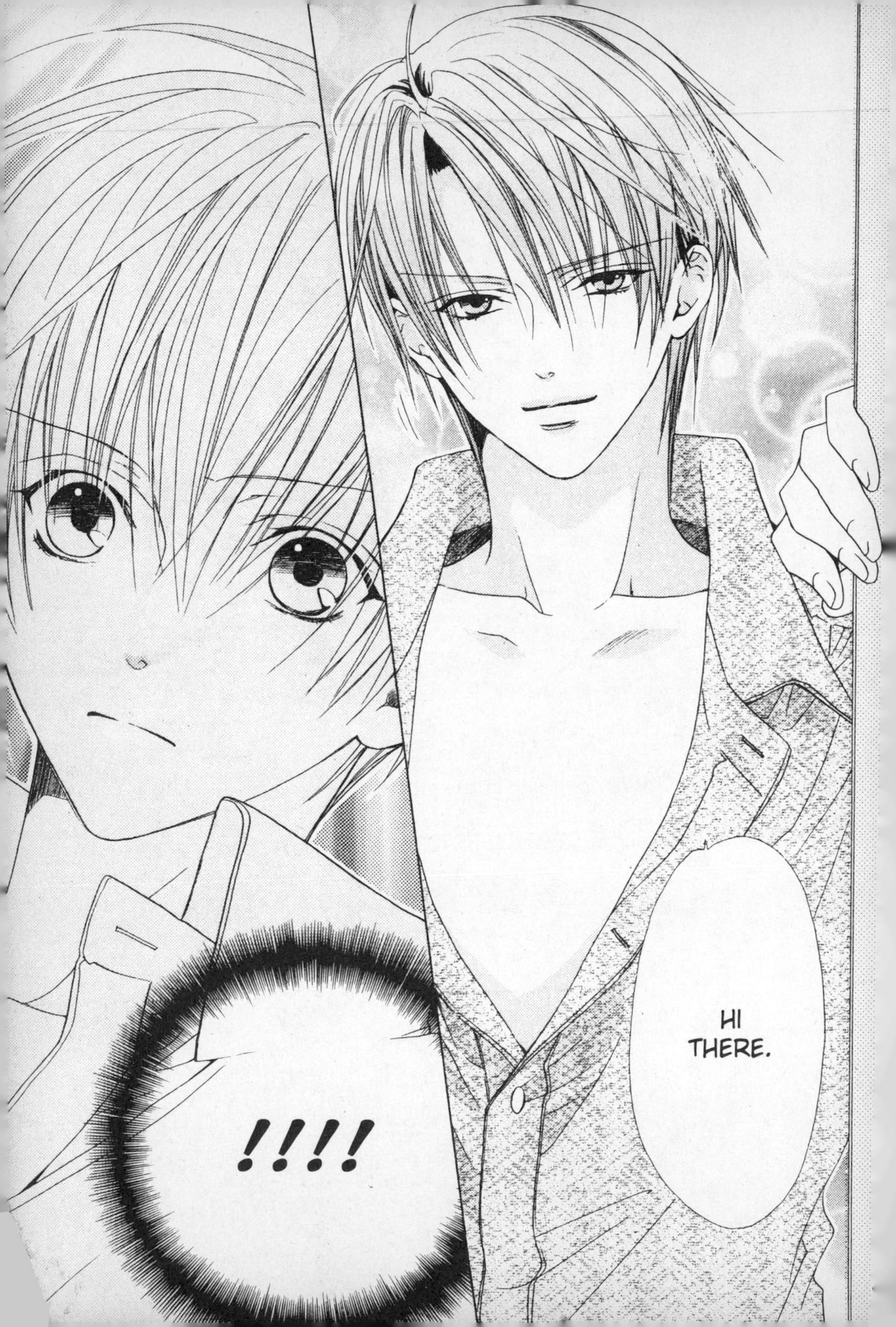
HI THERE.
!!!!

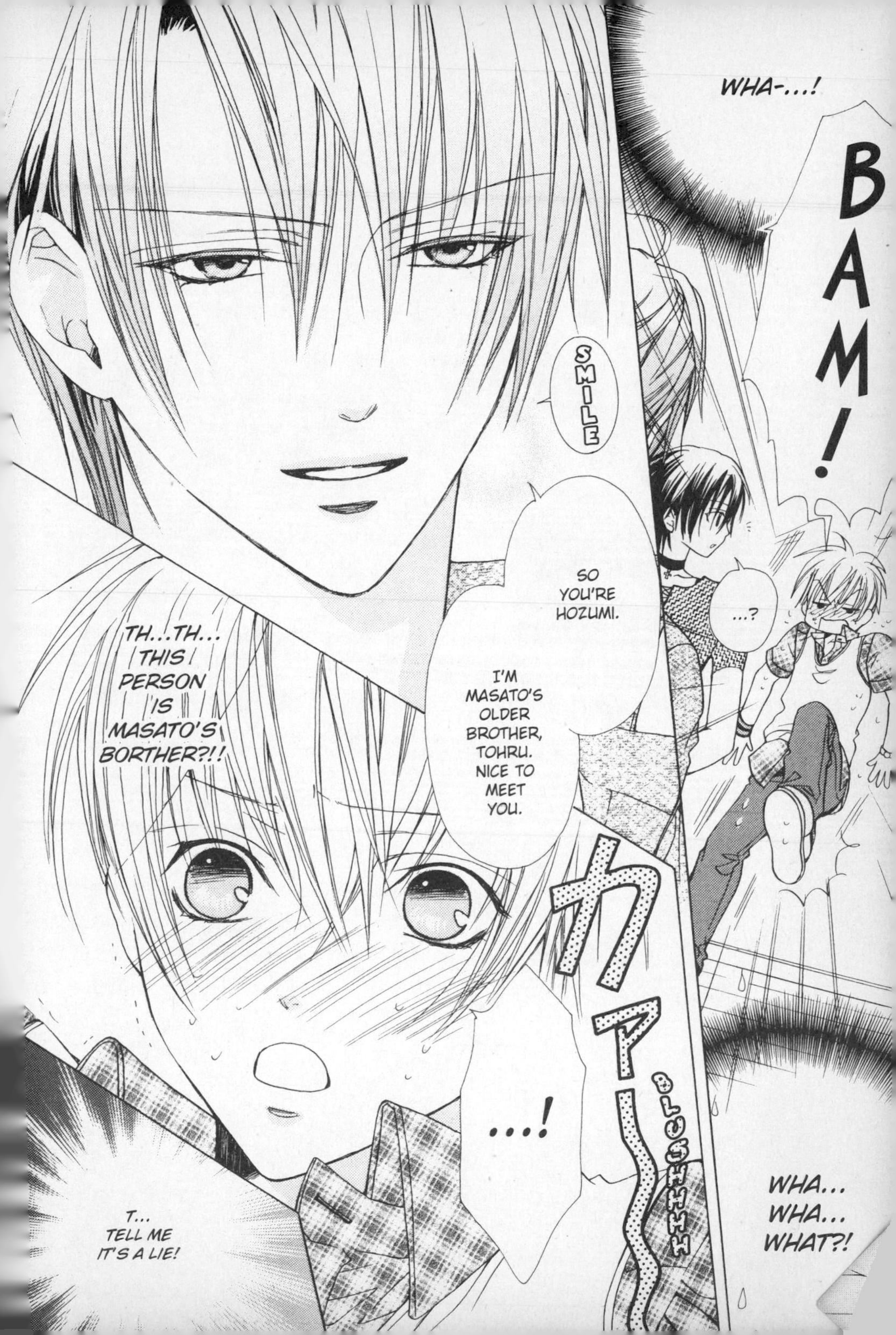
WHA-...!
BAM!
...?
WHA... WHA... WHAT?!
SMILE
SO YOU'RE HOZUMI.
I'M MASATO'S OLDER BROTHER, TOHRU. NICE TO MEET YOU.
TH...TH... THIS PERSON IS MASATO'S BORTHER?!!
カァー
BLUSHHHH
...!
T... TELL ME IT'S A LIE!

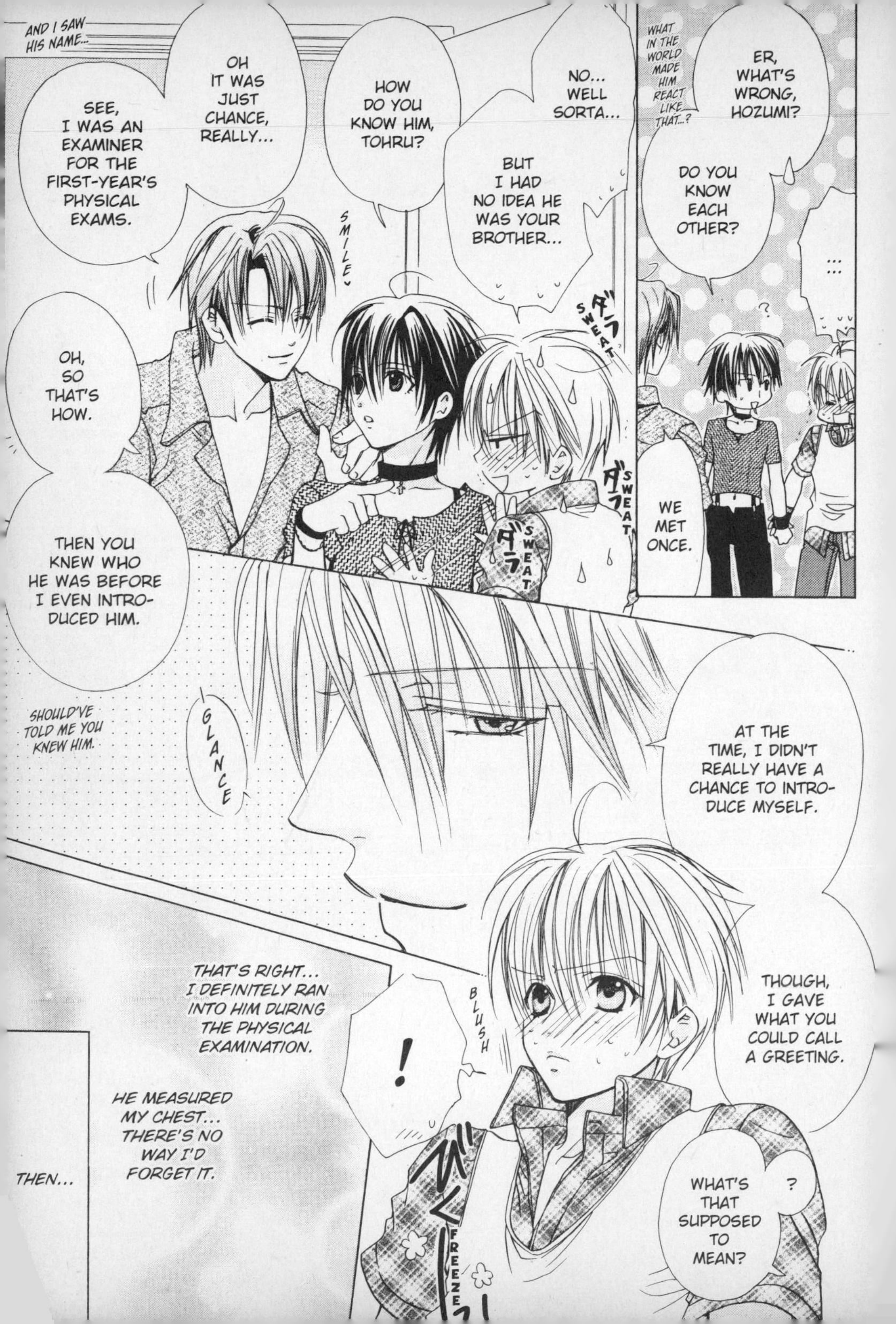
WHAT IN THE WORLD MADE HIM REACT LIKE THAT...?
ER, WHAT'S WRONG, HOZUMI?
DO YOU KNOW EACH OTHER?
...
...
?
WE MET ONCE.
NO... WELL SORTA...
BUT I HAD NO IDEA HE WAS YOUR BROTHER...
SWEAT
SWEAT
SWEAT
HOW DO YOU KNOW HIM, TOHRU?
SMILE
OH IT WAS JUST CHANCE, REALLY...
SEE, I WAS AN EXAMINER FOR THE FIRST-YEAR'S PHYSICAL EXAMS.
AND I SAW HIS NAME...
OH, SO THAT'S HOW.
THEN YOU KNEW WHO HE WAS BEFORE I EVEN INTRODUCED HIM.
AT THE TIME, I DIDN'T REALLY HAVE A CHANCE TO INTRODUCE MYSELF.
GLANCE
SHOULD'VE TOLD ME YOU KNEW HIM.
THOUGH, I GAVE WHAT YOU COULD CALL A GREETING.
WHAT'S THAT SUPPOSED TO MEAN?
?
BLUSH
!
FREEZE
THAT'S RIGHT... I DEFINITELY RAN INTO HIM DURING THE PHYSICAL EXAMINATION.
HE MEASURED MY CHEST... THERE'S NO WAY I'D FORGET IT.
THEN...

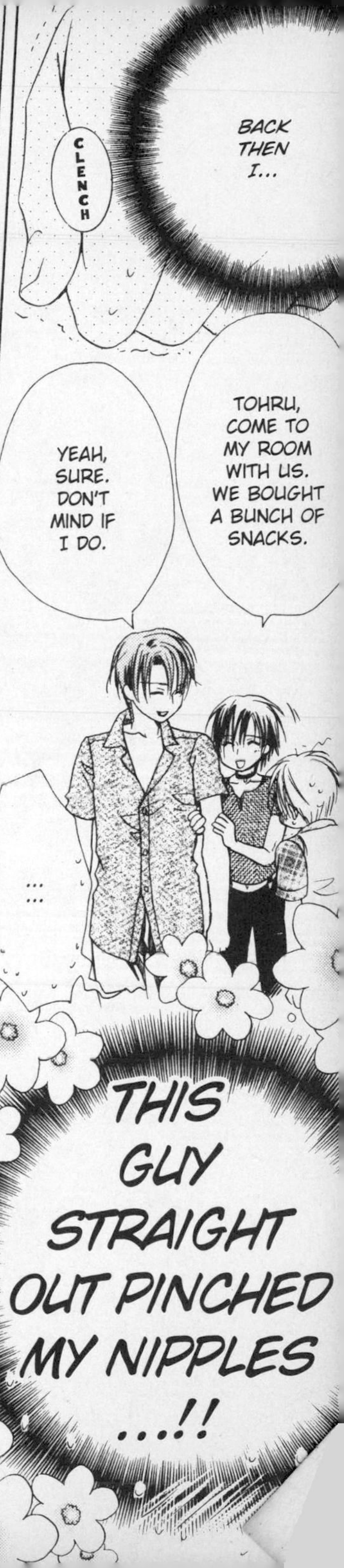
BACK THEN I...
CLENCH
TOHRU, COME TO MY ROOM WITH US. WE BOUGHT A BUNCH OF SNACKS.
YEAH, SURE. DON'T MIND IF I DO.
... ...
THIS GUY STRAIGHT OUT PINCHED MY NIPPLES ...!!
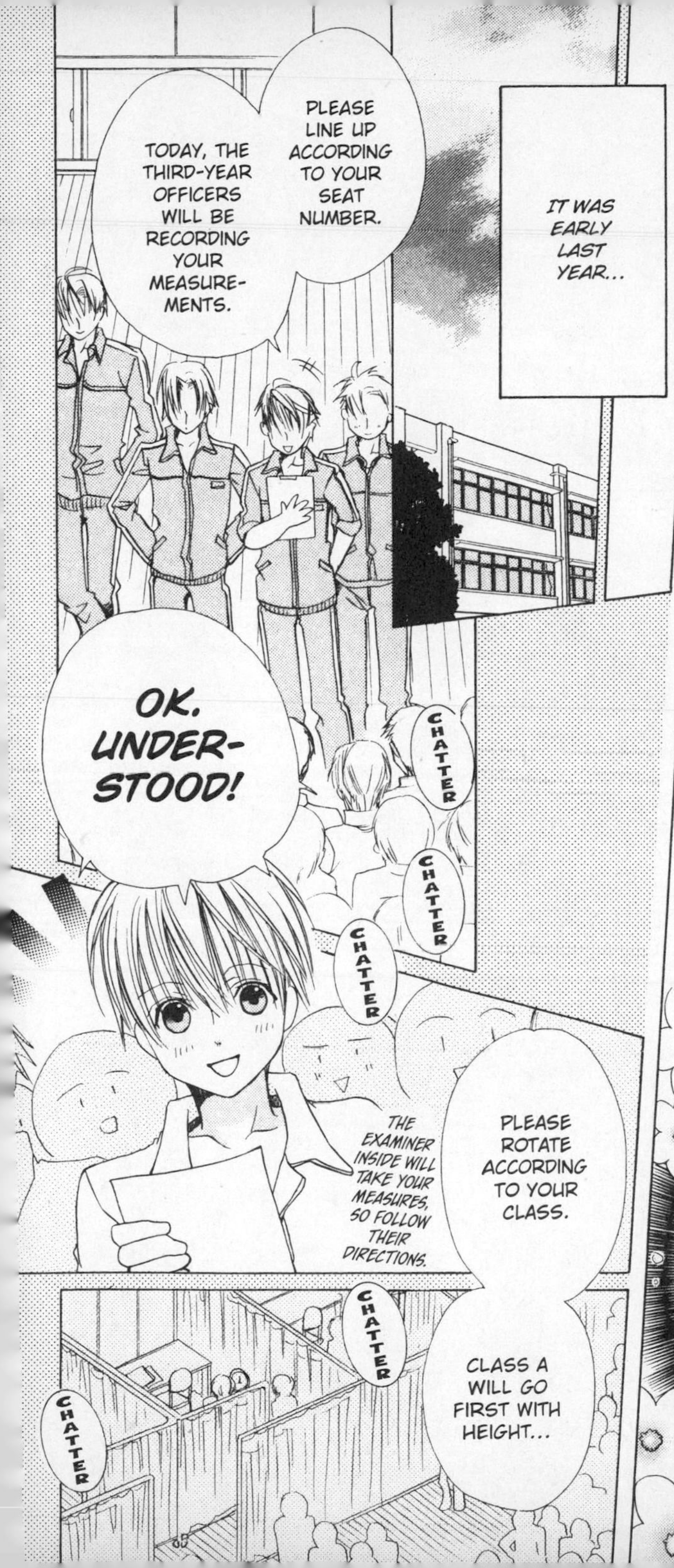
IT WAS EARLY LAST YEAR...
PLEASE LINE UP ACCORDING TO YOUR SEAT NUMBER.
TODAY, THE THIRD-YEAR OFFICERS WILL BE RECORDING YOUR MEASURE-MENTS.
CHATTER
OK. UNDER-STOOD!
CHATTER
CHATTER
PLEASE ROTATE ACCORDING TO YOUR CLASS.
THE EXAMINER INSIDE WILL TAKE YOUR MEASURES, SO FOLLOW THEIR DIRECTIONS.
CHATTER
CLASS A WILL GO FIRST WITH HEIGHT...
CHATTER

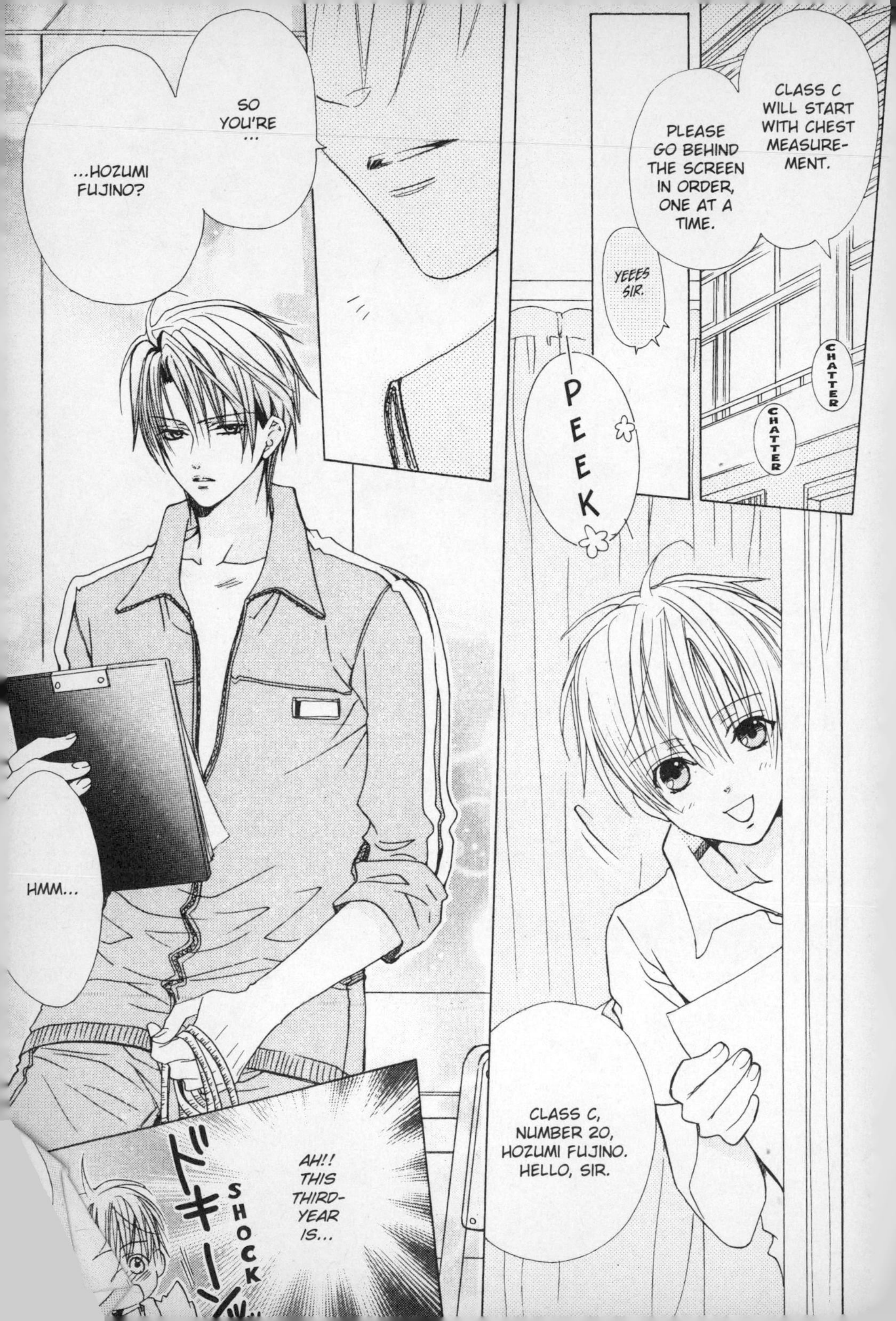
CLASS C WILL START WITH CHEST MEASUREMENT.
PLEASE GO BEHIND THE SCREEN IN ORDER, ONE AT A TIME.
YEEES SIR.
CHATTER
CHATTER
PEEK
CLASS C, NUMBER 20, HOZUMI FUJINO. HELLO, SIR.
SO YOU'RE ...
...HOZUMI FUJINO?
HMM...
AH!! THIS THIRD-YEAR IS...
ドキーン
SHOCK

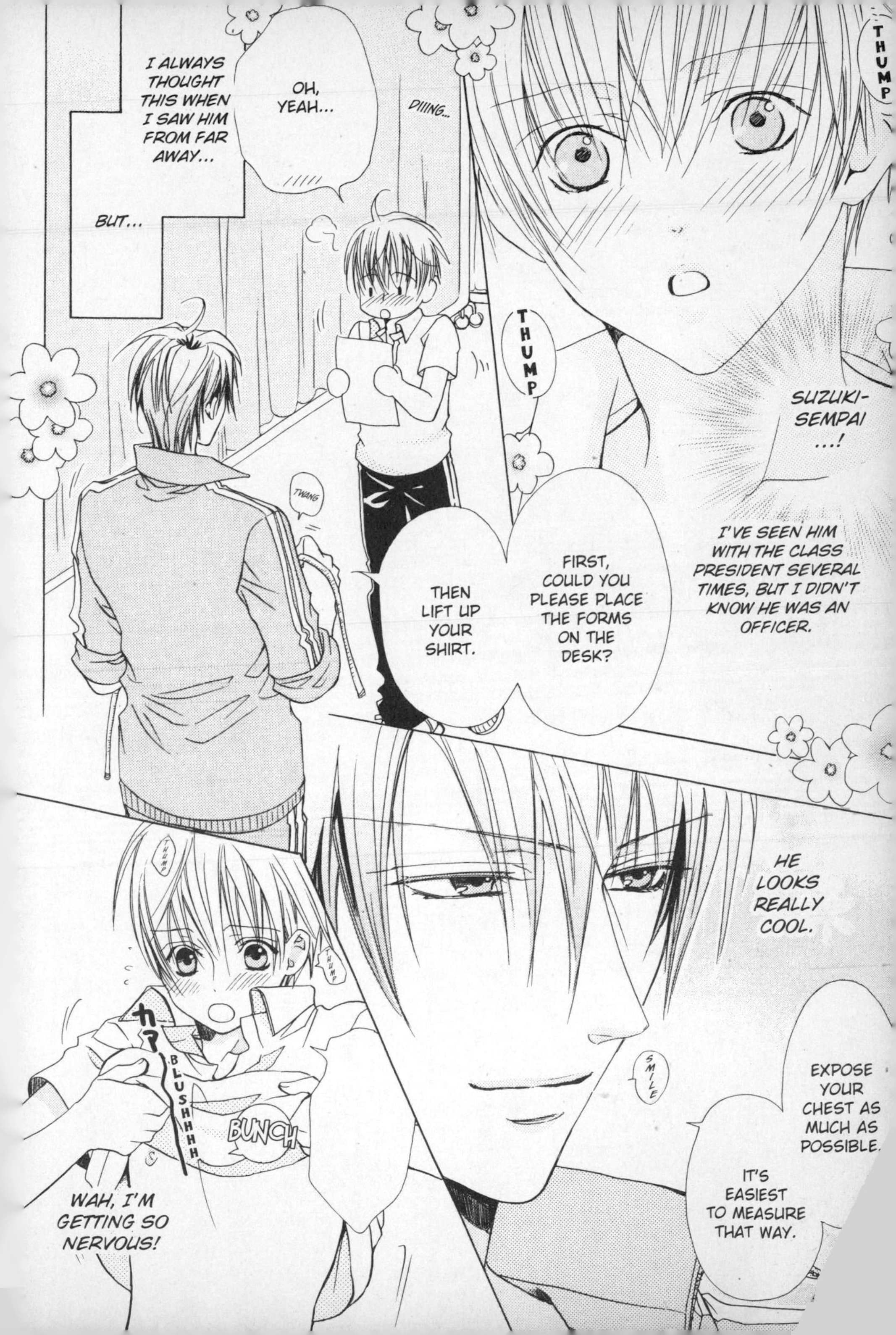
THUMP
SUZUKI-SEMPAI ...!
I'VE SEEN HIM WITH THE CLASS PRESIDENT SEVERAL TIMES, BUT I DIDN'T KNOW HE WAS AN OFFICER.
DIIING..
OH, YEAH...
I ALWAYS THOUGHT THIS WHEN I SAW HIM FROM FAR AWAY...
BUT...
THUMP
FIRST, COULD YOU PLEASE PLACE THE FORMS ON THE DESK?
THEN LIFT UP YOUR SHIRT.
TWANG
HE LOOKS REALLY COOL.
EXPOSE YOUR CHEST AS MUCH AS POSSIBLE.
IT'S EASIEST TO MEASURE THAT WAY.
SMILE
THUMP
THUMP
カァ
BLUSHHHH
BUNCH
WAH, I'M GETTING SO NERVOUS!

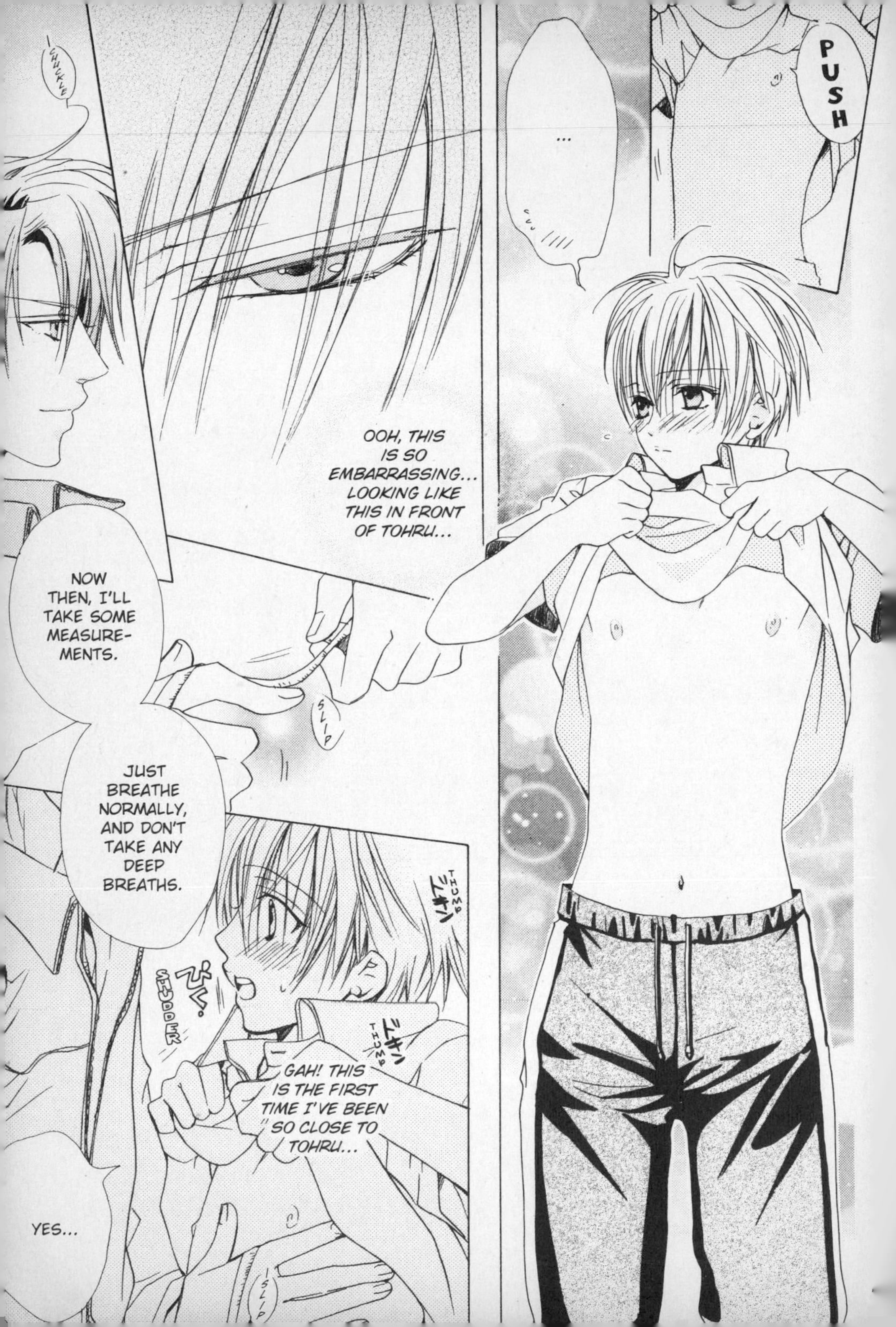
PUSH
...
OOH, THIS IS SO EMBARRASSING... LOOKING LIKE THIS IN FRONT OF TOHRU...
CHUCKLE
NOW THEN, I'LL TAKE SOME MEASUREMENTS.
SLIP
JUST BREATHE NORMALLY, AND DON'T TAKE ANY DEEP BREATHS.
THUMP
SHUDDER
THUMP
GAH! THIS IS THE FIRST TIME I'VE BEEN SO CLOSE TO TOHRU...
YES...
SLIP

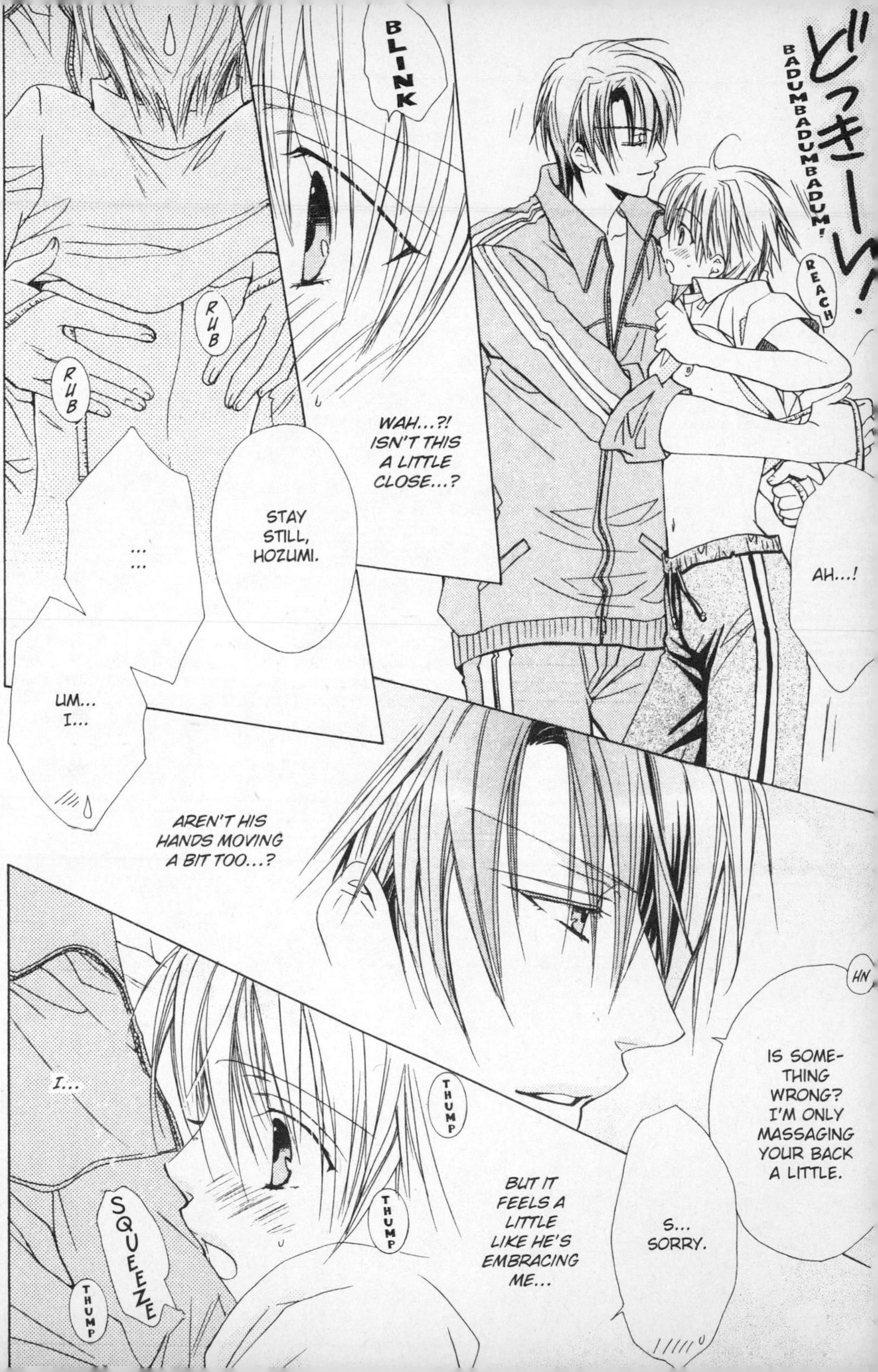
どっきーん!
BADUMBADUMBADUM!
REACH
AH...!
BLINK
WAH...?! ISN'T THIS A LITTLE CLOSE...?
STAY STILL, HOZUMI.
RUB
RUB
... ...
UM... I...
AREN'T HIS HANDS MOVING A BIT TOO...?
HN
IS SOME-THING WRONG? I'M ONLY MASSAGING YOUR BACK A LITTLE.
S... SORRY.
BUT IT FEELS A LITTLE LIKE HE'S EMBRACING ME...
THUMP
THUMP
I...
SQUEEZE
THUMP

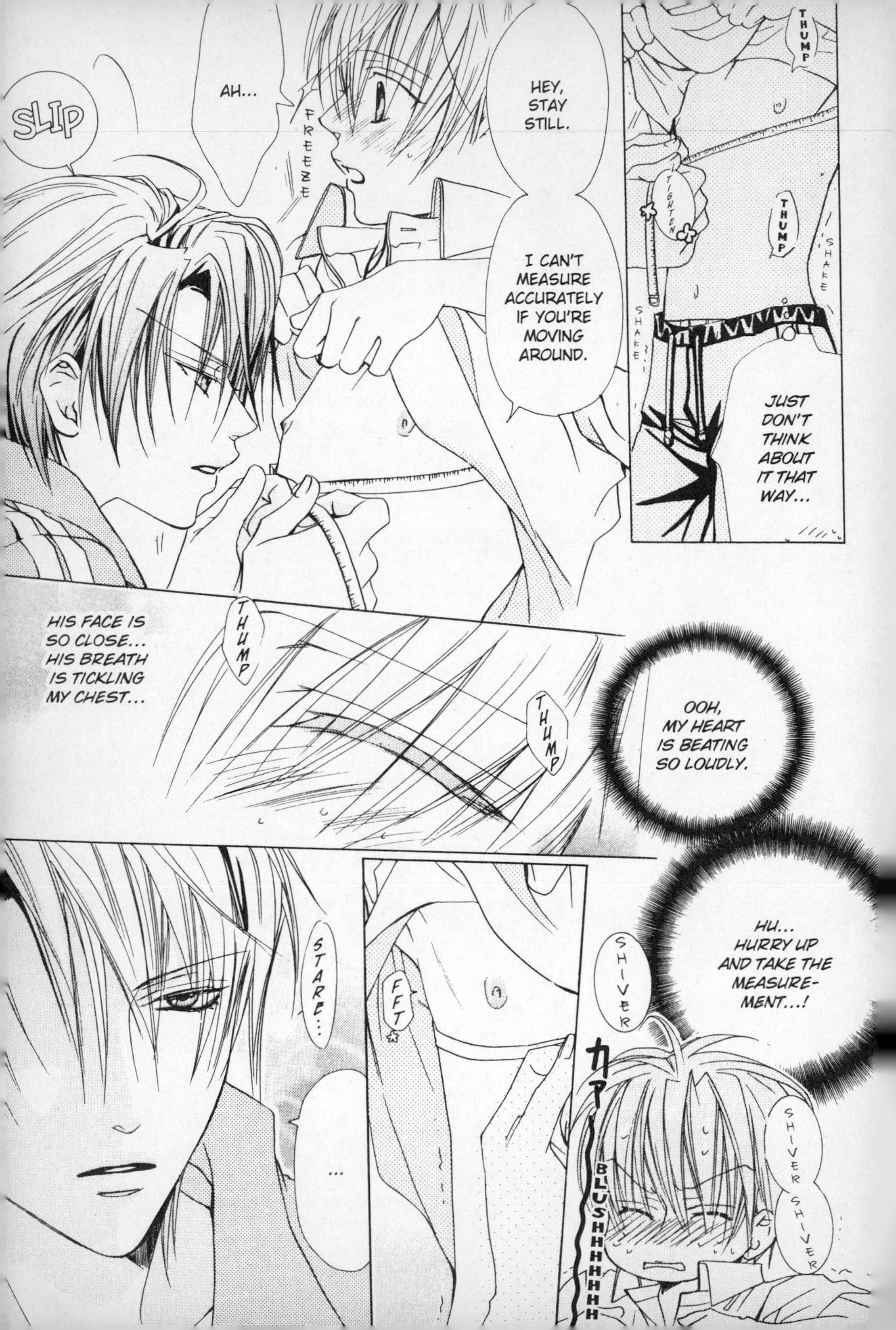
THUMP
TIGHTEN
THUMP
SHAKE
SHAKE
JUST DON'T THINK ABOUT IT THAT WAY...
HEY, STAY STILL.
I CAN'T MEASURE ACCURATELY IF YOU'RE MOVING AROUND.
FREEZE
AH...
SLIP
OOH, MY HEART IS BEATING SO LOUDLY.
THUMP
THUMP
HIS FACE IS SO CLOSE... HIS BREATH IS TICKLING MY CHEST...
HU... HURRY UP AND TAKE THE MEASUREMENT...!
SHIVER
カァー
BLUSHHHHHHH
SHIVER SHIVER
FFT
STARE...
...

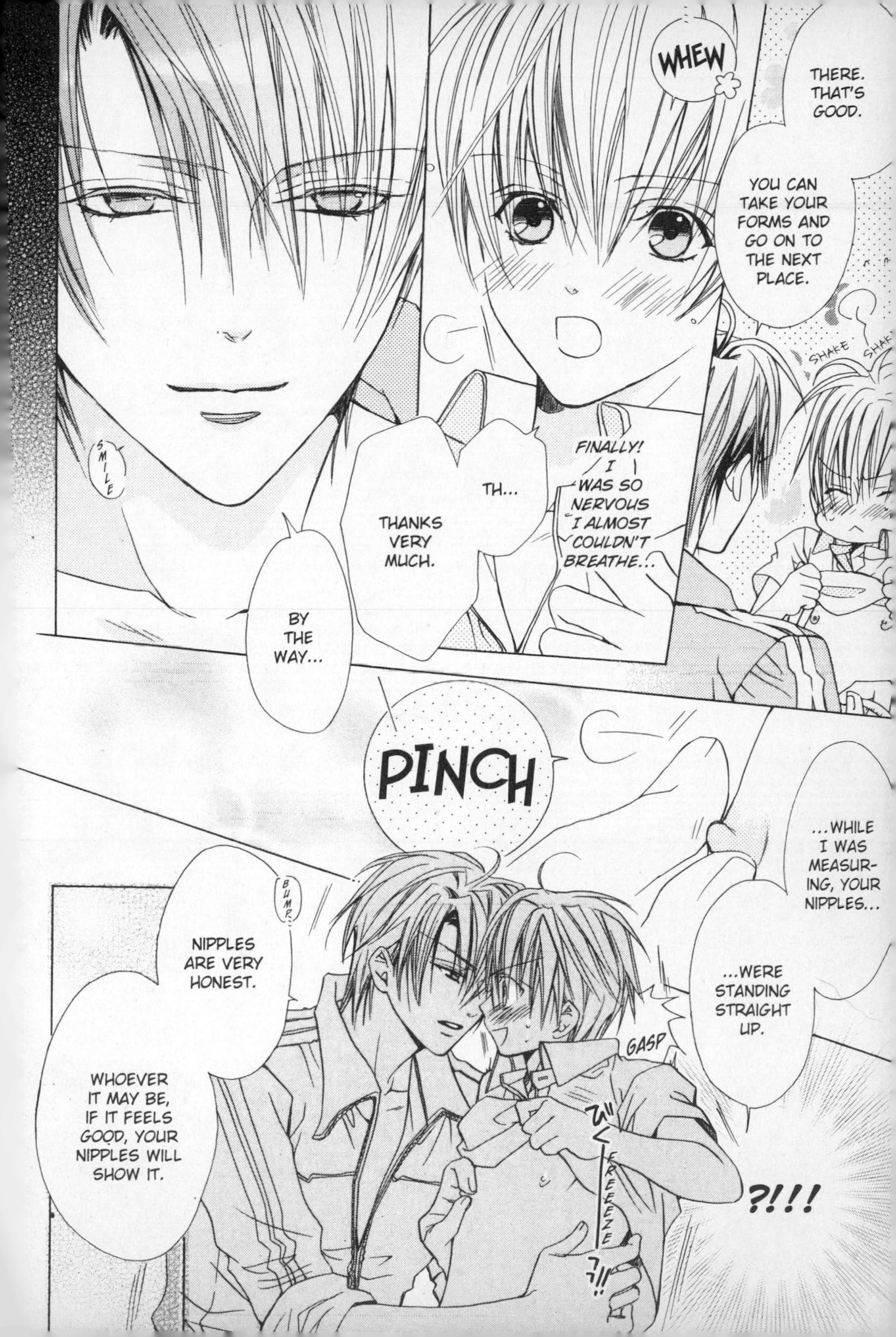
WHEW
THERE. THAT'S GOOD.
YOU CAN TAKE YOUR FORMS AND GO ON TO THE NEXT PLACE.
SHAKE SHAKE
FINALLY! I WAS SO NERVOUS I ALMOST COULDN'T BREATHE...
TH...
THANKS VERY MUCH.
SMILE
BY THE WAY...
PINCH
...WHILE I WAS MEASURING, YOUR NIPPLES...
...WERE STANDING STRAIGHT UP.
?!!!
GASP
FREEEZE
BUMP
NIPPLES ARE VERY HONEST.
WHOEVER IT MAY BE, IF IT FEELS GOOD, YOUR NIPPLES WILL SHOW IT.

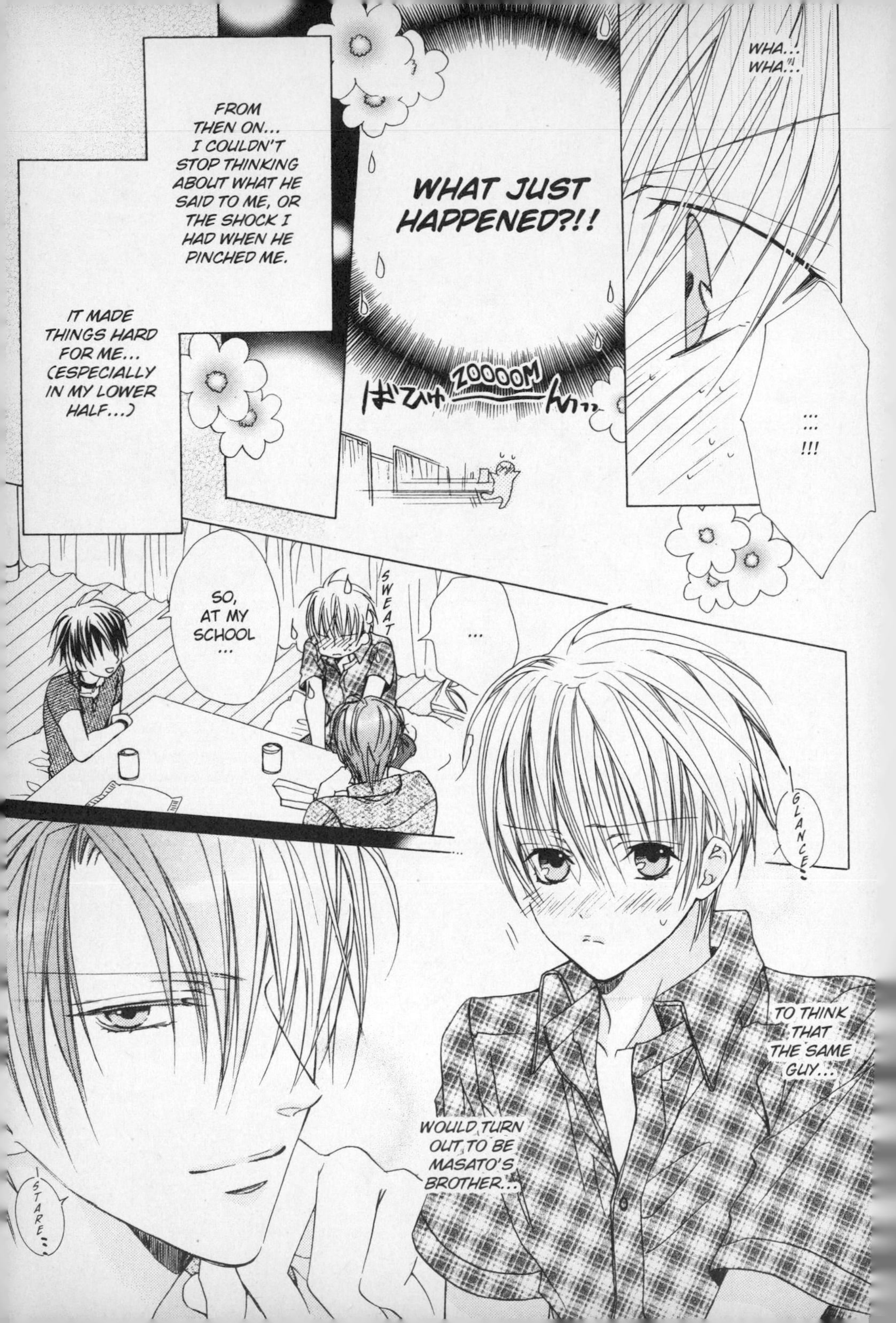
WHA... WHA...
...
...
!!!
WHAT JUST HAPPENED?!!
ZOOOOM
FROM THEN ON... I COULDN'T STOP THINKING ABOUT WHAT HE SAID TO ME, OR THE SHOCK I HAD WHEN HE PINCHED ME.
IT MADE THINGS HARD FOR ME... (ESPECIALLY IN MY LOWER HALF...)
SWEAT
SO, AT MY SCHOOL ...
...
GLANCE
TO THINK THAT THE SAME GUY...
WOULD TURN OUT TO BE MASATO'S BROTHER...
STARE

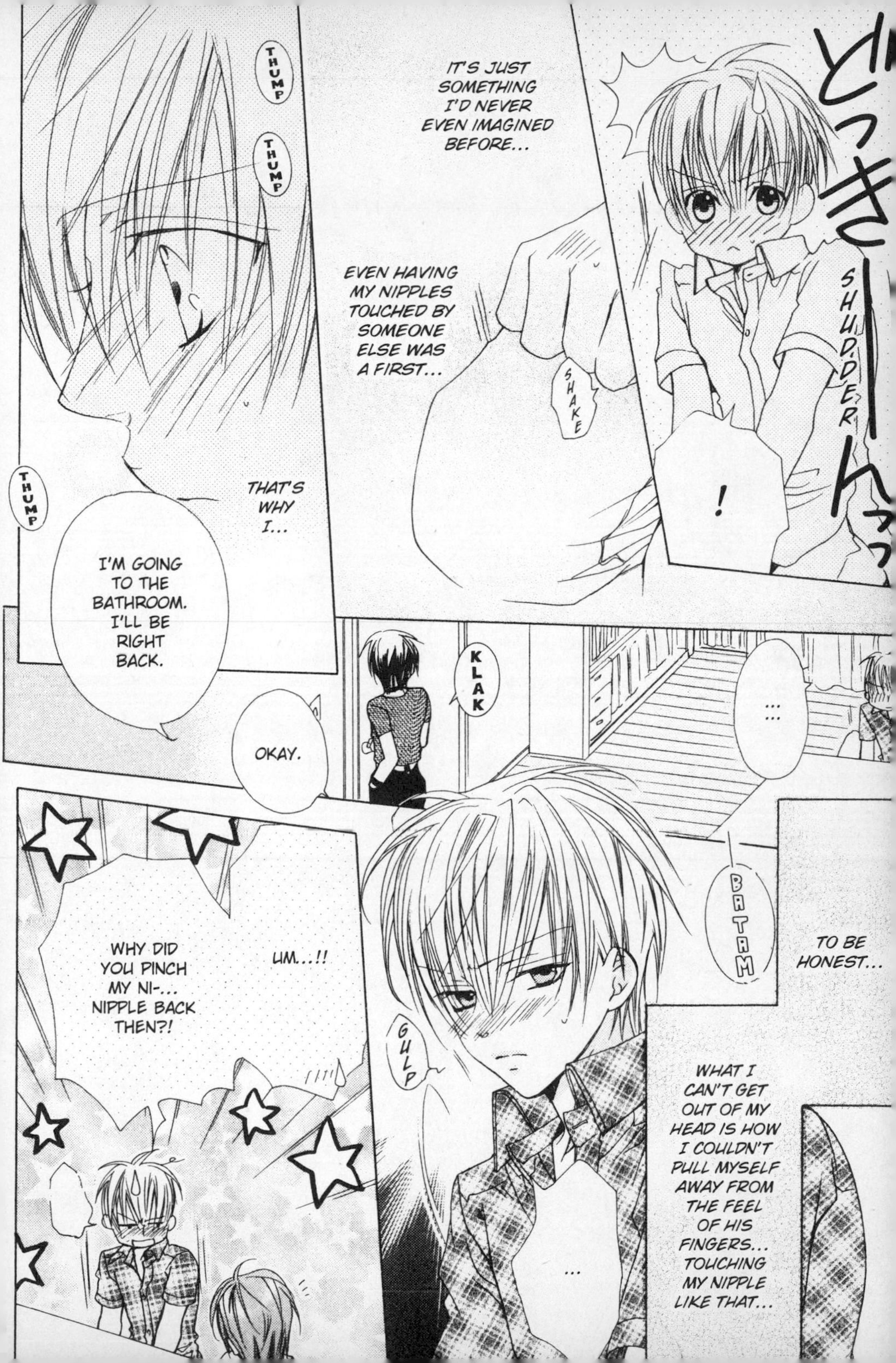

どっきーんっ
SHUDDER
!
IT'S JUST SOMETHING I'D NEVER EVEN IMAGINED BEFORE...
EVEN HAVING MY NIPPLES TOUCHED BY SOMEONE ELSE WAS A FIRST...
SHAKE
THUMP
THUMP
THUMP
THAT'S WHY I...
I'M GOING TO THE BATHROOM. I'LL BE RIGHT BACK.
...
...
KLAK
OKAY.
BATAM
TO BE HONEST...
WHAT I CAN'T GET OUT OF MY HEAD IS HOW I COULDN'T PULL MYSELF AWAY FROM THE FEEL OF HIS FINGERS... TOUCHING MY NIPPLE LIKE THAT...
...
GULP
UM...!!
WHY DID YOU PINCH MY NI-... NIPPLE BACK THEN?!

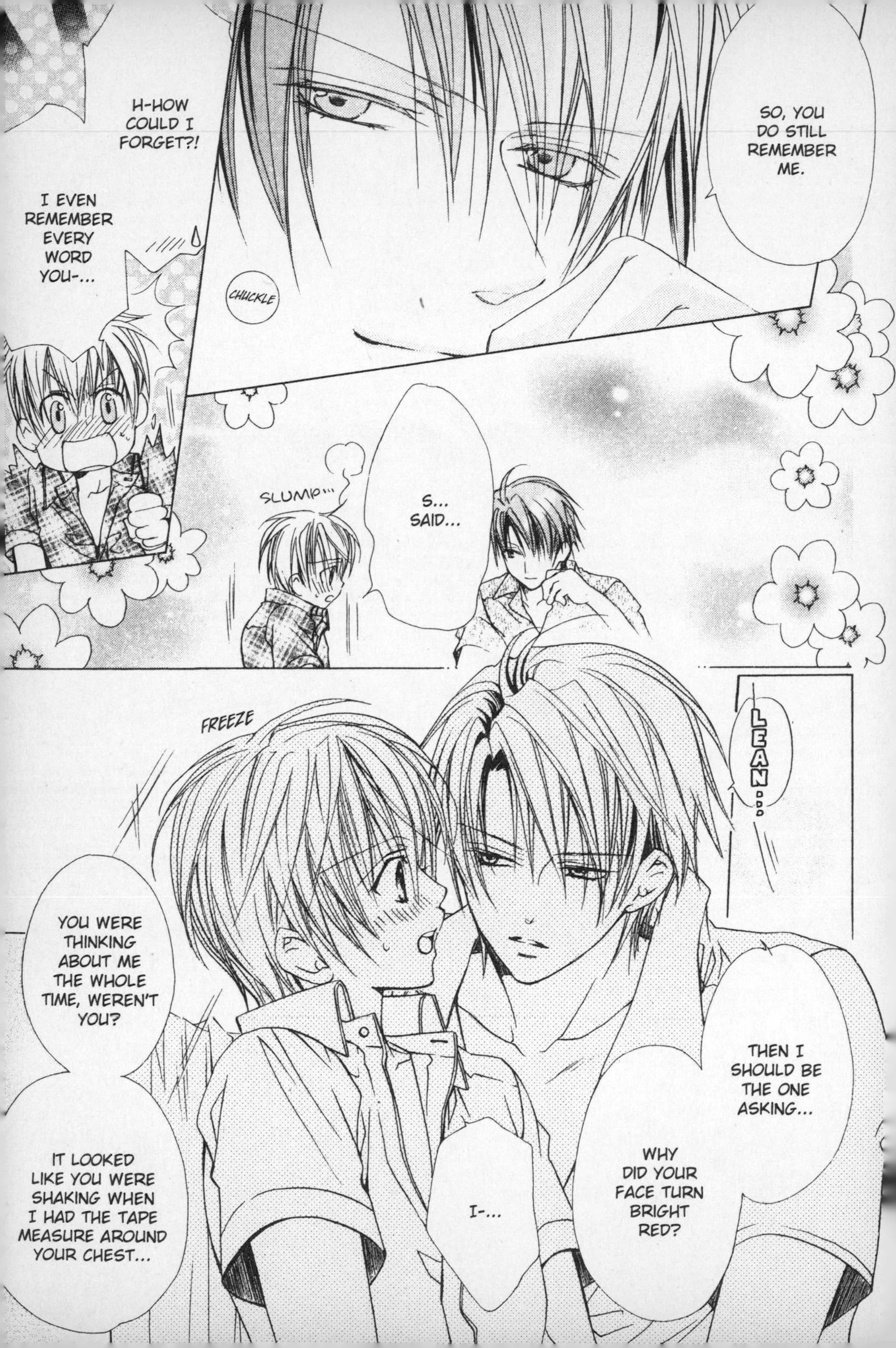
SO, YOU DO STILL REMEMBER ME.
CHUCKLE
H-HOW COULD I FORGET?!
I EVEN REMEMBER EVERY WORD YOU-...
S... SAID...
SLUMP...
LEAN...
FREEZE
THEN I SHOULD BE THE ONE ASKING...
WHY DID YOUR FACE TURN BRIGHT RED?
I-...
YOU WERE THINKING ABOUT ME THE WHOLE TIME, WEREN'T YOU?
IT LOOKED LIKE YOU WERE SHAKING WHEN I HAD THE TAPE MEASURE AROUND YOUR CHEST...

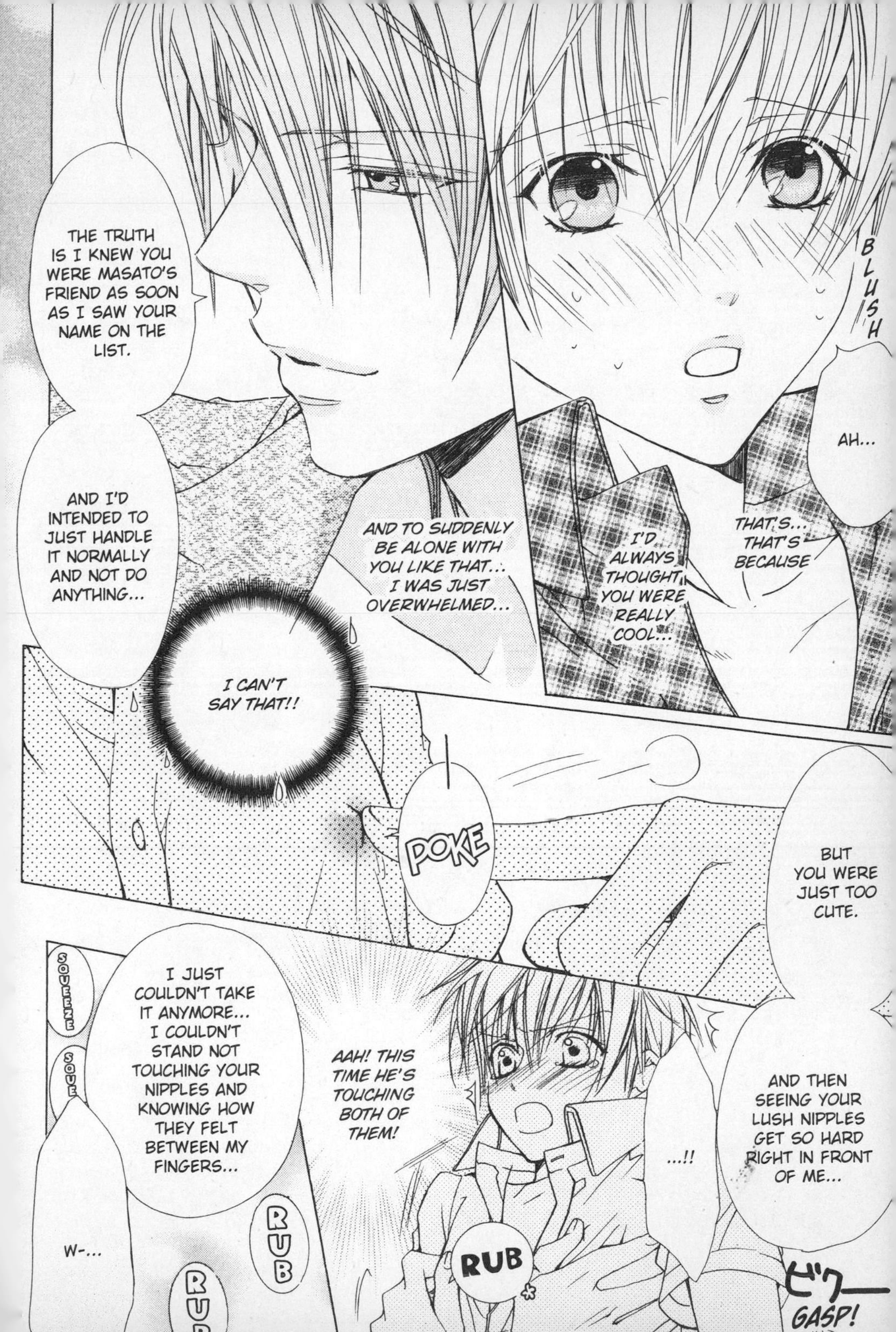

BLUSH
AH...
THAT'S... THAT'S BECAUSE
I'D ALWAYS THOUGHT YOU WERE REALLY COOL...
AND TO SUDDENLY BE ALONE WITH YOU LIKE THAT... I WAS JUST OVERWHELMED...
THE TRUTH IS I KNEW YOU WERE MASATO'S FRIEND AS SOON AS I SAW YOUR NAME ON THE LIST.
AND I'D INTENDED TO JUST HANDLE IT NORMALLY AND NOT DO ANYTHING...
BUT YOU WERE JUST TOO CUTE.
POKE
I CAN'T SAY THAT!!
AND THEN SEEING YOUR LUSH NIPPLES GET SO HARD RIGHT IN FRONT OF ME...
ビクー
GASP!
...!!
AAH! THIS TIME HE'S TOUCHING BOTH OF THEM!
I JUST COULDN'T TAKE IT ANYMORE... I COULDN'T STAND NOT TOUCHING YOUR NIPPLES AND KNOWING HOW THEY FELT BETWEEN MY FINGERS...
SQUEEZE
SQUE
RUB
RUB
RUB
W-...

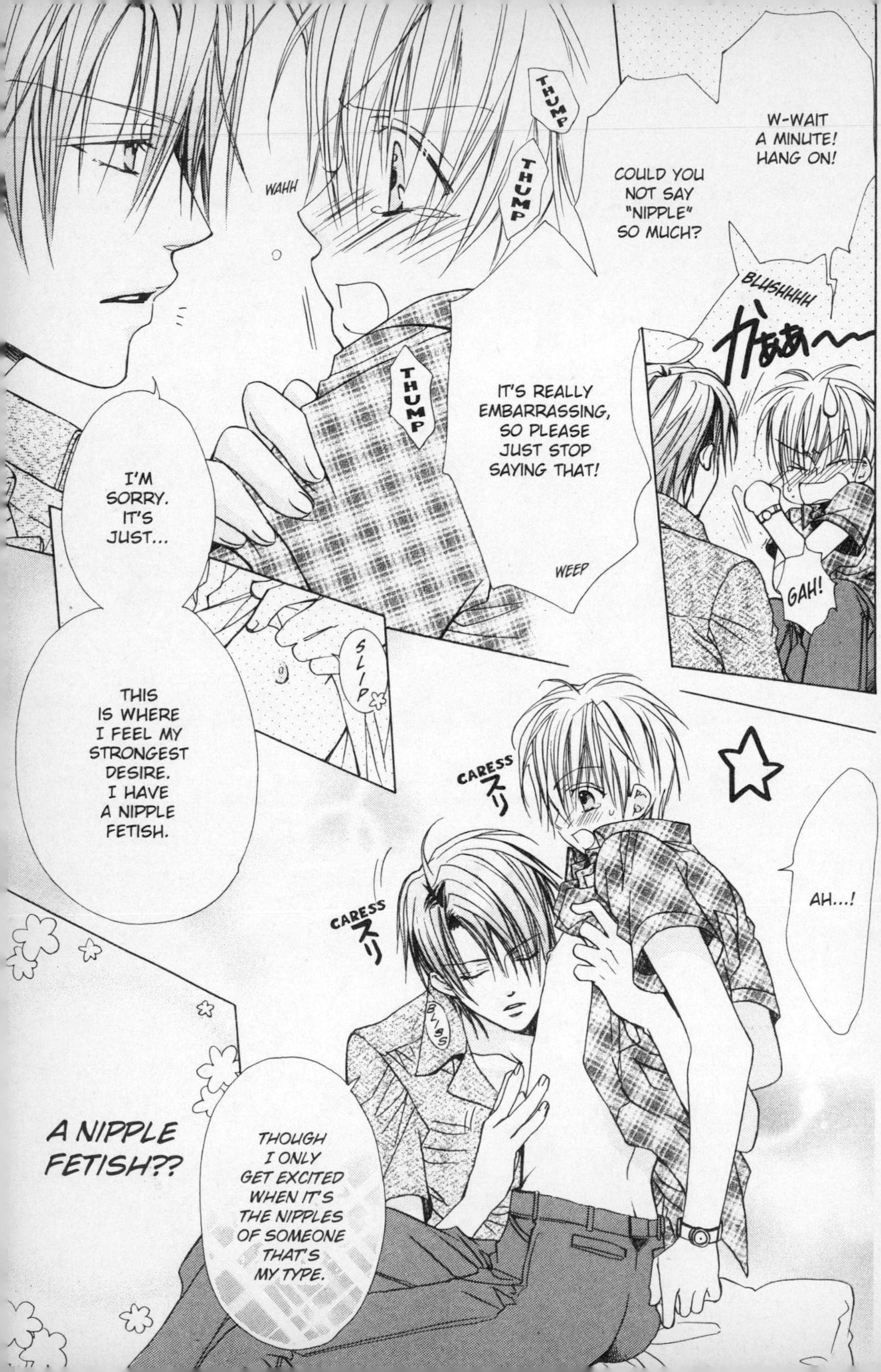
W-WAIT A MINUTE! HANG ON!
COULD YOU NOT SAY "NIPPLE" SO MUCH?
BLUSHHHH
GAH!
IT'S REALLY EMBARRASSING, SO PLEASE JUST STOP SAYING THAT!
WEEP
THUMP
THUMP
THUMP
WAHH
I'M SORRY. IT'S JUST...
SLIP
THIS IS WHERE I FEEL MY STRONGEST DESIRE. I HAVE A NIPPLE FETISH.
CARESS スリ
AH...!
CARESS スリ
BLISS
A NIPPLE FETISH??
THOUGH I ONLY GET EXCITED WHEN IT'S THE NIPPLES OF SOMEONE THAT'S MY TYPE.

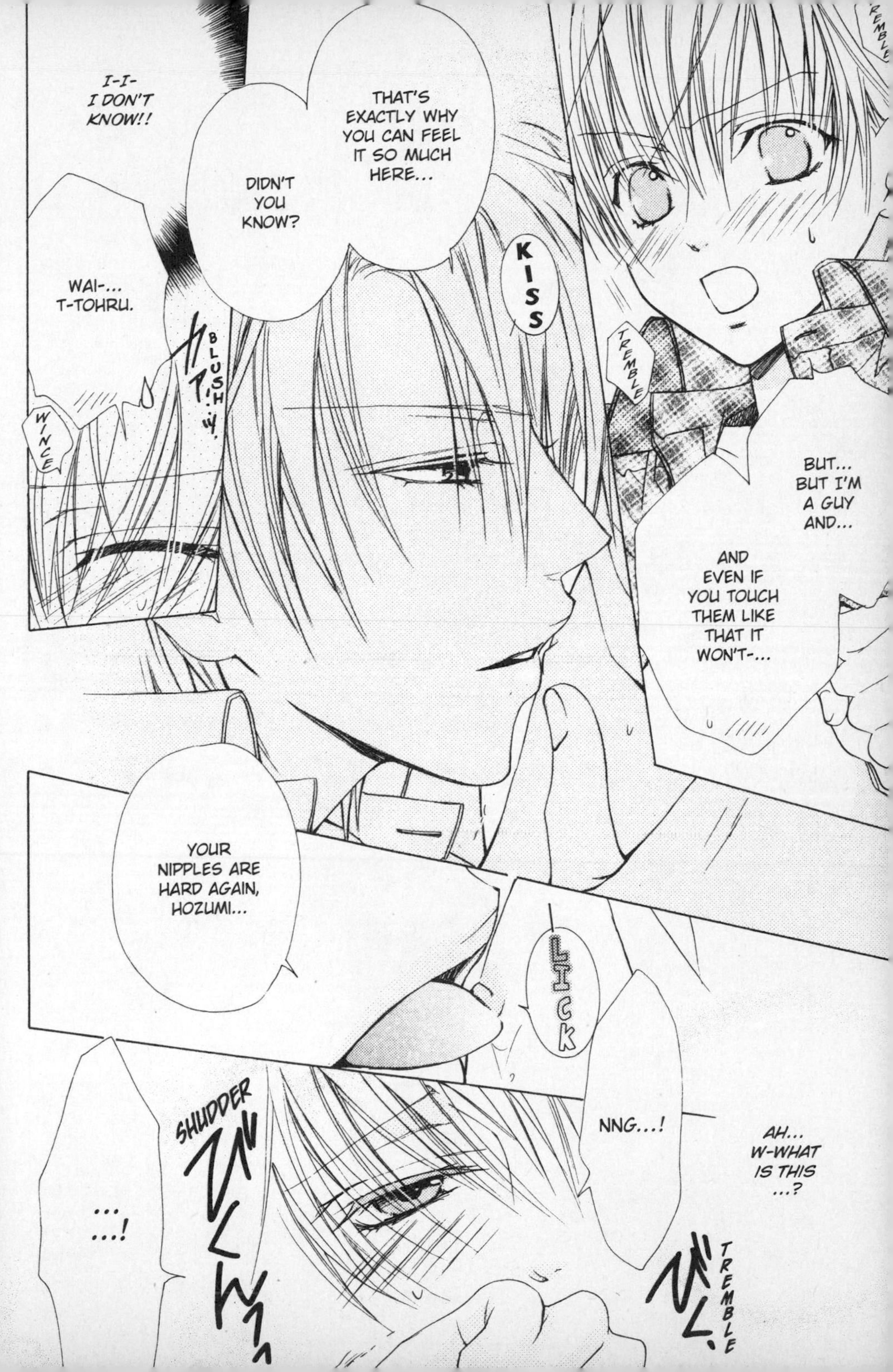
TREMBLE
BUT... BUT I'M A GUY AND...
AND EVEN IF YOU TOUCH THEM LIKE THAT IT WON'T-...
TREMBLE
THAT'S EXACTLY WHY YOU CAN FEEL IT SO MUCH HERE...
DIDN'T YOU KNOW?
KISS
I-I- I DON'T KNOW!!
WAI-... T-TOHRU.
BLUSH
WINCE
YOUR NIPPLES ARE HARD AGAIN, HOZUMI...
LICK
AH... W-WHAT IS THIS ...?
TREMBLE
NNG...!
SHUDDER
... ...!

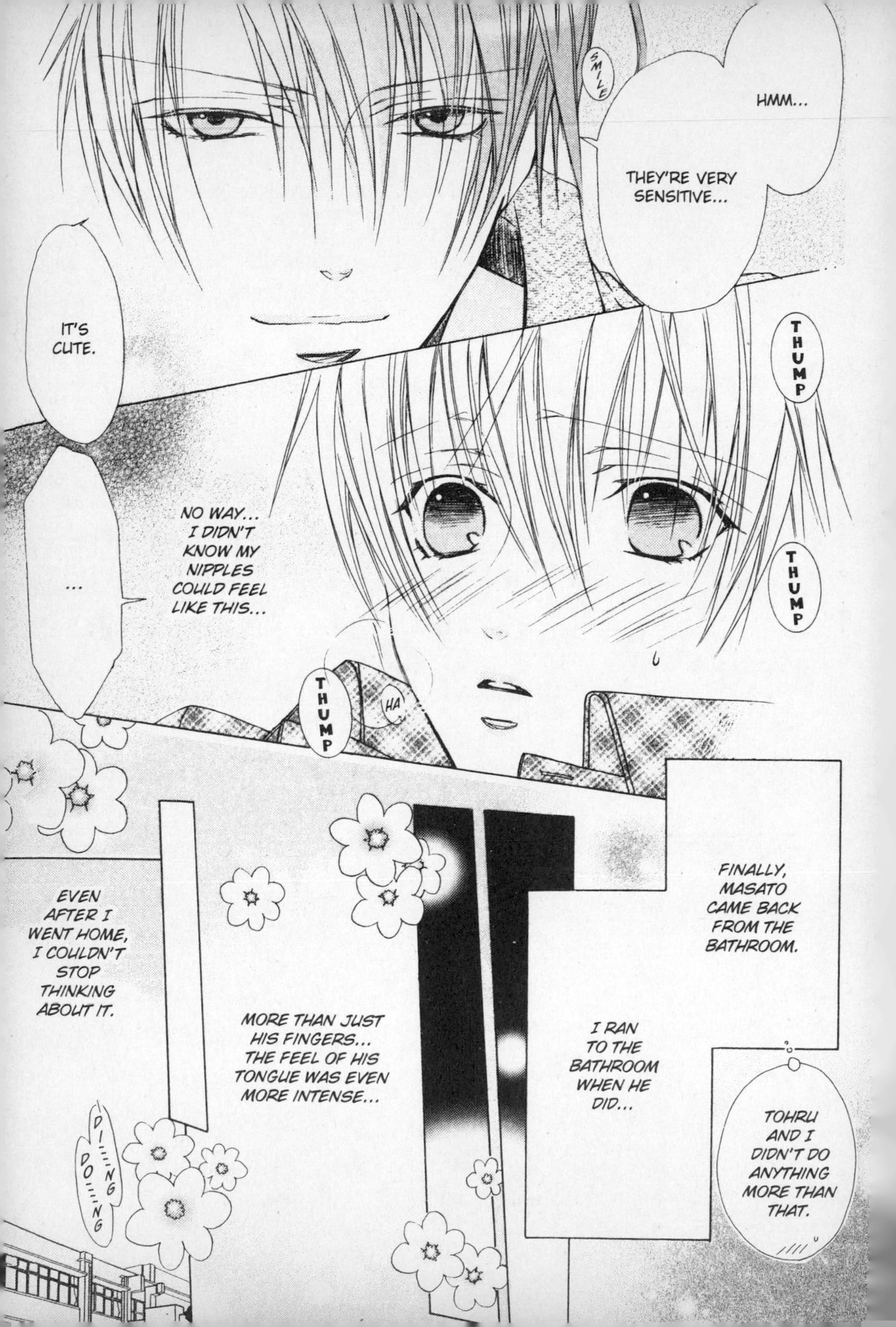
SMILE
HMM...
THEY'RE VERY SENSITIVE...
IT'S CUTE.
THUMP
THUMP
NO WAY... I DIDN'T KNOW MY NIPPLES COULD FEEL LIKE THIS...
...
THUMP
HA
FINALLY, MASATO CAME BACK FROM THE BATHROOM.
TOHRU AND I DIDN'T DO ANYTHING MORE THAN THAT.
I RAN TO THE BATHROOM WHEN HE DID...
MORE THAN JUST HIS FINGERS... THE FEEL OF HIS TONGUE WAS EVEN MORE INTENSE...
EVEN AFTER I WENT HOME, I COULDN'T STOP THINKING ABOUT IT.
DI-I-NG
DO-O-NG

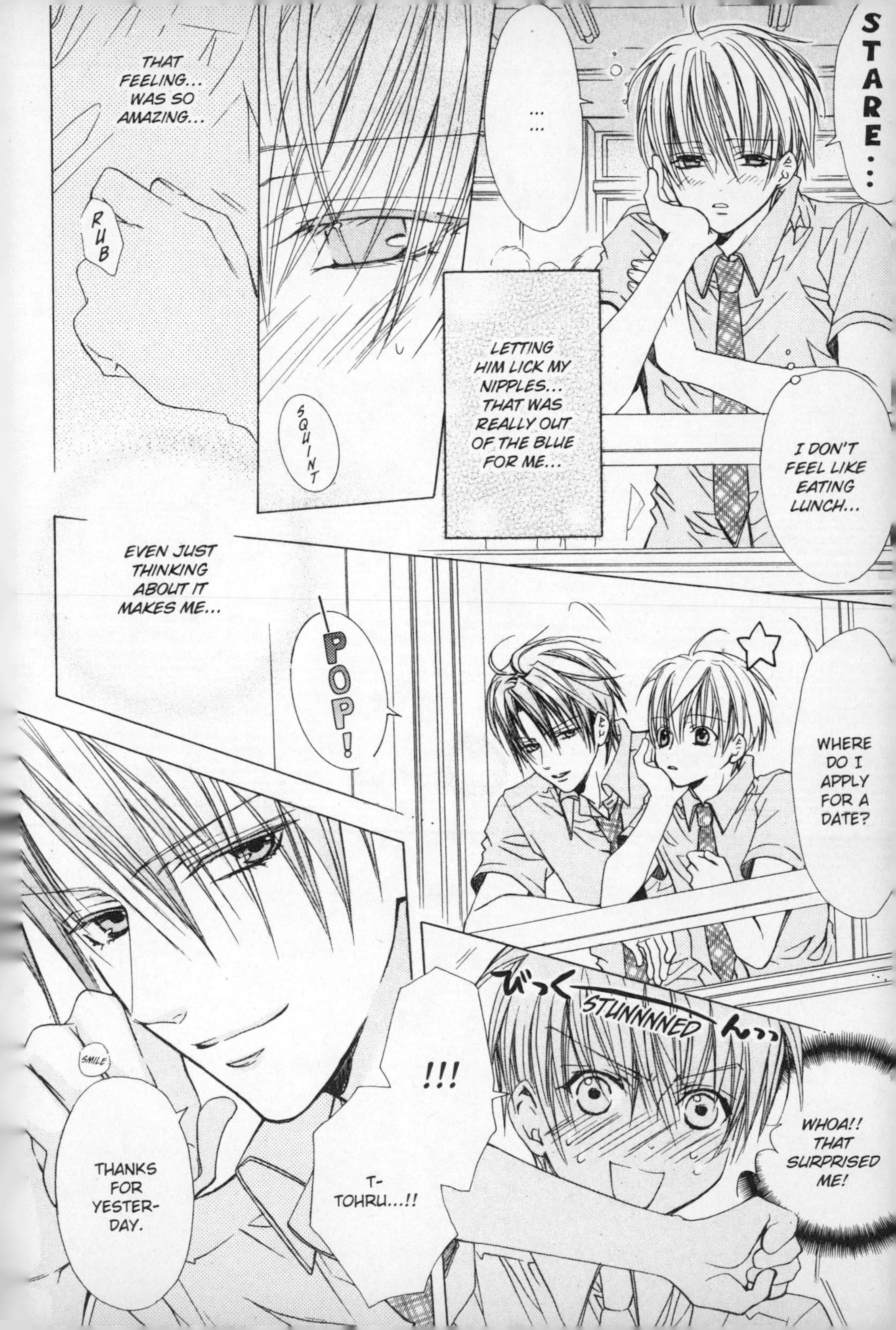
STARE...
I DON'T FEEL LIKE EATING LUNCH...
LETTING HIM LICK MY NIPPLES... THAT WAS REALLY OUT OF THE BLUE FOR ME...
......
SQUINT
THAT FEELING... WAS SO AMAZING...
RUB
WHERE DO I APPLY FOR A DATE?
EVEN JUST THINKING ABOUT IT MAKES ME...
POP!
びっく STUNNNNED んっ
WHOA!! THAT SURPRISED ME!
!!!
T-TOHRU...!!
SMILE
THANKS FOR YESTER-DAY.

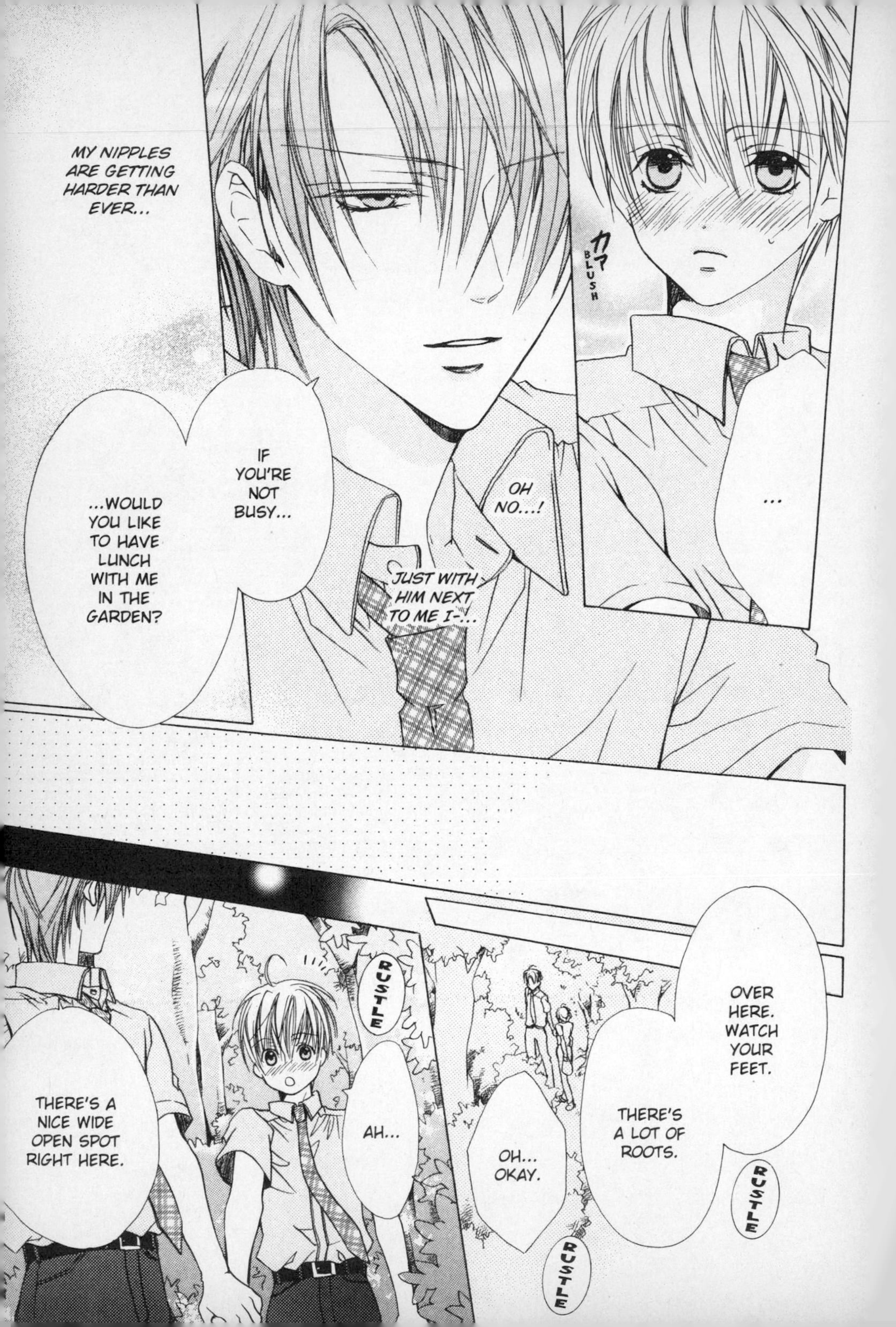

カァ
BLUSH
...
OH NO...!
JUST WITH HIM NEXT TO ME I-...
MY NIPPLES ARE GETTING HARDER THAN EVER...
IF YOU'RE NOT BUSY...
...WOULD YOU LIKE TO HAVE LUNCH WITH ME IN THE GARDEN?
OVER HERE. WATCH YOUR FEET.
THERE'S A LOT OF ROOTS.
RUSTLE
OH... OKAY.
RUSTLE
RUSTLE
AH...
THERE'S A NICE WIDE OPEN SPOT RIGHT HERE.

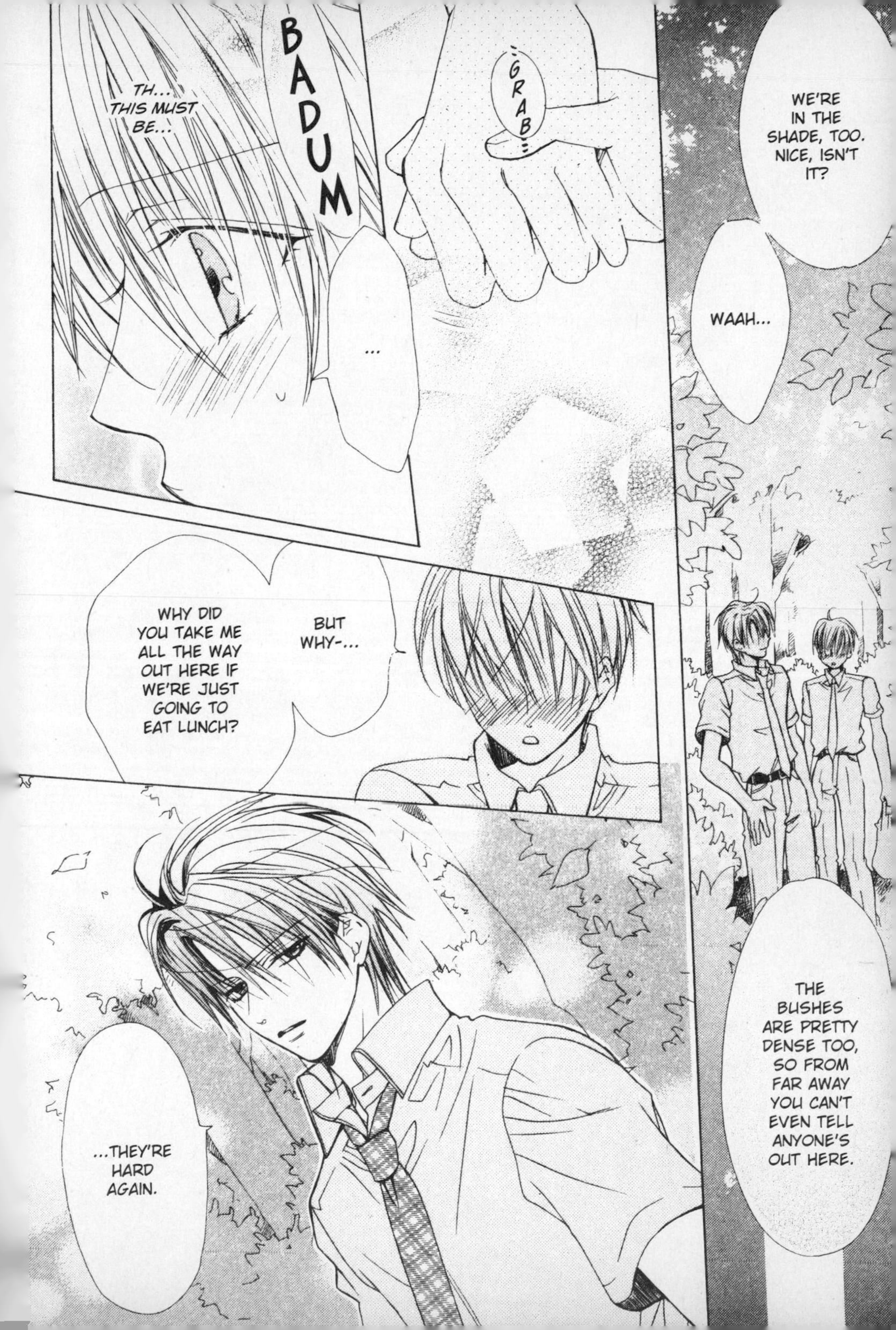
WE'RE IN THE SHADE, TOO. NICE, ISN'T IT?
WAAH...
THE BUSHES ARE PRETTY DENSE TOO, SO FROM FAR AWAY YOU CAN'T EVEN TELL ANYONE'S OUT HERE.
...GRAB...
BADUM
TH... THIS MUST BE...
...
BUT WHY-...
WHY DID YOU TAKE ME ALL THE WAY OUT HERE IF WE'RE JUST GOING TO EAT LUNCH?
...THEY'RE HARD AGAIN.

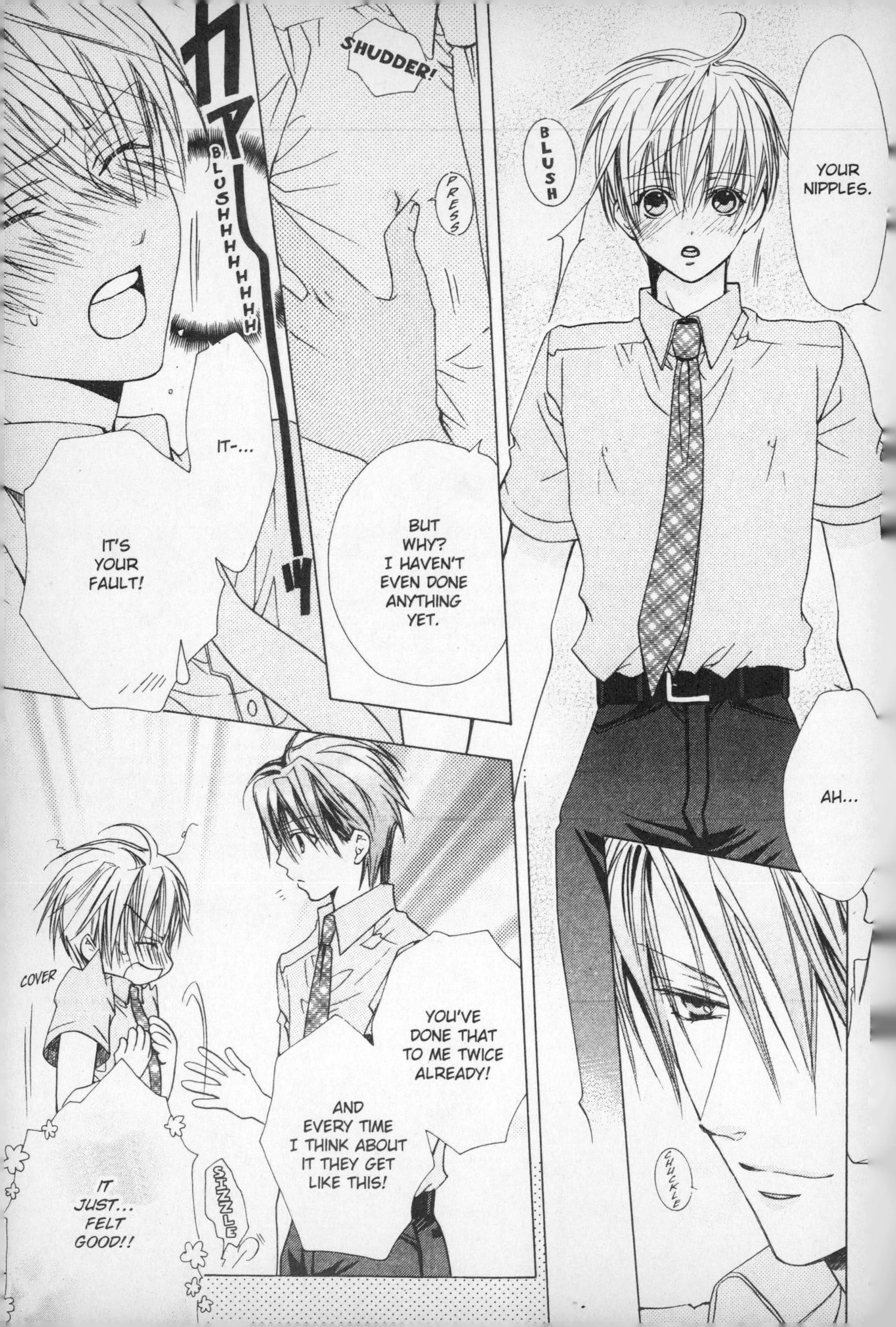
YOUR NIPPLES.
BLUSH
AH...
CHUCKLE
SHUDDER!
PRESS
BUT WHY? I HAVEN'T EVEN DONE ANYTHING YET.
BLUSHHHHHHHH
IT-...
IT'S YOUR FAULT!
YOU'VE DONE THAT TO ME TWICE ALREADY!
AND EVERY TIME I THINK ABOUT IT THEY GET LIKE THIS!
SIZZLE
COVER
IT JUST... FELT GOOD!!

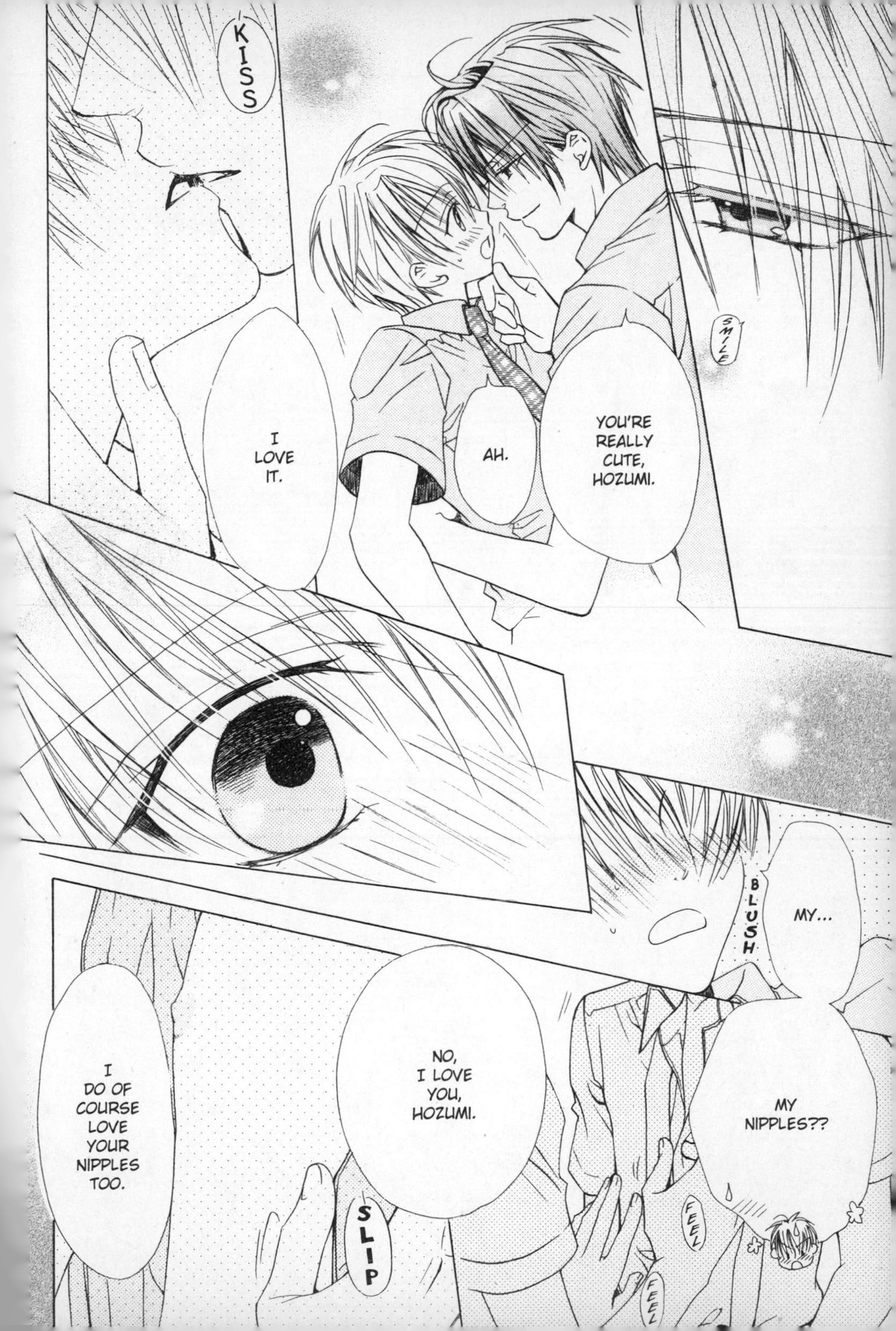
SMILE
YOU'RE REALLY CUTE, HOZUMI.
AH.
KISS
I LOVE IT.
BLUSH
MY...
MY NIPPLES??
FEEL
FEEL
NO, I LOVE YOU, HOZUMI.
SLIP
I DO OF COURSE LOVE YOUR NIPPLES TOO.

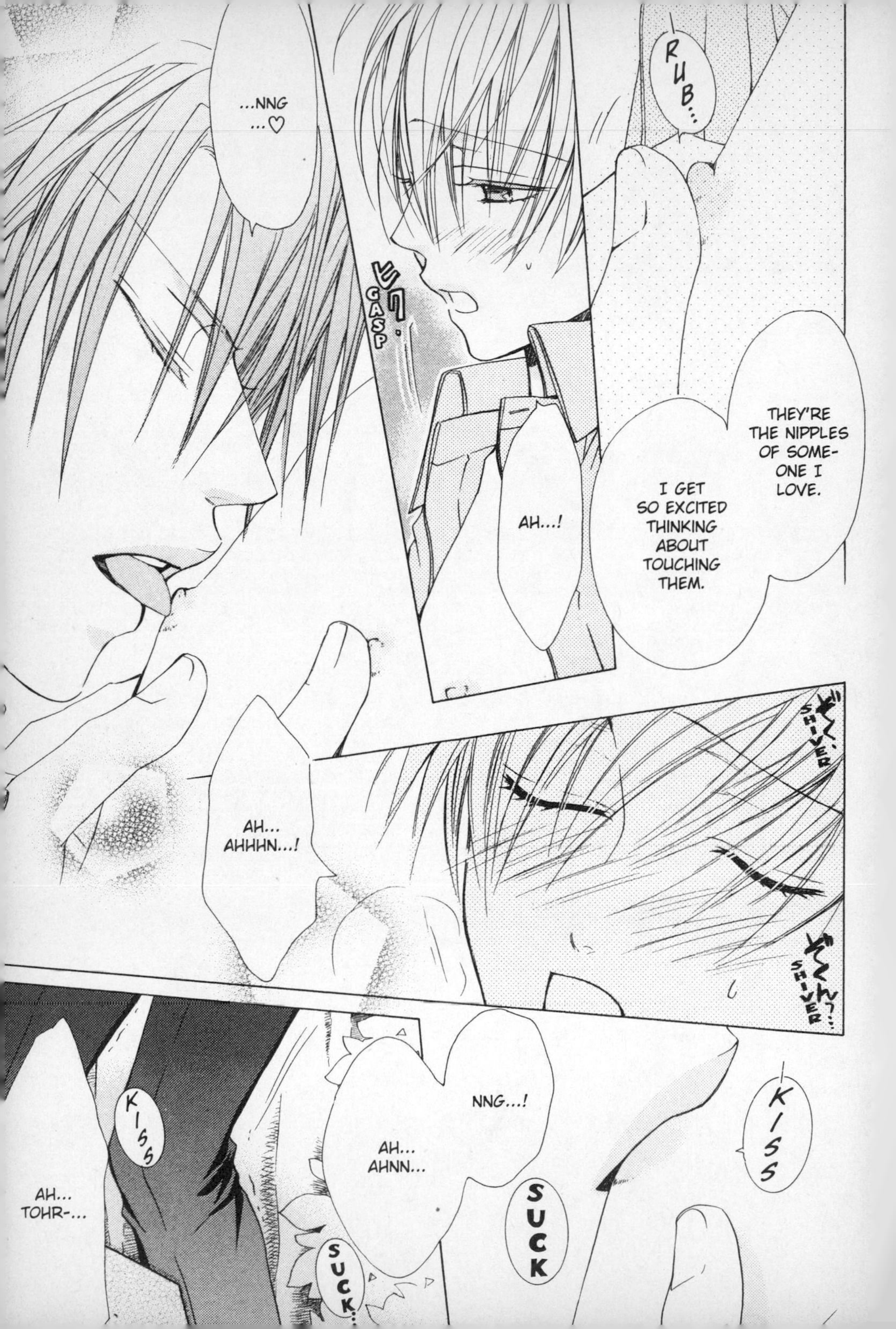

RUB...
THEY'RE THE NIPPLES OF SOME-ONE I LOVE.
I GET SO EXCITED THINKING ABOUT TOUCHING THEM.
GASP
AH...!
...NNG ...♡
SHIVER
SHIVER...
AH... AHHHN...!
KISS
NNG...!
SUCK
AH... AHNN...
SUCK...
KISS
AH... TOHR-...

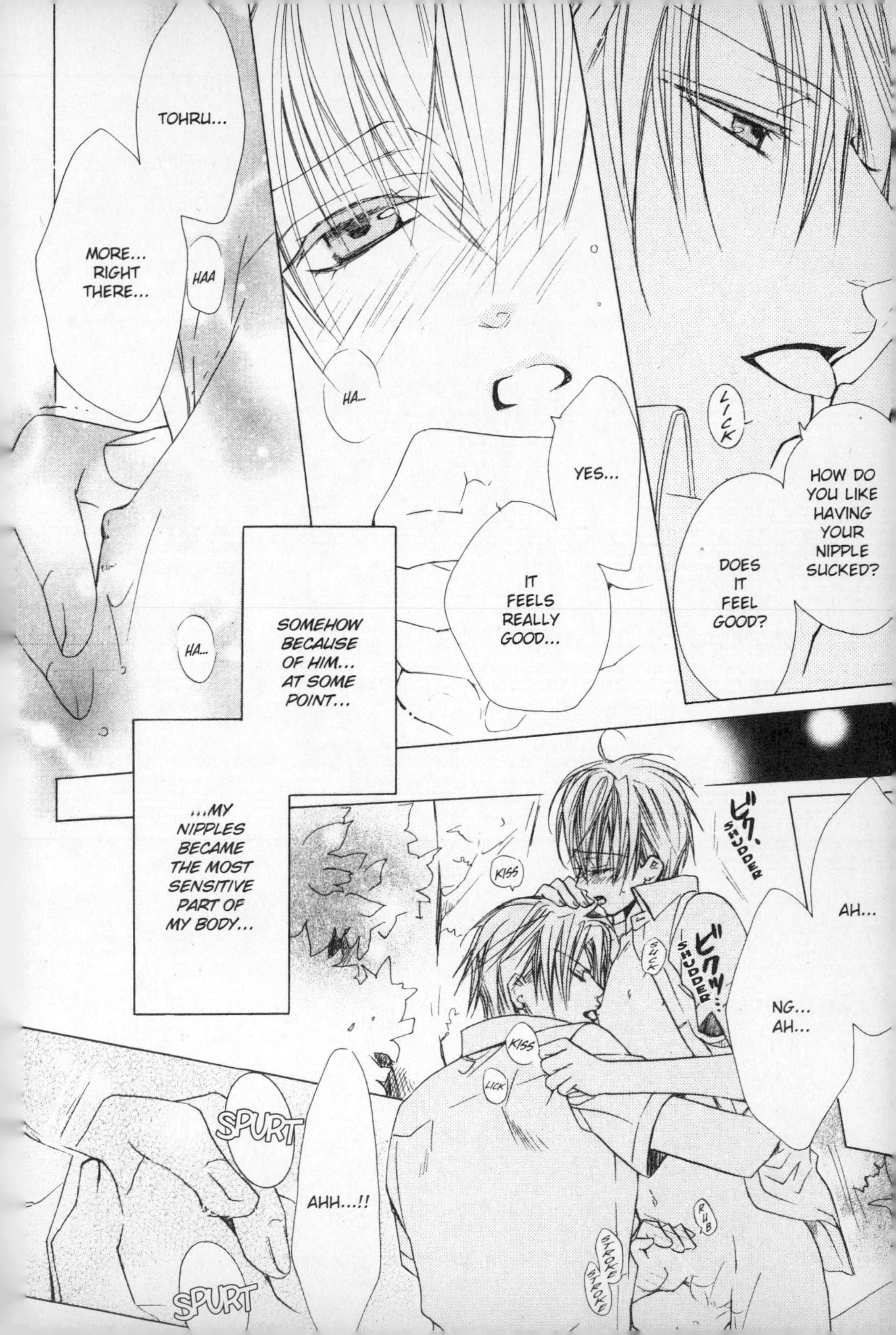

LICK
HOW DO YOU LIKE HAVING YOUR NIPPLE SUCKED?
DOES IT FEEL GOOD?
YES...
IT FEELS REALLY GOOD...
HA...
TOHRU...
HAA
MORE... RIGHT THERE...
HA...
SOMEHOW BECAUSE OF HIM... AT SOME POINT...
...MY NIPPLES BECAME THE MOST SENSITIVE PART OF MY BODY...
SHUDDER
AH...
SHUDDER
NG... AH...
KISS
SUCK
KISS
LICK
RUB
STROKE
STROKE
SPURT
AHH...!!
SPURT

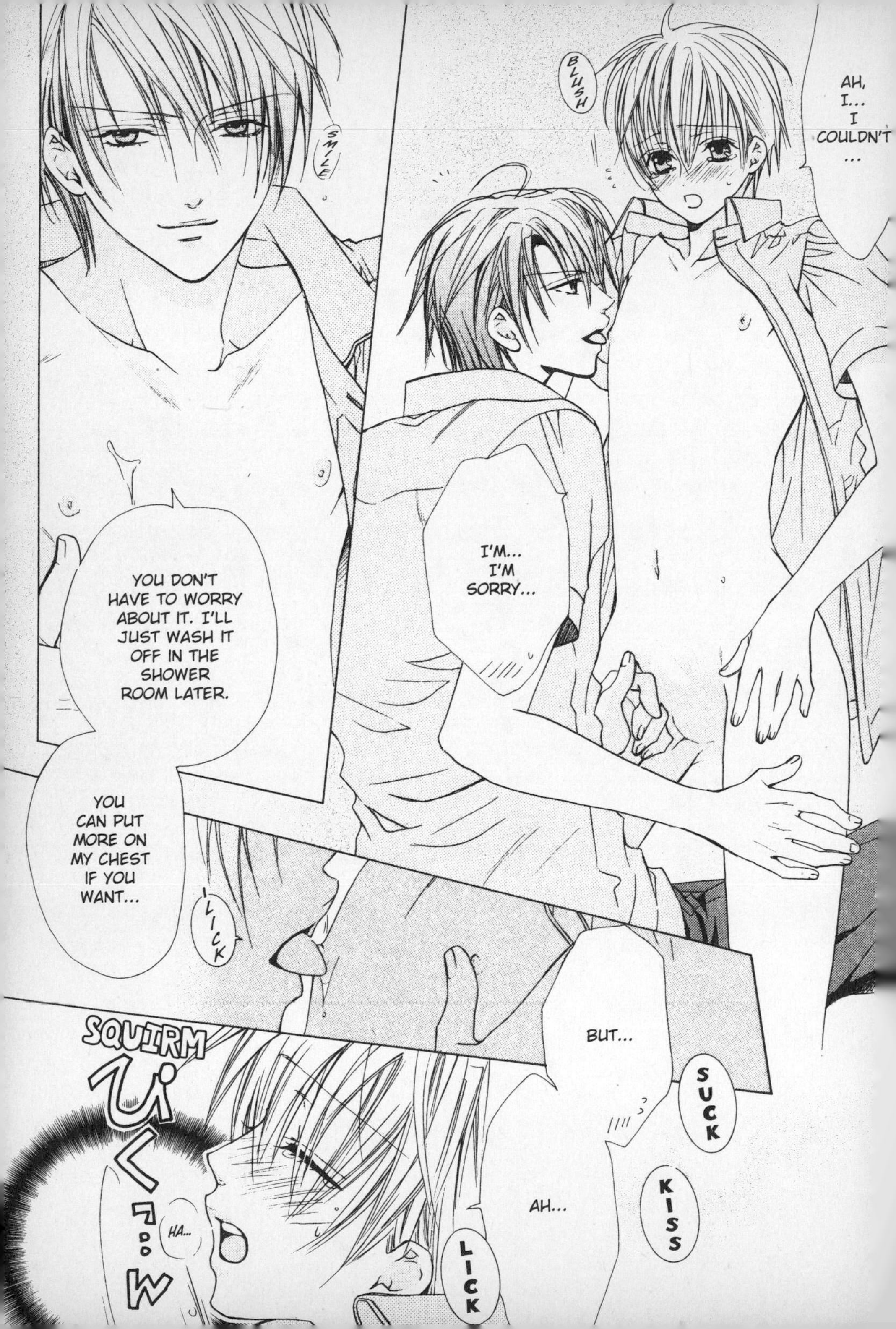
AH, I... I COULDN'T ...
BLUSH
I'M... I'M SORRY...
SMILE
YOU DON'T HAVE TO WORRY ABOUT IT. I'LL JUST WASH IT OFF IN THE SHOWER ROOM LATER.
YOU CAN PUT MORE ON MY CHEST IF YOU WANT...
LICK
BUT...
SUCK
KISS
AH...
LICK
HA...
SQUIRM

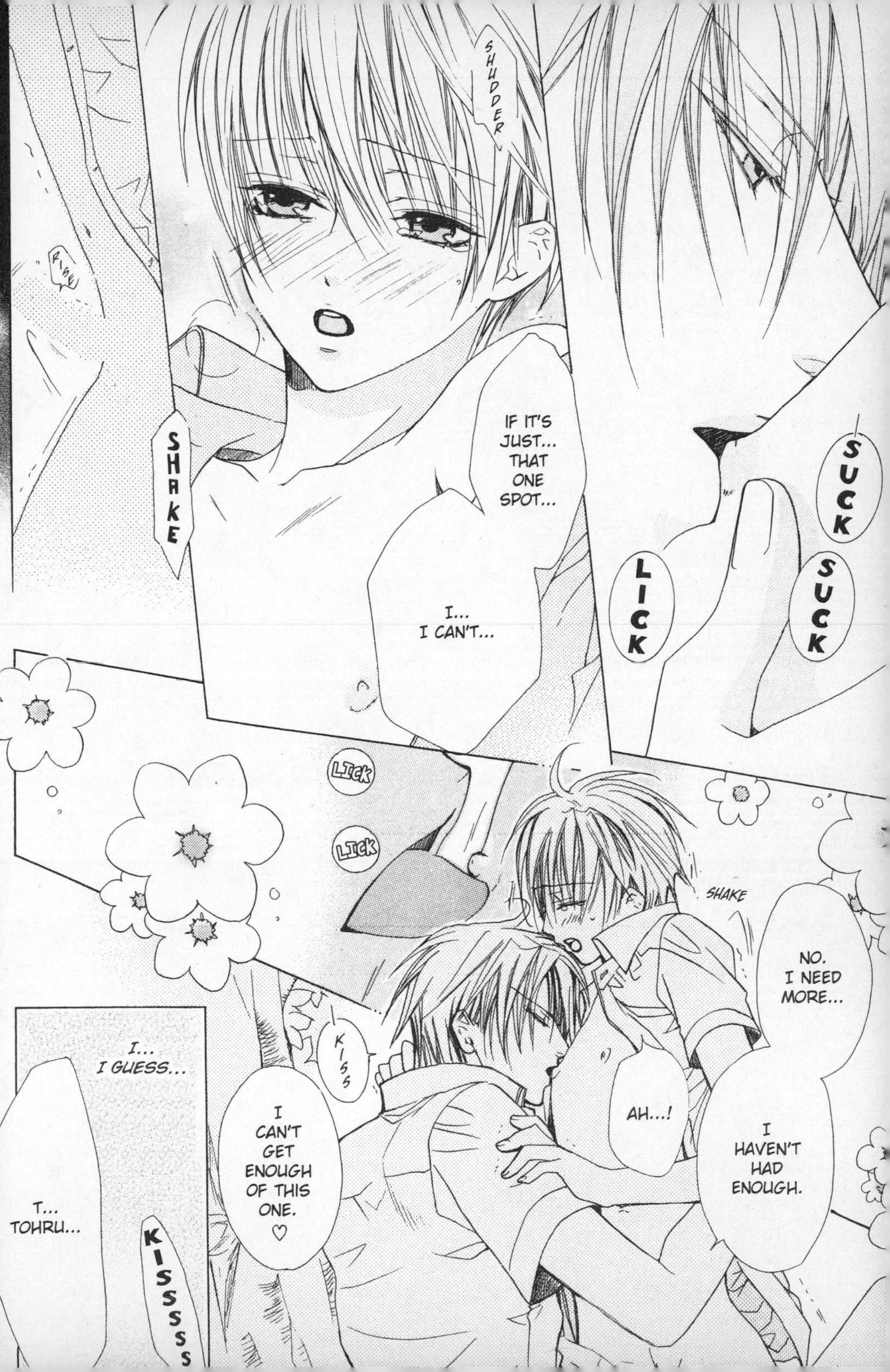
SUCK
SUCK
LICK
SHUDDER
IF IT'S JUST... THAT ONE SPOT...
I... I CAN'T...
SHAKE
RISE
LICK
LICK
SHAKE
NO. I NEED MORE...
I HAVEN'T HAD ENOUGH.
AH...!
KISS
I CAN'T GET ENOUGH OF THIS ONE. ♡
I... I GUESS...
T... TOHRU...
KISSSSS

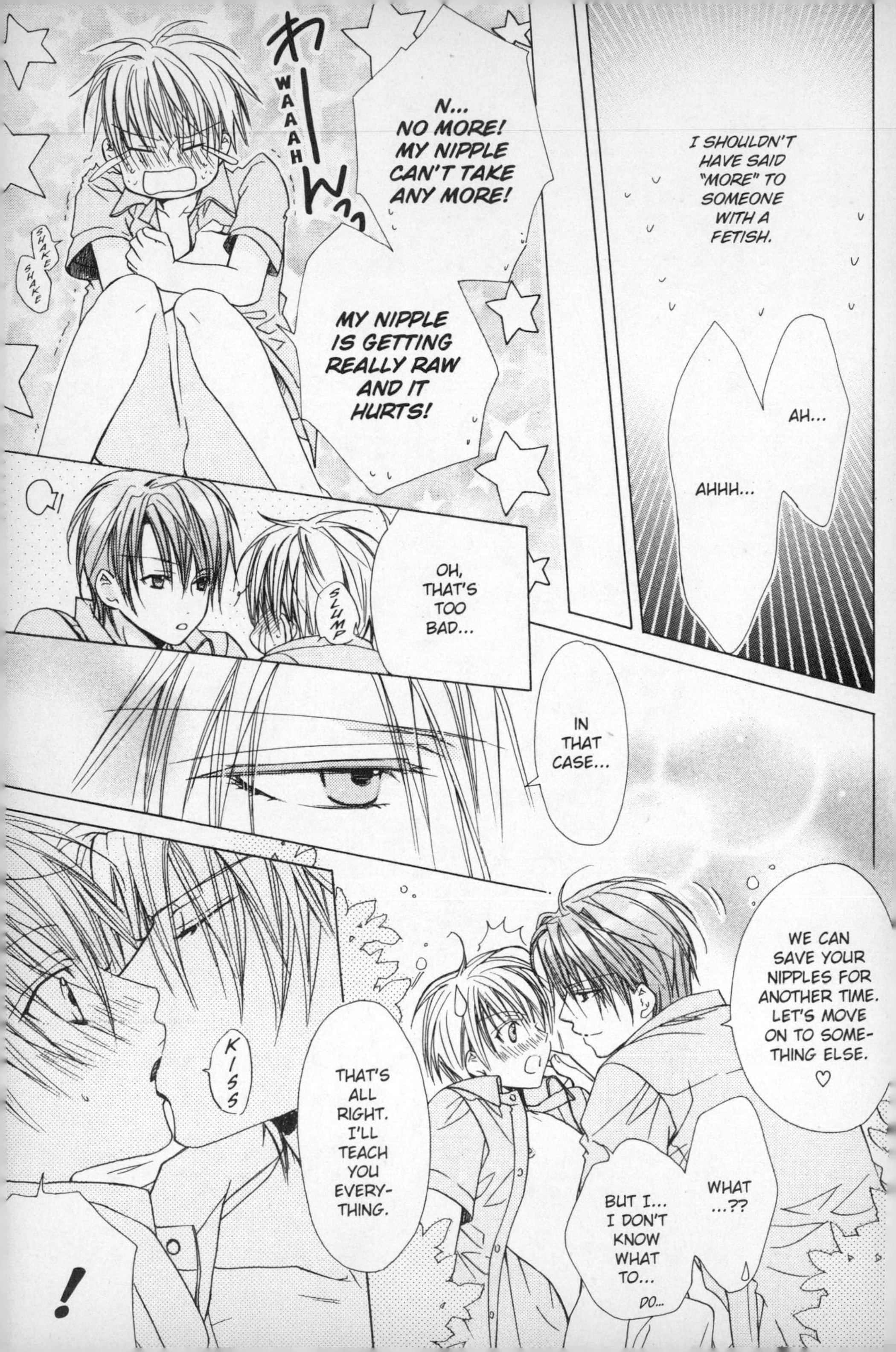
I SHOULDN'T HAVE SAID "MORE" TO SOMEONE WITH A FETISH.
AH...
AHHH...
わー
WAAAH
SHAKE SHAKE
N... NO MORE! MY NIPPLE CAN'T TAKE ANY MORE!
MY NIPPLE IS GETTING REALLY RAW AND IT HURTS!
OH, THAT'S TOO BAD...
SLUMP
IN THAT CASE...
WE CAN SAVE YOUR NIPPLES FOR ANOTHER TIME. LET'S MOVE ON TO SOMETHING ELSE. ♡
WHAT ...??
BUT I... I DON'T KNOW WHAT TO...
DO...
THAT'S ALL RIGHT. I'LL TEACH YOU EVERYTHING.
KISS
!

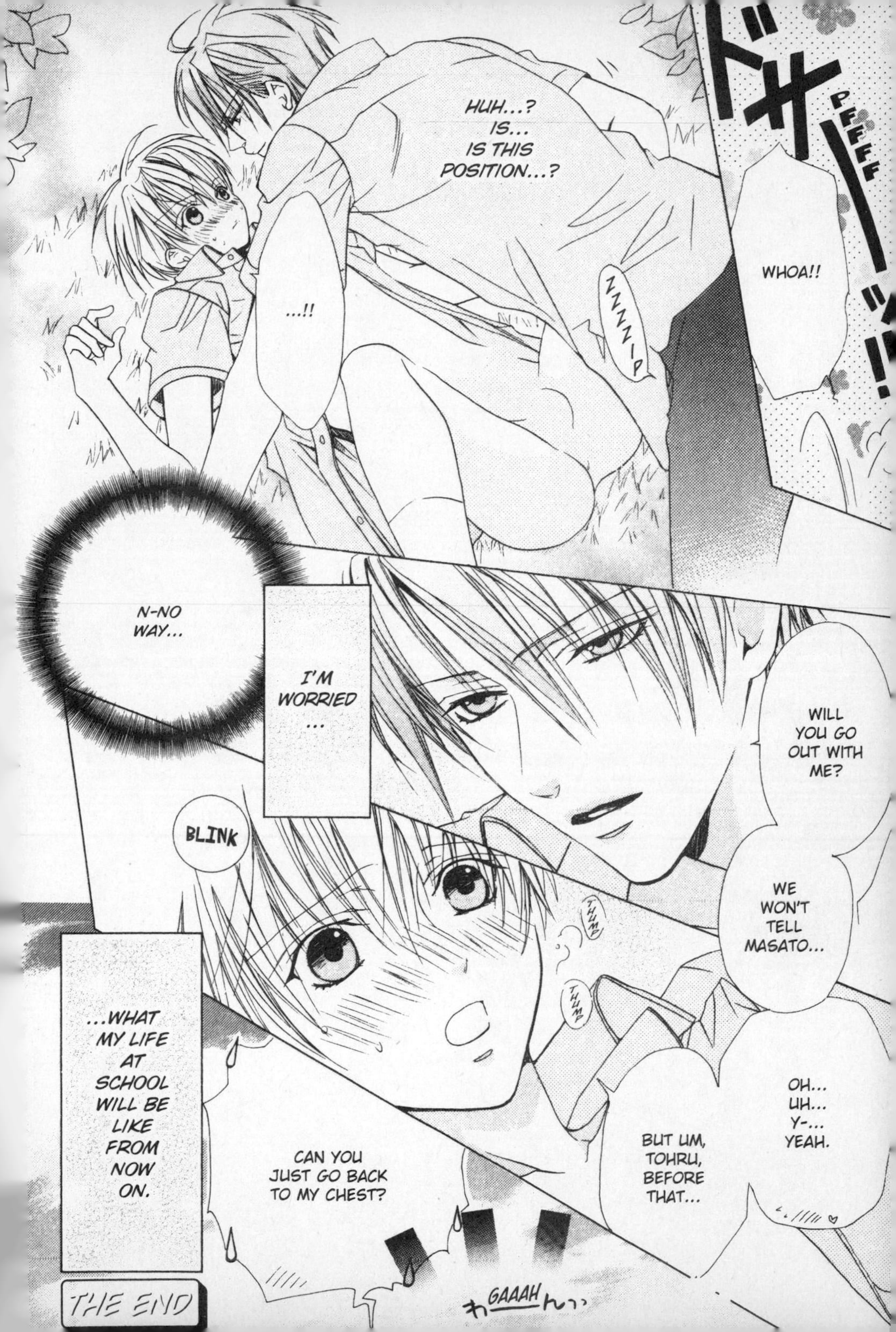
PFFFF!!
WHOA!!
ZZZZIP
HUH...? IS... IS THIS POSITION...?
...!!
N-NO WAY...
I'M WORRIED...
WILL YOU GO OUT WITH ME?
WE WON'T TELL MASATO...
BLINK
THUMP
THUMP
OH... UH... Y-... YEAH.
BUT UM, TOHRU, BEFORE THAT...
CAN YOU JUST GO BACK TO MY CHEST?
GAAAH
...WHAT MY LIFE AT SCHOOL WILL BE LIKE FROM NOW ON.
THE END

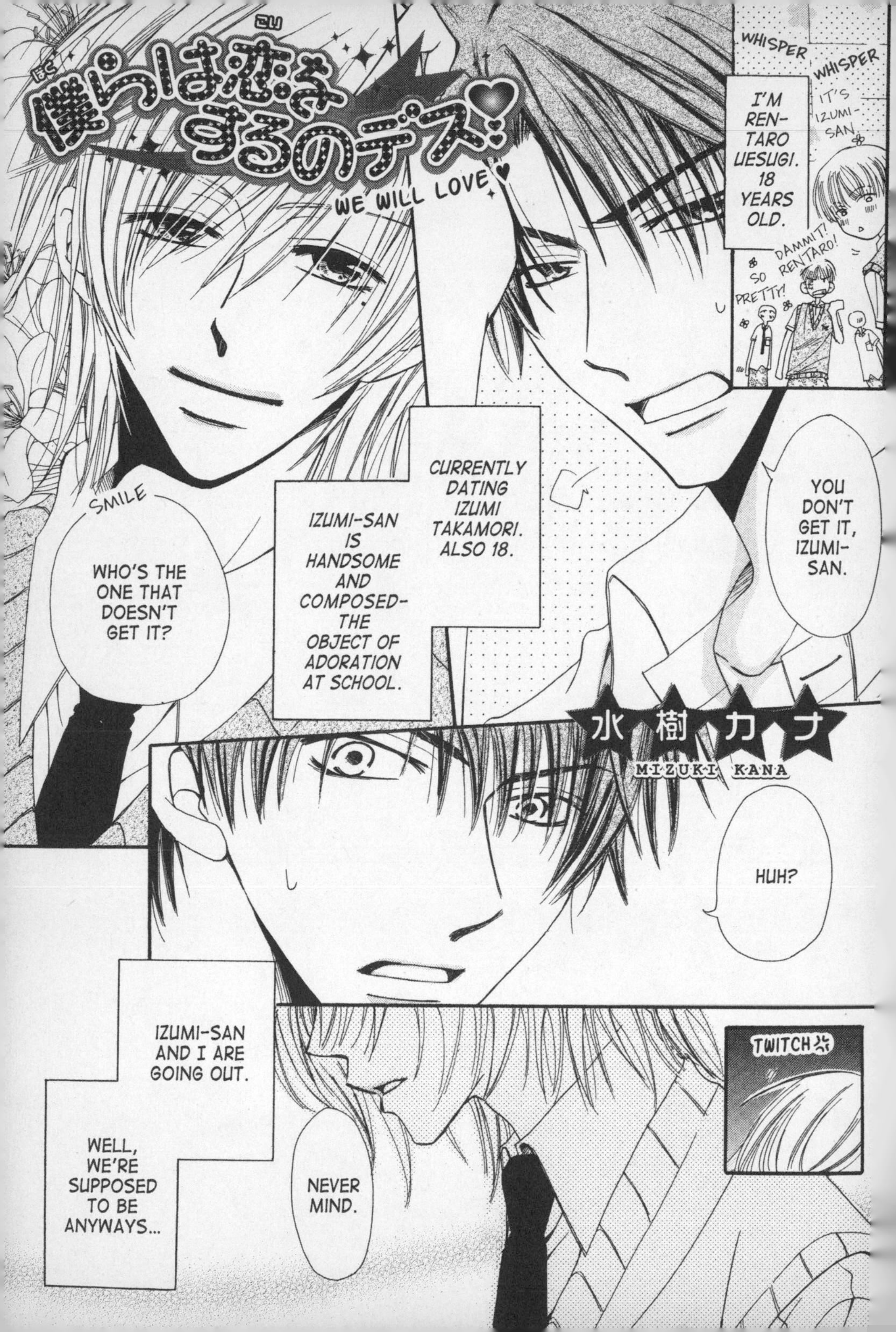
WHISPER
WHISPER
I'M RENTARO UESUGI. 18 YEARS OLD.
IT'S IZUMI-SAN
DAMMIT! RENTARO!
SO PRETTY!
僕らは恋をするのデス!
WE WILL LOVE
CURRENTLY DATING IZUMI TAKAMORI. ALSO 18.
IZUMI-SAN IS HANDSOME AND COMPOSED- THE OBJECT OF ADORATION AT SCHOOL.
YOU DON'T GET IT, IZUMI-SAN.
SMILE
WHO'S THE ONE THAT DOESN'T GET IT?
水樹カナ
MIZUKI KANA
HUH?
TWITCH
NEVER MIND.
IZUMI-SAN AND I ARE GOING OUT.
WELL, WE'RE SUPPOSED TO BE ANYWAYS...

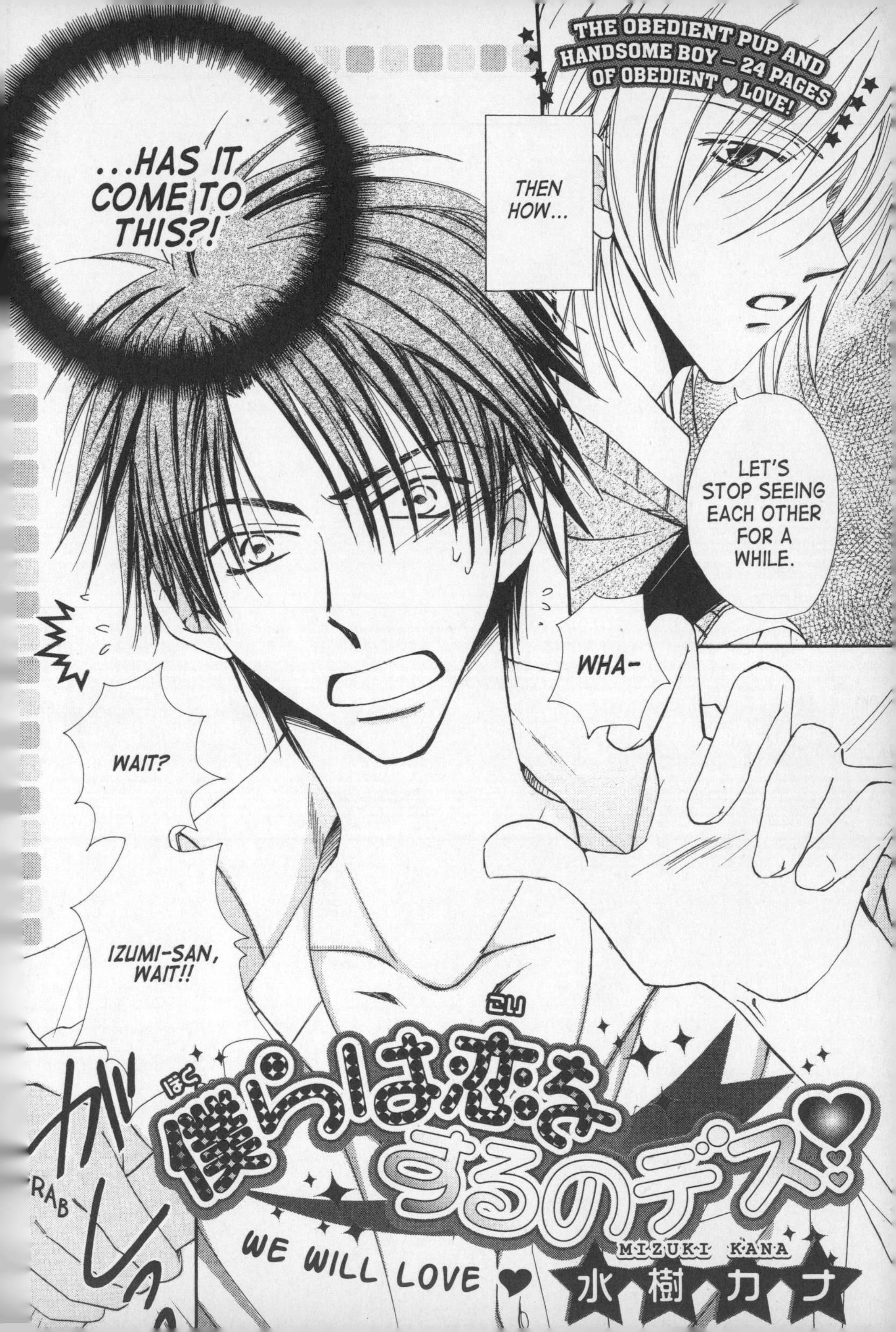

THE OBEDIENT PUP AND HANDSOME BOY – 24 PAGES OF OBEDIENT ♥ LOVE!
THEN HOW...
LET'S STOP SEEING EACH OTHER FOR A WHILE.
...HAS IT COME TO THIS?!
WHA-
WAIT?
IZUMI-SAN, WAIT!!
がし
RAB
僕らは恋をするのデス!
WE WILL LOVE ♥
MIZUKI KANA
水樹カナ

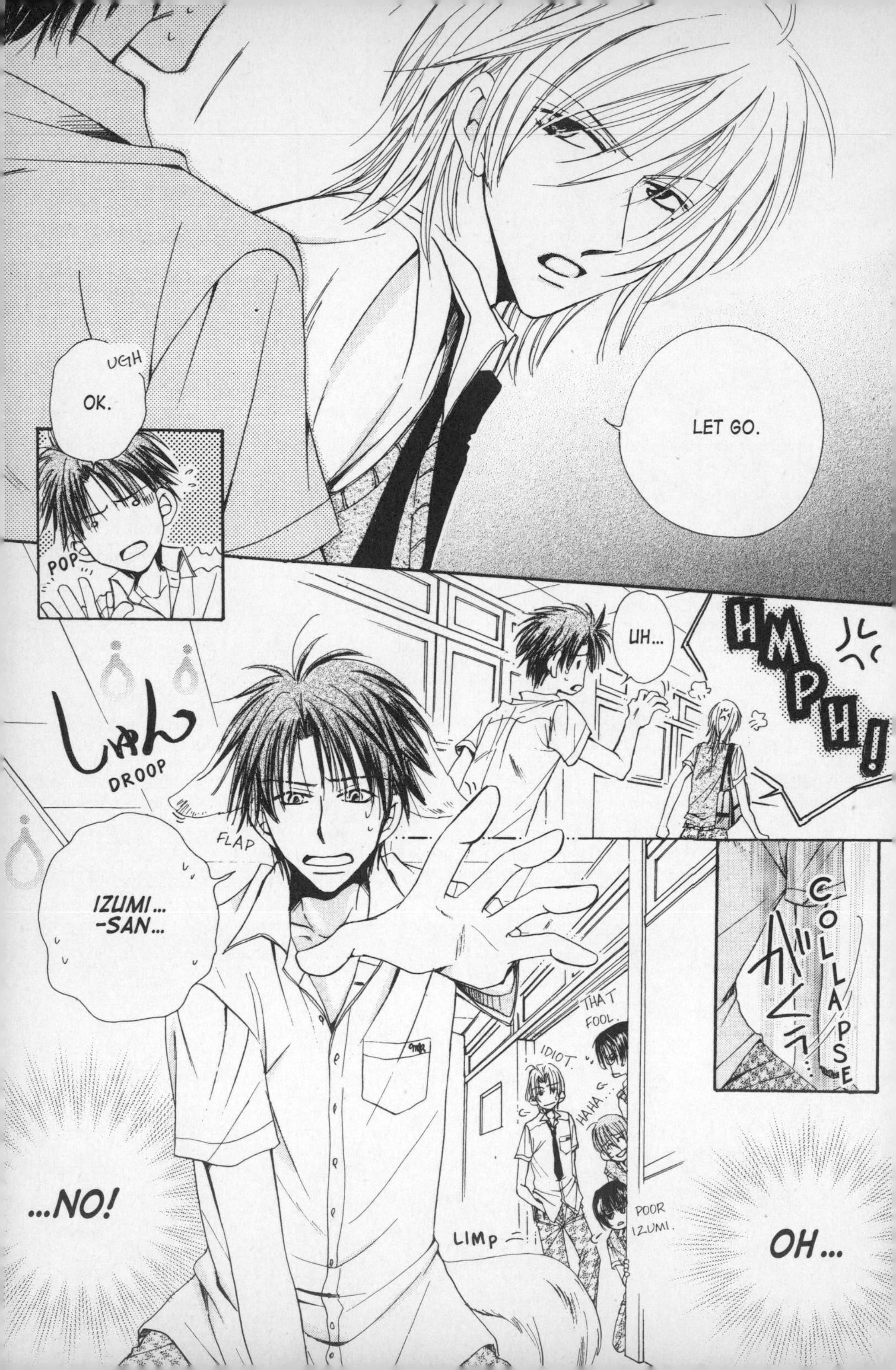
LET GO.
UGH
OK.
POP
HMPH!
UH...
COLLAPSE
THAT FOOL.
IDIOT.
HAHA
POOR IZUMI.
LIMP
OH...
しゅん
DROOP
FLAP
IZUMI... -SAN...
...NO!

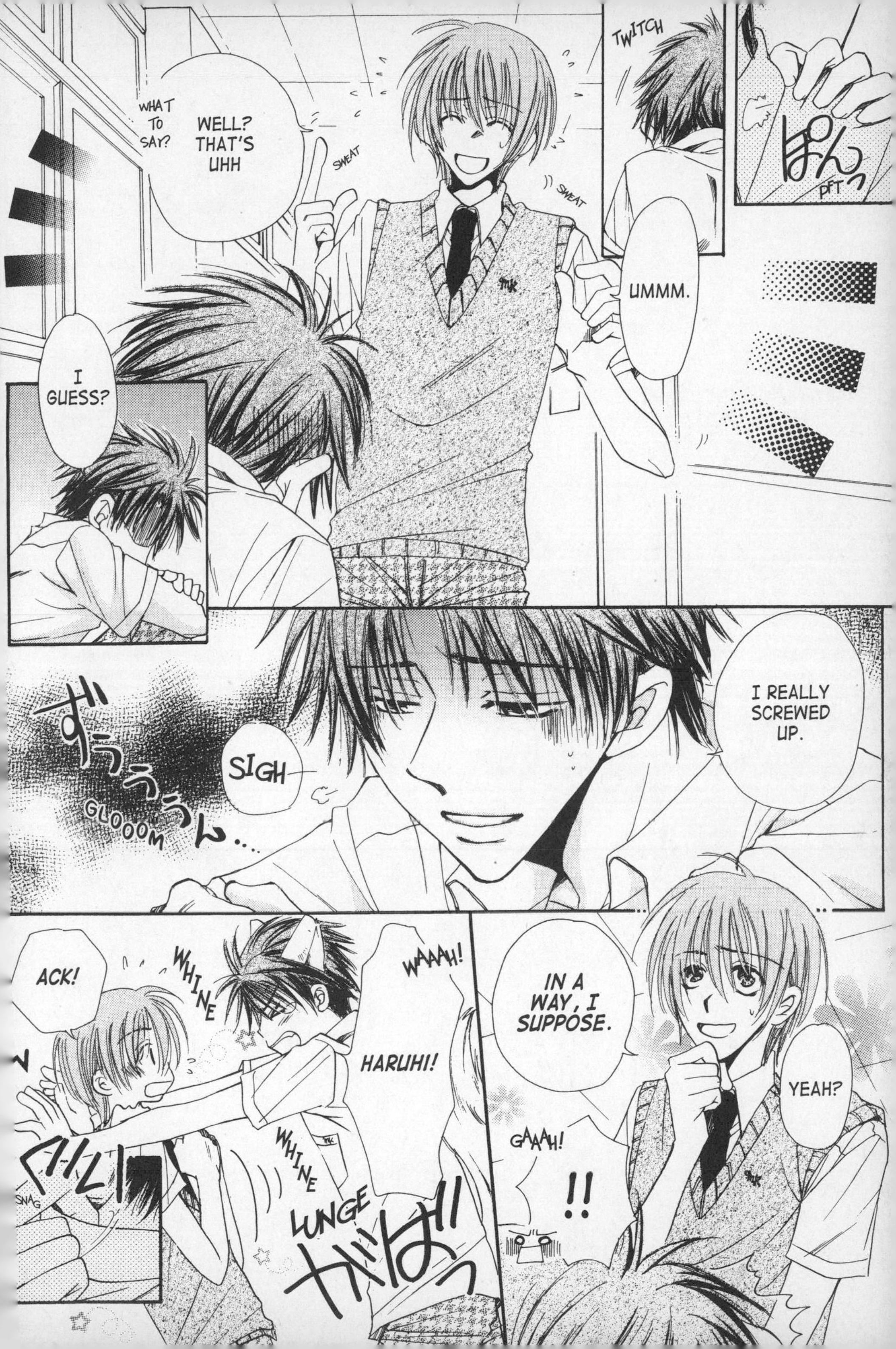
TWITCH
ぽんっ
PFT
UMMM.
WELL? THAT'S UHH
WHAT TO SAY?
SWEAT
SWEAT
I GUESS?
I REALLY SCREWED UP.
SIGH
GLOOOM
YEAH?
IN A WAY, I SUPPOSE.
GAAAH!
!!
WAAAH!
HARUHI!
WHINE
ACK!
WHINE
LUNGE
がばっ
SWAG

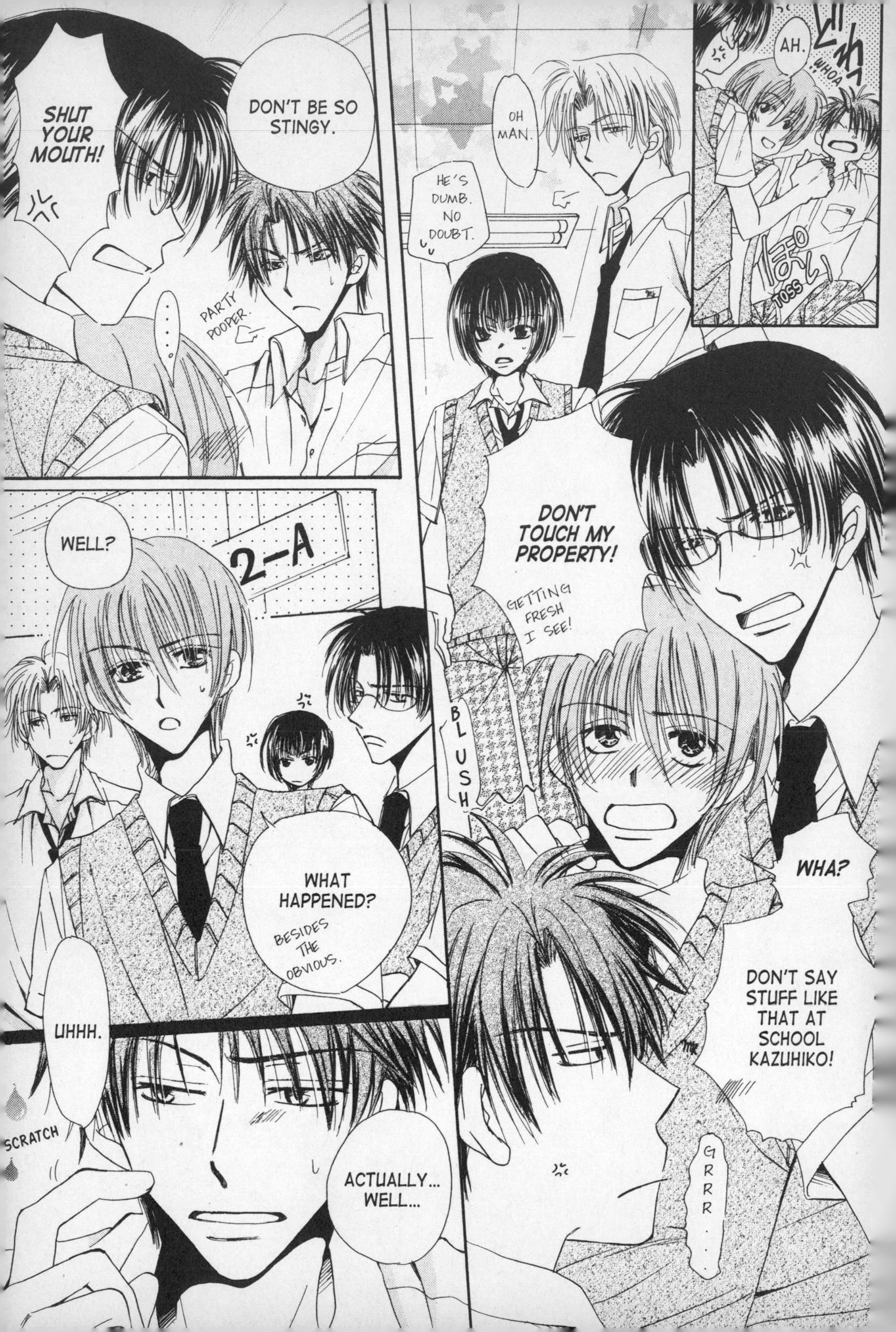
AH.
WHOA
TOSS
OH MAN.
HE'S DUMB. NO DOUBT.
DON'T BE SO STINGY.
SHUT YOUR MOUTH!
...
PARTY POOPER.
DON'T TOUCH MY PROPERTY!
GETTING FRESH I SEE!
BLUSH
WHA?
DON'T SAY STUFF LIKE THAT AT SCHOOL KAZUHIKO!
GRRR...
WELL?
2-A
WHAT HAPPENED?
BESIDES THE OBVIOUS.
UHHH.
SCRATCH
ACTUALLY... WELL...

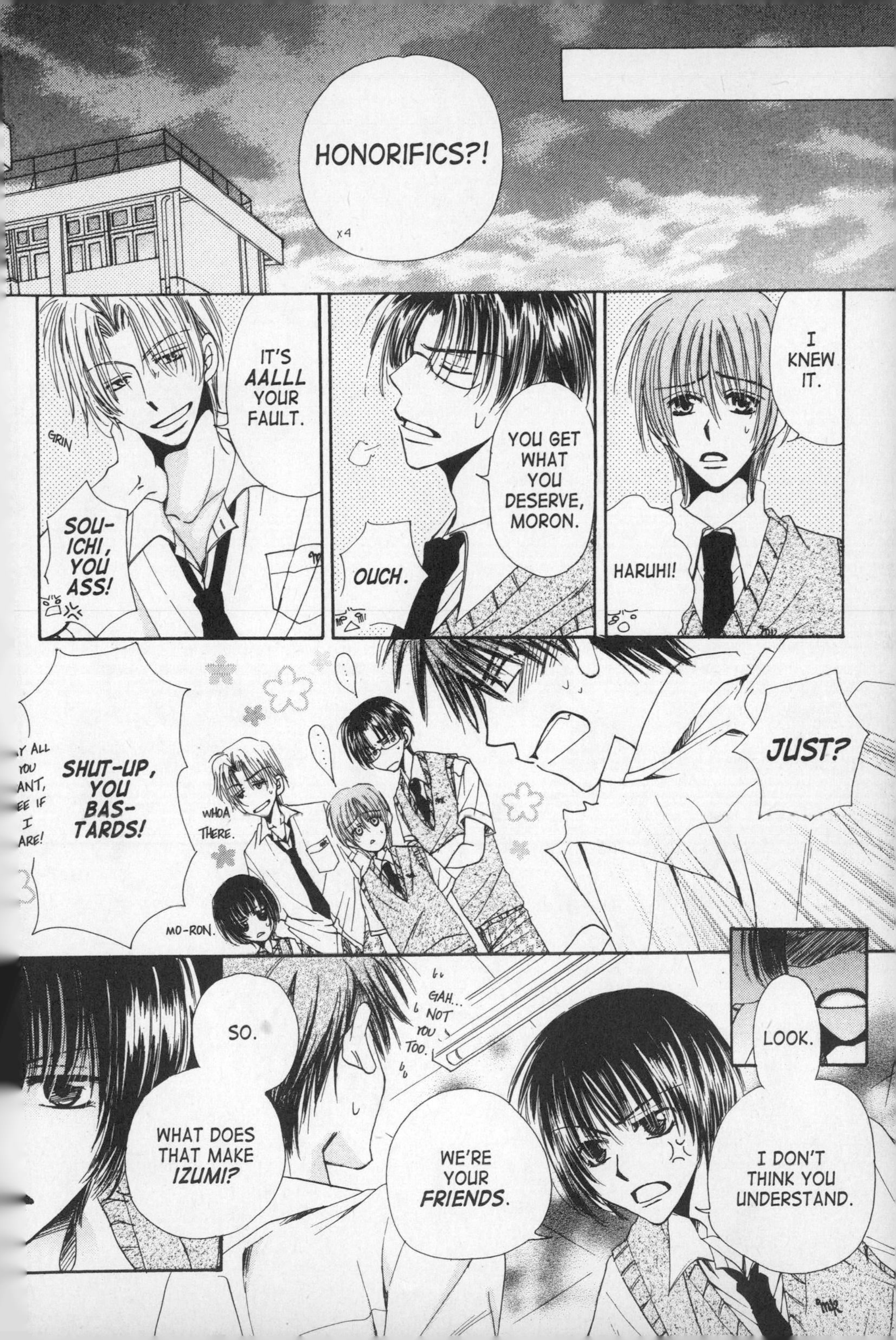
HONORIFICS?!
x4
I KNEW IT.
HARUHI!
YOU GET WHAT YOU DESERVE, MORON.
OUCH.
IT'S AALLL YOUR FAULT.
GRIN
SOU-ICHI, YOU ASS!
JUST?
...
...
SHUT-UP, YOU BASTARDS!
WHOA THERE.
MO-RON.
LOOK.
I DON'T THINK YOU UNDERSTAND.
WE'RE YOUR FRIENDS.
GAH... NOT YOU TOO.
SO.
WHAT DOES THAT MAKE IZUMI?

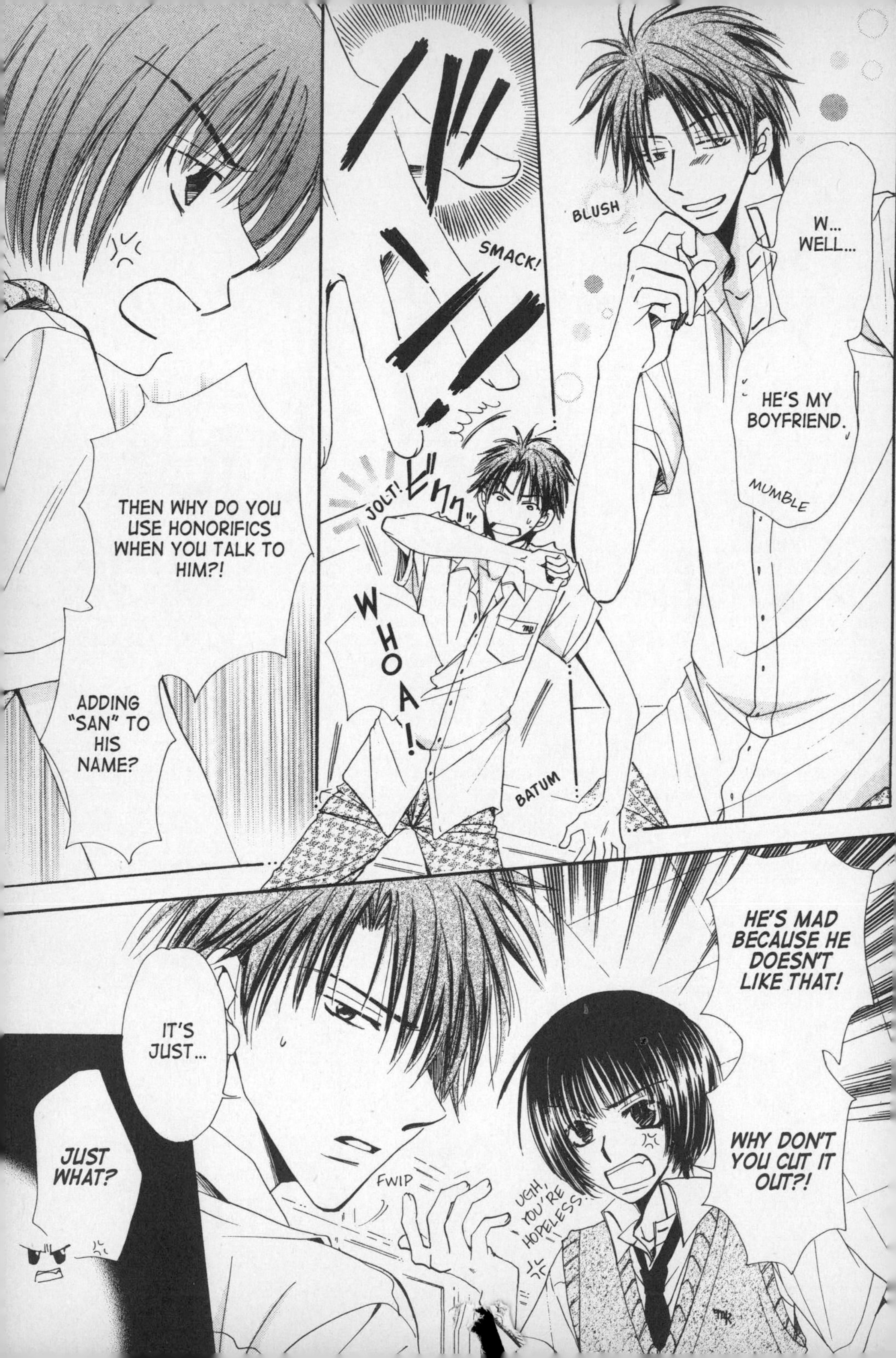
W... WELL...
BLUSH
HE'S MY BOYFRIEND.
MUMBLE
SMACK!
JOLT!
WHOA!
BATUM
THEN WHY DO YOU USE HONORIFICS WHEN YOU TALK TO HIM?!
ADDING "SAN" TO HIS NAME?
HE'S MAD BECAUSE HE DOESN'T LIKE THAT!
WHY DON'T YOU CUT IT OUT?!
UGH, YOU'RE HOPELESS...
IT'S JUST...
FWIP
JUST WHAT?

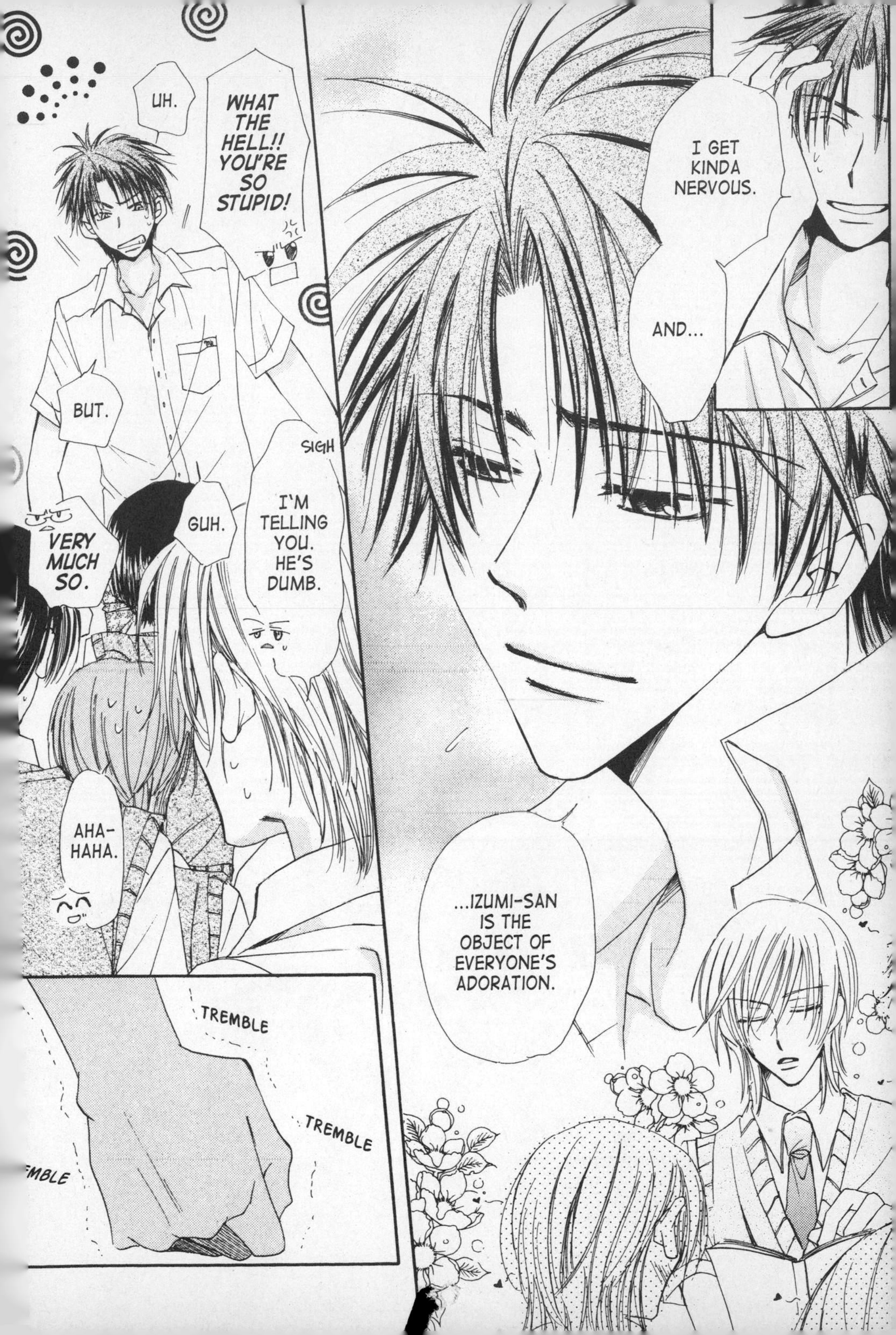
I GET KINDA NERVOUS.
AND...
...IZUMI-SAN IS THE OBJECT OF EVERYONE'S ADORATION.
WHAT THE HELL!! YOU'RE SO STUPID!
UH.
BUT.
SIGH
I'M TELLING YOU. HE'S DUMB.
GUH.
VERY MUCH SO.
AHA-HAHA.
TREMBLE
TREMBLE

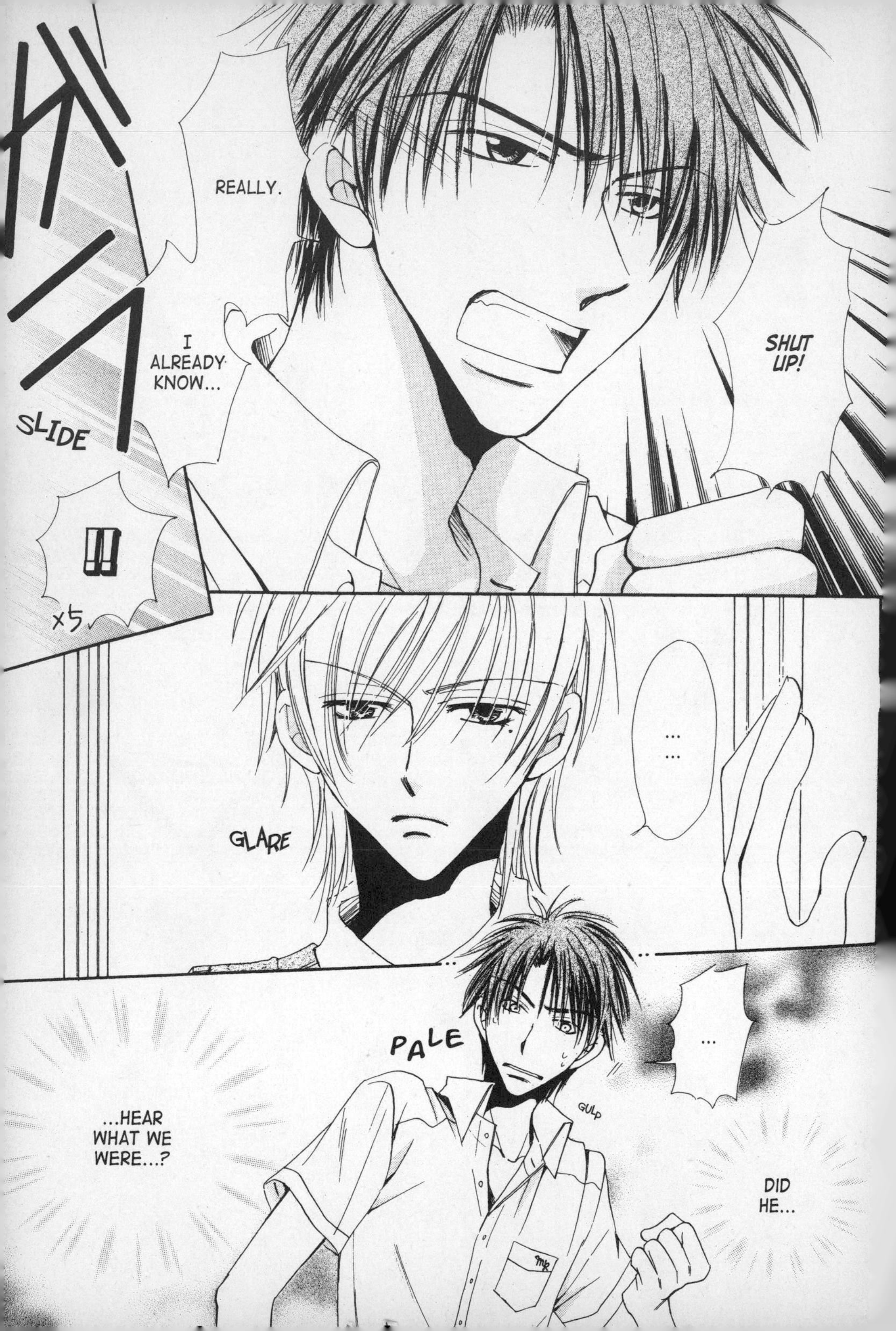

SHUT UP!
REALLY.
I ALREADY KNOW...
SLIDE
!!
x5
......
GLARE
...
PALE
GULP
DID HE...
...HEAR WHAT WE WERE...?

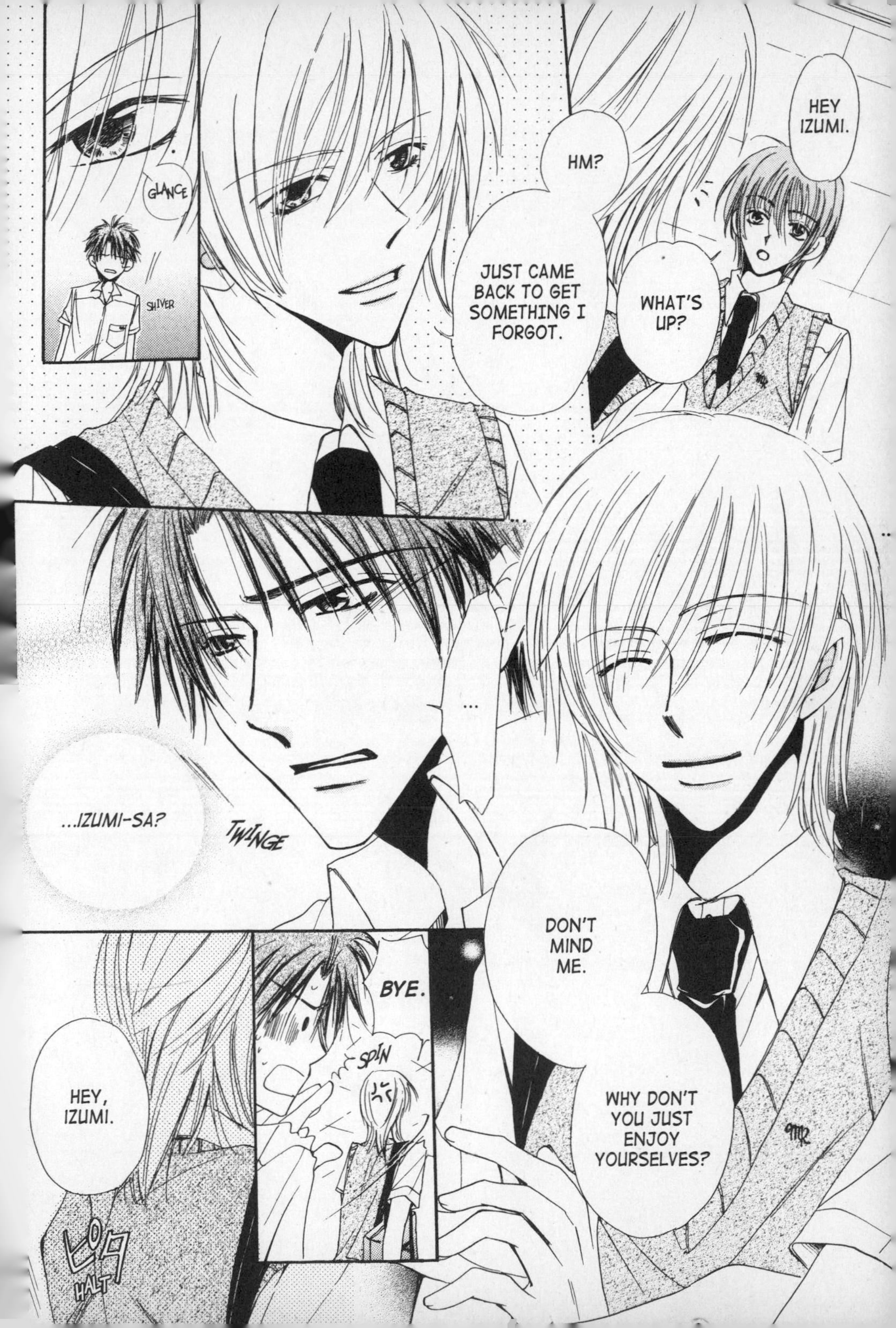
HEY IZUMI.
HM?
WHAT'S UP?
JUST CAME BACK TO GET SOMETHING I FORGOT.
GLANCE
SHIVER
...
DON'T MIND ME.
WHY DON'T YOU JUST ENJOY YOURSELVES?
...IZUMI-SA?
TWINGE
BYE.
SPIN
HEY, IZUMI.
ピタ
HALT!

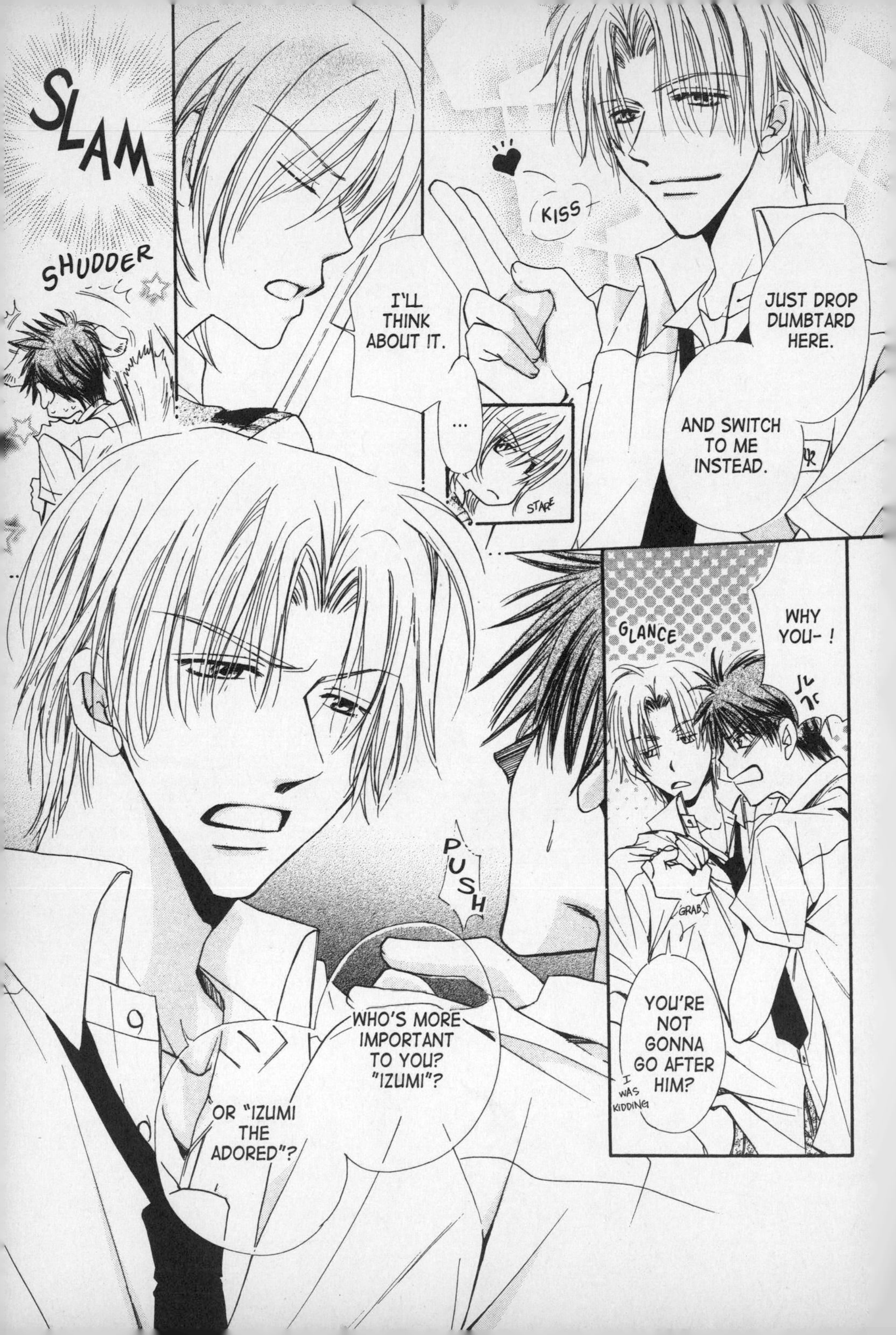
KISS
JUST DROP DUMBTARD HERE.
AND SWITCH TO ME INSTEAD.
...
STARE
I'LL THINK ABOUT IT.
SLAM
SHUDDER
GLANCE
WHY YOU- !
GRAB
YOU'RE NOT GONNA GO AFTER HIM?
I WAS KIDDING
PUSH
WHO'S MORE IMPORTANT TO YOU? "IZUMI"?
OR "IZUMI THE ADORED"?

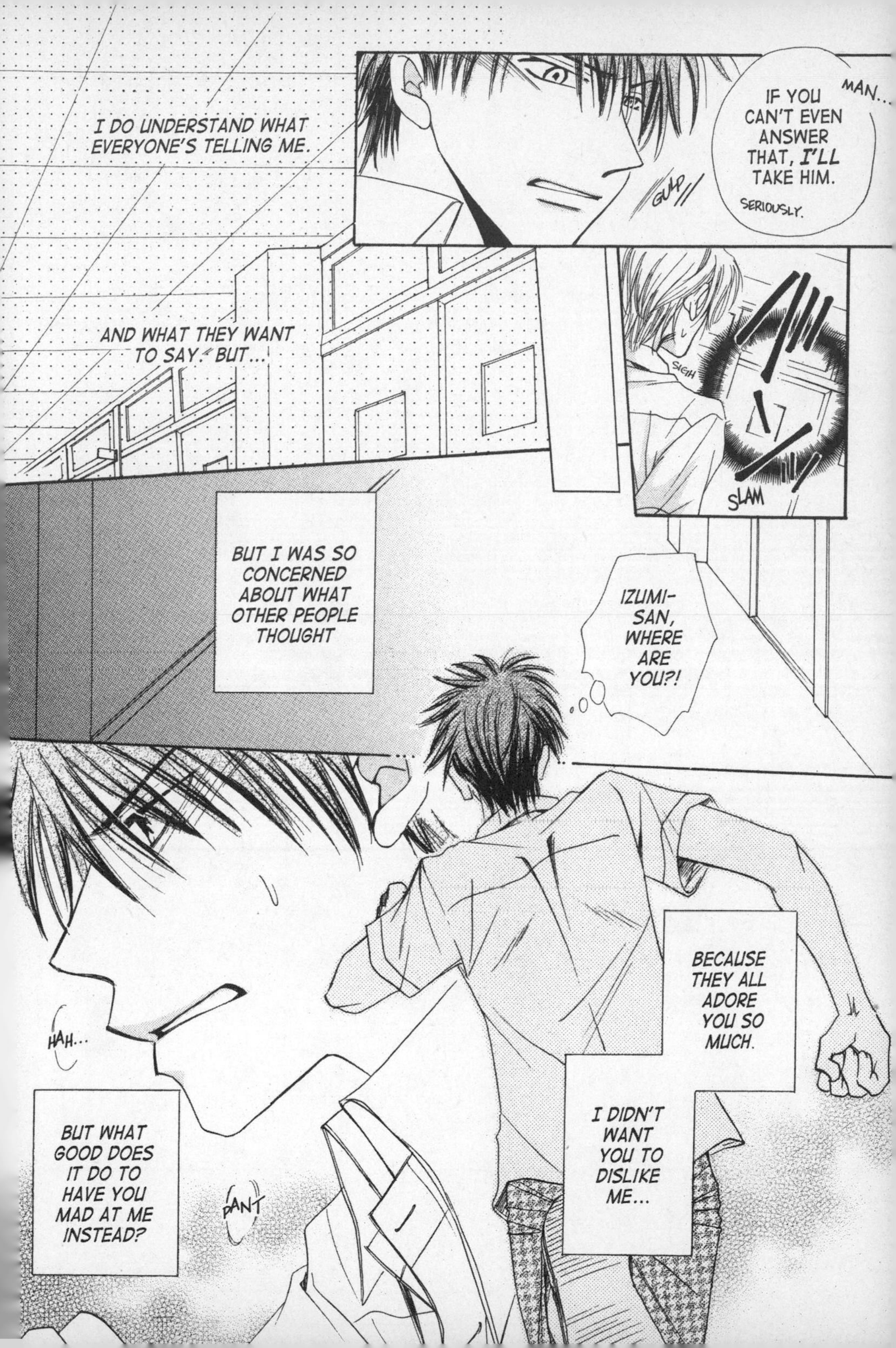
MAN...
IF YOU CAN'T EVEN ANSWER THAT, I'LL TAKE HIM.
SERIOUSLY.
GULP
SIGH
SLAM
I DO UNDERSTAND WHAT EVERYONE'S TELLING ME.
AND WHAT THEY WANT TO SAY. BUT...
IZUMI-SAN, WHERE ARE YOU?!
BUT I WAS SO CONCERNED ABOUT WHAT OTHER PEOPLE THOUGHT
BECAUSE THEY ALL ADORE YOU SO MUCH.
I DIDN'T WANT YOU TO DISLIKE ME...
PANT
HAH...
BUT WHAT GOOD DOES IT DO TO HAVE YOU MAD AT ME INSTEAD?

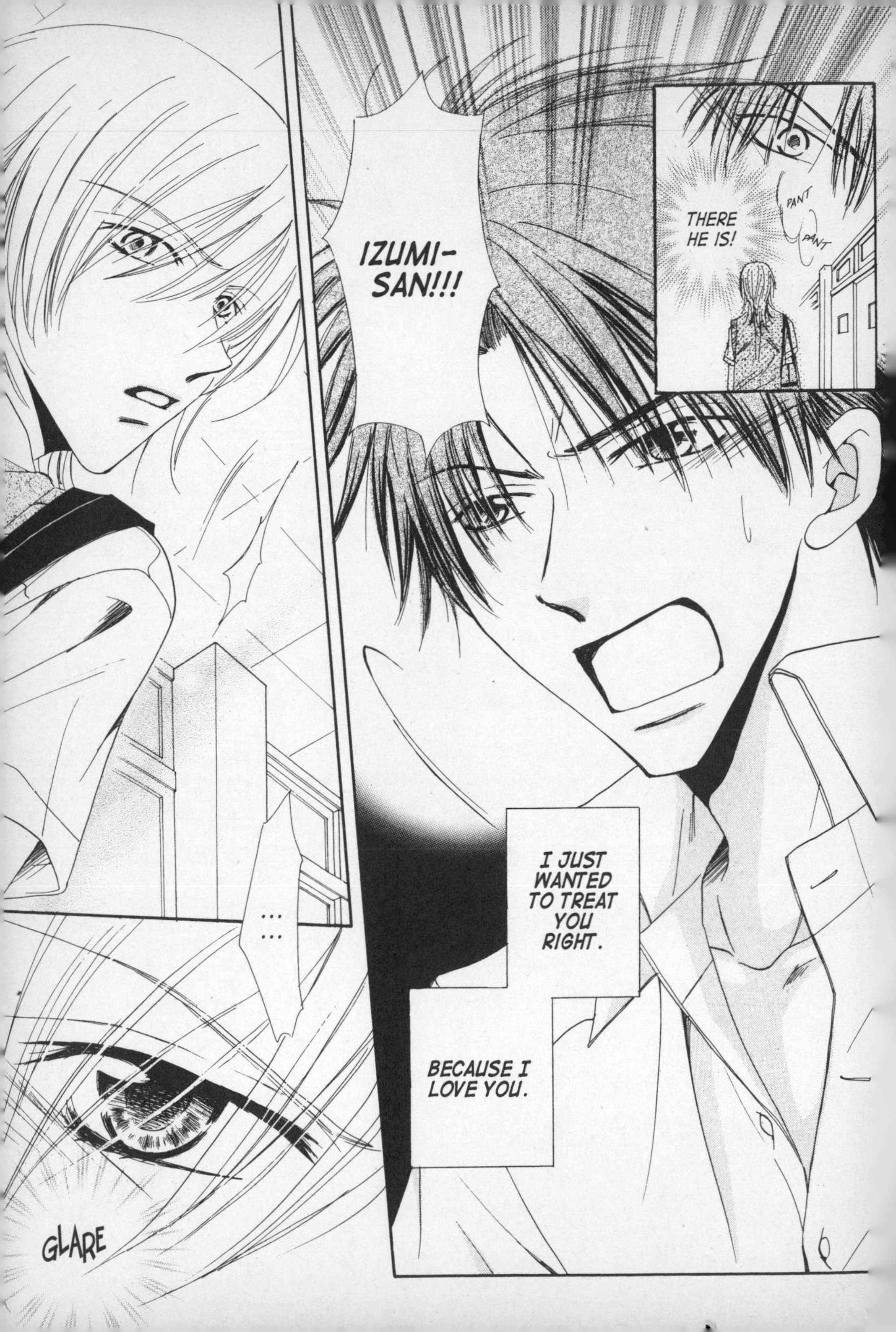
THERE HE IS!
PANT PANT
IZUMI-SAN!!!
I JUST WANTED TO TREAT YOU RIGHT.
BECAUSE I LOVE YOU.
...
...
GLARE

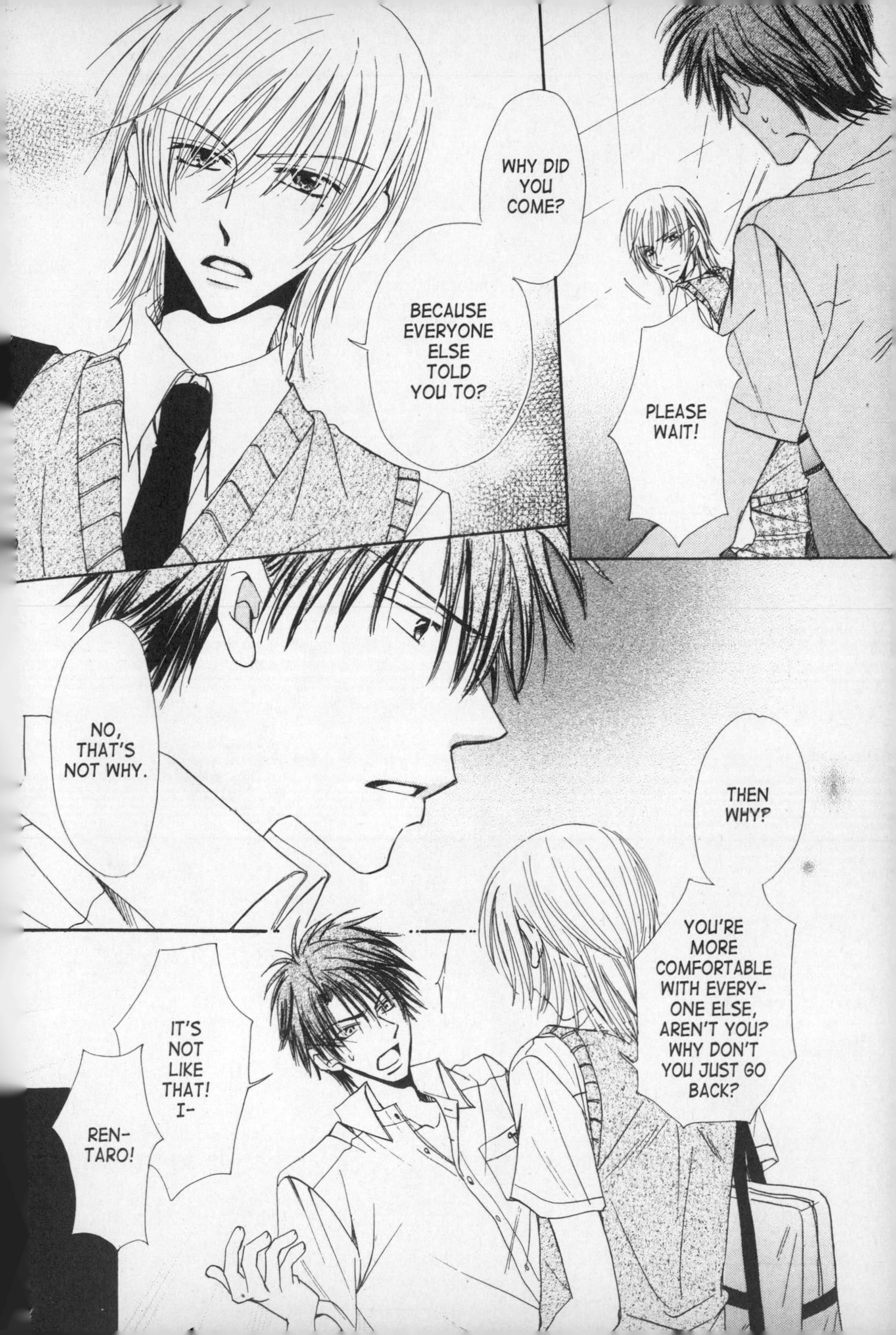
PLEASE WAIT!
WHY DID YOU COME?
BECAUSE EVERYONE ELSE TOLD YOU TO?
NO, THAT'S NOT WHY.
THEN WHY?
YOU'RE MORE COMFORTABLE WITH EVERY-ONE ELSE, AREN'T YOU? WHY DON'T YOU JUST GO BACK?
IT'S NOT LIKE THAT! I-
REN-TARO!

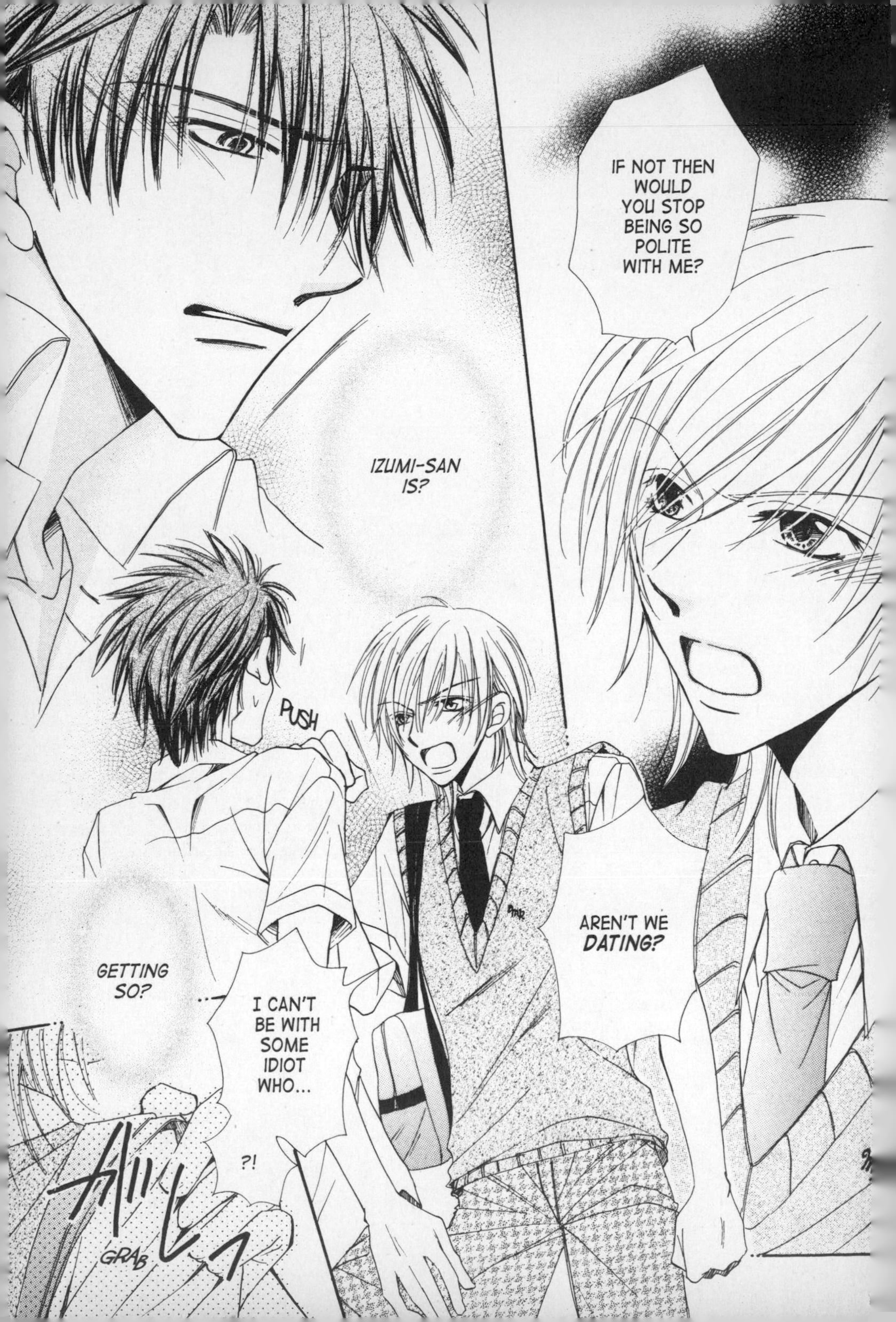
IF NOT THEN WOULD YOU STOP BEING SO POLITE WITH ME?
AREN'T WE *DATING?*
IZUMI-SAN IS?
PUSH
GETTING SO?
I CAN'T BE WITH SOME IDIOT WHO...
?!
GRAB

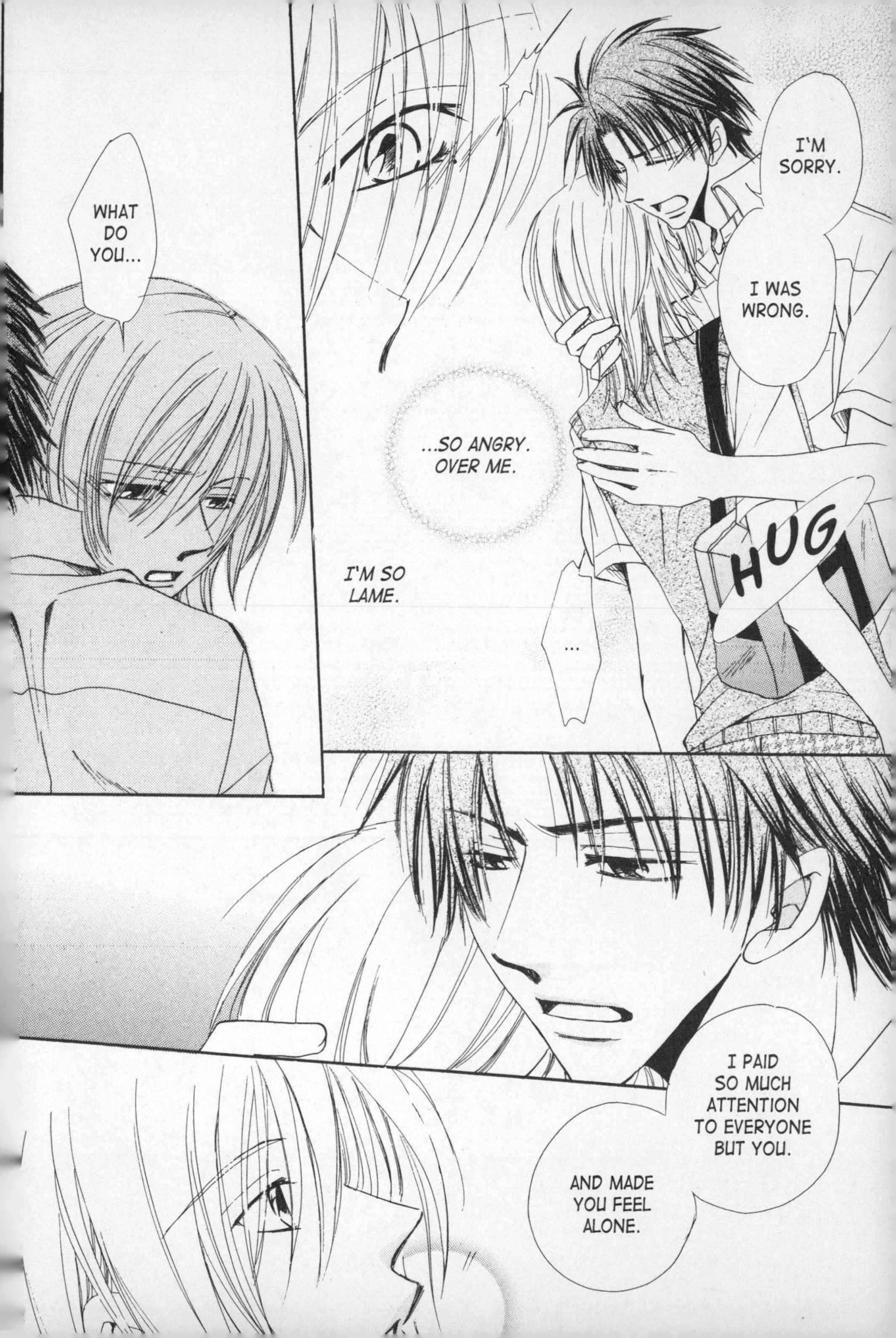
I'M SORRY.
I WAS WRONG.
HUG
...
...SO ANGRY. OVER ME.
I'M SO LAME.
WHAT DO YOU...
I PAID SO MUCH ATTENTION TO EVERYONE BUT YOU.
AND MADE YOU FEEL ALONE.

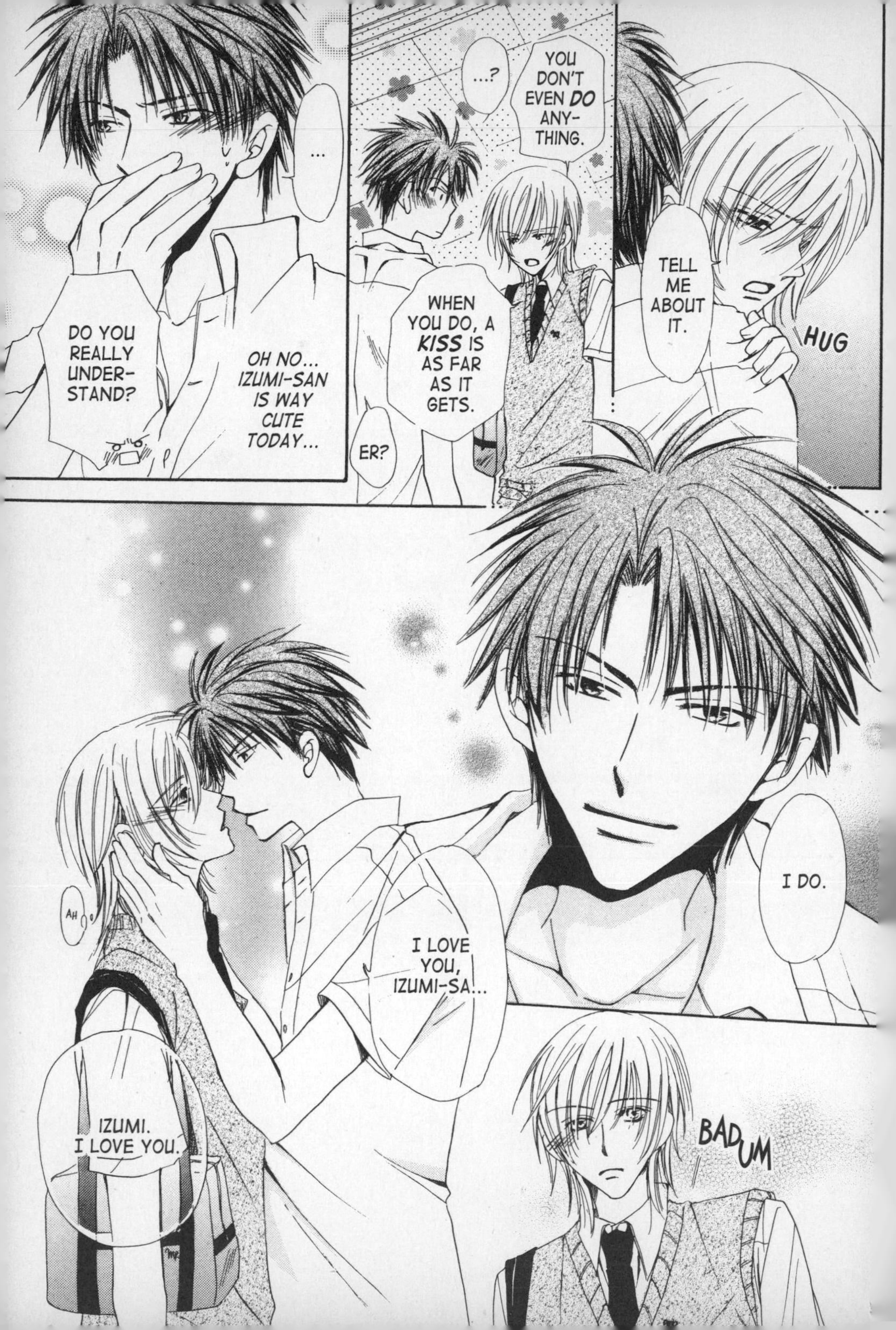
TELL ME ABOUT IT.
HUG
YOU DON'T EVEN DO ANY-THING.
...?
WHEN YOU DO, A KISS IS AS FAR AS IT GETS.
ER?
...
OH NO... IZUMI-SAN IS WAY CUTE TODAY...
DO YOU REALLY UNDER-STAND?
I DO.
BADUM
I LOVE YOU, IZUMI-SA...
AH
IZUMI. I LOVE YOU.

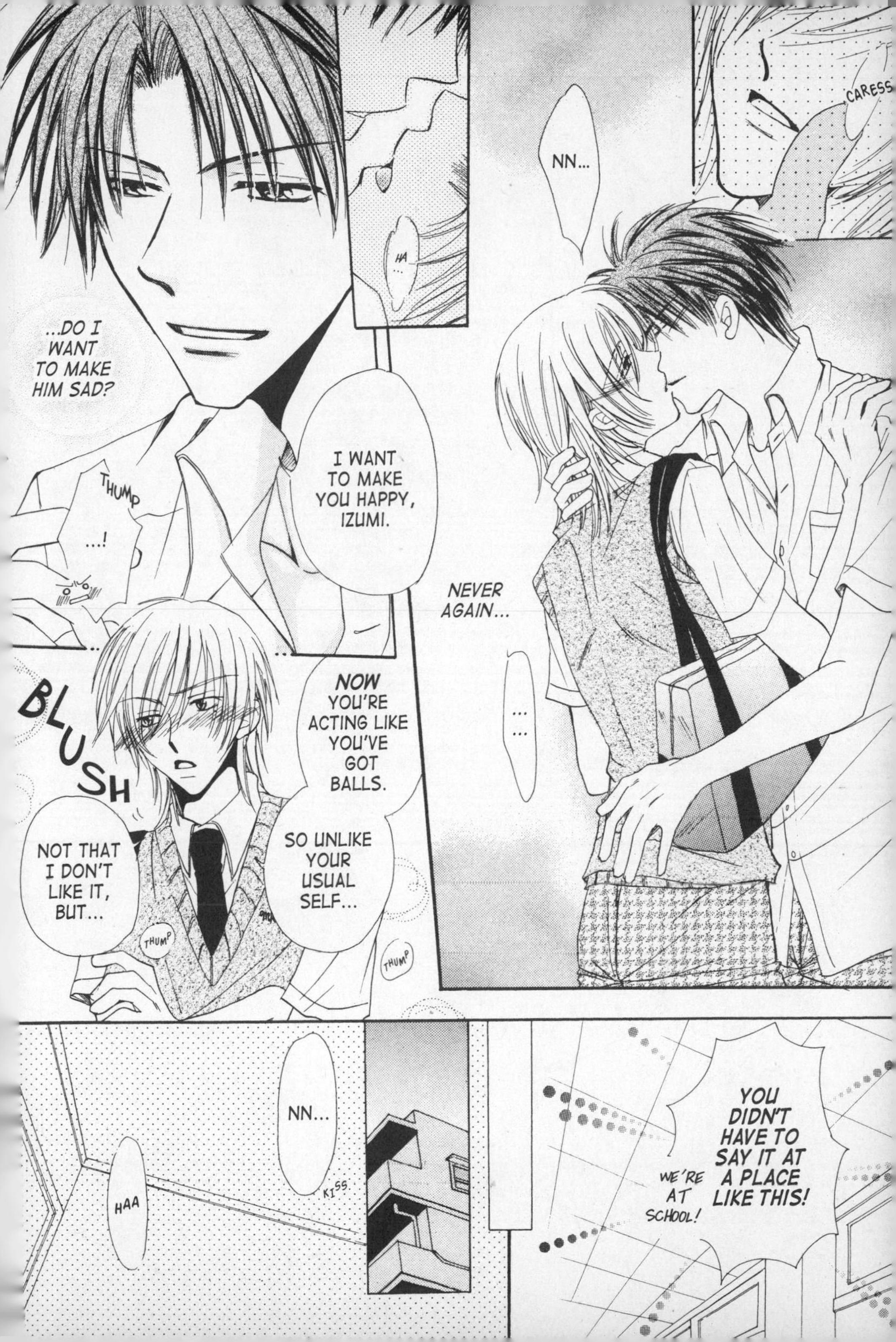
CARESS
NN...
NEVER AGAIN...
... ...
HA ...
...DO I WANT TO MAKE HIM SAD?
I WANT TO MAKE YOU HAPPY, IZUMI.
THUMP
...!
NOW YOU'RE ACTING LIKE YOU'VE GOT BALLS.
SO UNLIKE YOUR USUAL SELF...
BLUSH
NOT THAT I DON'T LIKE IT, BUT...
THUMP
THUMP
YOU DIDN'T HAVE TO SAY IT AT A PLACE LIKE THIS!
WE'RE AT SCHOOL!
NN...
KISS.
HAA

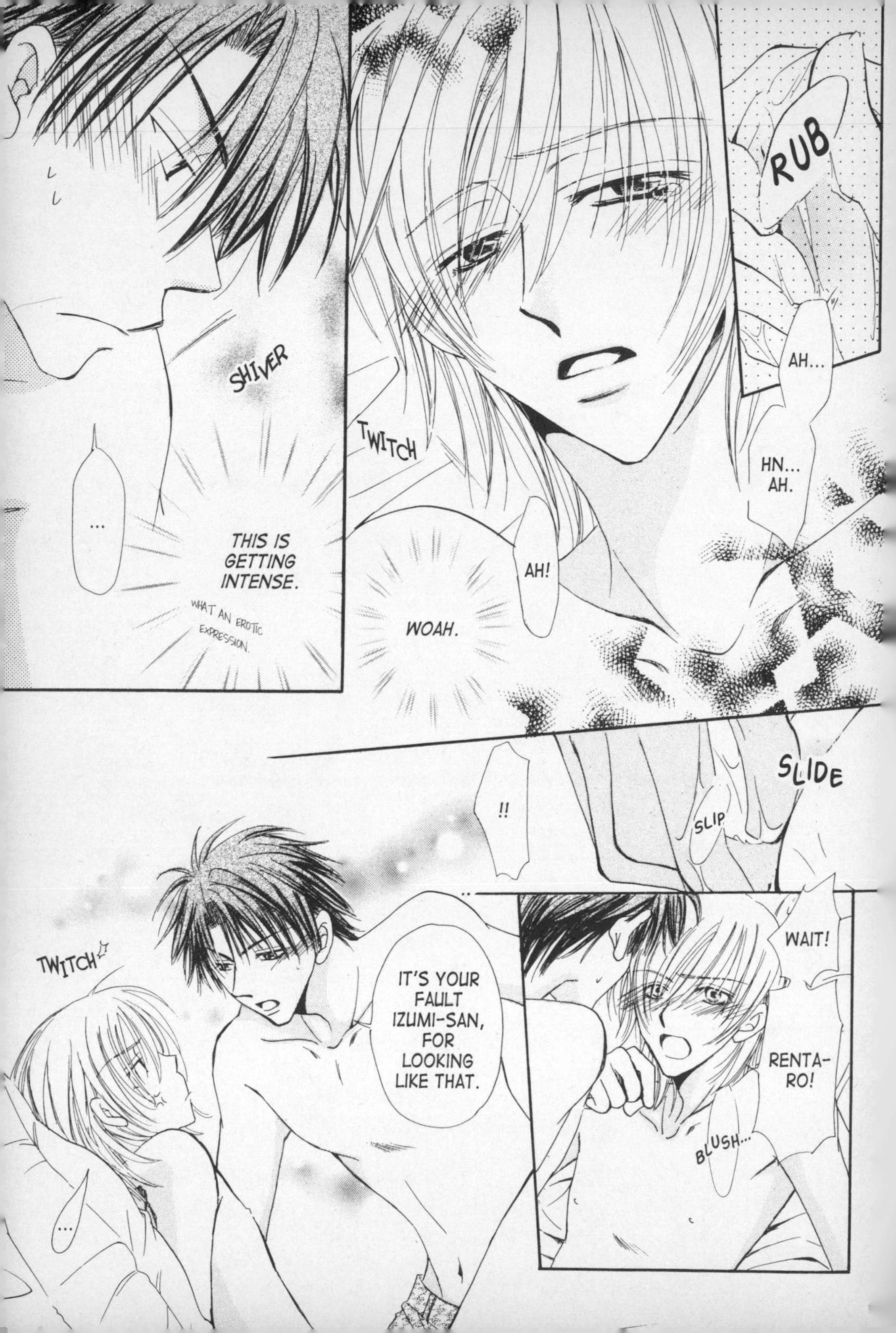
RUB
AH...
HN... AH.
TWITCH
AH!
WOAH.
SHIVER
...
THIS IS GETTING INTENSE.
WHAT AN EROTIC EXPRESSION.
SLIDE
SLIP
!!
WAIT!
RENTARO!
BLUSH...
TWITCH
IT'S YOUR FAULT IZUMI-SAN, FOR LOOKING LIKE THAT.
...

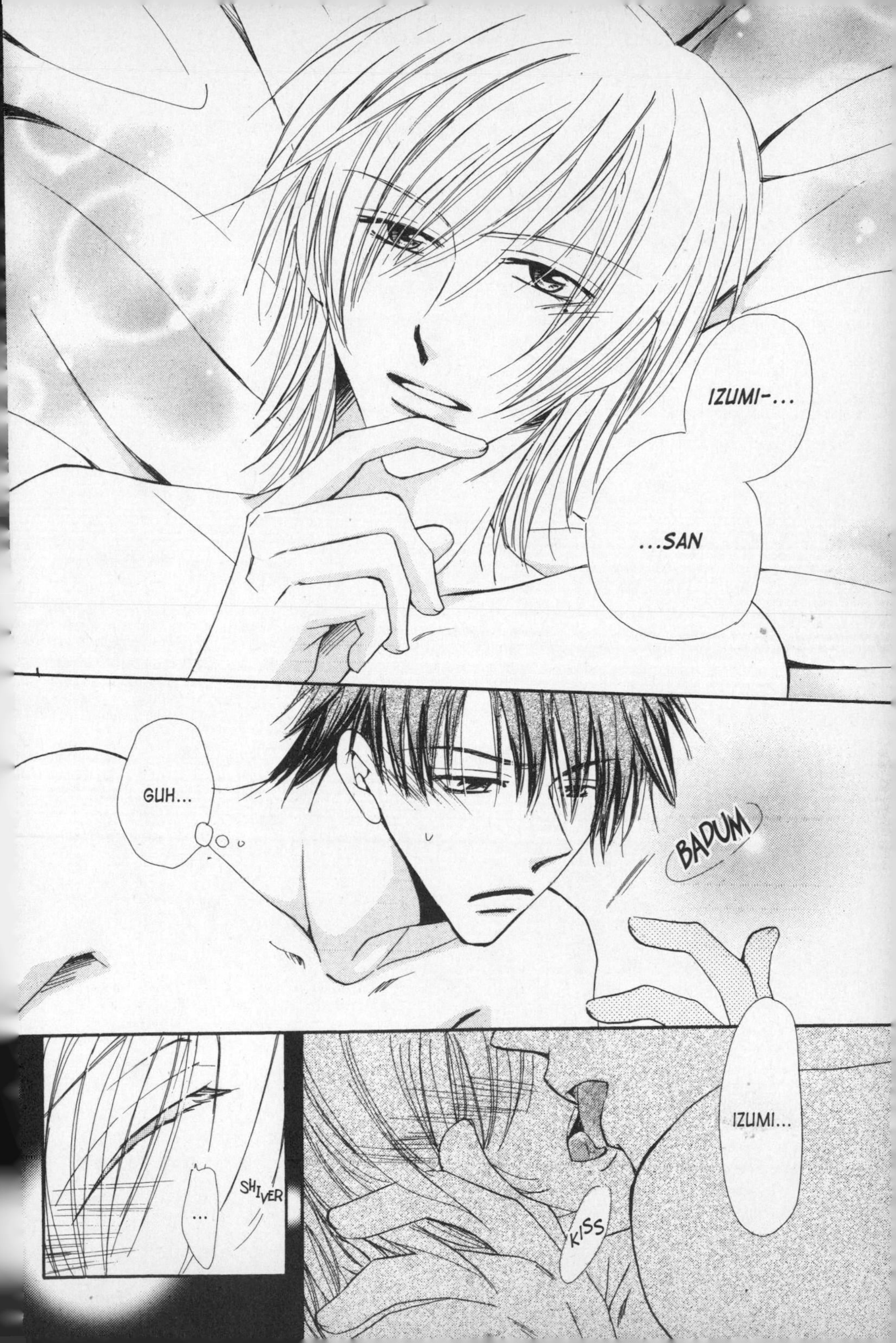
IZUMI-...
...SAN
BADUM
GUH...
IZUMI...
KISS
SHIVER
...

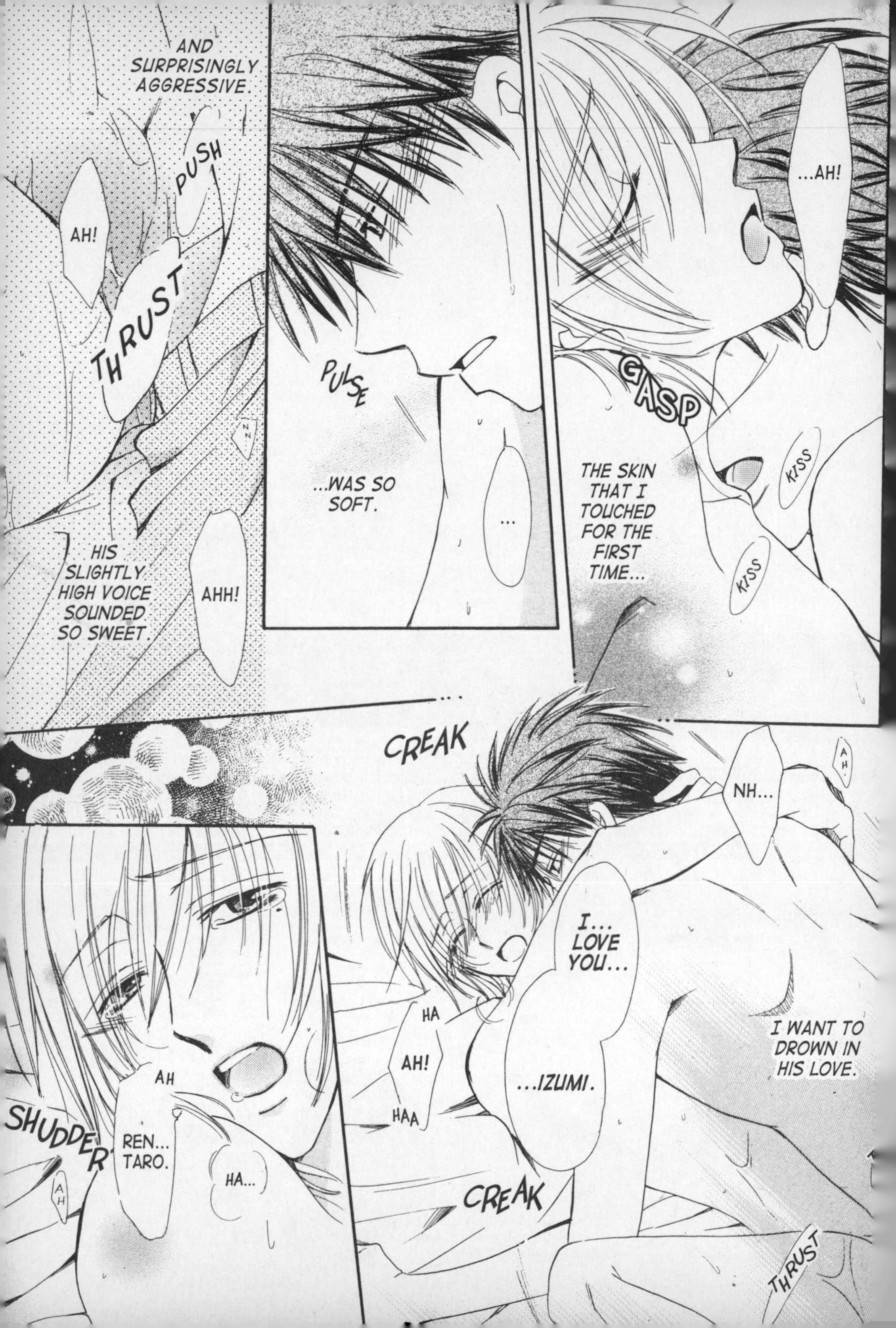
...AH!
GASP
THE SKIN THAT I TOUCHED FOR THE FIRST TIME...
KISS
KISS
PULSE
...WAS SO SOFT.
...
AND SURPRISINGLY AGGRESSIVE.
PUSH
AH!
THRUST
NN
HIS SLIGHTLY HIGH VOICE SOUNDED SO SWEET.
AHH!
...
AH
NH...
CREAK
I... LOVE YOU...
I WANT TO DROWN IN HIS LOVE.
HA
AH!
HAA
...IZUMI.
CREAK
THRUST
AH
SHUDDER
REN... TARO.
HA...
AH

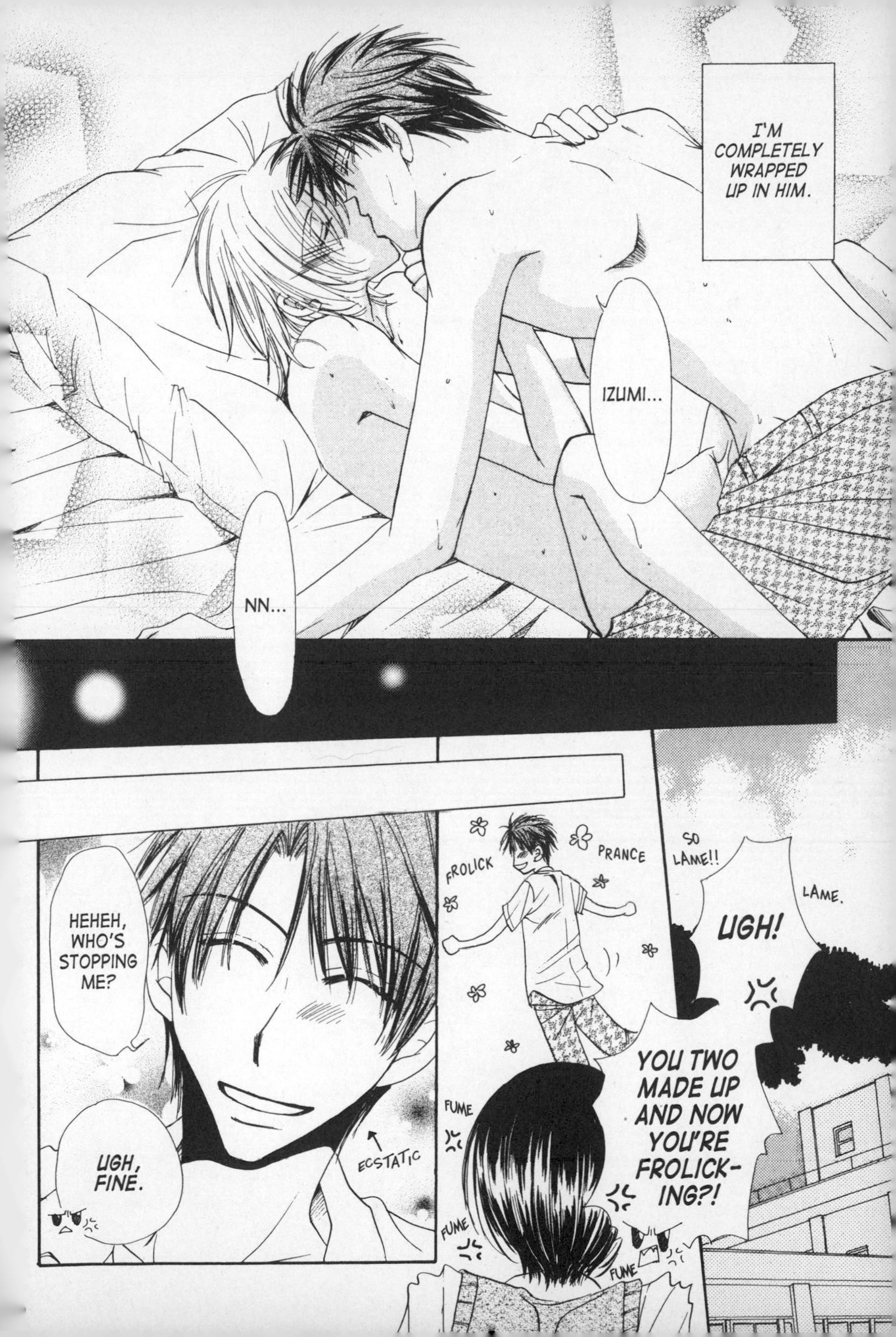
I'M COMPLETELY WRAPPED UP IN HIM.
IZUMI...
NN...
SO LAME!!
LAME.
UGH!
PRANCE
FROLICK
YOU TWO MADE UP AND NOW YOU'RE FROLICK-ING?!
FUME
FUME
FUME
HEHEH, WHO'S STOPPING ME?
ECSTATIC
UGH, FINE.

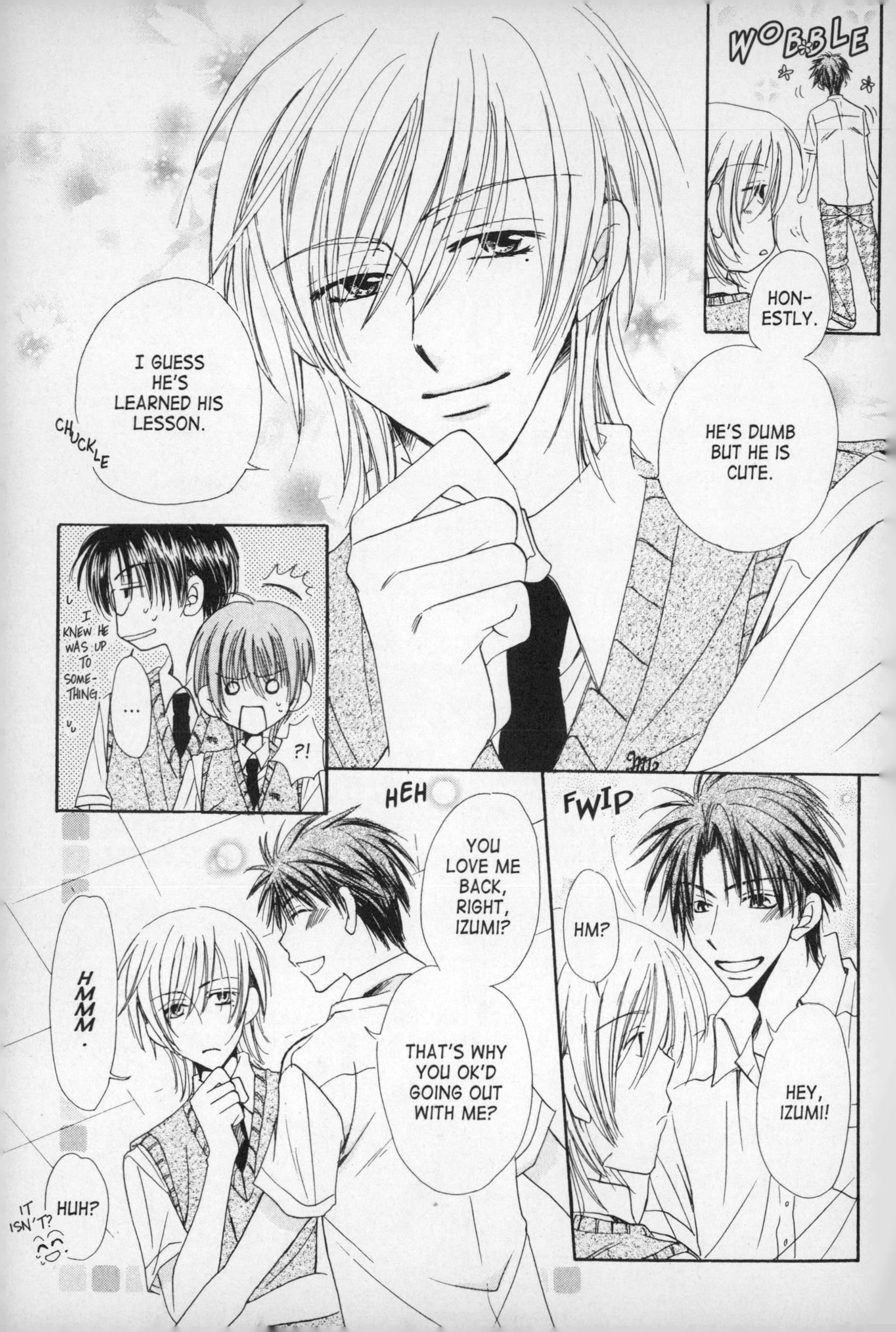
WOBBLE
HON-ESTLY.
HE'S DUMB BUT HE IS CUTE.
I GUESS HE'S LEARNED HIS LESSON.
CHUCKLE
?!
...
I KNEW HE WAS UP TO SOME-THING.
FWIP
HEY, IZUMI!
HM?
HEH
YOU LOVE ME BACK, RIGHT, IZUMI?
THAT'S WHY YOU OK'D GOING OUT WITH ME?
HMMM.
HUH?
IT ISN'T?

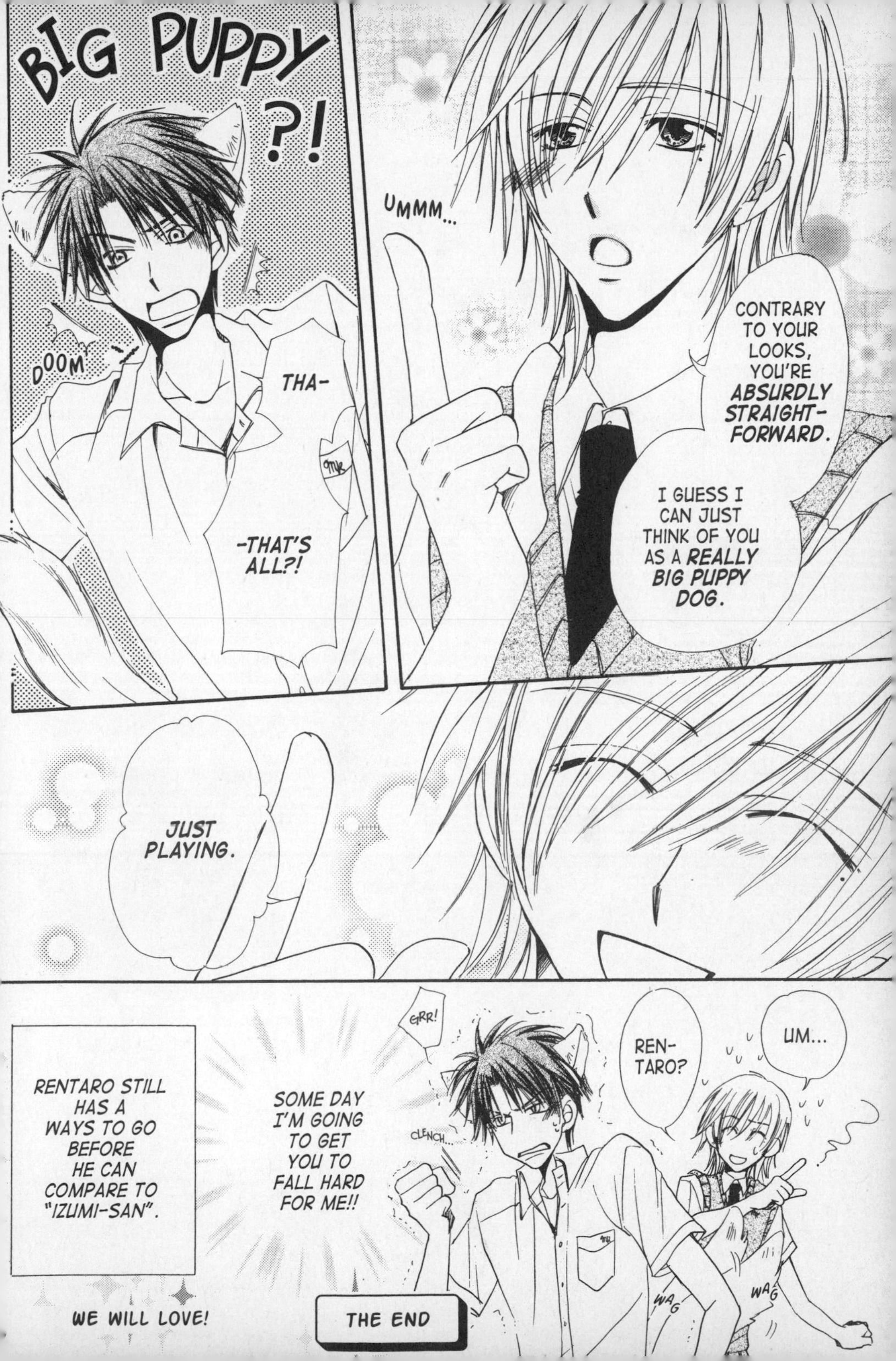
UMMM...
CONTRARY TO YOUR LOOKS, YOU'RE ABSURDLY STRAIGHT-FORWARD.
I GUESS I CAN JUST THINK OF YOU AS A REALLY BIG PUPPY DOG.
BIG PUPPY ?!
DOOM
THA-
-THAT'S ALL?!
JUST PLAYING.
UM...
REN-TARO?
GRR!
CLENCH...
WAG
WAG
SOME DAY I'M GOING TO GET YOU TO FALL HARD FOR ME!!
RENTARO STILL HAS A WAYS TO GO BEFORE HE CAN COMPARE TO "IZUMI-SAN".
THE END
WE WILL LOVE!

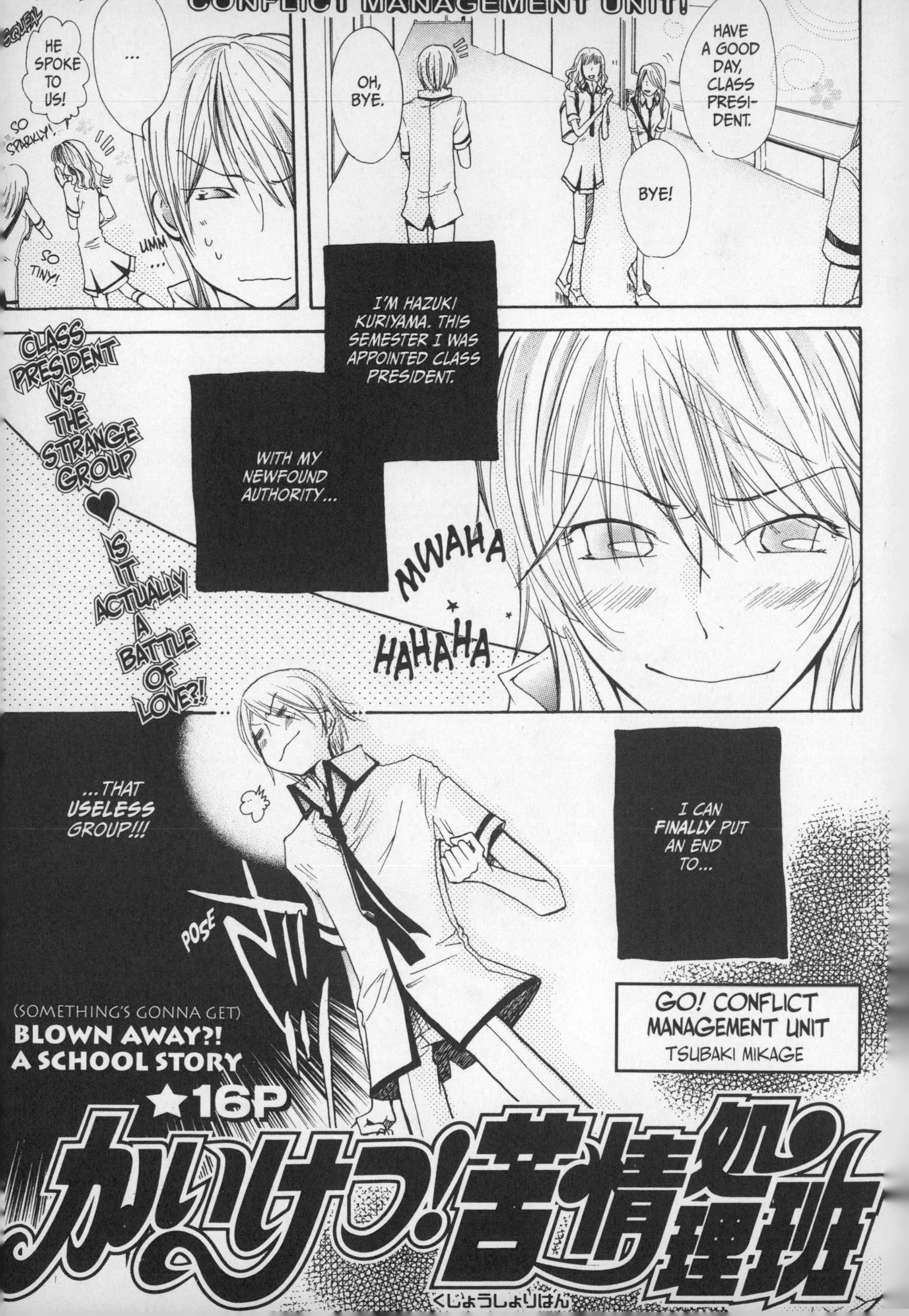
HAVE A GOOD DAY, CLASS PRESI-DENT.
BYE!
OH, BYE.
...
SQUEAL
SQUEAL
HE SPOKE TO US!
SO SPARKLY!
SO TINY!
UMM ...
I'M HAZUKI KURIYAMA. THIS SEMESTER I WAS APPOINTED CLASS PRESIDENT.
WITH MY NEWFOUND AUTHORITY...
MWAHA
HAHAHA
CLASS PRESIDENT VS. THE STRANGE GROUP ♥ IS IT ACTUALLY A BATTLE OF LOVE?!
I CAN FINALLY PUT AN END TO...
...THAT USELESS GROUP!!!
POSE
GO! CONFLICT MANAGEMENT UNIT
TSUBAKI MIKAGE
(SOMETHING'S GONNA GET) BLOWN AWAY?! A SCHOOL STORY
★16P
かいけつ!苦情処理班
くじょうしょりはん

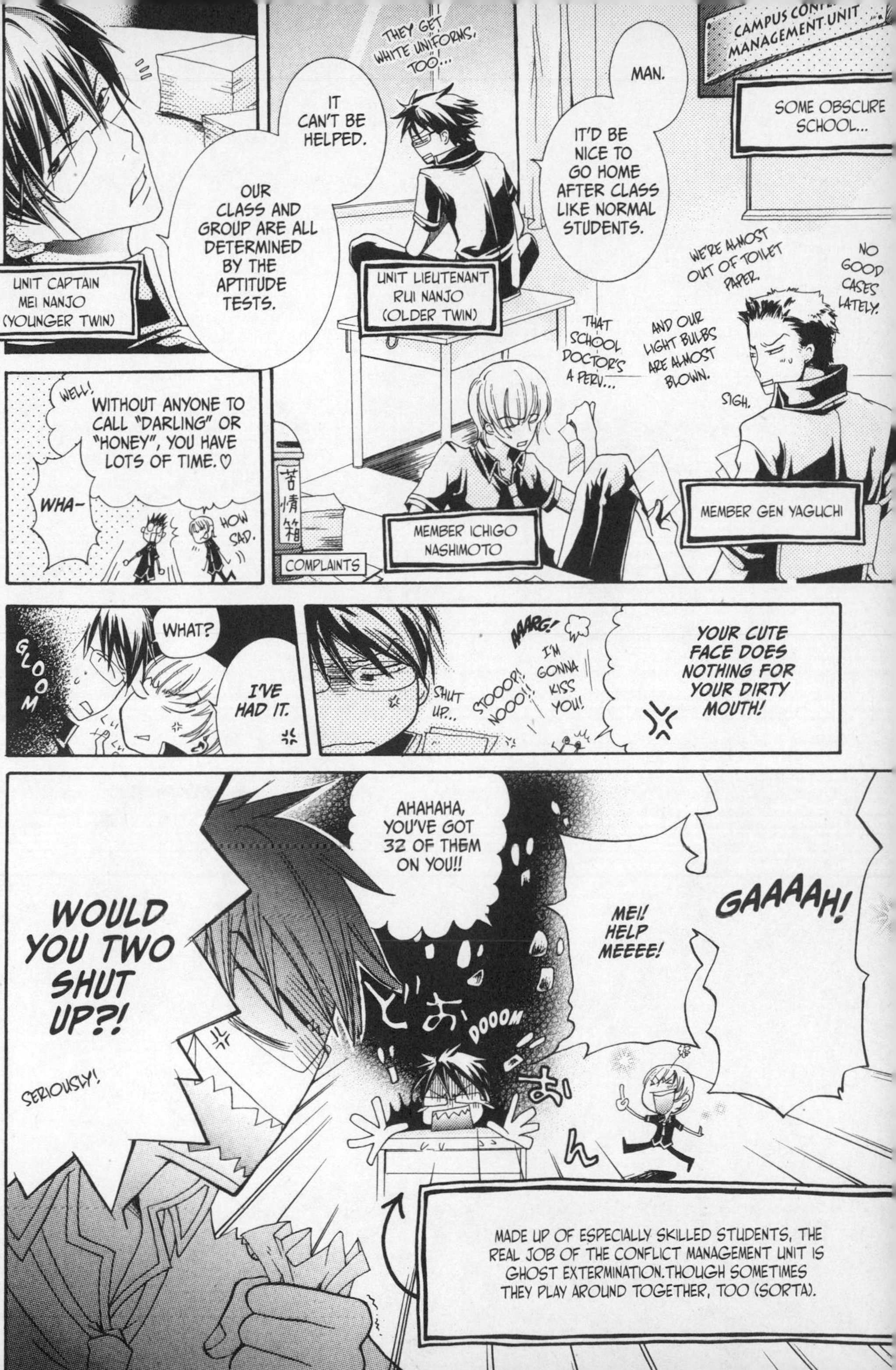
CAMPUS CON... MANAGEMENT UNIT
SOME OBSCURE SCHOOL...
MAN.
IT'D BE NICE TO GO HOME AFTER CLASS LIKE NORMAL STUDENTS.
THEY GET WHITE UNIFORMS, TOO...
IT CAN'T BE HELPED.
OUR CLASS AND GROUP ARE ALL DETERMINED BY THE APTITUDE TESTS.
NO GOOD CASES LATELY.
WE'RE ALMOST OUT OF TOILET PAPER.
UNIT LIEUTENANT RUI NANJO (OLDER TWIN)
AND OUR LIGHT BULBS ARE ALMOST BLOWN.
THAT SCHOOL DOCTOR'S A PERV...
SIGH.
MEMBER GEN YAGUCHI
MEMBER ICHIGO NASHIMOTO
苦情箱
COMPLAINTS
UNIT CAPTAIN MEI NANJO (YOUNGER TWIN)
WELL! WITHOUT ANYONE TO CALL "DARLING" OR "HONEY", YOU HAVE LOTS OF TIME. ♡
HOW SAD.
WHA-
YOUR CUTE FACE DOES NOTHING FOR YOUR DIRTY MOUTH!
AAARG!
I'M GONNA KISS YOU!
STOOOP!! NOOO!!
SHUT UP...
WHAT?
I'VE HAD IT.
GLOOM
GAAAAH!
AHAHAHA, YOU'VE GOT 32 OF THEM ON YOU!!
MEI! HELP MEEEE!
WOULD YOU TWO SHUT UP?!
DOOOM
SERIOUSLY!
MADE UP OF ESPECIALLY SKILLED STUDENTS, THE REAL JOB OF THE CONFLICT MANAGEMENT UNIT IS GHOST EXTERMINATION. THOUGH SOMETIMES THEY PLAY AROUND TOGETHER, TOO (SORTA).

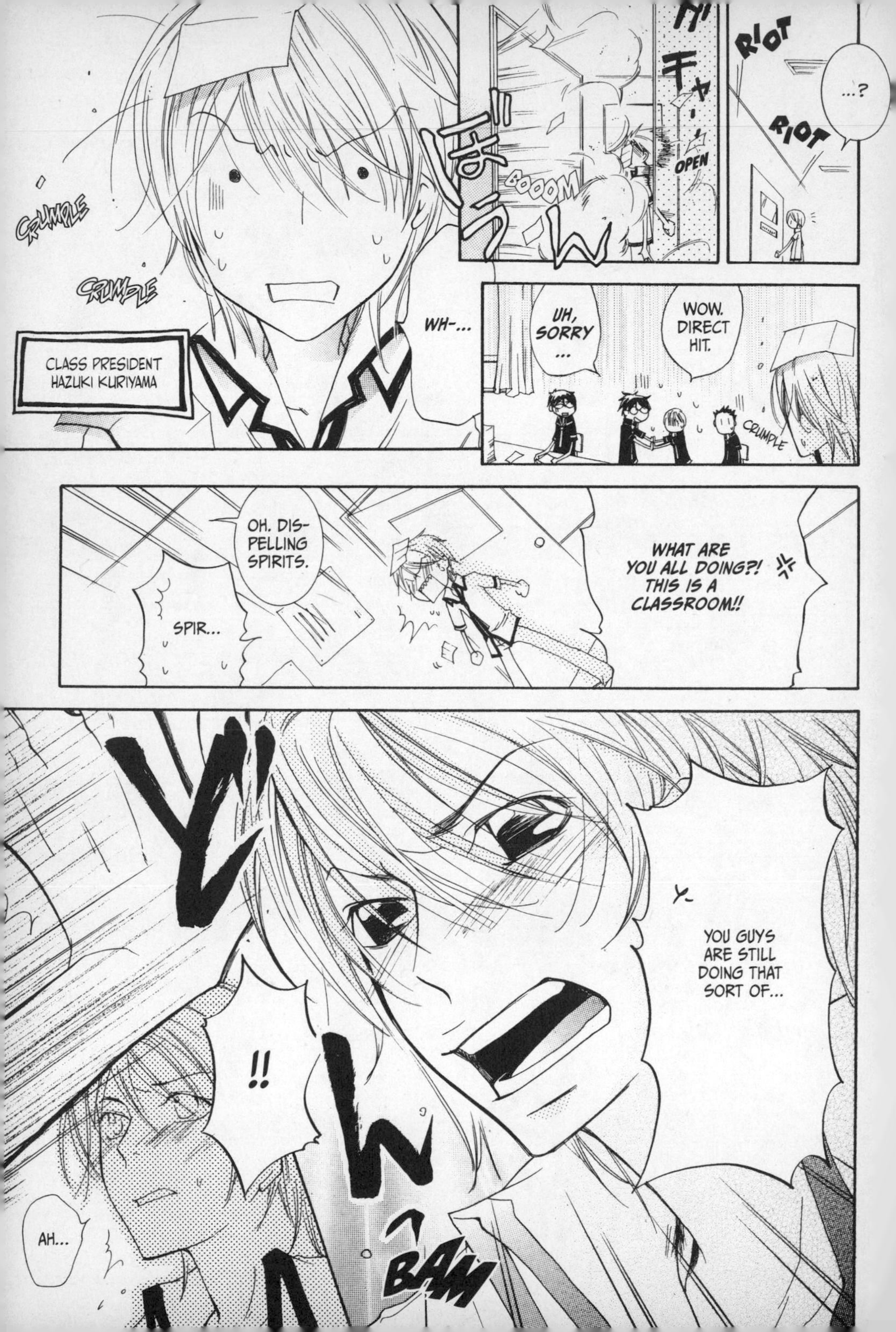
RIOT
RIOT
...?
ガチャ
OPEN
ぼうん
BOOOM
WOW. DIRECT HIT.
UH, SORRY ...
CRUMPLE
WH-...
CRUMPLE
CRUMPLE
CLASS PRESIDENT HAZUKI KURIYAMA
WHAT ARE YOU ALL DOING?! THIS IS A CLASSROOM!!
OH. DIS-PELLING SPIRITS.
SPIR...
Y-
YOU GUYS ARE STILL DOING THAT SORT OF...
!!
BAM
AH...

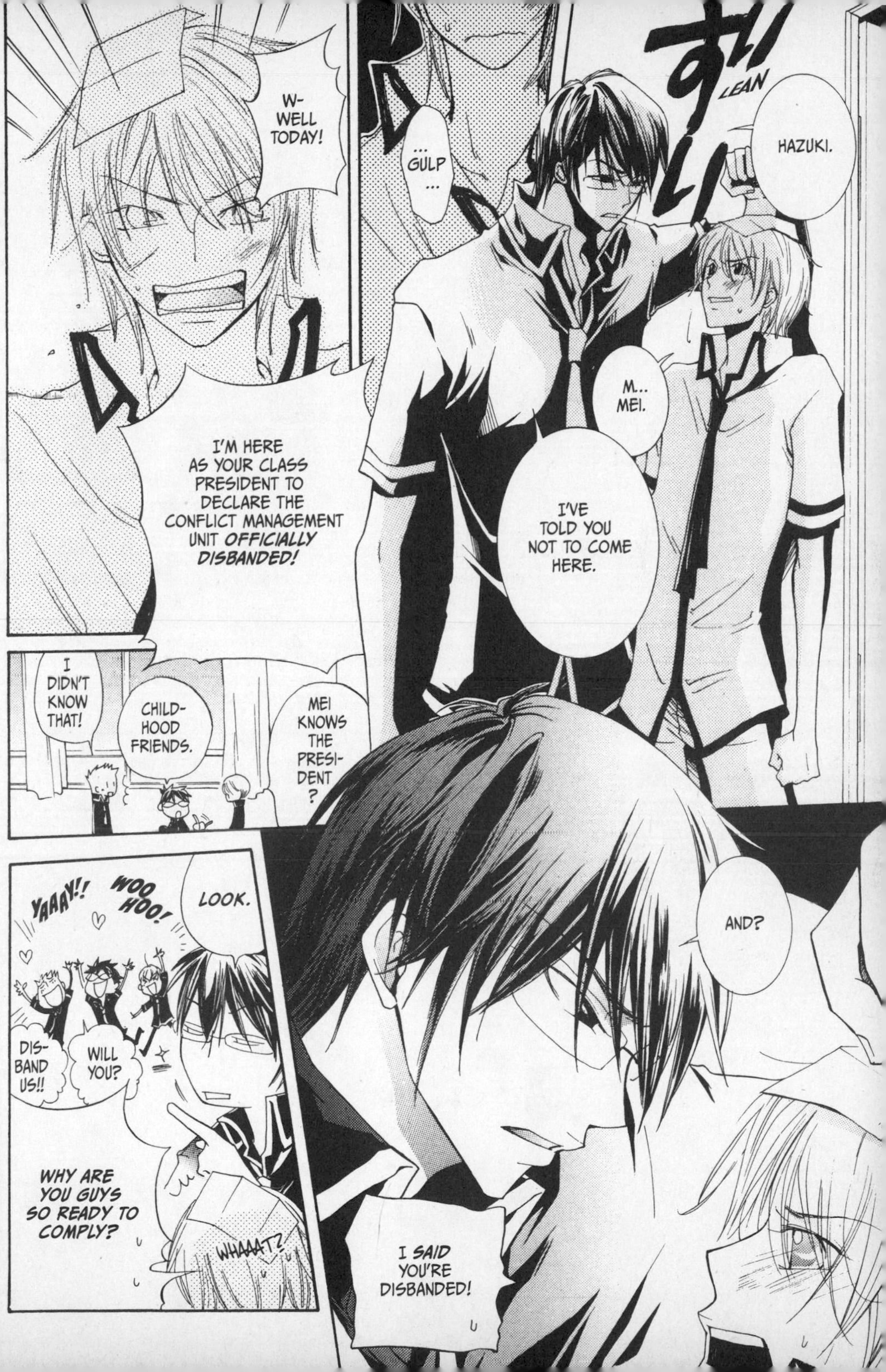

LEAN
HAZUKI.
... GULP ...
M... MEI.
I'VE TOLD YOU NOT TO COME HERE.
W-WELL TODAY!
I'M HERE AS YOUR CLASS PRESIDENT TO DECLARE THE CONFLICT MANAGEMENT UNIT *OFFICIALLY DISBANDED!*
MEI KNOWS THE PRESI-DENT?
CHILD-HOOD FRIENDS.
I DIDN'T KNOW THAT!
AND?
I SAID YOU'RE DISBANDED!
LOOK.
WOO HOO!
YAAAY!!
WILL YOU?
DIS-BAND US!!
WHY ARE YOU GUYS SO READY TO COMPLY?
WHAAAT?

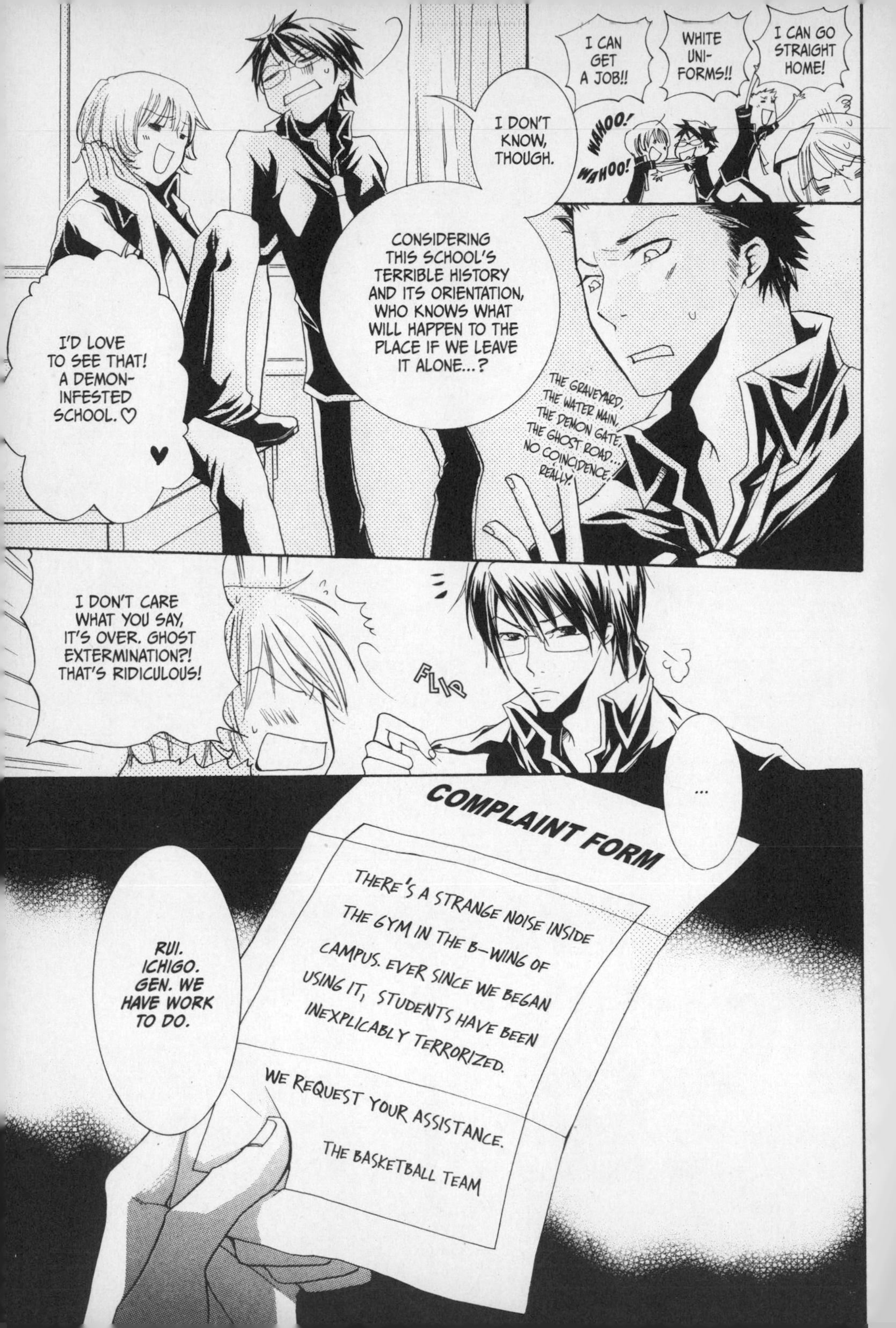
I CAN GO STRAIGHT HOME!
WHITE UNI-FORMS!!
I CAN GET A JOB!!
WAHOO!
WAHOO!
I DON'T KNOW, THOUGH.
CONSIDERING THIS SCHOOL'S TERRIBLE HISTORY AND ITS ORIENTATION, WHO KNOWS WHAT WILL HAPPEN TO THE PLACE IF WE LEAVE IT ALONE...?
THE GRAVEYARD, THE WATER MAIN, THE DEMON GATE, THE GHOST ROAD... NO COINCIDENCE, REALLY.
I'D LOVE TO SEE THAT! A DEMON-INFESTED SCHOOL. ♡
I DON'T CARE WHAT YOU SAY, IT'S OVER. GHOST EXTERMINATION?! THAT'S RIDICULOUS!
FLIP
...
COMPLAINT FORM
THERE'S A STRANGE NOISE INSIDE THE GYM IN THE B-WING OF CAMPUS. EVER SINCE WE BEGAN USING IT, STUDENTS HAVE BEEN INEXPLICABLY TERRORIZED.
WE REQUEST YOUR ASSISTANCE.
THE BASKETBALL TEAM
RUI. ICHIGO. GEN. WE HAVE WORK TO DO.

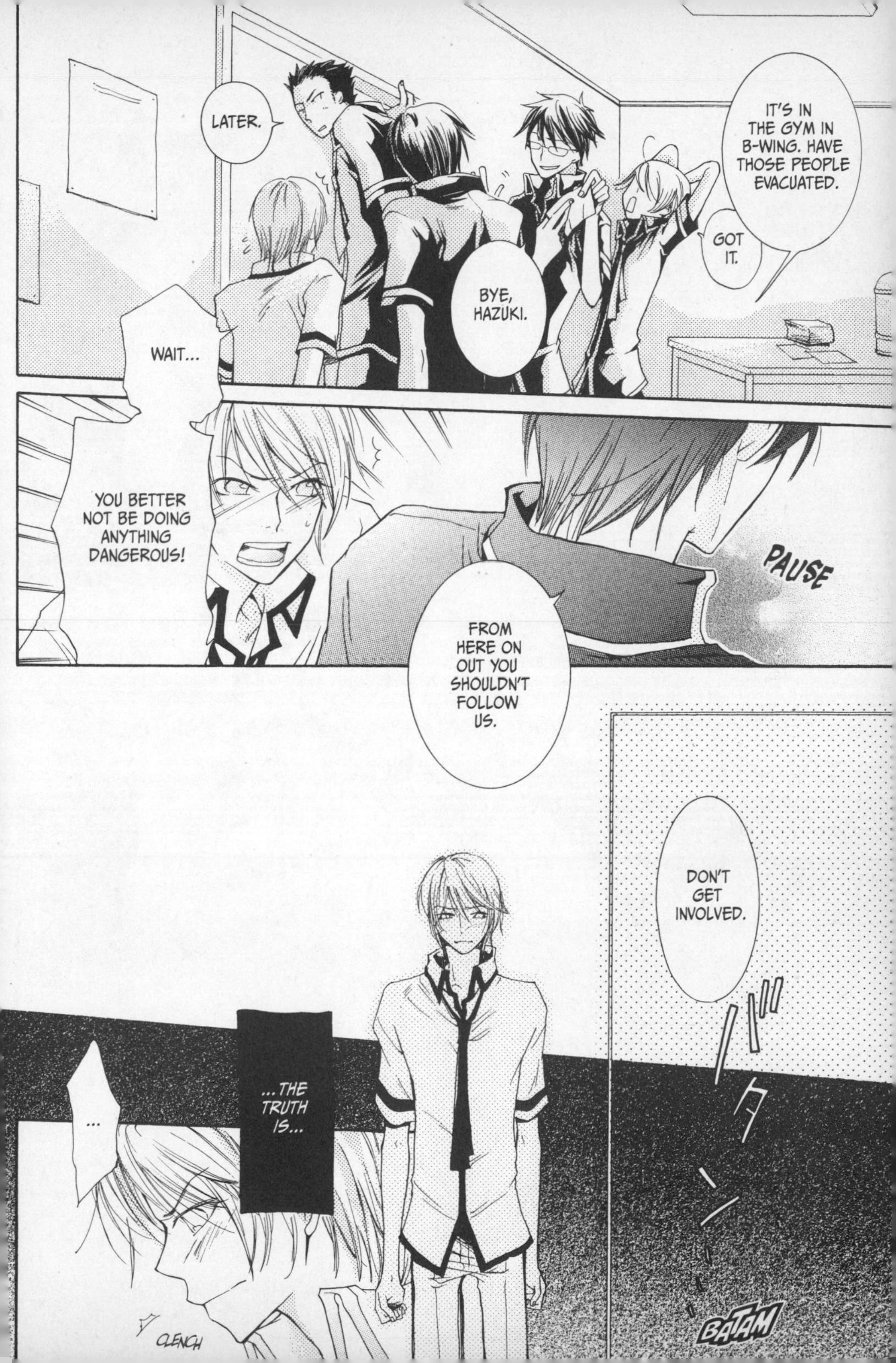
IT'S IN THE GYM IN B-WING. HAVE THOSE PEOPLE EVACUATED.
GOT IT.
BYE, HAZUKI.
LATER.
WAIT...
PAUSE
YOU BETTER NOT BE DOING ANYTHING DANGEROUS!
FROM HERE ON OUT YOU SHOULDN'T FOLLOW US.
DON'T GET INVOLVED.
BATAM
...THE TRUTH IS...
...
CLENCH

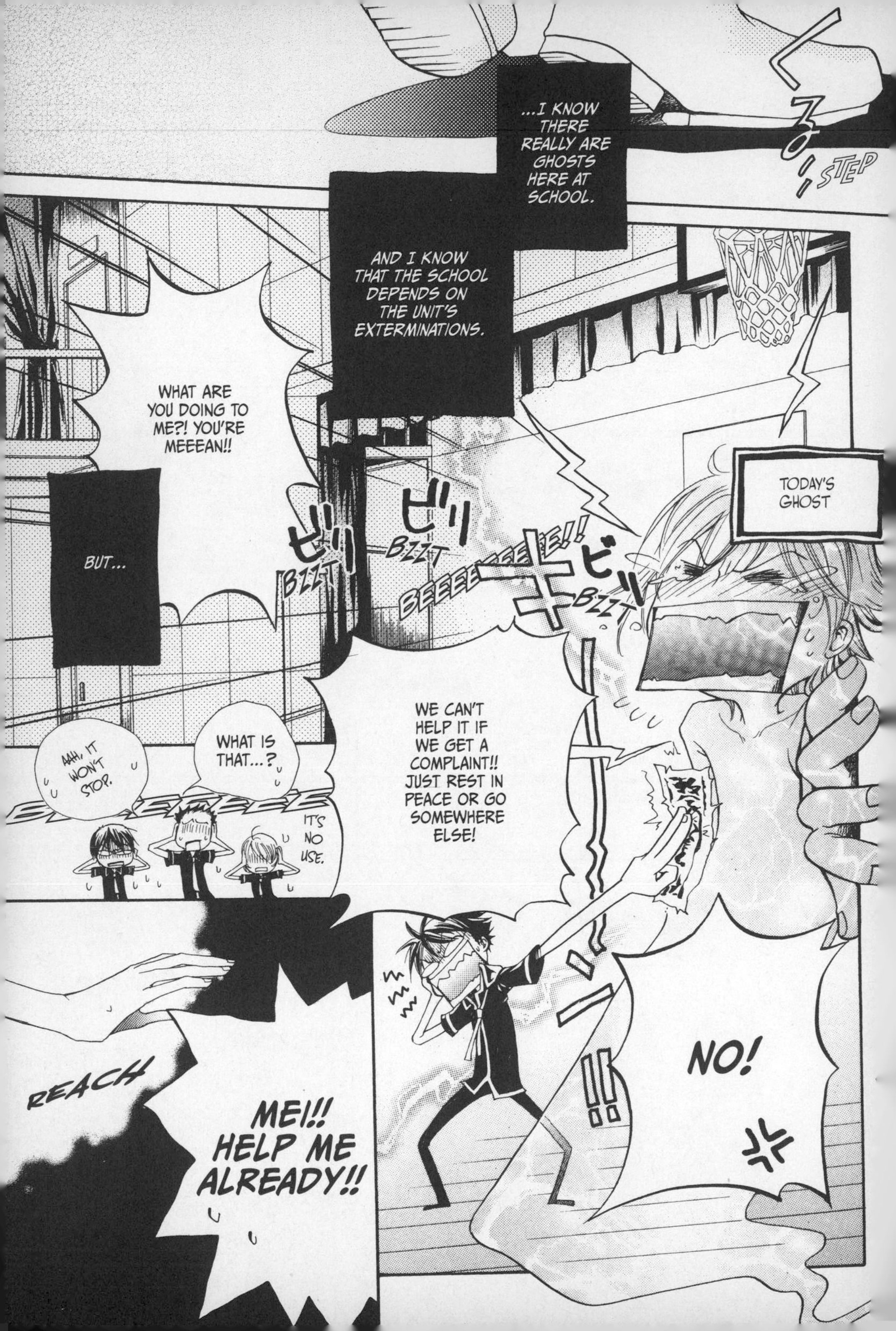

STEP
...I KNOW THERE REALLY ARE GHOSTS HERE AT SCHOOL.
AND I KNOW THAT THE SCHOOL DEPENDS ON THE UNIT'S EXTERMINATIONS.
TODAY'S GHOST
ビリ BZZT
BEEEEEEEEE!!
ビリ BZZT
ビリ BZZT
WHAT ARE YOU DOING TO ME?! YOU'RE MEEEAN!!
BUT...
WE CAN'T HELP IT IF WE GET A COMPLAINT!! JUST REST IN PEACE OR GO SOMEWHERE ELSE!
WHAT IS THAT...?
AAH, IT WON'T STOP.
IT'S NO USE.
NO!
!!
MEI!! HELP ME ALREADY!!
REACH

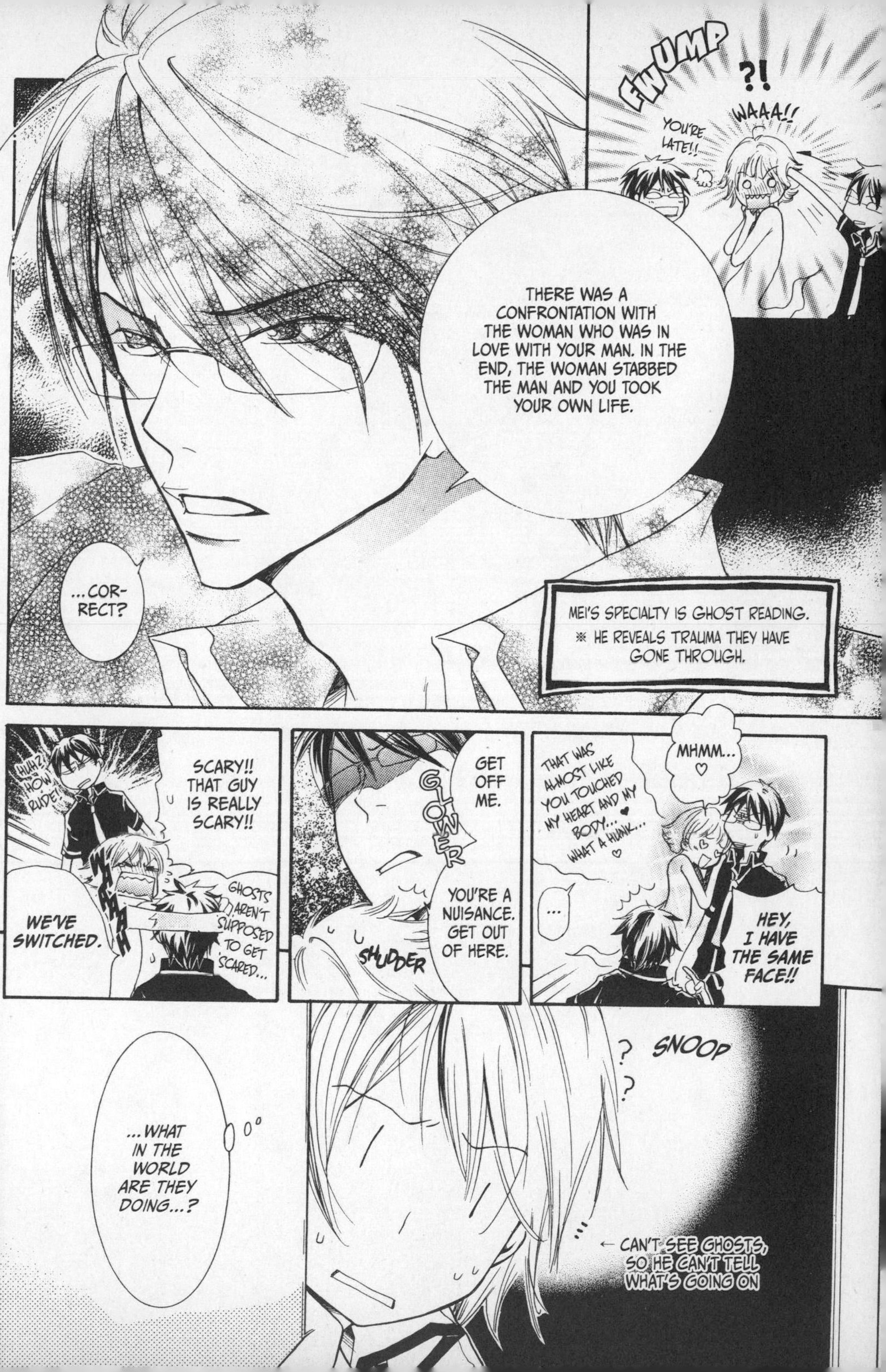
FWUMP
?!
WAAA!!
YOU'RE LATE!!
THERE WAS A CONFRONTATION WITH THE WOMAN WHO WAS IN LOVE WITH YOUR MAN. IN THE END, THE WOMAN STABBED THE MAN AND YOU TOOK YOUR OWN LIFE.
...CORRECT?
MEI'S SPECIALTY IS GHOST READING.
※ HE REVEALS TRAUMA THEY HAVE GONE THROUGH.
MHMM... ♡
THAT WAS ALMOST LIKE YOU TOUCHED MY HEART AND MY BODY... ♥ WHAT A HUNK... ♡
...
HEY, I HAVE THE SAME FACE!!
GET OFF ME.
GLOWER
YOU'RE A NUISANCE. GET OUT OF HERE.
SHUDDER
SCARY!! THAT GUY IS REALLY SCARY!!
HUH? HOW RUDE!
GHOSTS AREN'T SUPPOSED TO GET SCARED...
WE'VE SWITCHED.
SNOOP
??
...WHAT IN THE WORLD ARE THEY DOING...?
...
← CAN'T SEE GHOSTS, SO HE CAN'T TELL WHAT'S GOING ON

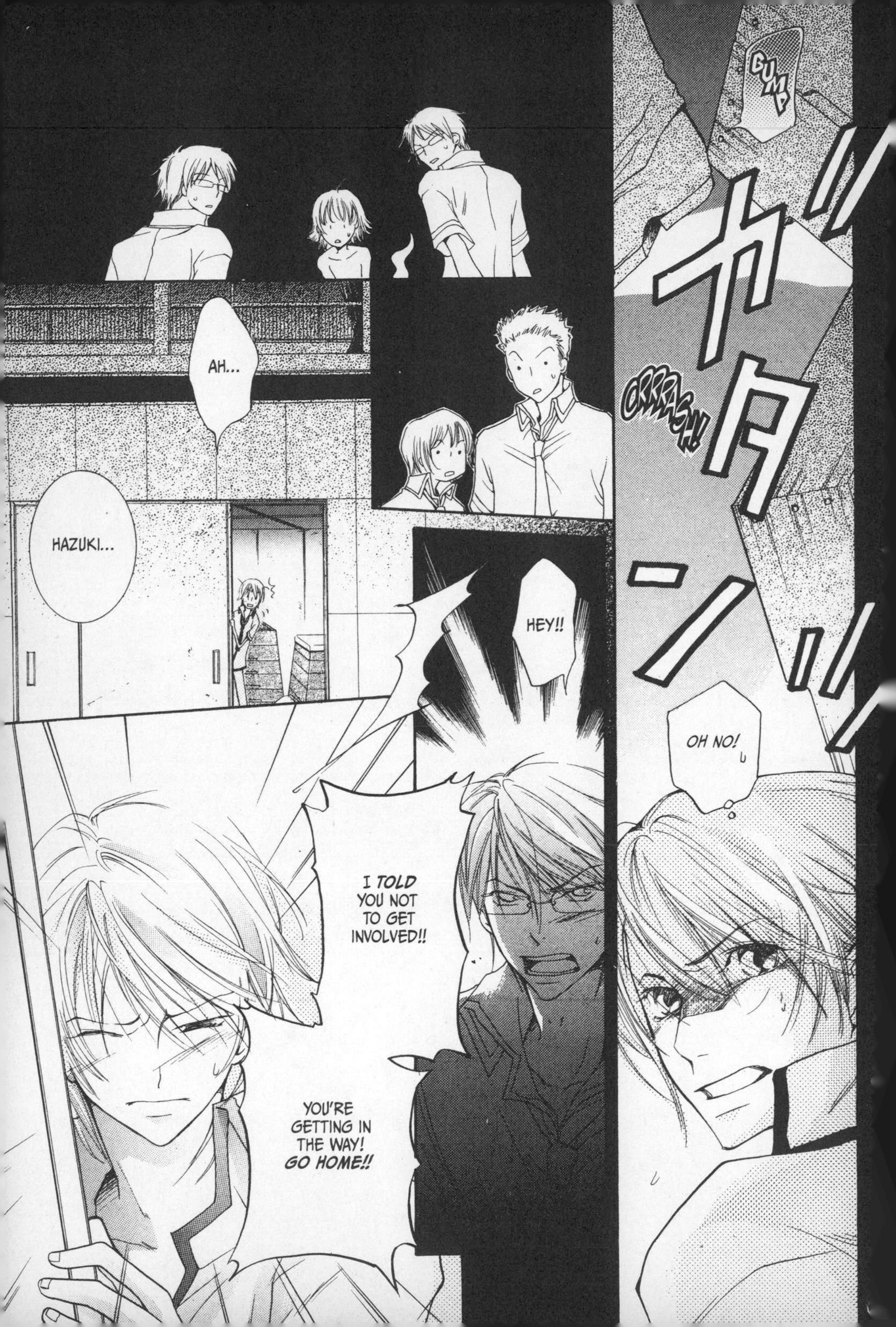
GUMP
CRRRASH!!
ガターン
OH NO!
AH...
HAZUKI...
HEY!!
I TOLD YOU NOT TO GET INVOLVED!!
YOU'RE GETTING IN THE WAY! GO HOME!!

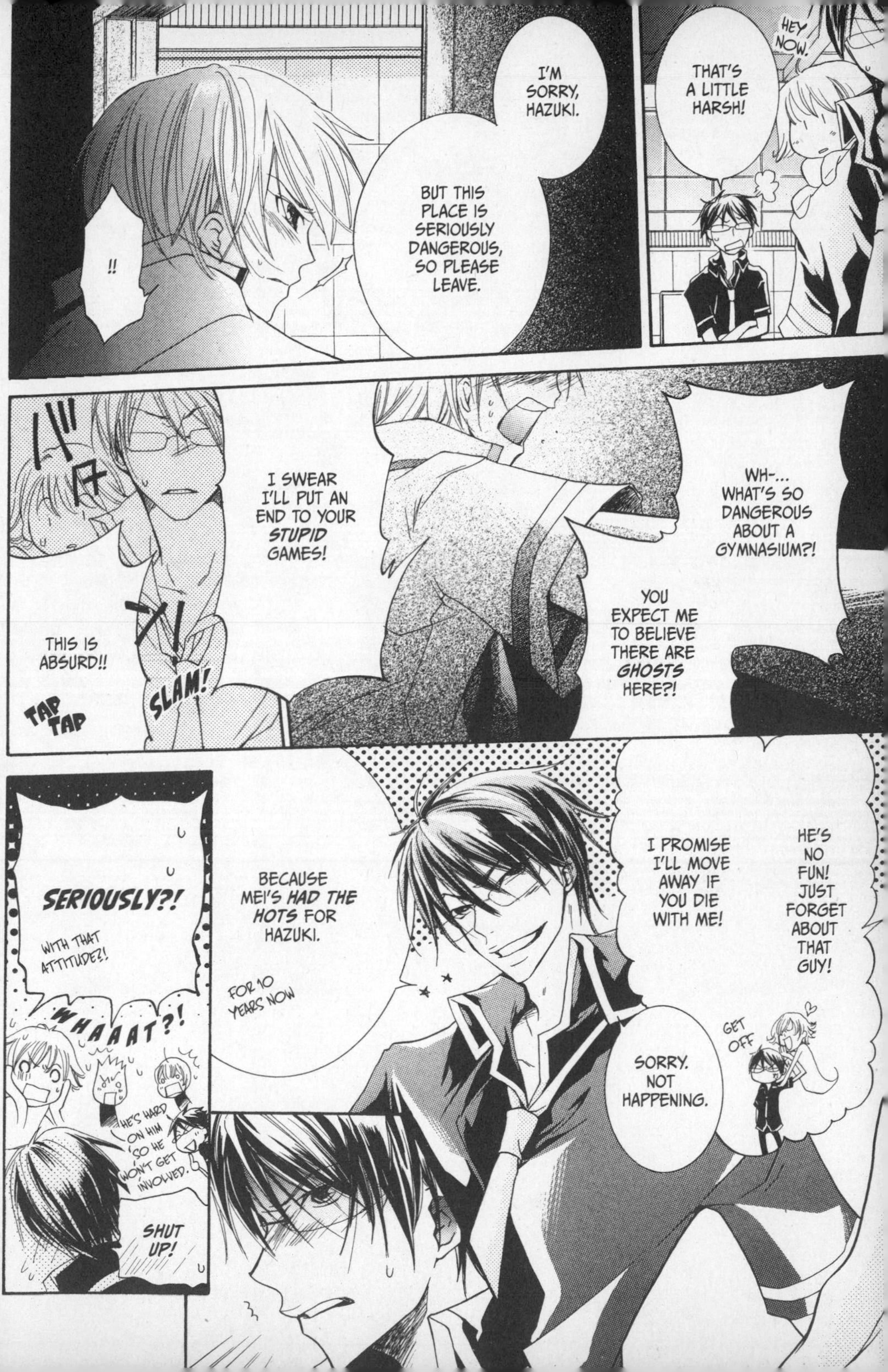
HEY NOW!
THAT'S A LITTLE HARSH!
I'M SORRY, HAZUKI.
BUT THIS PLACE IS SERIOUSLY DANGEROUS, SO PLEASE LEAVE.
!!
WH-... WHAT'S SO DANGEROUS ABOUT A GYMNASIUM?!
YOU EXPECT ME TO BELIEVE THERE ARE *GHOSTS* HERE?!
I SWEAR I'LL PUT AN END TO YOUR *STUPID* GAMES!
THIS IS ABSURD!!
SLAM!
TAP TAP
HE'S NO FUN! JUST FORGET ABOUT THAT GUY!
I PROMISE I'LL MOVE AWAY IF YOU DIE WITH ME!
GET OFF
SORRY. NOT HAPPENING.
BECAUSE MEI'S *HAD THE HOTS* FOR HAZUKI.
FOR 10 YEARS NOW
SERIOUSLY?!
WITH THAT ATTITUDE?!
WHAAAT?!
HE'S HARD ON HIM SO HE WON'T GET INVOLVED.
SHUT UP!

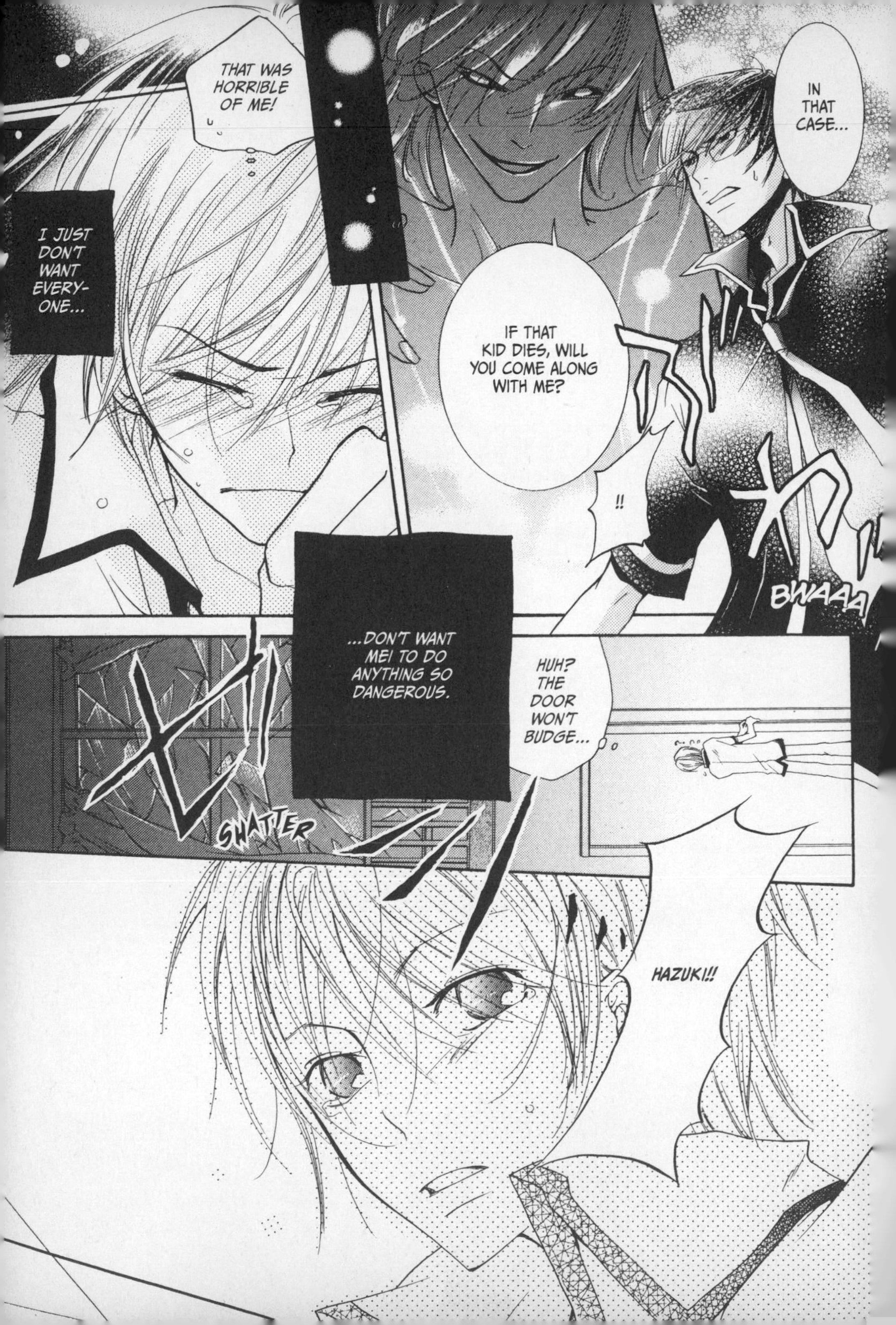
IN THAT CASE...
IF THAT KID DIES, WILL YOU COME ALONG WITH ME?
!!
BWAAA
THAT WAS HORRIBLE OF ME!
I JUST DON'T WANT EVERY-ONE...
...DON'T WANT MEI TO DO ANYTHING SO DANGEROUS.
HUH? THE DOOR WON'T BUDGE...
SHATTER
HAZUKI!!

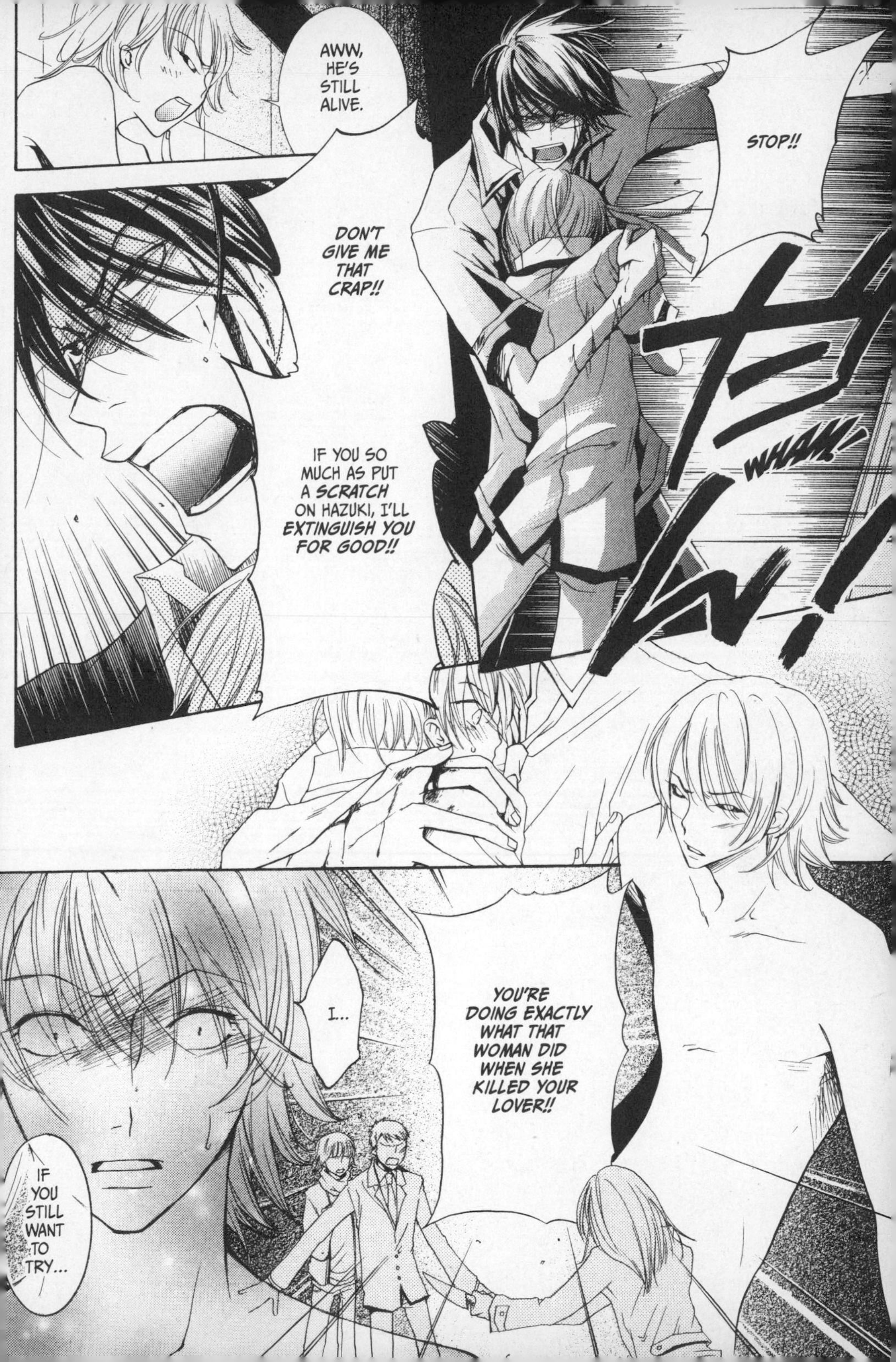
STOP!!
WHAM!
AWW, HE'S STILL ALIVE.
DON'T GIVE ME THAT CRAP!!
IF YOU SO MUCH AS PUT A SCRATCH ON HAZUKI, I'LL EXTINGUISH YOU FOR GOOD!!
YOU'RE DOING EXACTLY WHAT THAT WOMAN DID WHEN SHE KILLED YOUR LOVER!!
I...
IF YOU STILL WANT TO TRY...

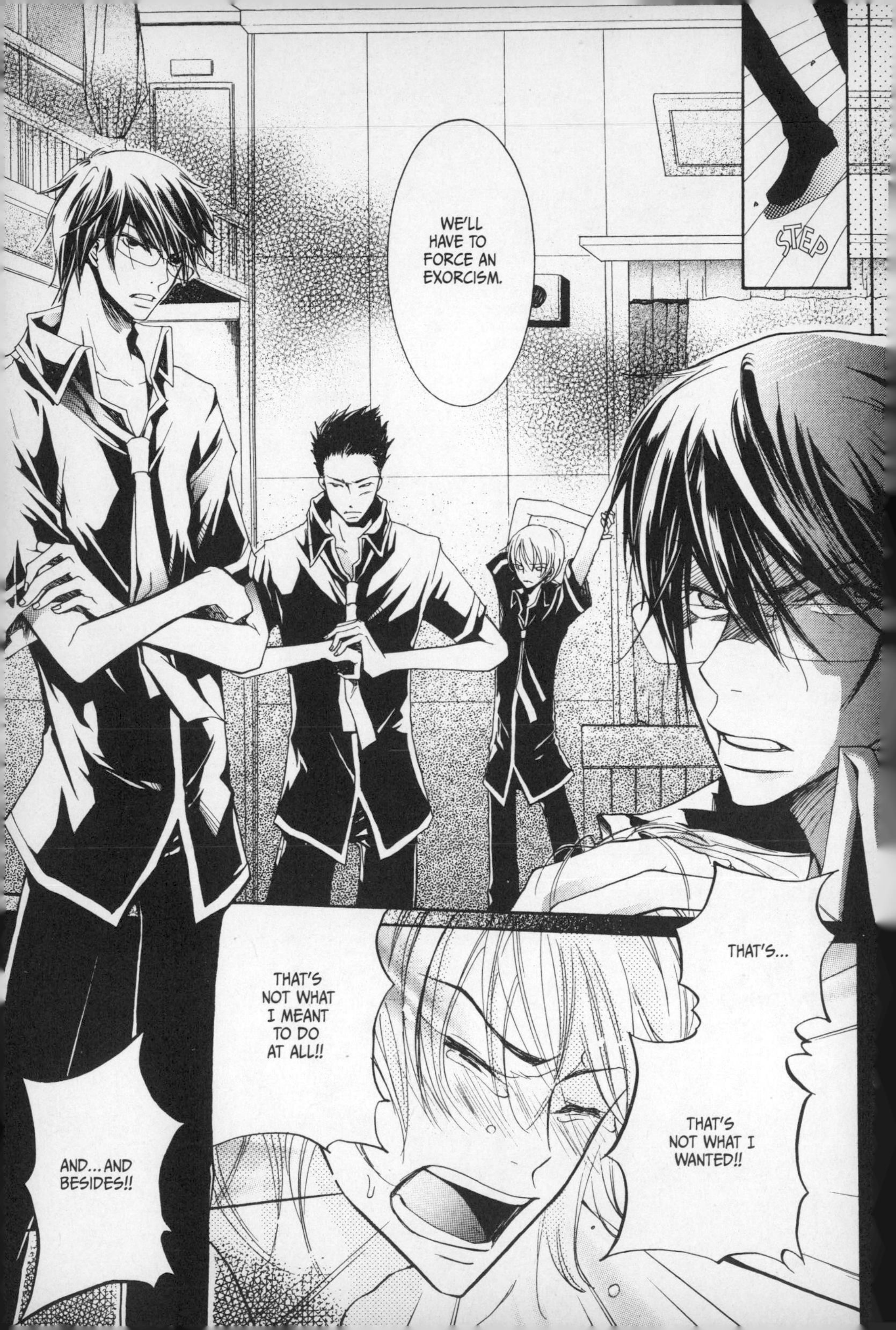
STEP
WE'LL HAVE TO FORCE AN EXORCISM.
THAT'S...
THAT'S NOT WHAT I WANTED!!
THAT'S NOT WHAT I MEANT TO DO AT ALL!!
AND...AND BESIDES!!

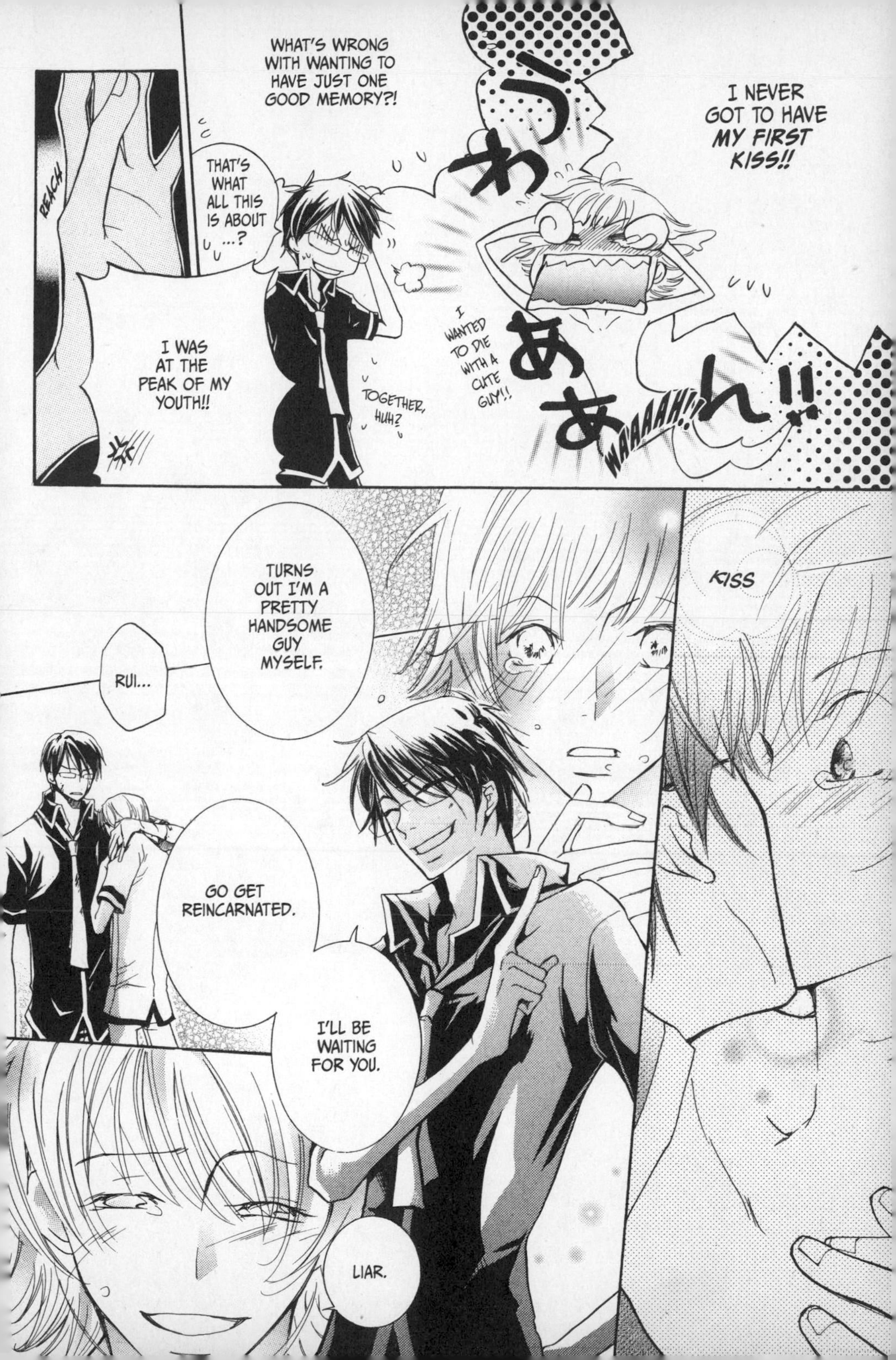
I NEVER GOT TO HAVE MY FIRST KISS!!
うわああん!!
WAAAAH!!
I WANTED TO DIE WITH A CUTE GUY!!
TOGETHER, HUH?
WHAT'S WRONG WITH WANTING TO HAVE JUST ONE GOOD MEMORY?!
THAT'S WHAT ALL THIS IS ABOUT ...?
REACH
I WAS AT THE PEAK OF MY YOUTH!!
KISS
TURNS OUT I'M A PRETTY HANDSOME GUY MYSELF.
RUI...
GO GET REINCARNATED.
I'LL BE WAITING FOR YOU.
LIAR.

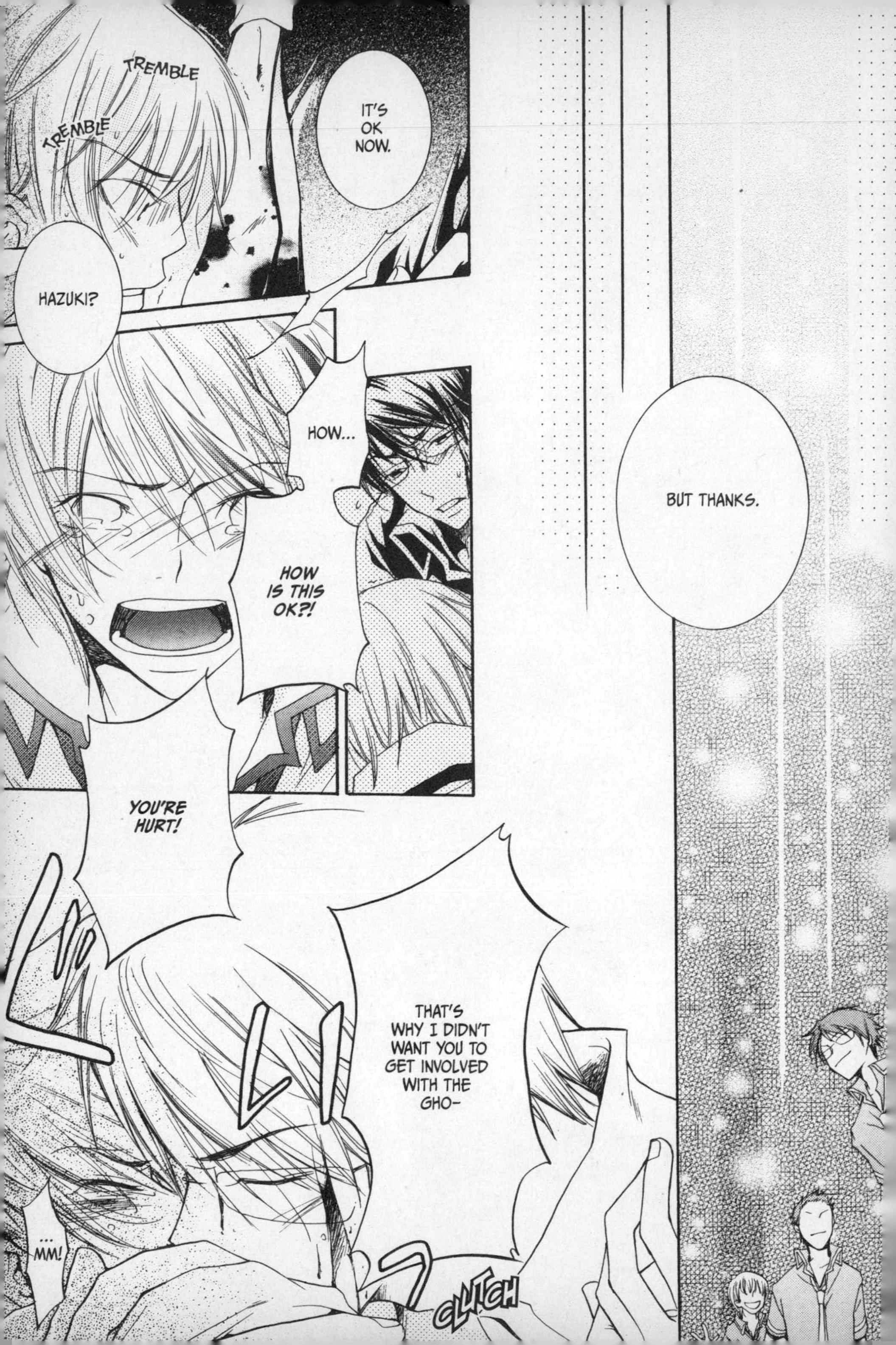
BUT THANKS.
IT'S OK NOW.
TREMBLE
TREMBLE
HAZUKI?
HOW...
HOW IS THIS OK?!
YOU'RE HURT!
THAT'S WHY I DIDN'T WANT YOU TO GET INVOLVED WITH THE GHO-
...MM!
CLUTCH

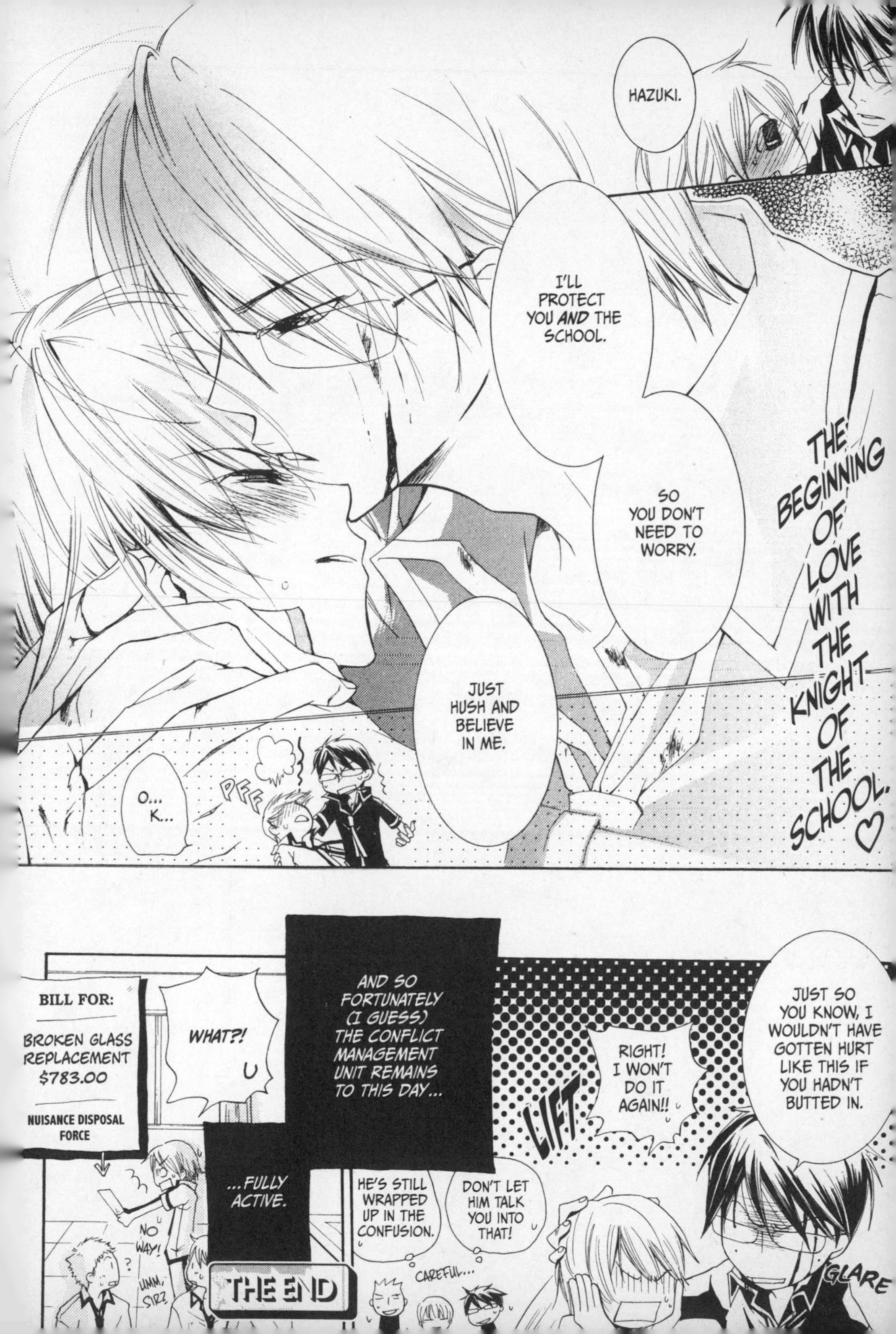
HAZUKI.
I'LL PROTECT YOU *AND* THE SCHOOL.
SO YOU DON'T NEED TO WORRY.
THE BEGINNING OF LOVE WITH THE KNIGHT OF THE SCHOOL. ♡
JUST HUSH AND BELIEVE IN ME.
PFF
O... K...
JUST SO YOU KNOW, I WOULDN'T HAVE GOTTEN HURT LIKE THIS IF YOU HADN'T BUTTED IN.
LIFT
RIGHT! I WON'T DO IT AGAIN!!
GLARE
AND SO FORTUNATELY (I GUESS) THE CONFLICT MANAGEMENT UNIT REMAINS TO THIS DAY...
WHAT?!
BILL FOR:
BROKEN GLASS REPLACEMENT $783.00
NUISANCE DISPOSAL FORCE
...FULLY ACTIVE.
DON'T LET HIM TALK YOU INTO THAT!
HE'S STILL WRAPPED UP IN THE CONFUSION.
CAREFUL...
NO WAY!
UMM, SIR?
THE END

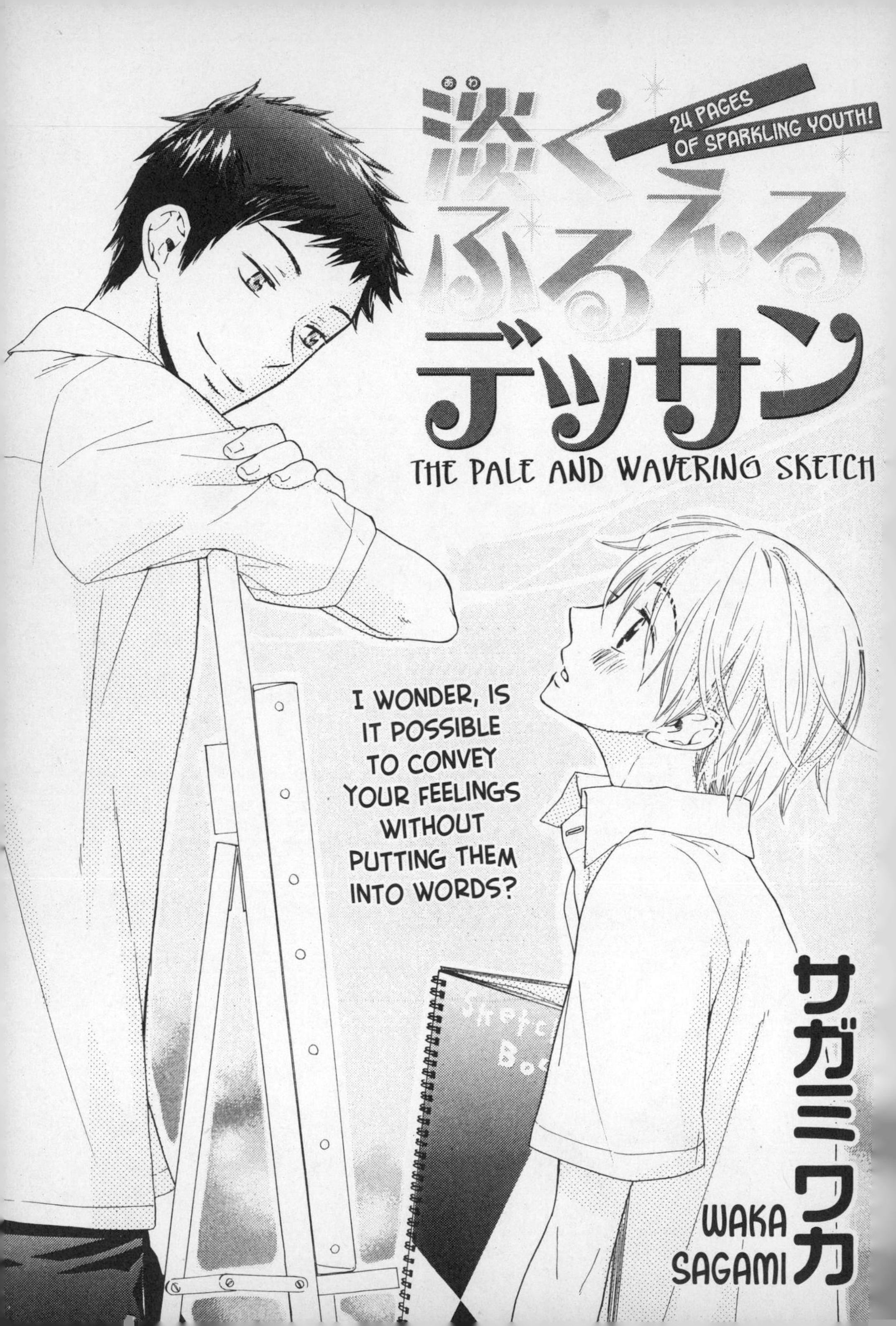

淡くふるえるデッサン
24 PAGES OF SPARKLING YOUTH!
THE PALE AND WAVERING SKETCH
サガミワカ
WAKA SAGAMI
I WONDER, IS IT POSSIBLE TO CONVEY YOUR FEELINGS WITHOUT PUTTING THEM INTO WORDS?

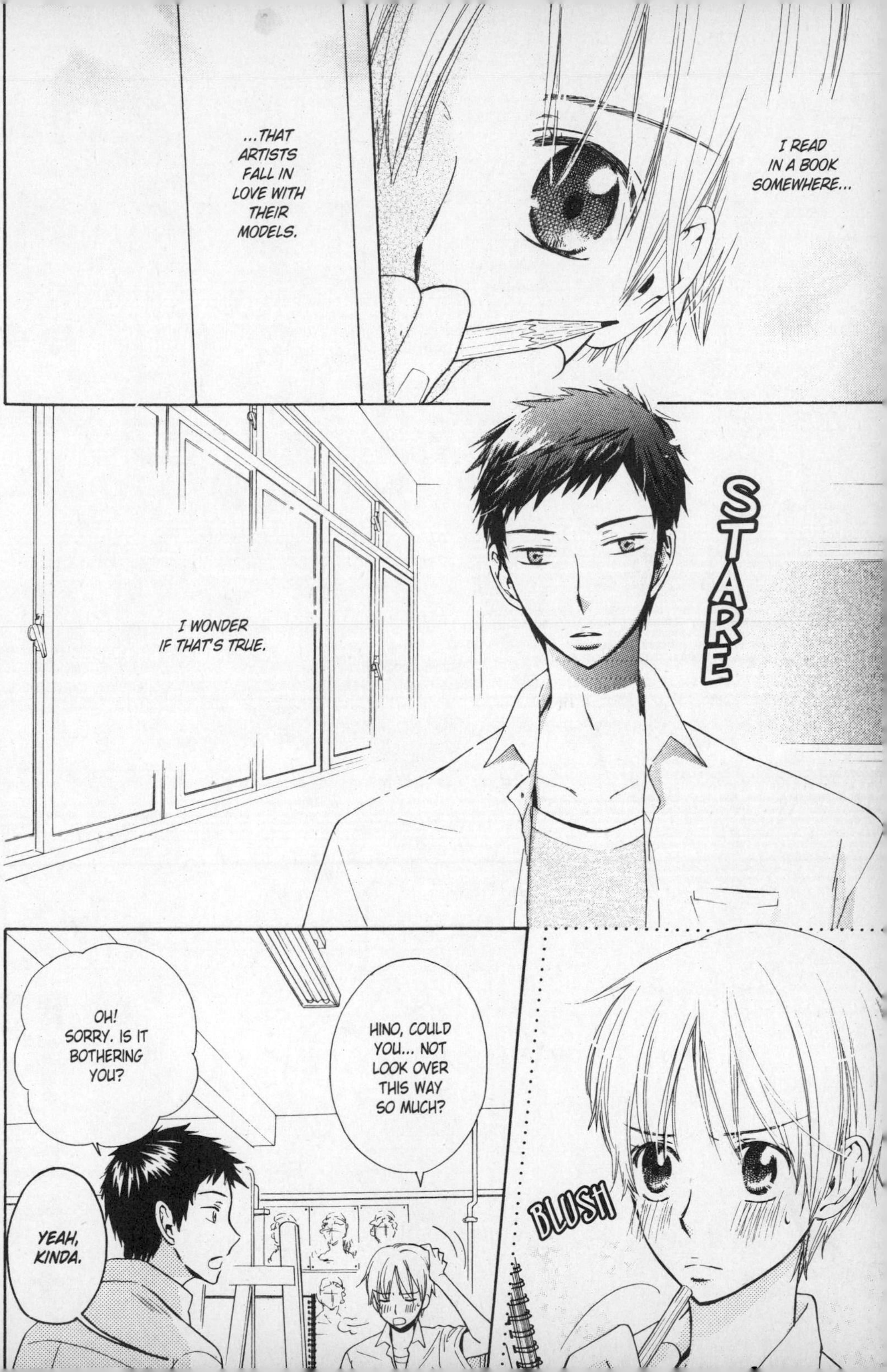
I READ IN A BOOK SOMEWHERE...
...THAT ARTISTS FALL IN LOVE WITH THEIR MODELS.
STARE
I WONDER IF THAT'S TRUE.
BLUSH
HINO, COULD YOU... NOT LOOK OVER THIS WAY SO MUCH?
OH! SORRY. IS IT BOTHERING YOU?
YEAH, KINDA.

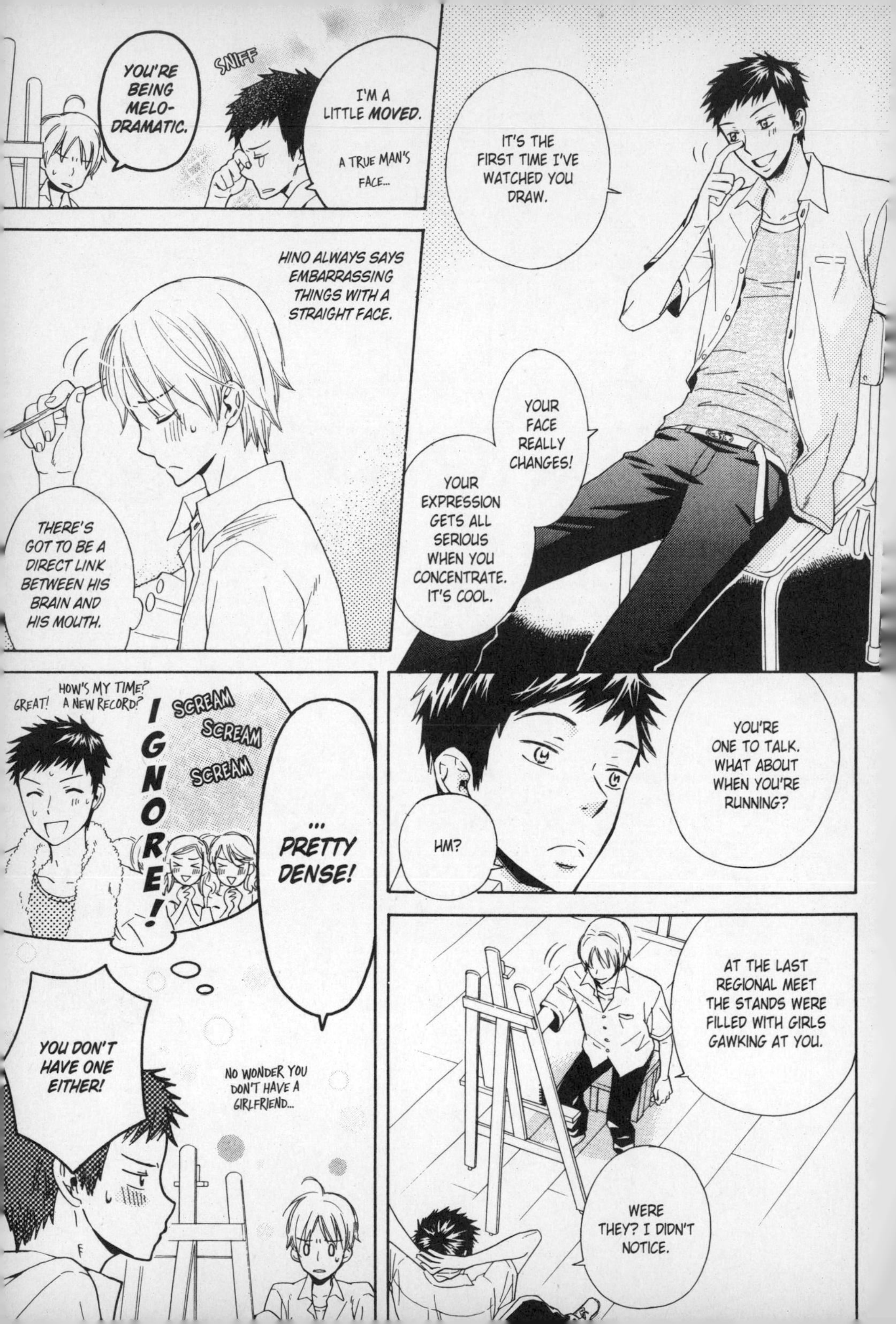
IT'S THE FIRST TIME I'VE WATCHED YOU DRAW.
YOUR FACE REALLY CHANGES!
YOUR EXPRESSION GETS ALL SERIOUS WHEN YOU CONCENTRATE. IT'S COOL.
I'M A LITTLE MOVED.
A TRUE MAN'S FACE...
SNIFF
YOU'RE BEING MELO-DRAMATIC.
HINO ALWAYS SAYS EMBARRASSING THINGS WITH A STRAIGHT FACE.
THERE'S GOT TO BE A DIRECT LINK BETWEEN HIS BRAIN AND HIS MOUTH.
YOU'RE ONE TO TALK. WHAT ABOUT WHEN YOU'RE RUNNING?
HM?
AT THE LAST REGIONAL MEET THE STANDS WERE FILLED WITH GIRLS GAWKING AT YOU.
WERE THEY? I DIDN'T NOTICE.
... PRETTY DENSE!
SCREAM
SCREAM
SCREAM
IGNORE!
HOW'S MY TIME? A NEW RECORD?
GREAT!
NO WONDER YOU DON'T HAVE A GIRLFRIEND...
YOU DON'T HAVE ONE EITHER!

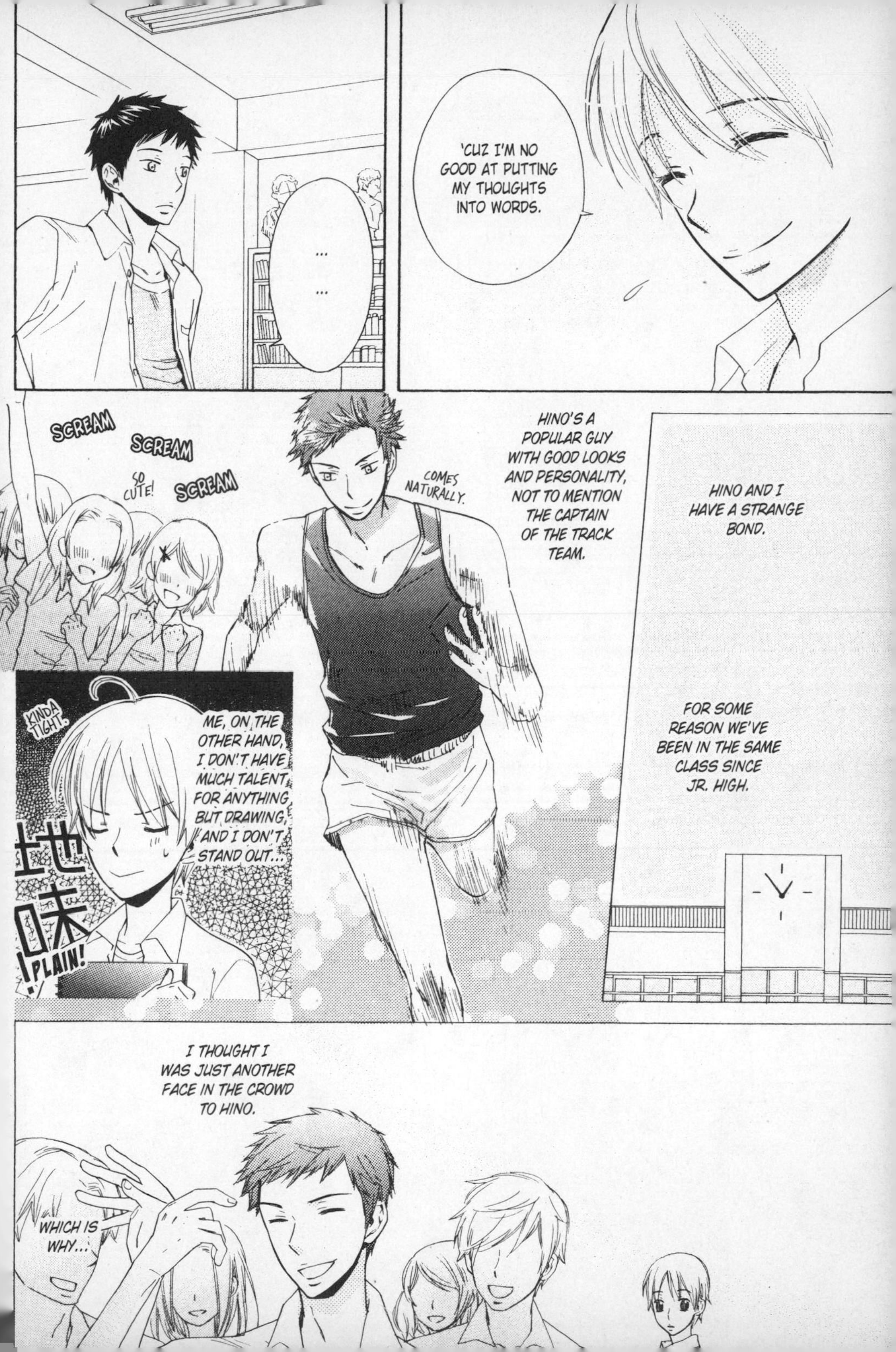
'CUZ I'M NO GOOD AT PUTTING MY THOUGHTS INTO WORDS.
... ...
HINO AND I HAVE A STRANGE BOND.
FOR SOME REASON WE'VE BEEN IN THE SAME CLASS SINCE JR. HIGH.
HINO'S A POPULAR GUY WITH GOOD LOOKS AND PERSONALITY, NOT TO MENTION THE CAPTAIN OF THE TRACK TEAM.
COMES NATURALLY.
SCREAM
SCREAM
SO CUTE!
SCREAM
ME, ON THE OTHER HAND, I DON'T HAVE MUCH TALENT FOR ANYTHING BUT DRAWING, AND I DON'T STAND OUT...
KINDA TIGHT.
地味
PLAIN!
I THOUGHT I WAS JUST ANOTHER FACE IN THE CROWD TO HINO.
WHICH IS WHY...

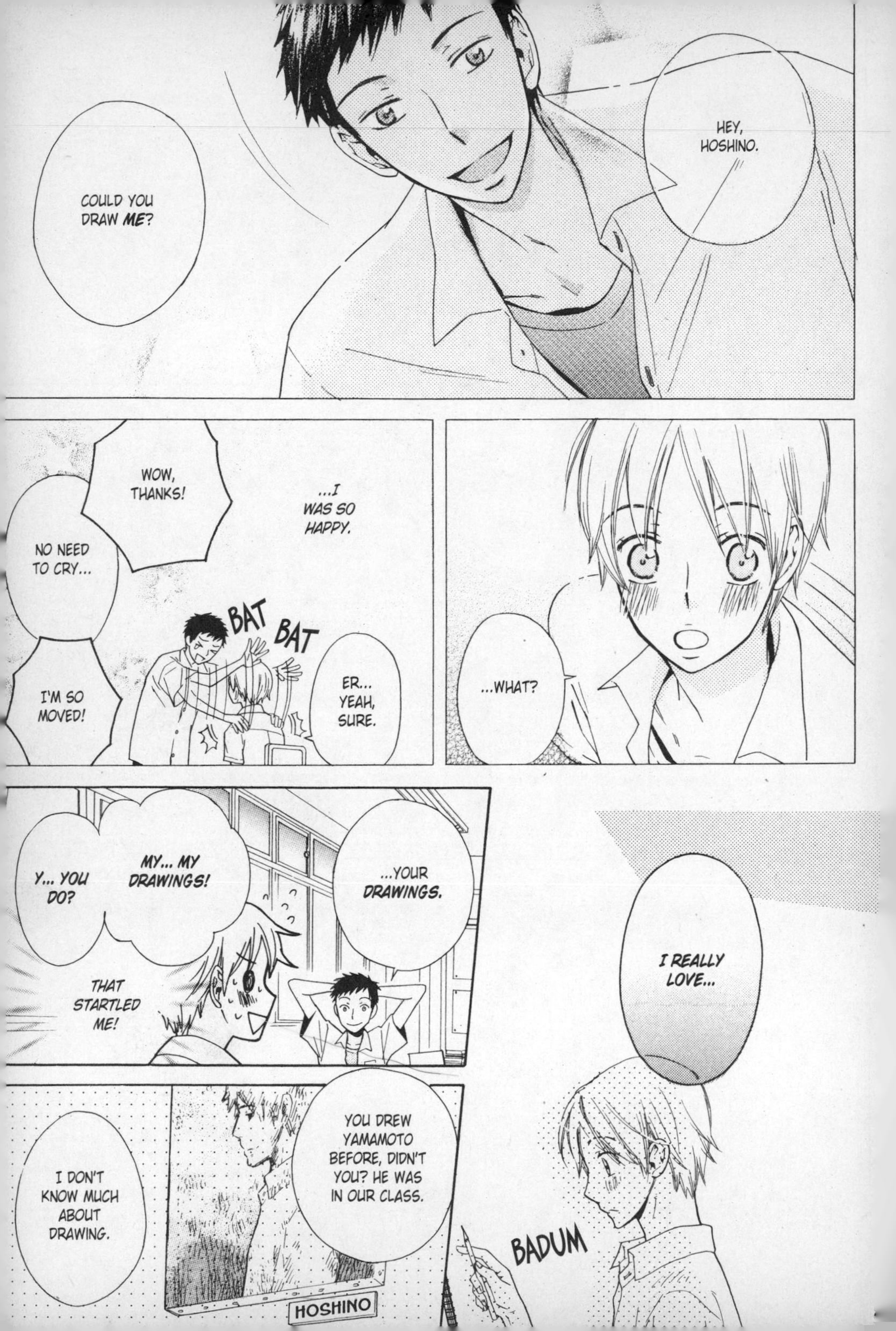

HEY, HOSHINO.
COULD YOU DRAW ME?
...WHAT?
ER... YEAH, SURE.
...I WAS SO HAPPY.
WOW, THANKS!
BAT
BAT
NO NEED TO CRY...
I'M SO MOVED!
I REALLY LOVE...
BADUM
...YOUR DRAWINGS.
MY... MY DRAWINGS!
Y... YOU DO?
THAT STARTLED ME!
YOU DREW YAMAMOTO BEFORE, DIDN'T YOU? HE WAS IN OUR CLASS.
I DON'T KNOW MUCH ABOUT DRAWING.
HOSHINO

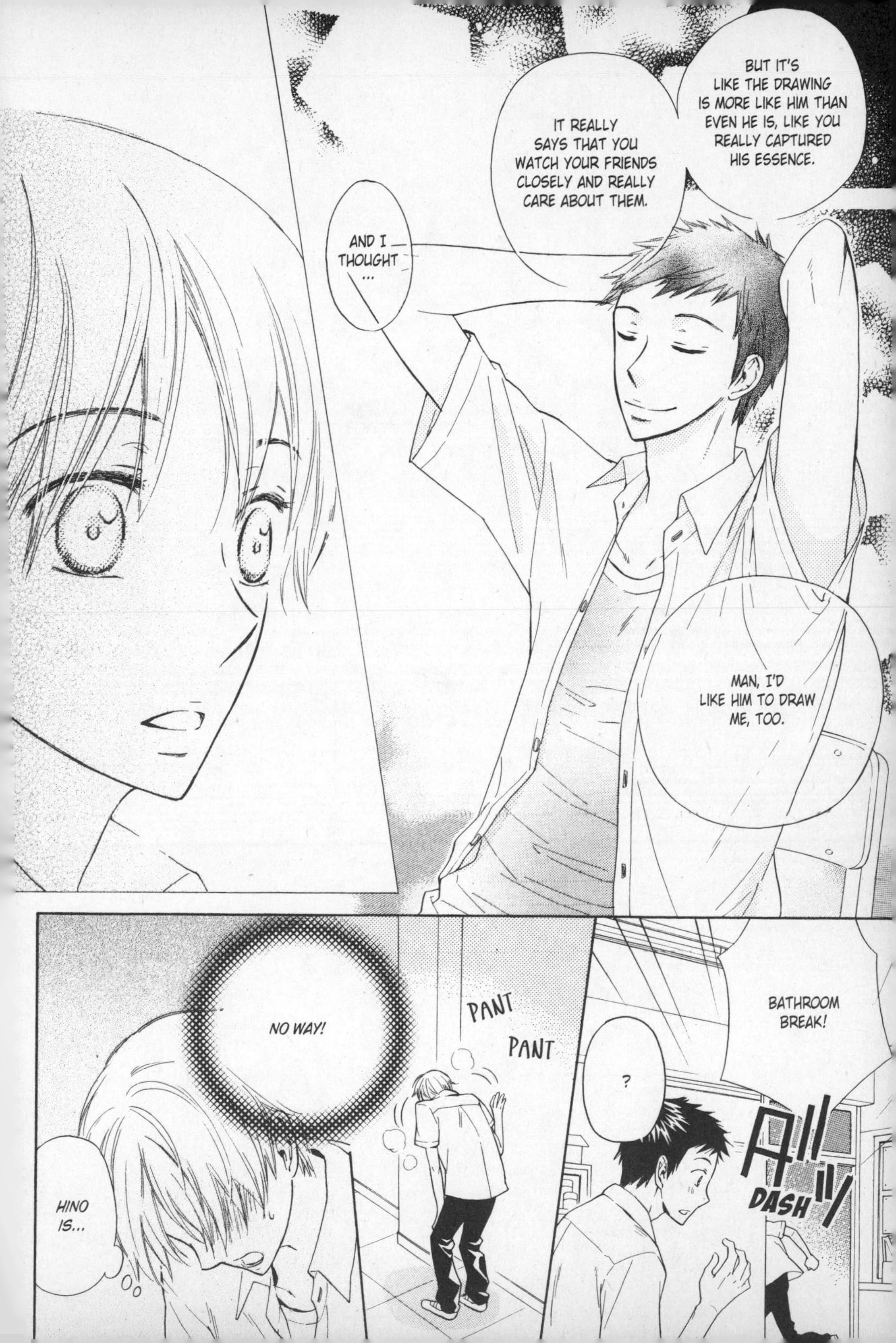
BUT IT'S LIKE THE DRAWING IS MORE LIKE HIM THAN EVEN HE IS, LIKE YOU REALLY CAPTURED HIS ESSENCE.
IT REALLY SAYS THAT YOU WATCH YOUR FRIENDS CLOSELY AND REALLY CARE ABOUT THEM.
MAN, I'D LIKE HIM TO DRAW ME, TOO.
AND I THOUGHT ...
BATHROOM BREAK!
?
DASH
PANT
PANT
NO WAY!
HINO IS...

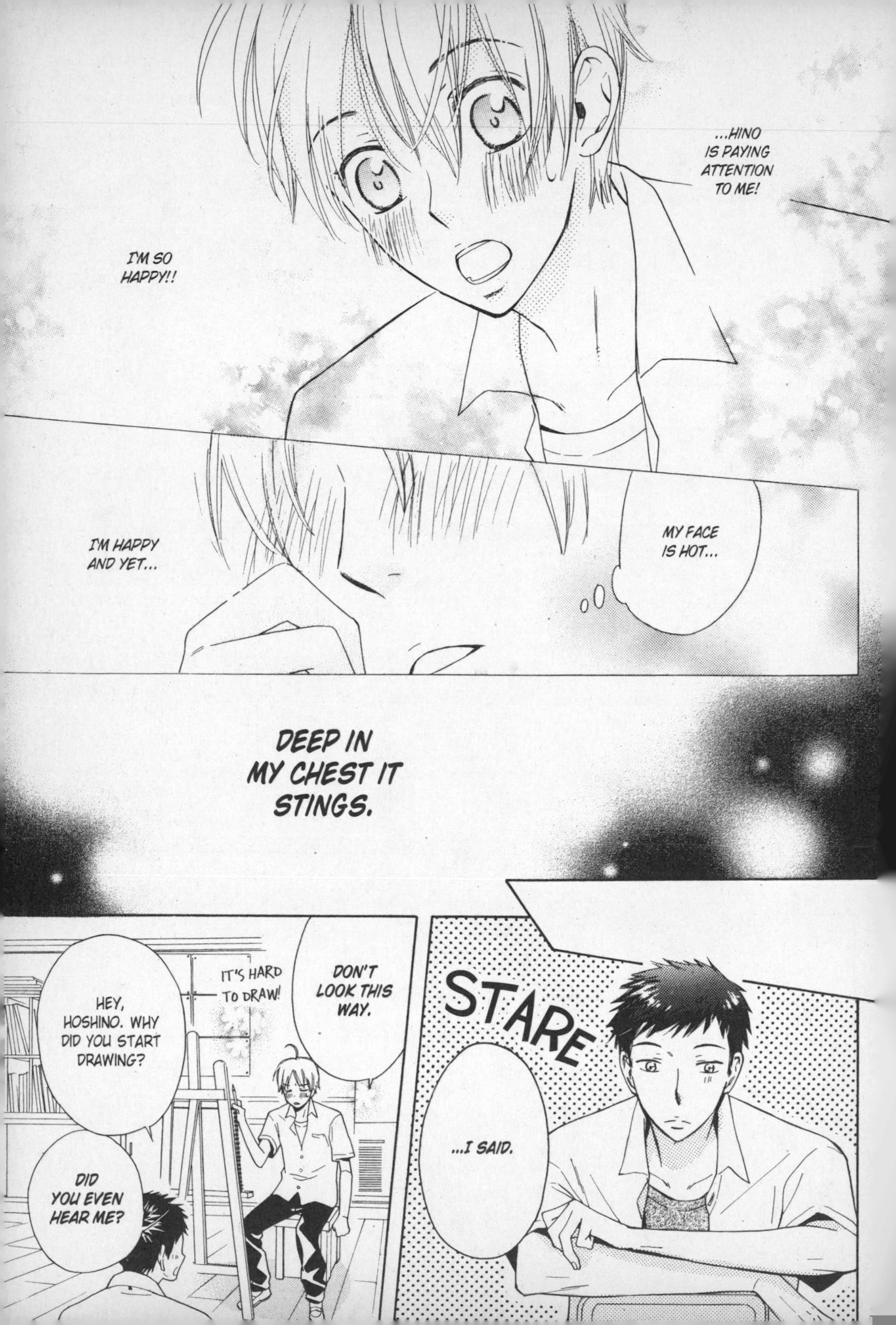
...HINO IS PAYING ATTENTION TO ME!
I'M SO HAPPY!!
MY FACE IS HOT...
I'M HAPPY AND YET...
DEEP IN MY CHEST IT STINGS.
STARE
...I SAID.
DON'T LOOK THIS WAY.
IT'S HARD TO DRAW!
HEY, HOSHINO. WHY DID YOU START DRAWING?
DID YOU EVEN HEAR ME?

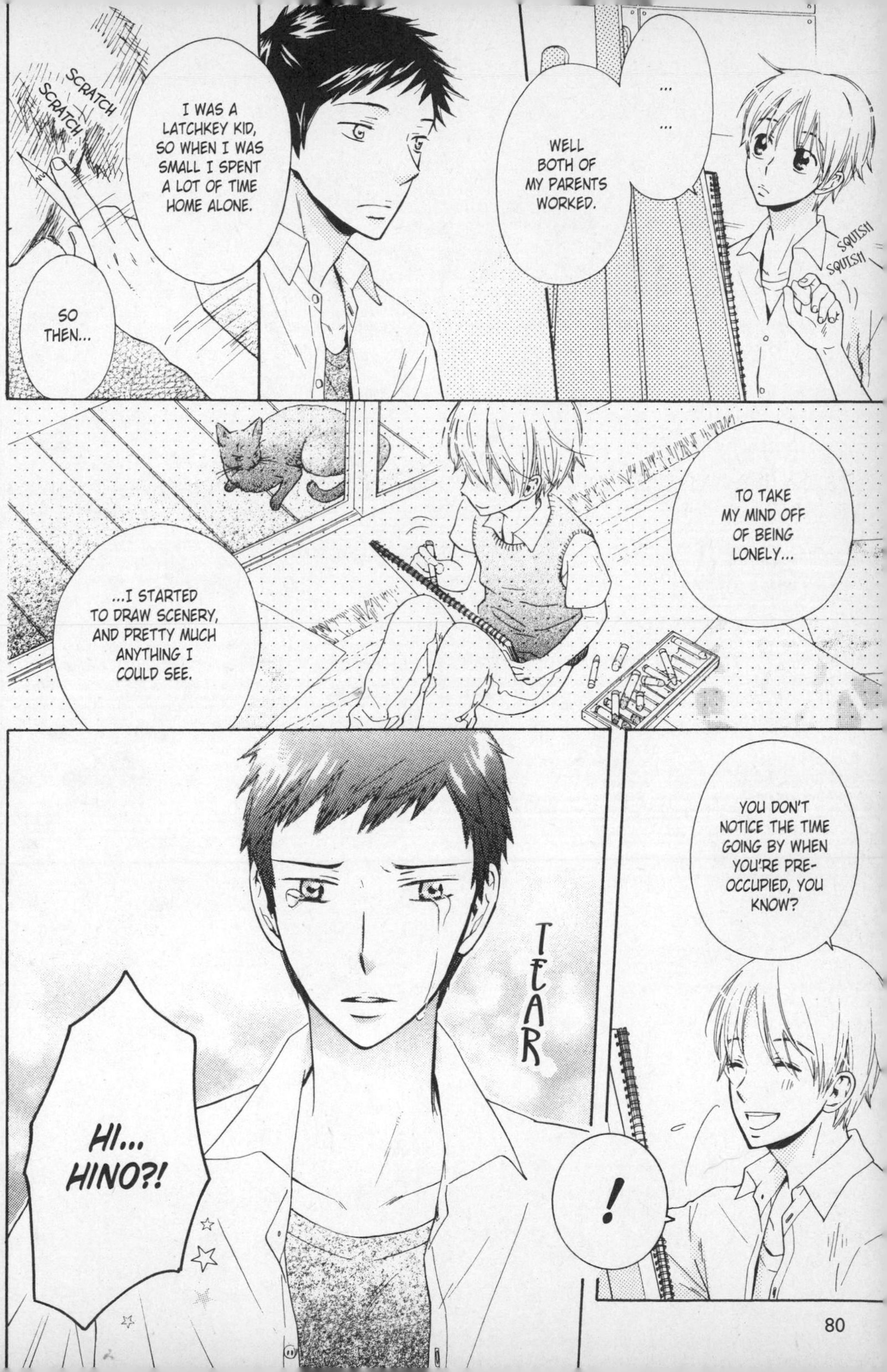
...
...
WELL BOTH OF MY PARENTS WORKED.
SQUISH SQUISH
I WAS A LATCHKEY KID, SO WHEN I WAS SMALL I SPENT A LOT OF TIME HOME ALONE.
SCRATCH SCRATCH
SO THEN...
TO TAKE MY MIND OFF OF BEING LONELY...
...I STARTED TO DRAW SCENERY, AND PRETTY MUCH ANYTHING I COULD SEE.
YOU DON'T NOTICE THE TIME GOING BY WHEN YOU'RE PRE-OCCUPIED, YOU KNOW?
!
TEAR
HI... HINO?!

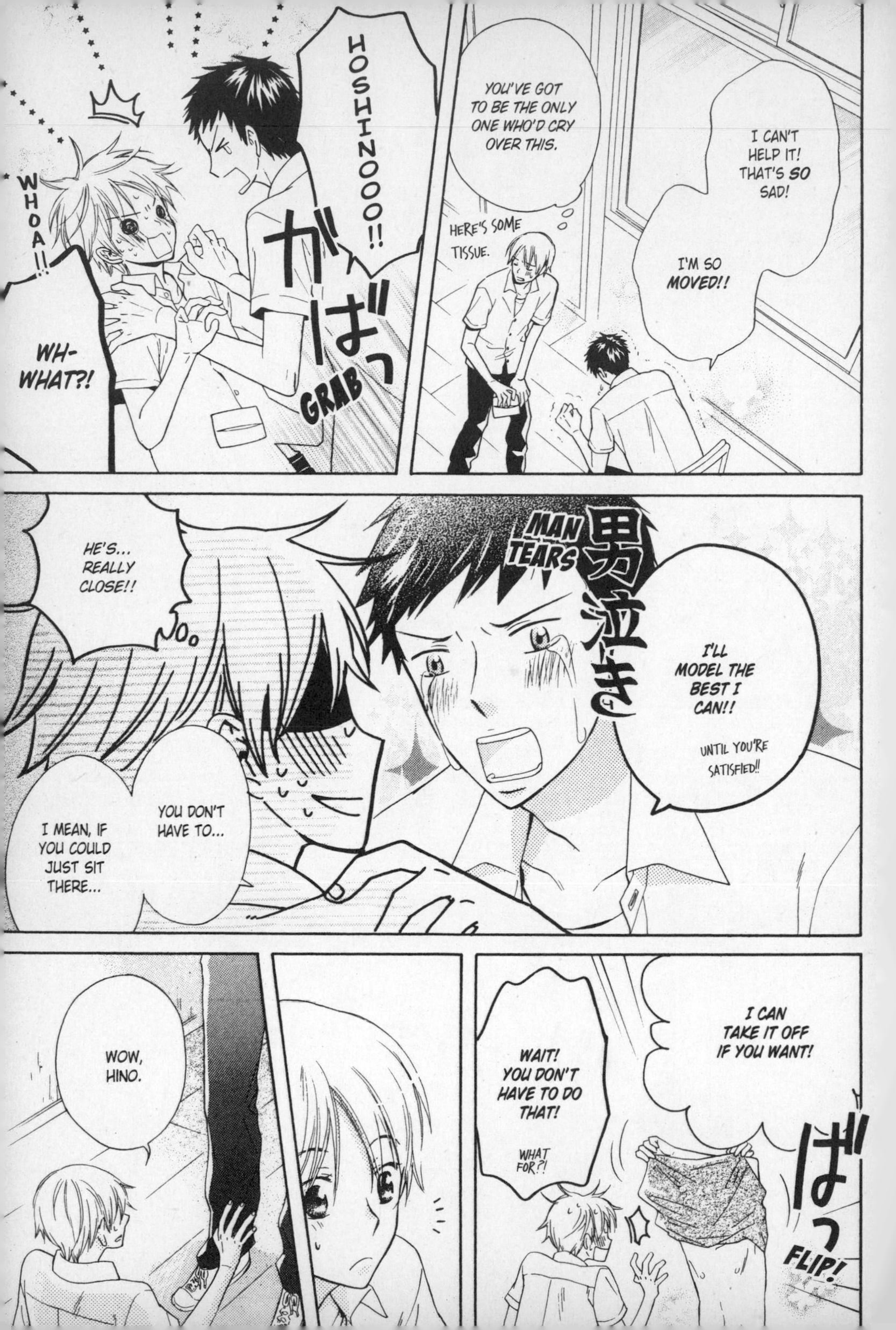
I CAN'T HELP IT! THAT'S SO SAD!
YOU'VE GOT TO BE THE ONLY ONE WHO'D CRY OVER THIS.
I'M SO MOVED!!
HERE'S SOME TISSUE.
HOSHINOOOO!!
がばっ
GRAB
WHOA!!
WH-WHAT?!
MAN TEARS
男泣き
I'LL MODEL THE BEST I CAN!!
UNTIL YOU'RE SATISFIED!!
HE'S... REALLY CLOSE!!
YOU DON'T HAVE TO...
I MEAN, IF YOU COULD JUST SIT THERE...
I CAN TAKE IT OFF IF YOU WANT!
ぱっ
FLIP!
WAIT! YOU DON'T HAVE TO DO THAT!
WHAT FOR?!
WOW, HINO.

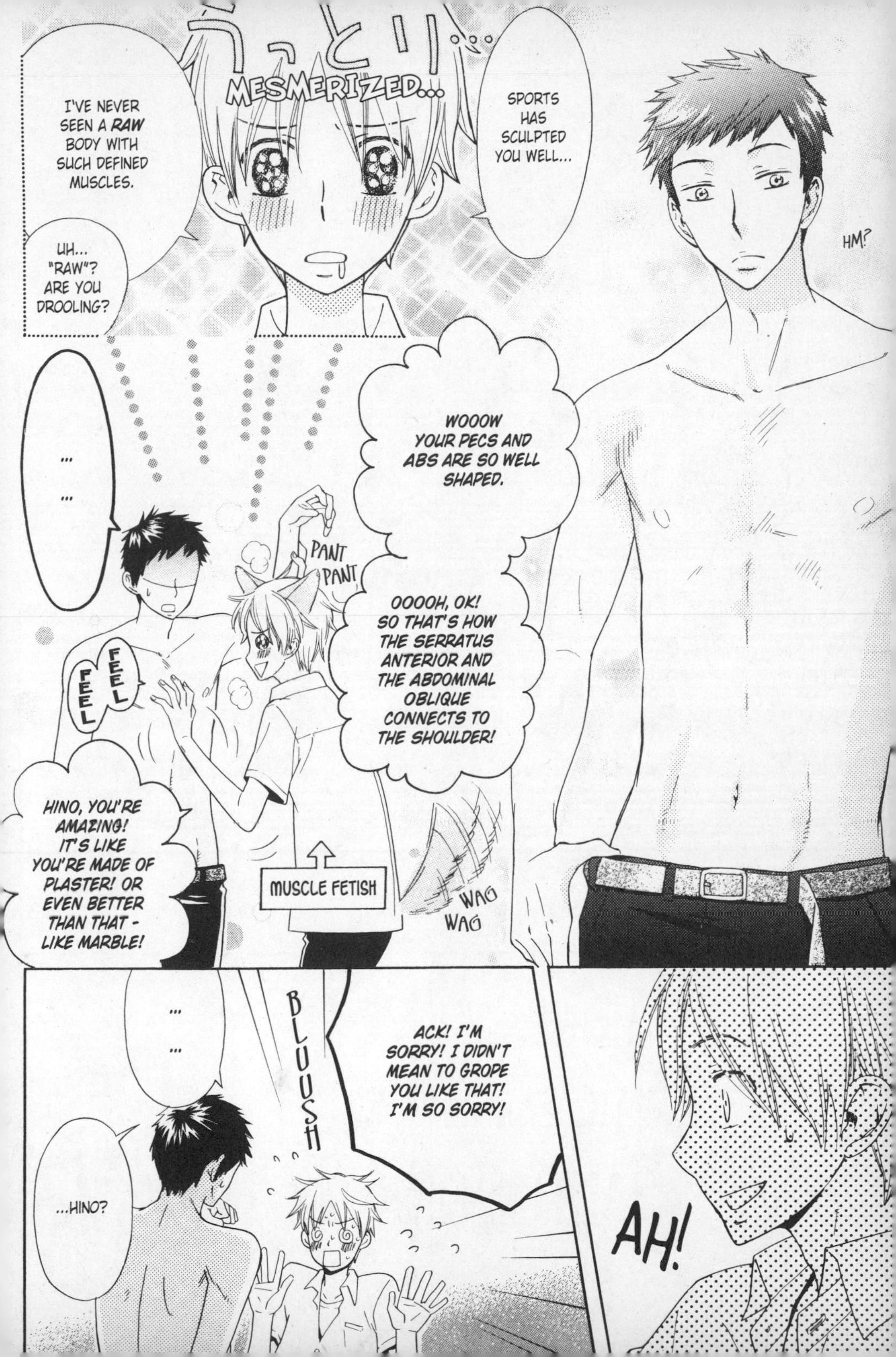
HM?
SPORTS HAS SCULPTED YOU WELL...
うっとり…
MESMERIZED...
I'VE NEVER SEEN A *RAW* BODY WITH SUCH DEFINED MUSCLES.
UH... "RAW"? ARE YOU DROOLING?
WOOOW YOUR PECS AND ABS ARE SO WELL SHAPED.
... ...
PANT PANT
OOOOH, OK! SO THAT'S HOW THE SERRATUS ANTERIOR AND THE ABDOMINAL OBLIQUE CONNECTS TO THE SHOULDER!
FEEL FEEL
HINO, YOU'RE AMAZING! IT'S LIKE YOU'RE MADE OF PLASTER! OR EVEN BETTER THAN THAT - LIKE MARBLE!
MUSCLE FETISH
WAG WAG
AH!
ACK! I'M SORRY! I DIDN'T MEAN TO GROPE YOU LIKE THAT! I'M SO SORRY!
BLUUSH
... ...
...HINO?

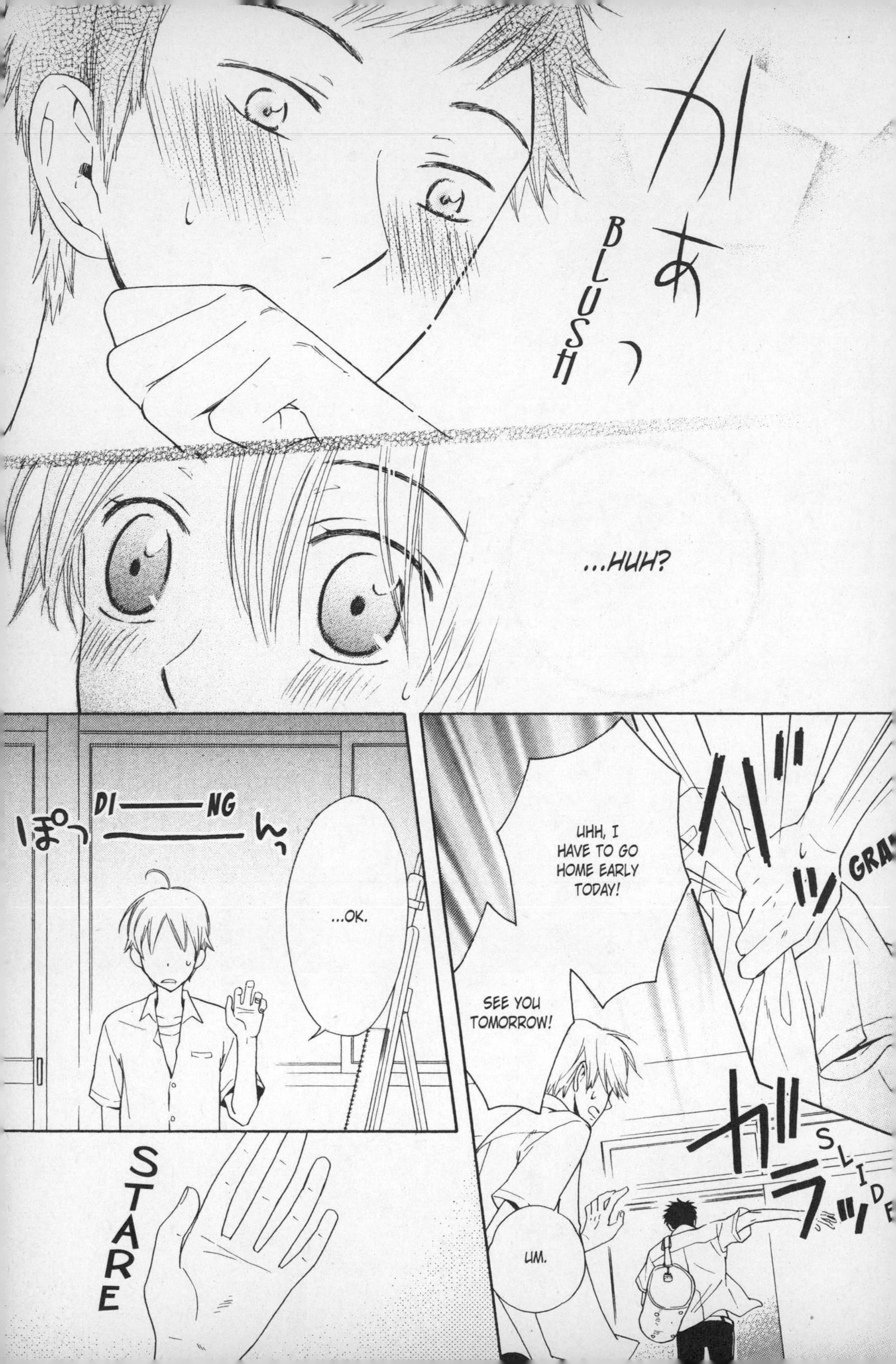
カあっ
BLUSH
...HUH?
バッ
GRA
UHH, I HAVE TO GO HOME EARLY TODAY!
SEE YOU TOMORROW!
ガラッ
SLIDE
UM.
ぽっ———ん
DI———NG
...OK.
STARE

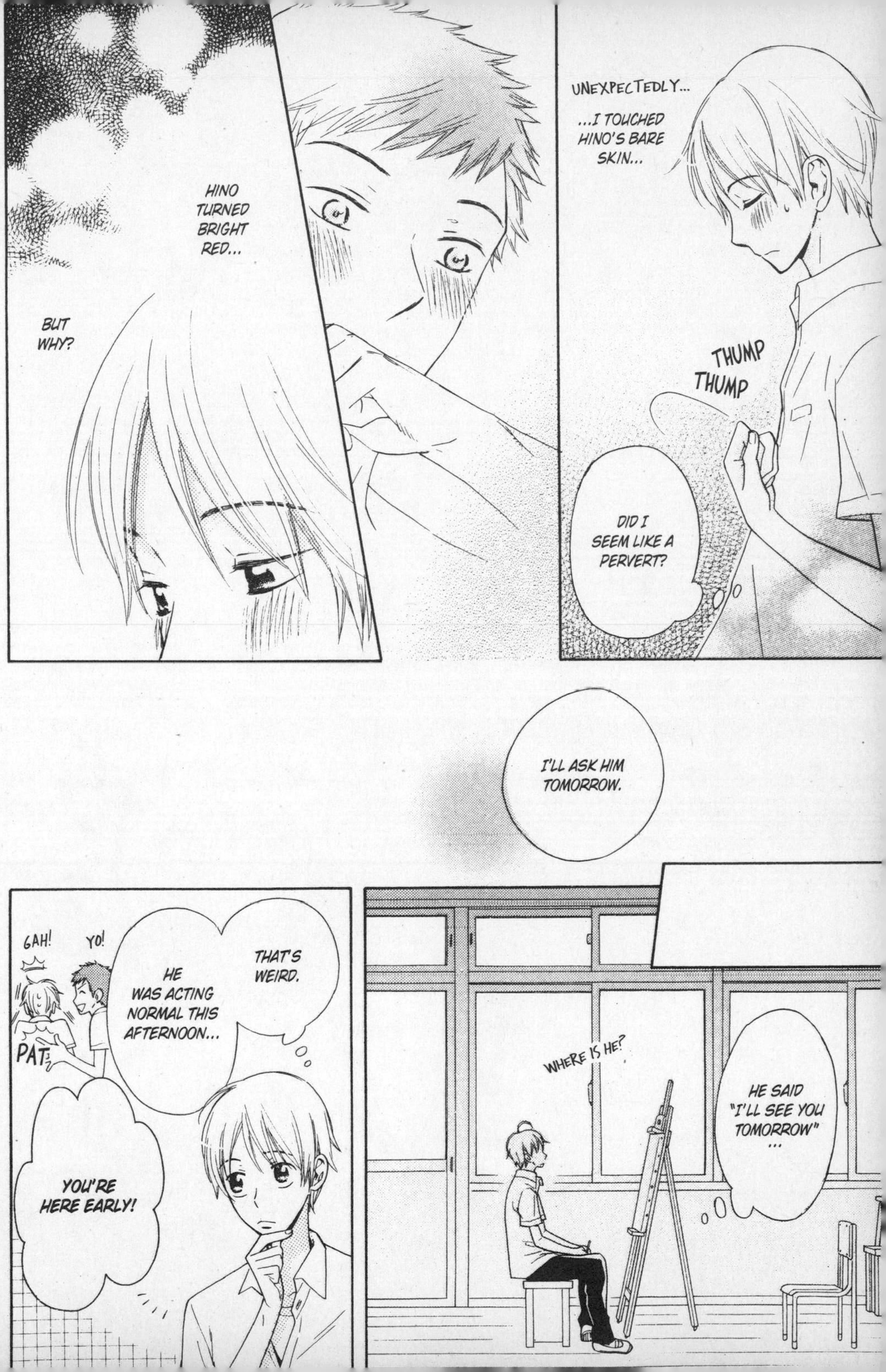
UNEXPECTEDLY...
...I TOUCHED HINO'S BARE SKIN...
THUMP THUMP
DID I SEEM LIKE A PERVERT?
HINO TURNED BRIGHT RED...
BUT WHY?
I'LL ASK HIM TOMORROW.
HE SAID "I'LL SEE YOU TOMORROW" ...
WHERE IS HE?
THAT'S WEIRD.
HE WAS ACTING NORMAL THIS AFTERNOON...
YO!
GAH!
PAT
YOU'RE HERE EARLY!

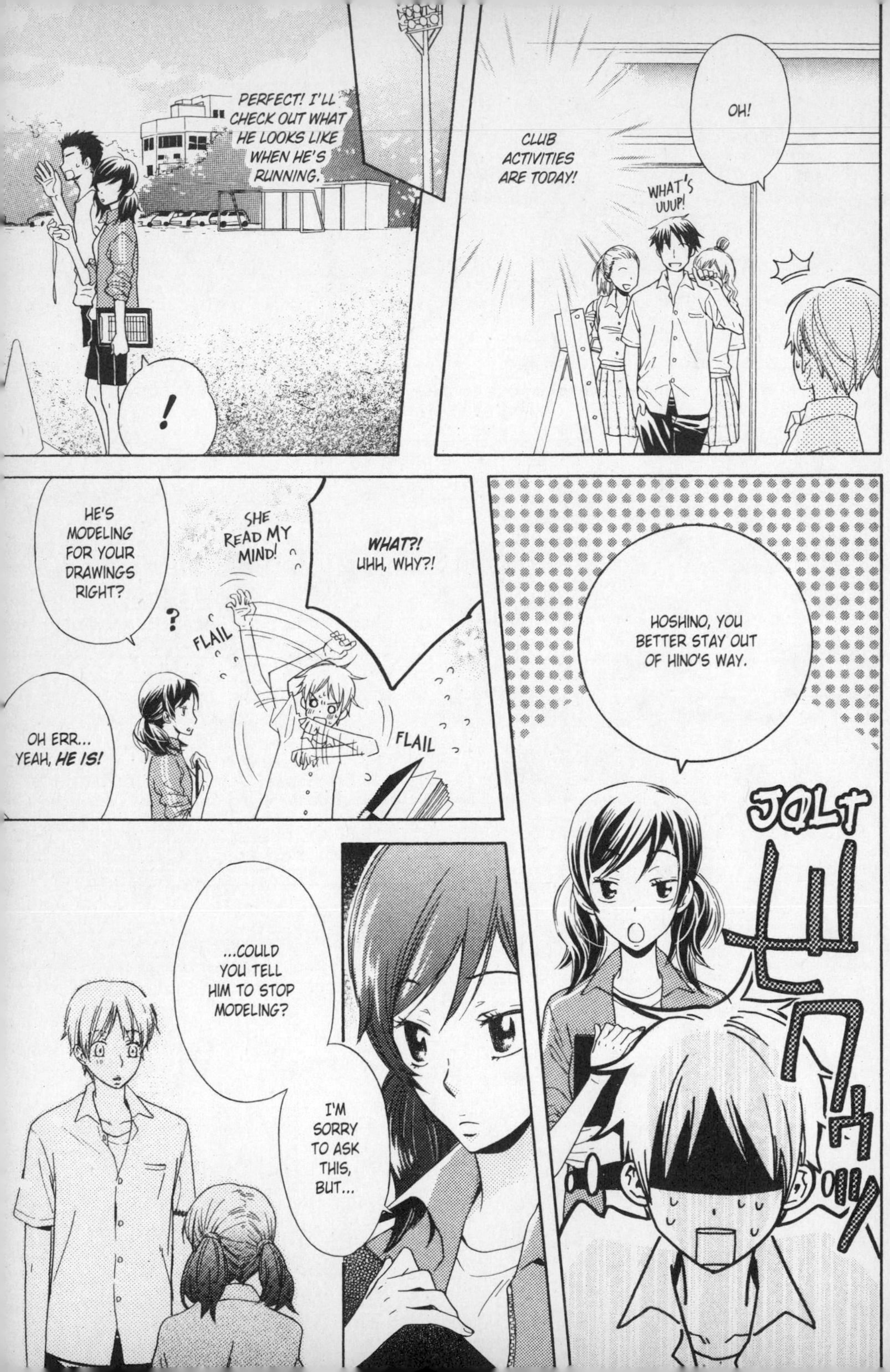
OH!
CLUB ACTIVITIES ARE TODAY!
WHAT'S UUUP!
PERFECT! I'LL CHECK OUT WHAT HE LOOKS LIKE WHEN HE'S RUNNING.
!
HOSHINO, YOU BETTER STAY OUT OF HINO'S WAY.
JOLT
WHAT?! UHH, WHY?!
SHE READ MY MIND!
HE'S MODELING FOR YOUR DRAWINGS RIGHT?
?
FLAIL
FLAIL
OH ERR... YEAH, HE IS!
I'M SORRY TO ASK THIS, BUT...
...COULD YOU TELL HIM TO STOP MODELING?

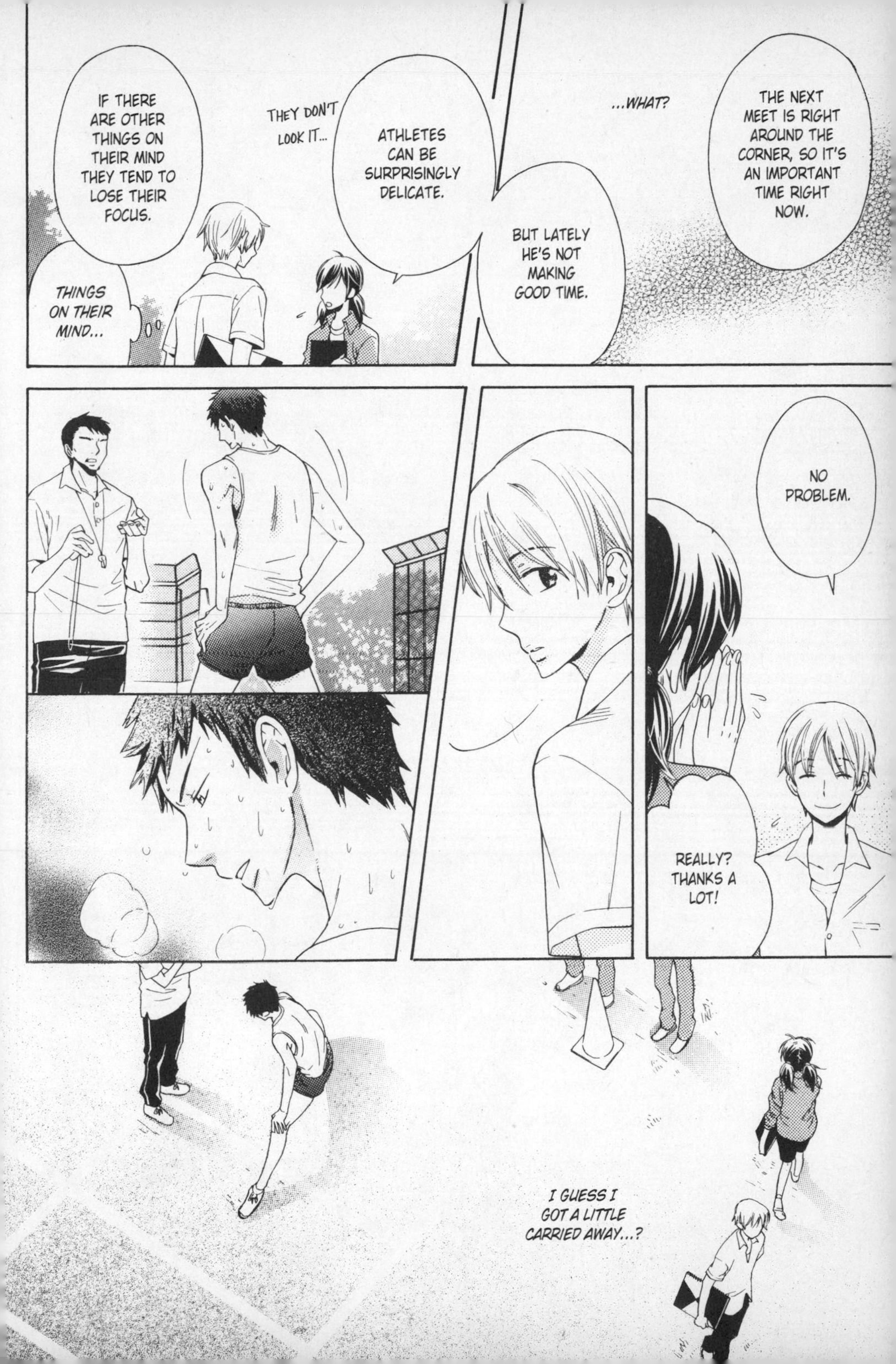
THE NEXT MEET IS RIGHT AROUND THE CORNER, SO IT'S AN IMPORTANT TIME RIGHT NOW.
...WHAT?
BUT LATELY HE'S NOT MAKING GOOD TIME.
ATHLETES CAN BE SURPRISINGLY DELICATE.
THEY DON'T LOOK IT...
IF THERE ARE OTHER THINGS ON THEIR MIND THEY TEND TO LOSE THEIR FOCUS.
THINGS ON THEIR MIND...
NO PROBLEM.
REALLY? THANKS A LOT!
I GUESS I GOT A LITTLE CARRIED AWAY...?

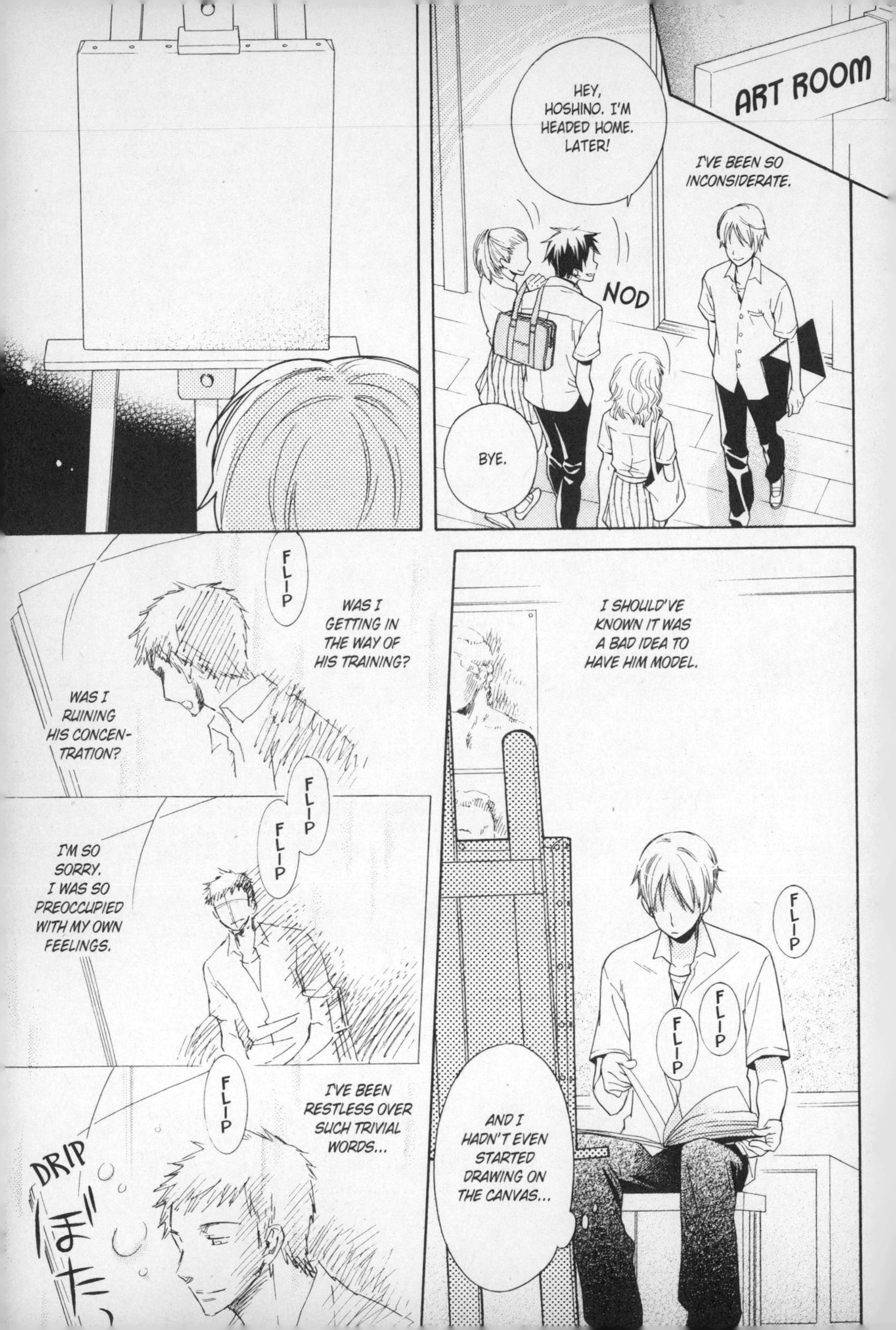
ART ROOM
HEY, HOSHINO. I'M HEADED HOME. LATER!
I'VE BEEN SO INCONSIDERATE.
NOD
BYE.
I SHOULD'VE KNOWN IT WAS A BAD IDEA TO HAVE HIM MODEL.
FLIP
FLIP
FLIP
AND I HADN'T EVEN STARTED DRAWING ON THE CANVAS...
FLIP
WAS I GETTING IN THE WAY OF HIS TRAINING?
WAS I RUINING HIS CONCENTRATION?
FLIP
FLIP
I'M SO SORRY. I WAS SO PREOCCUPIED WITH MY OWN FEELINGS.
FLIP
I'VE BEEN RESTLESS OVER SUCH TRIVIAL WORDS...
DRIP
ぽた、

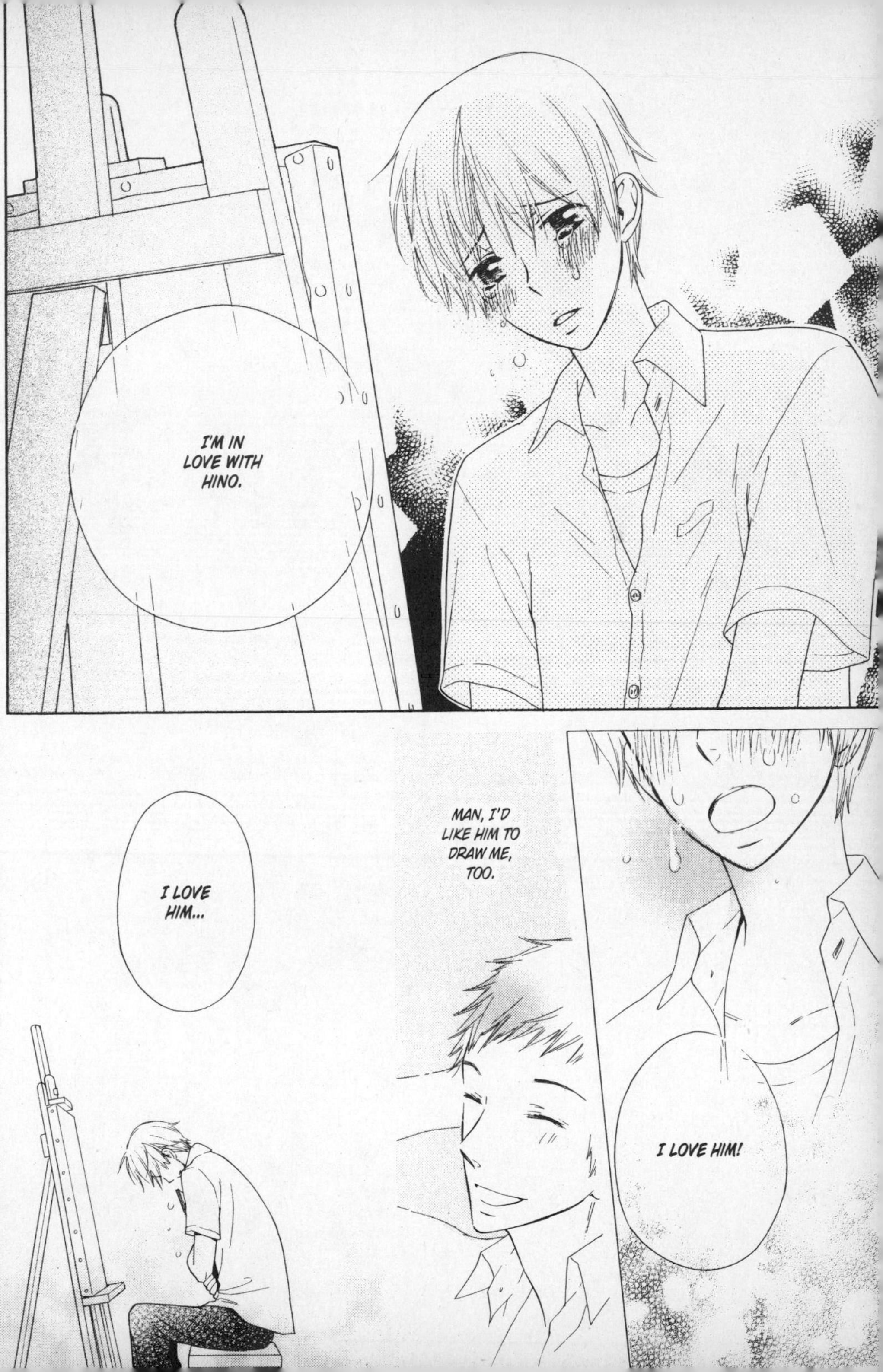
I'M IN LOVE WITH HINO.
I LOVE HIM!
MAN, I'D LIKE HIM TO DRAW ME, TOO.
I LOVE HIM...

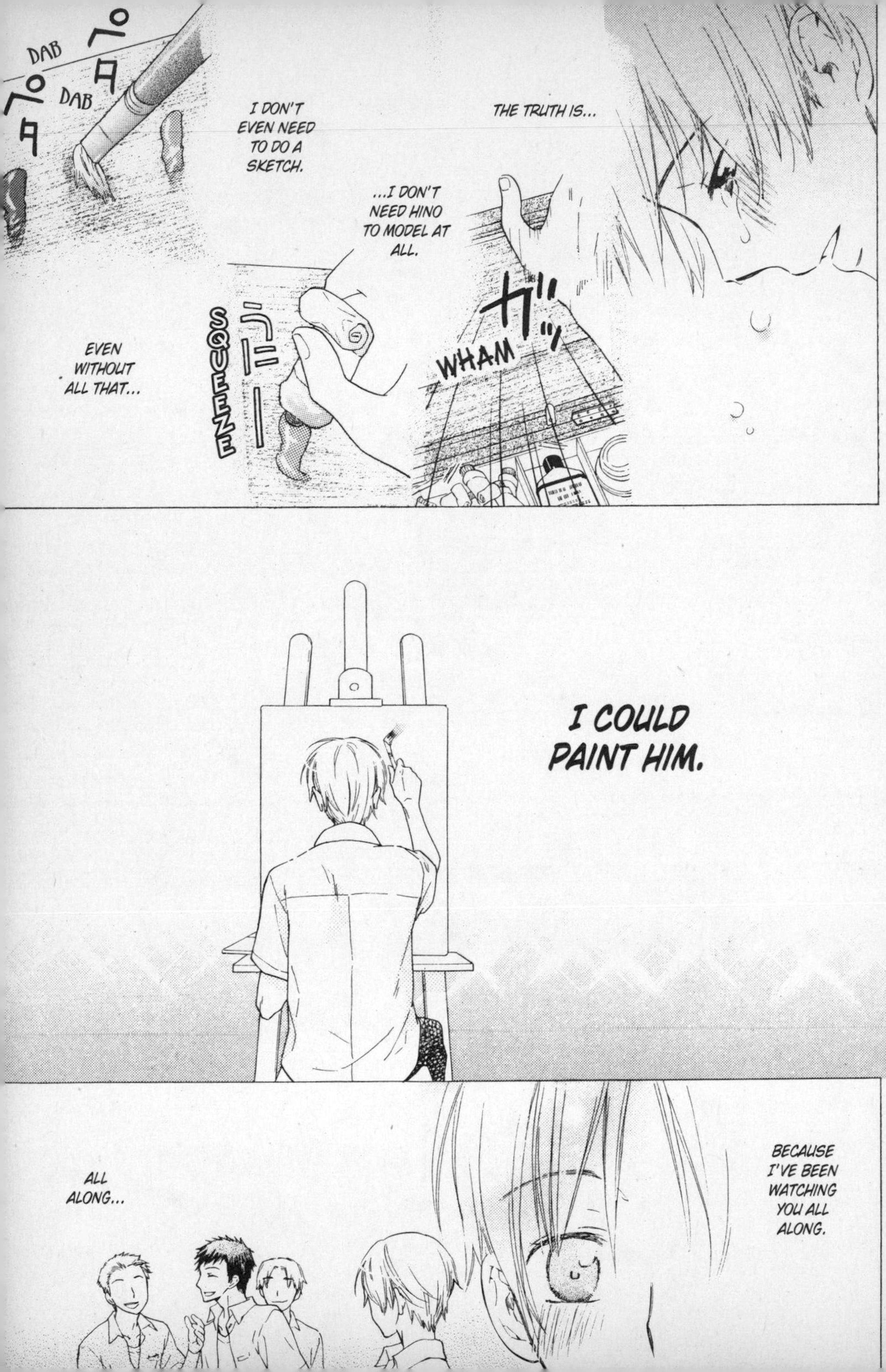
THE TRUTH IS...
ガッ
WHAM
I DON'T EVEN NEED TO DO A SKETCH.
...I DON'T NEED HINO TO MODEL AT ALL.
うにー
SQUEEZE
ペタ
DAB
ペタ
DAB
EVEN WITHOUT ALL THAT...
I COULD PAINT HIM.
BECAUSE I'VE BEEN WATCHING YOU ALL ALONG.
ALL ALONG...

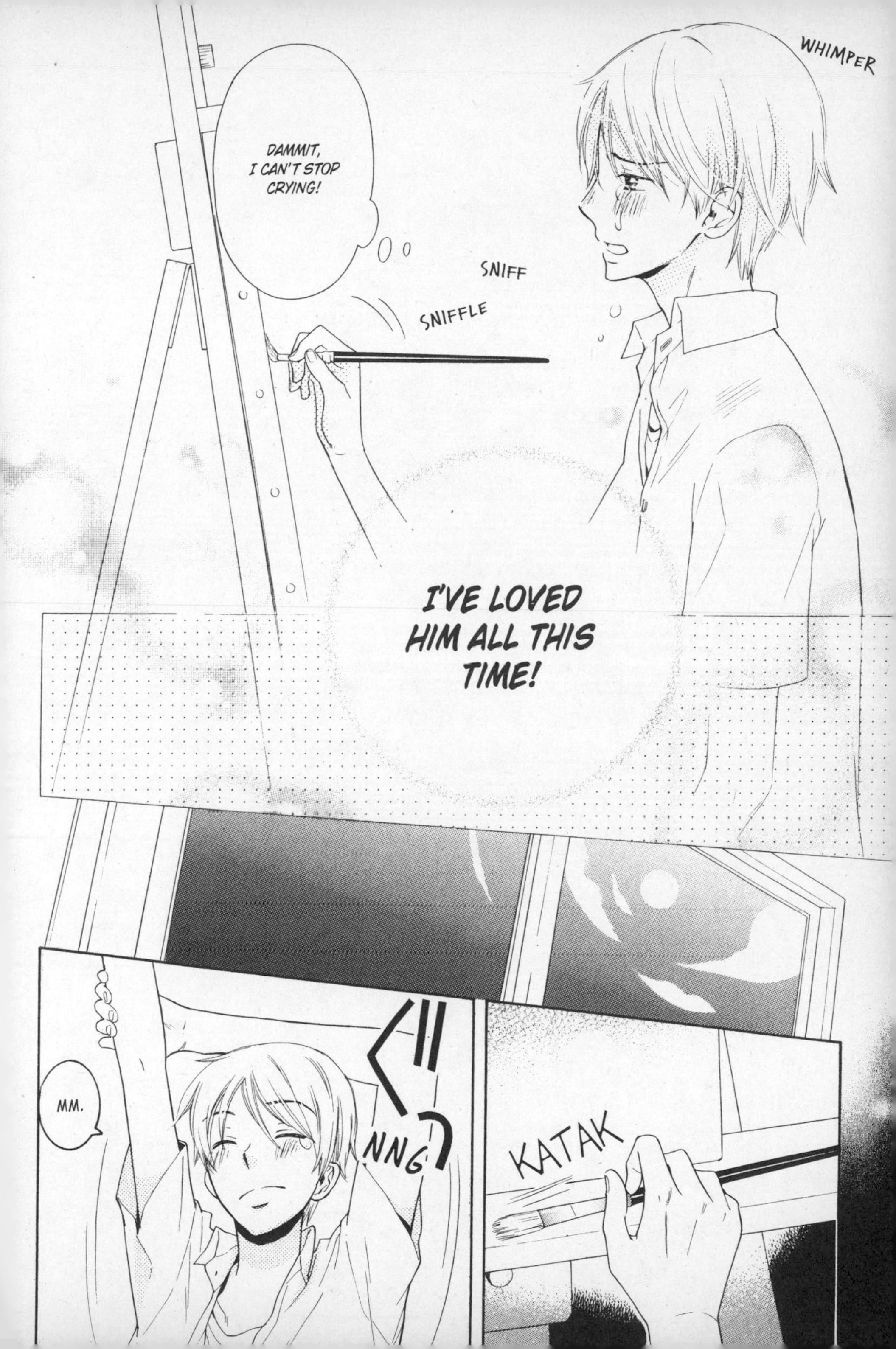

WHIMPER
SNIFF
SNIFFLE
DAMMIT, I CAN'T STOP CRYING!
I'VE LOVED HIM ALL THIS TIME!
KATAK
NNG
MM.

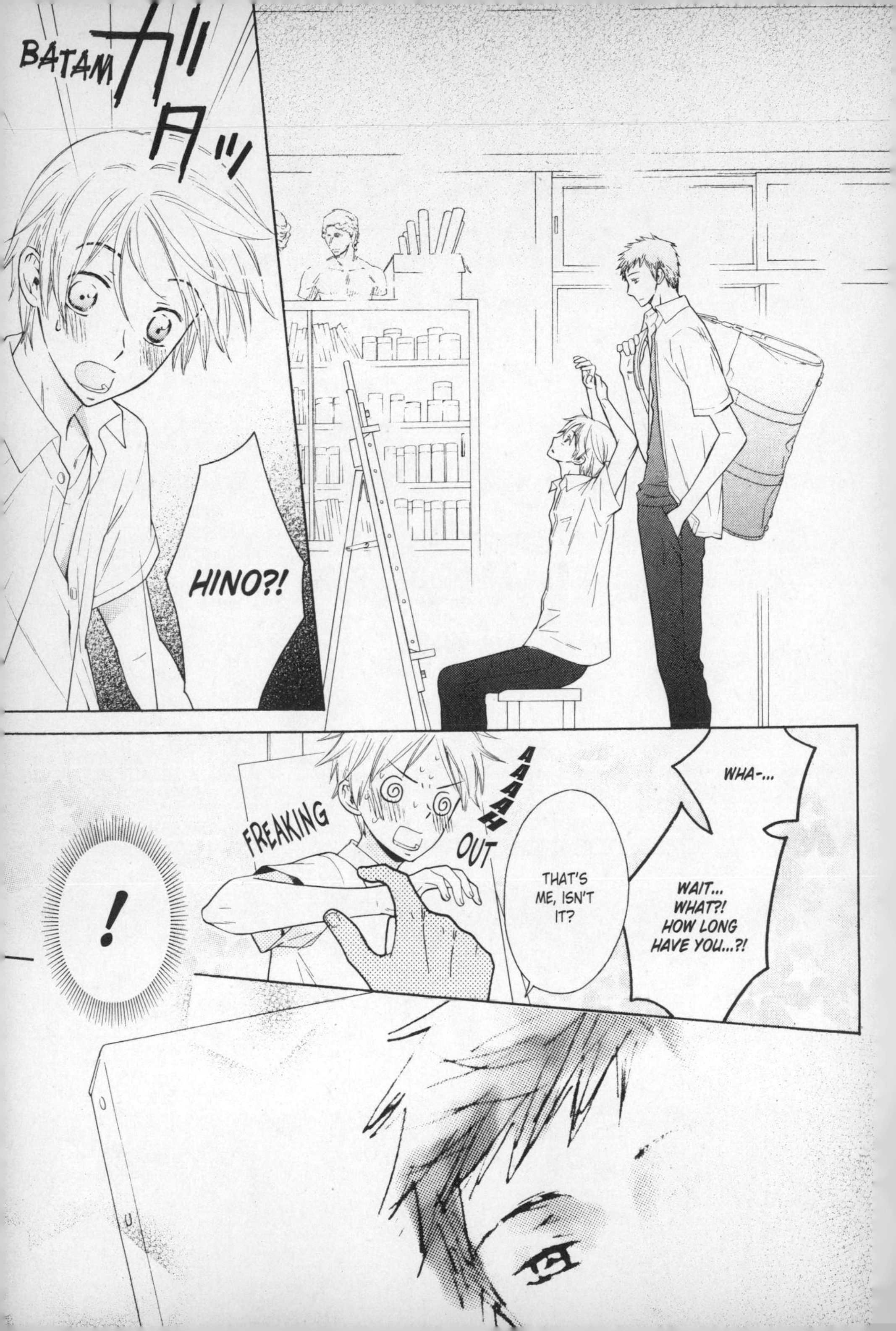
BATAM
ガタッ
HINO?!
WHA-...
WAIT... WHAT?! HOW LONG HAVE YOU...?!
THAT'S ME, ISN'T IT?
AAAAH
FREAKING OUT
!

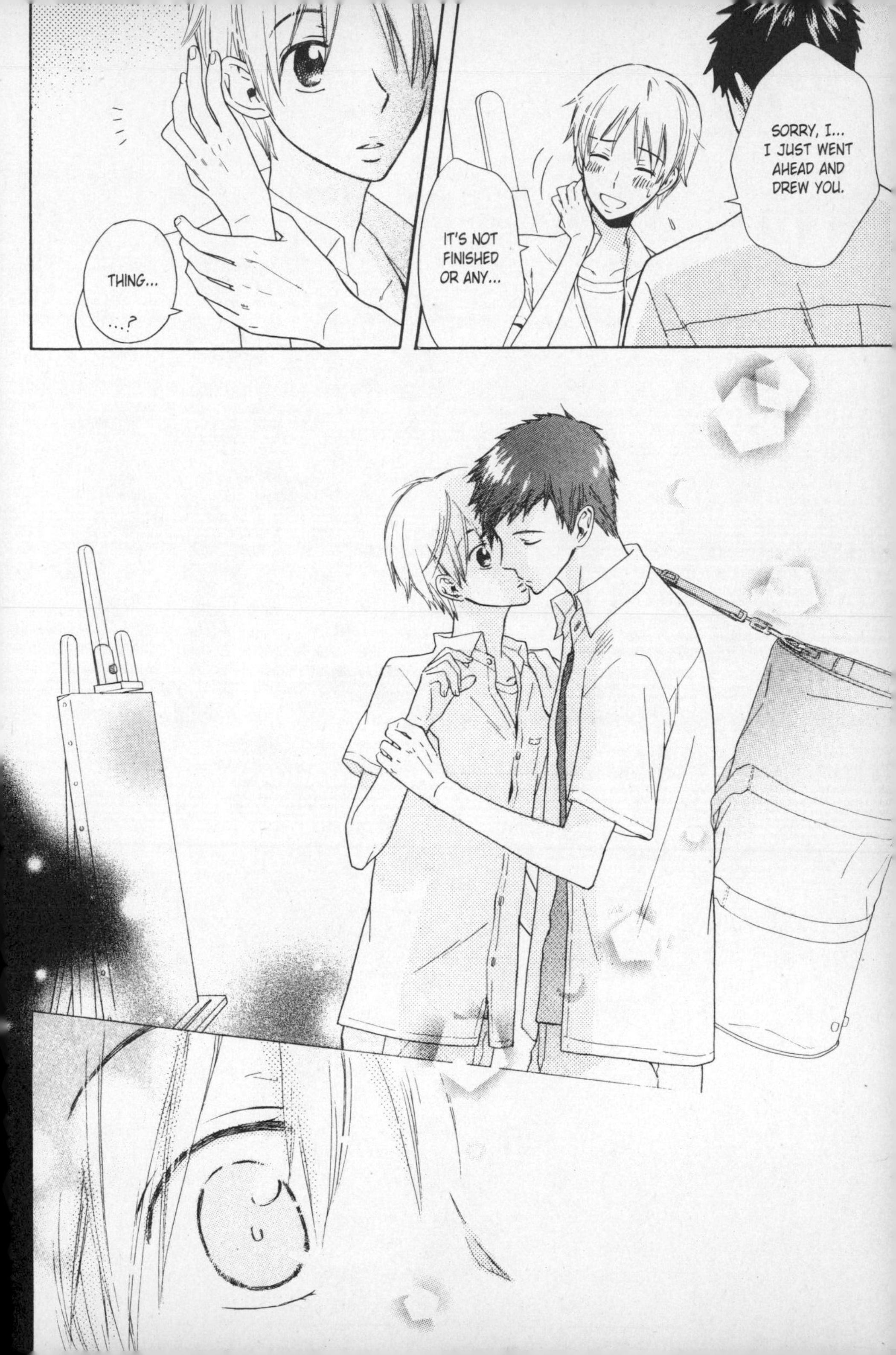
SORRY, I... I JUST WENT AHEAD AND DREW YOU.
IT'S NOT FINISHED OR ANY...
THING...
...?

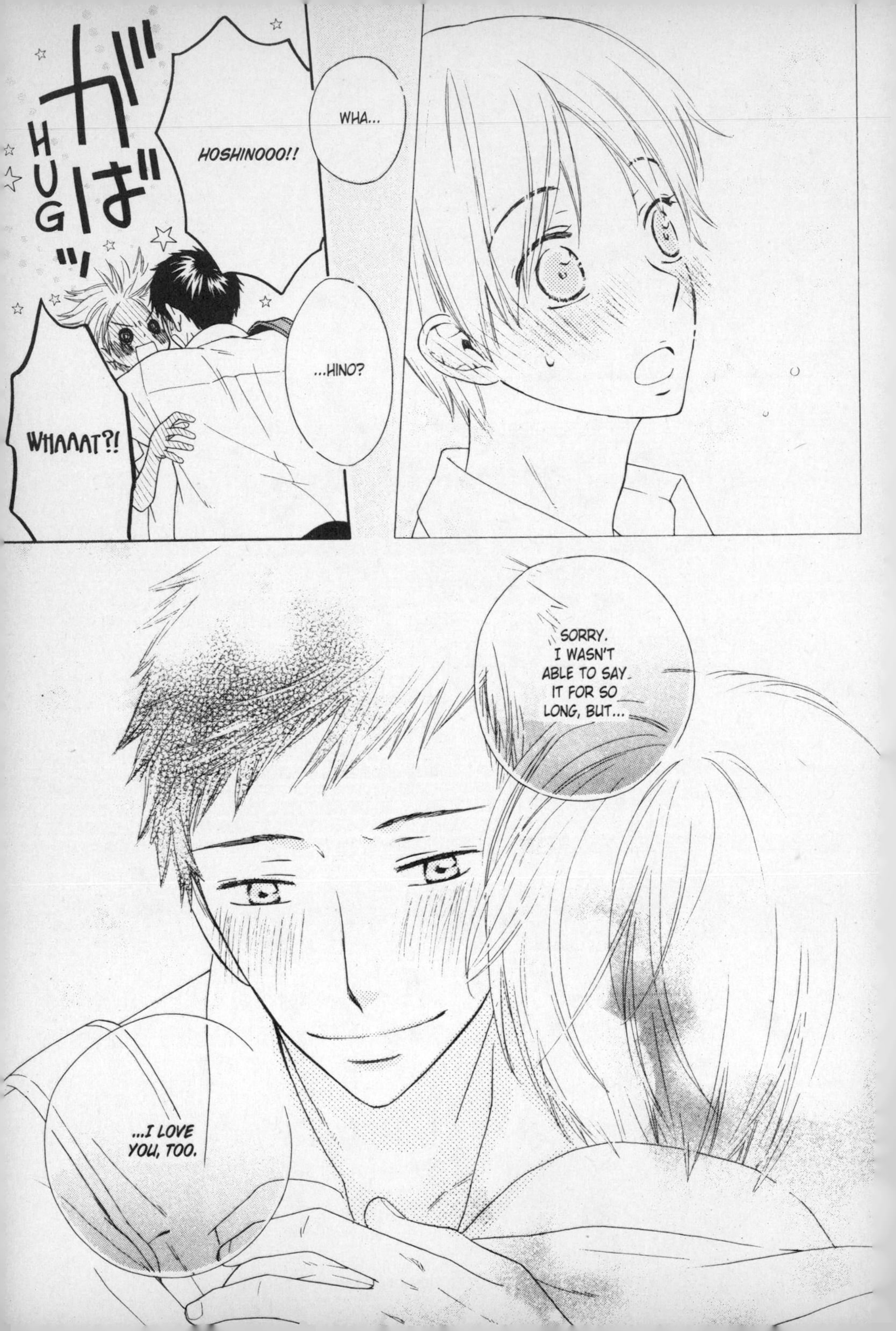
WHA...
...HINO?
HOSHINOOO!!
ガばッ
HUG
WHAAAT?!
SORRY. I WASN'T ABLE TO SAY IT FOR SO LONG, BUT...
...I LOVE YOU, TOO.

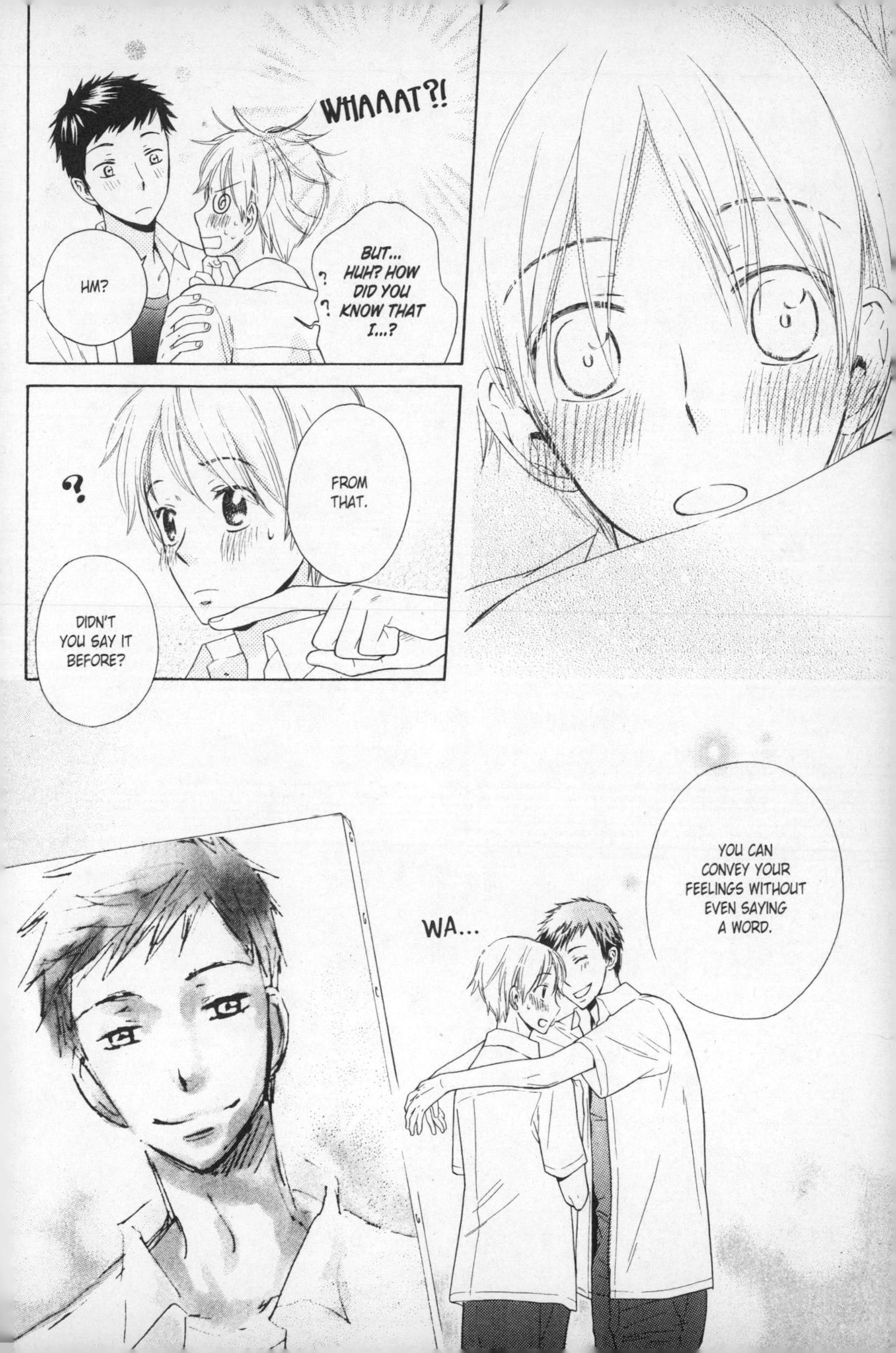
WHAAAT?!
BUT... HUH? HOW DID YOU KNOW THAT I...?
? ?
HM?
FROM THAT.
?
DIDN'T YOU SAY IT BEFORE?
YOU CAN CONVEY YOUR FEELINGS WITHOUT EVEN SAYING A WORD.
WA...

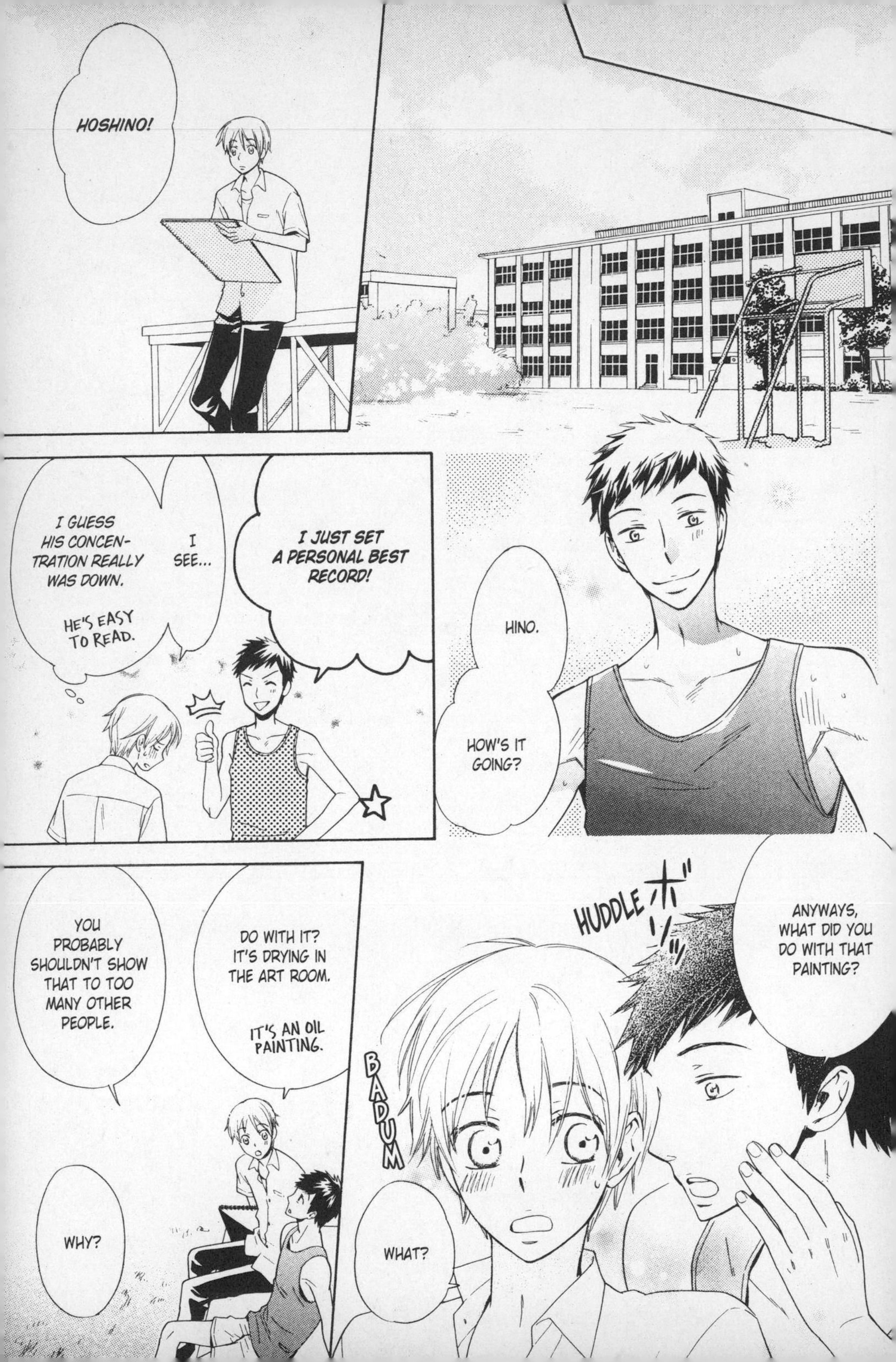

HOSHINO!
HINO.
HOW'S IT GOING?
I JUST SET A PERSONAL BEST RECORD!
I SEE...
I GUESS HIS CONCENTRATION REALLY WAS DOWN.
HE'S EASY TO READ.
ANYWAYS, WHAT DID YOU DO WITH THAT PAINTING?
HUDDLE
ボ
BADUM
WHAT?
DO WITH IT? IT'S DRYING IN THE ART ROOM.
IT'S AN OIL PAINTING.
YOU PROBABLY SHOULDN'T SHOW THAT TO TOO MANY OTHER PEOPLE.
WHY?

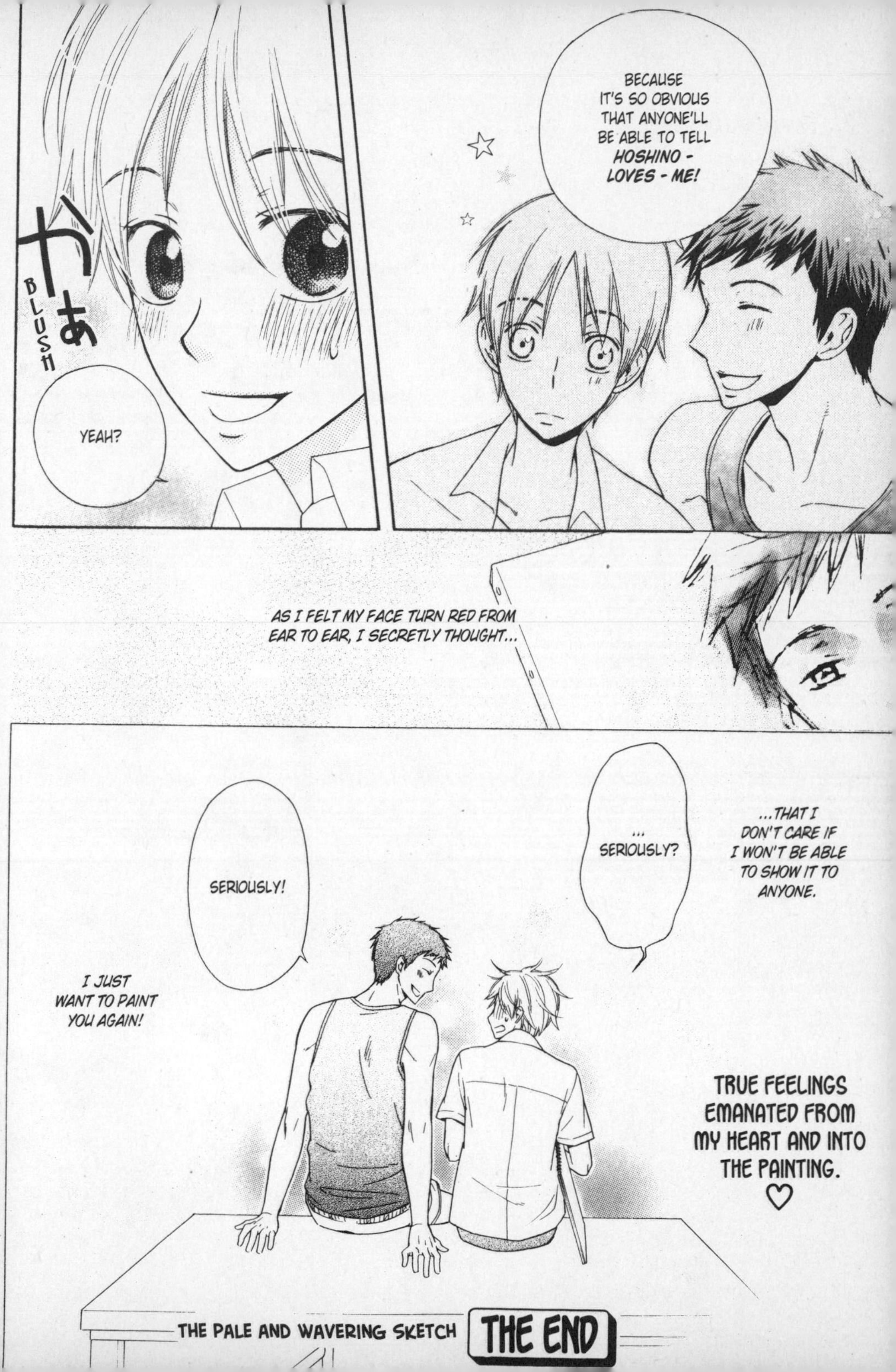
BECAUSE IT'S SO OBVIOUS THAT ANYONE'LL BE ABLE TO TELL ***HOSHINO - LOVES - ME!***
かあ
BLUSH
YEAH?
AS I FELT MY FACE TURN RED FROM EAR TO EAR, I SECRETLY THOUGHT...
...THAT I DON'T CARE IF I WON'T BE ABLE TO SHOW IT TO ANYONE.
... SERIOUSLY?
SERIOUSLY!
I JUST WANT TO PAINT YOU AGAIN!
TRUE FEELINGS EMANATED FROM MY HEART AND INTO THE PAINTING. ♡
THE PALE AND WAVERING SKETCH
THE END

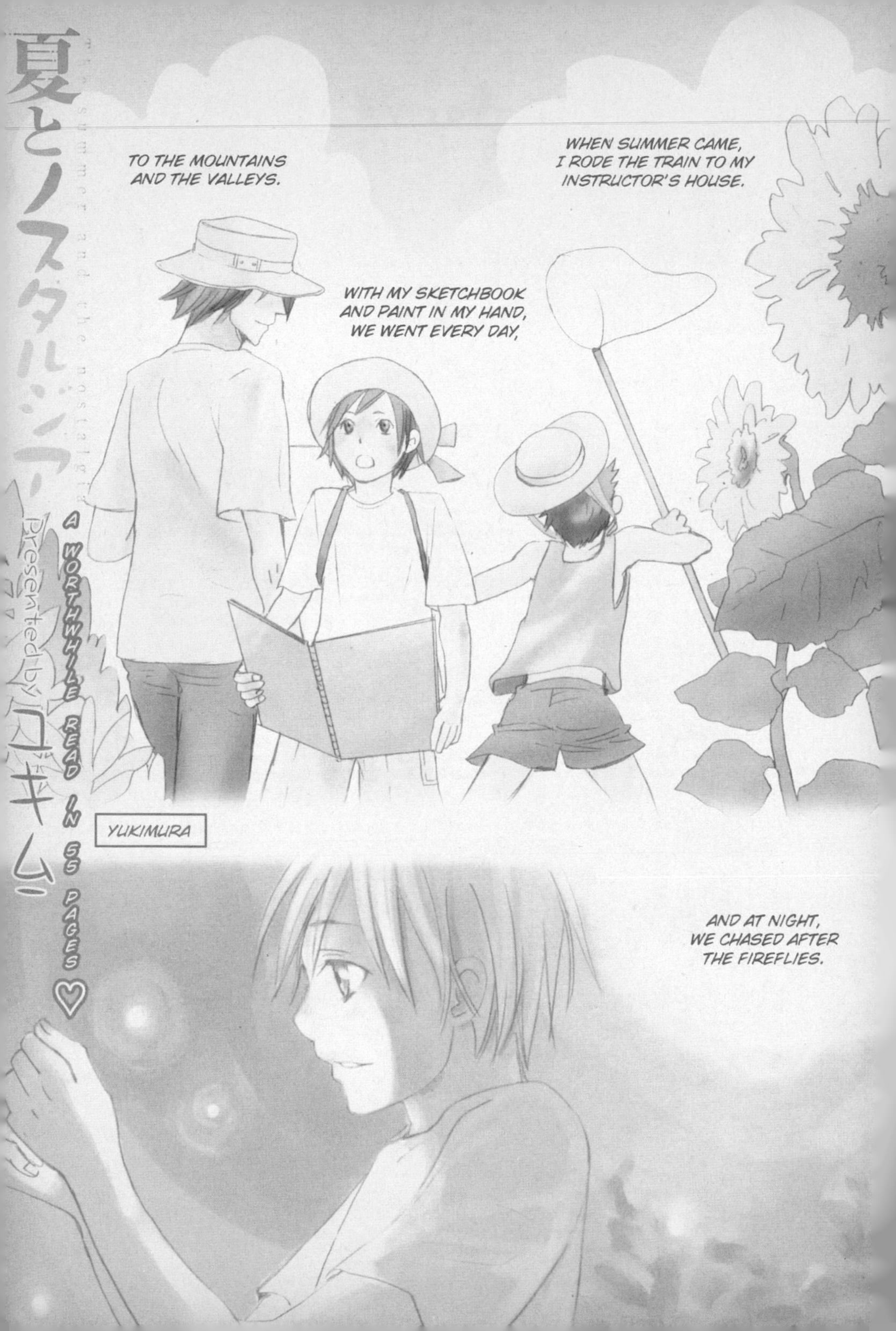
夏とノスタルジア
the summer and the nostalgia
A WORTHWHILE READ IN 55 PAGES ♡
Presented by
WHEN SUMMER CAME, I RODE THE TRAIN TO MY INSTRUCTOR'S HOUSE.
TO THE MOUNTAINS AND THE VALLEYS.
WITH MY SKETCHBOOK AND PAINT IN MY HAND, WE WENT EVERY DAY,
YUKIMURA
AND AT NIGHT, WE CHASED AFTER THE FIREFLIES.

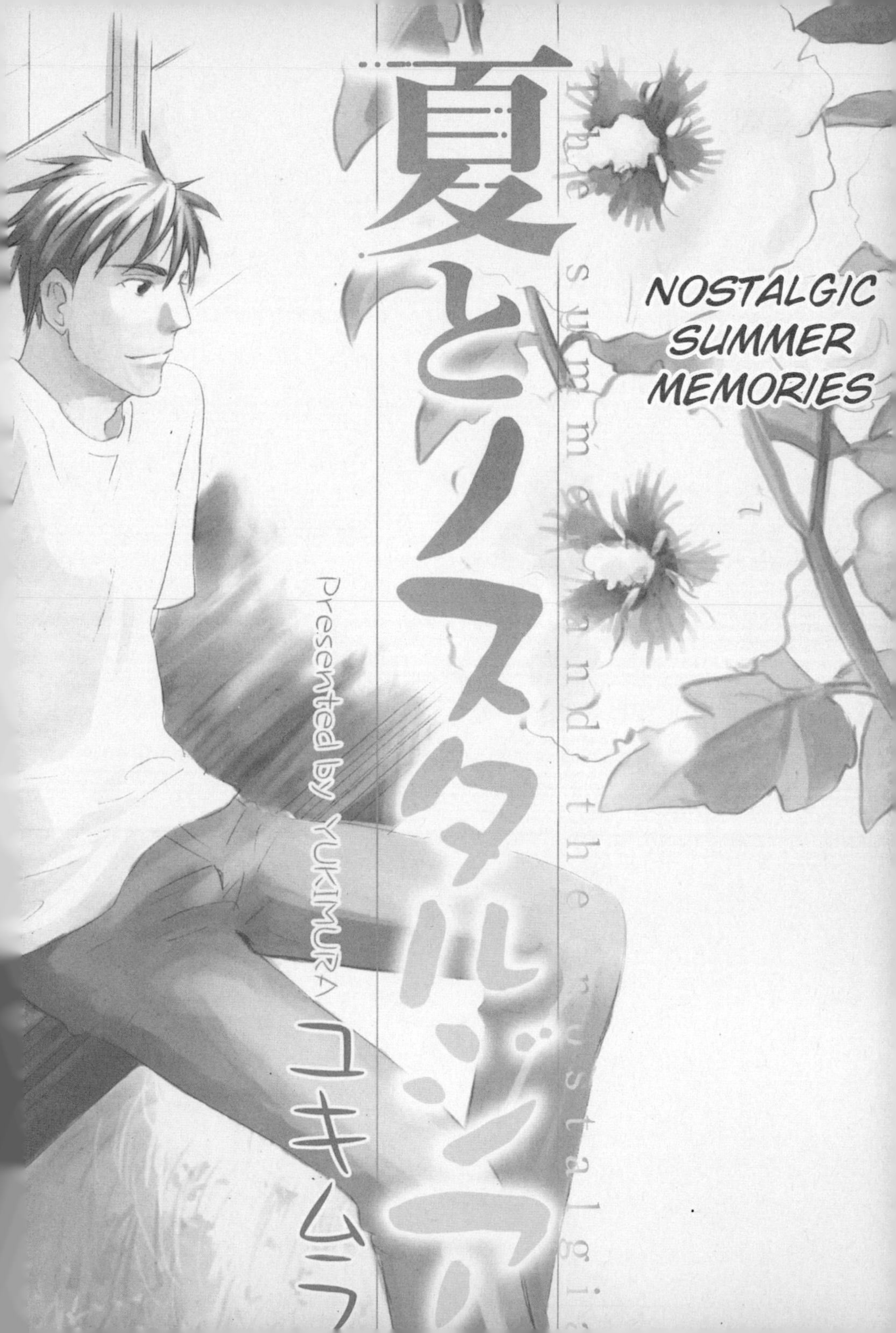
夏とノスタルジア
the summer and the nostalgi
NOSTALGIC SUMMER MEMORIES
Presented by YUKIMURA
ユキムラ

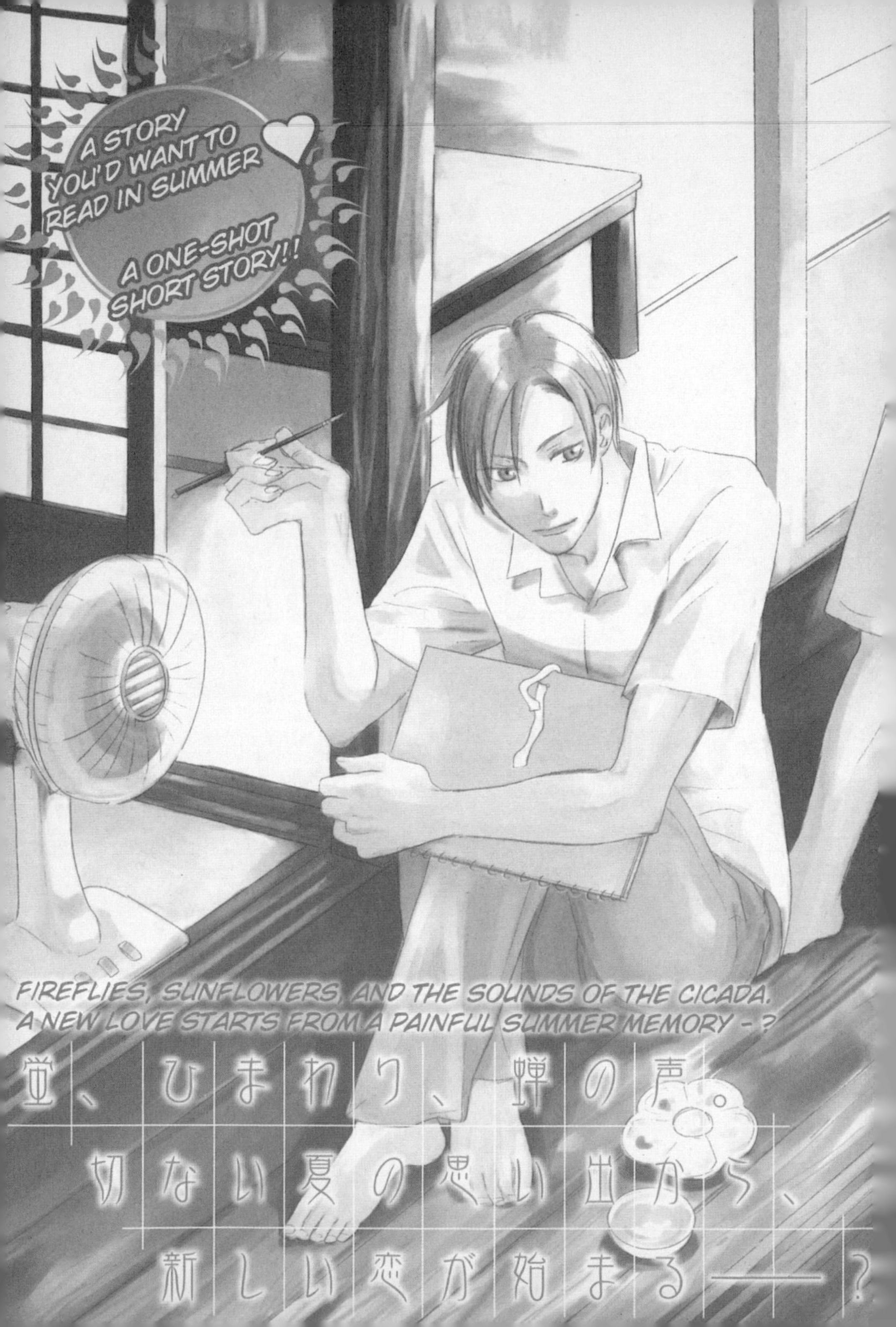
A STORY YOU'D WANT TO READ IN SUMMER
A ONE-SHOT SHORT STORY!!
FIREFLIES, SUNFLOWERS, AND THE SOUNDS OF THE CICADA.
A NEW LOVE STARTS FROM A PAINFUL SUMMER MEMORY - ?
蛍、ひまわり、蝉の声。
切ない夏の思い出から、
新しい恋が始まる——？

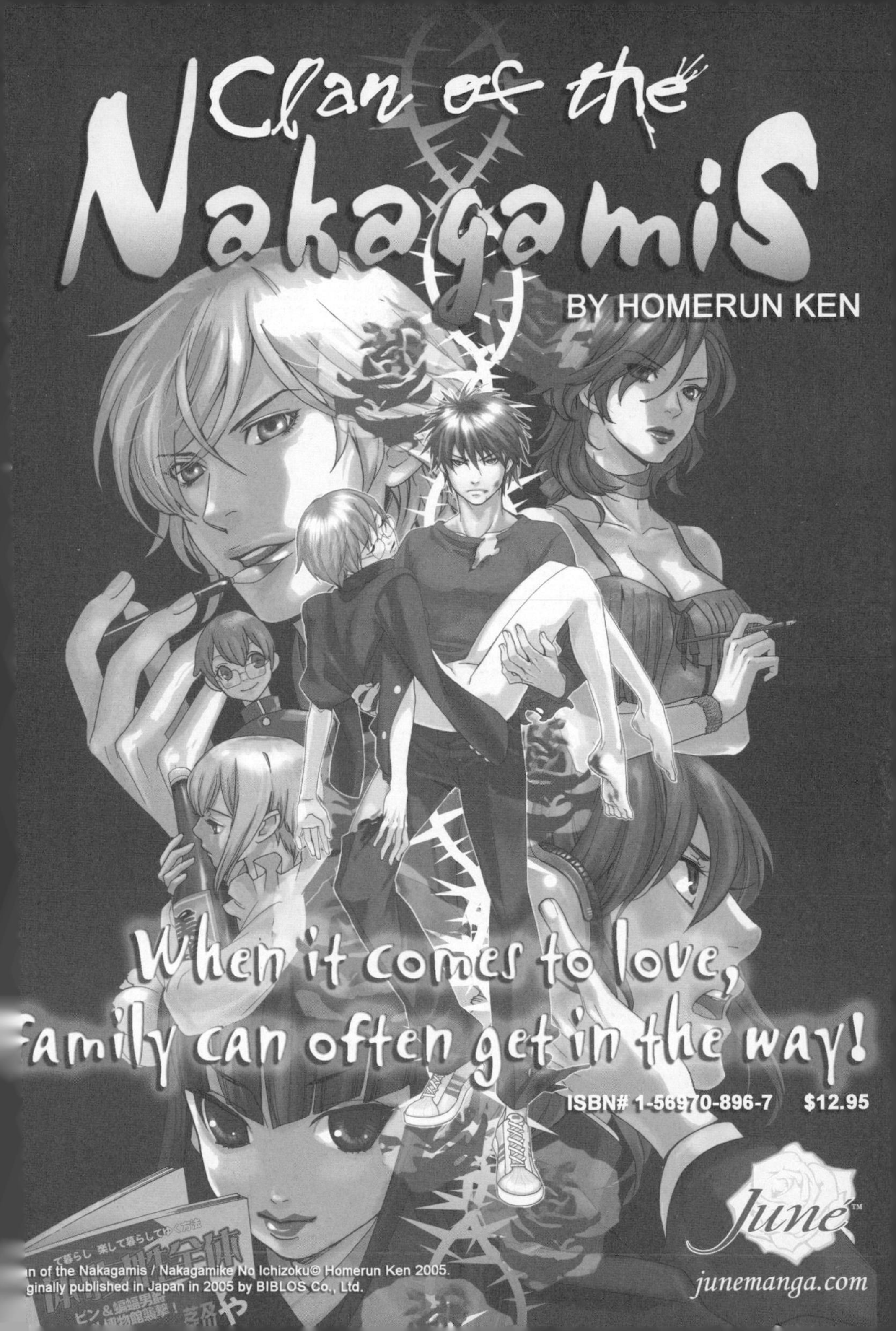
Clan of the Nakagamis
BY HOMERUN KEN
When it comes to love, family can often get in the way!
ISBN# 1-56970-896-7 $12.95
June™
an of the Nakagamis / Nakagamike No Ichizoku© Homerun Ken 2005.
ginally published in Japan in 2005 by BIBLOS Co., Ltd.
junemanga.com

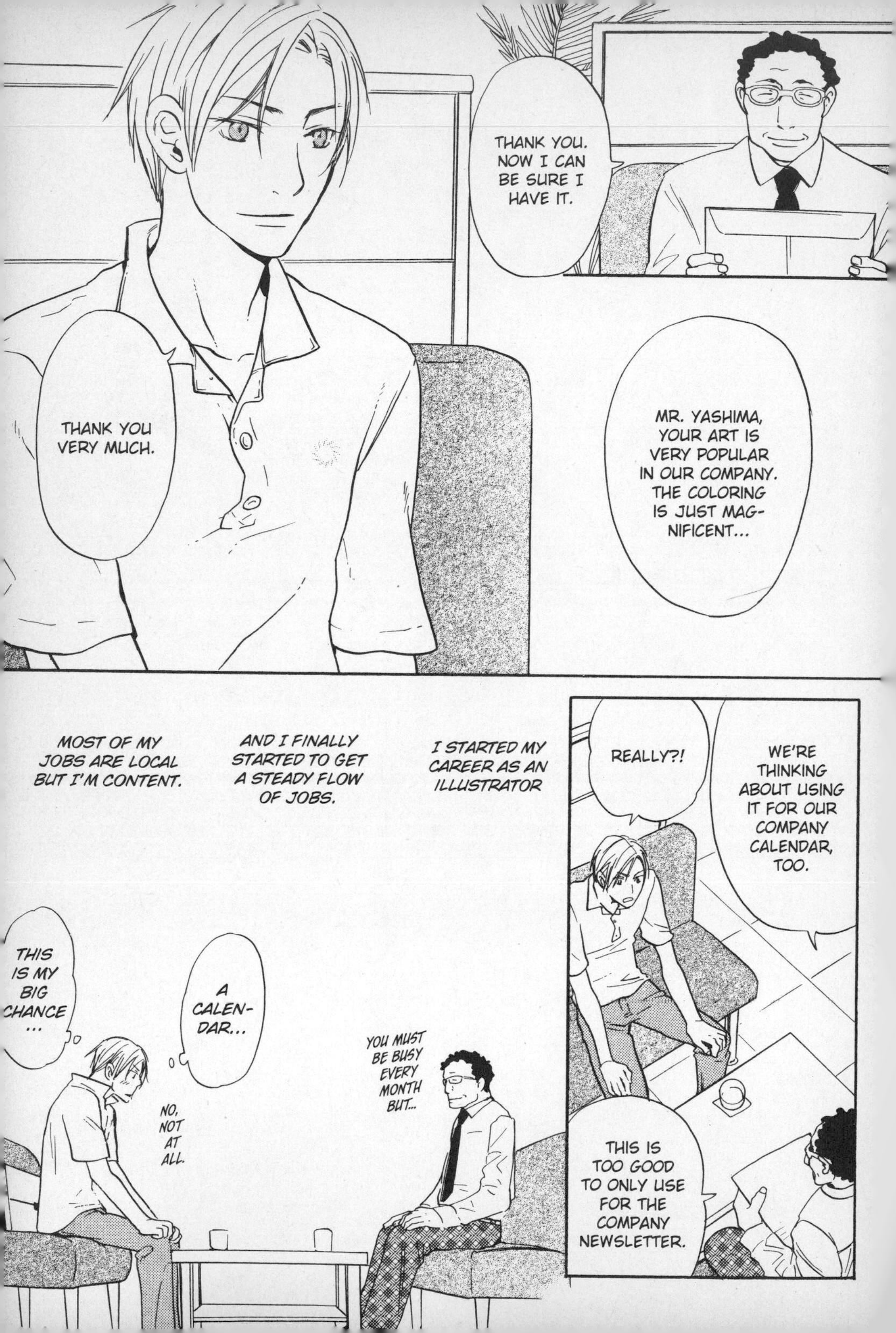
THANK YOU. NOW I CAN BE SURE I HAVE IT.
MR. YASHIMA, YOUR ART IS VERY POPULAR IN OUR COMPANY. THE COLORING IS JUST MAG-NIFICENT...
THANK YOU VERY MUCH.
WE'RE THINKING ABOUT USING IT FOR OUR COMPANY CALENDAR, TOO.
REALLY?!
THIS IS TOO GOOD TO ONLY USE FOR THE COMPANY NEWSLETTER.
I STARTED MY CAREER AS AN ILLUSTRATOR
AND I FINALLY STARTED TO GET A STEADY FLOW OF JOBS.
MOST OF MY JOBS ARE LOCAL BUT I'M CONTENT.
YOU MUST BE BUSY EVERY MONTH BUT...
NO, NOT AT ALL.
A CALEN-DAR...
THIS IS MY BIG CHANCE...

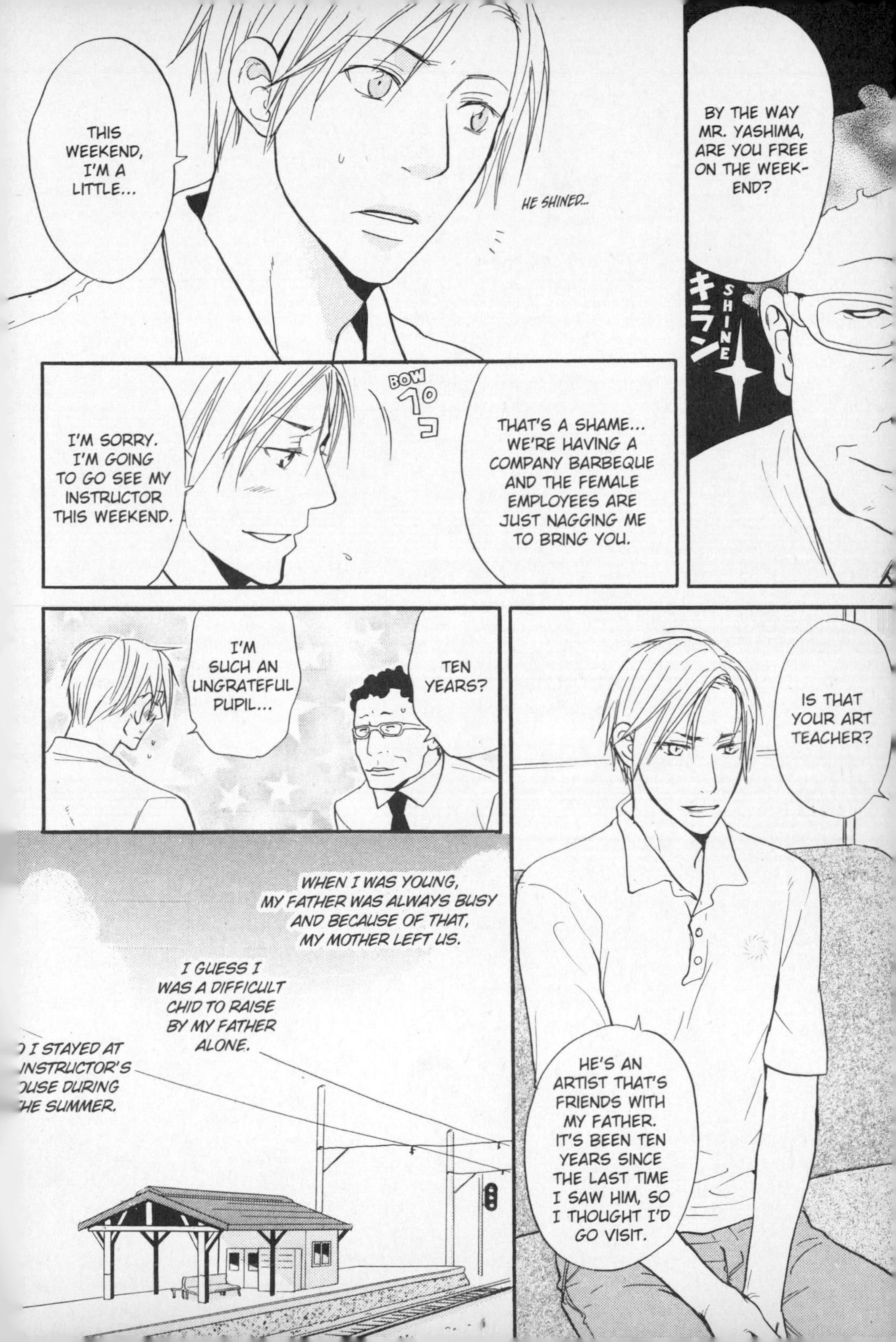
BY THE WAY MR. YASHIMA, ARE YOU FREE ON THE WEEK-END?
キラン
SHINE
HE SHINED...
THIS WEEKEND, I'M A LITTLE...
THAT'S A SHAME... WE'RE HAVING A COMPANY BARBEQUE AND THE FEMALE EMPLOYEES ARE JUST NAGGING ME TO BRING YOU.
BOW
ペコ
I'M SORRY. I'M GOING TO GO SEE MY INSTRUCTOR THIS WEEKEND.
IS THAT YOUR ART TEACHER?
HE'S AN ARTIST THAT'S FRIENDS WITH MY FATHER. IT'S BEEN TEN YEARS SINCE THE LAST TIME I SAW HIM, SO I THOUGHT I'D GO VISIT.
TEN YEARS?
I'M SUCH AN UNGRATEFUL PUPIL...
WHEN I WAS YOUNG, MY FATHER WAS ALWAYS BUSY AND BECAUSE OF THAT, MY MOTHER LEFT US.
I GUESS I WAS A DIFFICULT CHID TO RAISE BY MY FATHER ALONE.
O I STAYED AT INSTRUCTOR'S OUSE DURING HE SUMMER.

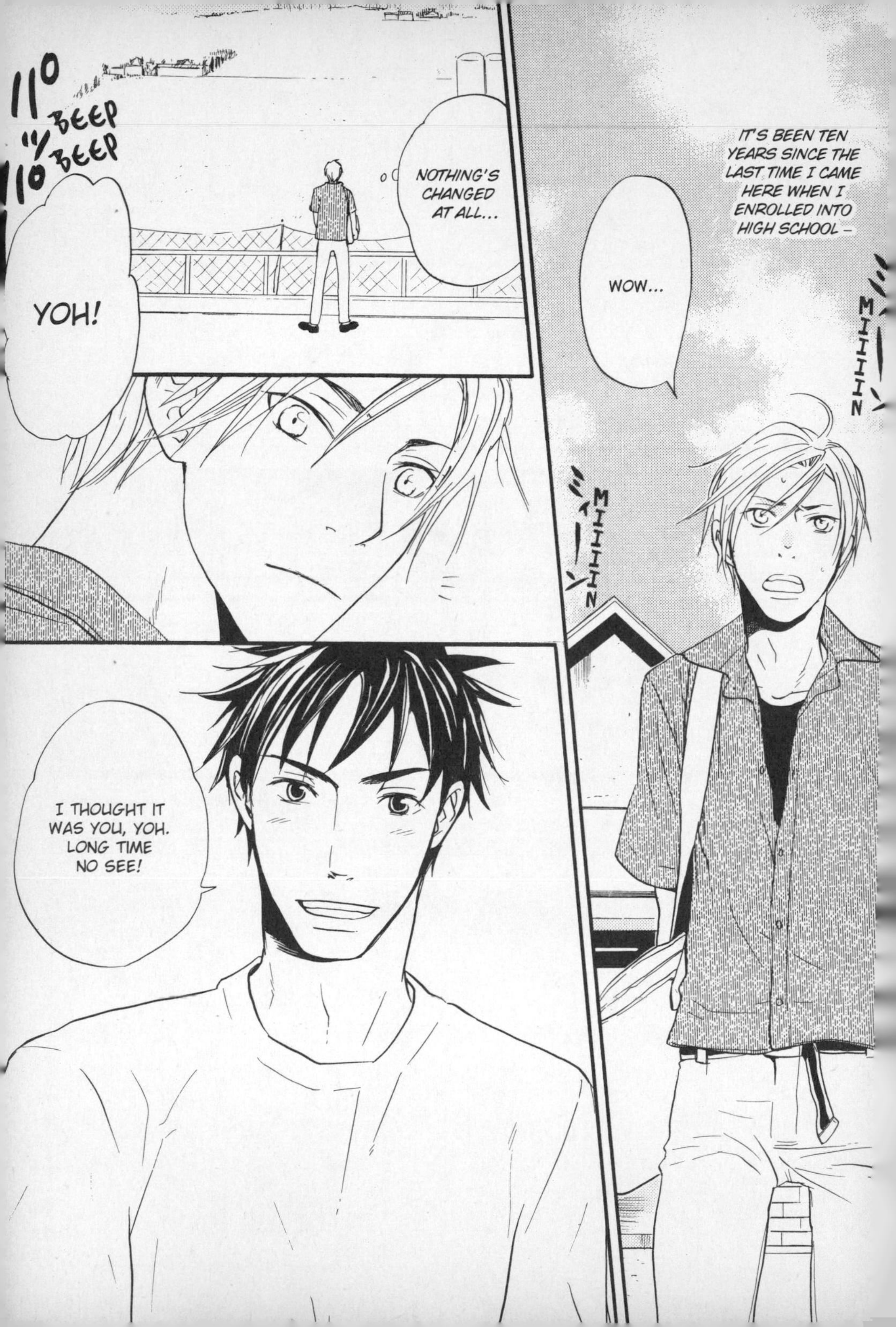
IT'S BEEN TEN YEARS SINCE THE LAST TIME I CAME HERE WHEN I ENROLLED INTO HIGH SCHOOL –
WOW...
MIIIIIN
MIIIIIN
NOTHING'S CHANGED AT ALL...
BEEP BEEP
YOH!
I THOUGHT IT WAS YOU, YOH. LONG TIME NO SEE!

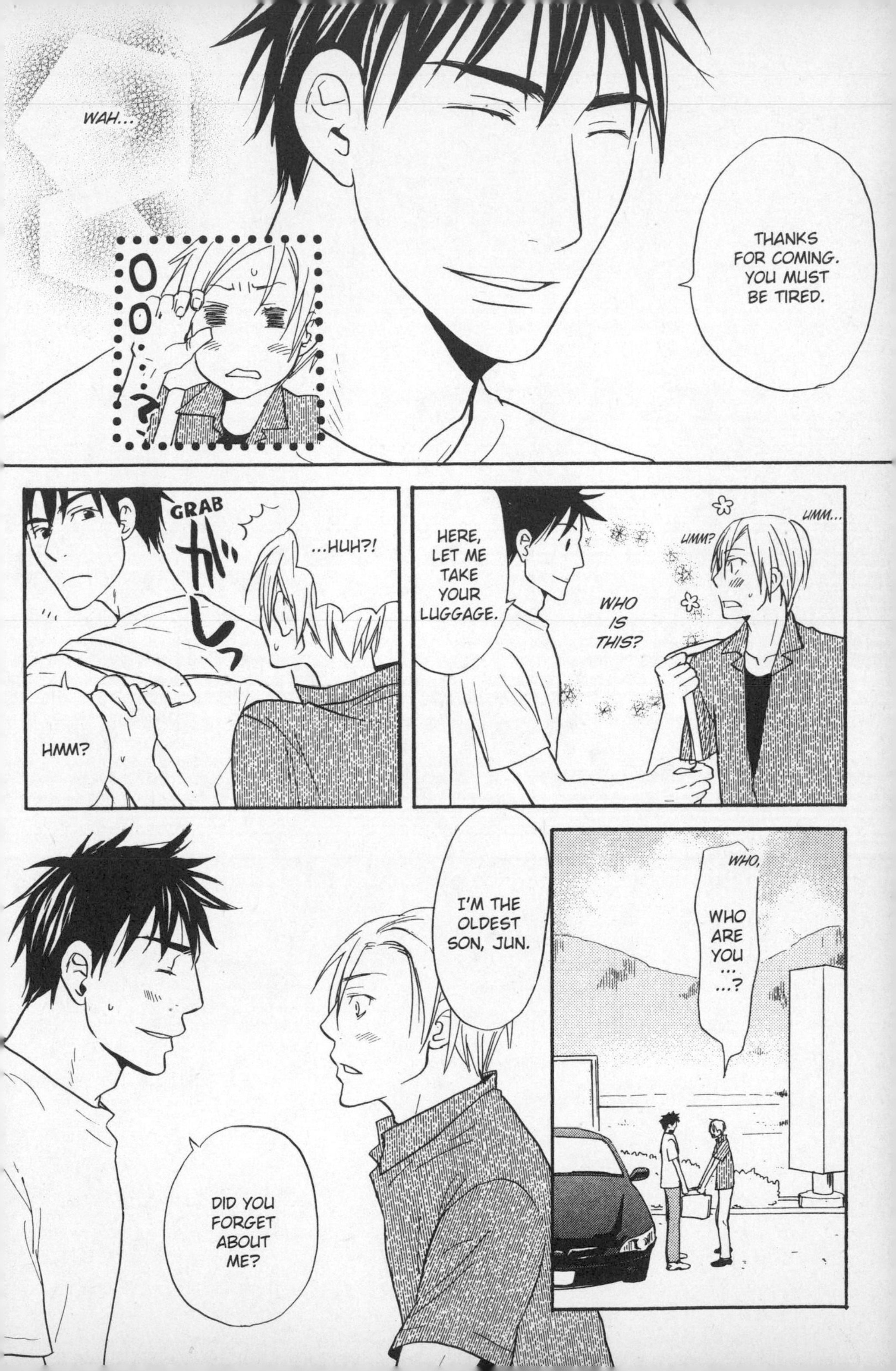
THANKS FOR COMING. YOU MUST BE TIRED.
WAH...
UMM...
UMM?
WHO IS THIS?
HERE, LET ME TAKE YOUR LUGGAGE.
...HUH?!
GRAB
がしっ
HMM?
WHO,
WHO ARE YOU ......?
I'M THE OLDEST SON, JUN.
DID YOU FORGET ABOUT ME?

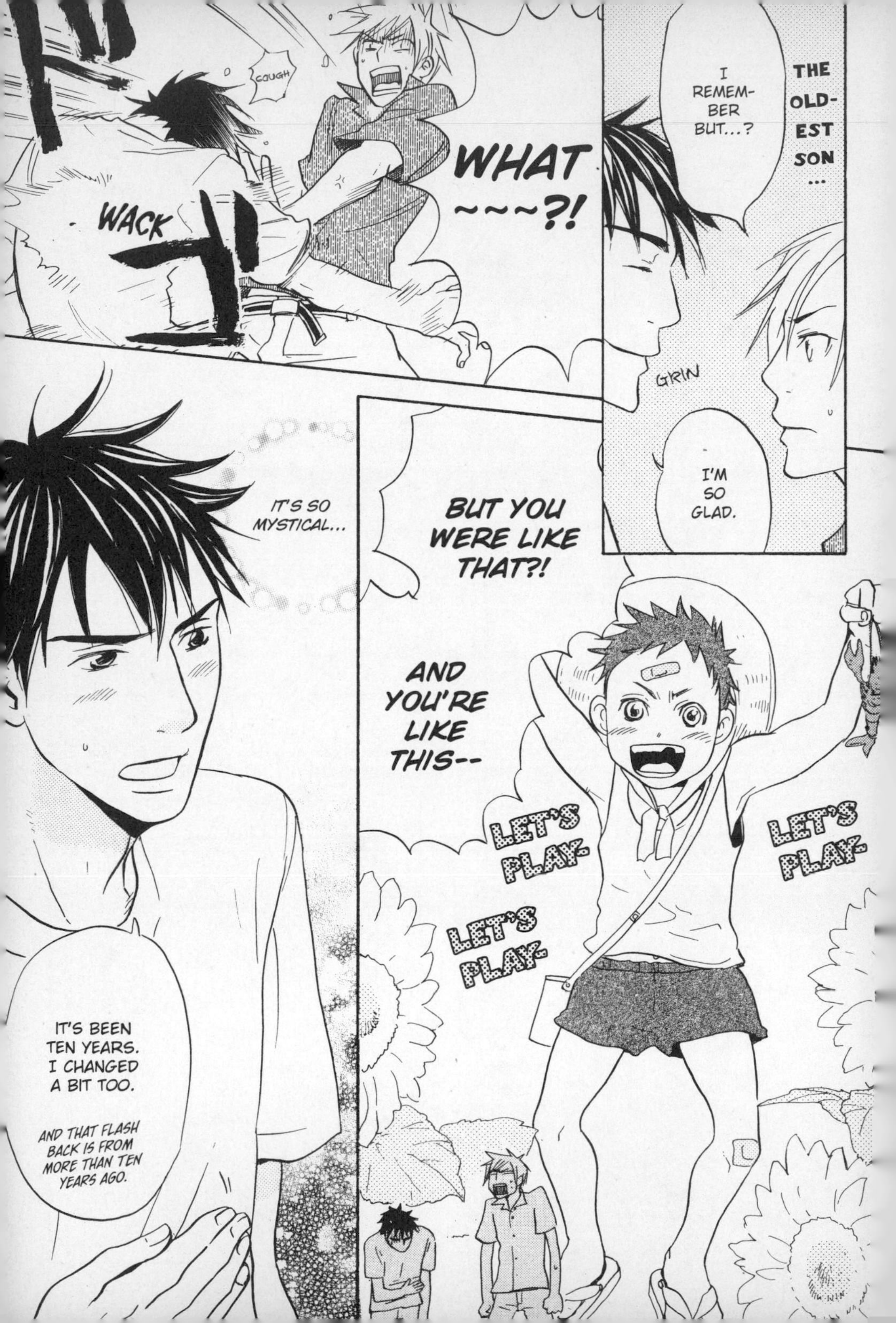
THE OLDEST SON...
I REMEMBER BUT...?
GRIN
I'M SO GLAD.
COUGH
WACK
WHAT~~~?!
BUT YOU WERE LIKE THAT?!
AND YOU'RE LIKE THIS--
LET'S PLAY
LET'S PLAY
LET'S PLAY
IT'S SO MYSTICAL...
IT'S BEEN TEN YEARS. I CHANGED A BIT TOO.
AND THAT FLASH BACK IS FROM MORE THAN TEN YEARS AGO.

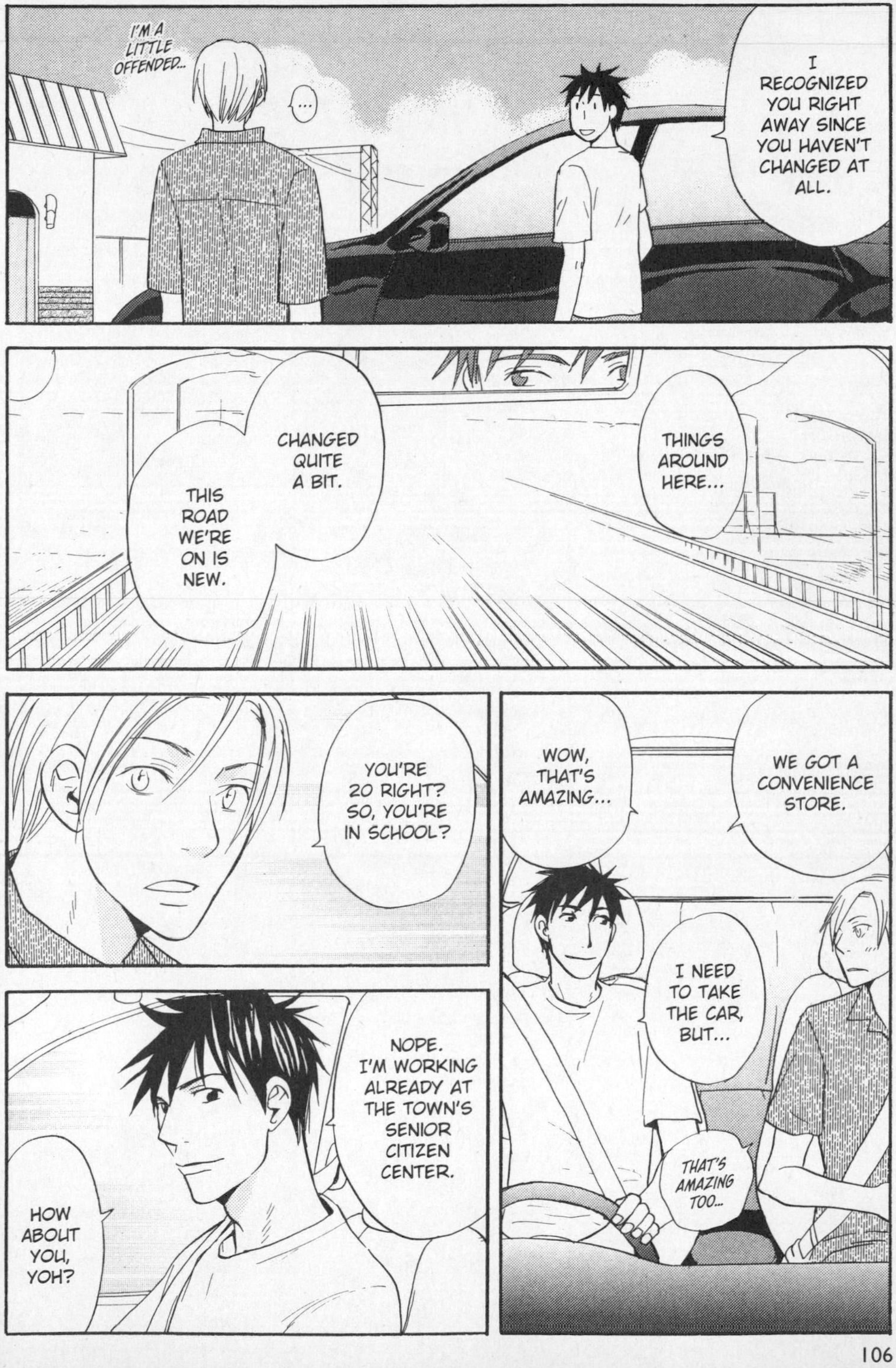
I RECOGNIZED YOU RIGHT AWAY SINCE YOU HAVEN'T CHANGED AT ALL.
...
I'M A LITTLE OFFENDED...
THINGS AROUND HERE...
CHANGED QUITE A BIT.
THIS ROAD WE'RE ON IS NEW.
WE GOT A CONVENIENCE STORE.
WOW, THAT'S AMAZING...
I NEED TO TAKE THE CAR, BUT...
THAT'S AMAZING TOO...
YOU'RE 20 RIGHT? SO, YOU'RE IN SCHOOL?
NOPE. I'M WORKING ALREADY AT THE TOWN'S SENIOR CITIZEN CENTER.
HOW ABOUT YOU, YOH?

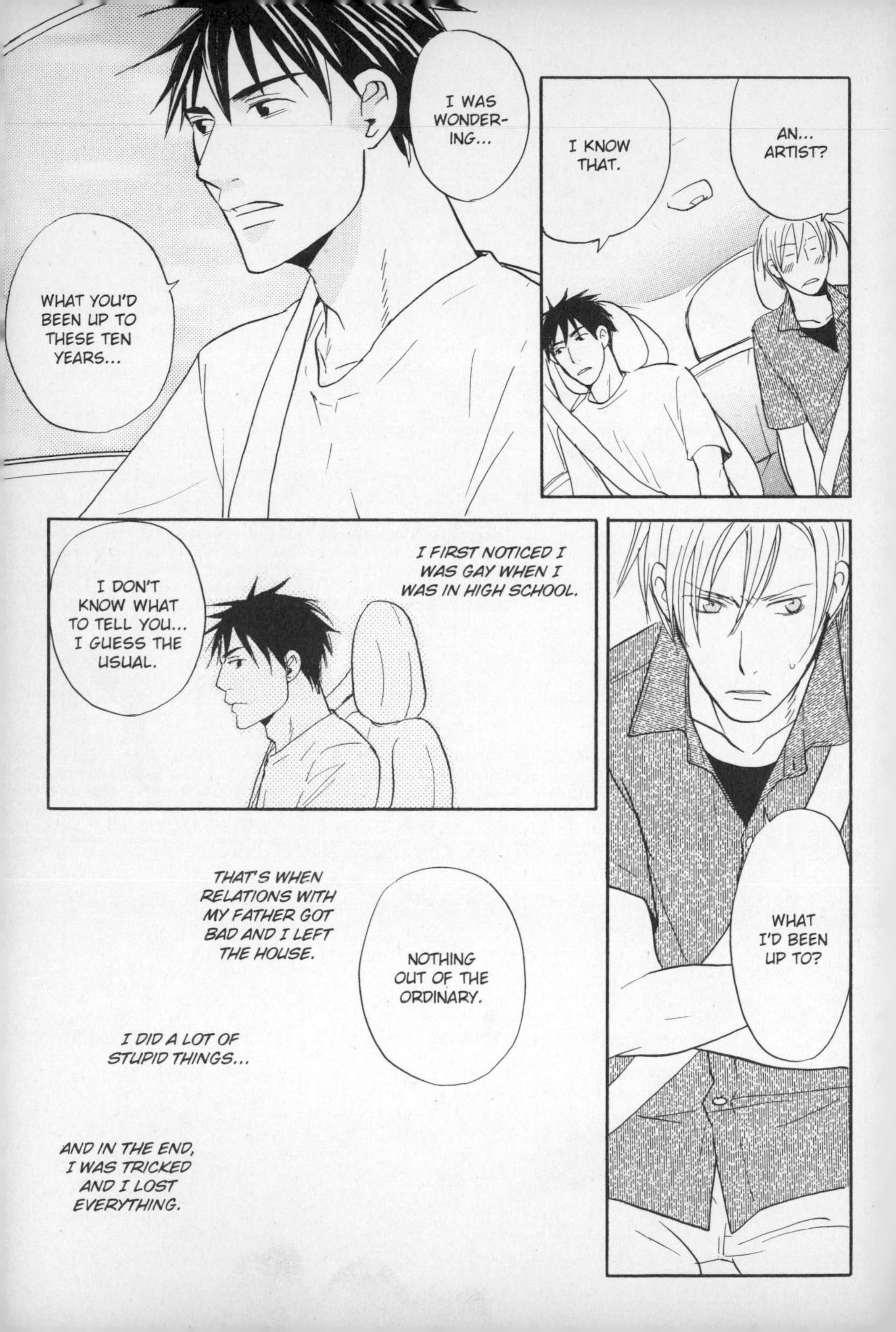
AN... ARTIST?
I KNOW THAT.
I WAS WONDER-ING...
WHAT YOU'D BEEN UP TO THESE TEN YEARS...
WHAT I'D BEEN UP TO?
I FIRST NOTICED I WAS GAY WHEN I WAS IN HIGH SCHOOL.
I DON'T KNOW WHAT TO TELL YOU... I GUESS THE USUAL.
NOTHING OUT OF THE ORDINARY.
THAT'S WHEN RELATIONS WITH MY FATHER GOT BAD AND I LEFT THE HOUSE.
I DID A LOT OF STUPID THINGS...
AND IN THE END, I WAS TRICKED AND I LOST EVERYTHING.

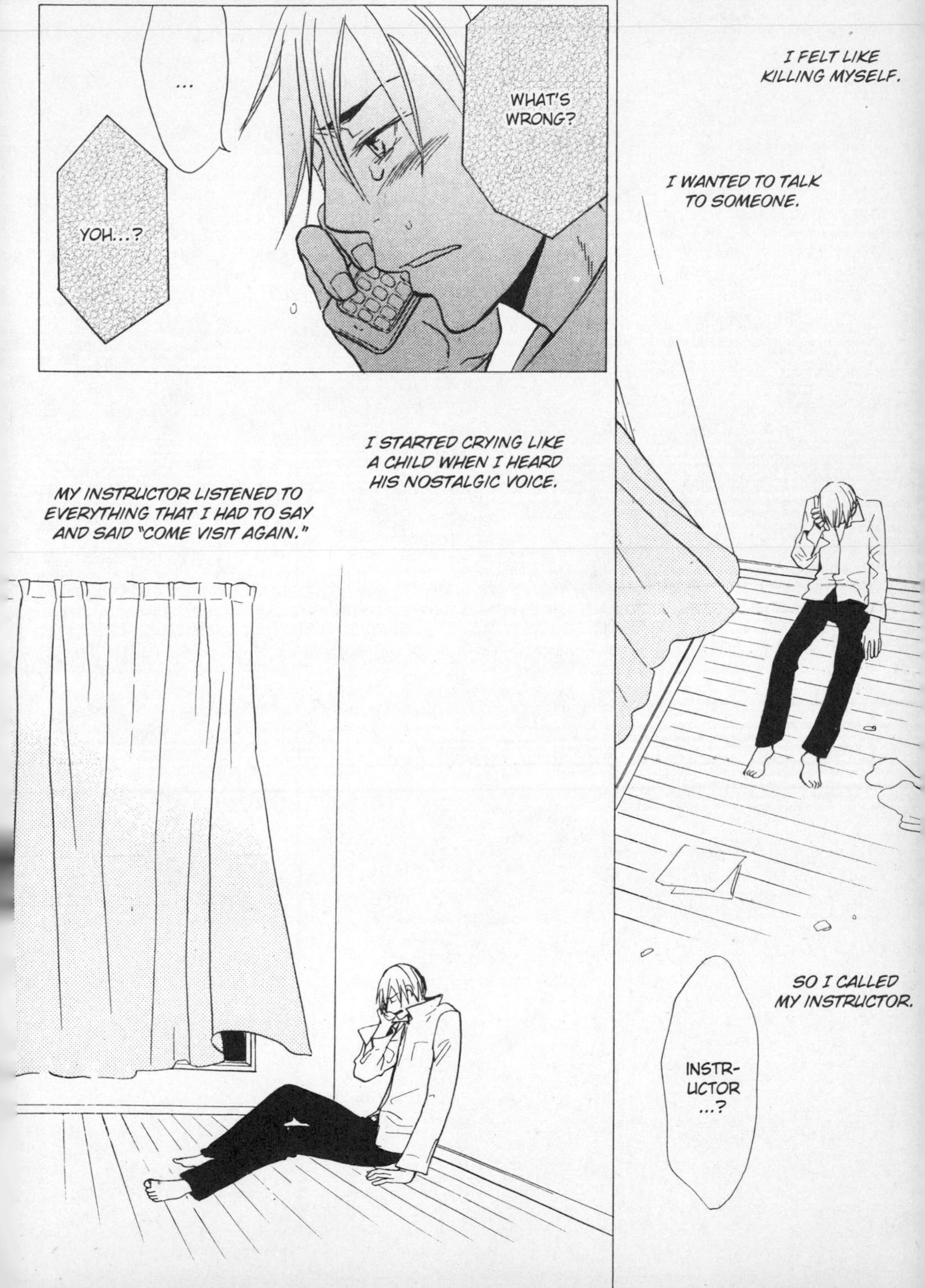
I FELT LIKE KILLING MYSELF.
I WANTED TO TALK TO SOMEONE.
SO I CALLED MY INSTRUCTOR.
INSTR-UCTOR ...?
WHAT'S WRONG?
...
YOH...?
I STARTED CRYING LIKE A CHILD WHEN I HEARD HIS NOSTALGIC VOICE.
MY INSTRUCTOR LISTENED TO EVERYTHING THAT I HAD TO SAY AND SAID "COME VISIT AGAIN."

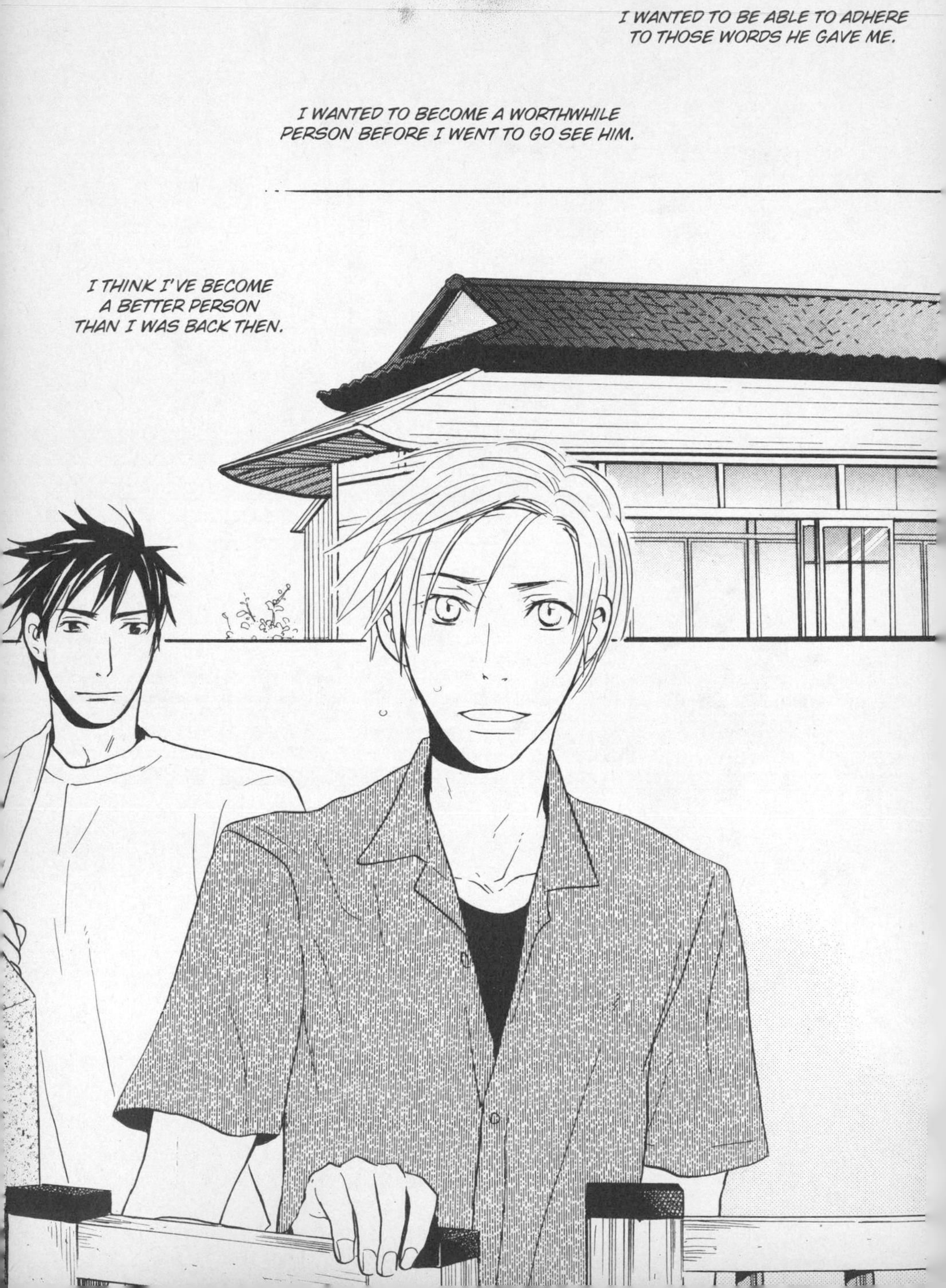
I WANTED TO BE ABLE TO ADHERE TO THOSE WORDS HE GAVE ME.
I WANTED TO BECOME A WORTHWHILE PERSON BEFORE I WENT TO GO SEE HIM.
I THINK I'VE BECOME A BETTER PERSON THAN I WAS BACK THEN.

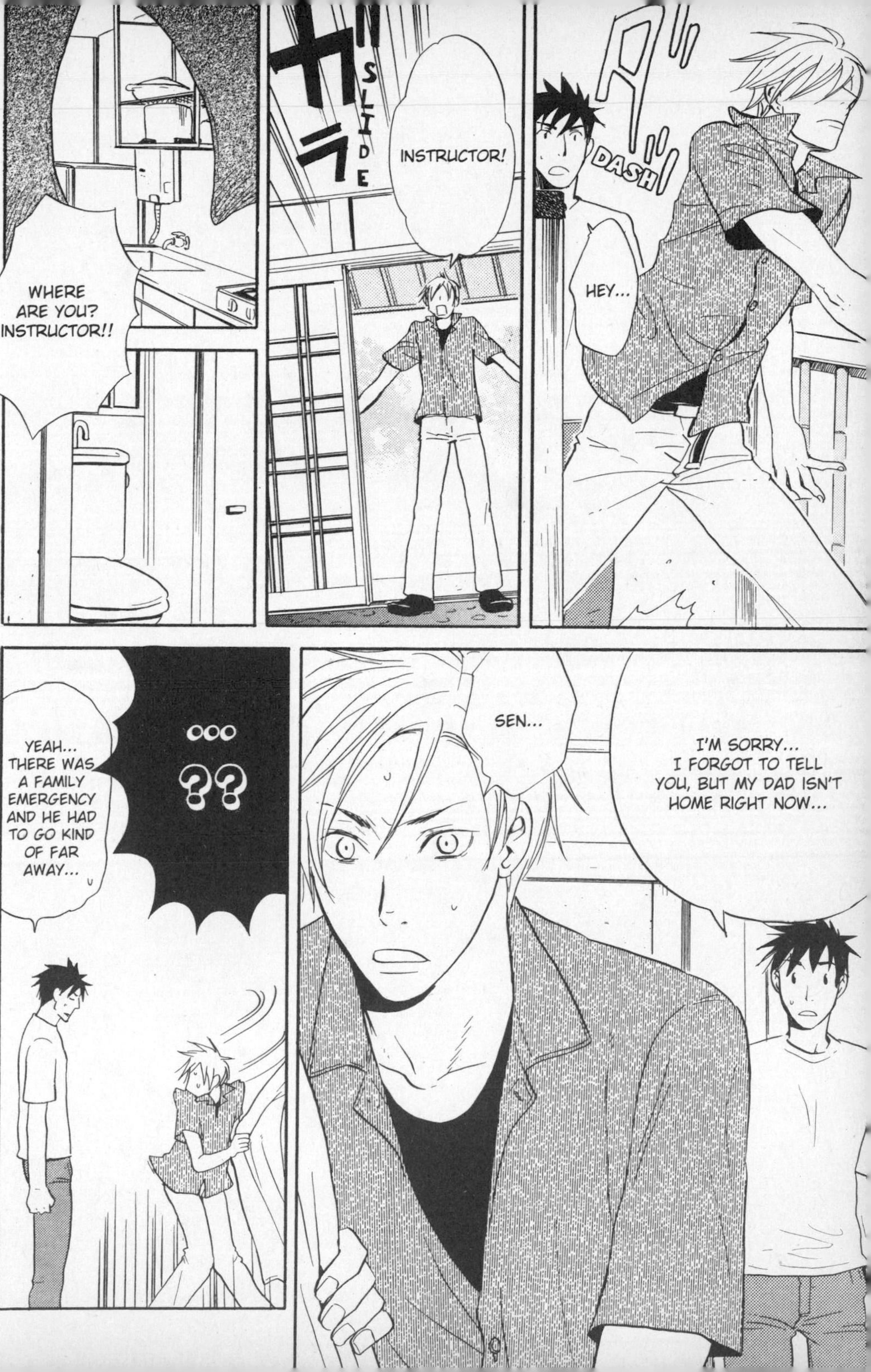
DASH
HEY...
SLIDE
INSTRUCTOR!
WHERE ARE YOU? INSTRUCTOR!!
I'M SORRY... I FORGOT TO TELL YOU, BUT MY DAD ISN'T HOME RIGHT NOW...
SEN...
??
YEAH... THERE WAS A FAMILY EMERGENCY AND HE HAD TO GO KIND OF FAR AWAY...

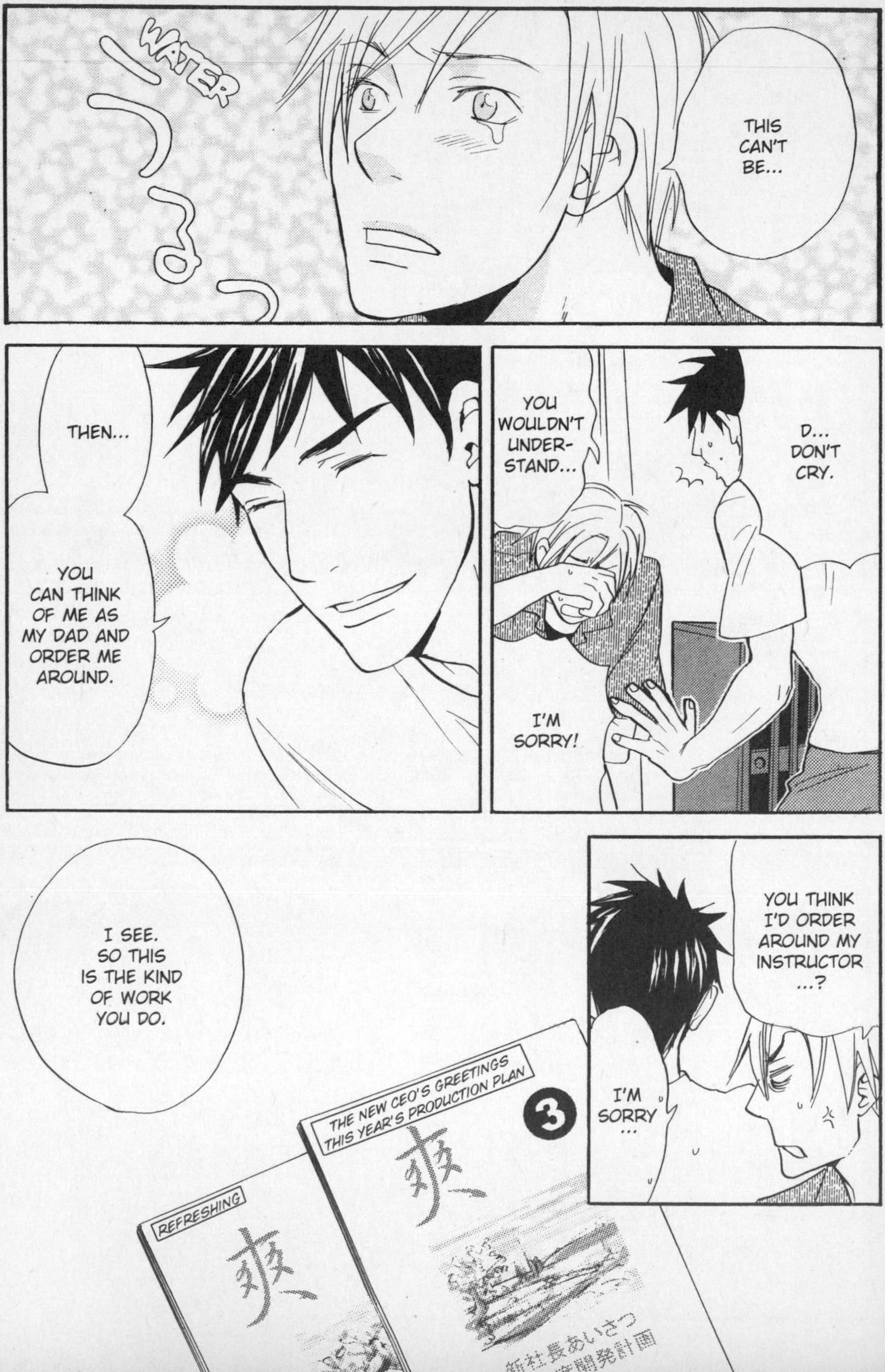
WATER
つるっ
THIS CAN'T BE...
D... DON'T CRY.
YOU WOULDN'T UNDER-STAND...
I'M SORRY!
THEN...
YOU CAN THINK OF ME AS MY DAD AND ORDER ME AROUND.
YOU THINK I'D ORDER AROUND MY INSTRUCTOR ...?
I'M SORRY ...
I SEE. SO THIS IS THE KIND OF WORK YOU DO.
THE NEW CEO'S GREETINGS
THIS YEAR'S PRODUCTION PLAN
3
REFRESHING
新社長あいさつ

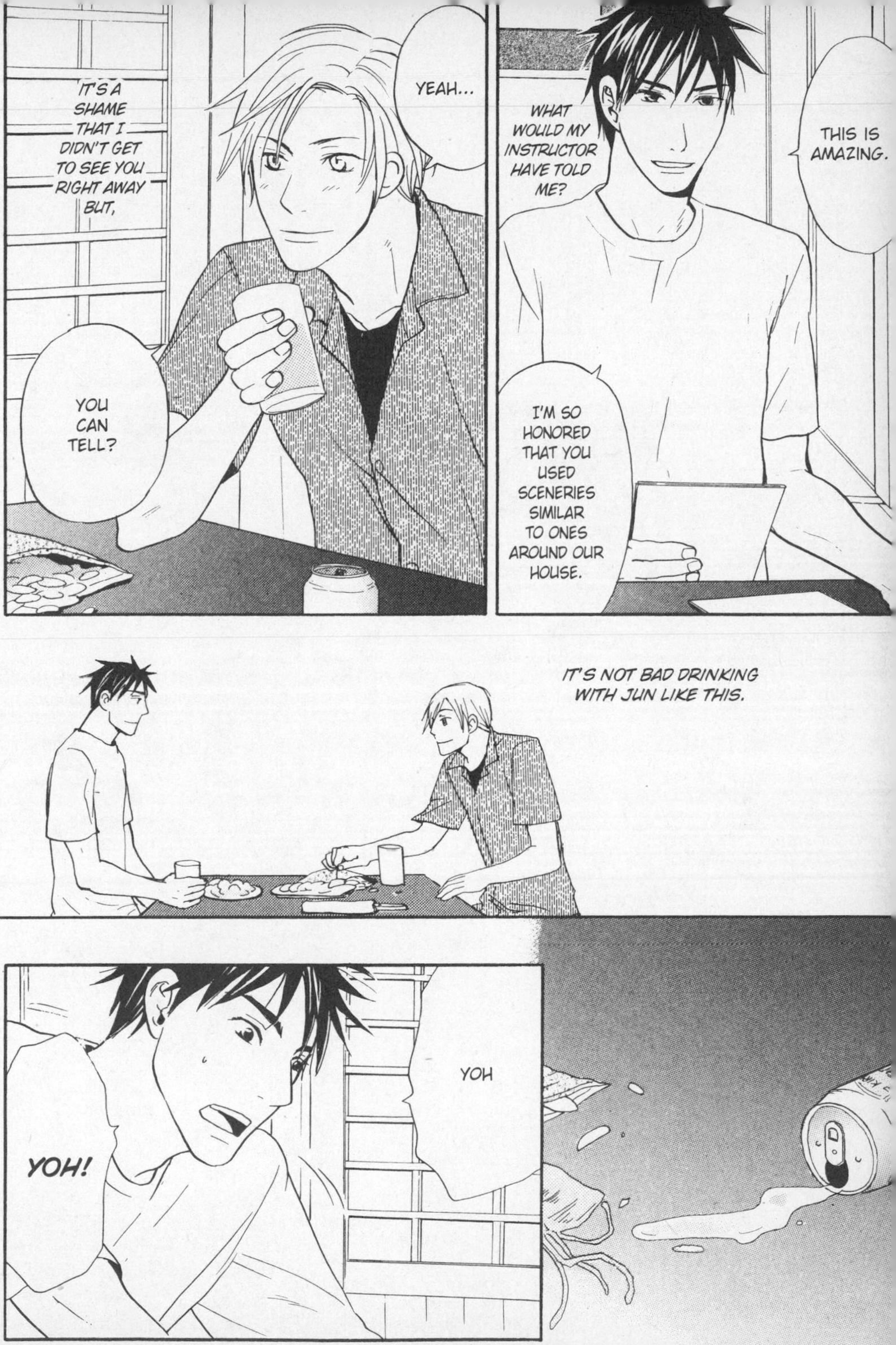
THIS IS AMAZING.
WHAT WOULD MY INSTRUCTOR HAVE TOLD ME?
I'M SO HONORED THAT YOU USED SCENERIES SIMILAR TO ONES AROUND OUR HOUSE.
YEAH...
IT'S A SHAME THAT I DIDN'T GET TO SEE YOU RIGHT AWAY BUT,
YOU CAN TELL?
IT'S NOT BAD DRINKING WITH JUN LIKE THIS.
YOH
YOH!

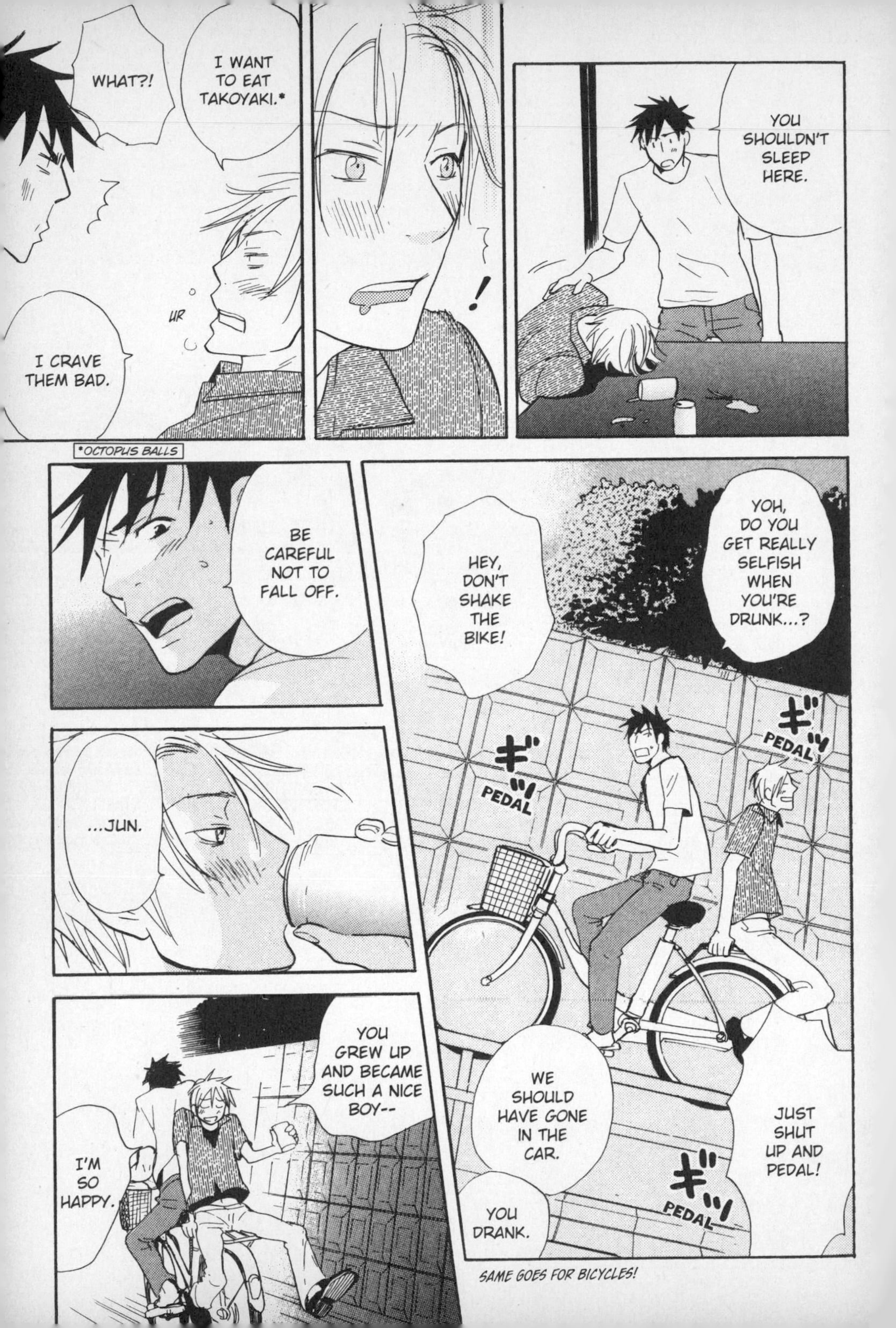
YOU SHOULDN'T SLEEP HERE.
!
I WANT TO EAT TAKOYAKI.*
WHAT?!
UR
I CRAVE THEM BAD.
YOH, DO YOU GET REALLY SELFISH WHEN YOU'RE DRUNK...?
HEY, DON'T SHAKE THE BIKE!
PEDAL
PEDAL
JUST SHUT UP AND PEDAL!
WE SHOULD HAVE GONE IN THE CAR.
YOU DRANK.
PEDAL
BE CAREFUL NOT TO FALL OFF.
...JUN.
YOU GREW UP AND BECAME SUCH A NICE BOY--
I'M SO HAPPY.

*OCTOPUS BALLS

SAME GOES FOR BICYCLES!

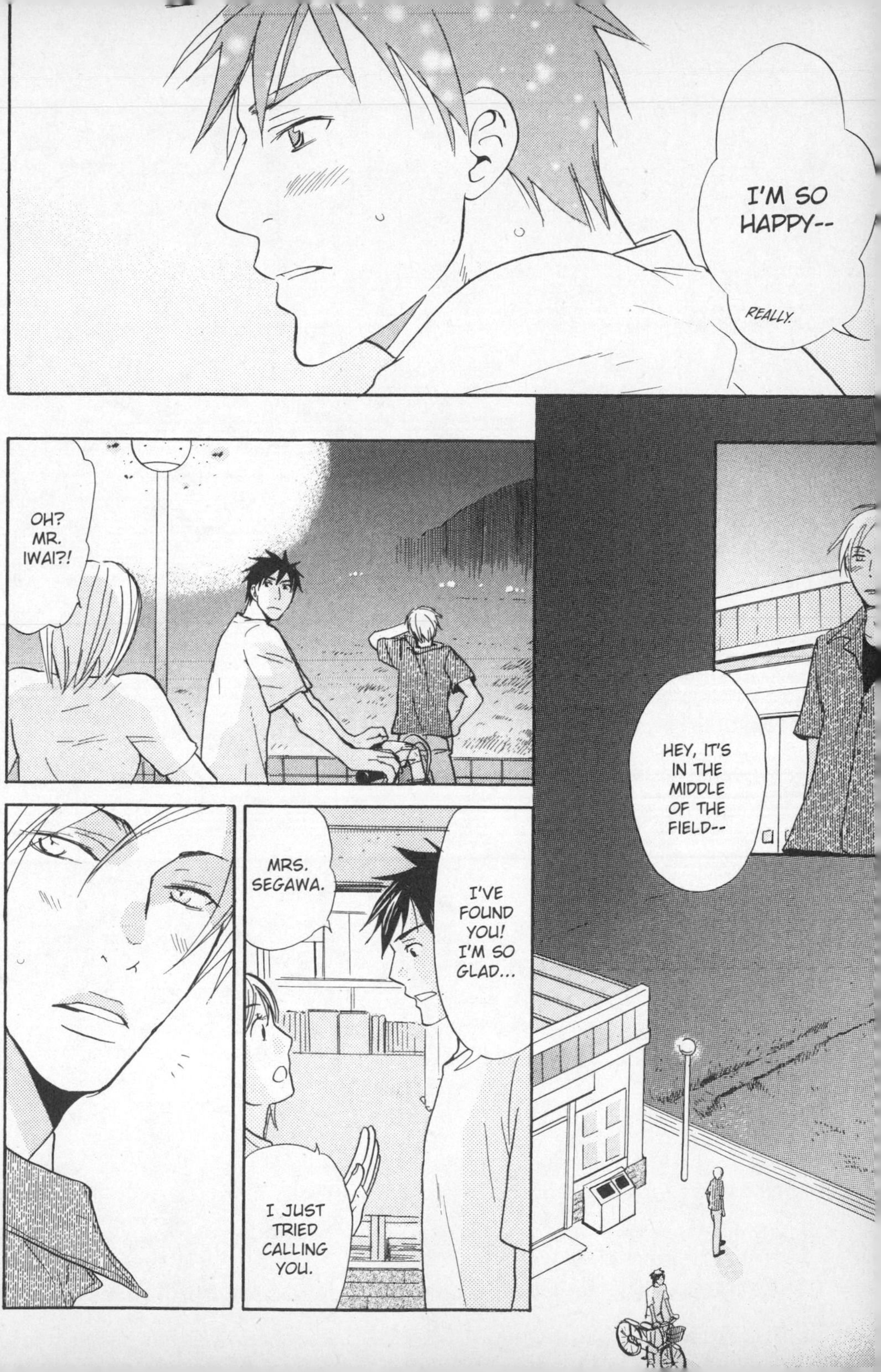
I'M SO HAPPY--
REALLY.
HEY, IT'S IN THE MIDDLE OF THE FIELD--
OH? MR. IWAI?!
I'VE FOUND YOU! I'M SO GLAD...
MRS. SEGAWA.
I JUST TRIED CALLING YOU.

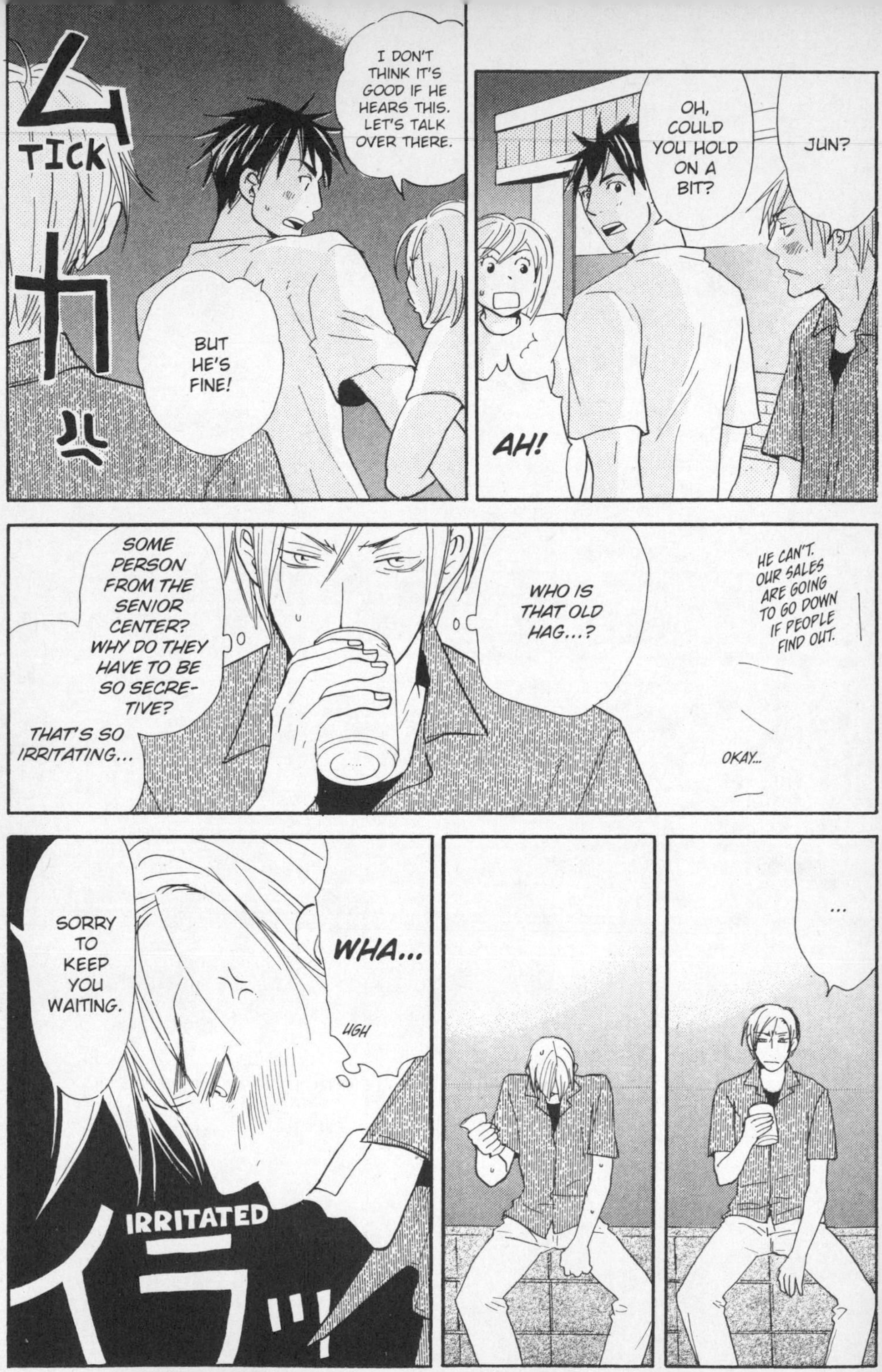
JUN?
OH, COULD YOU HOLD ON A BIT?
AH!
I DON'T THINK IT'S GOOD IF HE HEARS THIS. LET'S TALK OVER THERE.
ムカ
TICK
BUT HE'S FINE!
HE CAN'T. OUR SALES ARE GOING TO GO DOWN IF PEOPLE FIND OUT.
OKAY...
WHO IS THAT OLD HAG...?
SOME PERSON FROM THE SENIOR CENTER? WHY DO THEY HAVE TO BE SO SECRETIVE?
THAT'S SO IRRITATING...
...
WHA...
SORRY TO KEEP YOU WAITING.
UGH
IRRITATED
イラッ

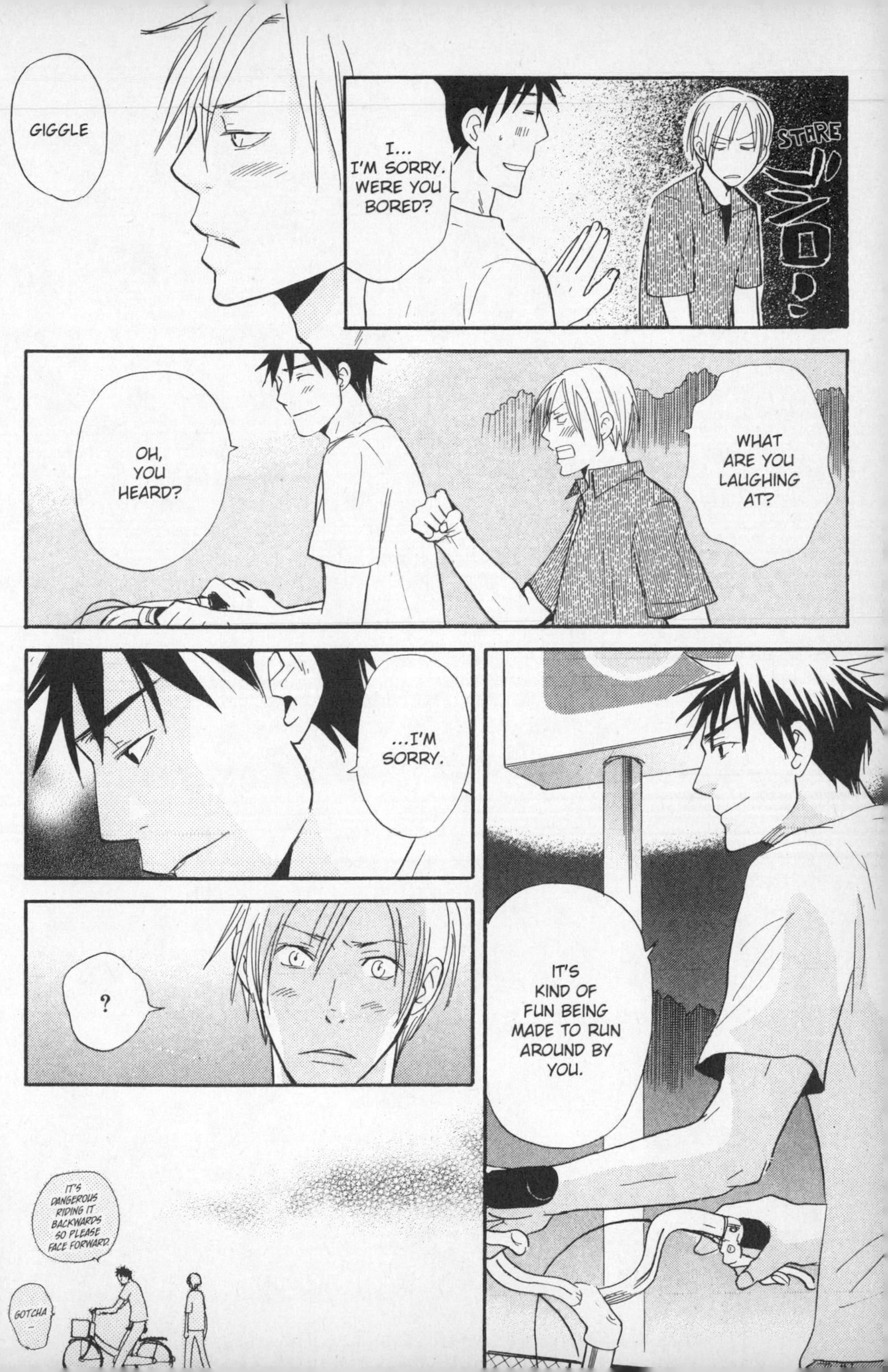
STARE
I... I'M SORRY. WERE YOU BORED?
GIGGLE
WHAT ARE YOU LAUGHING AT?
OH, YOU HEARD?
IT'S KIND OF FUN BEING MADE TO RUN AROUND BY YOU.
...I'M SORRY.
?
IT'S DANGEROUS RIDING IT BACKWARDS SO PLEASE FACE FORWARD.
GOTCHA —

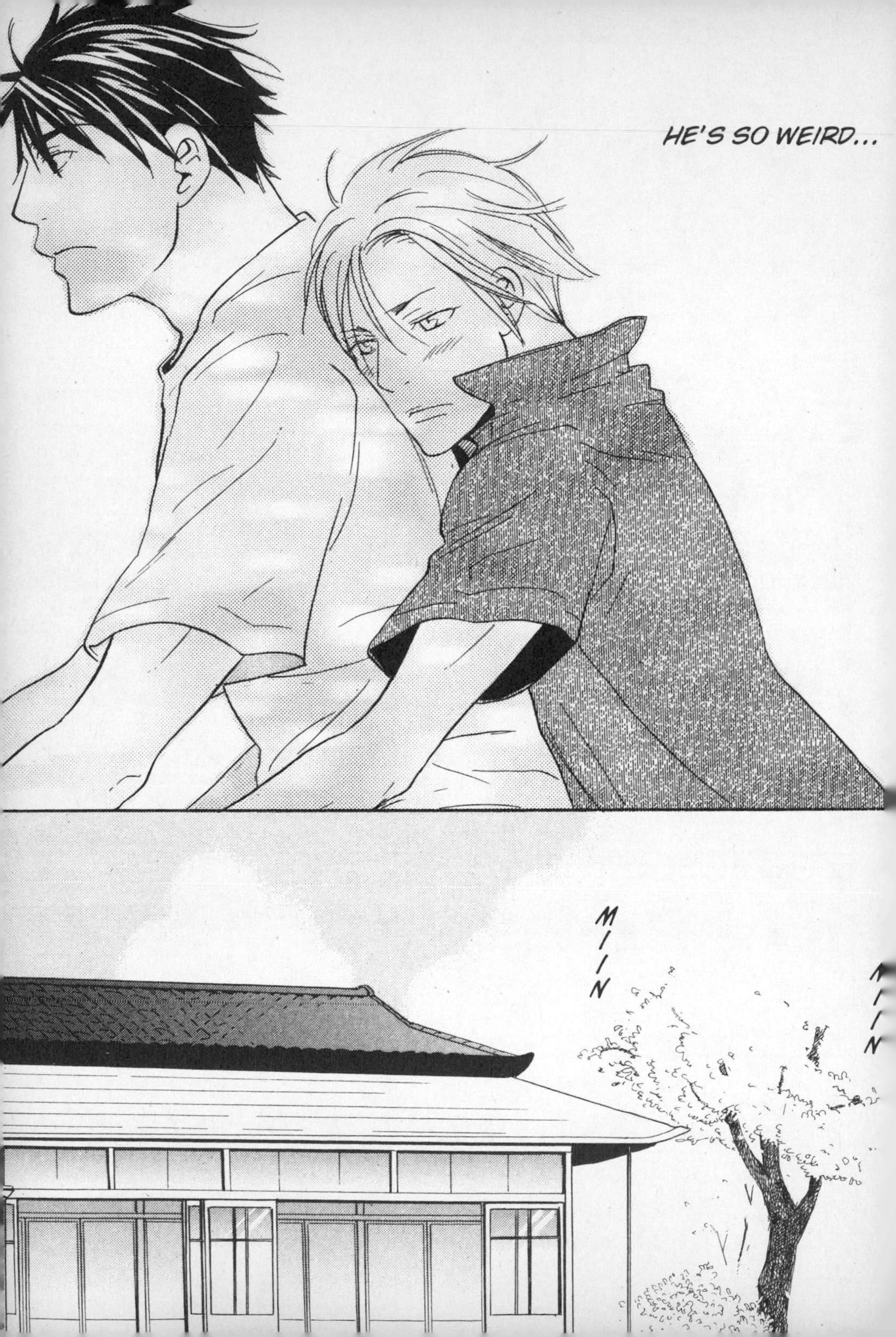
HE'S SO WEIRD...
MIIN
MIIN

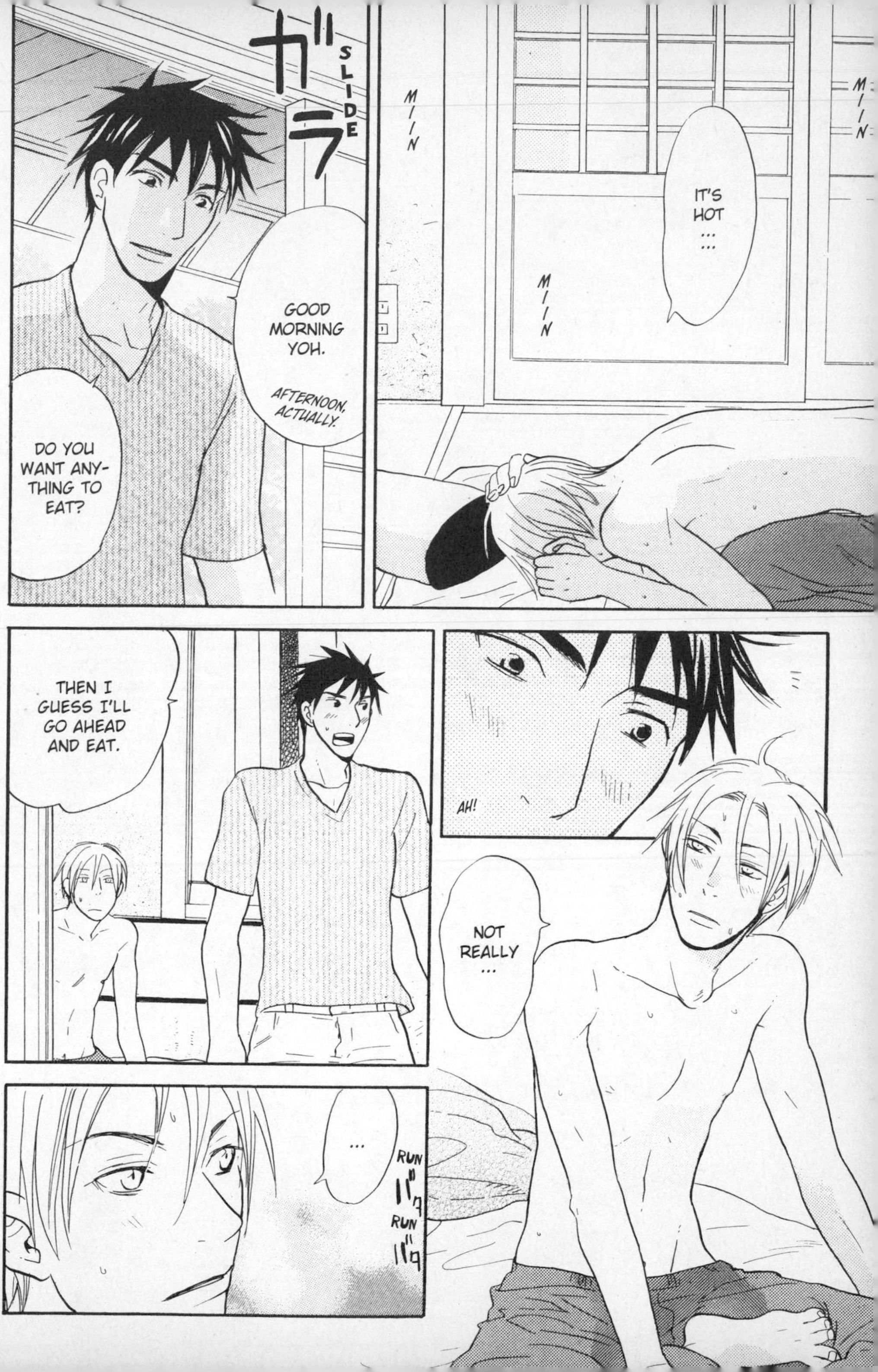

MIIN
IT'S HOT ......
MIIN
MIIN
ガラ
SLIDE
GOOD MORNING YOH.
AFTERNOON, ACTUALLY.
DO YOU WANT ANY-THING TO EAT?
AH!
NOT REALLY ...
THEN I GUESS I'LL GO AHEAD AND EAT.
...
RUN
パタ
RUN
パタ

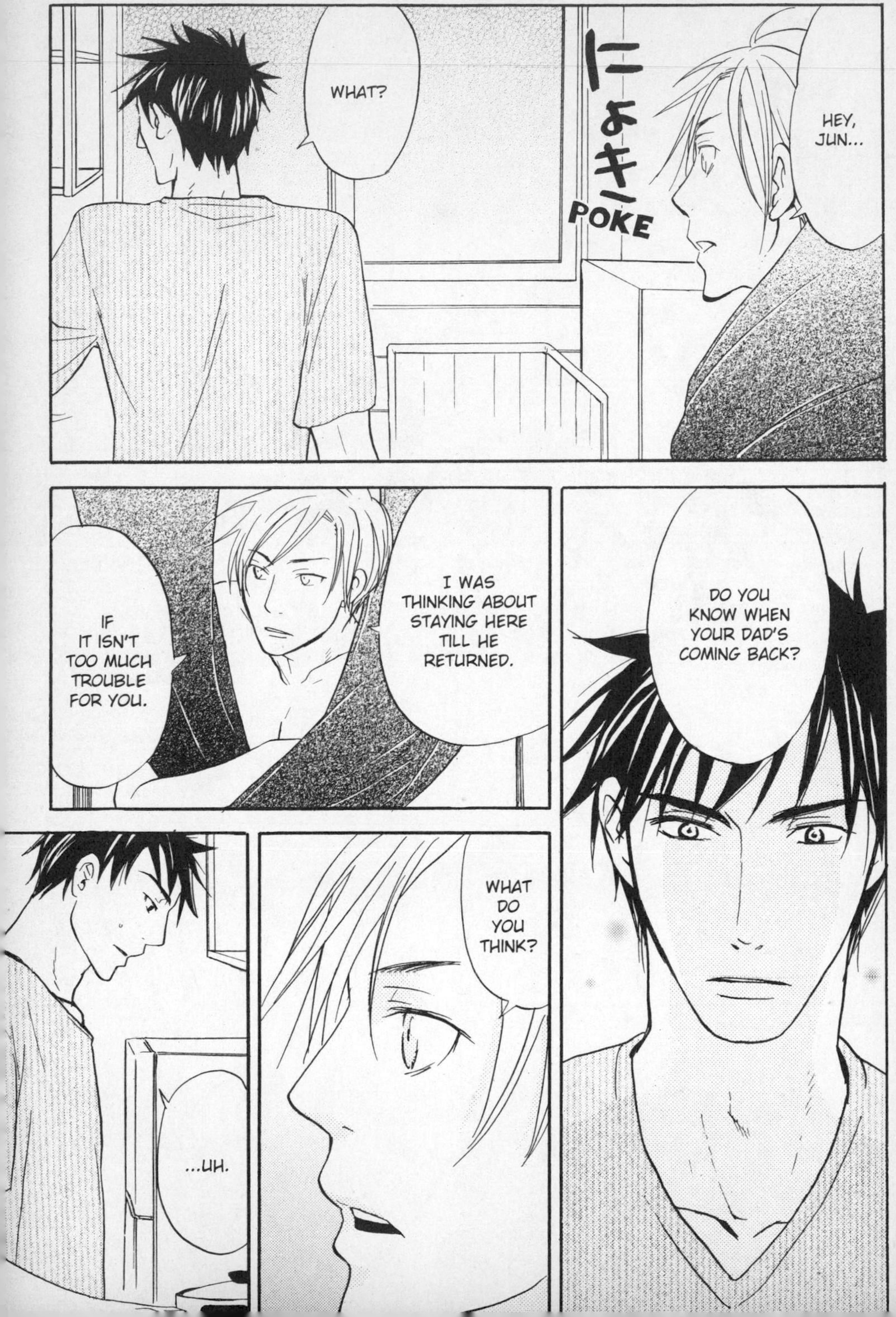
HEY, JUN...
にょき
POKE
WHAT?
DO YOU KNOW WHEN YOUR DAD'S COMING BACK?
I WAS THINKING ABOUT STAYING HERE TILL HE RETURNED.
IF IT ISN'T TOO MUCH TROUBLE FOR YOU.
WHAT DO YOU THINK?
...UH.

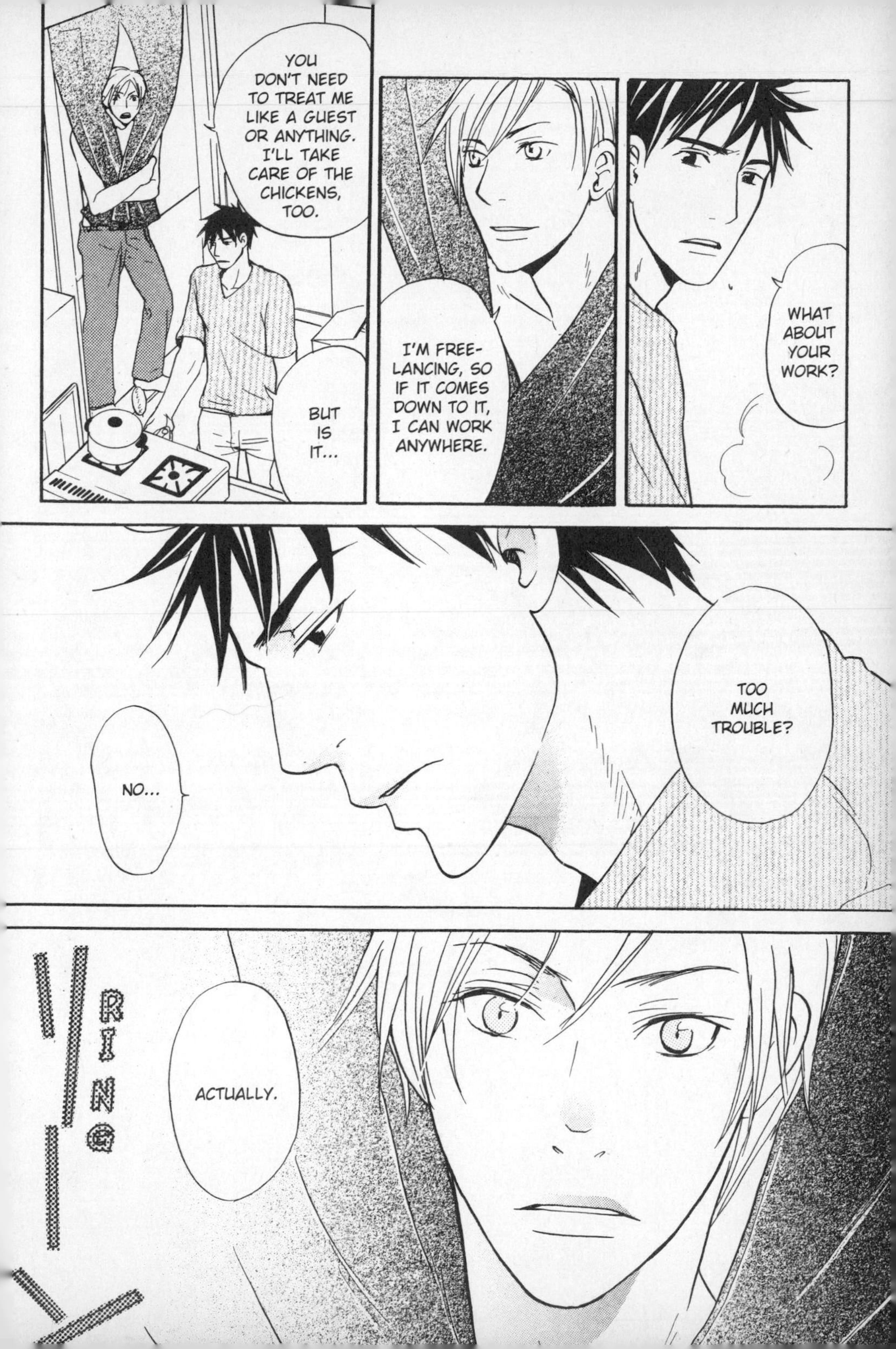
WHAT ABOUT YOUR WORK?
I'M FREE-LANCING, SO IF IT COMES DOWN TO IT, I CAN WORK ANYWHERE.
YOU DON'T NEED TO TREAT ME LIKE A GUEST OR ANYTHING. I'LL TAKE CARE OF THE CHICKENS, TOO.
BUT IS IT...
TOO MUCH TROUBLE?
NO...
RING
ACTUALLY.

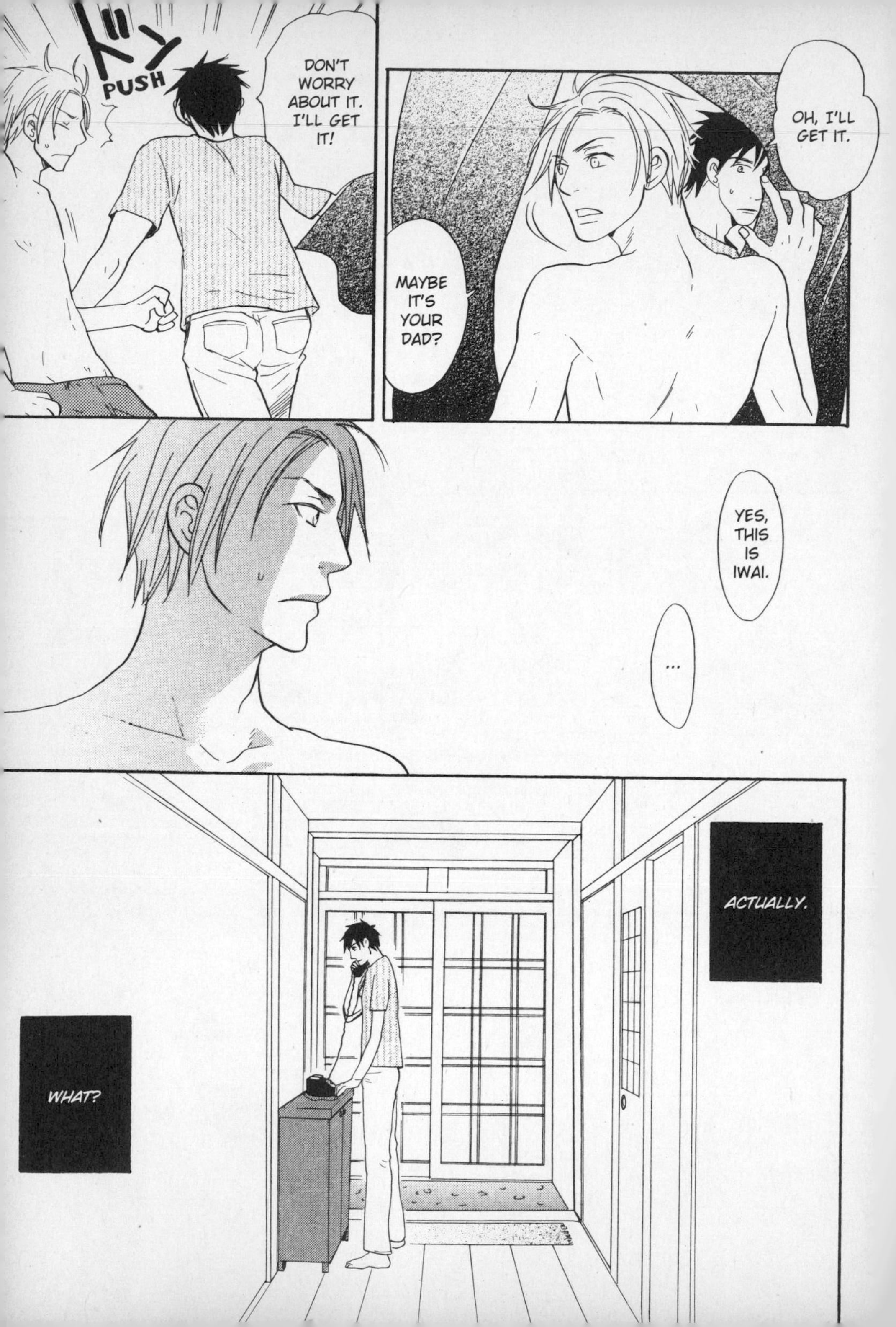
OH, I'LL GET IT.
MAYBE IT'S YOUR DAD?
DON'T WORRY ABOUT IT. I'LL GET IT!
ドン
PUSH
YES, THIS IS IWAI.
...
ACTUALLY.
WHAT?

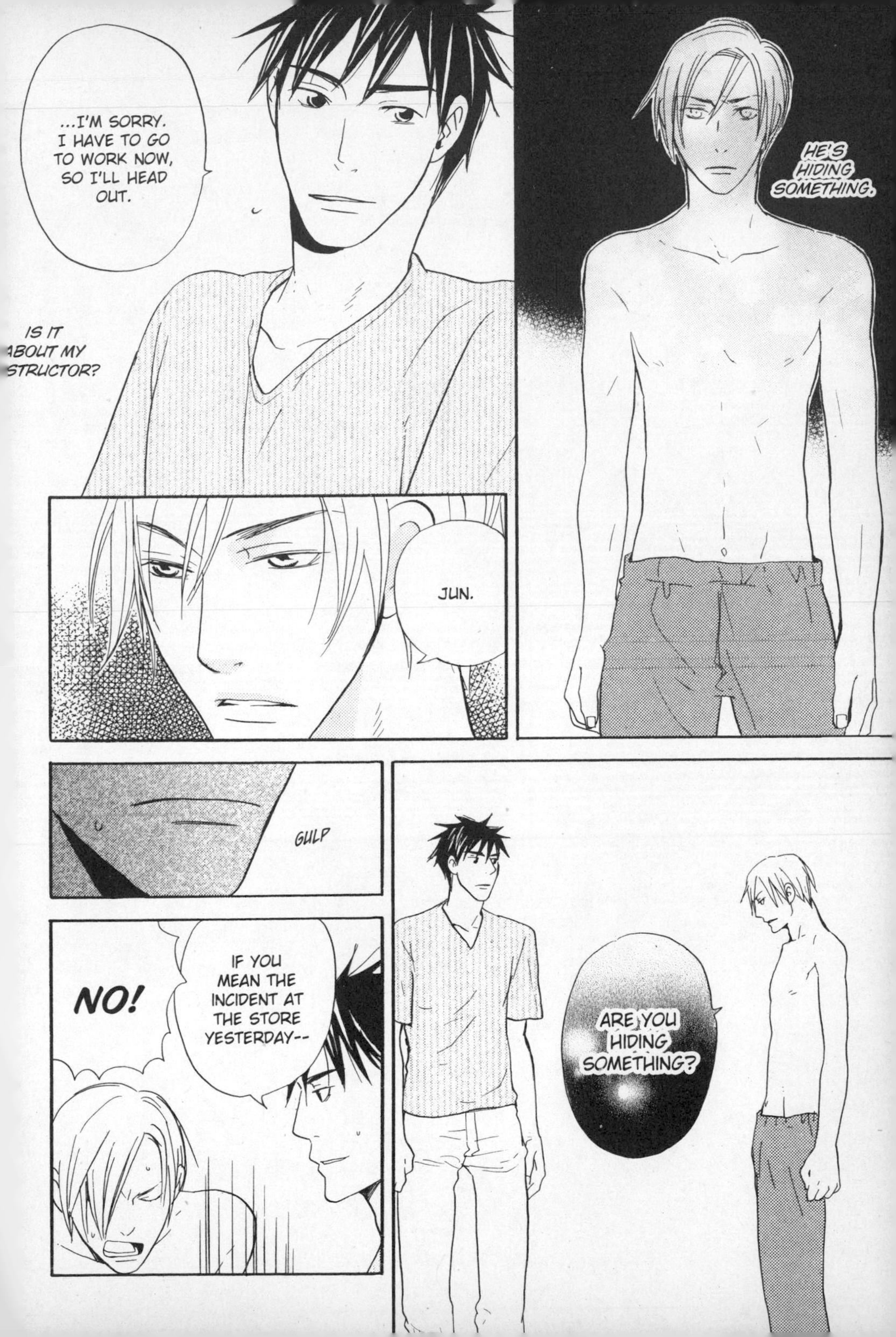
HE'S HIDING SOMETHING.
...I'M SORRY. I HAVE TO GO TO WORK NOW, SO I'LL HEAD OUT.
IS IT ABOUT MY STRUCTOR?
JUN.
ARE YOU HIDING SOMETHING?
GULP
IF YOU MEAN THE INCIDENT AT THE STORE YESTERDAY--
NO!

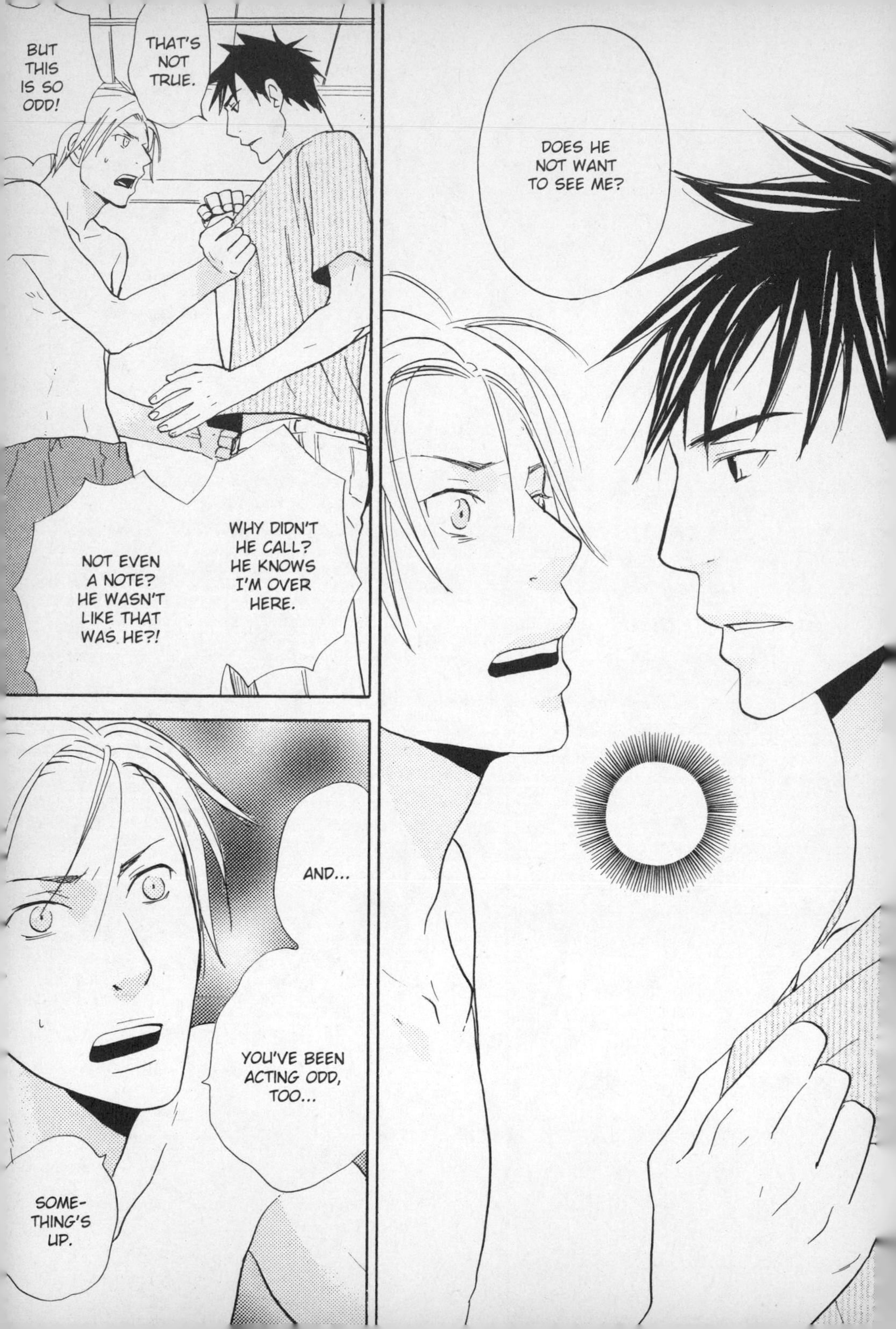
DOES HE NOT WANT TO SEE ME?
THAT'S NOT TRUE.
BUT THIS IS SO ODD!
WHY DIDN'T HE CALL? HE KNOWS I'M OVER HERE.
NOT EVEN A NOTE? HE WASN'T LIKE THAT WAS HE?!
AND...
YOU'VE BEEN ACTING ODD, TOO...
SOME-THING'S UP.

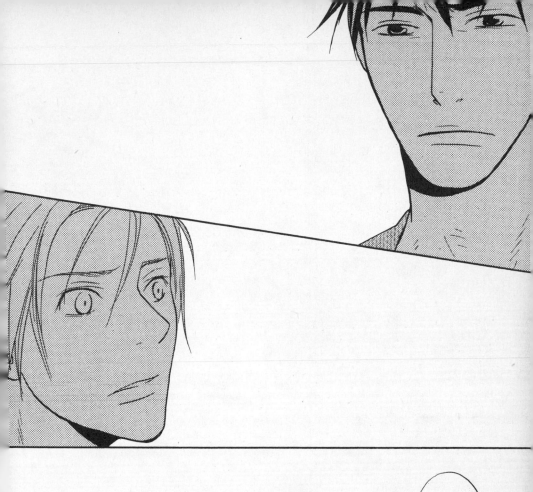

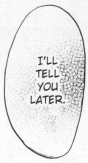

I'LL
TELL
YOU
LATER.

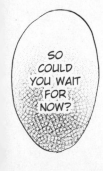

SO
COULD
YOU WAIT
FOR
NOW?

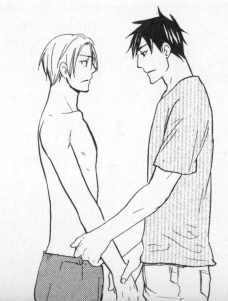

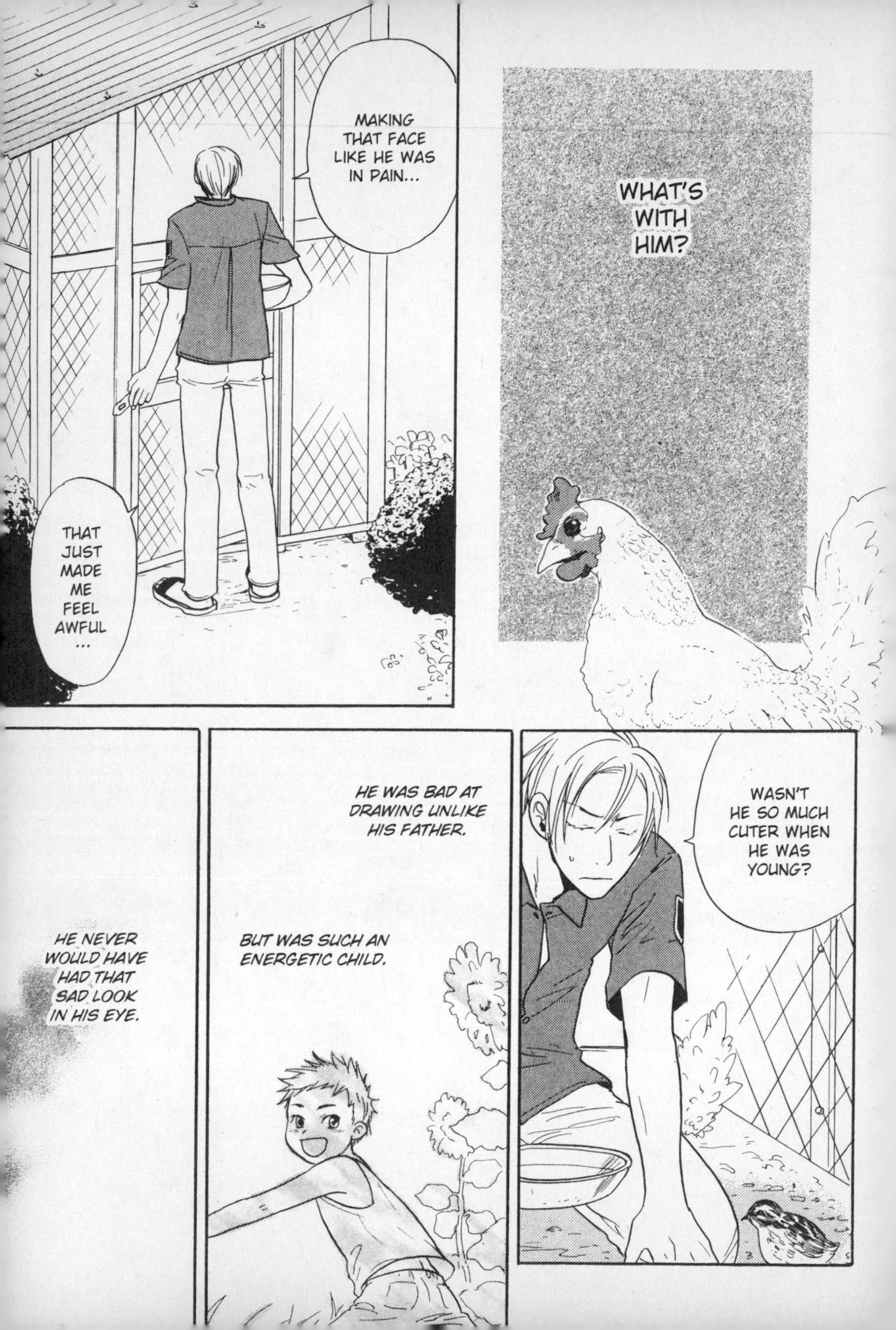
WHAT'S WITH HIM?
MAKING THAT FACE LIKE HE WAS IN PAIN...
THAT JUST MADE ME FEEL AWFUL ...
WASN'T HE SO MUCH CUTER WHEN HE WAS YOUNG?
HE WAS BAD AT DRAWING UNLIKE HIS FATHER.
BUT WAS SUCH AN ENERGETIC CHILD.
HE NEVER WOULD HAVE HAD THAT SAD LOOK IN HIS EYE.

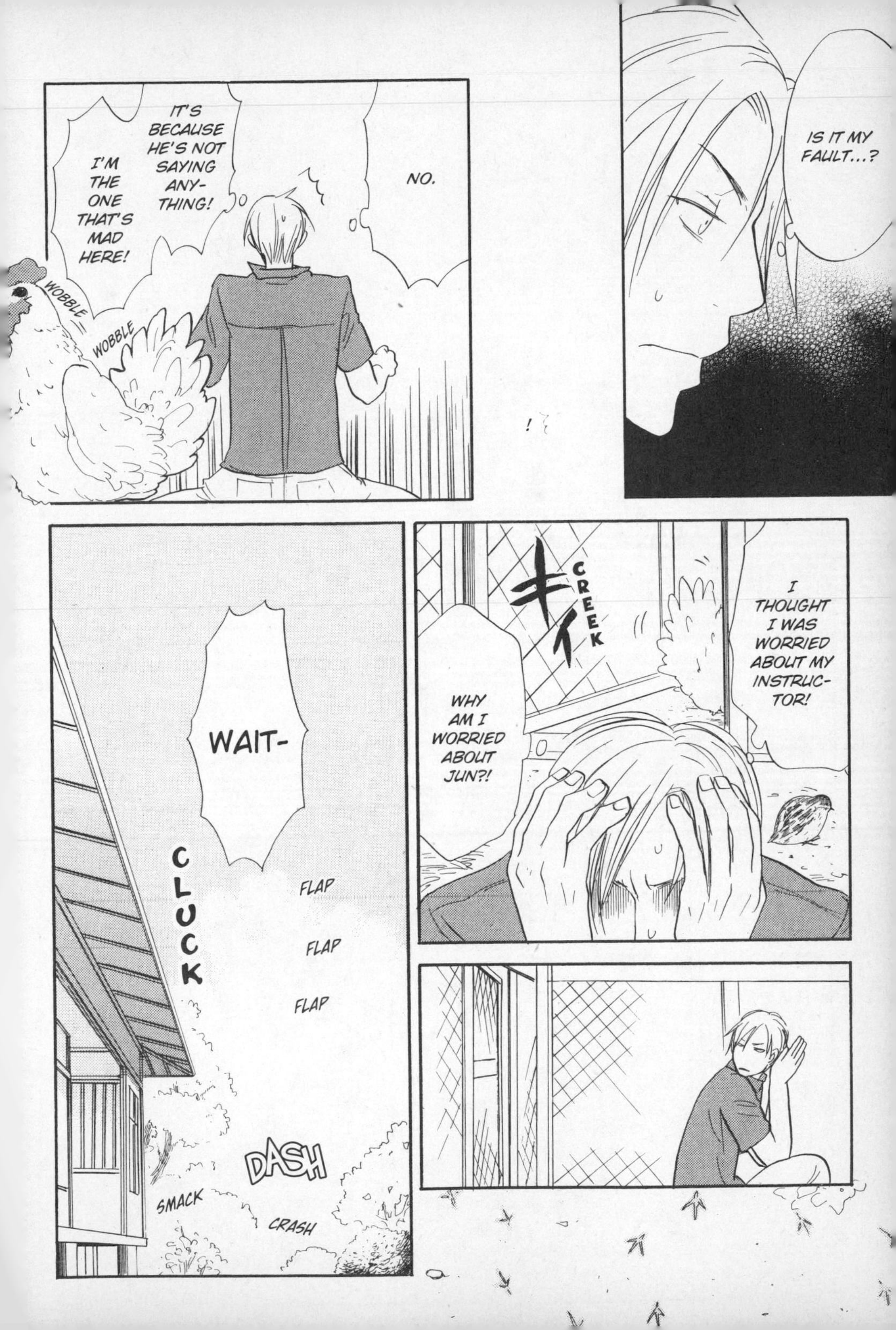
IS IT MY FAULT...?
NO.
IT'S BECAUSE HE'S NOT SAYING ANY-THING!
I'M THE ONE THAT'S MAD HERE!
WOBBLE
WOBBLE
!
キィ CREEK
I THOUGHT I WAS WORRIED ABOUT MY INSTRUC-TOR!
WHY AM I WORRIED ABOUT JUN?!
WAIT-
CLUCK
FLAP
FLAP
FLAP
DASH
SMACK
CRASH

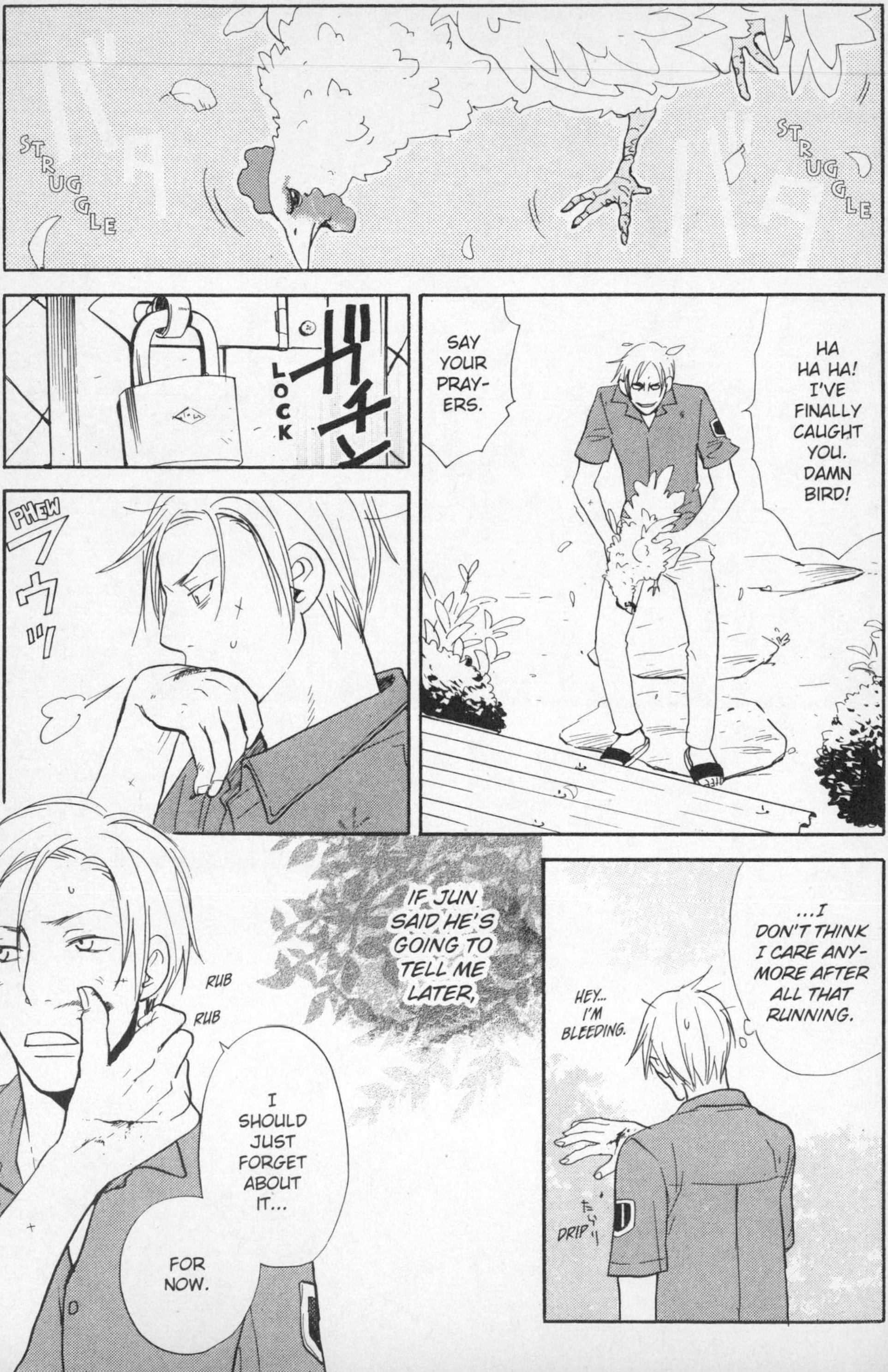
STRUGGLE
STRUGGLE
HA HA HA! I'VE FINALLY CAUGHT YOU. DAMN BIRD!
SAY YOUR PRAY-ERS.
LOCK
PHEW
...I DON'T THINK I CARE ANY-MORE AFTER ALL THAT RUNNING.
HEY... I'M BLEEDING.
DRIP
IF JUN SAID HE'S GOING TO TELL ME LATER,
RUB
RUB
IT GOT ON ME.
I SHOULD JUST FORGET ABOUT IT...
FOR NOW.

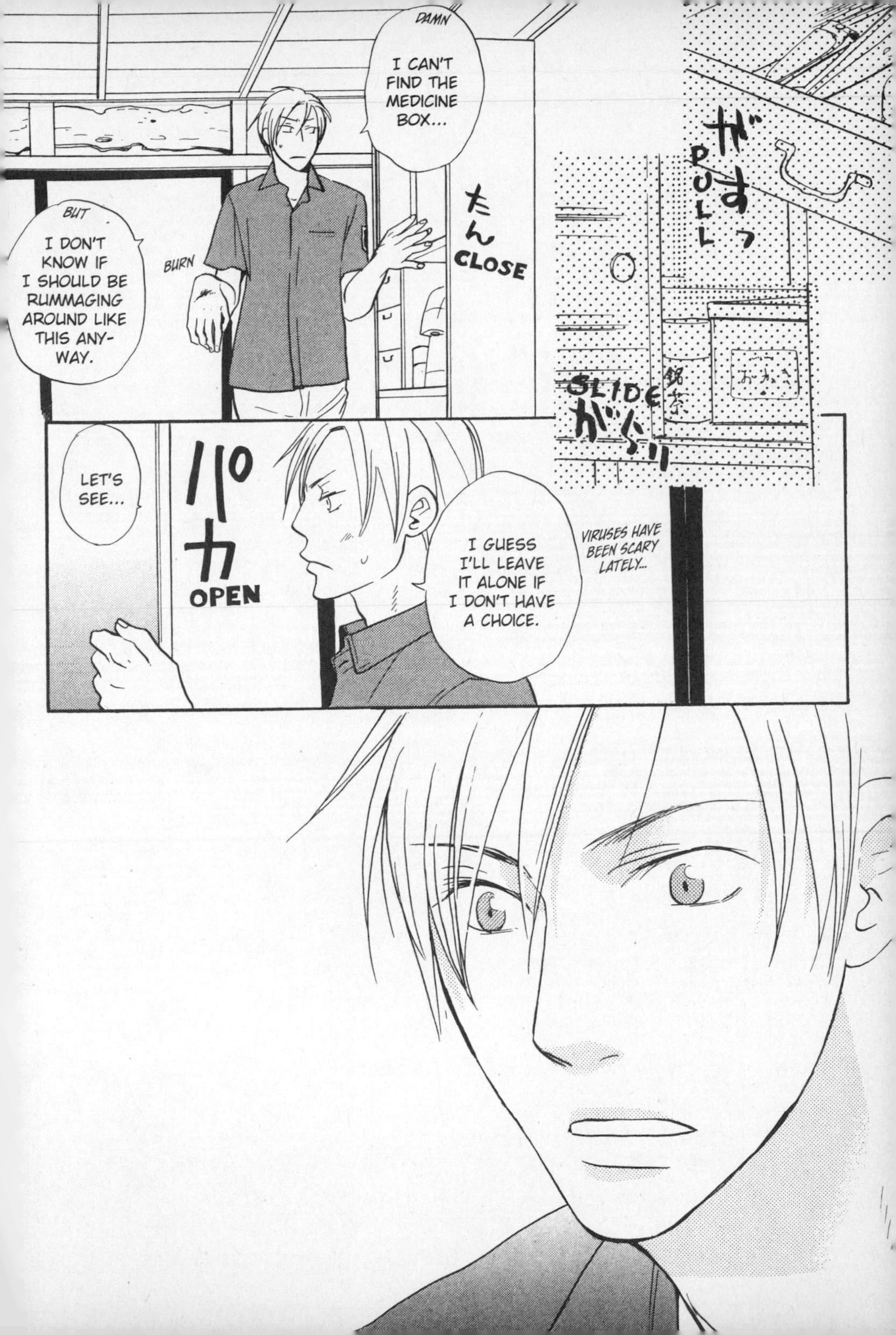

がすっ
PULL
SLIDE
がらり
銘茶
おかき
DAMN
I CAN'T FIND THE MEDICINE BOX...
たん
CLOSE
BUT
I DON'T KNOW IF I SHOULD BE RUMMAGING AROUND LIKE THIS ANYWAY.
BURN
VIRUSES HAVE BEEN SCARY LATELY...
I GUESS I'LL LEAVE IT ALONE IF I DON'T HAVE A CHOICE.
パカ
OPEN
LET'S SEE...

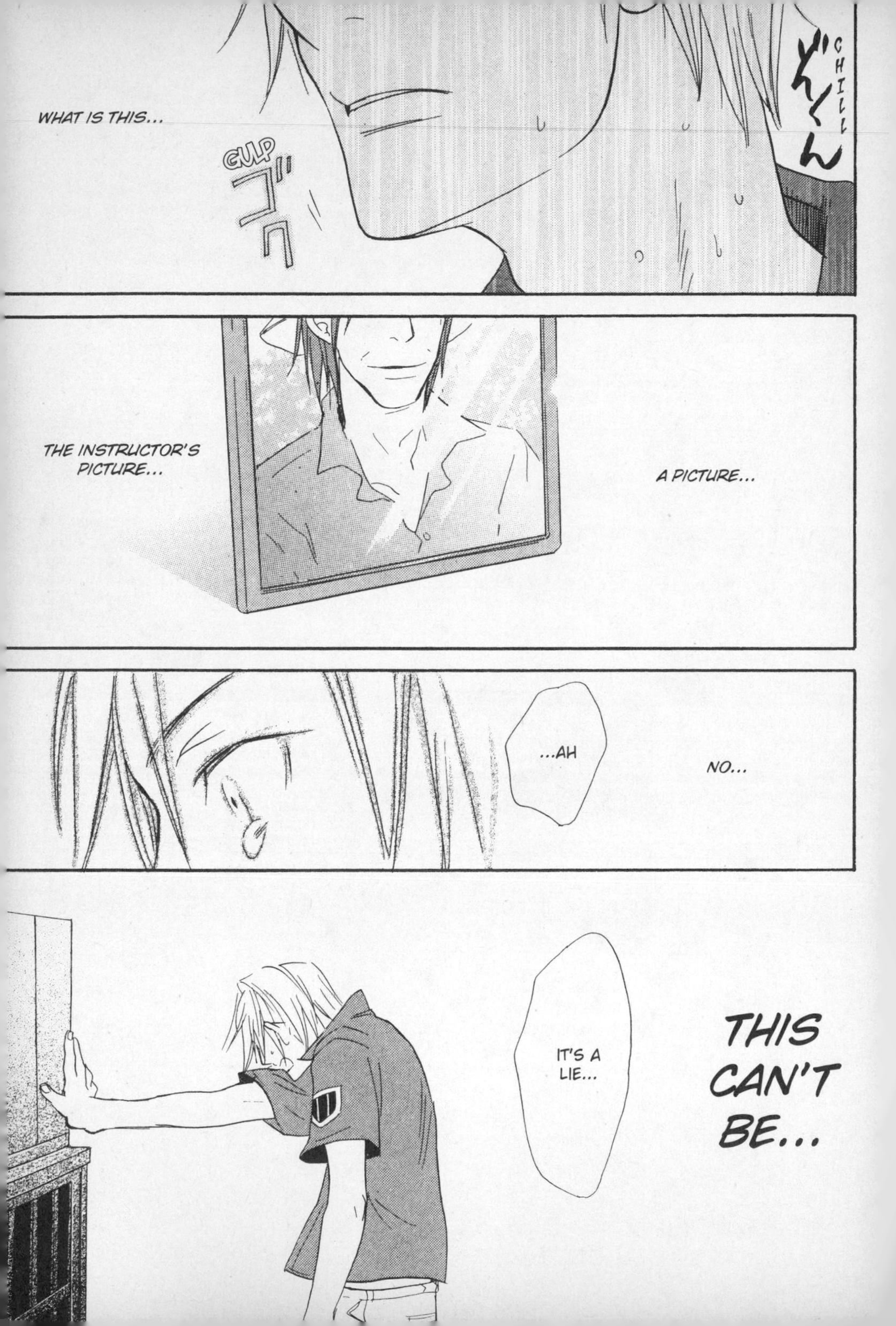
CHILL
GULP
WHAT IS THIS...
A PICTURE...
THE INSTRUCTOR'S PICTURE...
NO...
...AH
THIS CAN'T BE...
IT'S A LIE...

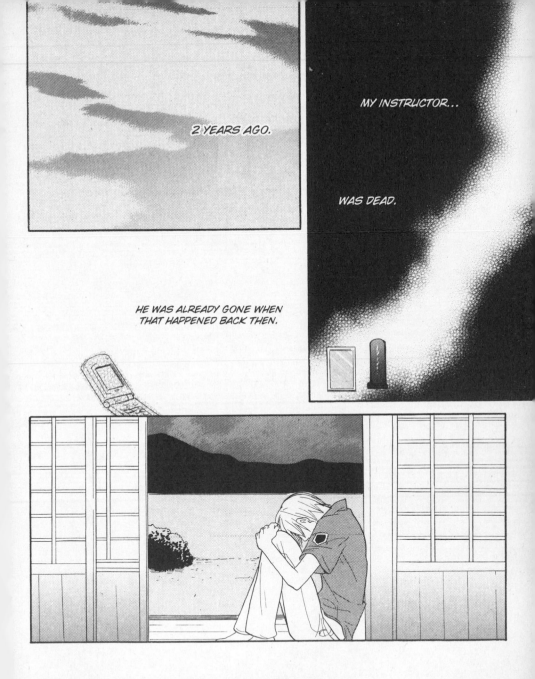

2 YEARS AGO.

MY INSTRUCTOR...

WAS DEAD.

HE WAS ALREADY GONE WHEN
THAT HAPPENED BACK THEN.

THE THING I WAS RELYING ON...

THE THING I WAS BEING SUPPORTED BY...

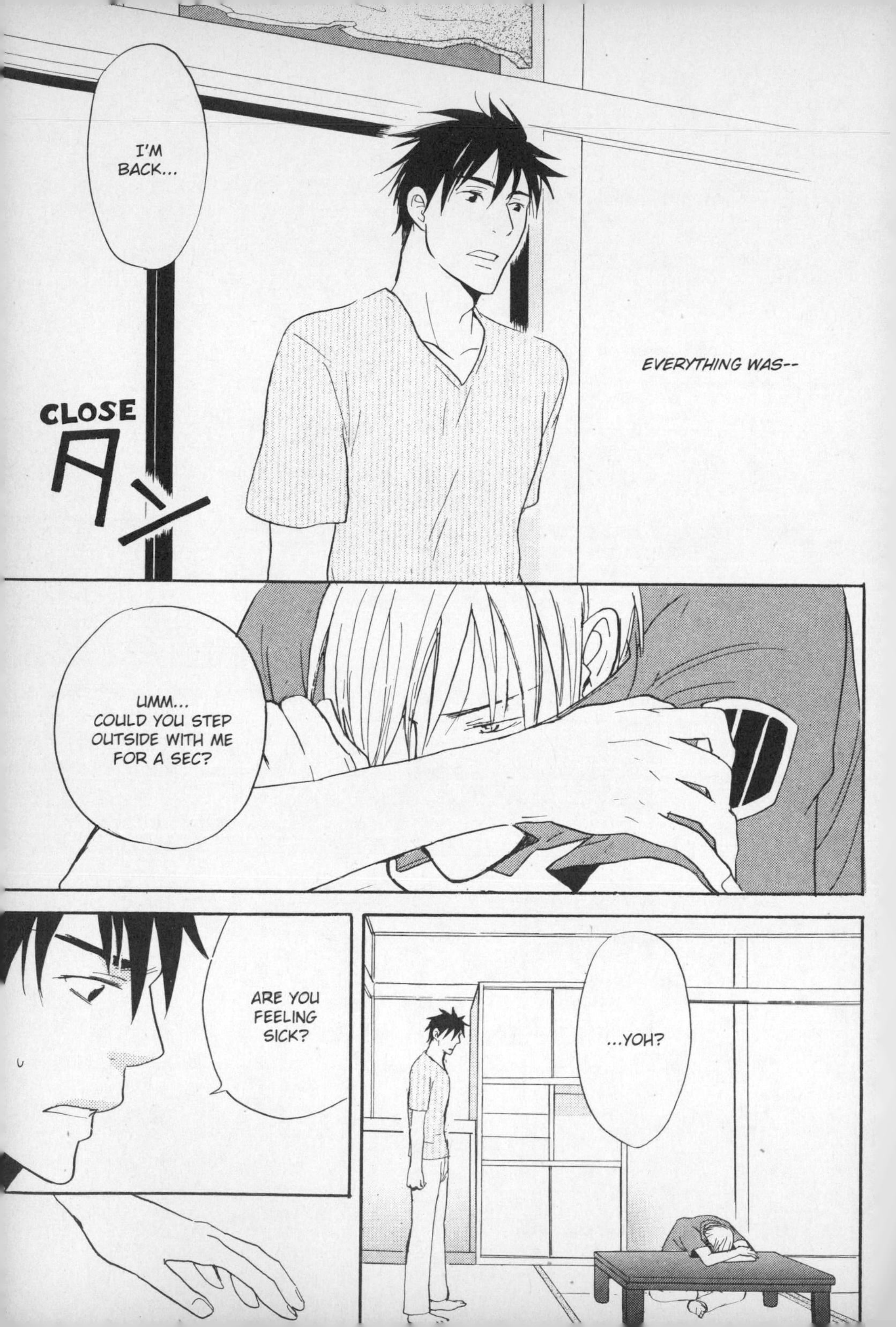
EVERYTHING WAS--
I'M BACK...
CLOSE
UMM... COULD YOU STEP OUTSIDE WITH ME FOR A SEC?
...YOH?
ARE YOU FEELING SICK?

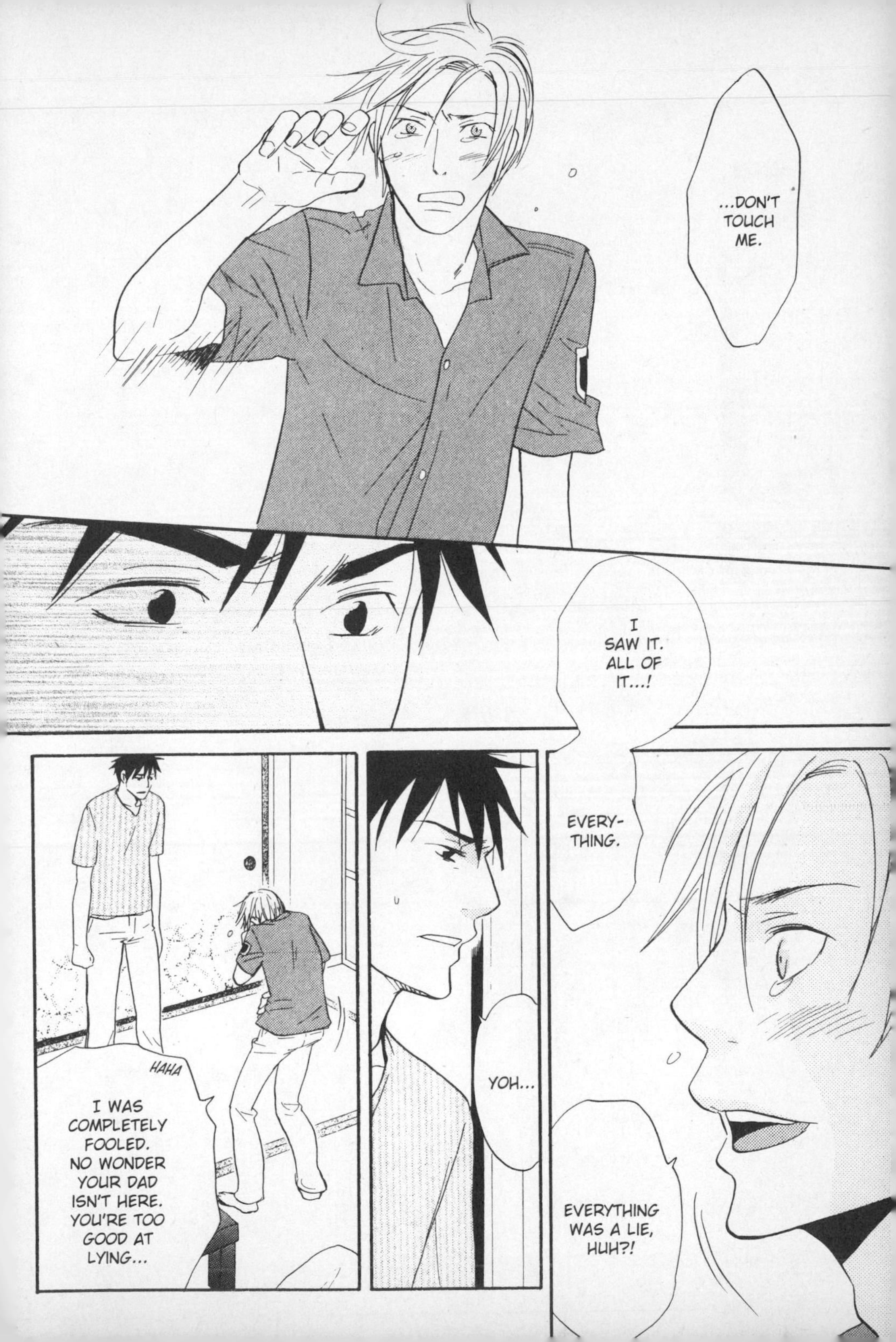
...DON'T TOUCH ME.
I SAW IT. ALL OF IT...!
EVERY-THING.
EVERYTHING WAS A LIE, HUH?!
YOH...
HAHA
I WAS COMPLETELY FOOLED. NO WONDER YOUR DAD ISN'T HERE. YOU'RE TOO GOOD AT LYING...

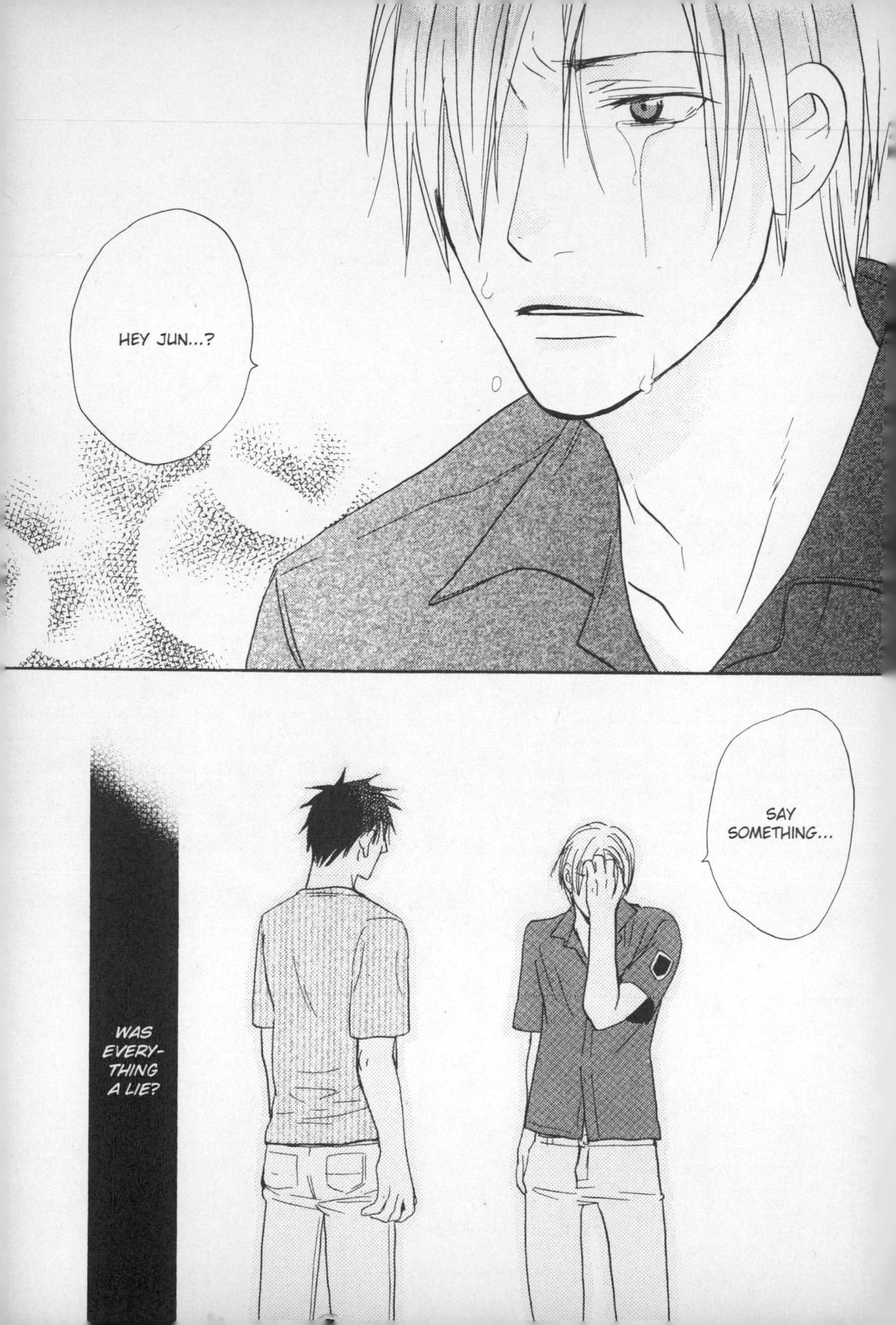
HEY JUN...?
SAY SOMETHING...
WAS EVERY-THING A LIE?

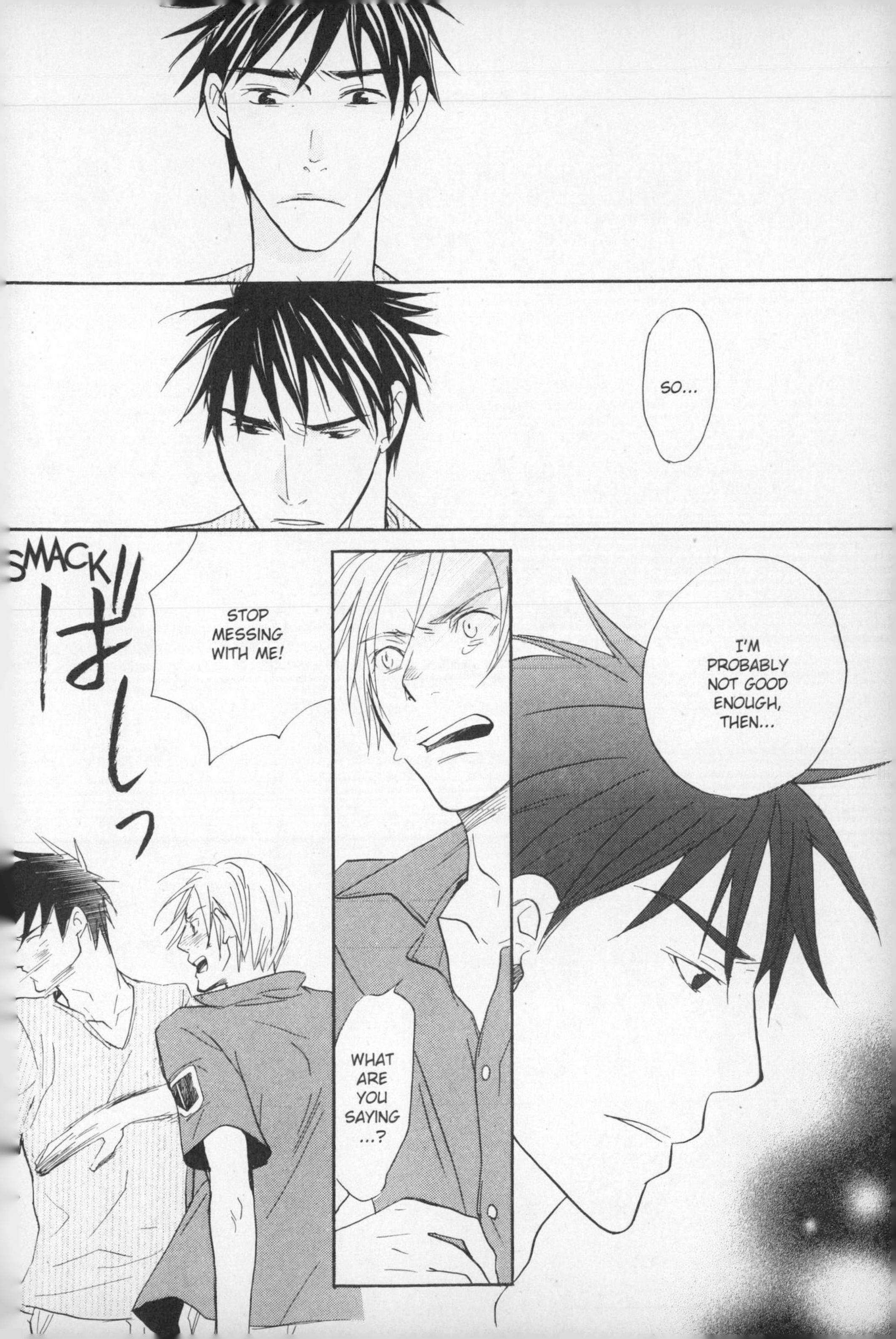
SO...
I'M PROBABLY NOT GOOD ENOUGH, THEN...
WHAT ARE YOU SAYING ...?
SMACK
ばしっ
STOP MESSING WITH ME!

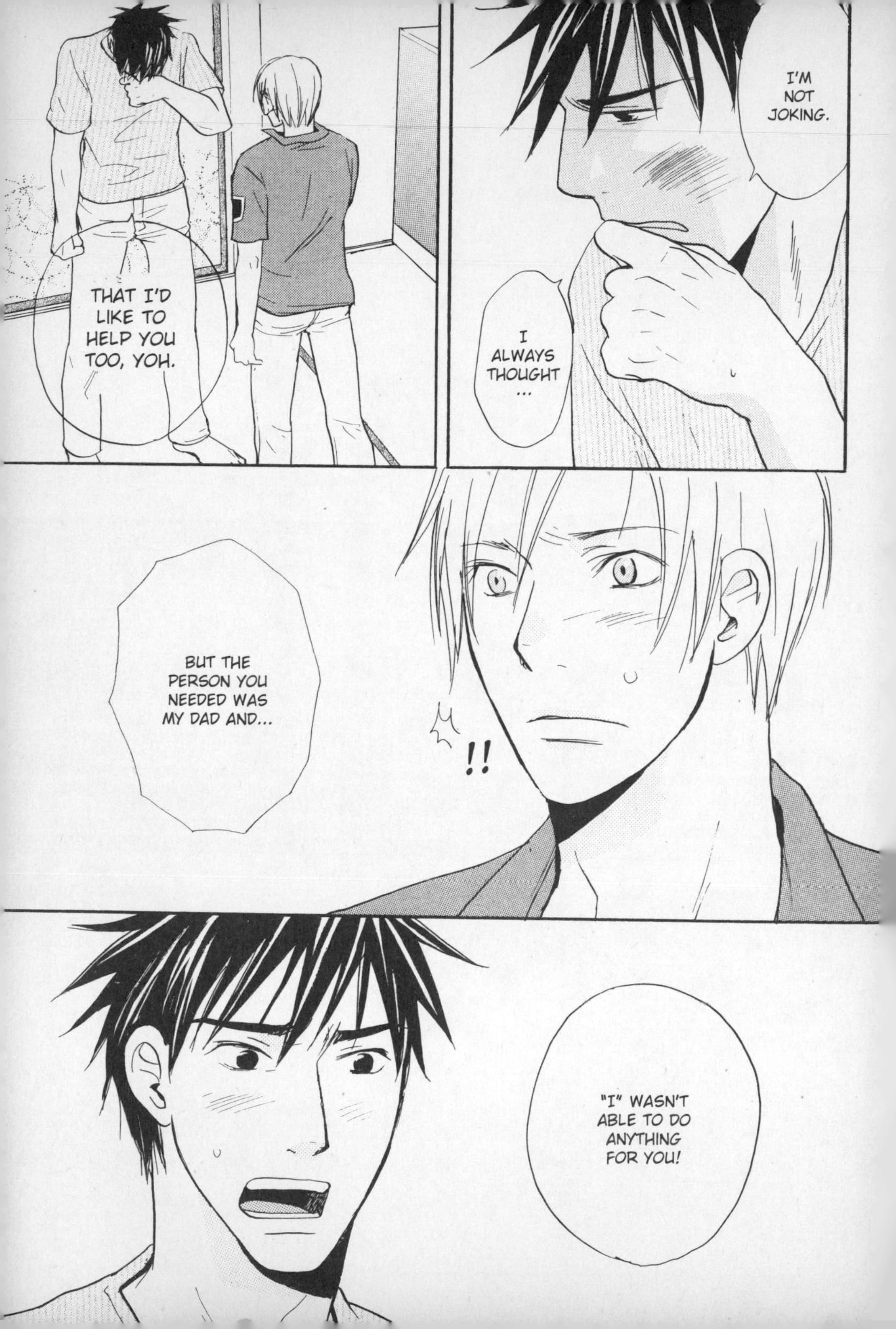
I'M NOT JOKING.
I ALWAYS THOUGHT ...
THAT I'D LIKE TO HELP YOU TOO, YOH.
BUT THE PERSON YOU NEEDED WAS MY DAD AND...
!!
"I" WASN'T ABLE TO DO ANYTHING FOR YOU!

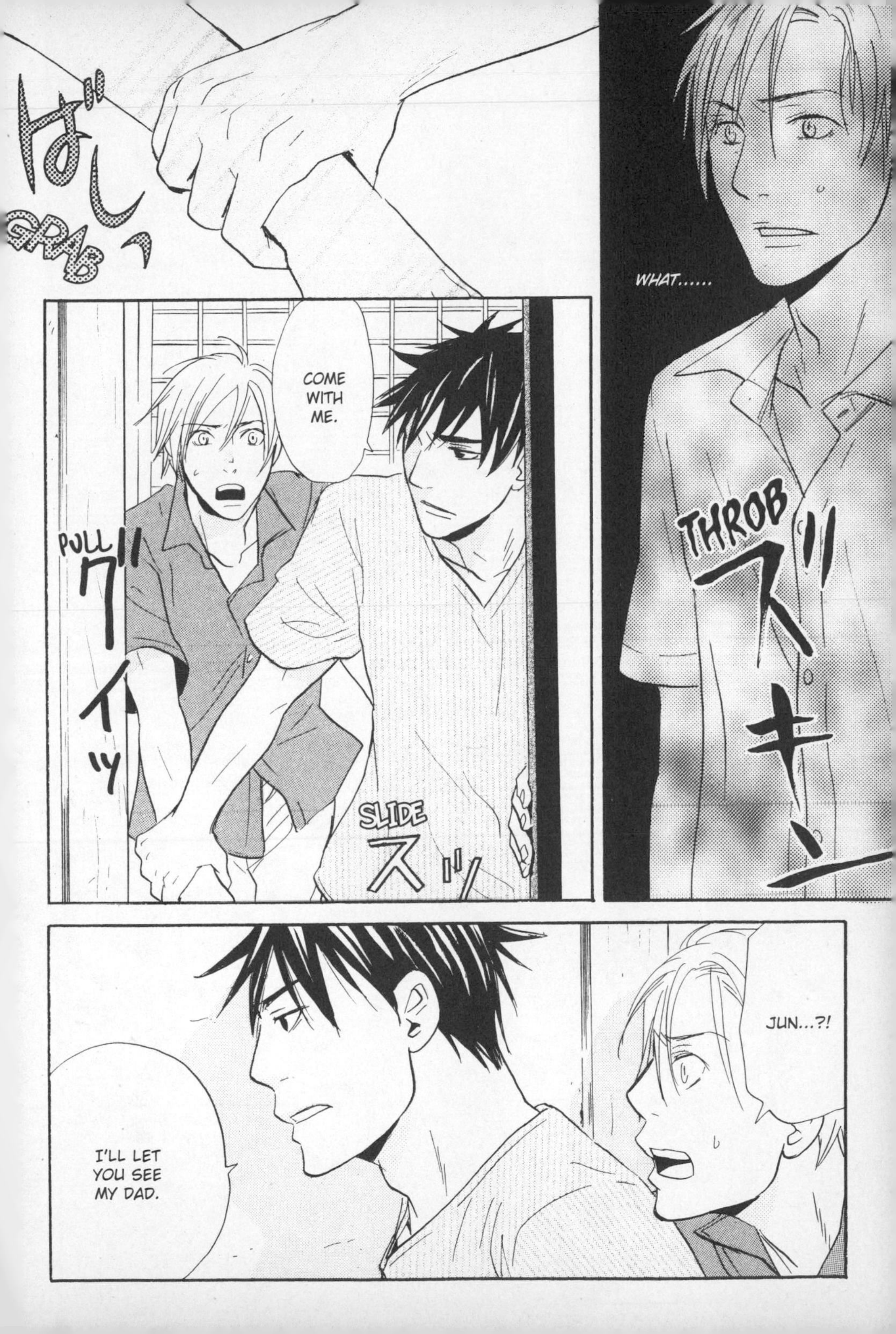

WHAT......
THROB
ズキン
ばしっ
GRAB
COME WITH ME.
PULL
グイッ
SLIDE
スッ
JUN...?!
I'LL LET YOU SEE MY DAD.

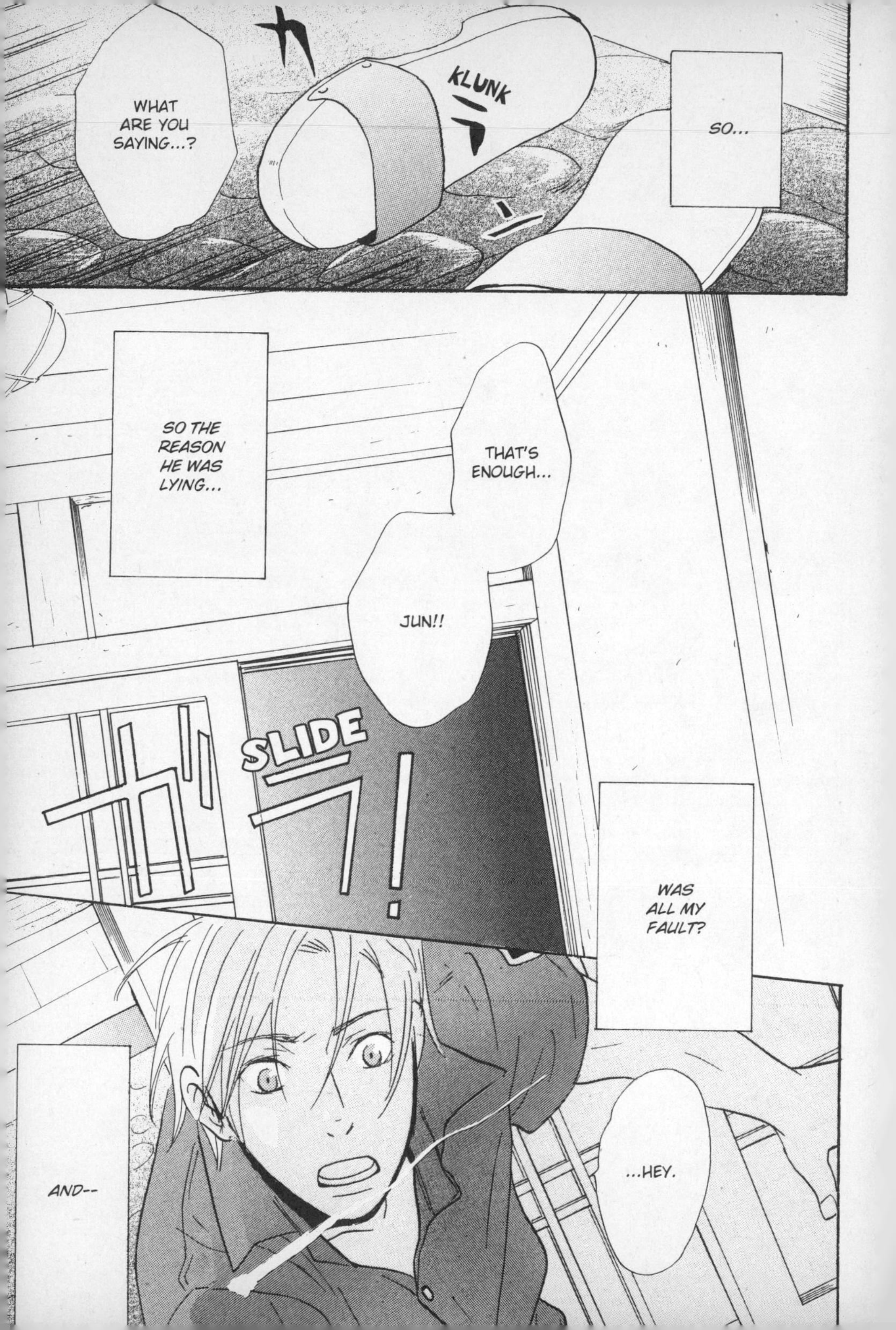
SO...
KLUNK
WHAT ARE YOU SAYING...?
THAT'S ENOUGH...
SO THE REASON HE WAS LYING...
JUN!!
SLIDE
WAS ALL MY FAULT?
...HEY.
AND--

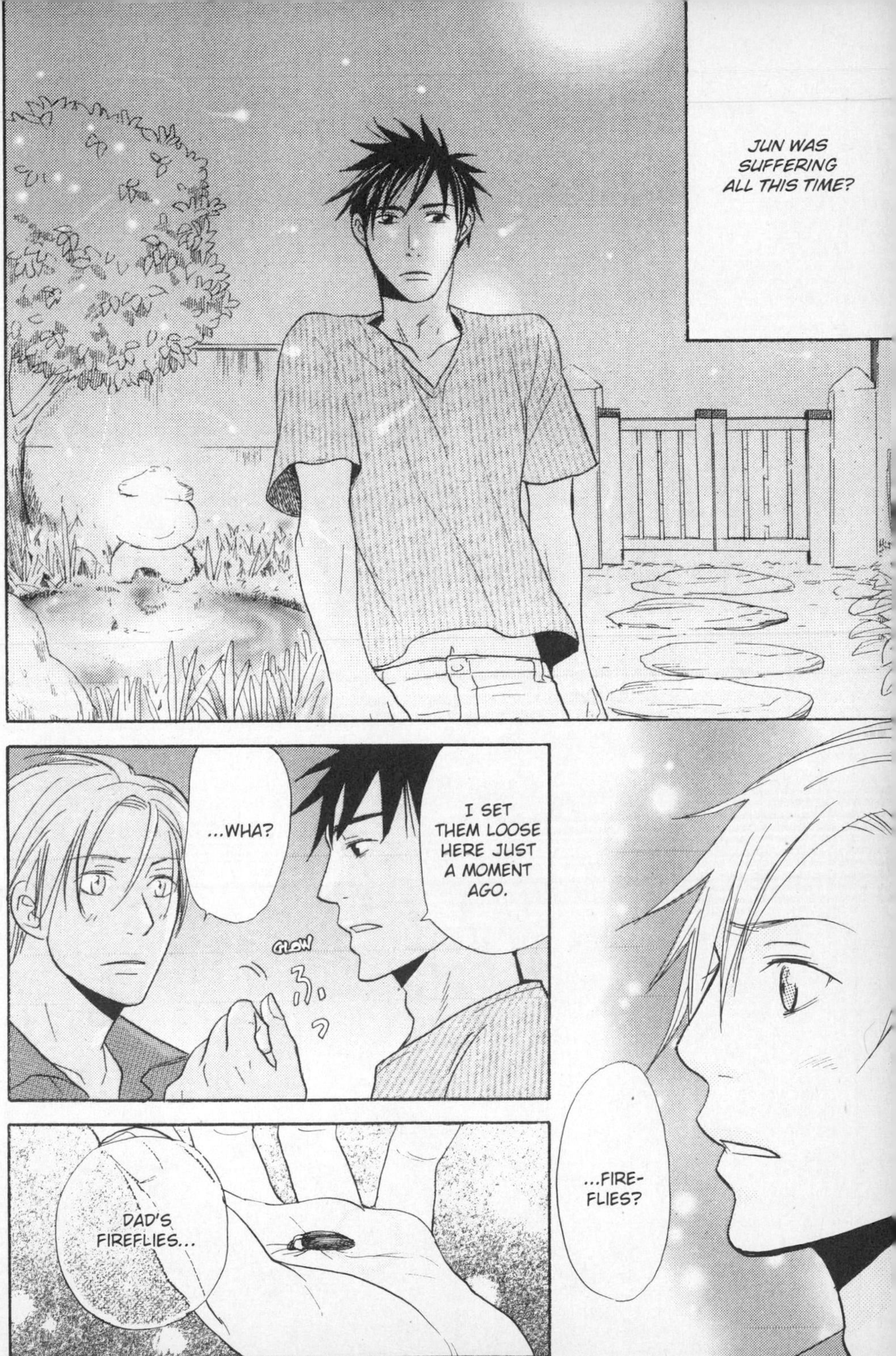
JUN WAS SUFFERING ALL THIS TIME?
...FIRE-FLIES?
I SET THEM LOOSE HERE JUST A MOMENT AGO.
...WHA?
GLOW
DAD'S FIREFLIES...

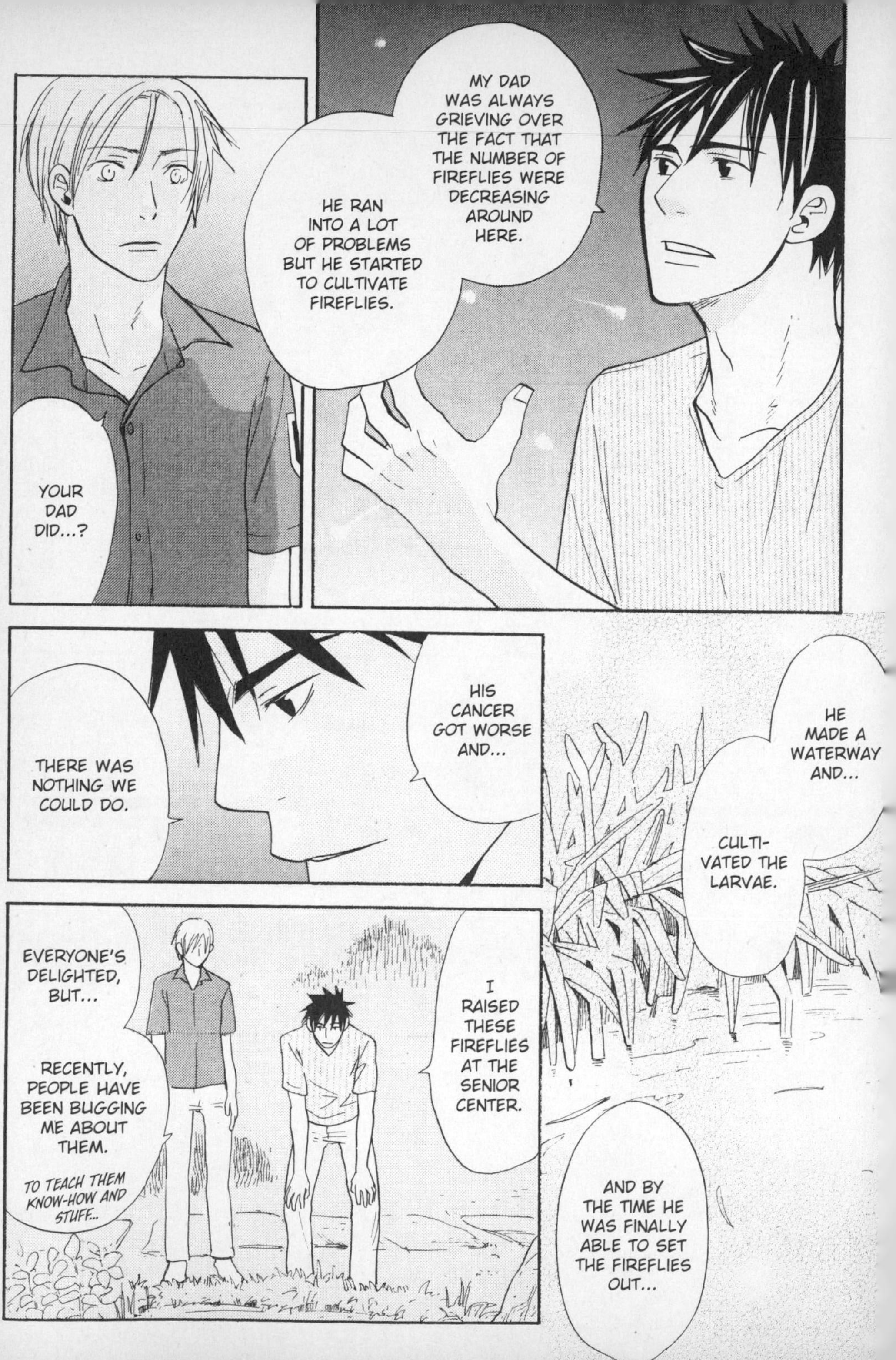
MY DAD WAS ALWAYS GRIEVING OVER THE FACT THAT THE NUMBER OF FIREFLIES WERE DECREASING AROUND HERE.
HE RAN INTO A LOT OF PROBLEMS BUT HE STARTED TO CULTIVATE FIREFLIES.
YOUR DAD DID...?
HE MADE A WATERWAY AND...
CULTI-VATED THE LARVAE.
AND BY THE TIME HE WAS FINALLY ABLE TO SET THE FIREFLIES OUT...
HIS CANCER GOT WORSE AND...
THERE WAS NOTHING WE COULD DO.
I RAISED THESE FIREFLIES AT THE SENIOR CENTER.
EVERYONE'S DELIGHTED, BUT...
RECENTLY, PEOPLE HAVE BEEN BUGGING ME ABOUT THEM.
TO TEACH THEM KNOW-HOW AND STUFF...

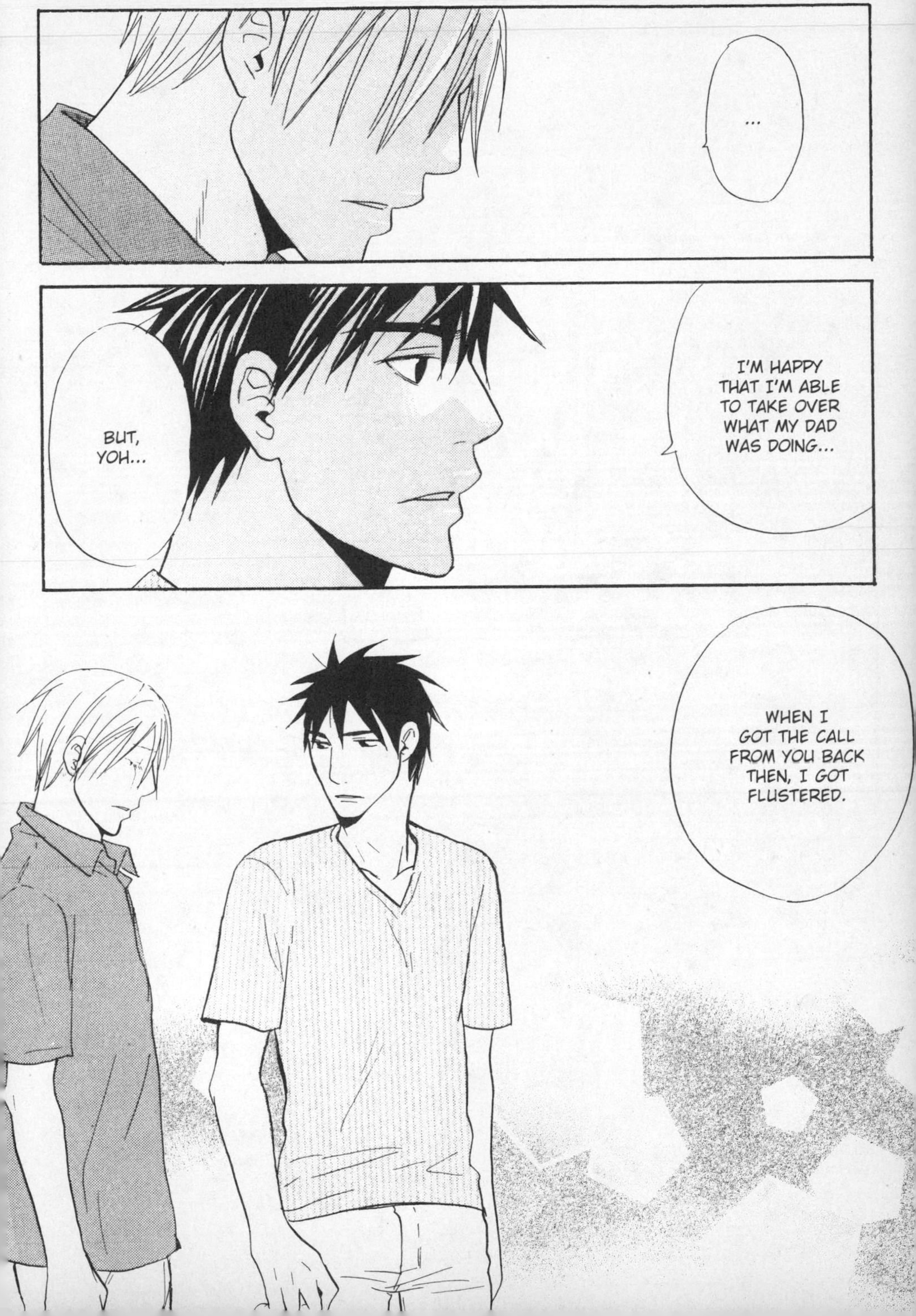
...
I'M HAPPY THAT I'M ABLE TO TAKE OVER WHAT MY DAD WAS DOING...
BUT, YOH...
WHEN I GOT THE CALL FROM YOU BACK THEN, I GOT FLUSTERED.

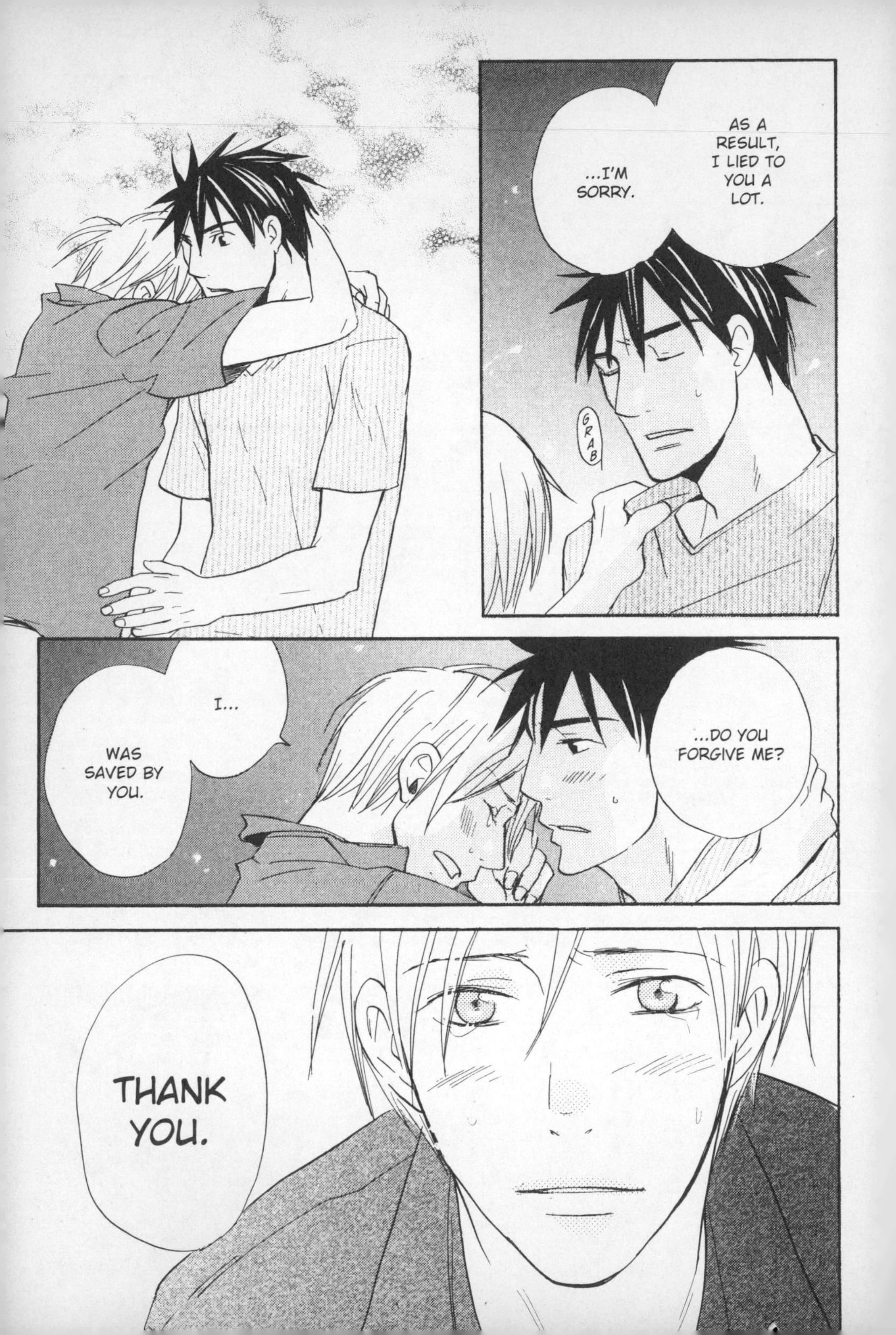
AS A RESULT, I LIED TO YOU A LOT.
...I'M SORRY.
GRAB
...DO YOU FORGIVE ME?
I...
WAS SAVED BY YOU.
THANK YOU.

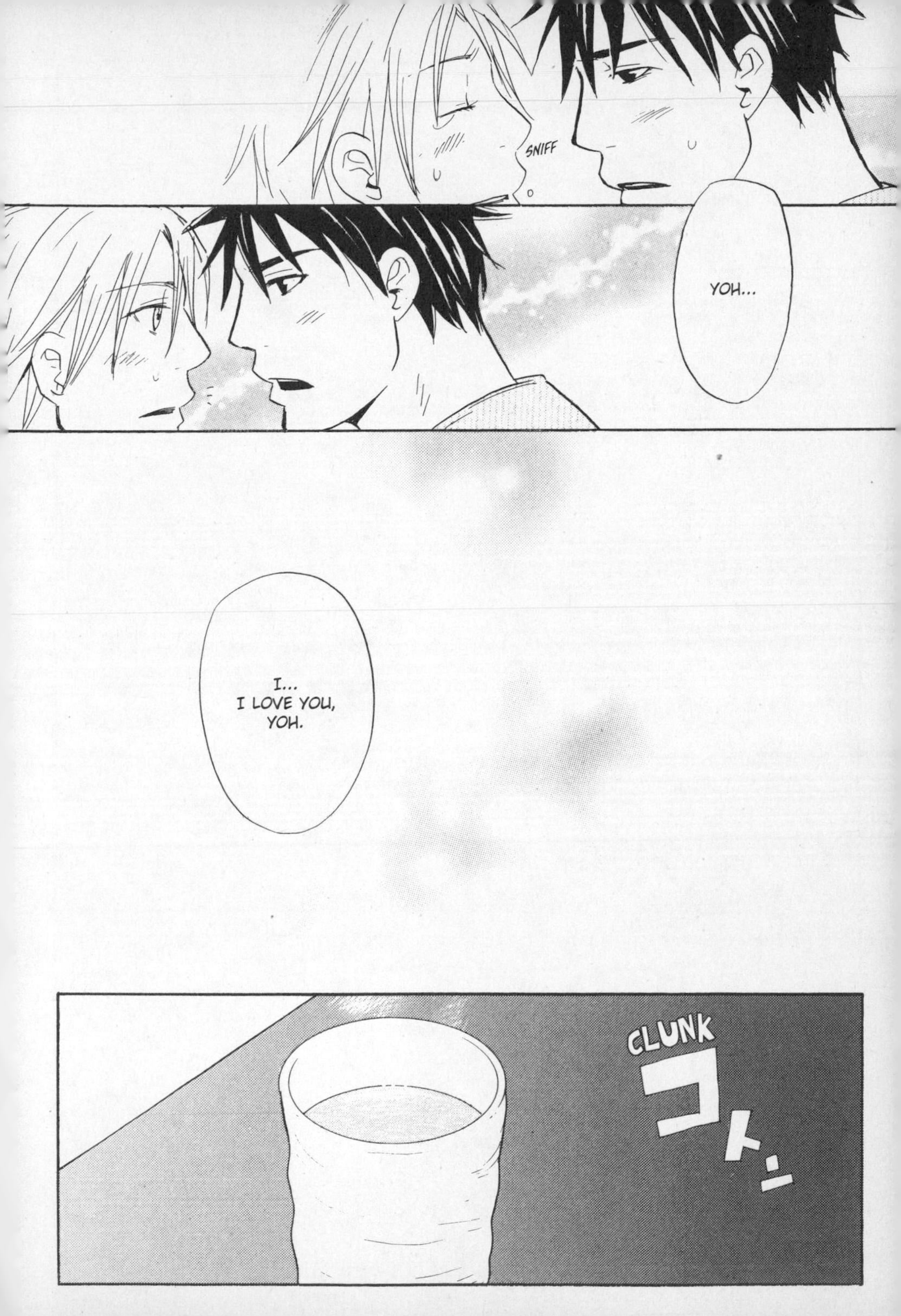
SNIFF
YOH...
I...
I LOVE YOU,
YOH.
CLUNK
コトン

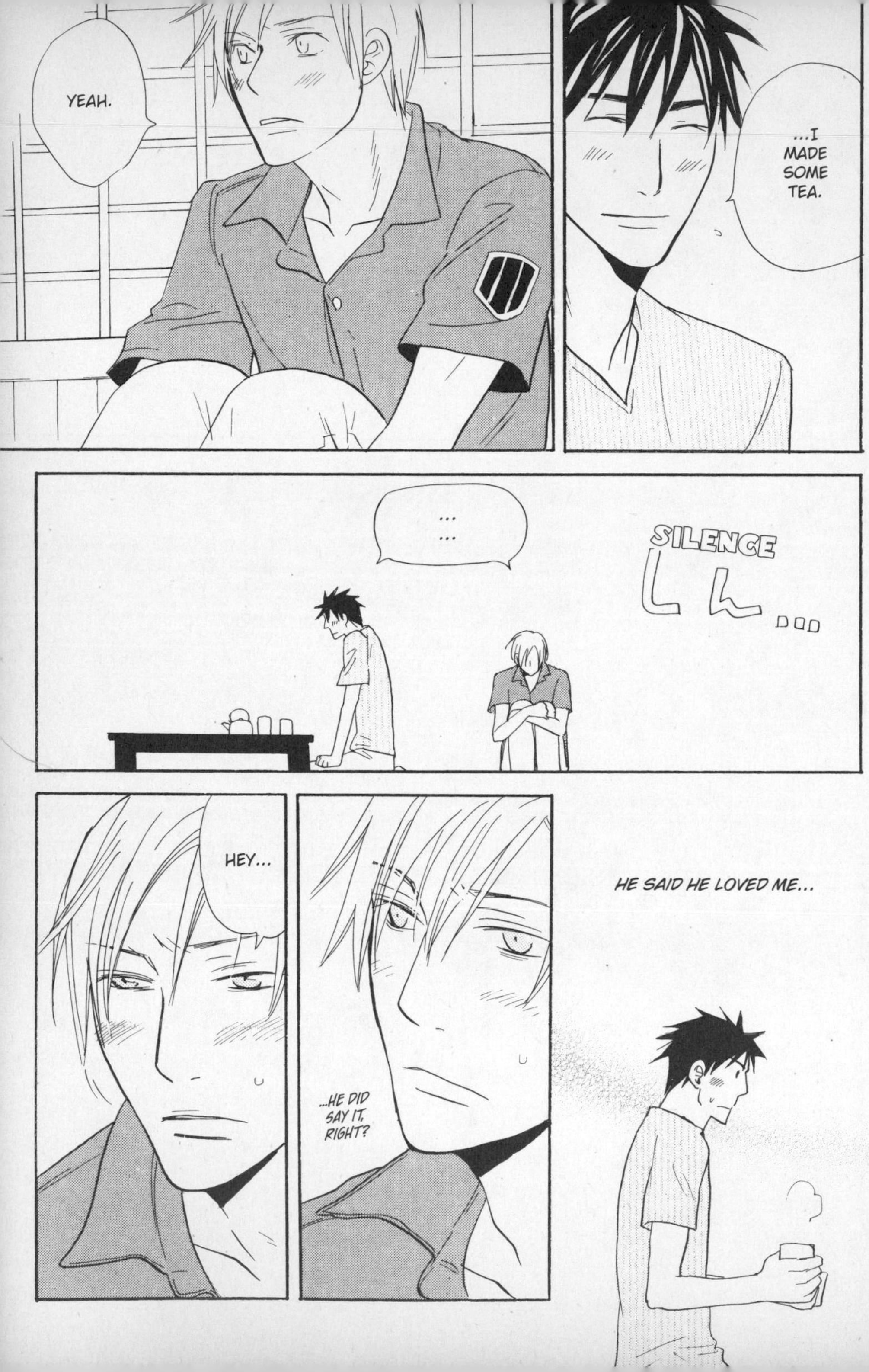
...I MADE SOME TEA.
YEAH.
... ...
SILENCE
HE SAID HE LOVED ME...
...HE DID SAY IT, RIGHT?
HEY...

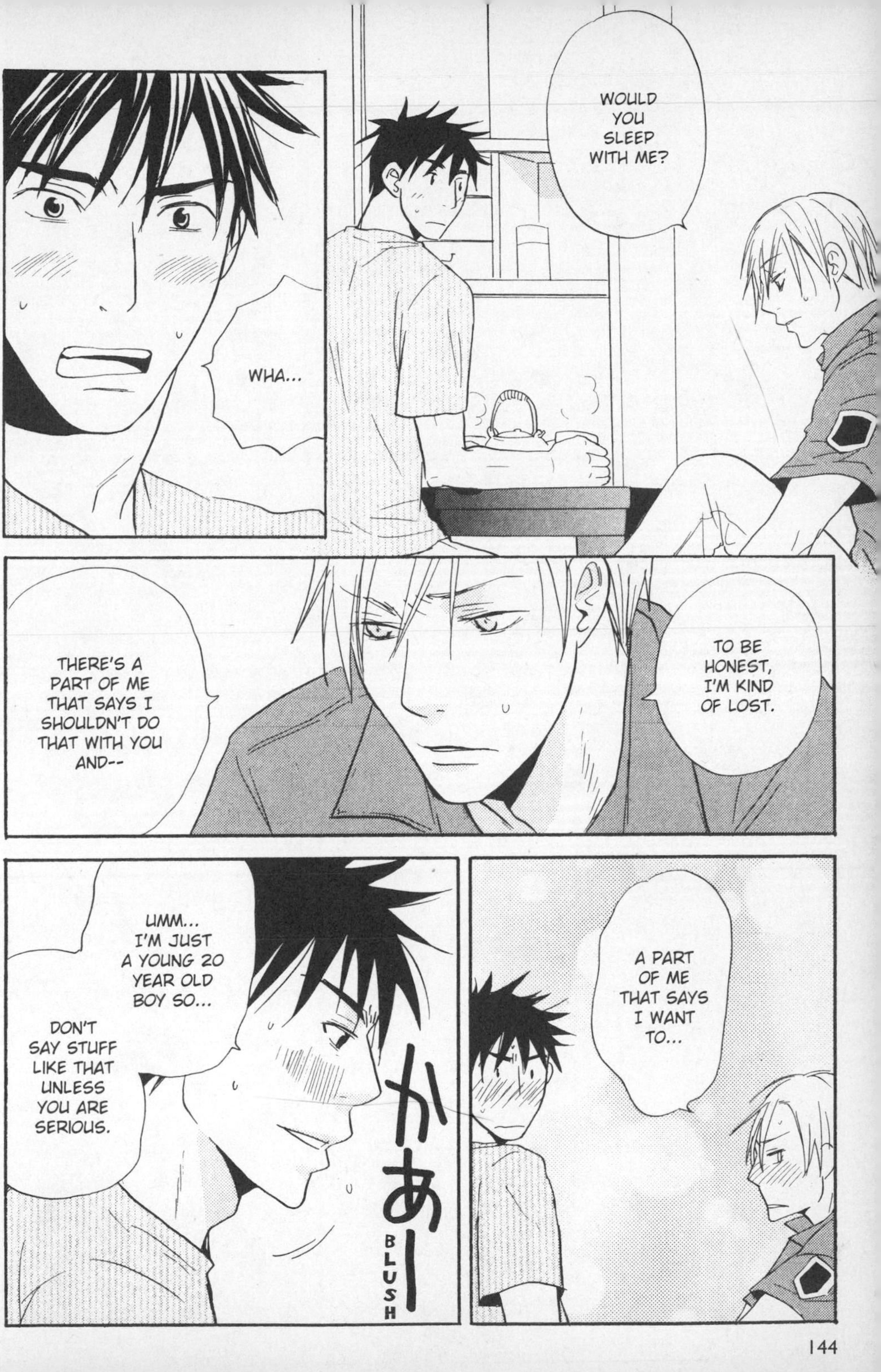
WOULD YOU SLEEP WITH ME?
WHA...
TO BE HONEST, I'M KIND OF LOST.
THERE'S A PART OF ME THAT SAYS I SHOULDN'T DO THAT WITH YOU AND--
A PART OF ME THAT SAYS I WANT TO...
UMM... I'M JUST A YOUNG 20 YEAR OLD BOY SO...
DON'T SAY STUFF LIKE THAT UNLESS YOU ARE SERIOUS.
かぁー
BLUSH

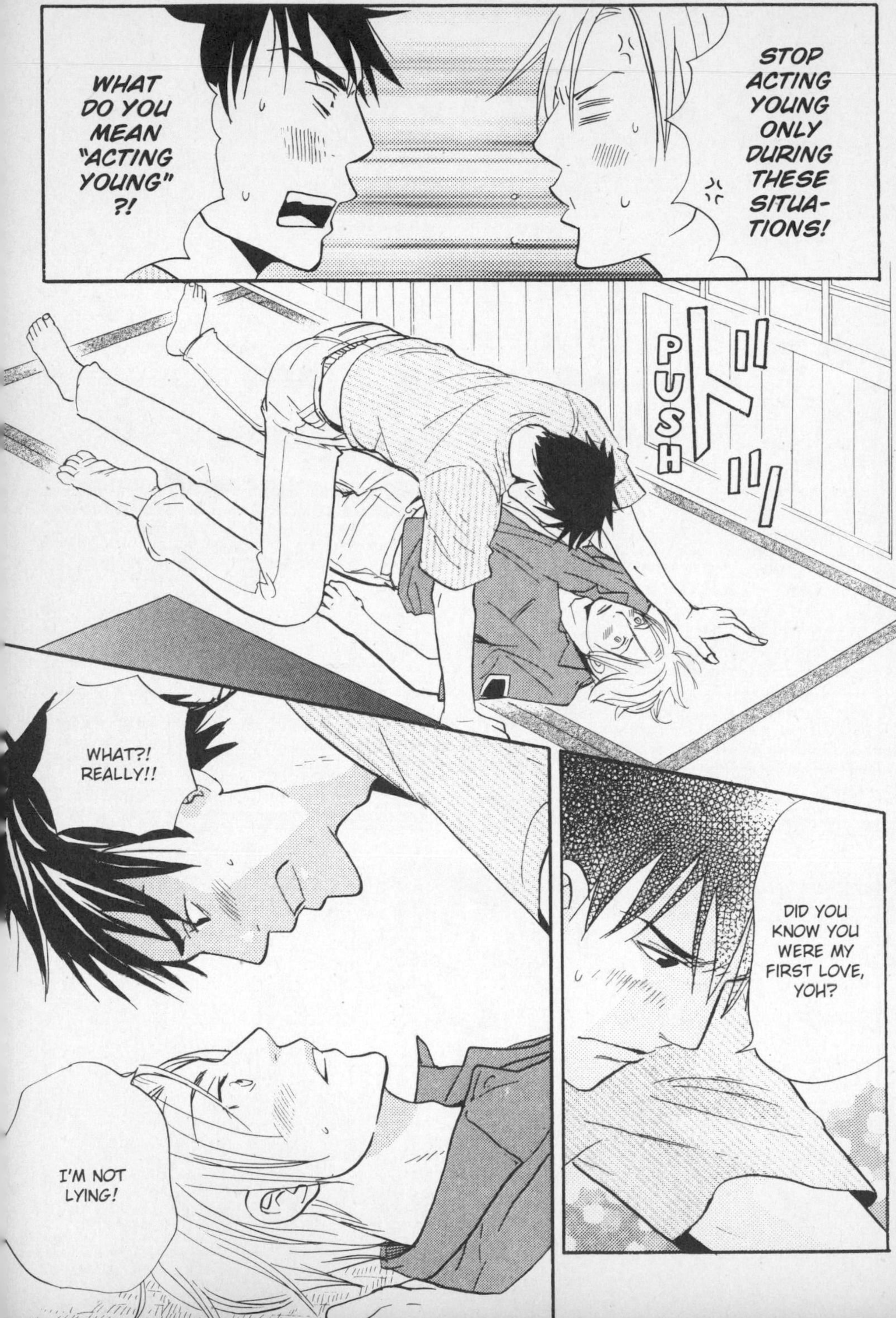
STOP ACTING YOUNG ONLY DURING THESE SITUA-TIONS!
WHAT DO YOU MEAN "ACTING YOUNG" ?!
PUSH
DID YOU KNOW YOU WERE MY FIRST LOVE, YOH?
WHAT?! REALLY!!
I'M NOT LYING!

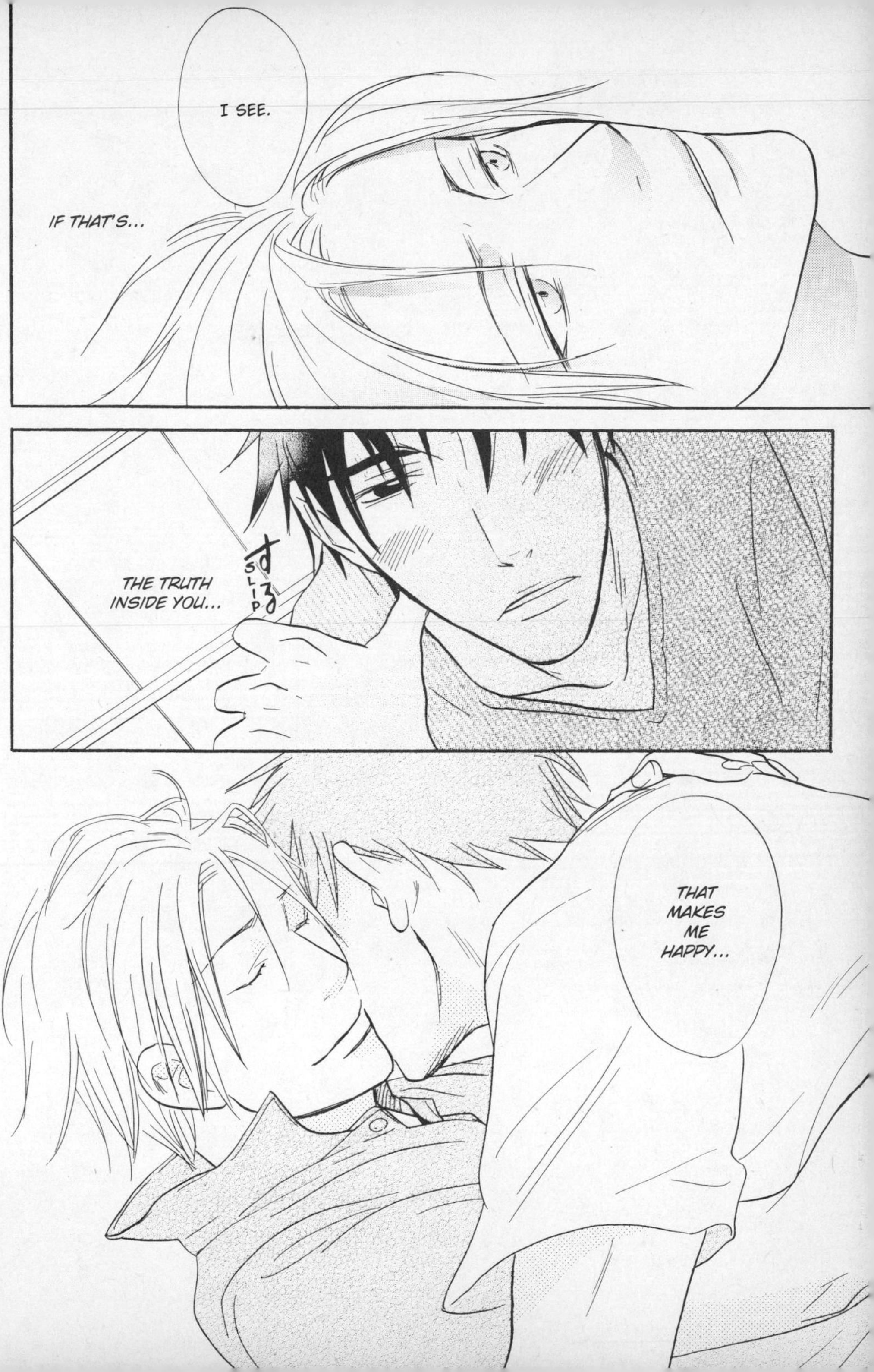
I SEE.
IF THAT'S...
THE TRUTH INSIDE YOU...
する
SLIP
THAT MAKES ME HAPPY...

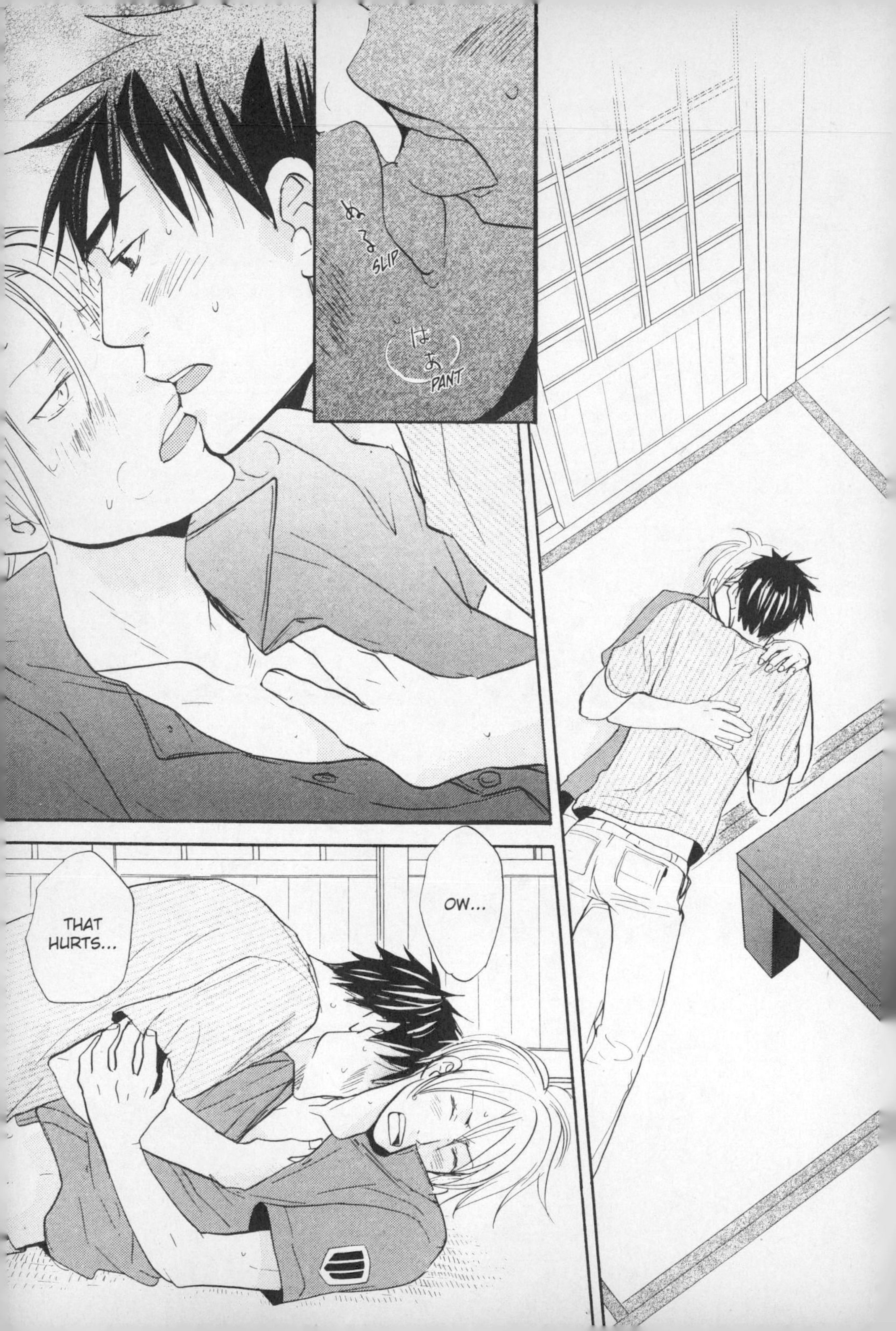
ぬる
SLIP
はぁ
PANT
OW...
THAT HURTS...

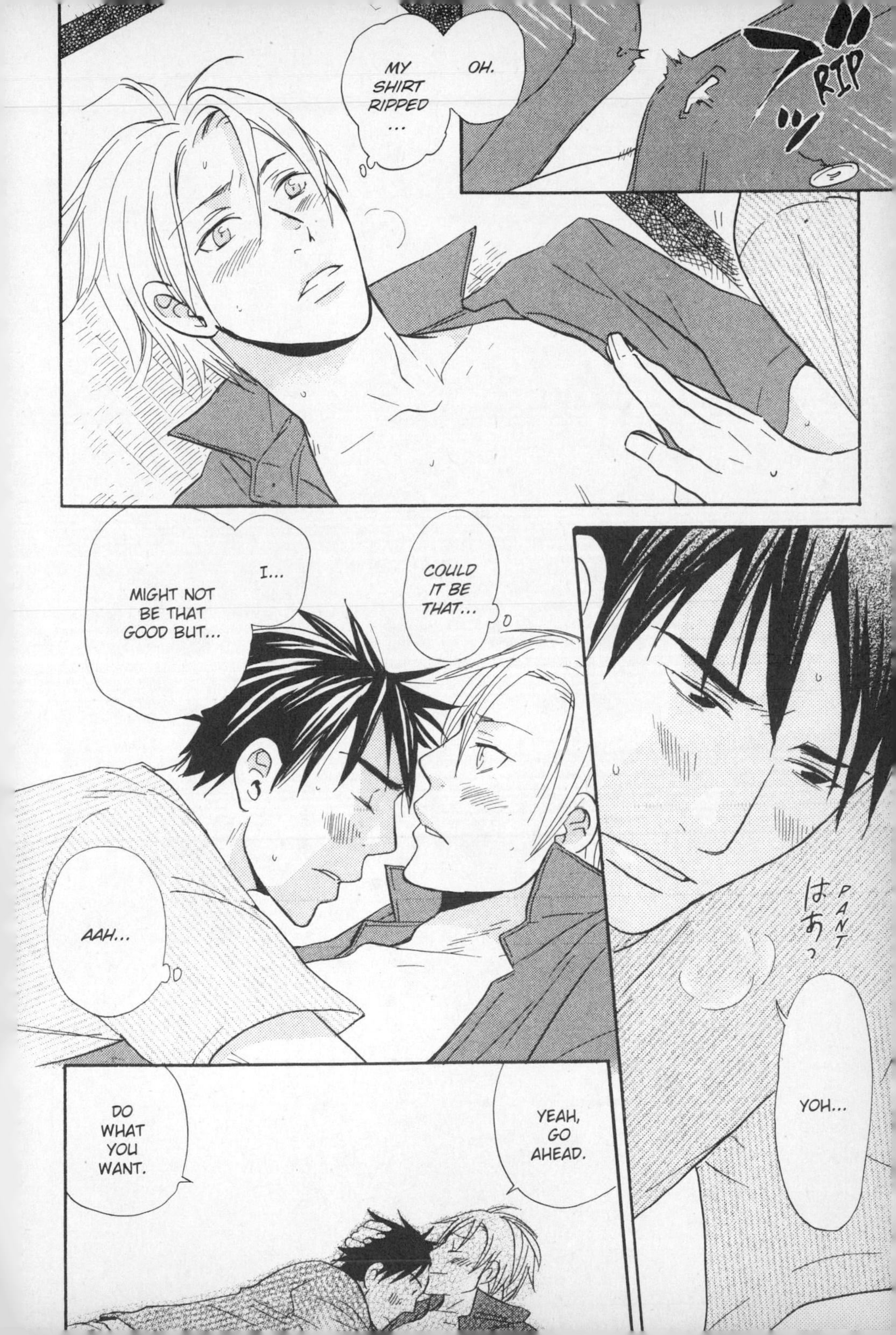
RIP
OH.
MY SHIRT RIPPED ...
はあっ PANT
YOH...
COULD IT BE THAT...
I...
MIGHT NOT BE THAT GOOD BUT...
AAH...
YEAH, GO AHEAD.
DO WHAT YOU WANT.

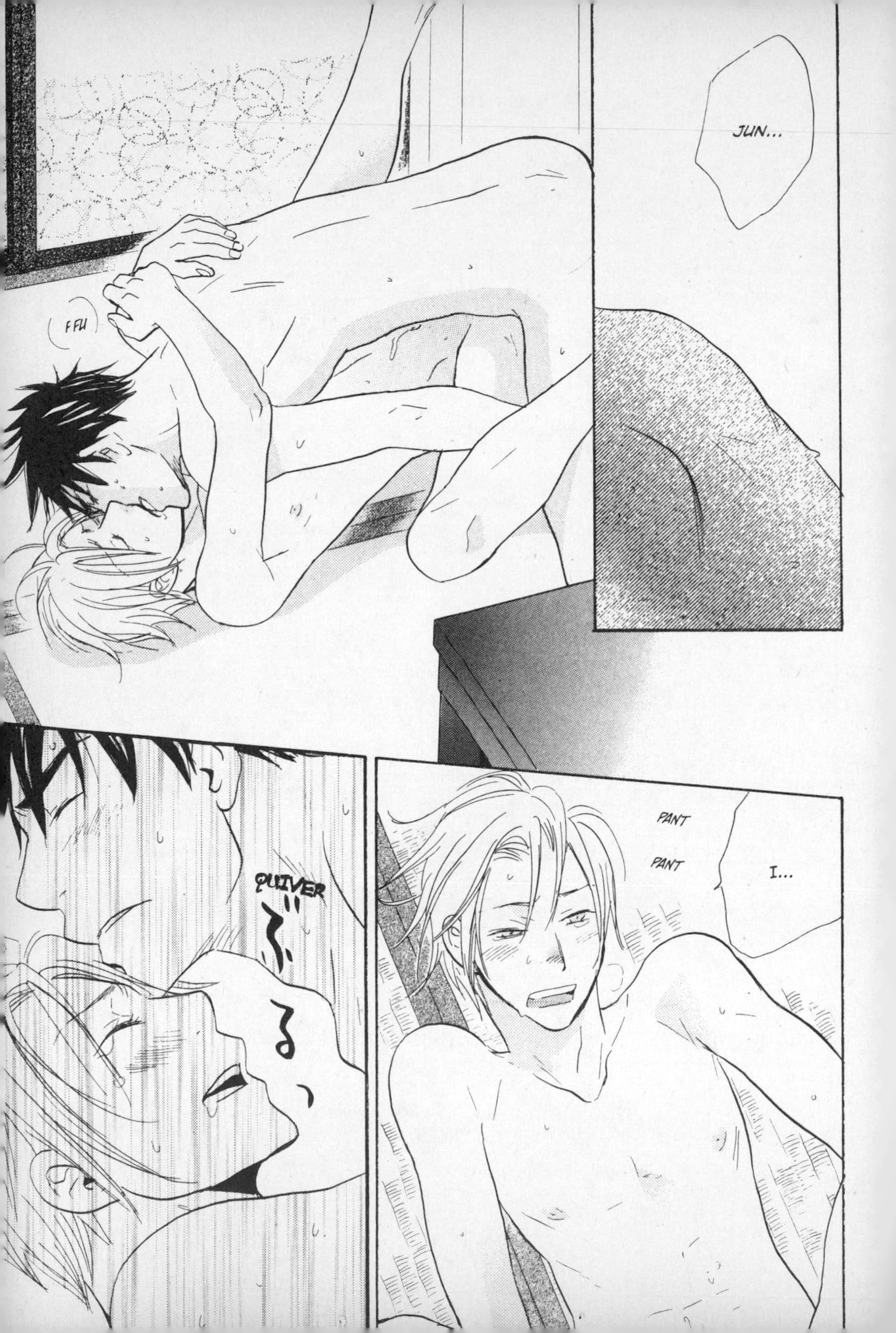
JUN...
FFU
PANT
PANT
I...
QUIVER
ぶる

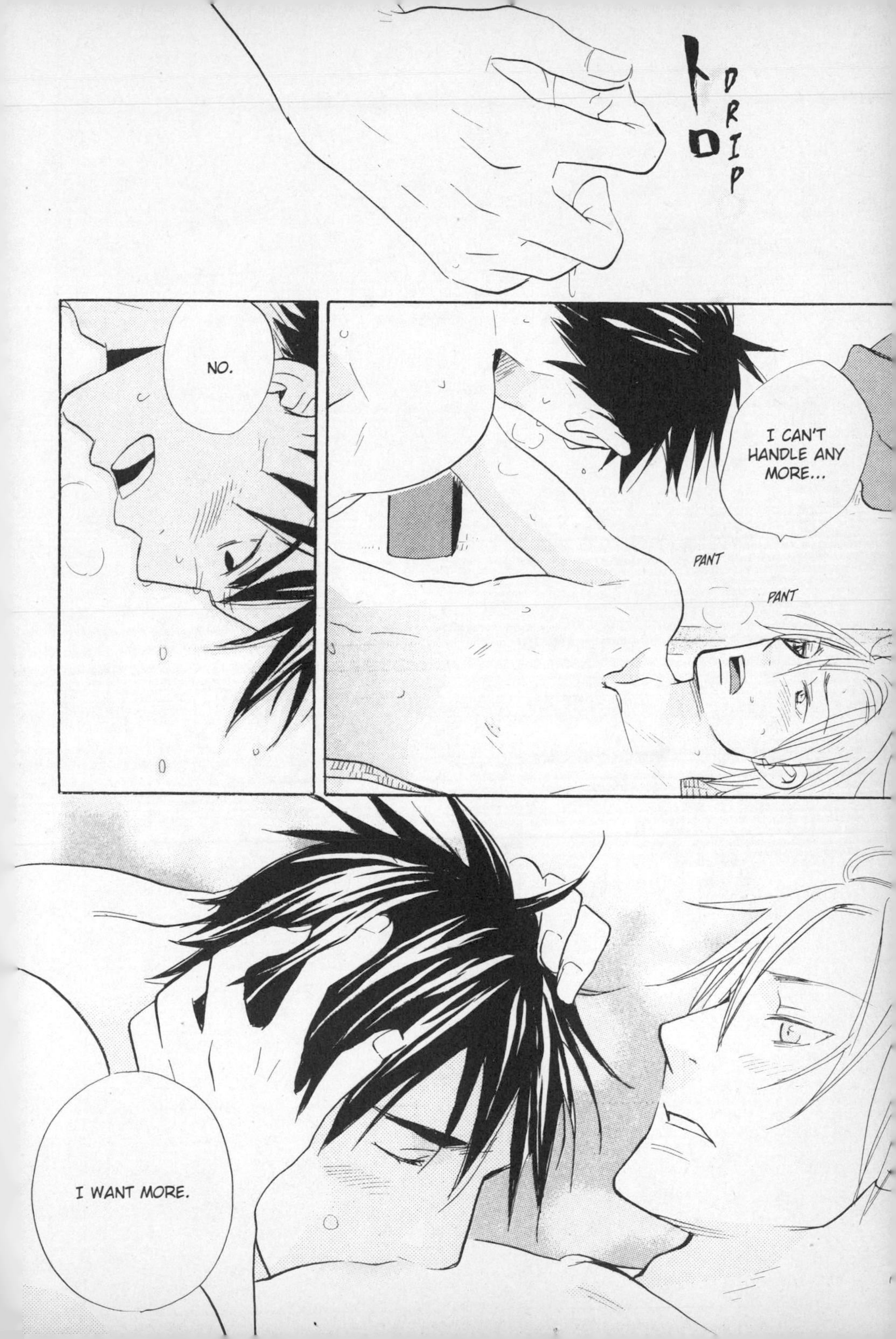
トロ
DRIP
I CAN'T HANDLE ANY MORE...
PANT
PANT
NO.
I WANT MORE.

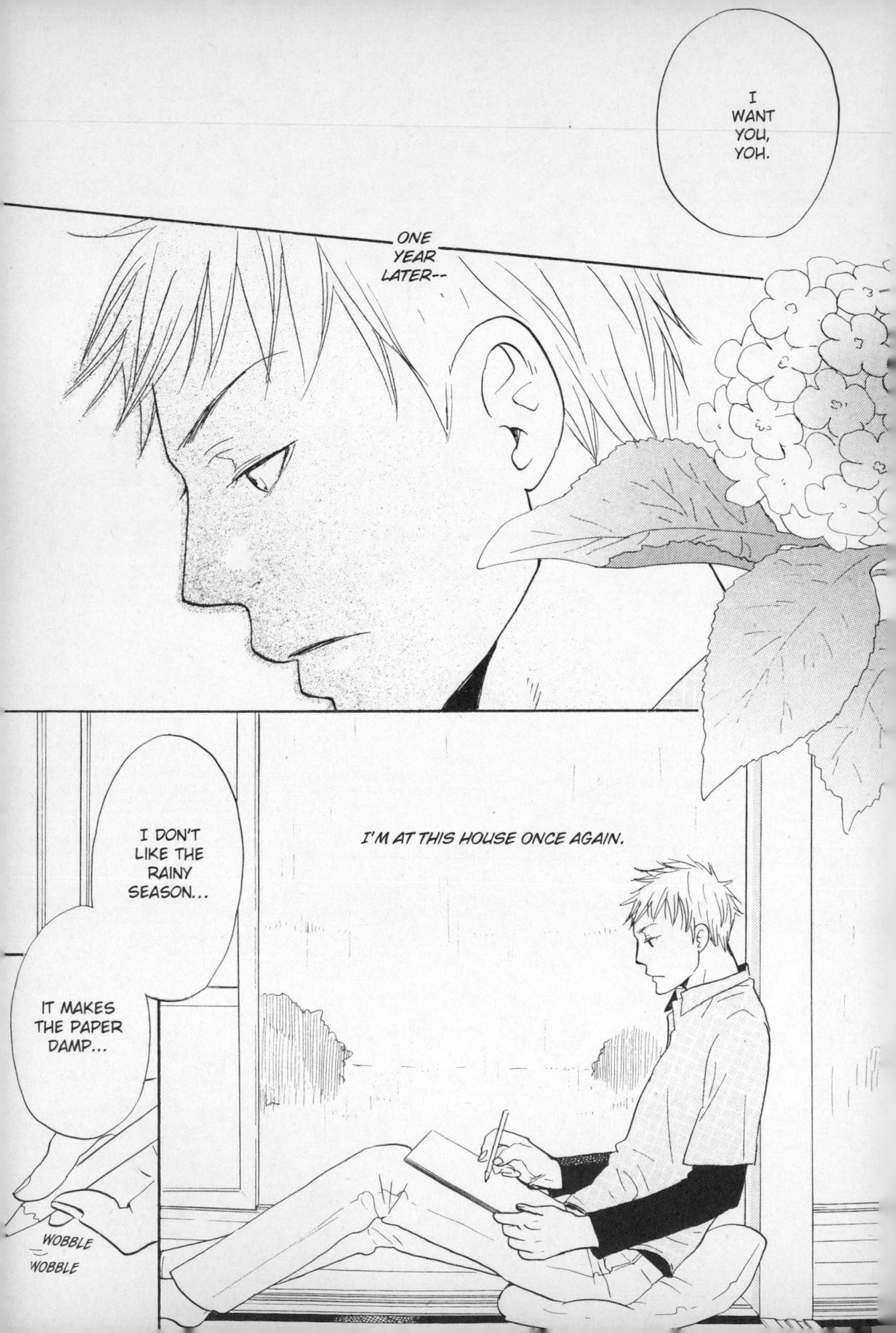
I WANT YOU, YOH.
ONE YEAR LATER--
I'M AT THIS HOUSE ONCE AGAIN.
I DON'T LIKE THE RAINY SEASON...
IT MAKES THE PAPER DAMP...
WOBBLE WOBBLE

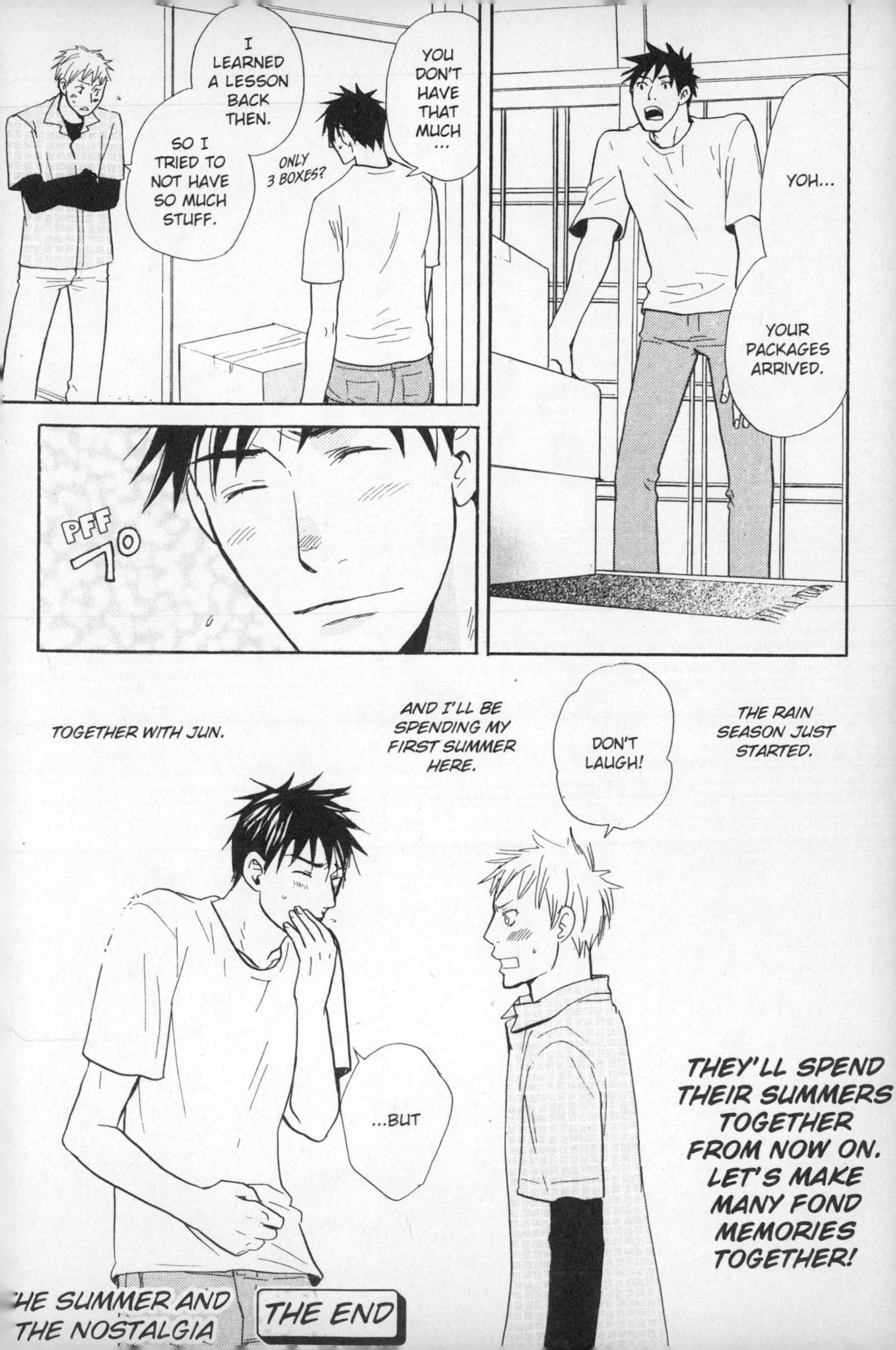
YOH...
YOUR PACKAGES ARRIVED.
YOU DON'T HAVE THAT MUCH ...
ONLY 3 BOXES?
I LEARNED A LESSON BACK THEN.
SO I TRIED TO NOT HAVE SO MUCH STUFF.
PFF
THE RAIN SEASON JUST STARTED.
DON'T LAUGH!
AND I'LL BE SPENDING MY FIRST SUMMER HERE.
TOGETHER WITH JUN.
...BUT
THEY'LL SPEND THEIR SUMMERS TOGETHER FROM NOW ON. LET'S MAKE MANY FOND MEMORIES TOGETHER!
HE SUMMER AND THE NOSTALGIA
THE END

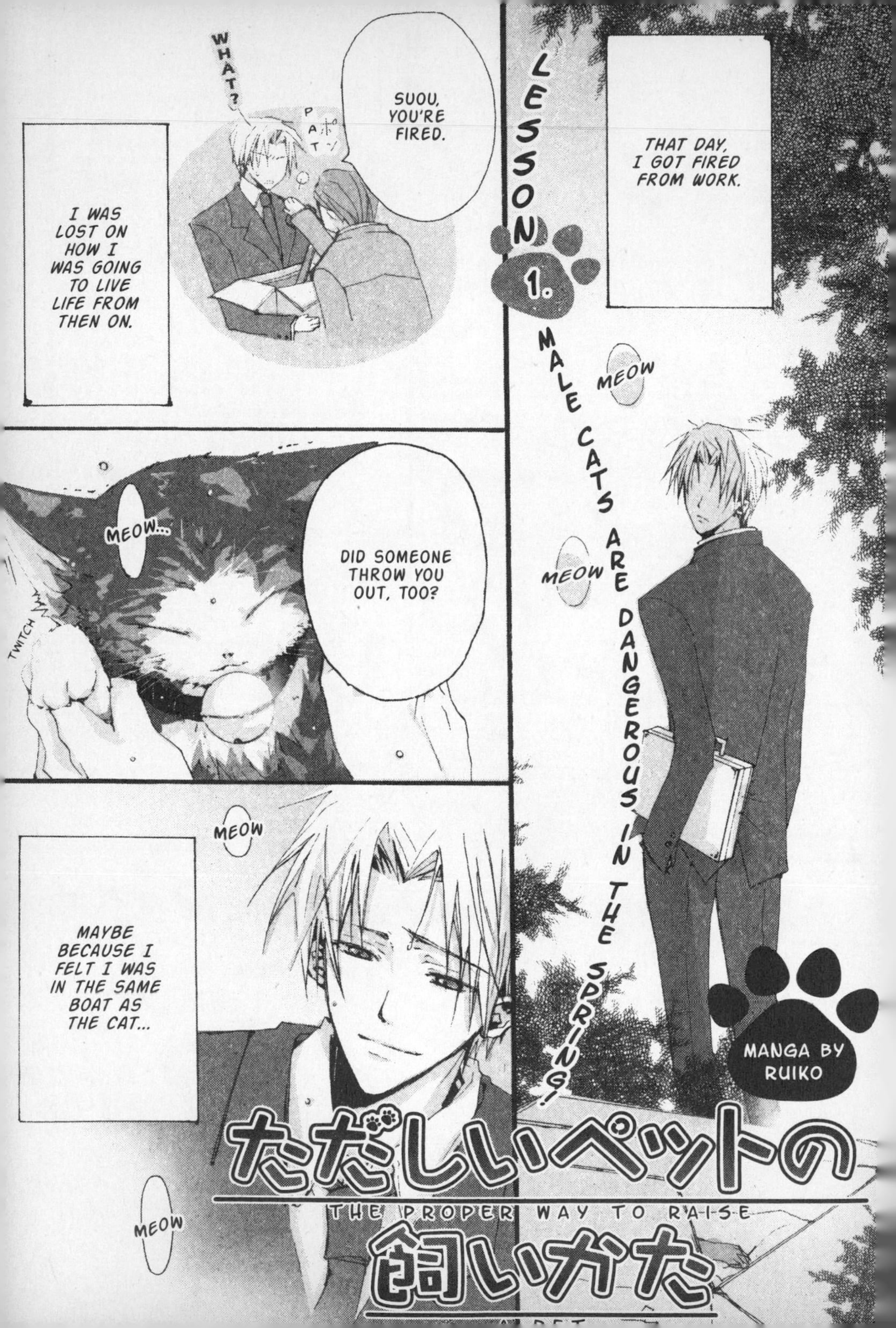
THAT DAY, I GOT FIRED FROM WORK.
LESSON 1. MALE CATS ARE DANGEROUS IN THE SPRING!
MEOW
MEOW
MANGA BY RUIKO
ただしいペットの飼いかた
THE PROPER WAY TO RAISE
SUOU, YOU'RE FIRED.
PAT PAT
WHAT?
I WAS LOST ON HOW I WAS GOING TO LIVE LIFE FROM THEN ON.
DID SOMEONE THROW YOU OUT, TOO?
MEOW...
TWITCH
MEOW
MAYBE BECAUSE I FELT I WAS IN THE SAME BOAT AS THE CAT...
MEOW

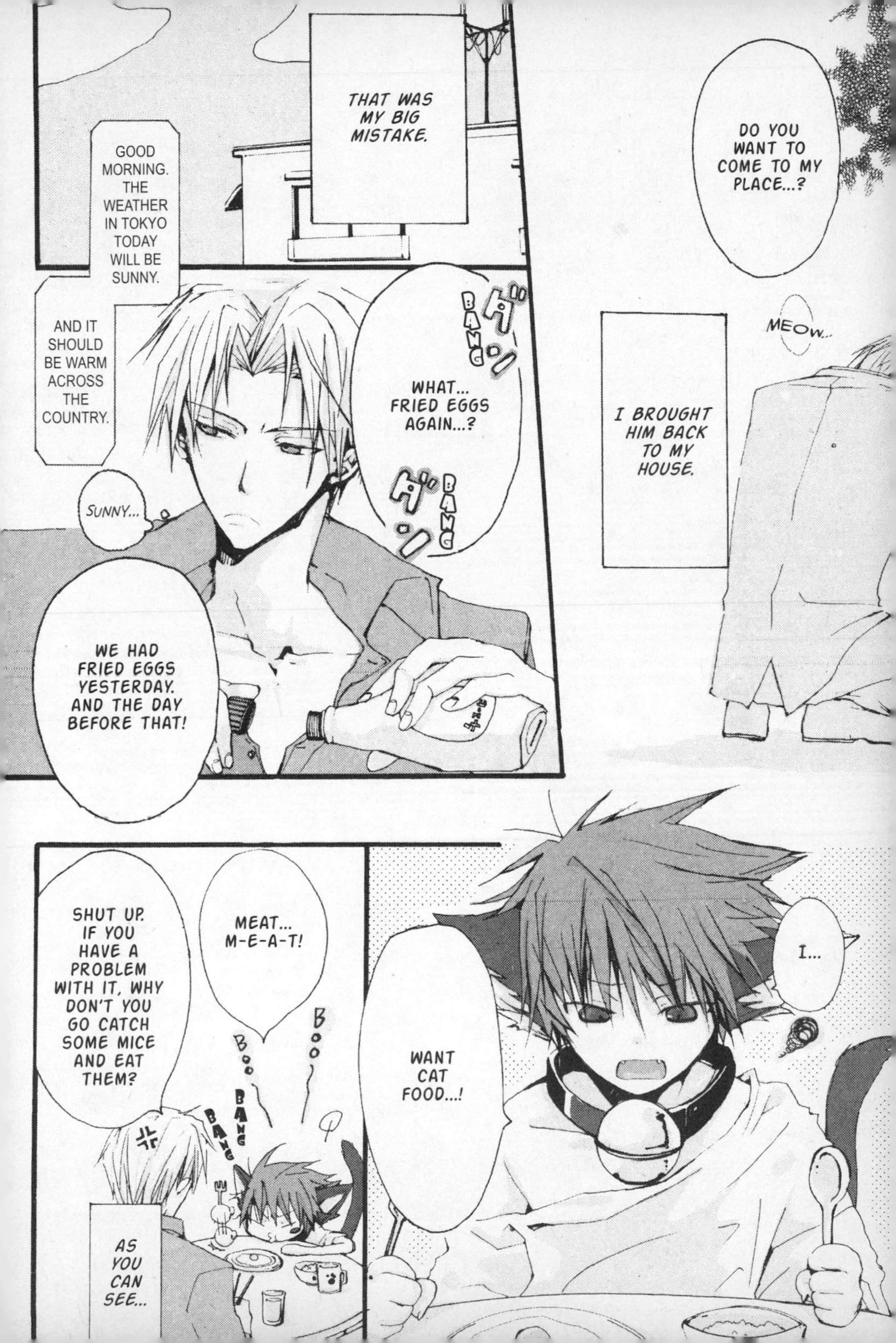

DO YOU WANT TO COME TO MY PLACE...?
MEOW...
I BROUGHT HIM BACK TO MY HOUSE.
THAT WAS MY BIG MISTAKE.
BANG
WHAT... FRIED EGGS AGAIN...?
BANG
GOOD MORNING. THE WEATHER IN TOKYO TODAY WILL BE SUNNY.
AND IT SHOULD BE WARM ACROSS THE COUNTRY.
SUNNY...
WE HAD FRIED EGGS YESTERDAY. AND THE DAY BEFORE THAT!
I...
WANT CAT FOOD...!
MEAT... M-E-A-T!
BOO
BOO
BANG
BANG
SHUT UP. IF YOU HAVE A PROBLEM WITH IT, WHY DON'T YOU GO CATCH SOME MICE AND EAT THEM?
AS YOU CAN SEE...

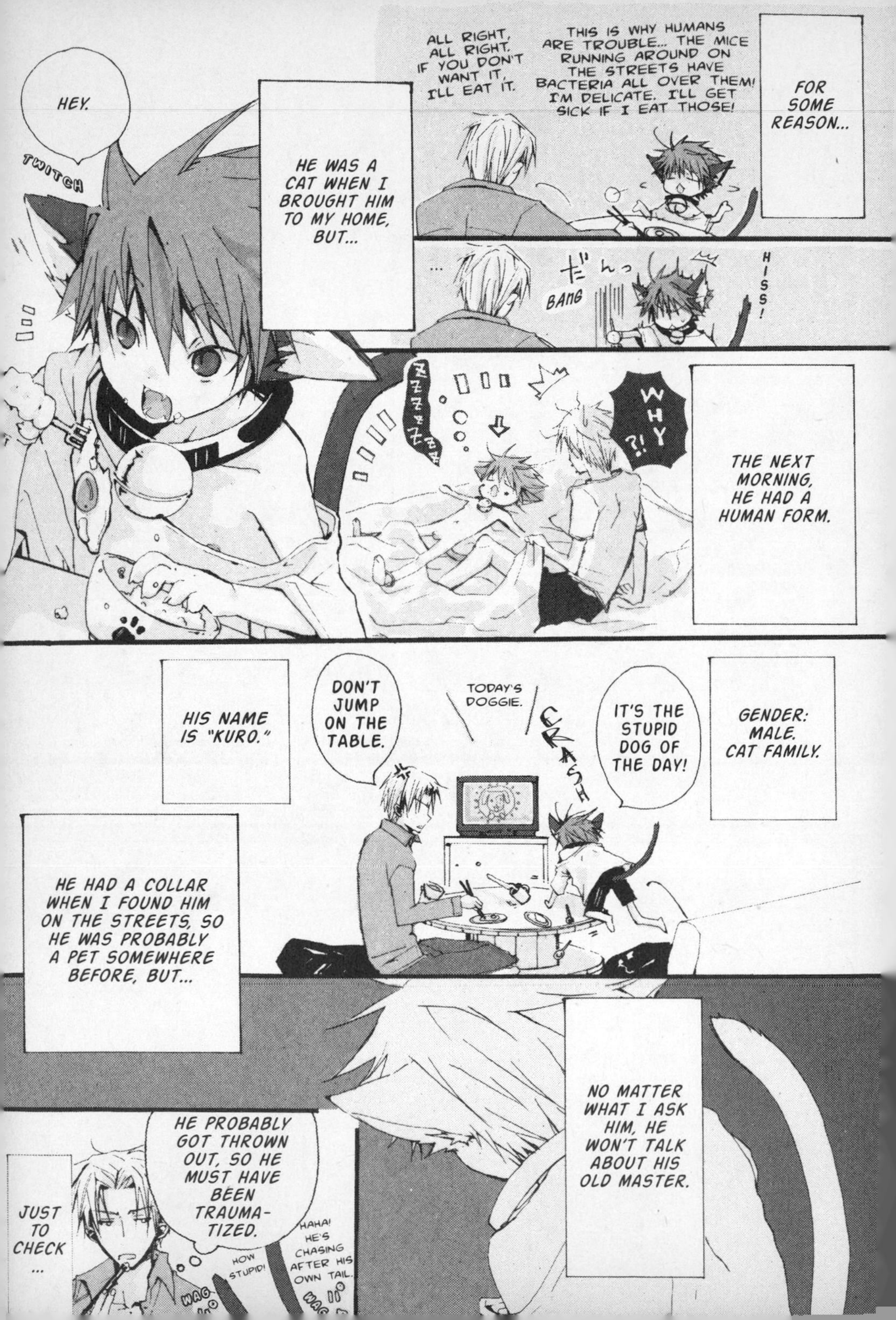
FOR SOME REASON...
THIS IS WHY HUMANS ARE TROUBLE... THE MICE RUNNING AROUND ON THE STREETS HAVE BACTERIA ALL OVER THEM! I'M DELICATE. I'LL GET SICK IF I EAT THOSE!
ALL RIGHT, ALL RIGHT. IF YOU DON'T WANT IT, I'LL EAT IT.
HISS!
...
だんっ
BANG
THE NEXT MORNING, HE HAD A HUMAN FORM.
WHY ?!
HE WAS A CAT WHEN I BROUGHT HIM TO MY HOME, BUT...
HEY.
TWITCH
GENDER: MALE. CAT FAMILY.
IT'S THE STUPID DOG OF THE DAY!
CRASH
TODAY'S DOGGIE.
DON'T JUMP ON THE TABLE.
HIS NAME IS "KURO."
HE HAD A COLLAR WHEN I FOUND HIM ON THE STREETS, SO HE WAS PROBABLY A PET SOMEWHERE BEFORE, BUT...
NO MATTER WHAT I ASK HIM, HE WON'T TALK ABOUT HIS OLD MASTER.
HAHA! HE'S CHASING AFTER HIS OWN TAIL.
HOW STUPID!
HE PROBABLY GOT THROWN OUT, SO HE MUST HAVE BEEN TRAUMATIZED.
JUST TO CHECK ...
WAG
WAG

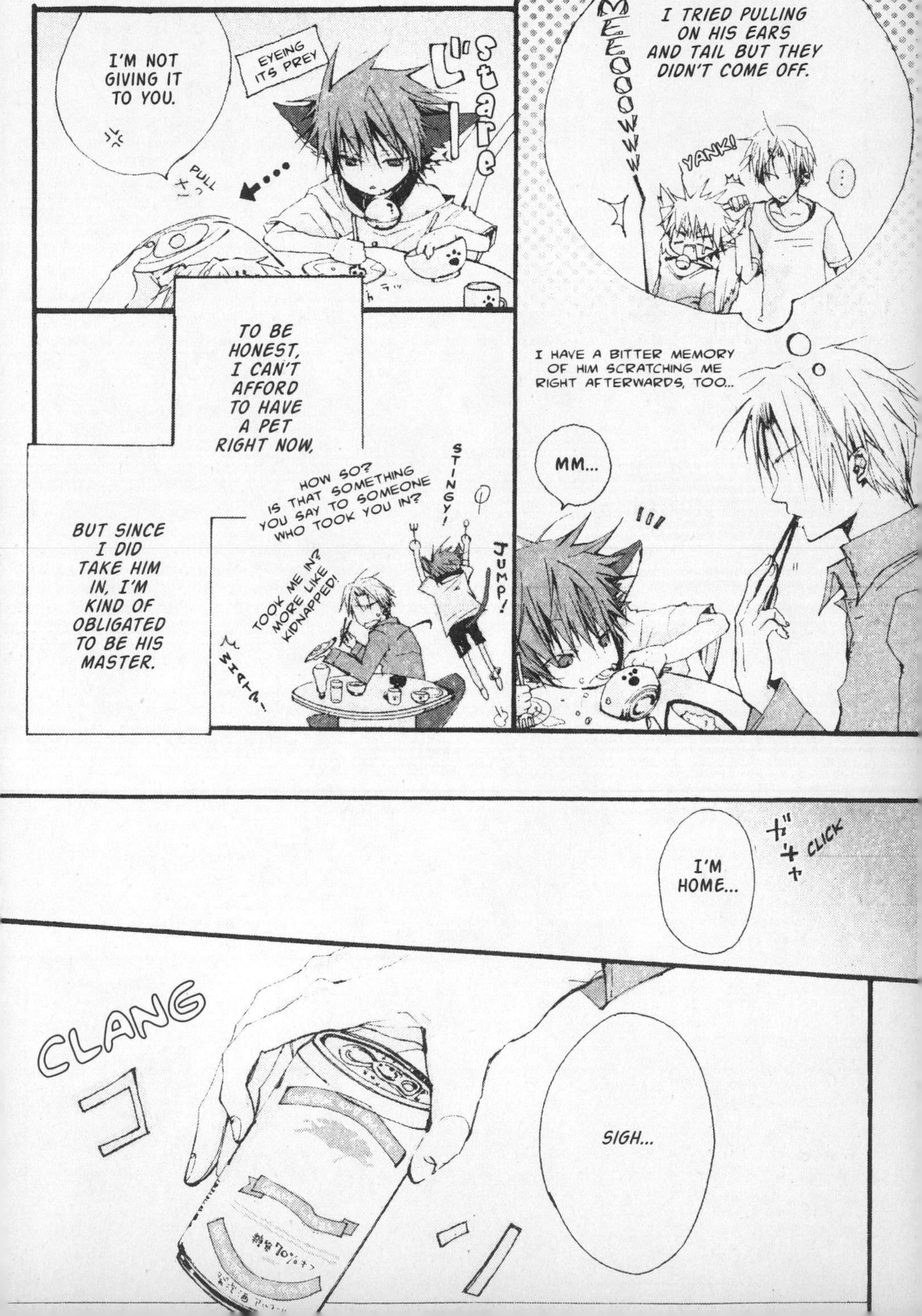
MEEOOOWWW
I TRIED PULLING ON HIS EARS AND TAIL BUT THEY DIDN'T COME OFF.
YANK!
I HAVE A BITTER MEMORY OF HIM SCRATCHING ME RIGHT AFTERWARDS, TOO...
MM...
Stare
EYEING ITS PREY
I'M NOT GIVING IT TO YOU.
PULL
TO BE HONEST, I CAN'T AFFORD TO HAVE A PET RIGHT NOW,
BUT SINCE I DID TAKE HIM IN, I'M KIND OF OBLIGATED TO BE HIS MASTER.
STINGY!
JUMP!
HOW SO? IS THAT SOMETHING YOU SAY TO SOMEONE WHO TOOK YOU IN?
TOOK ME IN? MORE LIKE KIDNAPPED!
CLICK
I'M HOME...
SIGH...
CLANG

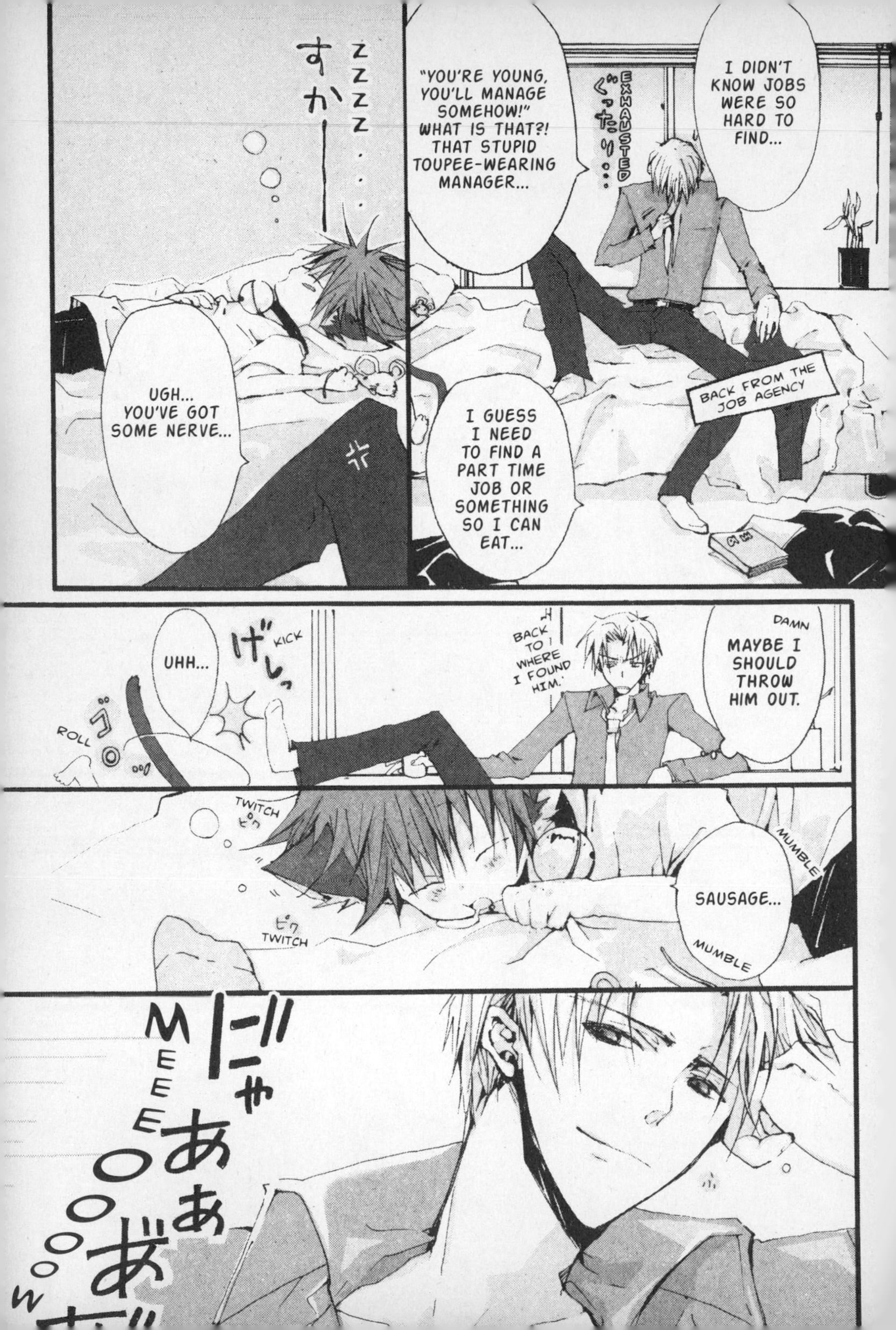
I DIDN'T KNOW JOBS WERE SO HARD TO FIND...
ぐったり…
EXHAUSTED
"YOU'RE YOUNG, YOU'LL MANAGE SOMEHOW!" WHAT IS THAT?! THAT STUPID TOUPEE-WEARING MANAGER...
BACK FROM THE JOB AGENCY
I GUESS I NEED TO FIND A PART TIME JOB OR SOMETHING SO I CAN EAT...
ZZZZ....
すかー
UGH... YOU'VE GOT SOME NERVE...
DAMN
MAYBE I SHOULD THROW HIM OUT.
BACK TO WHERE I FOUND HIM.
げしっ
KICK
UHH...
ゴ
ROLL
MUMBLE
SAUSAGE...
MUMBLE
TWITCH
ピク
ピク
TWITCH
にゃあぁあ
MEEEOOOOW

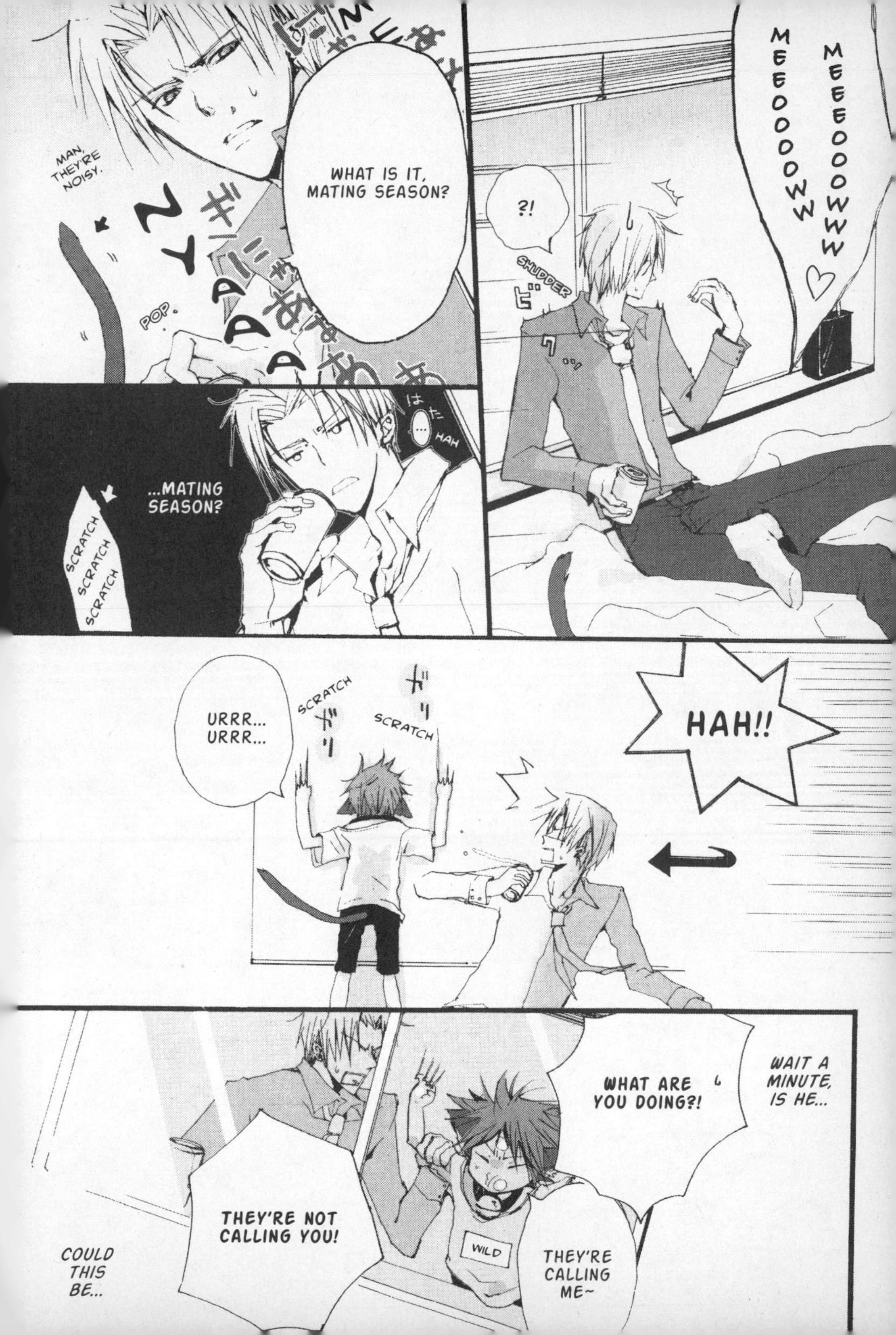
MEEEOOOWWW
MEEOOOOWW
?!
SHUDDER
WHAT IS IT, MATING SEASON?
MAN, THEY'RE NOISY.
NYAAAA
POP.
...
HAH
...MATING SEASON?
SCRATCH SCRATCH SCRATCH
HAH!!
SCRATCH
SCRATCH
URRR... URRR...
WAIT A MINUTE, IS HE...
WHAT ARE YOU DOING?!
THEY'RE CALLING ME~
THEY'RE NOT CALLING YOU!
WILD
COULD THIS BE...

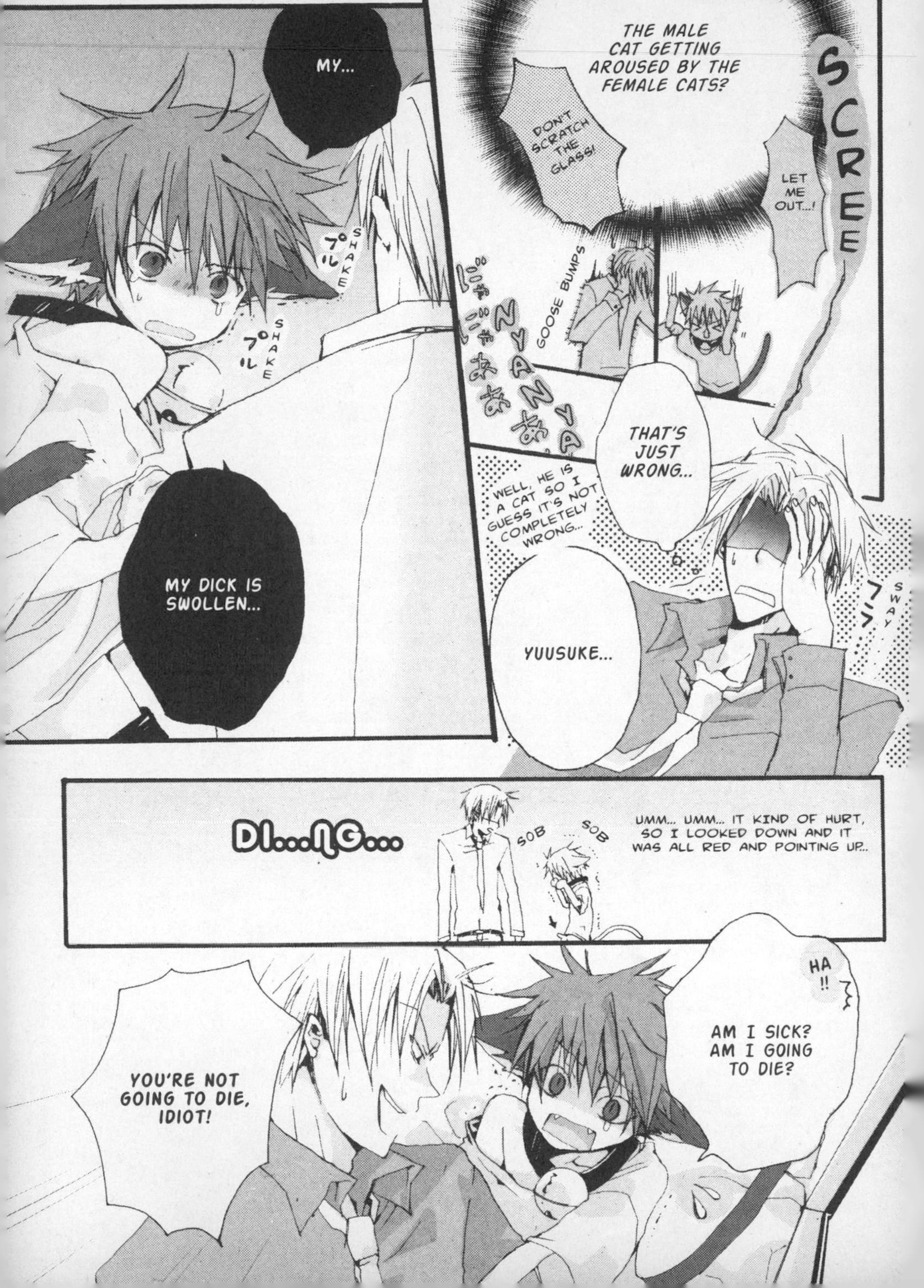
THE MALE CAT GETTING AROUSED BY THE FEMALE CATS?
SCREE
LET ME OUT...!
DON'T SCRATCH THE GLASS!
GOOSE BUMPS
NYANYA
THAT'S JUST WRONG...
WELL, HE IS A CAT SO I GUESS IT'S NOT COMPLETELY WRONG...
SWAY
YUUSUKE...
MY...
SHAKE
SHAKE
MY DICK IS SWOLLEN...
UMM... UMM... IT KIND OF HURT, SO I LOOKED DOWN AND IT WAS ALL RED AND POINTING UP...
SOB
SOB
DI...NG...
HA!!
AM I SICK? AM I GOING TO DIE?
YOU'RE NOT GOING TO DIE, IDIOT!

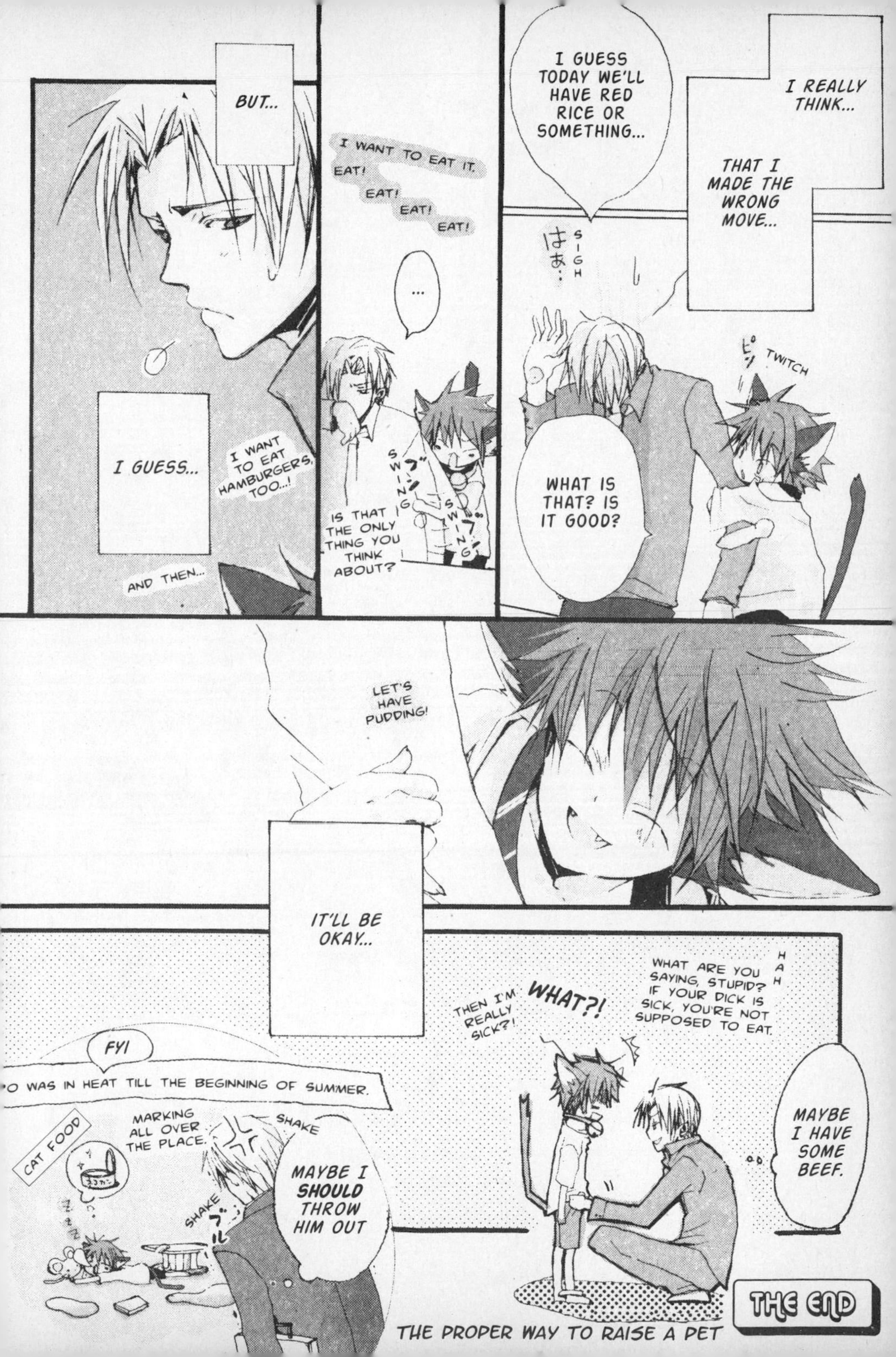
I REALLY THINK...
THAT I MADE THE WRONG MOVE...
I GUESS TODAY WE'LL HAVE RED RICE OR SOMETHING...
はぁ・ SIGH
ピッ TWITCH
WHAT IS THAT? IS IT GOOD?
I WANT TO EAT IT. EAT! EAT! EAT! EAT!
...
SWING SWING
IS THAT THE ONLY THING YOU THINK ABOUT?
BUT...
I GUESS...
I WANT TO EAT HAMBURGERS, TOO...!
AND THEN...
LET'S HAVE PUDDING!
IT'LL BE OKAY...
MAYBE I HAVE SOME BEEF.
WHAT ARE YOU SAYING, STUPID? IF YOUR DICK IS SICK, YOU'RE NOT SUPPOSED TO EAT.
HAH
WHAT?!
THEN I'M REALLY SICK?!
THE END
FYI
O WAS IN HEAT TILL THE BEGINNING OF SUMMER.
MARKING ALL OVER THE PLACE.
SHAKE
SHAKE
MAYBE I SHOULD THROW HIM OUT
CAT FOOD
THE PROPER WAY TO RAISE A PET

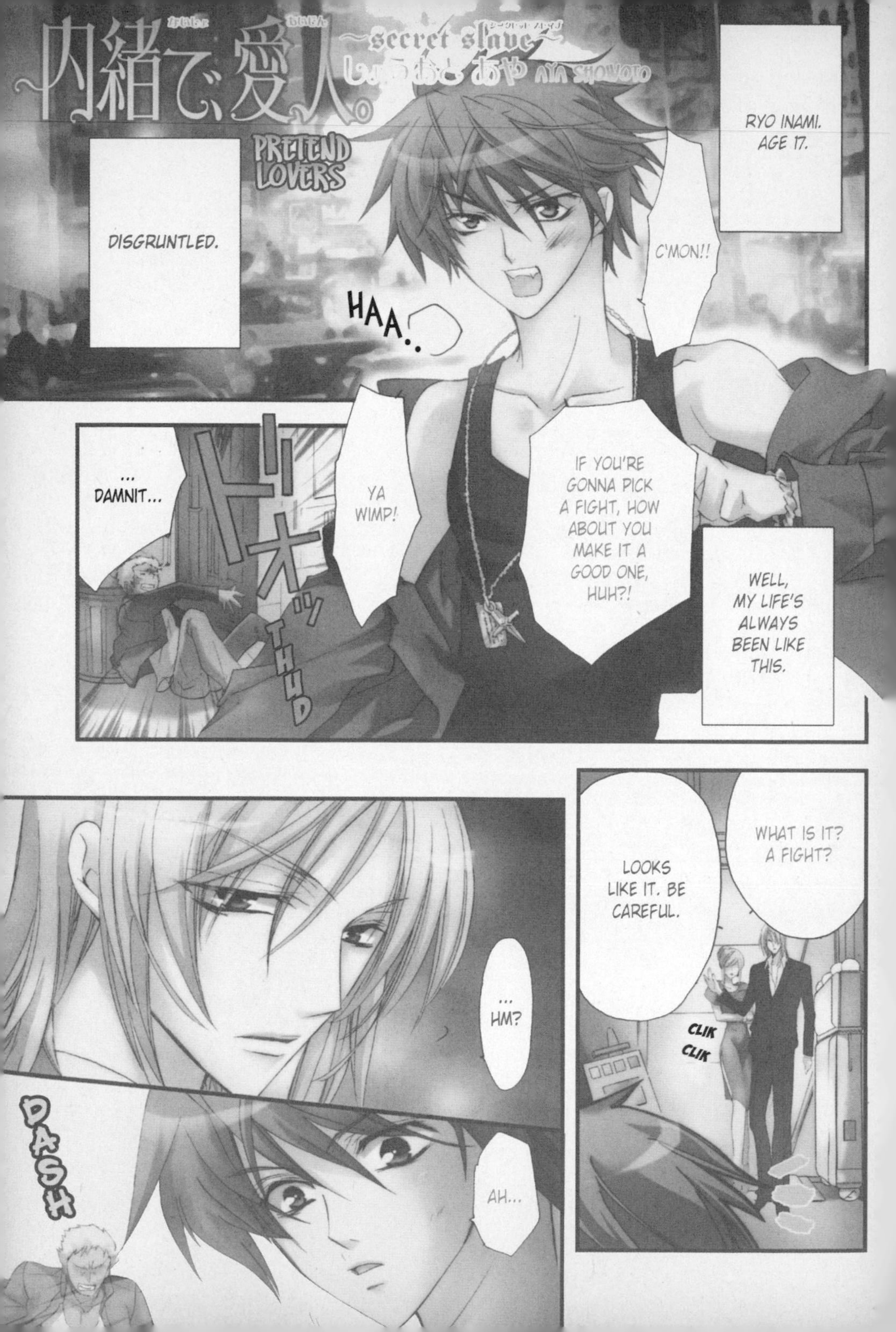

内緒で、愛人。
~secret slave~
しょうおとあや
AYA SHOUOTO
PRETEND LOVERS
RYO INAMI. AGE 17.
C'MON!!
HAA..
DISGRUNTLED.
WELL, MY LIFE'S ALWAYS BEEN LIKE THIS.
IF YOU'RE GONNA PICK A FIGHT, HOW ABOUT YOU MAKE IT A GOOD ONE, HUH?!
YA WIMP!
ドオッ
THUD
... DAMNIT...
WHAT IS IT? A FIGHT?
LOOKS LIKE IT. BE CAREFUL.
CLIK
CLIK
... HM?
AH...
DASH

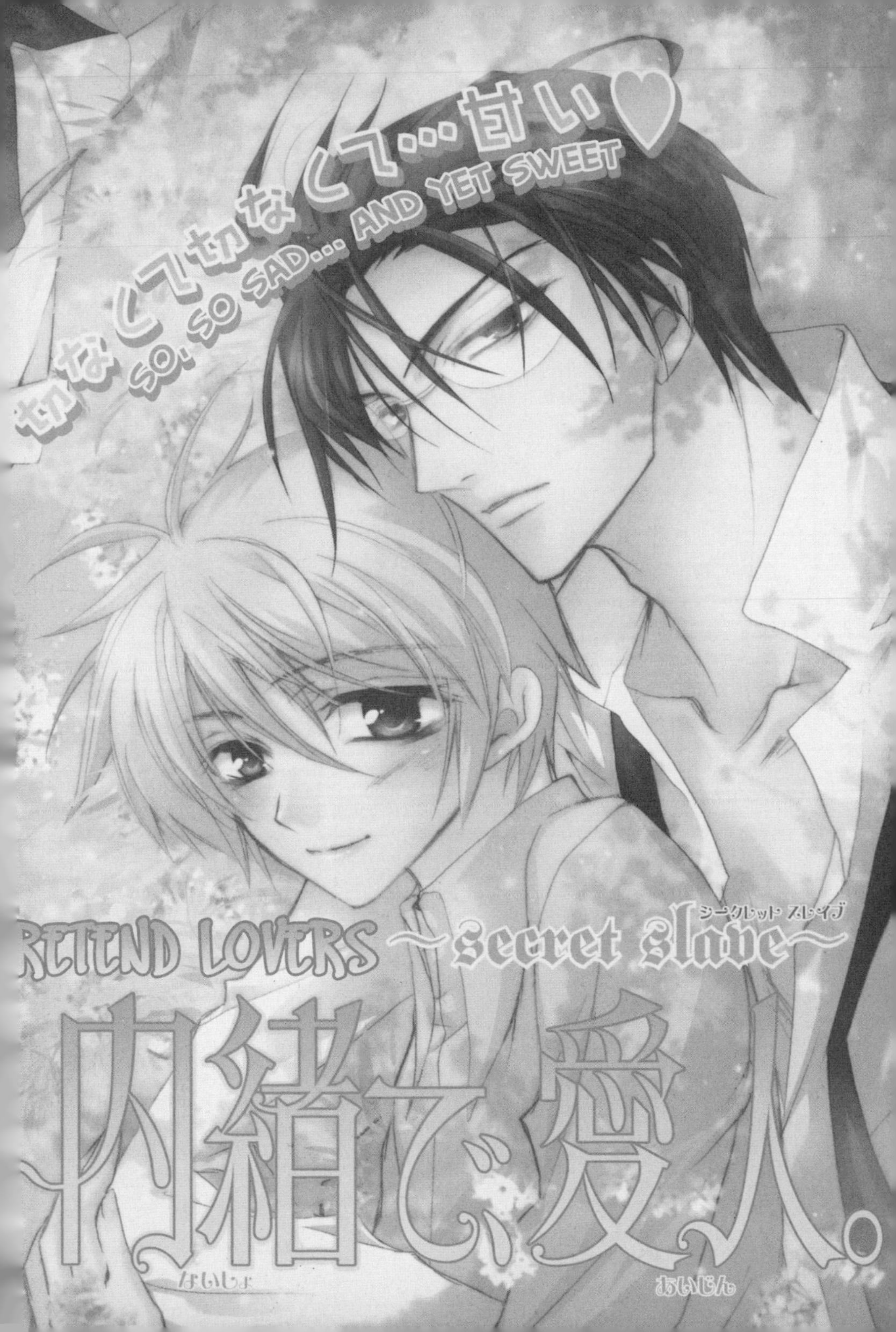

切なくて切なくて…甘い♥
SO, SO SAD... AND YET SWEET
RETEND LOVERS ~secret slave~
シークレットスレイブ
内緒で愛人。
ないしょ
あいじん

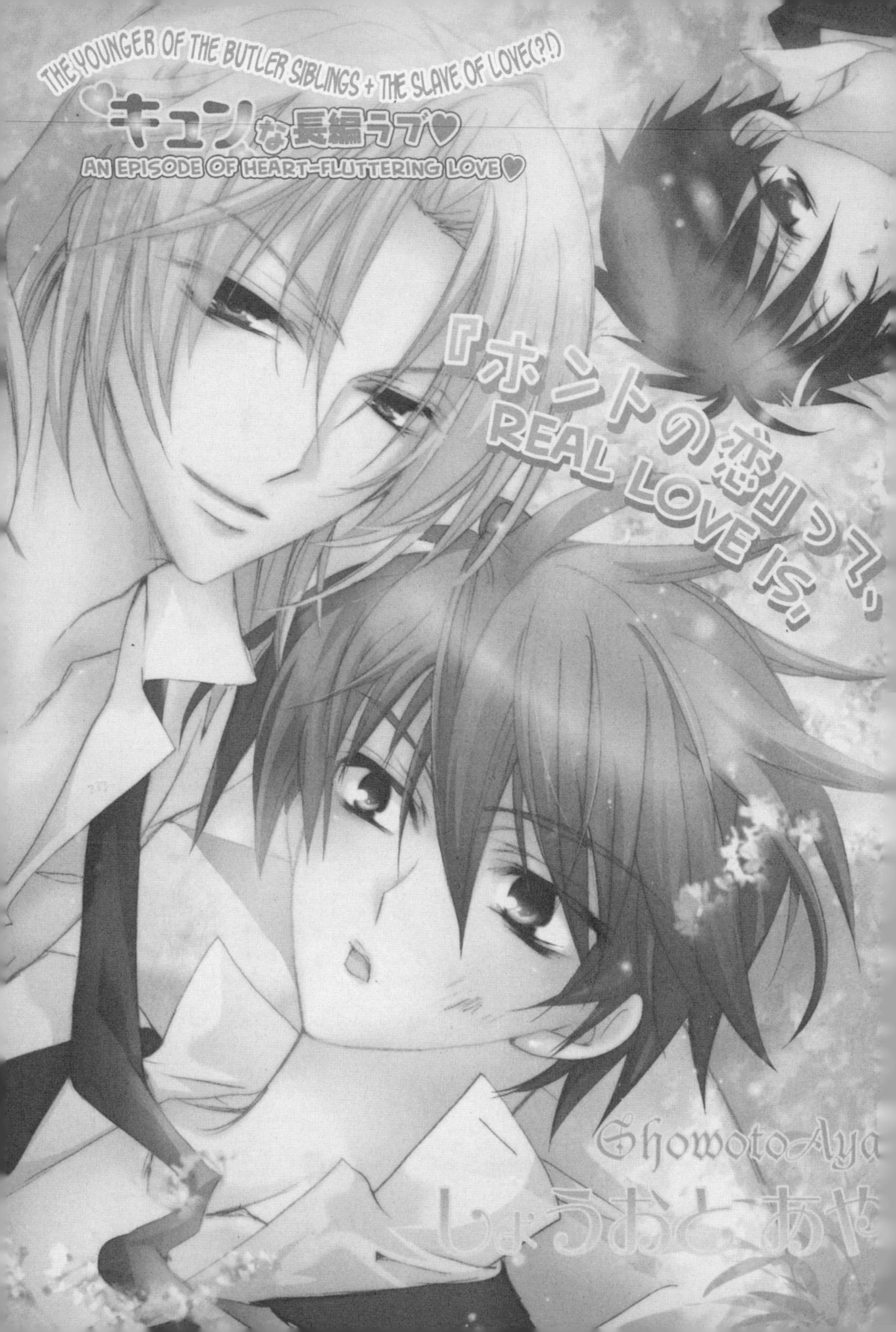
THE YOUNGER OF THE BUTLER SIBLINGS + THE SLAVE OF LOVE(?!)
♥キュンな長編ラブ♥
AN EPISODE OF HEART-FLUTTERING LOVE♥
『ホントの恋』って、
REAL LOVE IS,
Showoto Aya
しょうおとあや

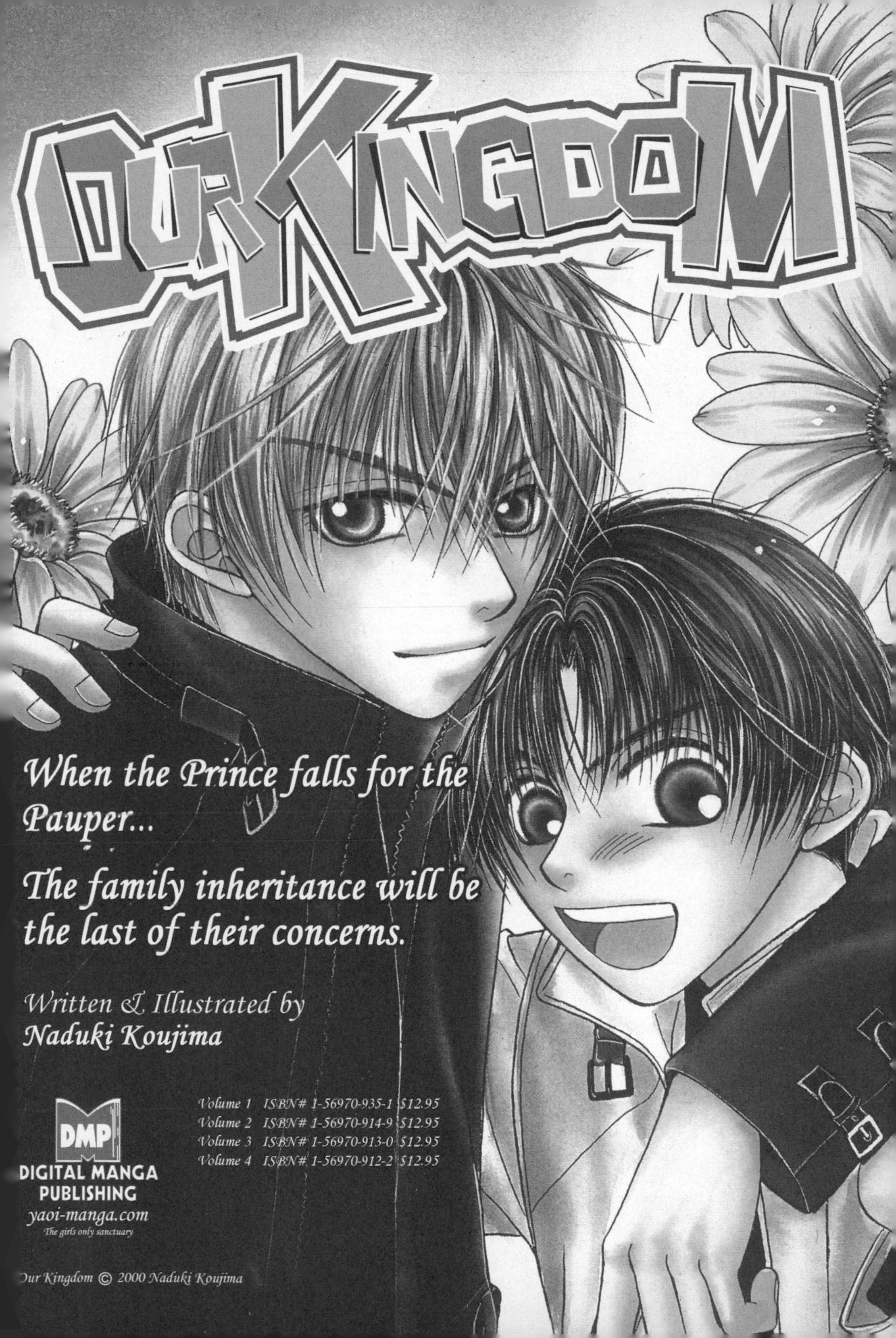
OUR KINGDOM
When the Prince falls for the Pauper...
The family inheritance will be the last of their concerns.
Written & Illustrated by
Naduki Koujima
Volume 1 ISBN# 1-56970-935-1 $12.95
Volume 2 ISBN# 1-56970-914-9 $12.95
Volume 3 ISBN# 1-56970-913-0 $12.95
Volume 4 ISBN# 1-56970-912-2 $12.95
DMP
DIGITAL MANGA PUBLISHING
yaoi-manga.com
The girls only sanctuary
Our Kingdom © 2000 Naduki Koujima

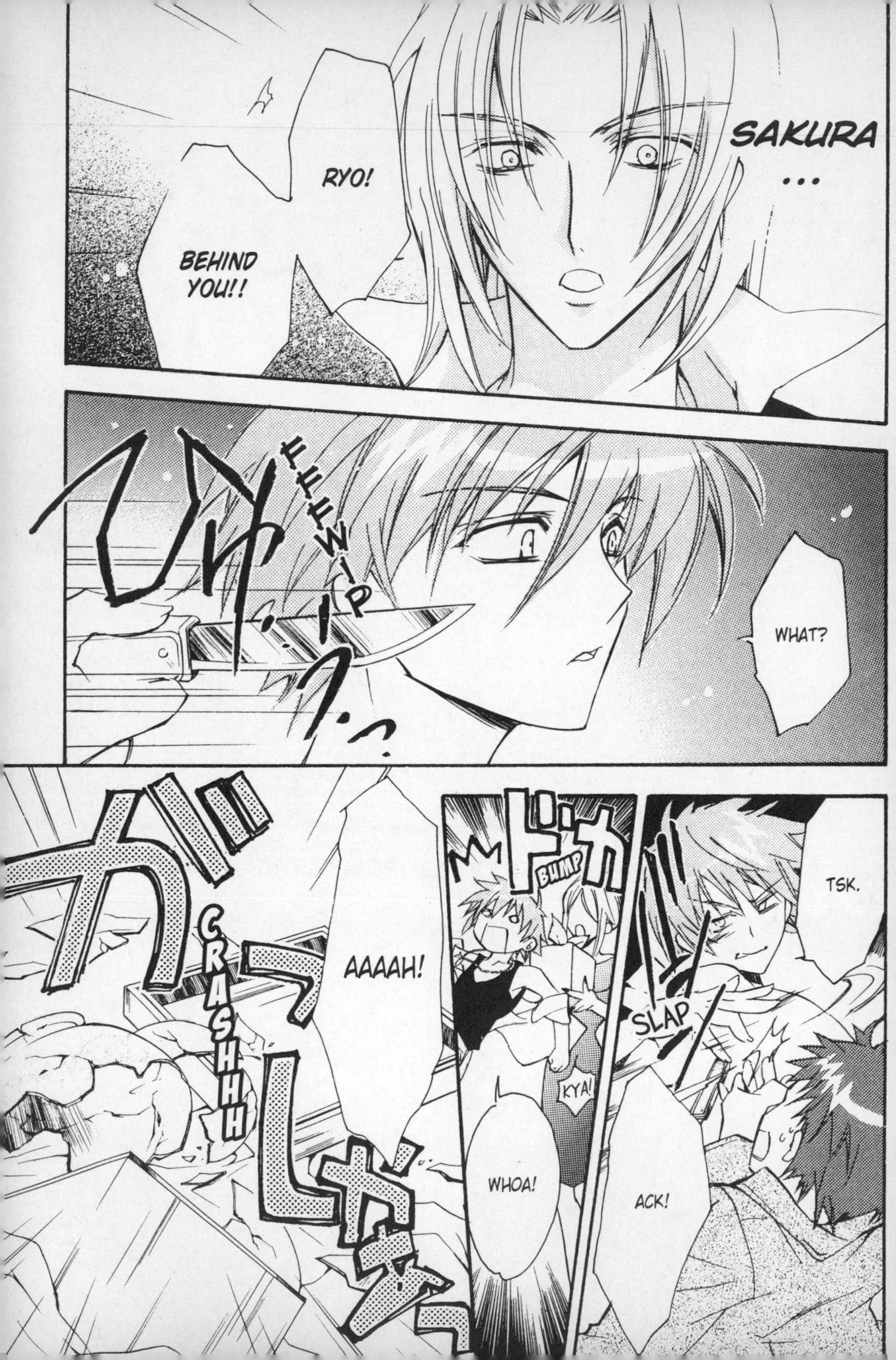
SAKURA ...
RYO!
BEHIND YOU!!
WHAT?
FFFWIP
TSK.
SLAP
ACK!
BUMP
KYA!
WHOA!
AAAAH!
CRASHHH

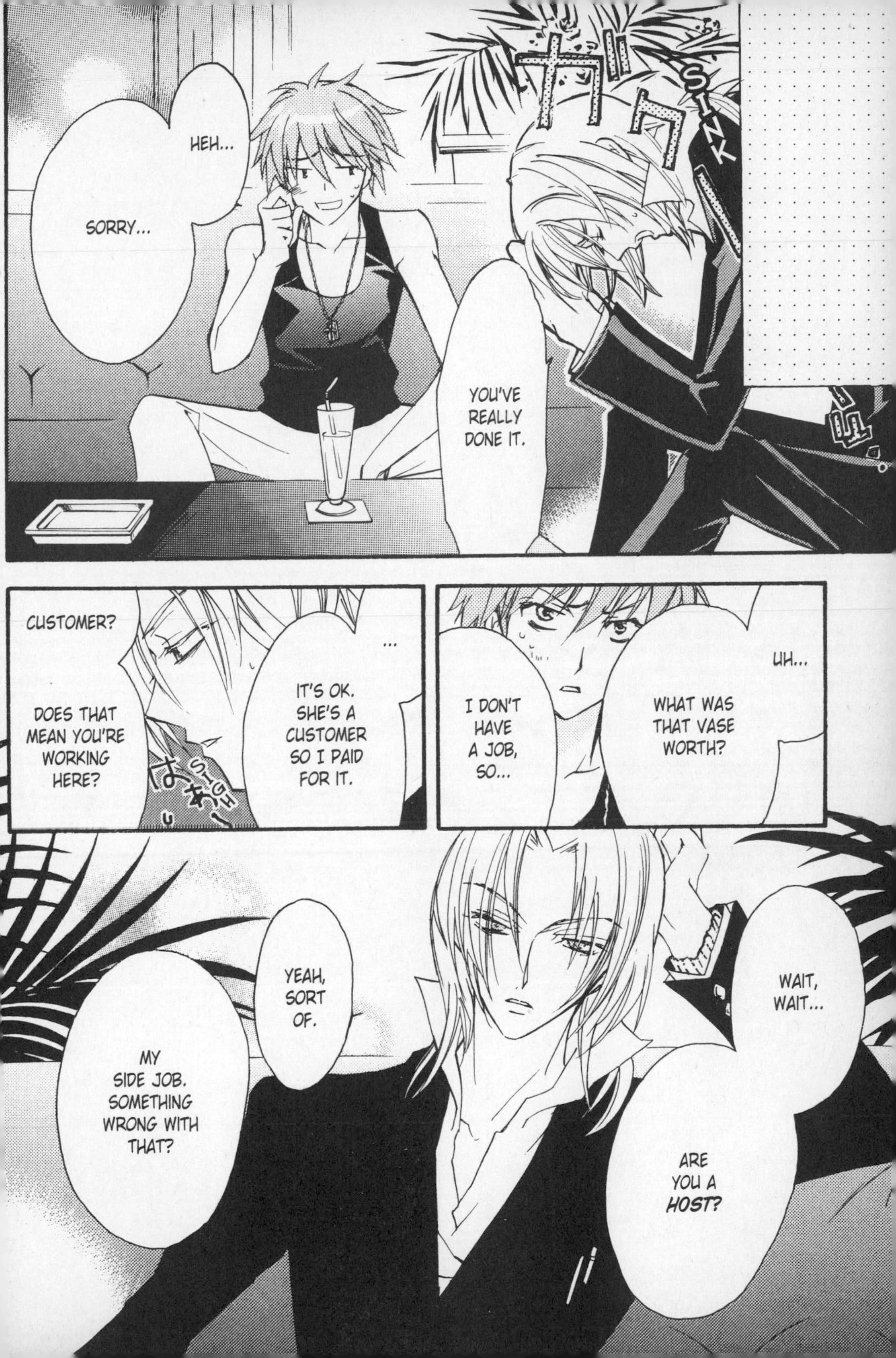
SINK
YOU'VE REALLY DONE IT.
HEH...
SORRY...
UH...
WHAT WAS THAT VASE WORTH?
I DON'T HAVE A JOB, SO...
...
IT'S OK. SHE'S A CUSTOMER SO I PAID FOR IT.
SIGH
CUSTOMER?
DOES THAT MEAN YOU'RE WORKING HERE?
WAIT, WAIT...
ARE YOU A *HOST*?
YEAH, SORT OF.
MY SIDE JOB. SOMETHING WRONG WITH THAT?

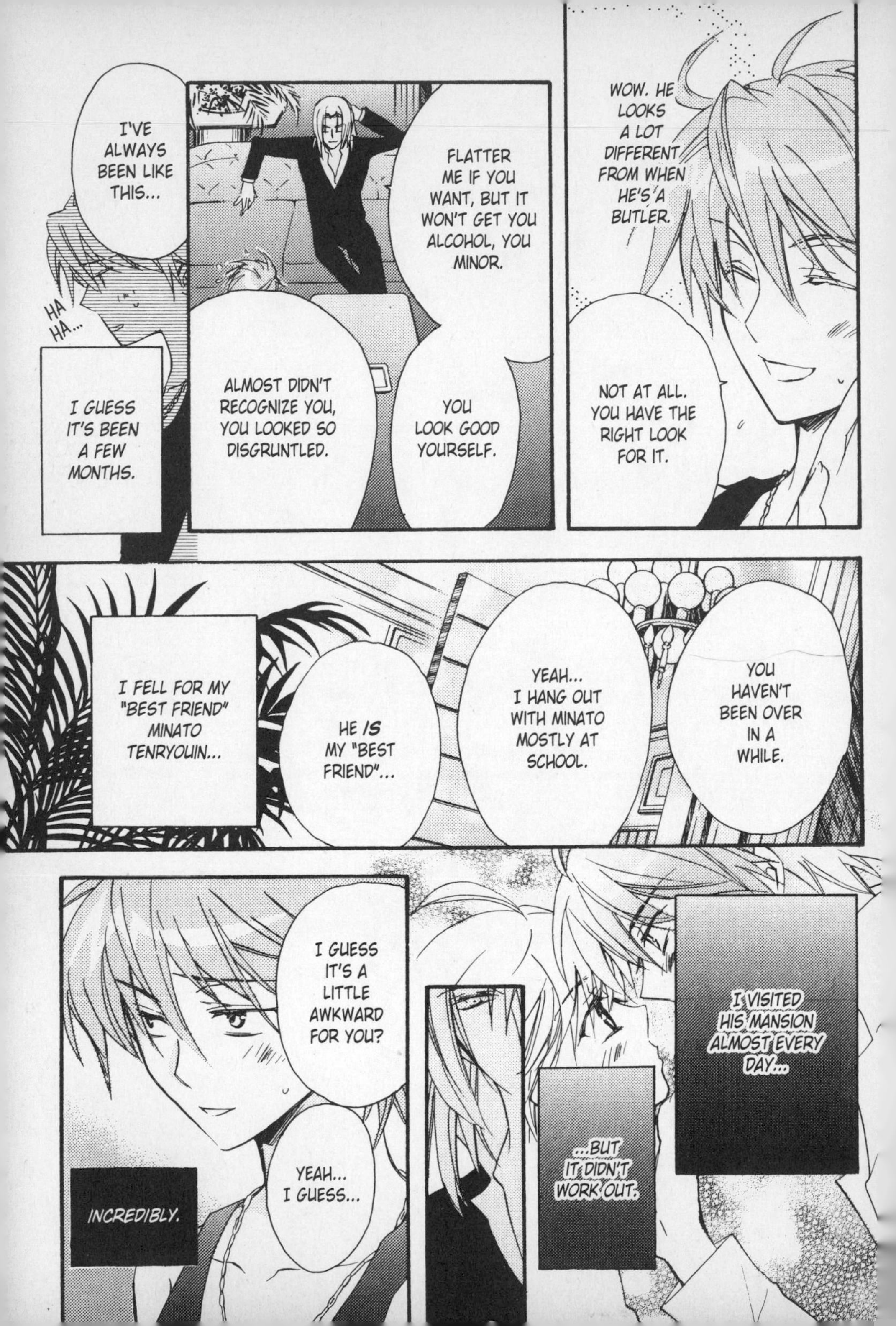
WOW. HE LOOKS A LOT DIFFERENT FROM WHEN HE'S A BUTLER.
NOT AT ALL. YOU HAVE THE RIGHT LOOK FOR IT.
FLATTER ME IF YOU WANT, BUT IT WON'T GET YOU ALCOHOL, YOU MINOR.
YOU LOOK GOOD YOURSELF.
ALMOST DIDN'T RECOGNIZE YOU, YOU LOOKED SO DISGRUNTLED.
I'VE ALWAYS BEEN LIKE THIS...
HA HA...
I GUESS IT'S BEEN A FEW MONTHS.
YOU HAVEN'T BEEN OVER IN A WHILE.
YEAH... I HANG OUT WITH MINATO MOSTLY AT SCHOOL.
HE *IS* MY "BEST FRIEND"...
I FELL FOR MY "BEST FRIEND" MINATO TENRYOUIN...
I VISITED HIS MANSION ALMOST EVERY DAY...
...BUT IT DIDN'T WORK OUT.
I GUESS IT'S A LITTLE AWKWARD FOR YOU?
YEAH... I GUESS...
INCREDIBLY.

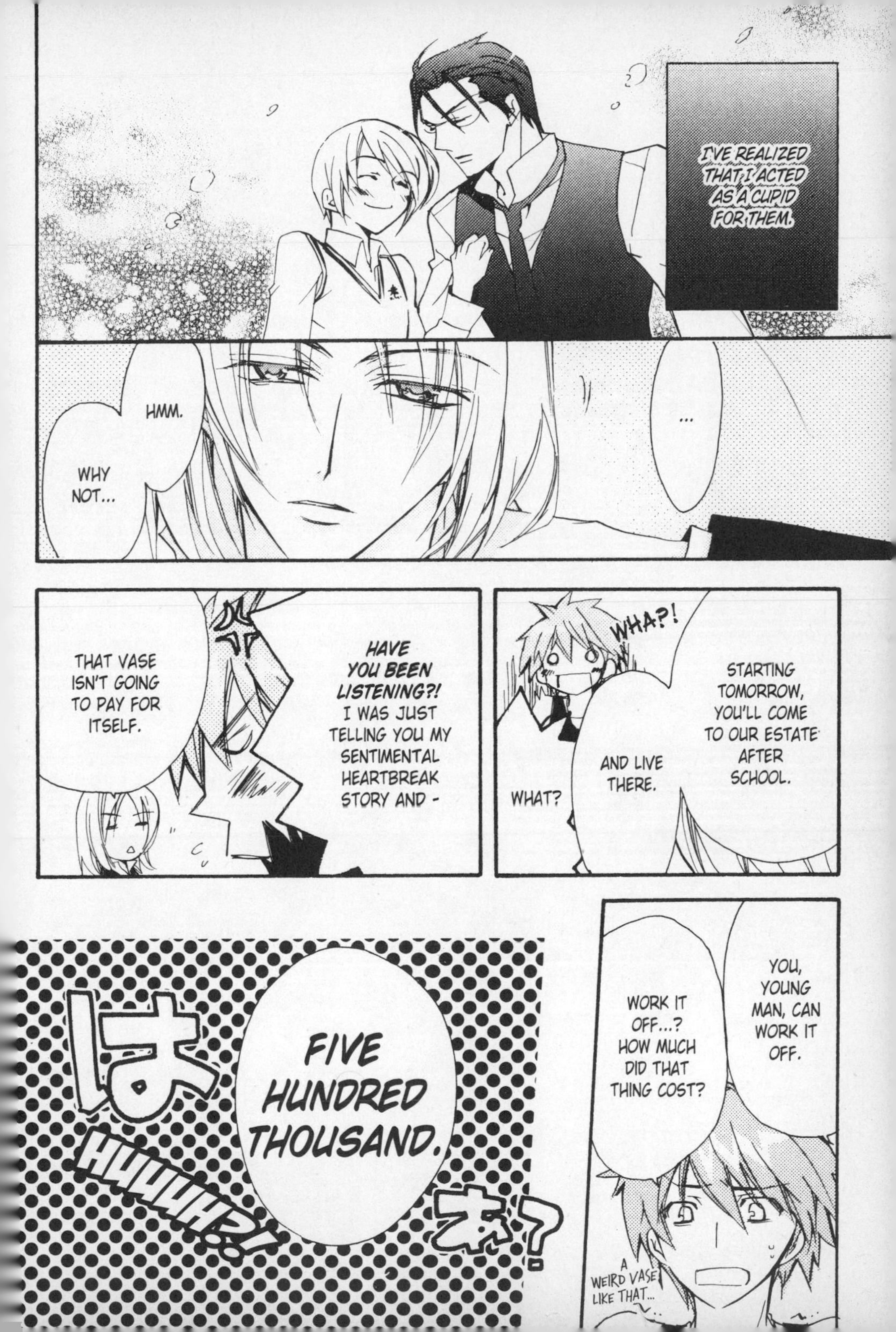
I'VE REALIZED THAT I ACTED AS A CUPID FOR THEM.
...
HMM.
WHY NOT...
STARTING TOMORROW, YOU'LL COME TO OUR ESTATE AFTER SCHOOL.
WHA?!
AND LIVE THERE.
WHAT?
HAVE YOU BEEN LISTENING?! I WAS JUST TELLING YOU MY SENTIMENTAL HEARTBREAK STORY AND -
THAT VASE ISN'T GOING TO PAY FOR ITSELF.
YOU, YOUNG MAN, CAN WORK IT OFF.
WORK IT OFF...? HOW MUCH DID THAT THING COST?
A WEIRD VASE LIKE THAT...
FIVE HUNDRED THOUSAND.
は
え?
HUUUH?!

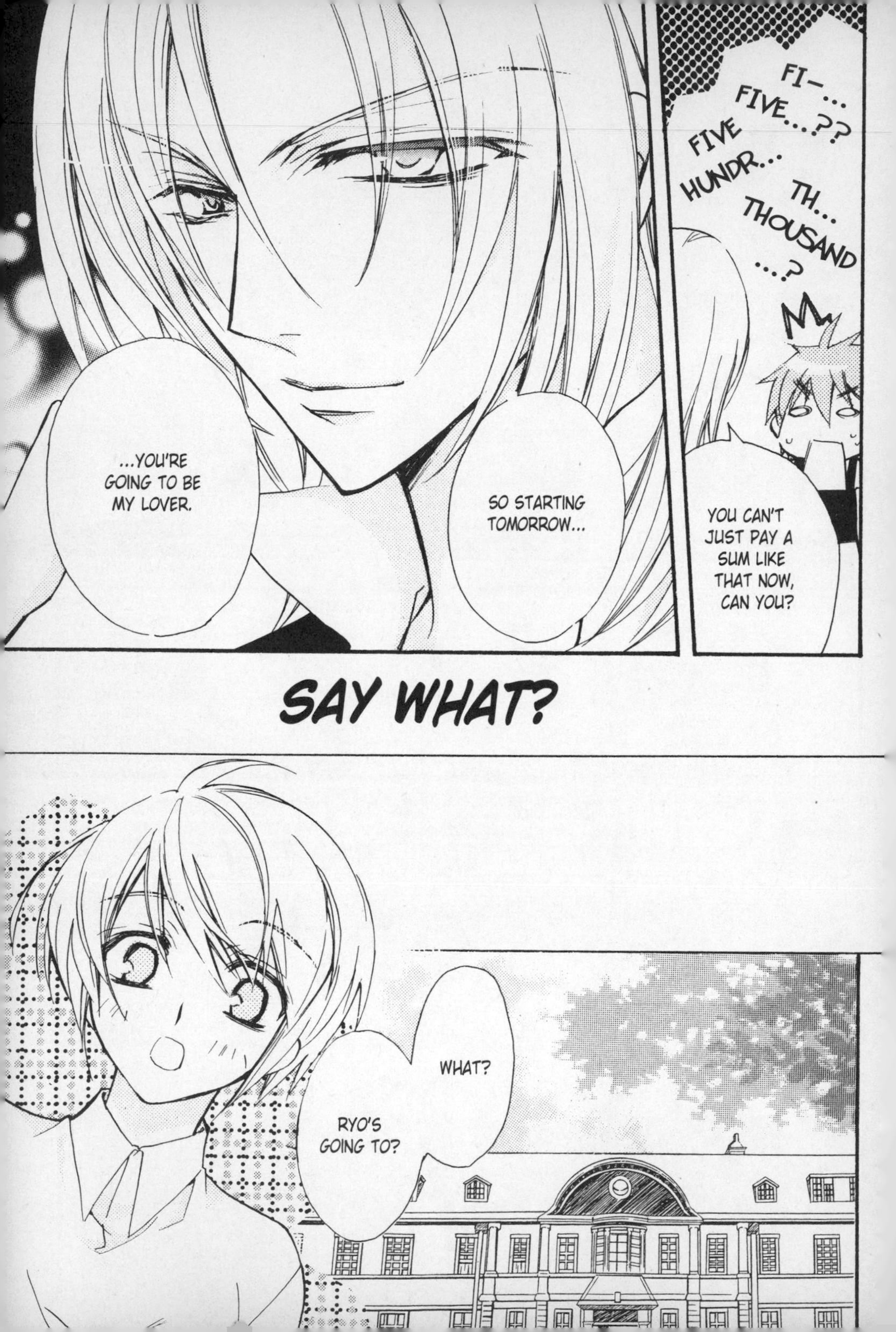
FI-... FIVE...??
FIVE HUNDR... TH... THOUSAND ...?
YOU CAN'T JUST PAY A SUM LIKE THAT NOW, CAN YOU?
SO STARTING TOMORROW...
...YOU'RE GOING TO BE MY LOVER.
SAY WHAT?
WHAT?
RYO'S GOING TO?

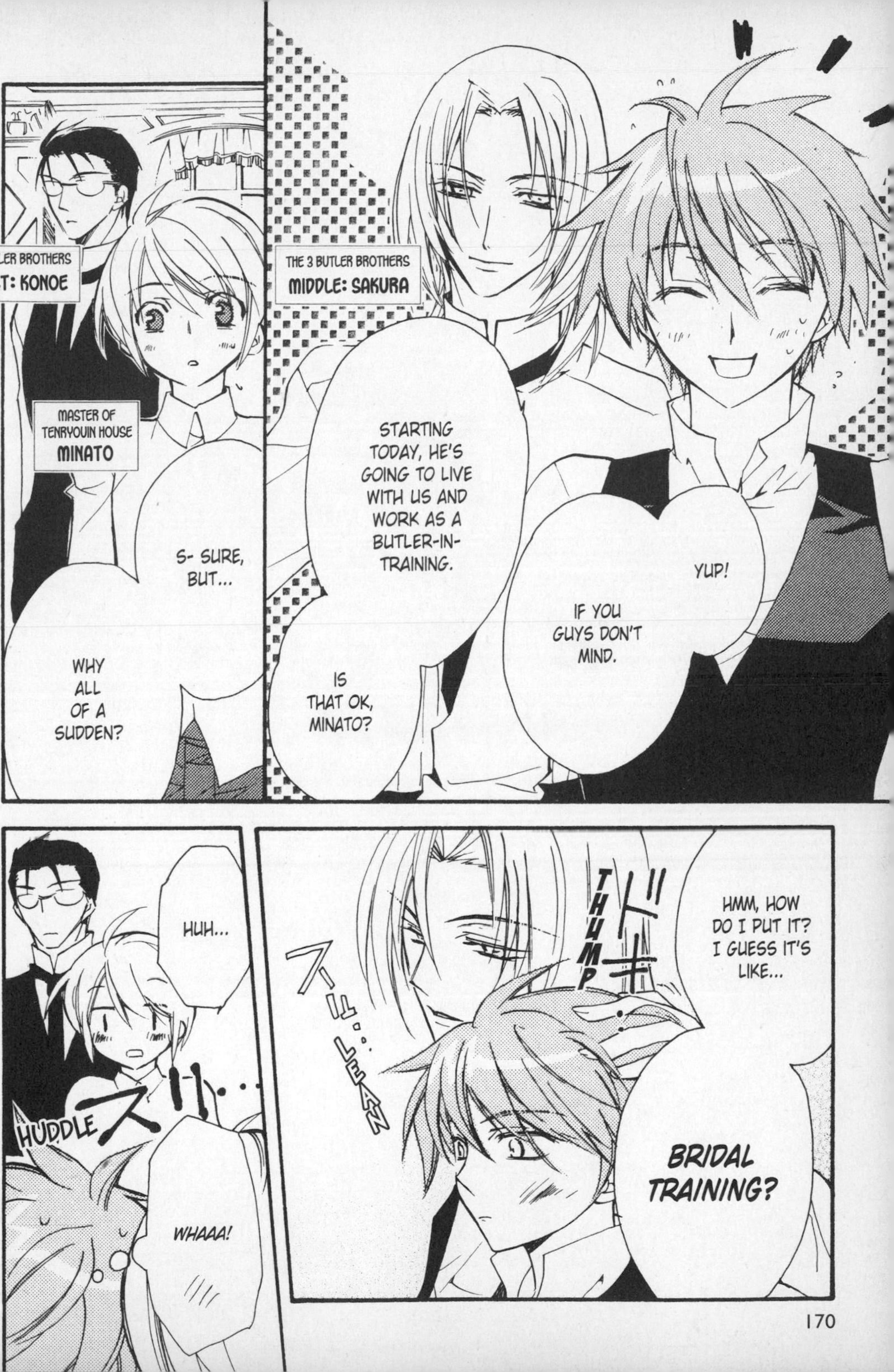
THE 3 BUTLER BROTHERS
MIDDLE: SAKURA
STARTING TODAY, HE'S GOING TO LIVE WITH US AND WORK AS A BUTLER-IN-TRAINING.
YUP!
IF YOU GUYS DON'T MIND.
IS THAT OK, MINATO?
3 BUTLER BROTHERS
DEST: KONOE
MASTER OF TENRYOUIN HOUSE
MINATO
S- SURE, BUT...
WHY ALL OF A SUDDEN?
HMM, HOW DO I PUT IT? I GUESS IT'S LIKE...
THUMP
LEAN
BRIDAL TRAINING?
HUH...
HUDDLE
WHAAA!

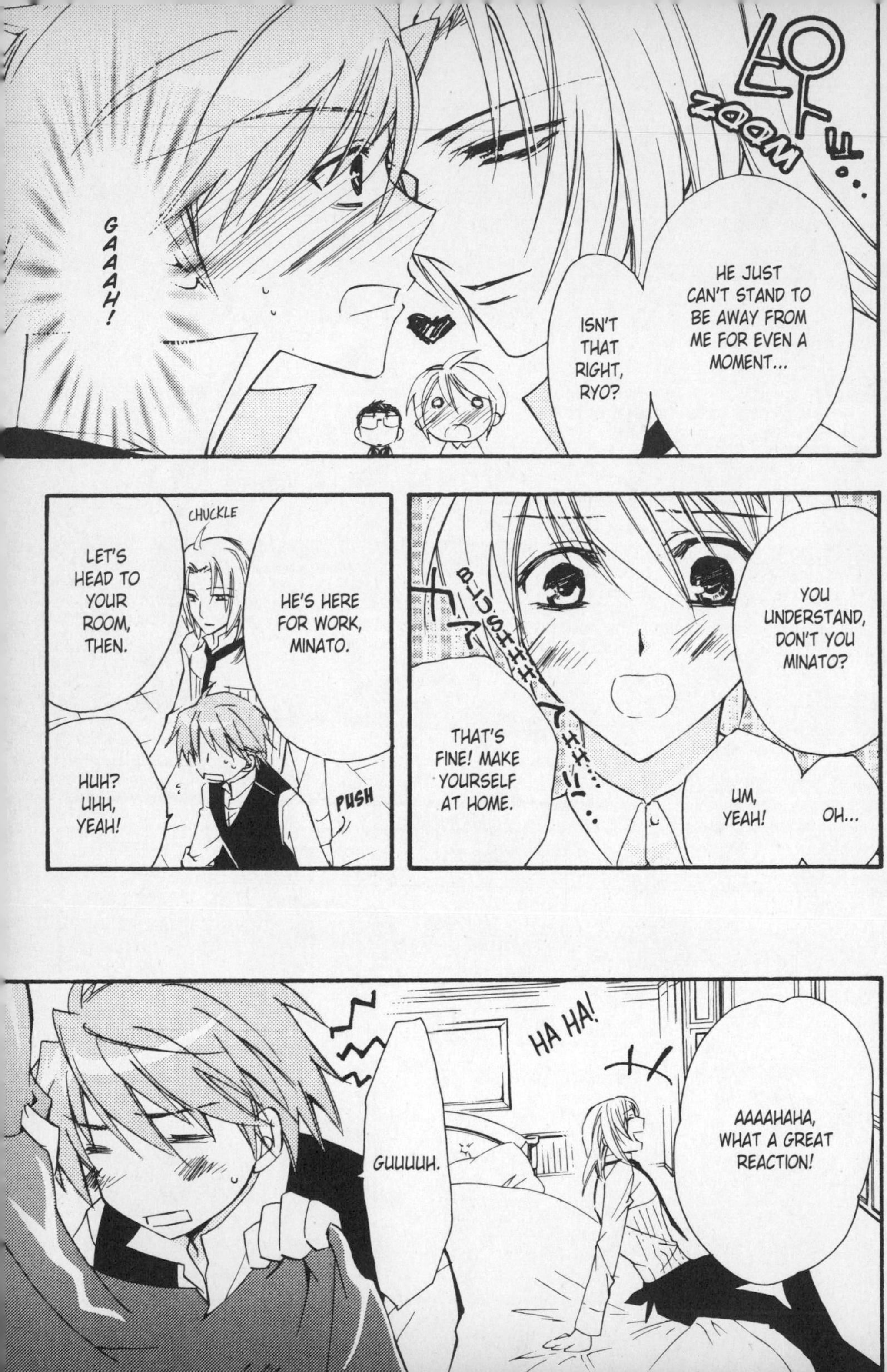
ZOOM
HE JUST CAN'T STAND TO BE AWAY FROM ME FOR EVEN A MOMENT...
ISN'T THAT RIGHT, RYO?
GAAAH!
YOU UNDERSTAND, DON'T YOU MINATO?
BLUSHHHH...
OH...
UM, YEAH!
THAT'S FINE! MAKE YOURSELF AT HOME.
CHUCKLE
HE'S HERE FOR WORK, MINATO.
LET'S HEAD TO YOUR ROOM, THEN.
PUSH
HUH? UHH, YEAH!
AAAAHAHA, WHAT A GREAT REACTION!
HA HA!
GUUUUH.

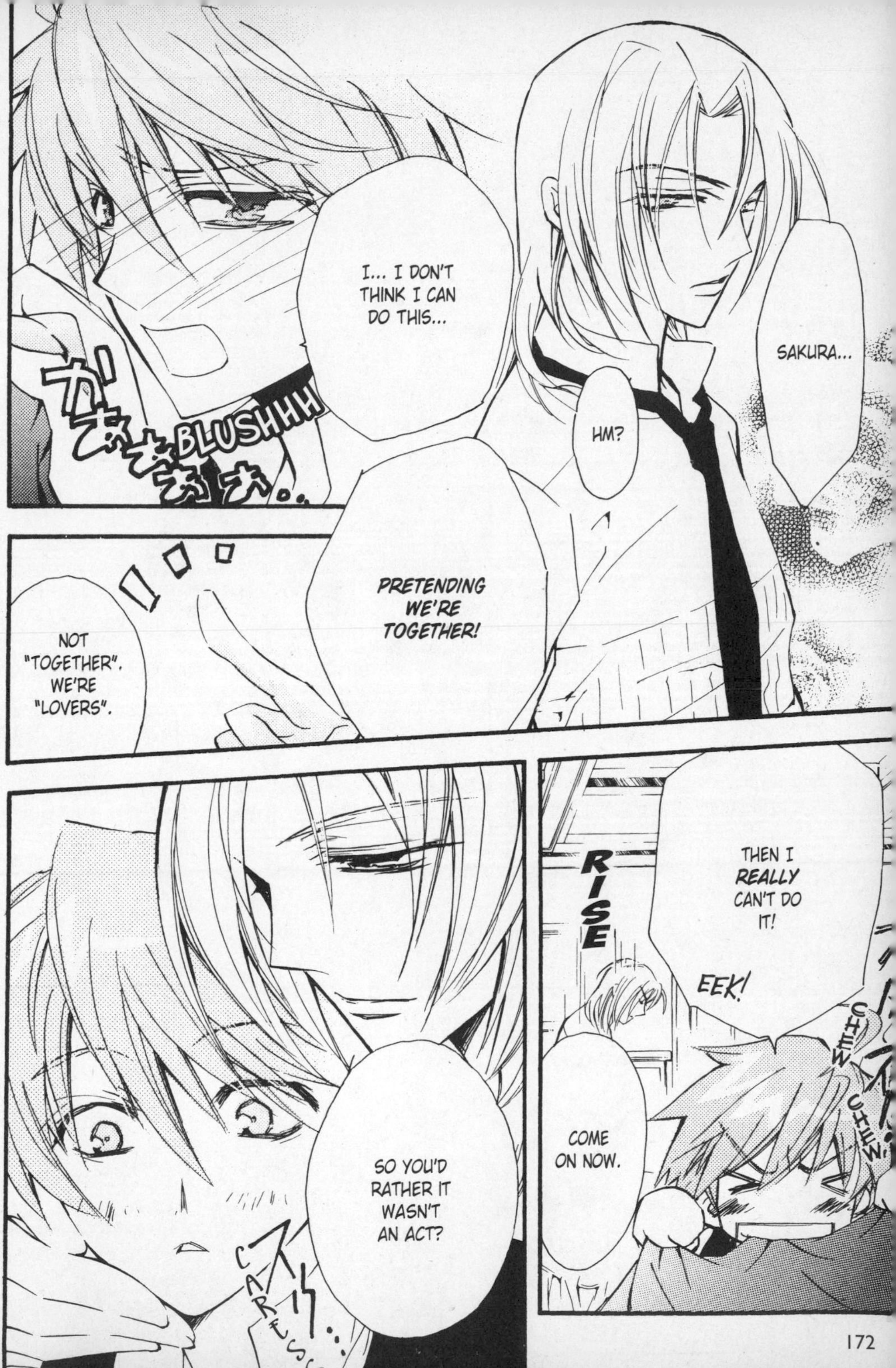
SAKURA...
HM?
I... I DON'T THINK I CAN DO THIS...
BLUSHHH
PRETENDING WE'RE TOGETHER!
NOT "TOGETHER". WE'RE "LOVERS".
THEN I REALLY CAN'T DO IT!
RISE
EEK!
CHEW CHEW
COME ON NOW.
SO YOU'D RATHER IT WASN'T AN ACT?
CARESSS...

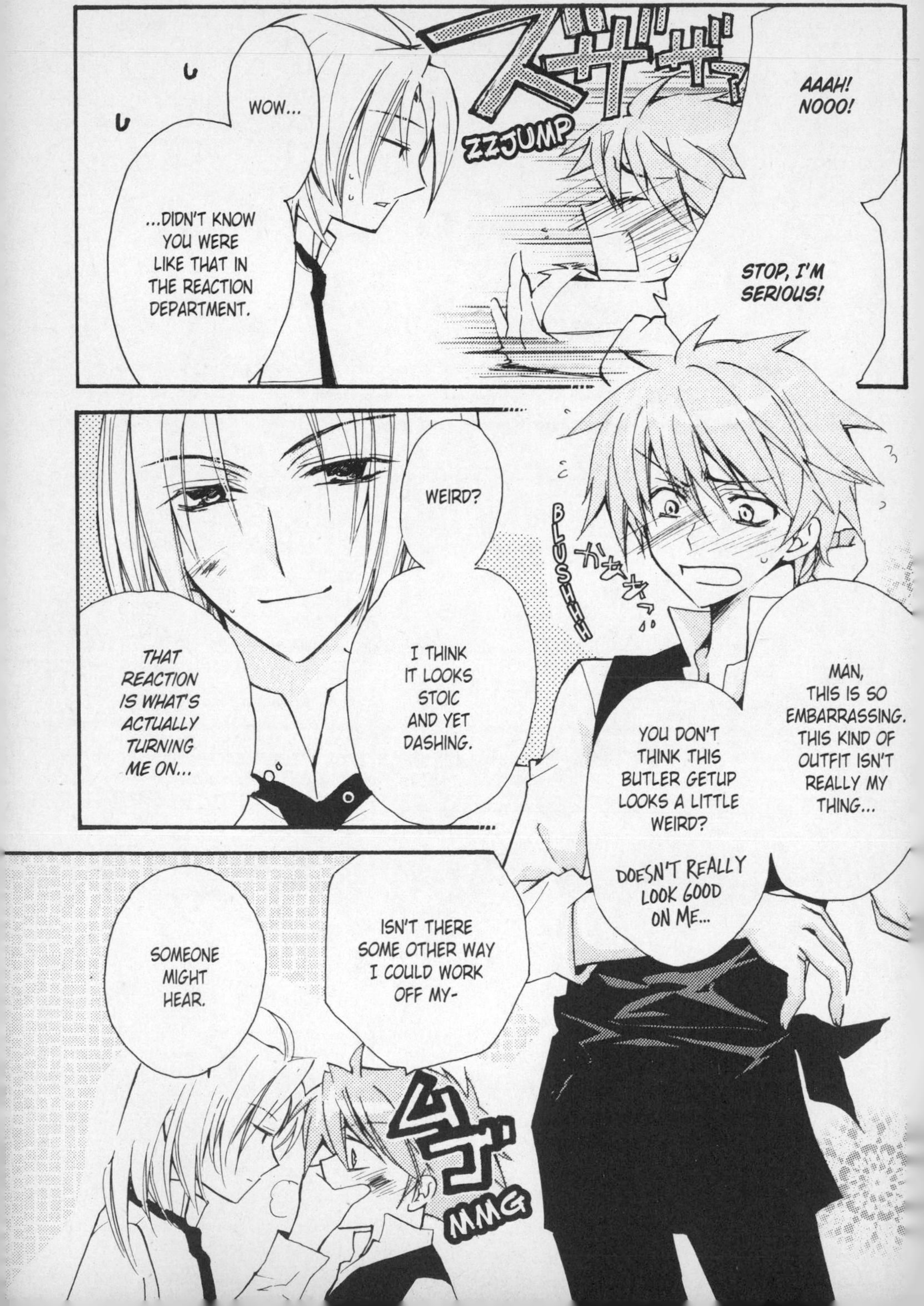
AAAH! NOOO!
STOP, I'M SERIOUS!
ZZJUMP
WOW...
...DIDN'T KNOW YOU WERE LIKE THAT IN THE REACTION DEPARTMENT.
MAN, THIS IS SO EMBARRASSING. THIS KIND OF OUTFIT ISN'T REALLY MY THING...
YOU DON'T THINK THIS BUTLER GETUP LOOKS A LITTLE WEIRD?
DOESN'T REALLY LOOK GOOD ON ME...
BLUSHHH
WEIRD?
I THINK IT LOOKS STOIC AND YET DASHING.
THAT REACTION IS WHAT'S ACTUALLY TURNING ME ON...
ISN'T THERE SOME OTHER WAY I COULD WORK OFF MY-
MMG
SOMEONE MIGHT HEAR.

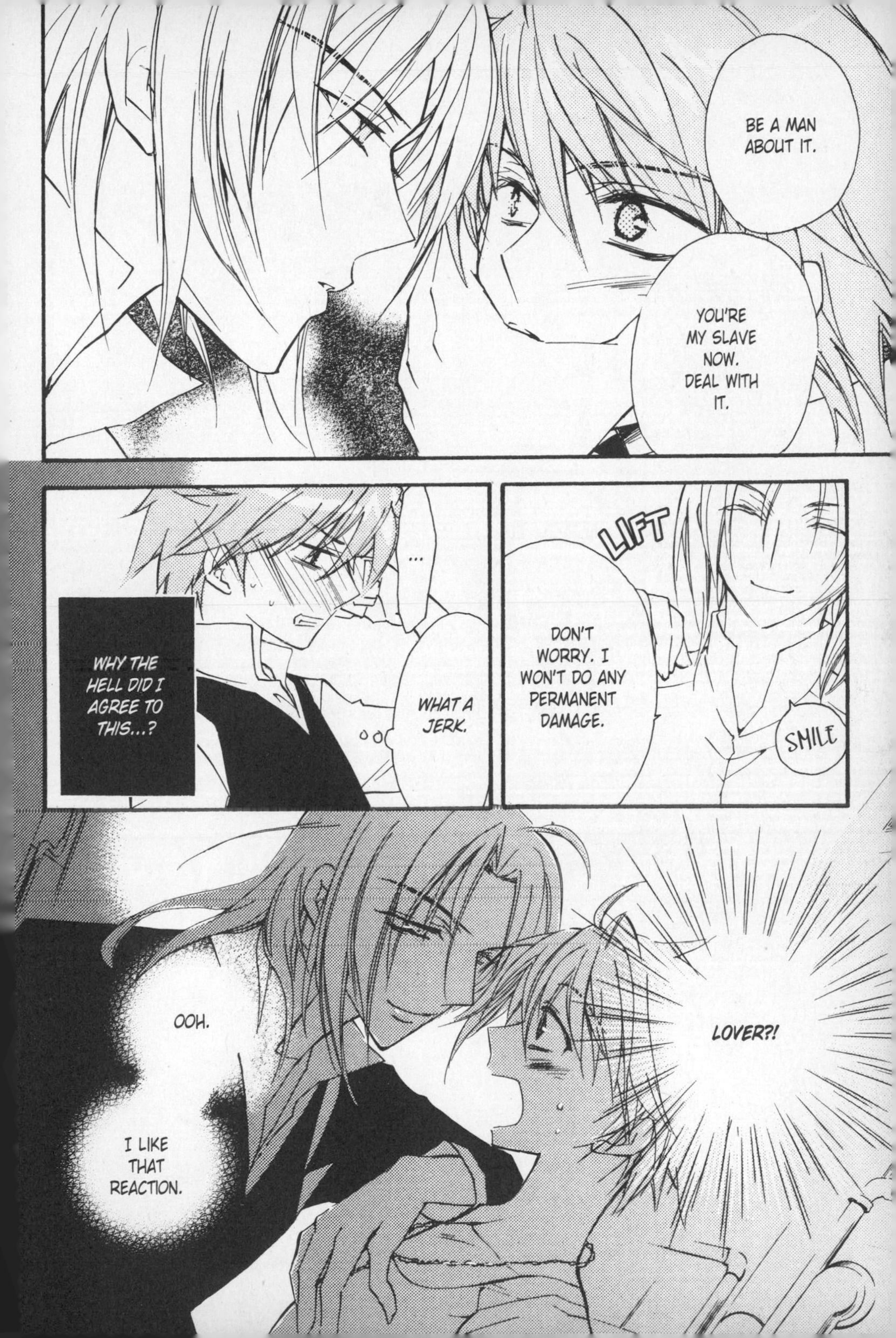
BE A MAN ABOUT IT.
YOU'RE MY SLAVE NOW. DEAL WITH IT.
LIFT
DON'T WORRY. I WON'T DO ANY PERMANENT DAMAGE.
SMILE
...
WHAT A JERK.
WHY THE HELL DID I AGREE TO THIS...?
LOVER?!
OOH.
I LIKE THAT REACTION.

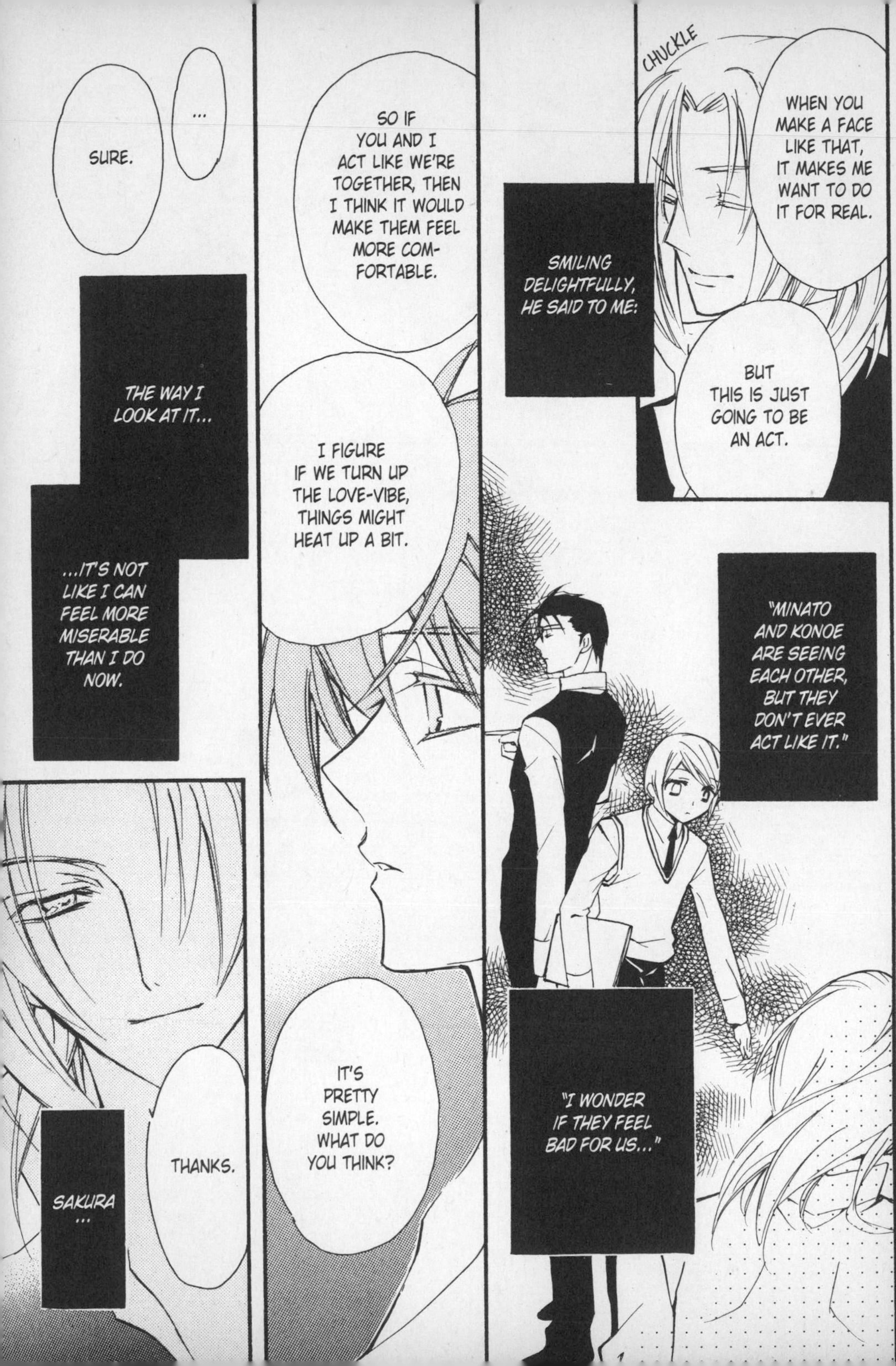
CHUCKLE
WHEN YOU MAKE A FACE LIKE THAT, IT MAKES ME WANT TO DO IT FOR REAL.
SMILING DELIGHTFULLY, HE SAID TO ME:
BUT THIS IS JUST GOING TO BE AN ACT.
"MINATO AND KONOE ARE SEEING EACH OTHER, BUT THEY DON'T EVER ACT LIKE IT."
"I WONDER IF THEY FEEL BAD FOR US..."
SO IF YOU AND I ACT LIKE WE'RE TOGETHER, THEN I THINK IT WOULD MAKE THEM FEEL MORE COM-FORTABLE.
I FIGURE IF WE TURN UP THE LOVE-VIBE, THINGS MIGHT HEAT UP A BIT.
IT'S PRETTY SIMPLE. WHAT DO YOU THINK?
...
SURE.
THE WAY I LOOK AT IT...
...IT'S NOT LIKE I CAN FEEL MORE MISERABLE THAN I DO NOW.
THANKS.
SAKURA ...

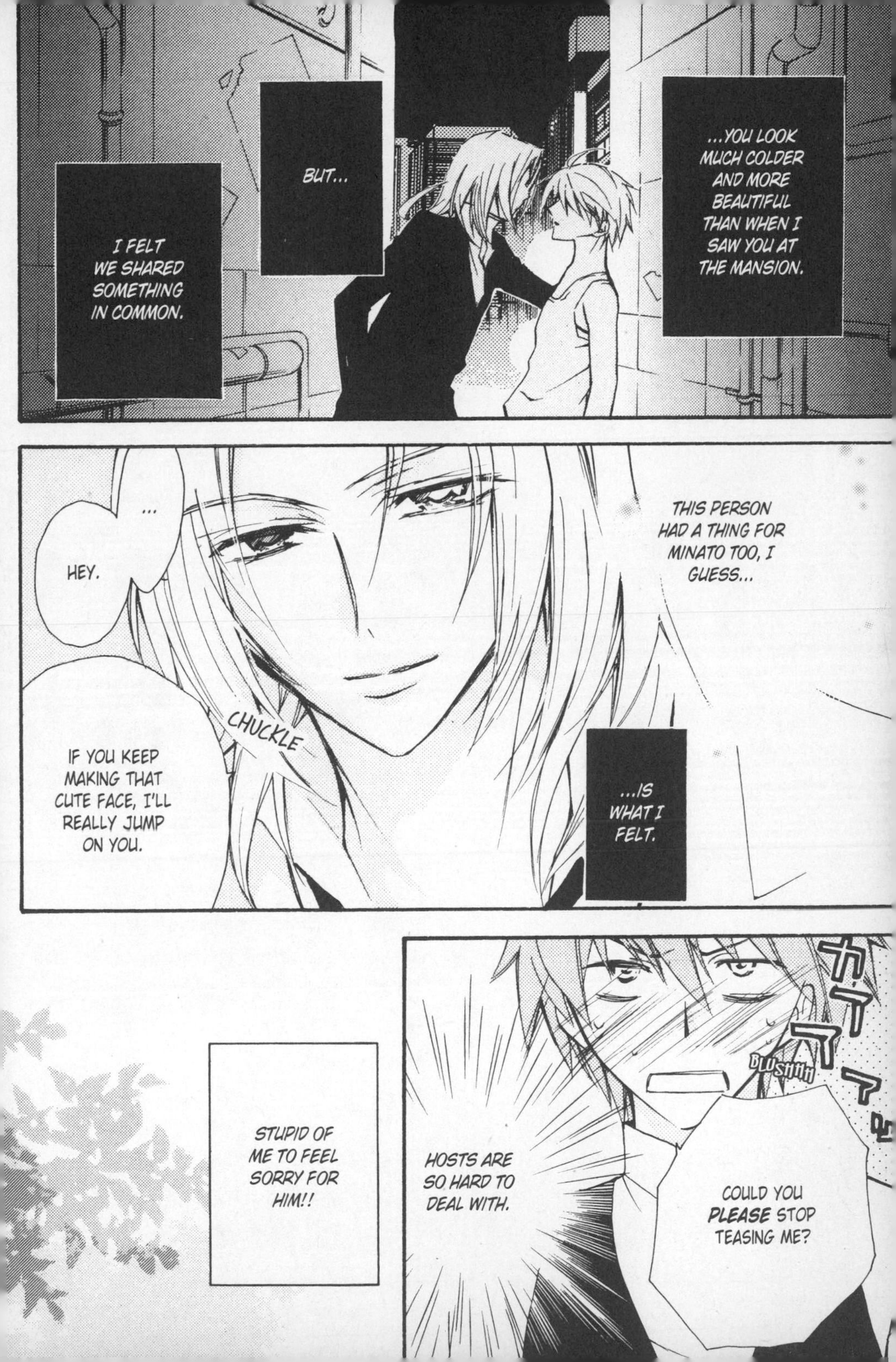
...YOU LOOK MUCH COLDER AND MORE BEAUTIFUL THAN WHEN I SAW YOU AT THE MANSION.
BUT...
I FELT WE SHARED SOMETHING IN COMMON.
THIS PERSON HAD A THING FOR MINATO TOO, I GUESS...
...IS WHAT I FELT.
...
HEY.
CHUCKLE
IF YOU KEEP MAKING THAT CUTE FACE, I'LL REALLY JUMP ON YOU.
BLUSHHH
COULD YOU PLEASE STOP TEASING ME?
HOSTS ARE SO HARD TO DEAL WITH.
STUPID OF ME TO FEEL SORRY FOR HIM!!

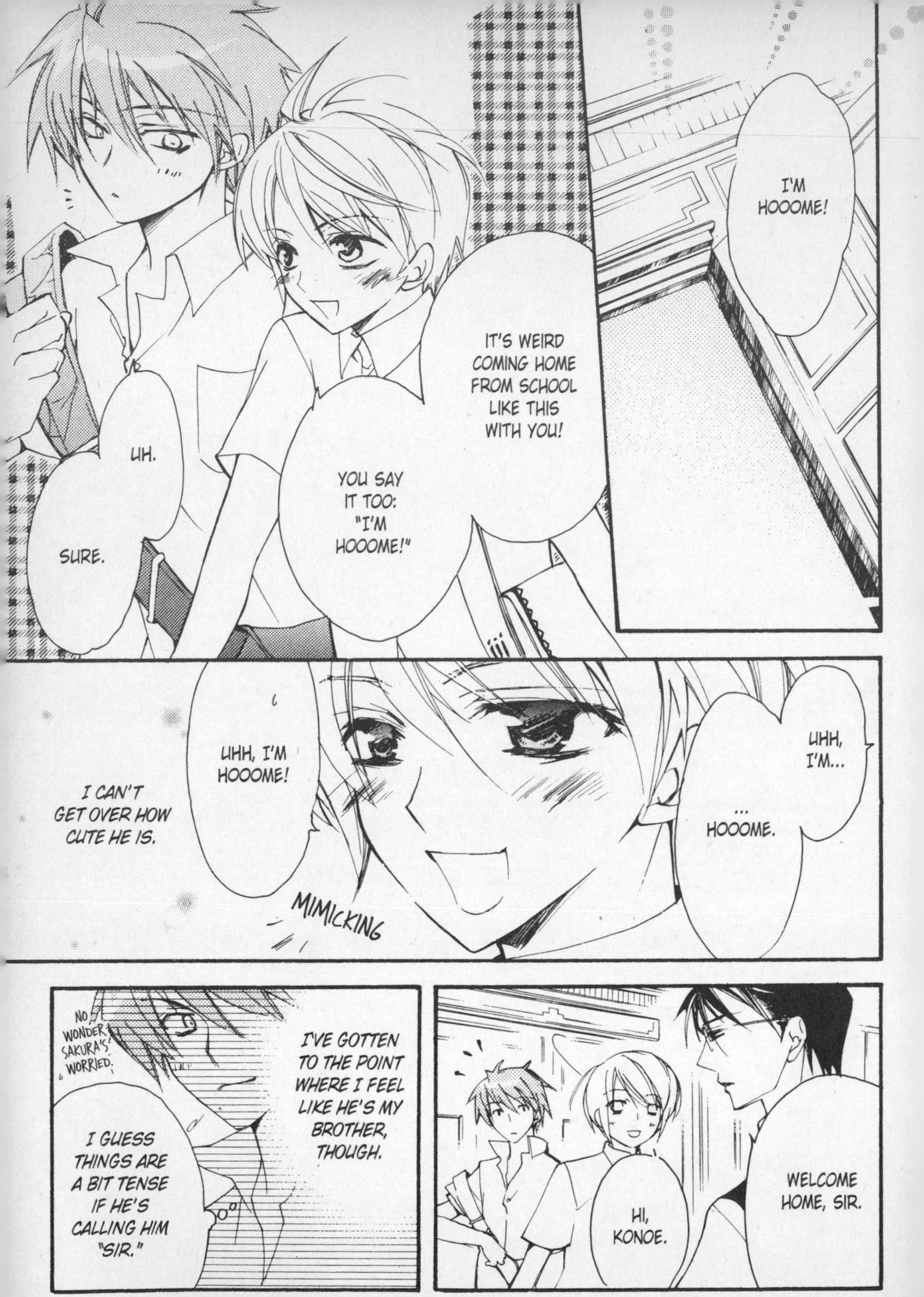

I'M HOOOME!
IT'S WEIRD COMING HOME FROM SCHOOL LIKE THIS WITH YOU!
YOU SAY IT TOO: "I'M HOOOME!"
UH.
SURE.
UHH, I'M...
... HOOOME.
UHH, I'M HOOOME!
MIMICKING
I CAN'T GET OVER HOW CUTE HE IS.
WELCOME HOME, SIR.
HI, KONOE.
I'VE GOTTEN TO THE POINT WHERE I FEEL LIKE HE'S MY BROTHER, THOUGH.
NO WONDER SAKURA'S WORRIED.
I GUESS THINGS ARE A BIT TENSE IF HE'S CALLING HIM "SIR."

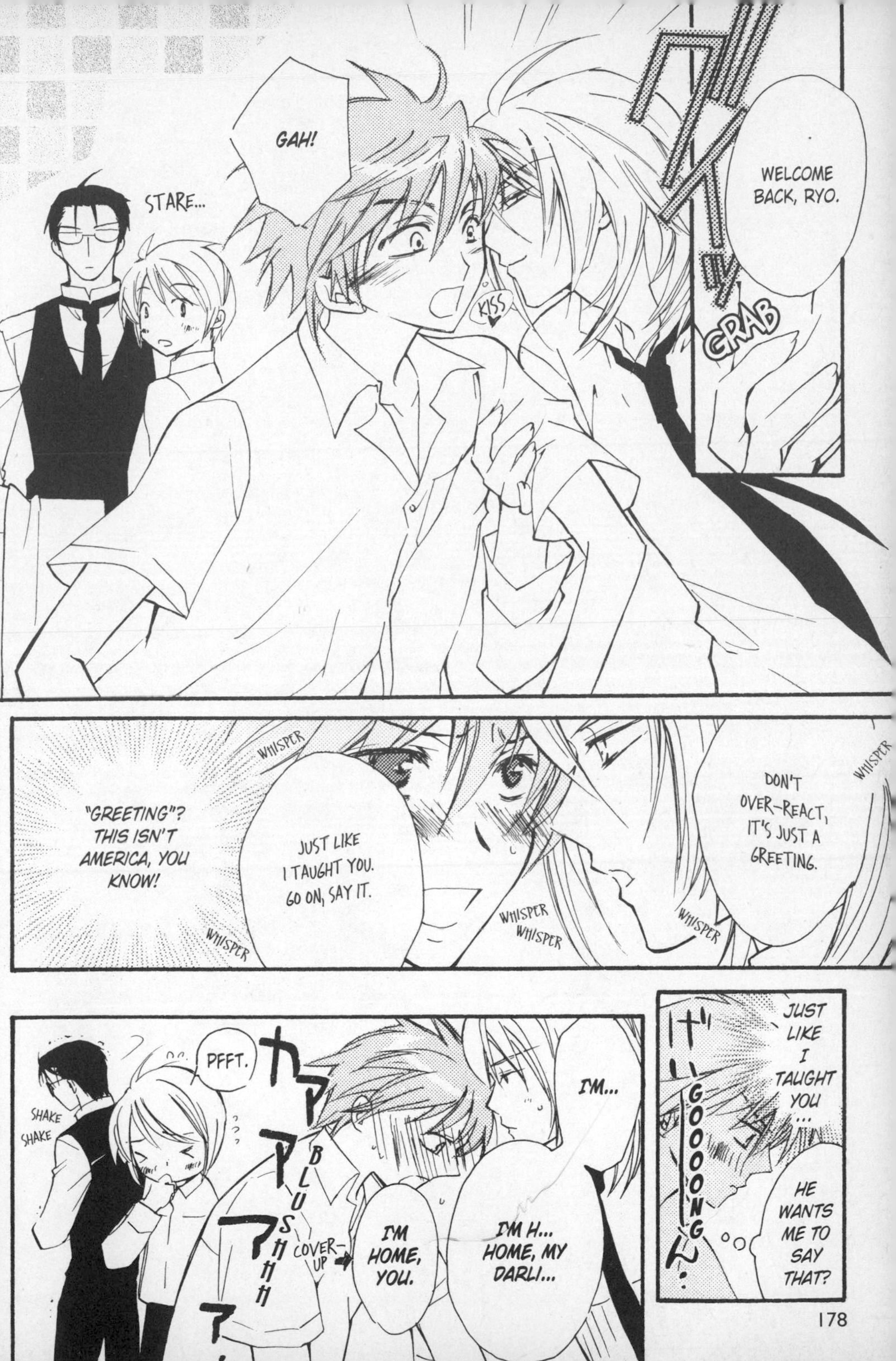
WELCOME BACK, RYO.
GRAB
KISS
GAH!
STARE...
WHISPER
DON'T OVER-REACT, IT'S JUST A GREETING.
WHISPER
WHISPER WHISPER
JUST LIKE I TAUGHT YOU. GO ON, SAY IT.
WHISPER
"GREETING"? THIS ISN'T AMERICA, YOU KNOW!
WHISPER
JUST LIKE I TAUGHT YOU...
GOOOOONG
HE WANTS ME TO SAY THAT?
I'M...
I'M H... HOME, MY DARLI...
I'M HOME, YOU.
COVER-UP
BLUSHHH
PFFT.
SHAKE SHAKE

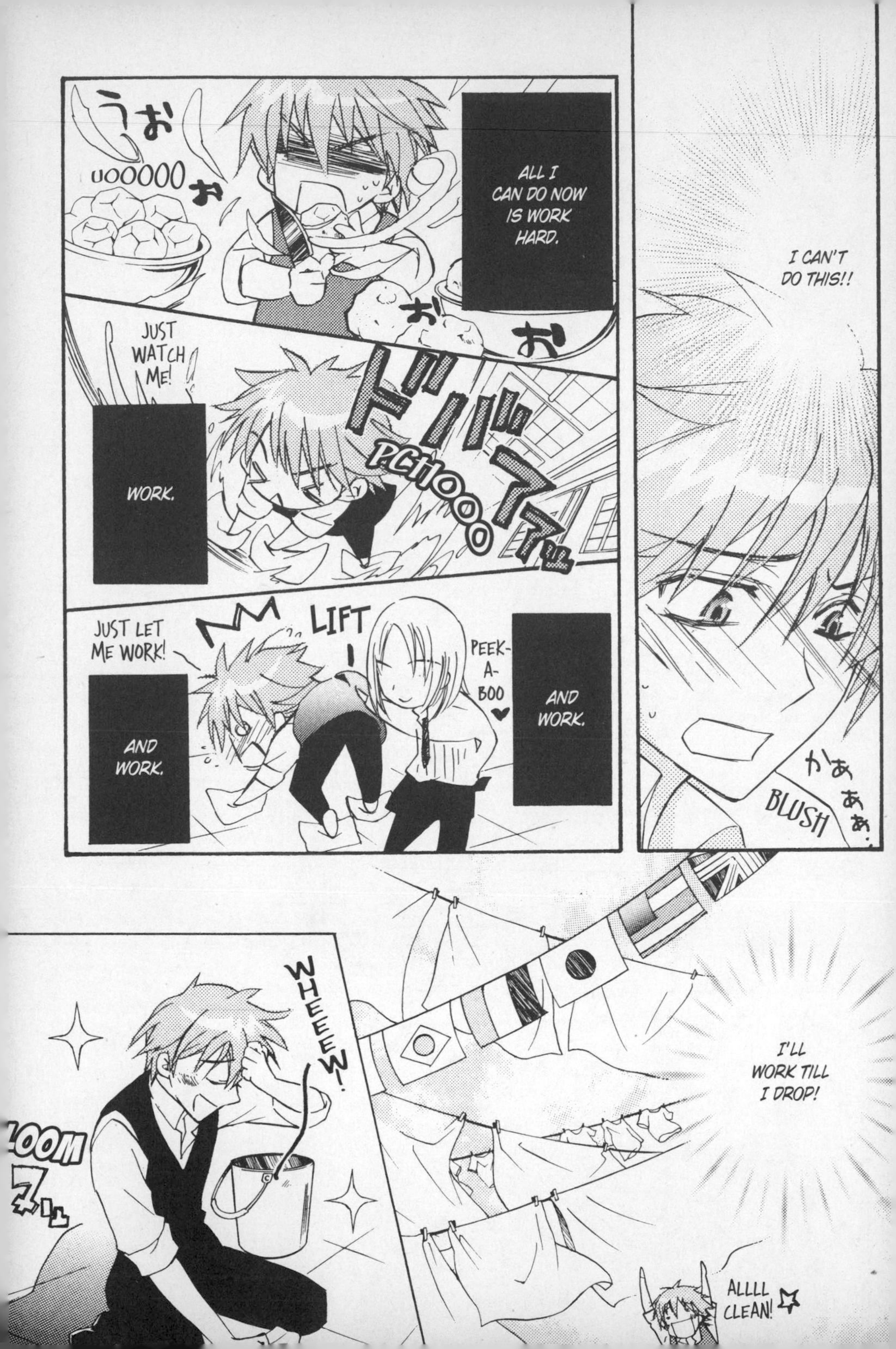
I CAN'T DO THIS!!
かあぁぁ
BLUSH
ALL I CAN DO NOW IS WORK HARD.
うおおおお
UOOOOO
JUST WATCH ME!
ドバァア
P.CHOOOO
WORK.
PEEK-A-BOO
LIFT
JUST LET ME WORK!
AND WORK.
AND WORK.
I'LL WORK TILL I DROP!
ALLLL CLEAN!
WHEEEW!
LOOM

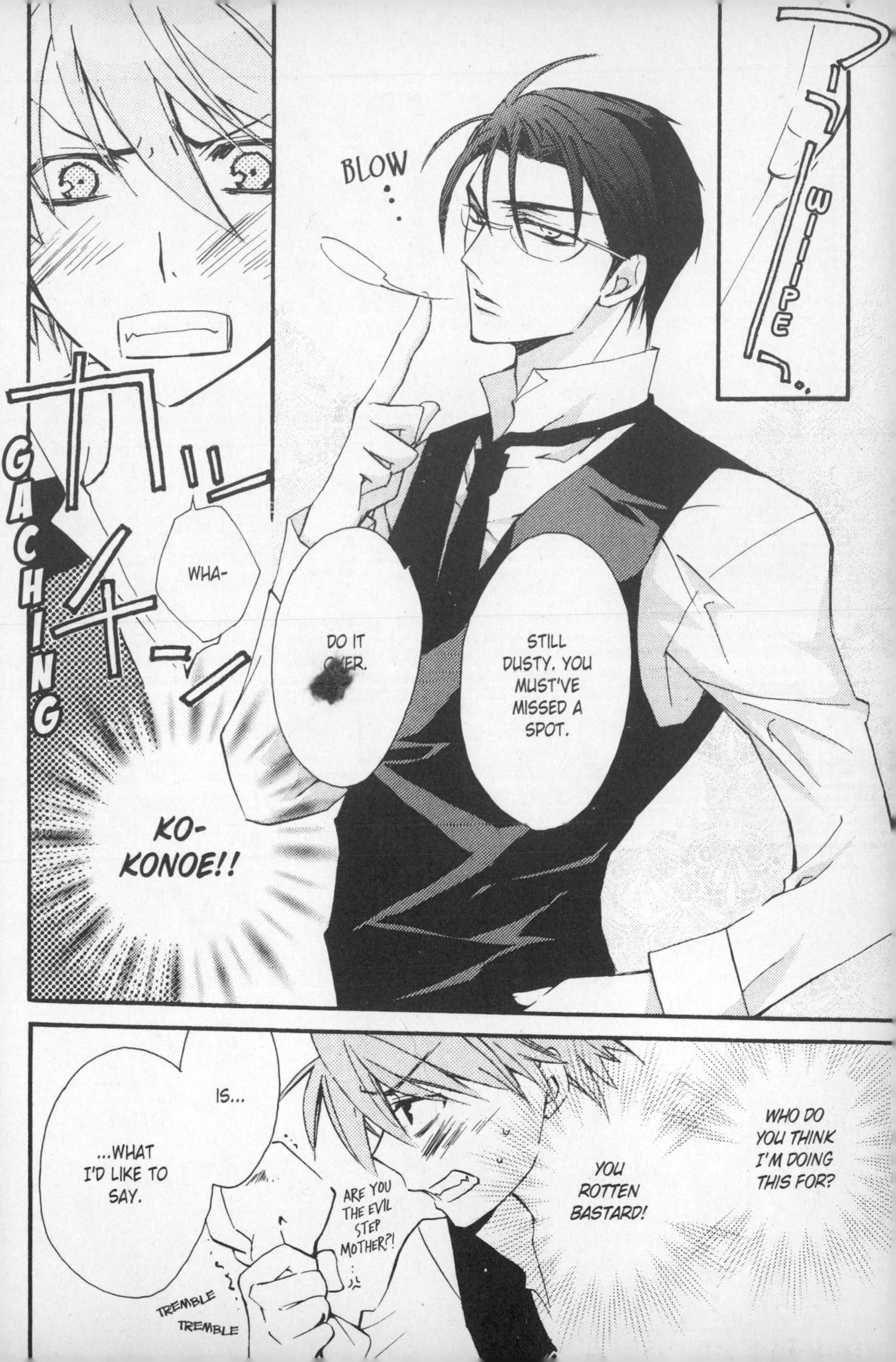
WIIIPE
BLOW...
STILL DUSTY. YOU MUST'VE MISSED A SPOT.
DO IT OVER.
GACHING
WHA-
KO-KONOE!!
WHO DO YOU THINK I'M DOING THIS FOR?
YOU ROTTEN BASTARD!
ARE YOU THE EVIL STEP MOTHER?!
IS...
...WHAT I'D LIKE TO SAY.
TREMBLE
TREMBLE

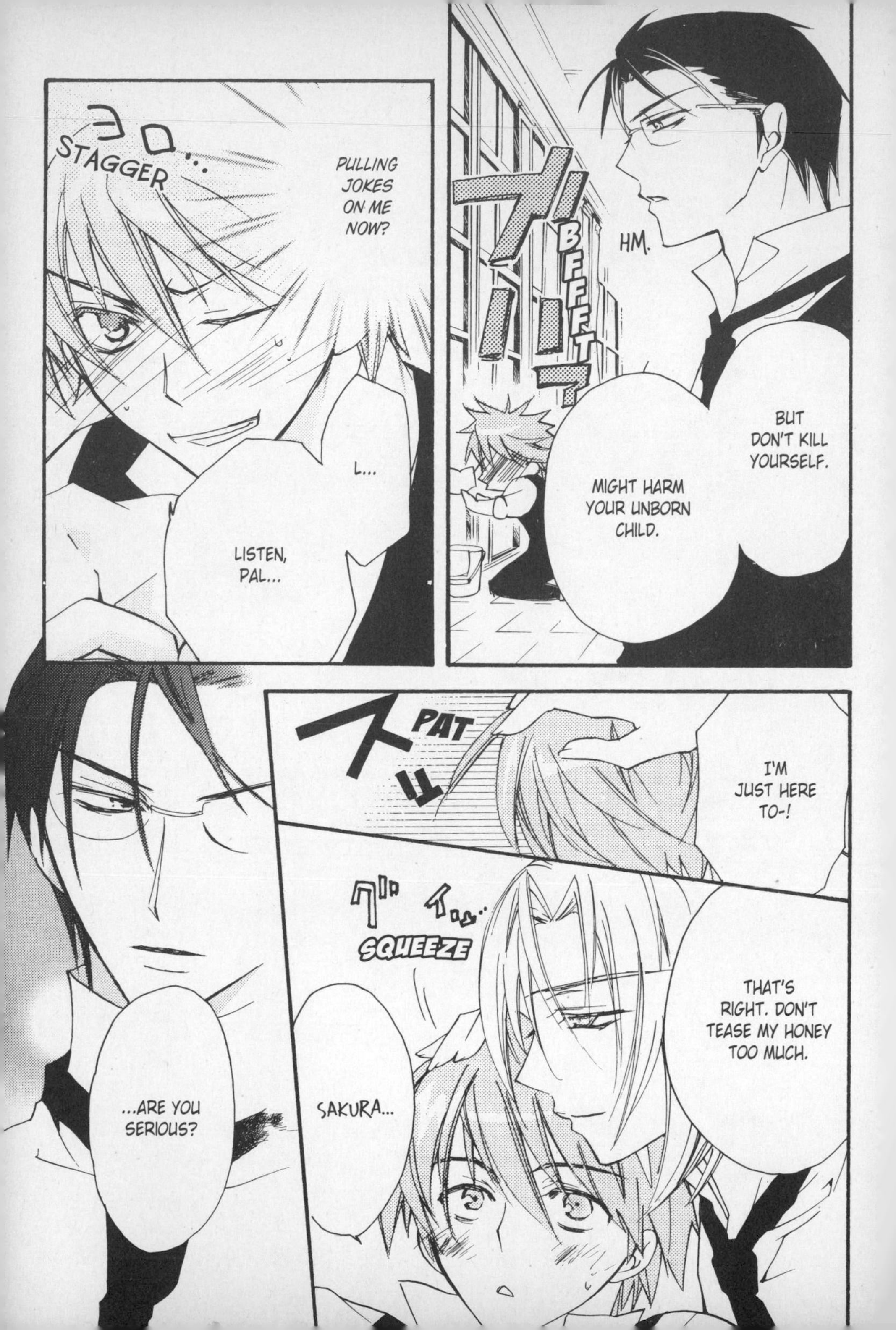
HM.
BFFFT
BUT DON'T KILL YOURSELF.
MIGHT HARM YOUR UNBORN CHILD.
STAGGER
PULLING JOKES ON ME NOW?
L...
LISTEN, PAL...
PAT
I'M JUST HERE TO-!
THAT'S RIGHT. DON'T TEASE MY HONEY TOO MUCH.
SQUEEZE
SAKURA...
...ARE YOU SERIOUS?

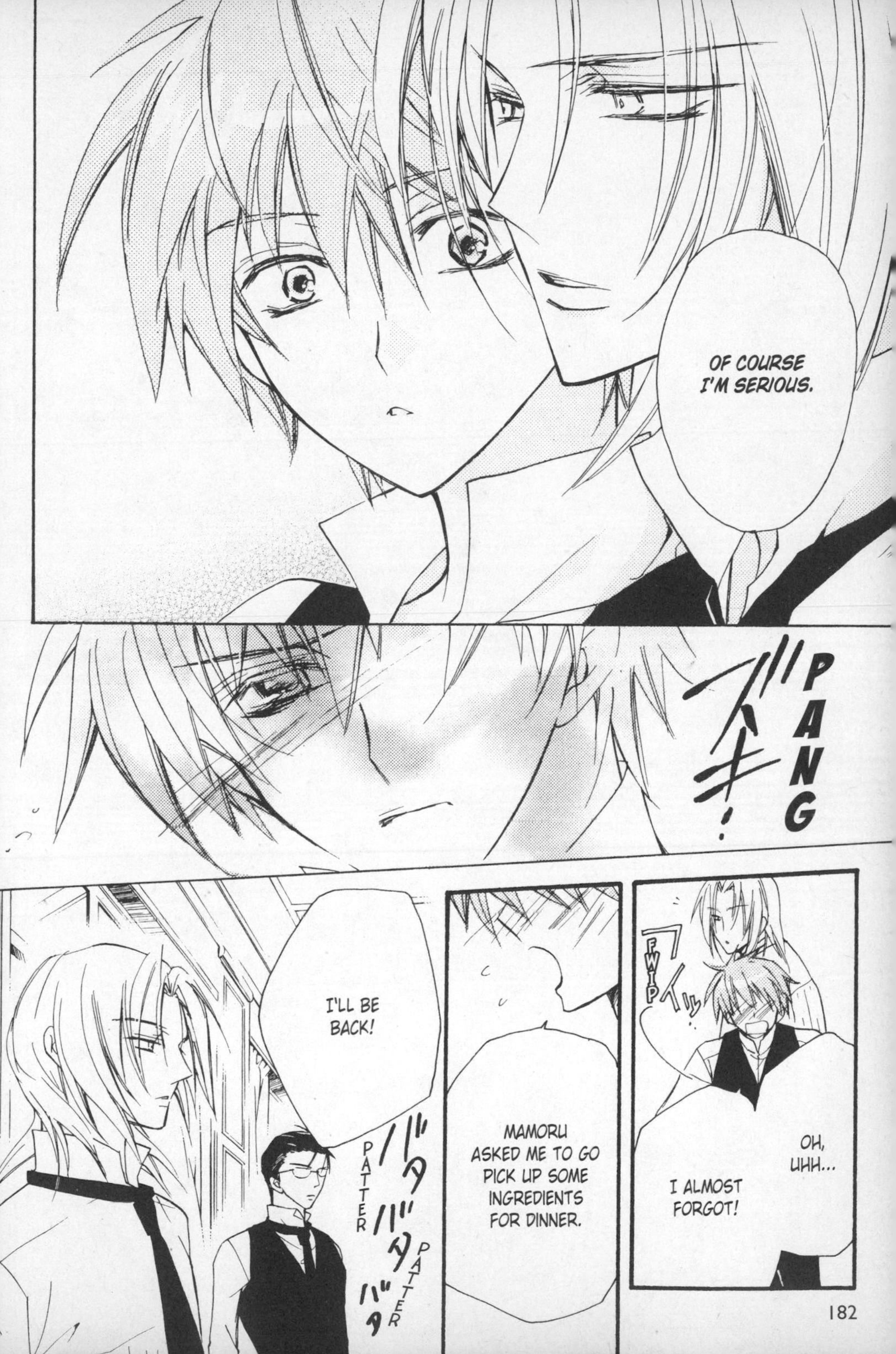
OF COURSE I'M SERIOUS.
PANG
FWIP
OH, UHH...
I ALMOST FORGOT!
MAMORU ASKED ME TO GO PICK UP SOME INGREDIENTS FOR DINNER.
I'LL BE BACK!
PATTER PATTER

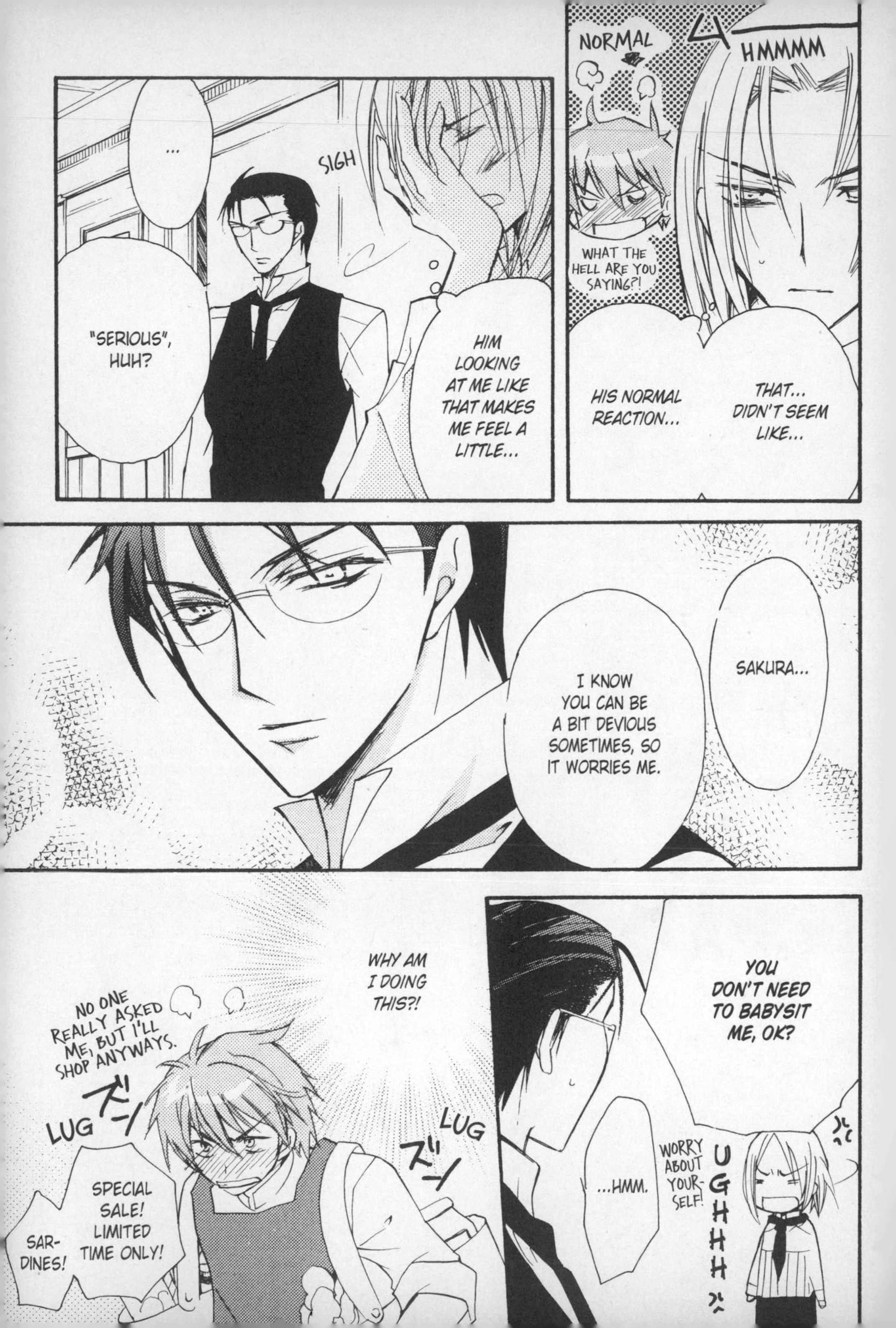
NORMAL
HMMMM
WHAT THE HELL ARE YOU SAYING?!
THAT... DIDN'T SEEM LIKE...
HIS NORMAL REACTION...
SIGH
...
HIM LOOKING AT ME LIKE THAT MAKES ME FEEL A LITTLE...
"SERIOUS", HUH?
SAKURA...
I KNOW YOU CAN BE A BIT DEVIOUS SOMETIMES, SO IT WORRIES ME.
YOU DON'T NEED TO BABYSIT ME, OK?
UGHHH
WORRY ABOUT YOUR-SELF!
...HMM.
WHY AM I DOING THIS?!
LUG
NO ONE REALLY ASKED ME, BUT I'LL SHOP ANYWAYS.
LUG
SPECIAL SALE! LIMITED TIME ONLY!
SAR-DINES!

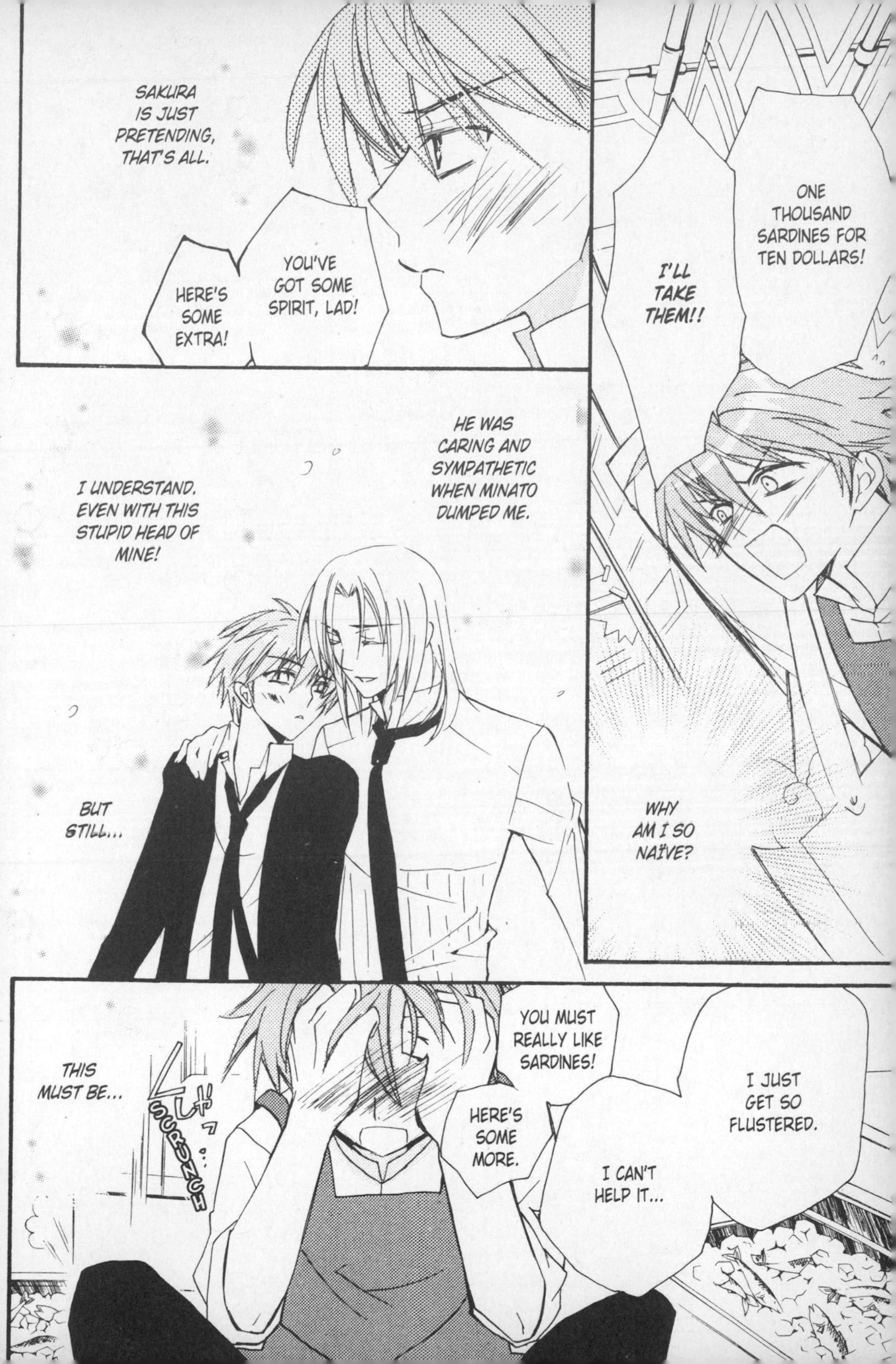
ONE THOUSAND SARDINES FOR TEN DOLLARS!
I'LL TAKE THEM!!
WHY AM I SO NAÏVE?
SAKURA IS JUST PRETENDING, THAT'S ALL.
YOU'VE GOT SOME SPIRIT, LAD!
HERE'S SOME EXTRA!
HE WAS CARING AND SYMPATHETIC WHEN MINATO DUMPED ME.
I UNDERSTAND. EVEN WITH THIS STUPID HEAD OF MINE!
BUT STILL...
I JUST GET SO FLUSTERED.
I CAN'T HELP IT...
YOU MUST REALLY LIKE SARDINES!
HERE'S SOME MORE.
SCRUNCH
THIS MUST BE...

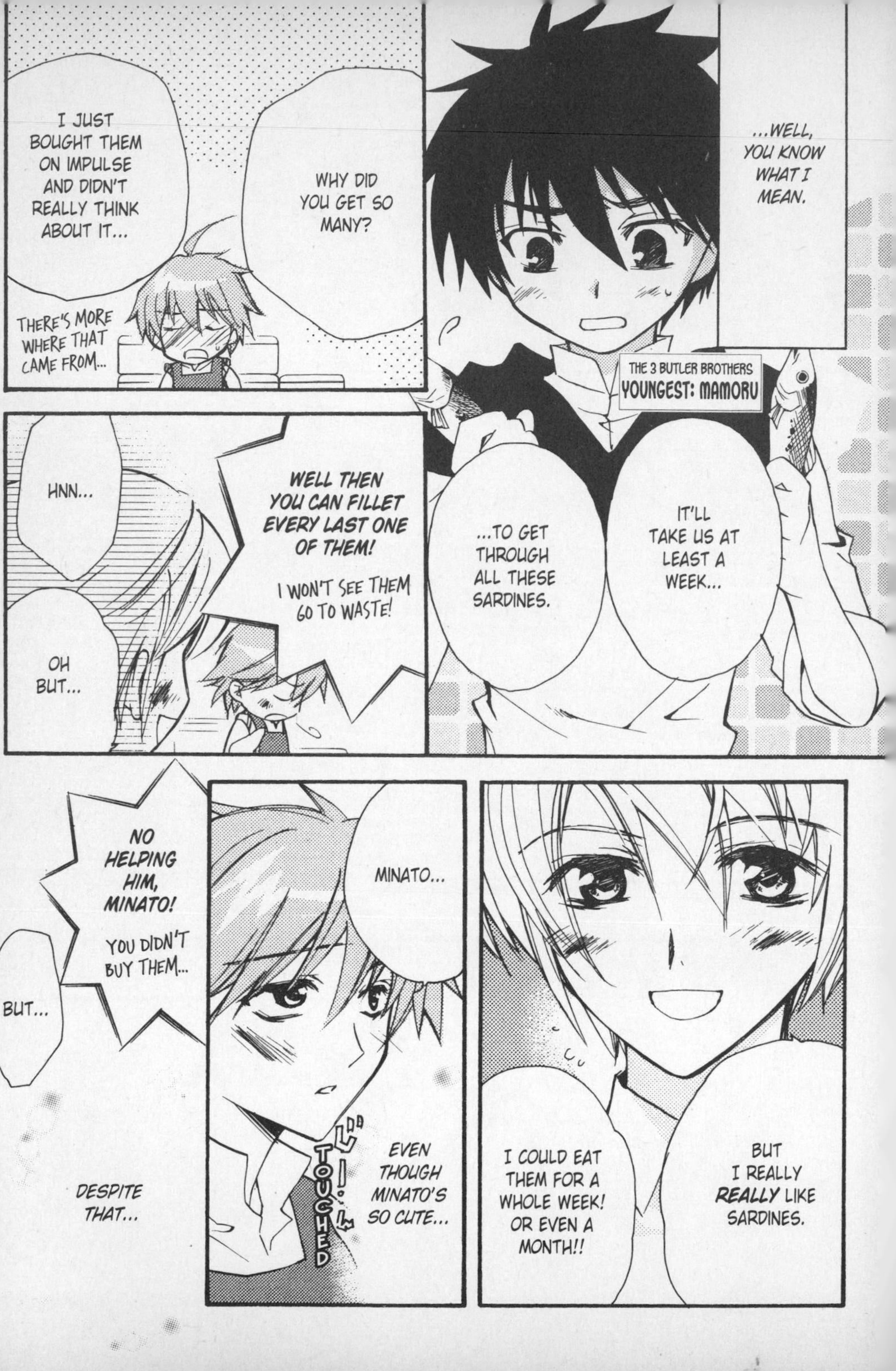
...WELL, YOU KNOW WHAT I MEAN.
THE 3 BUTLER BROTHERS YOUNGEST: MAMORU
IT'LL TAKE US AT LEAST A WEEK...
...TO GET THROUGH ALL THESE SARDINES.
WHY DID YOU GET SO MANY?
I JUST BOUGHT THEM ON IMPULSE AND DIDN'T REALLY THINK ABOUT IT...
THERE'S MORE WHERE THAT CAME FROM...
WELL THEN YOU CAN FILLET EVERY LAST ONE OF THEM!
I WON'T SEE THEM GO TO WASTE!
HNN...
OH BUT...
BUT I REALLY REALLY LIKE SARDINES.
I COULD EAT THEM FOR A WHOLE WEEK! OR EVEN A MONTH!!
MINATO...
EVEN THOUGH MINATO'S SO CUTE...
TOUCHED
NO HELPING HIM, MINATO!
YOU DIDN'T BUY THEM...
BUT...
DESPITE THAT...

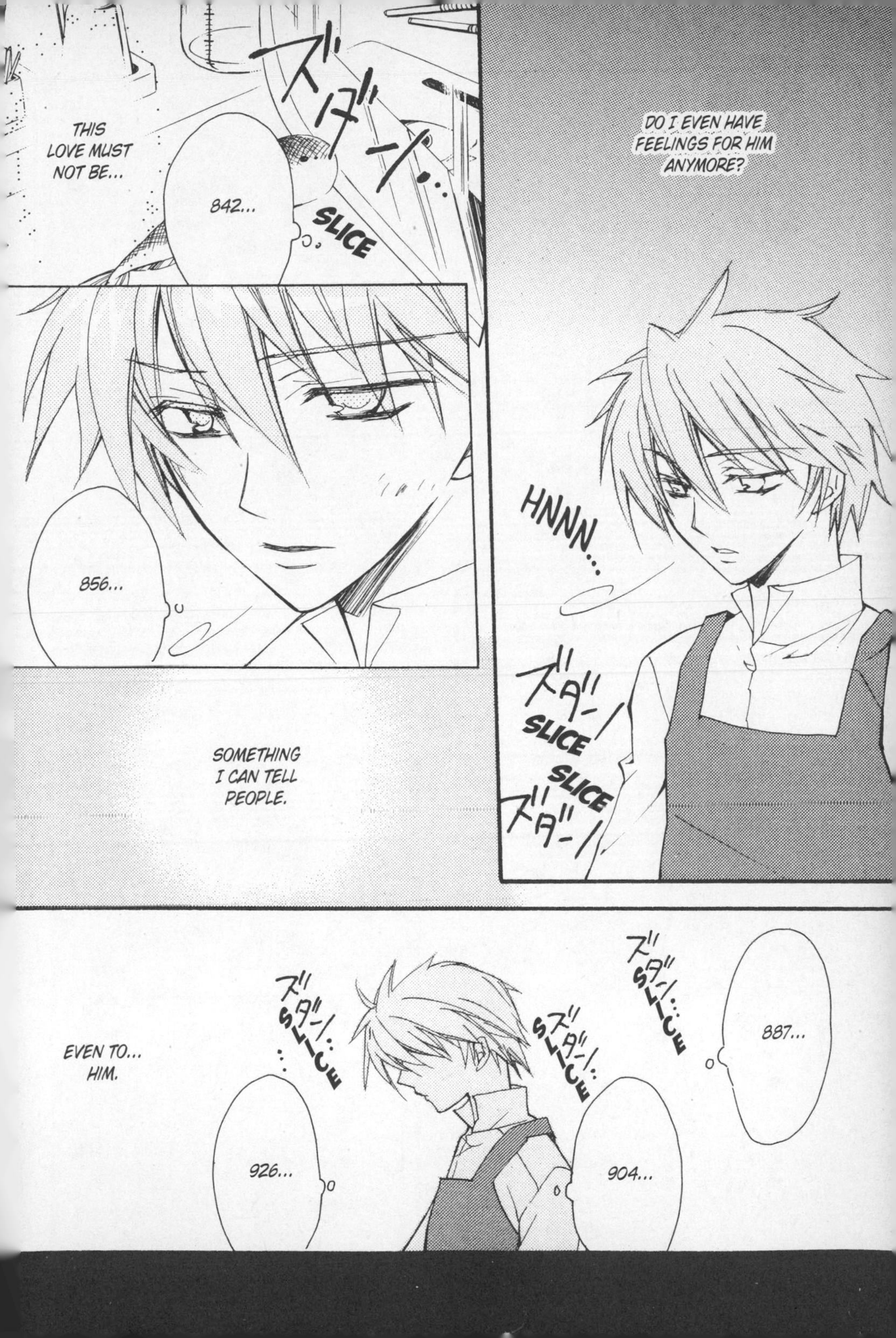
DO I EVEN HAVE FEELINGS FOR HIM ANYMORE?
HNNN...
SLICE
SLICE
THIS LOVE MUST NOT BE...
842...
SLICE
856...
SOMETHING I CAN TELL PEOPLE.
887...
SLICE
904...
SLICE
926...
SLICE
EVEN TO... HIM.

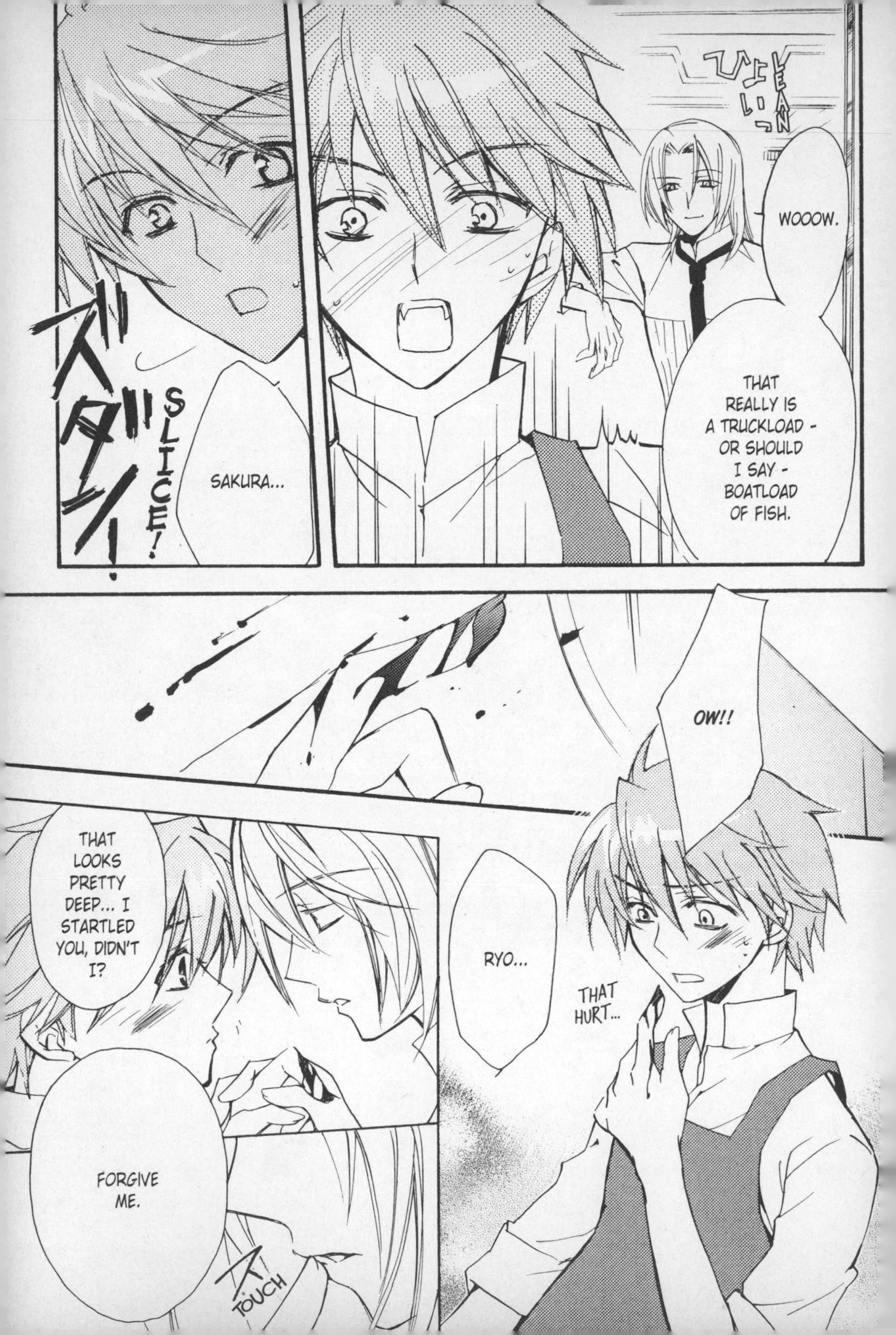
LEAN
WOOOW.
THAT REALLY IS A TRUCKLOAD - OR SHOULD I SAY - BOATLOAD OF FISH.
SLICE!
SAKURA...
OW!!
RYO...
THAT HURT...
THAT LOOKS PRETTY DEEP... I STARTLED YOU, DIDN'T I?
FORGIVE ME.
TOUCH

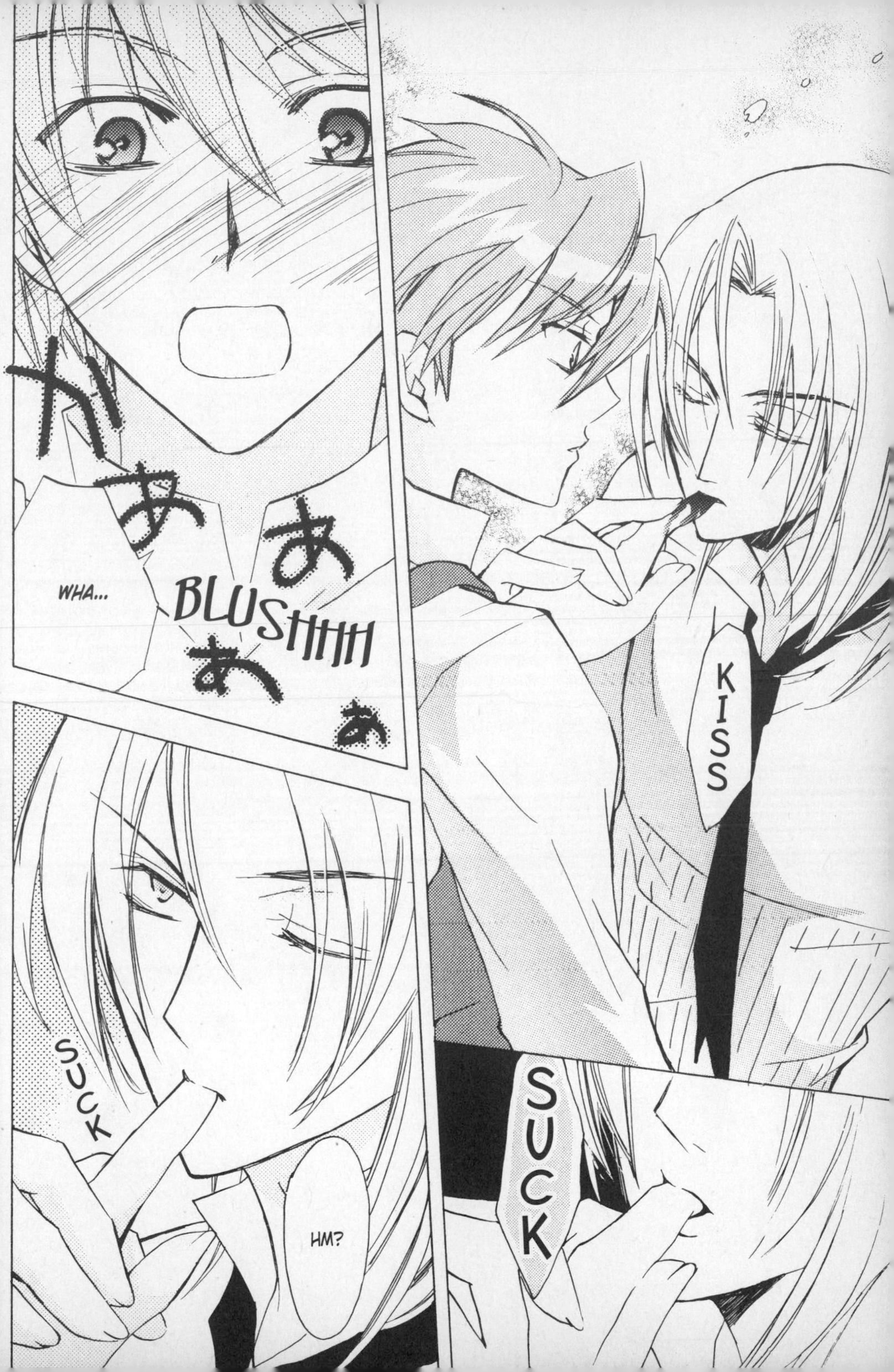
KISS
SUCK
かあああああ
BLUSHHHH
WHA...
SUCK
HM?

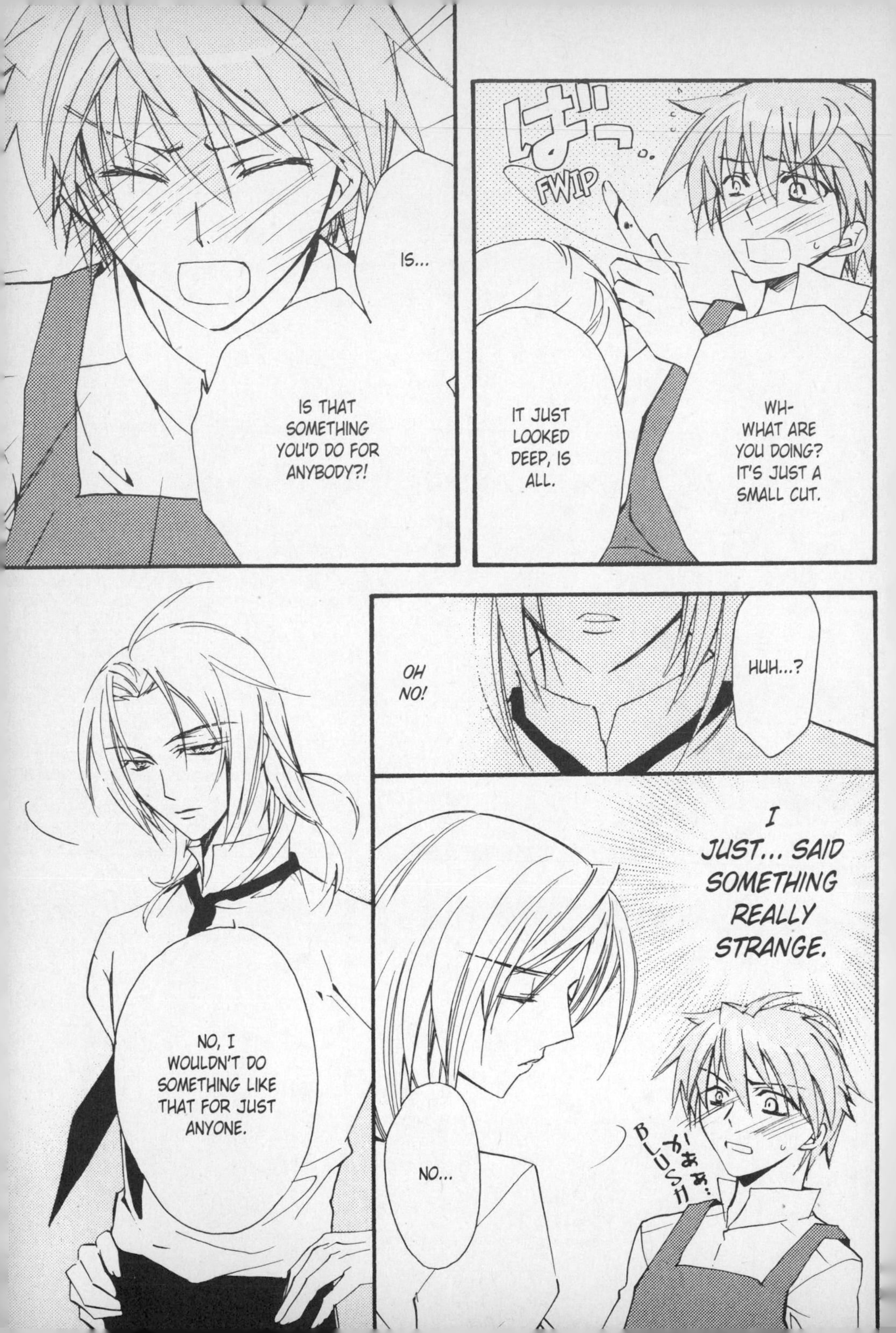
ばっ
FWIP
WH- WHAT ARE YOU DOING? IT'S JUST A SMALL CUT.
IT JUST LOOKED DEEP, IS ALL.
IS...
IS THAT SOMETHING YOU'D DO FOR ANYBODY?!
HUH...?
OH NO!
I JUST... SAID SOMETHING REALLY STRANGE.
かぁぁ…
BLUSH
NO...
NO, I WOULDN'T DO SOMETHING LIKE THAT FOR JUST ANYONE.

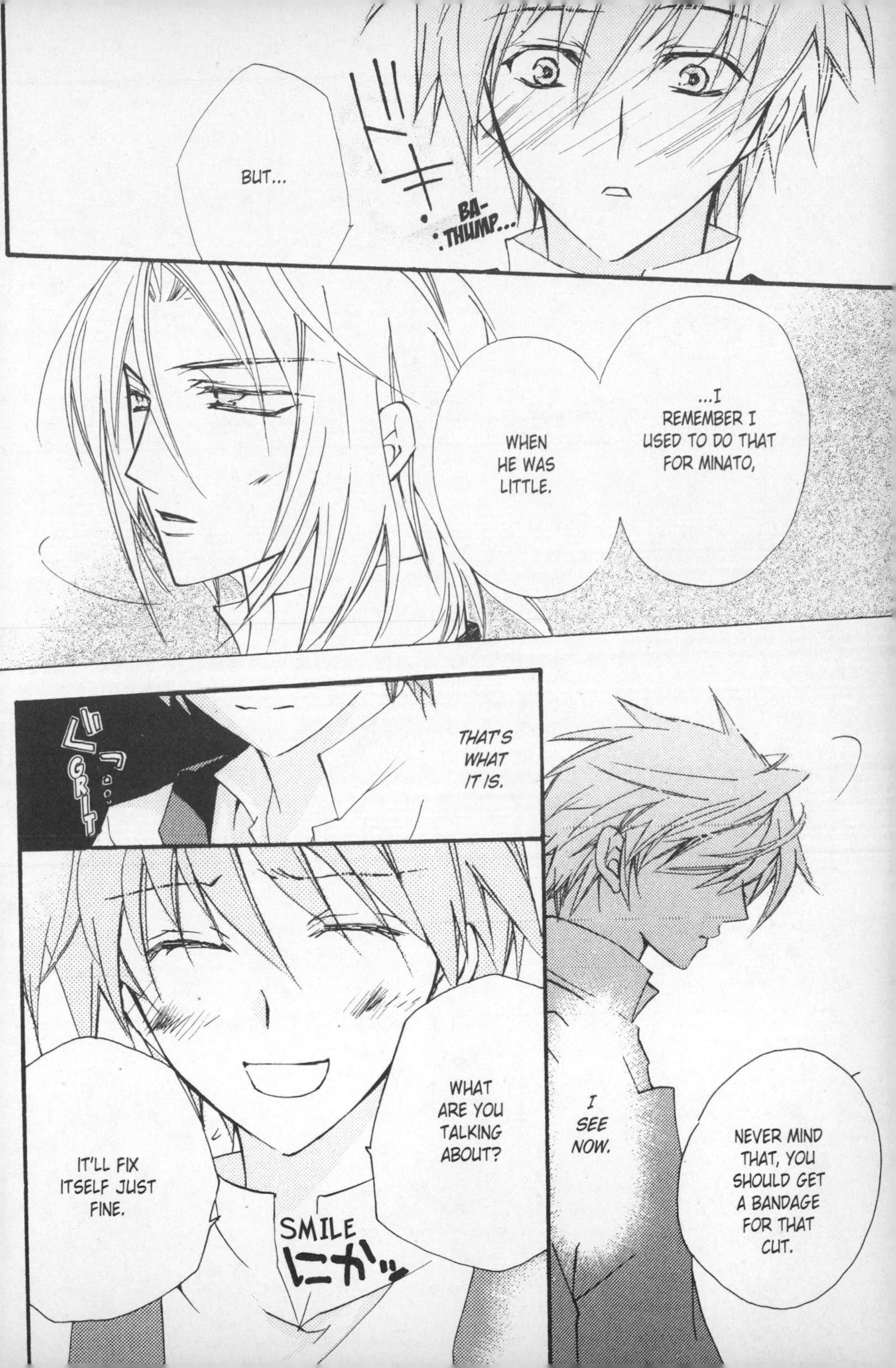
BA-THUMP...
BUT...
...I REMEMBER I USED TO DO THAT FOR MINATO,
WHEN HE WAS LITTLE.
NEVER MIND THAT, YOU SHOULD GET A BANDAGE FOR THAT CUT.
I SEE NOW.
THAT'S WHAT IT IS.
GRIT
WHAT ARE YOU TALKING ABOUT?
IT'LL FIX ITSELF JUST FINE.
SMILE
にかッ

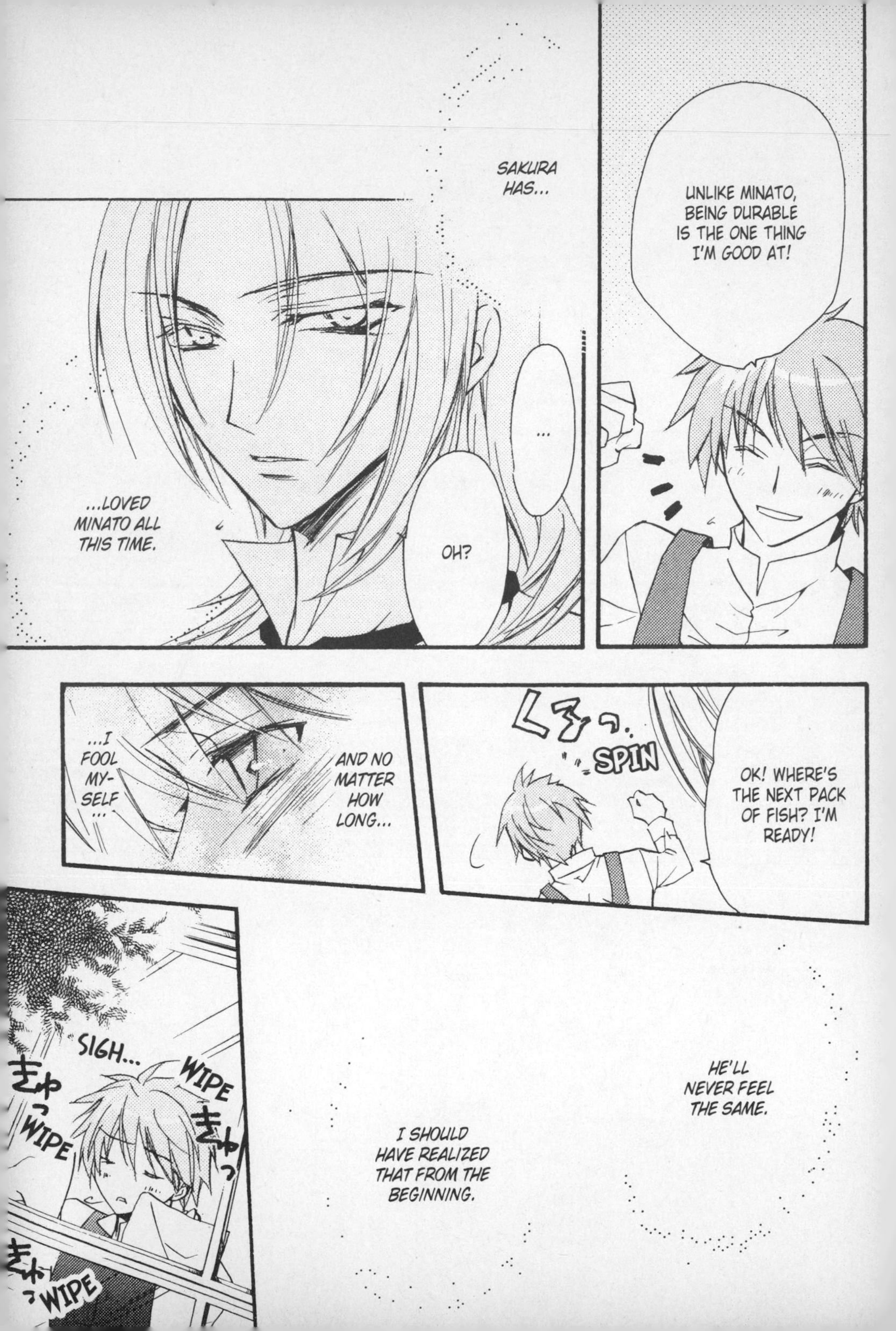
UNLIKE MINATO, BEING DURABLE IS THE ONE THING I'M GOOD AT!
SAKURA HAS...
...
OH?
...LOVED MINATO ALL THIS TIME.
くるっ
SPIN
OK! WHERE'S THE NEXT PACK OF FISH? I'M READY!
AND NO MATTER HOW LONG...
...I FOOL MY-SELF...
HE'LL NEVER FEEL THE SAME.
I SHOULD HAVE REALIZED THAT FROM THE BEGINNING.
WIPE
きゅっ
SIGH...
きゅっ
WIPE
きゅっ
WIPE

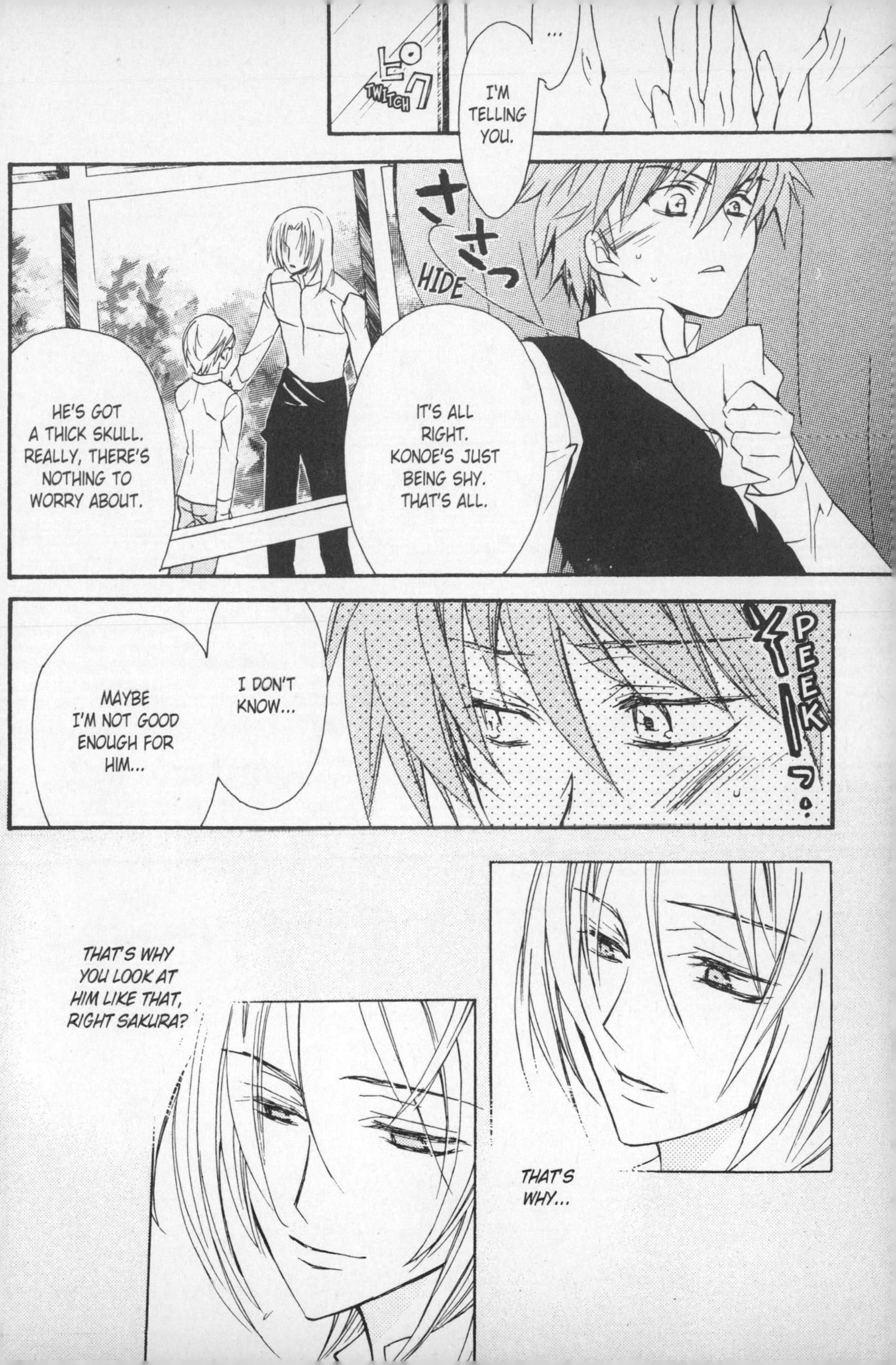

...
I'M TELLING YOU.
TWITCH
HIDE
IT'S ALL RIGHT. KONOE'S JUST BEING SHY. THAT'S ALL.
HE'S GOT A THICK SKULL. REALLY, THERE'S NOTHING TO WORRY ABOUT.
PEEK
I DON'T KNOW...
MAYBE I'M NOT GOOD ENOUGH FOR HIM...
THAT'S WHY...
THAT'S WHY YOU LOOK AT HIM LIKE THAT, RIGHT SAKURA?

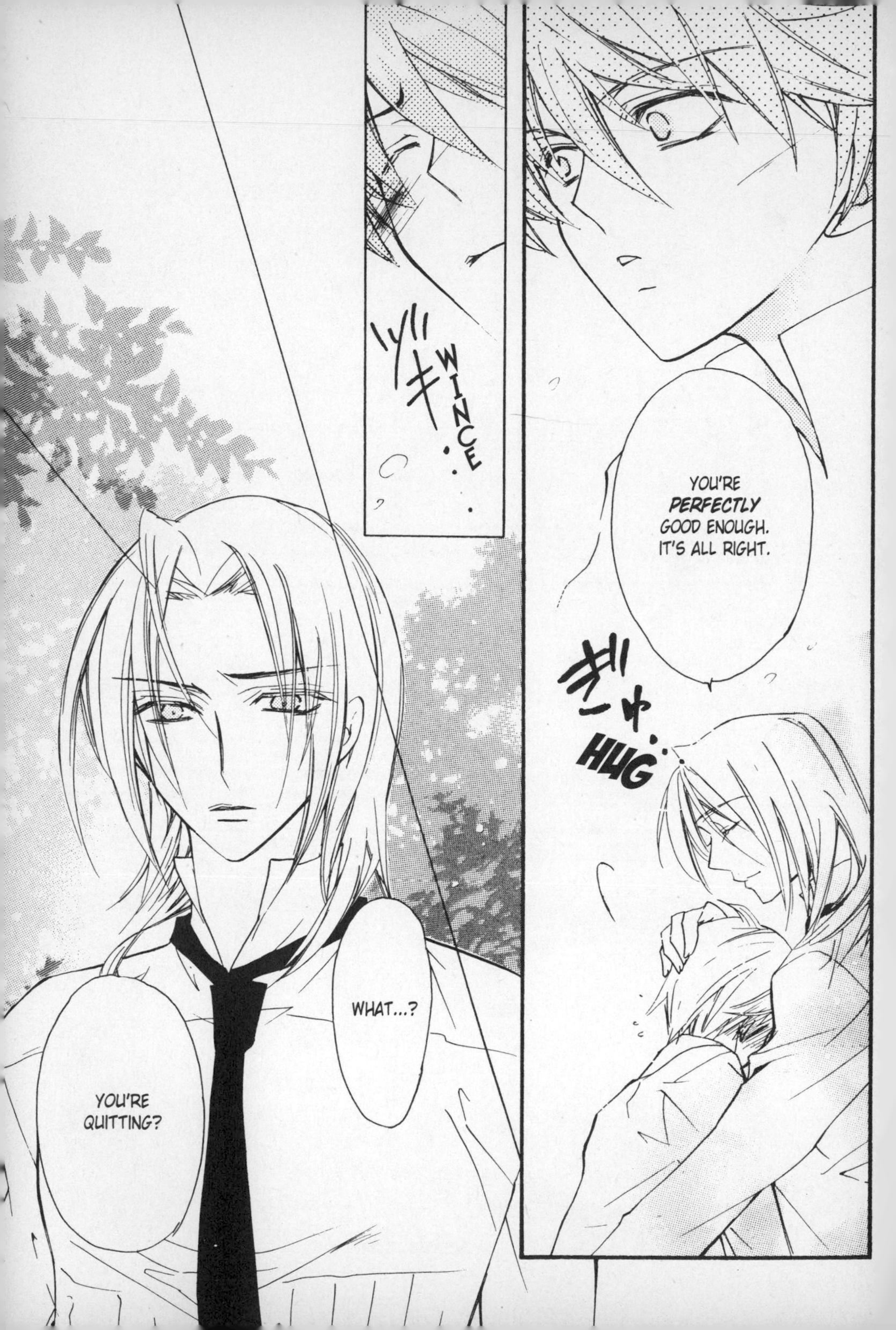
YOU'RE PERFECTLY GOOD ENOUGH. IT'S ALL RIGHT.
HUG
WINCE
WHAT...?
YOU'RE QUITTING?

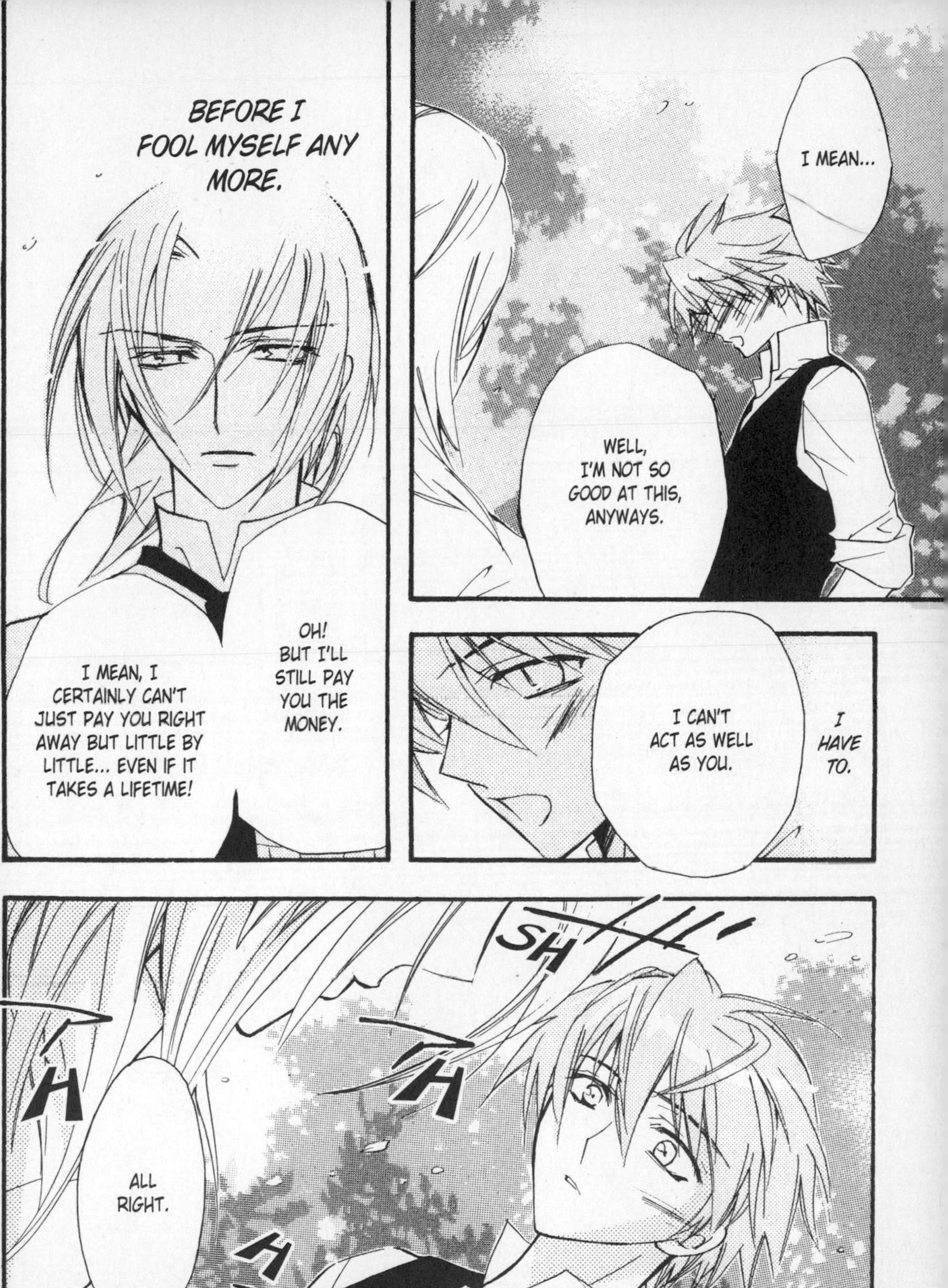
I MEAN...
WELL, I'M NOT SO GOOD AT THIS, ANYWAYS.
I HAVE TO.
I CAN'T ACT AS WELL AS YOU.
BEFORE I FOOL MYSELF ANY MORE.
OH! BUT I'LL STILL PAY YOU THE MONEY.
I MEAN, I CERTAINLY CAN'T JUST PAY YOU RIGHT AWAY BUT LITTLE BY LITTLE... EVEN IF IT TAKES A LIFETIME!
SH
H
H
H
ALL RIGHT.

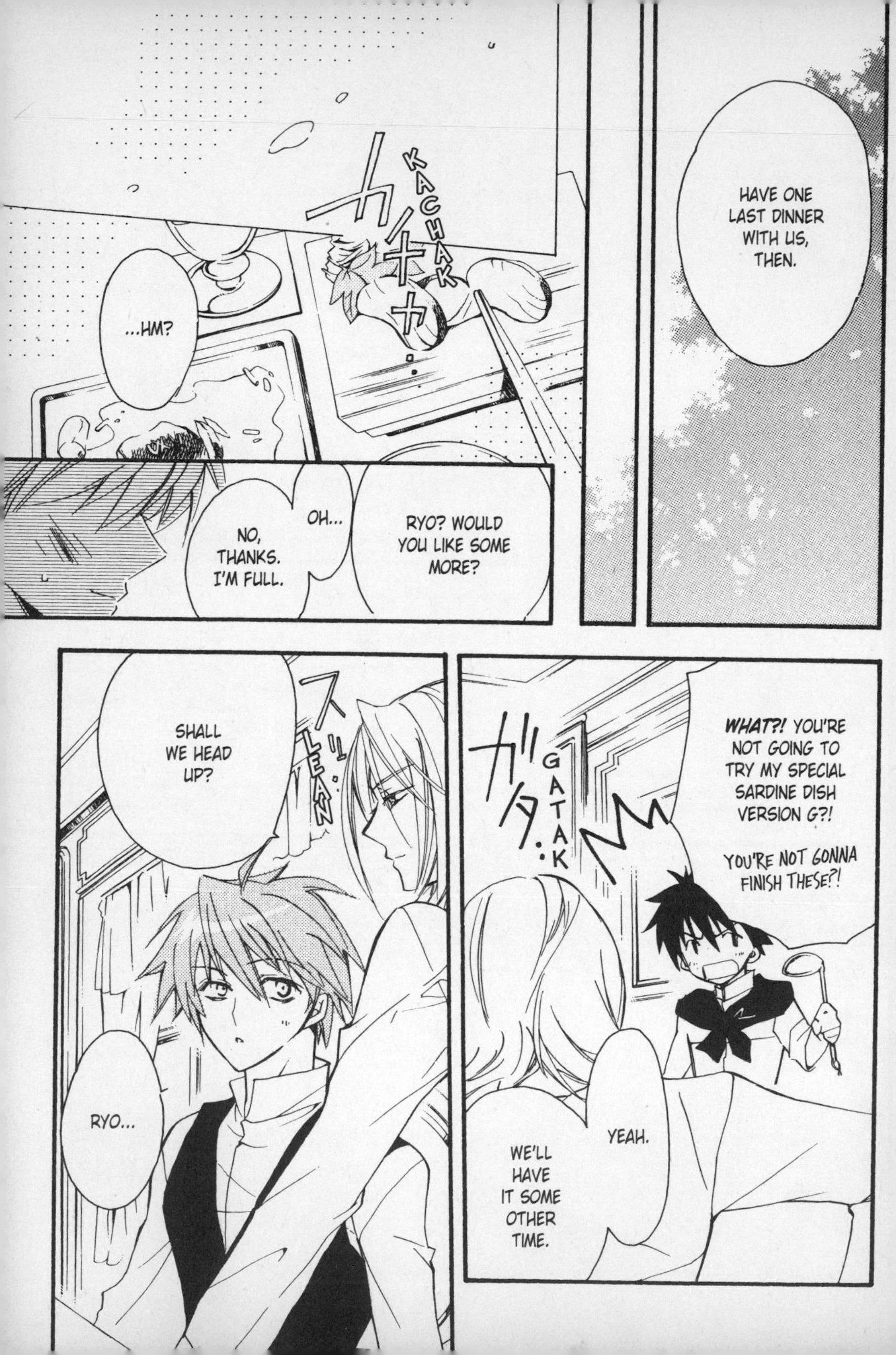
HAVE ONE LAST DINNER WITH US, THEN.
KACHAK
...HM?
RYO? WOULD YOU LIKE SOME MORE?
OH...
NO, THANKS. I'M FULL.
WHAT?! YOU'RE NOT GOING TO TRY MY SPECIAL SARDINE DISH VERSION G?!
YOU'RE NOT GONNA FINISH THESE?!
GATAK
YEAH.
WE'LL HAVE IT SOME OTHER TIME.
LEAN
SHALL WE HEAD UP?
RYO...

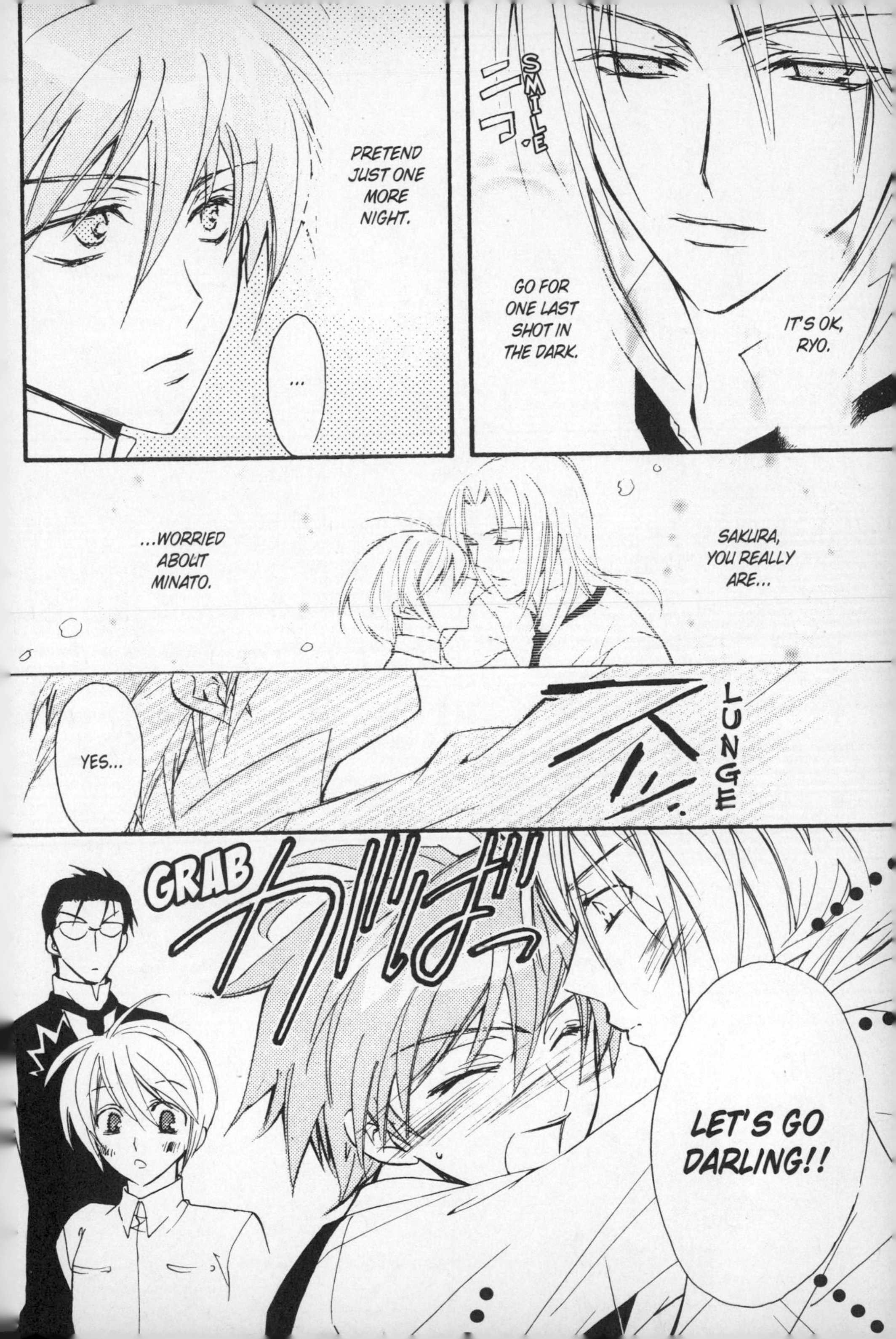
SMILE
IT'S OK, RYO.
GO FOR ONE LAST SHOT IN THE DARK.
PRETEND JUST ONE MORE NIGHT.
...
SAKURA, YOU REALLY ARE...
...WORRIED ABOUT MINATO.
LUNGE
YES...
LET'S GO DARLING!!
GRAB

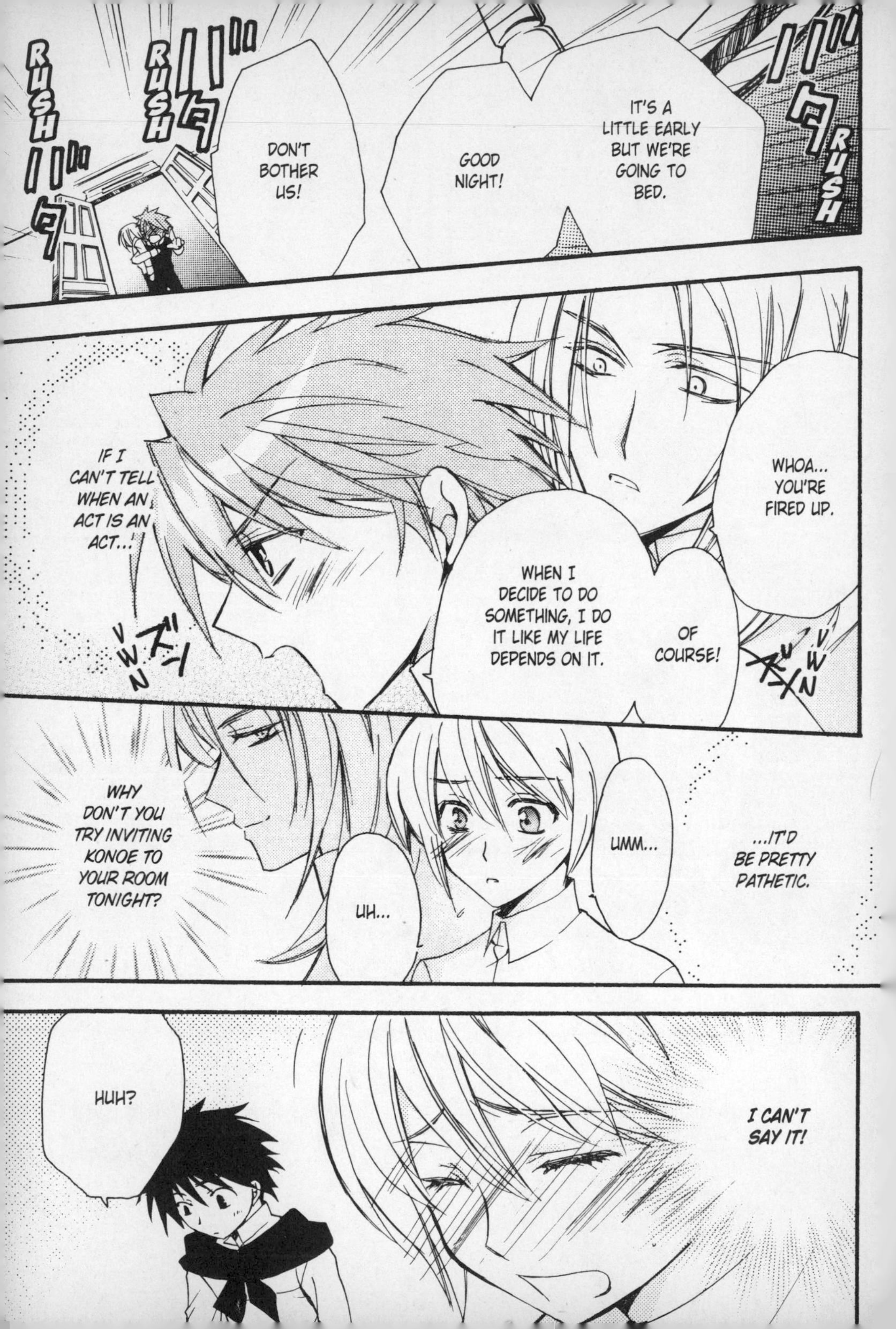
RUSH
IT'S A LITTLE EARLY BUT WE'RE GOING TO BED.
GOOD NIGHT!
DON'T BOTHER US!
RUSH
RUSH
WHOA... YOU'RE FIRED UP.
OF COURSE!
VWN
WHEN I DECIDE TO DO SOMETHING, I DO IT LIKE MY LIFE DEPENDS ON IT.
IF I CAN'T TELL WHEN AN ACT IS AN ACT...
VWN
...IT'D BE PRETTY PATHETIC.
UMM...
UH...
WHY DON'T YOU TRY INVITING KONOE TO YOUR ROOM TONIGHT?
I CAN'T SAY IT!
HUH?

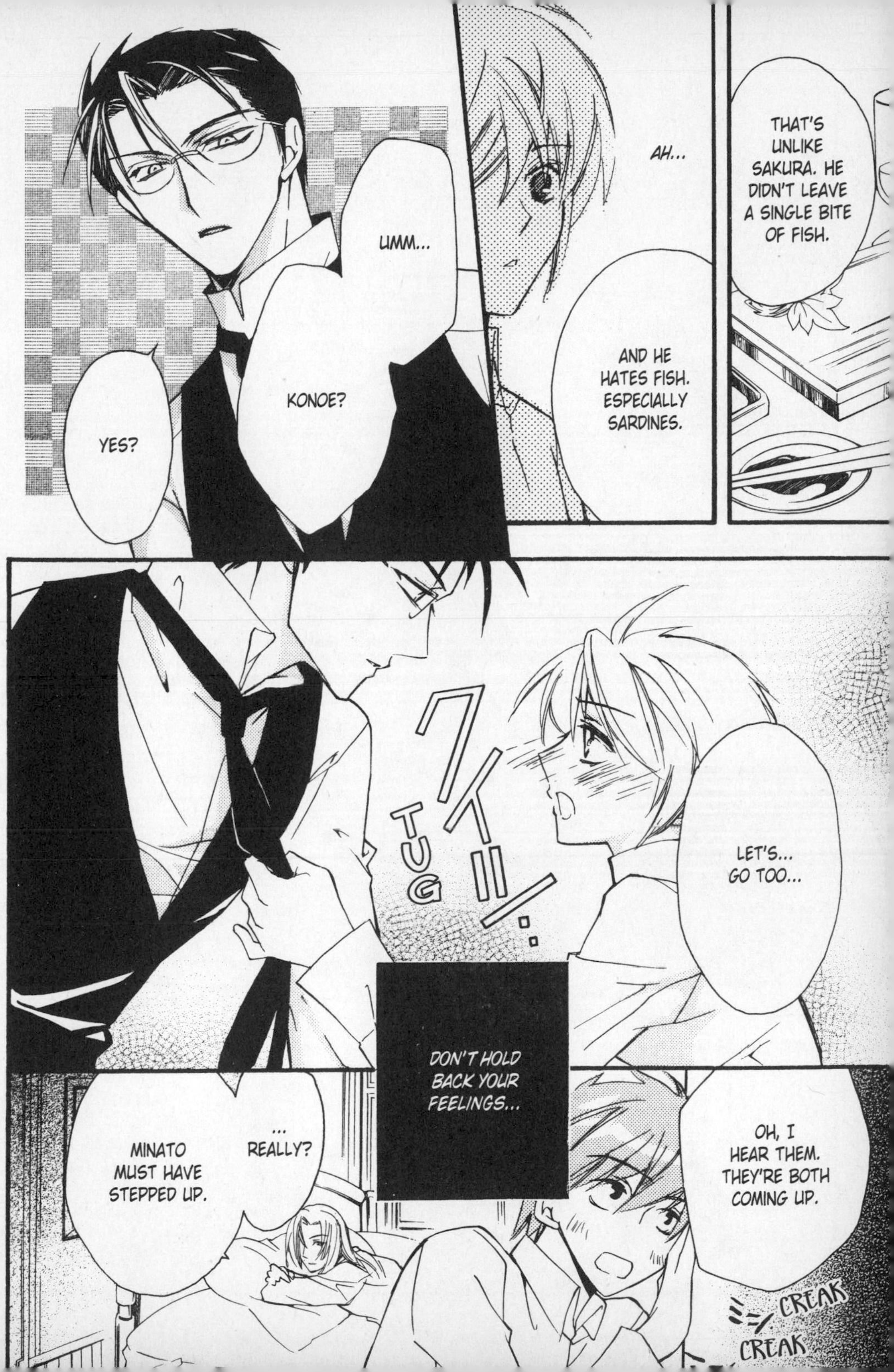
THAT'S UNLIKE SAKURA. HE DIDN'T LEAVE A SINGLE BITE OF FISH.
AH...
AND HE HATES FISH. ESPECIALLY SARDINES.
UMM...
KONOE?
YES?
LET'S... GO TOO...
TUG
DON'T HOLD BACK YOUR FEELINGS...
OH, I HEAR THEM. THEY'RE BOTH COMING UP.
CREAK
CREAK
... REALLY?
MINATO MUST HAVE STEPPED UP.

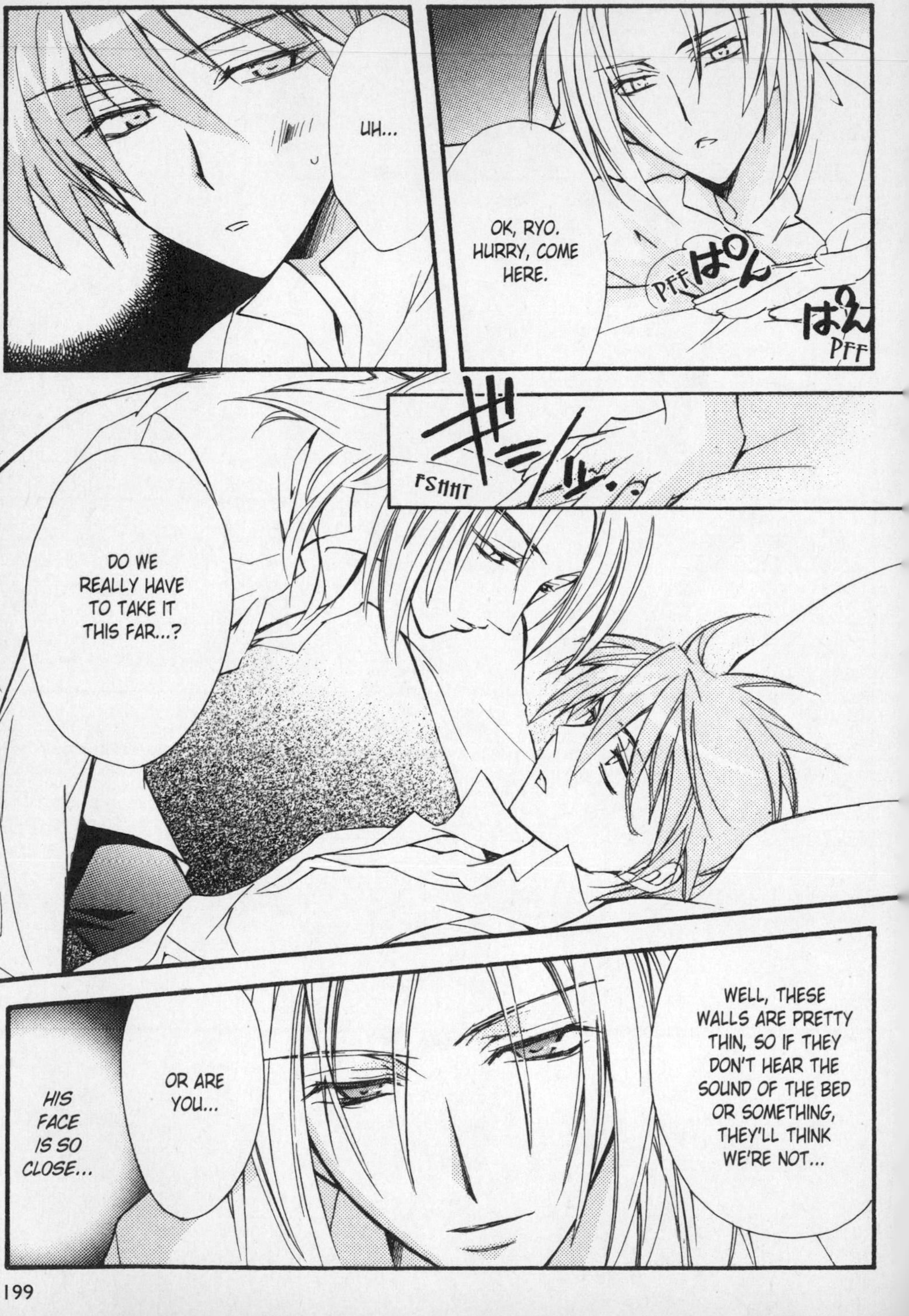
OK, RYO. HURRY, COME HERE.
PFF
ぱん
ぱん
PFF
UH...
FSHHT
ギシッ
DO WE REALLY HAVE TO TAKE IT THIS FAR...?
WELL, THESE WALLS ARE PRETTY THIN, SO IF THEY DON'T HEAR THE SOUND OF THE BED OR SOMETHING, THEY'LL THINK WE'RE NOT...
OR ARE YOU...
HIS FACE IS SO CLOSE...

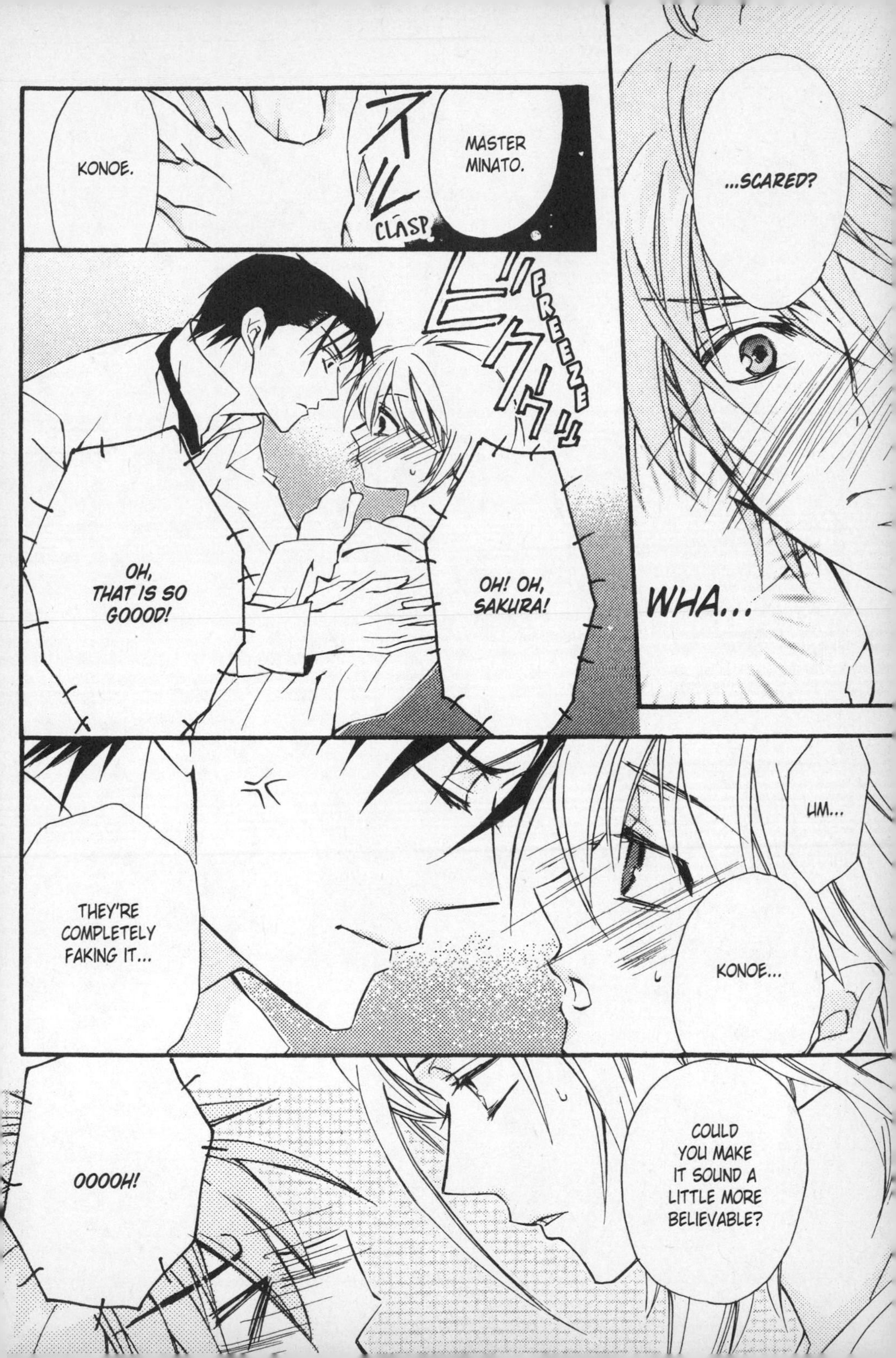
...SCARED?
WHA...
MASTER MINATO.
CLASP
KONOE.
FREEZE
OH! OH, SAKURA!
OH, THAT IS SO GOOOD!
UM...
KONOE...
THEY'RE COMPLETELY FAKING IT...
COULD YOU MAKE IT SOUND A LITTLE MORE BELIEVABLE?
OOOOH!

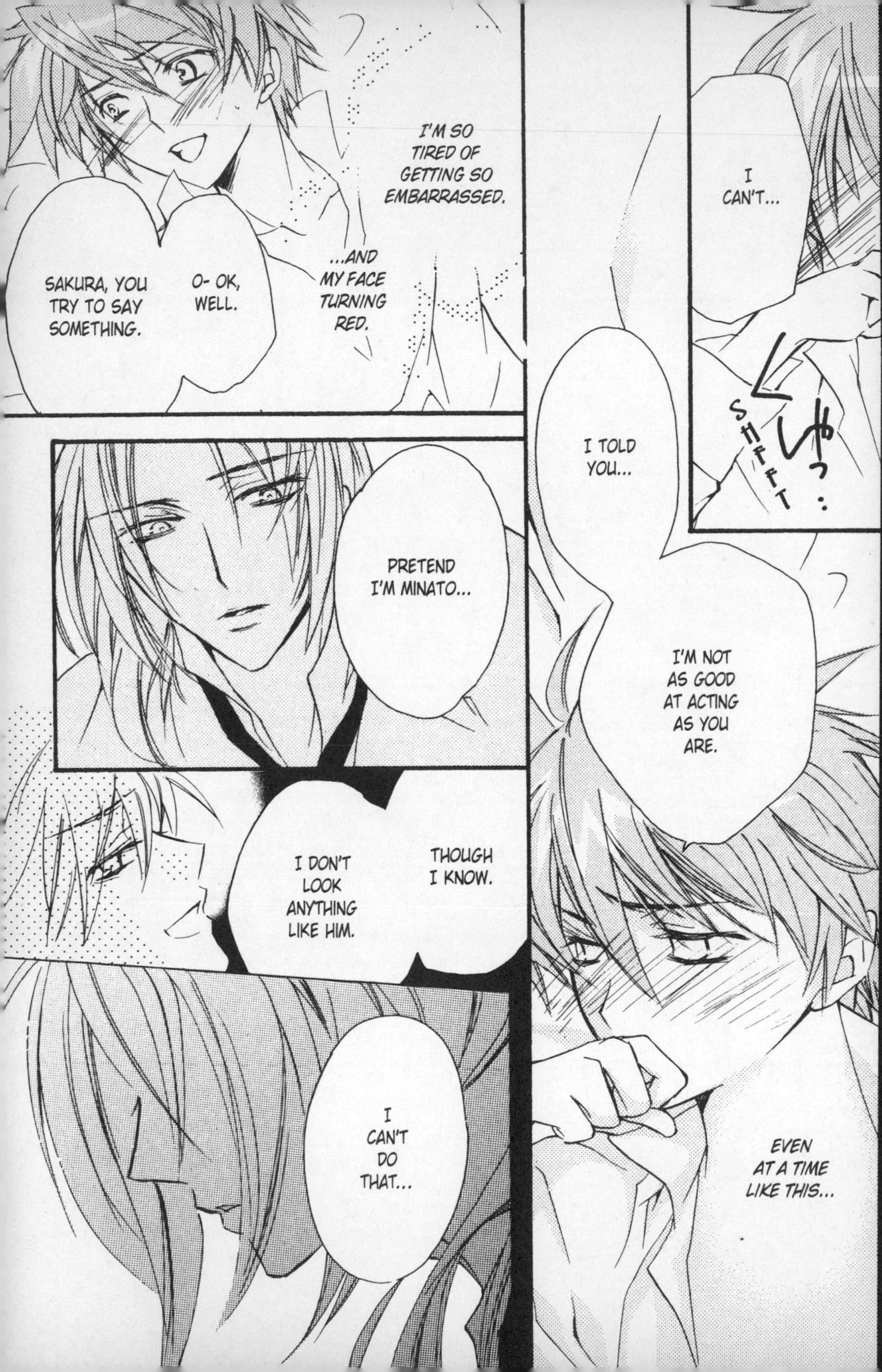
I CAN'T...
しゅっ
SHFFT
I TOLD YOU...
I'M NOT AS GOOD AT ACTING AS YOU ARE.
EVEN AT A TIME LIKE THIS...
I'M SO TIRED OF GETTING SO EMBARRASSED.
...AND MY FACE TURNING RED.
O- OK, WELL.
SAKURA, YOU TRY TO SAY SOMETHING.
PRETEND I'M MINATO...
THOUGH I KNOW.
I DON'T LOOK ANYTHING LIKE HIM.
I CAN'T DO THAT...

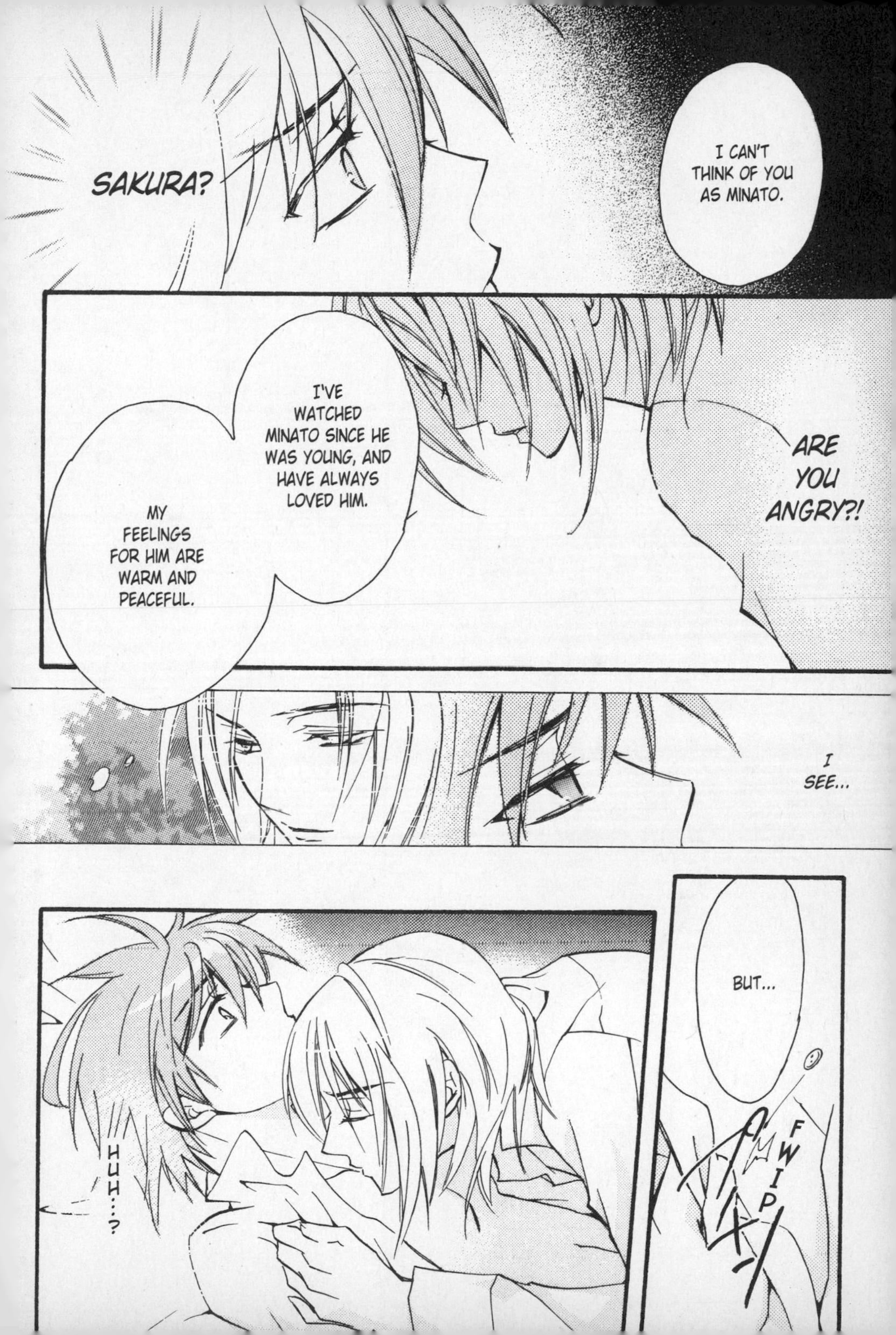
I CAN'T THINK OF YOU AS MINATO.
SAKURA?
ARE YOU ANGRY?!
I'VE WATCHED MINATO SINCE HE WAS YOUNG, AND HAVE ALWAYS LOVED HIM.
MY FEELINGS FOR HIM ARE WARM AND PEACEFUL.
I SEE...
BUT...
FWIP
HUH...?

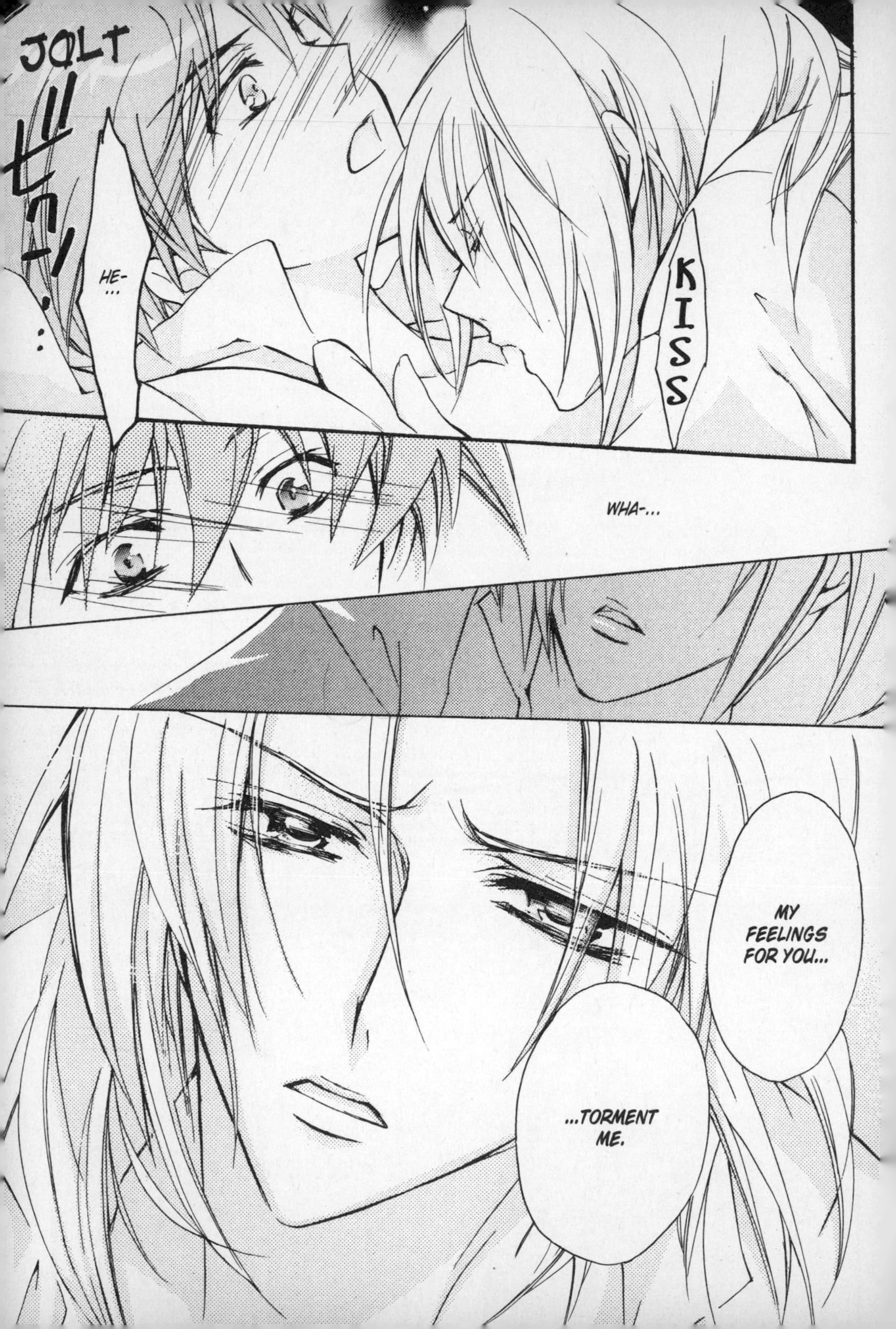
KISS
HE-...
JOLT
WHA-...
MY FEELINGS FOR YOU...
...TORMENT ME.

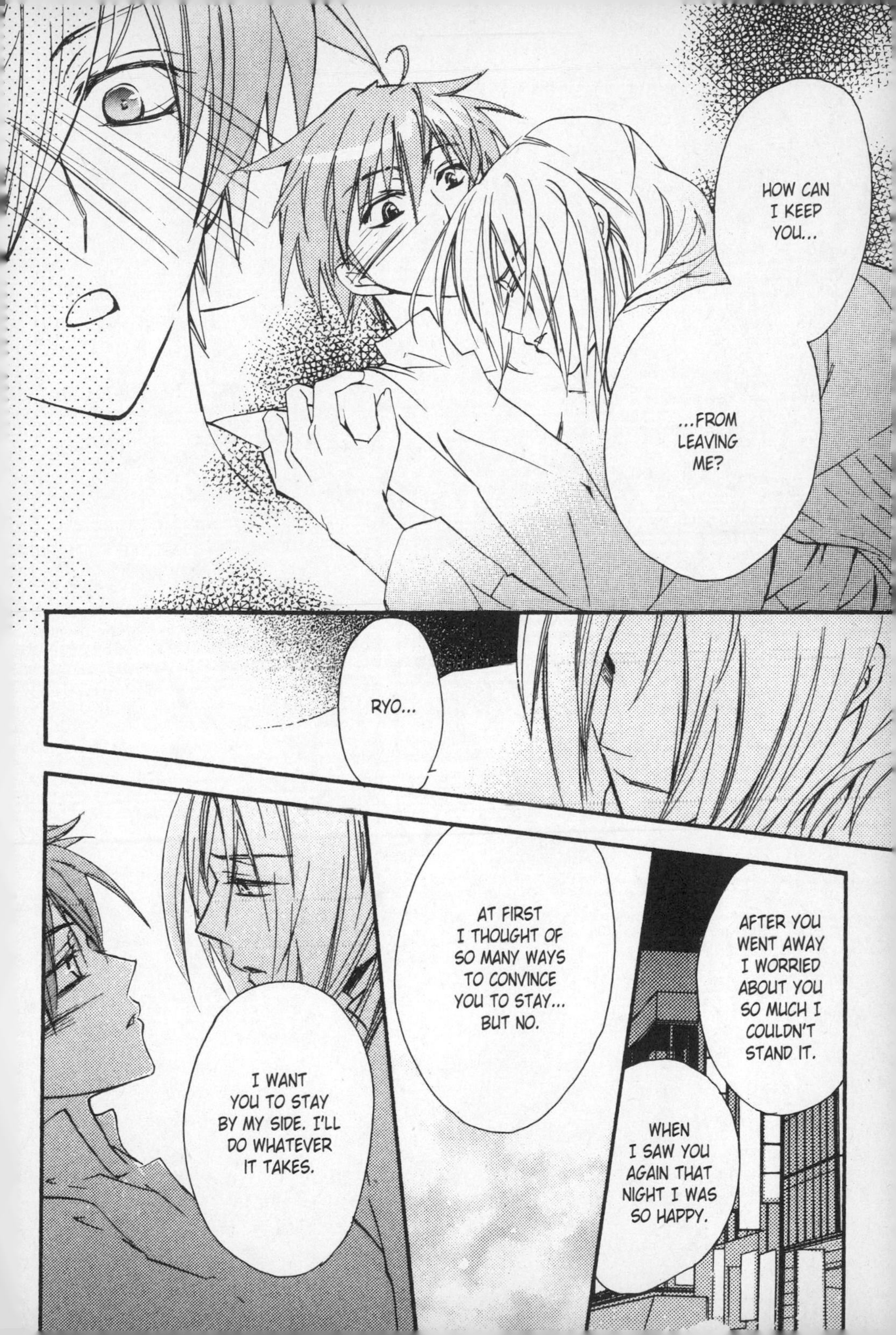
HOW CAN I KEEP YOU...
...FROM LEAVING ME?
RYO...
AFTER YOU WENT AWAY I WORRIED ABOUT YOU SO MUCH I COULDN'T STAND IT.
WHEN I SAW YOU AGAIN THAT NIGHT I WAS SO HAPPY.
AT FIRST I THOUGHT OF SO MANY WAYS TO CONVINCE YOU TO STAY... BUT NO.
I WANT YOU TO STAY BY MY SIDE. I'LL DO WHATEVER IT TAKES.

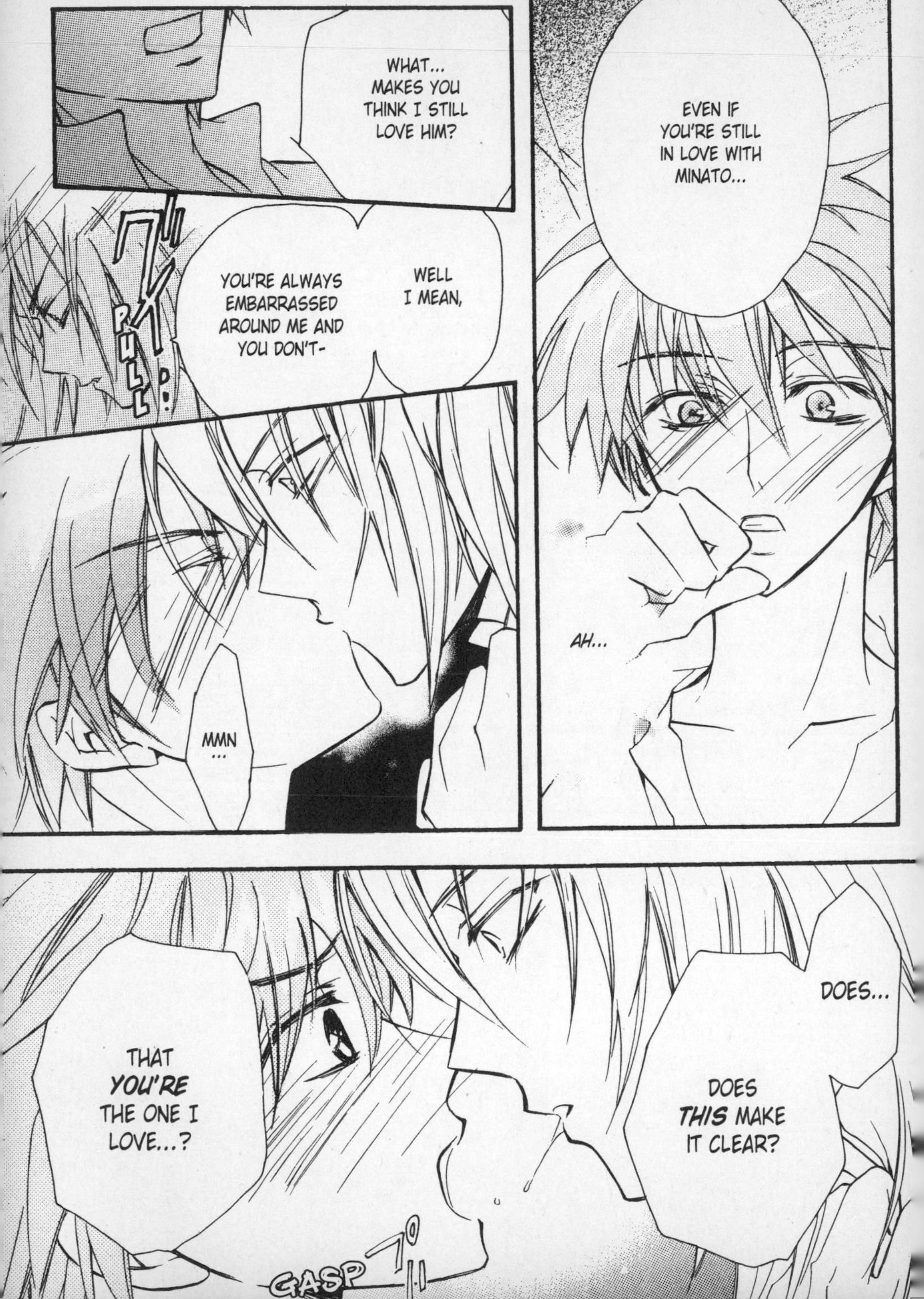
EVEN IF YOU'RE STILL IN LOVE WITH MINATO...
AH...
WHAT... MAKES YOU THINK I STILL LOVE HIM?
WELL I MEAN,
YOU'RE ALWAYS EMBARRASSED AROUND ME AND YOU DON'T-
PULL
MMN ...
DOES...
DOES THIS MAKE IT CLEAR?
THAT YOU'RE THE ONE I LOVE...?
GASP

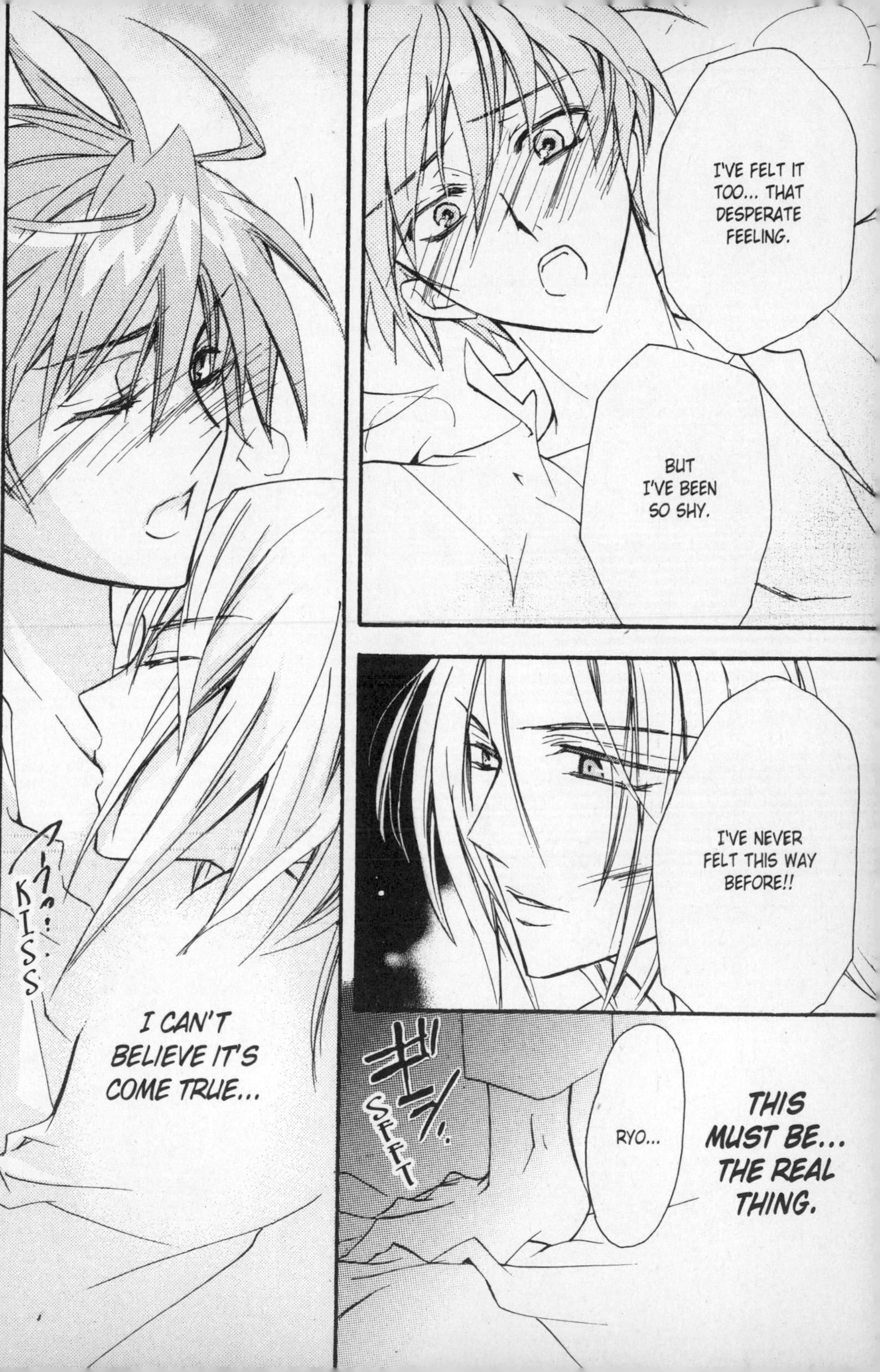
I'VE FELT IT TOO... THAT DESPERATE FEELING.
BUT I'VE BEEN SO SHY.
I'VE NEVER FELT THIS WAY BEFORE!!
THIS MUST BE... THE REAL THING.
RYO...
SFFT
KISS
I CAN'T BELIEVE IT'S COME TRUE...

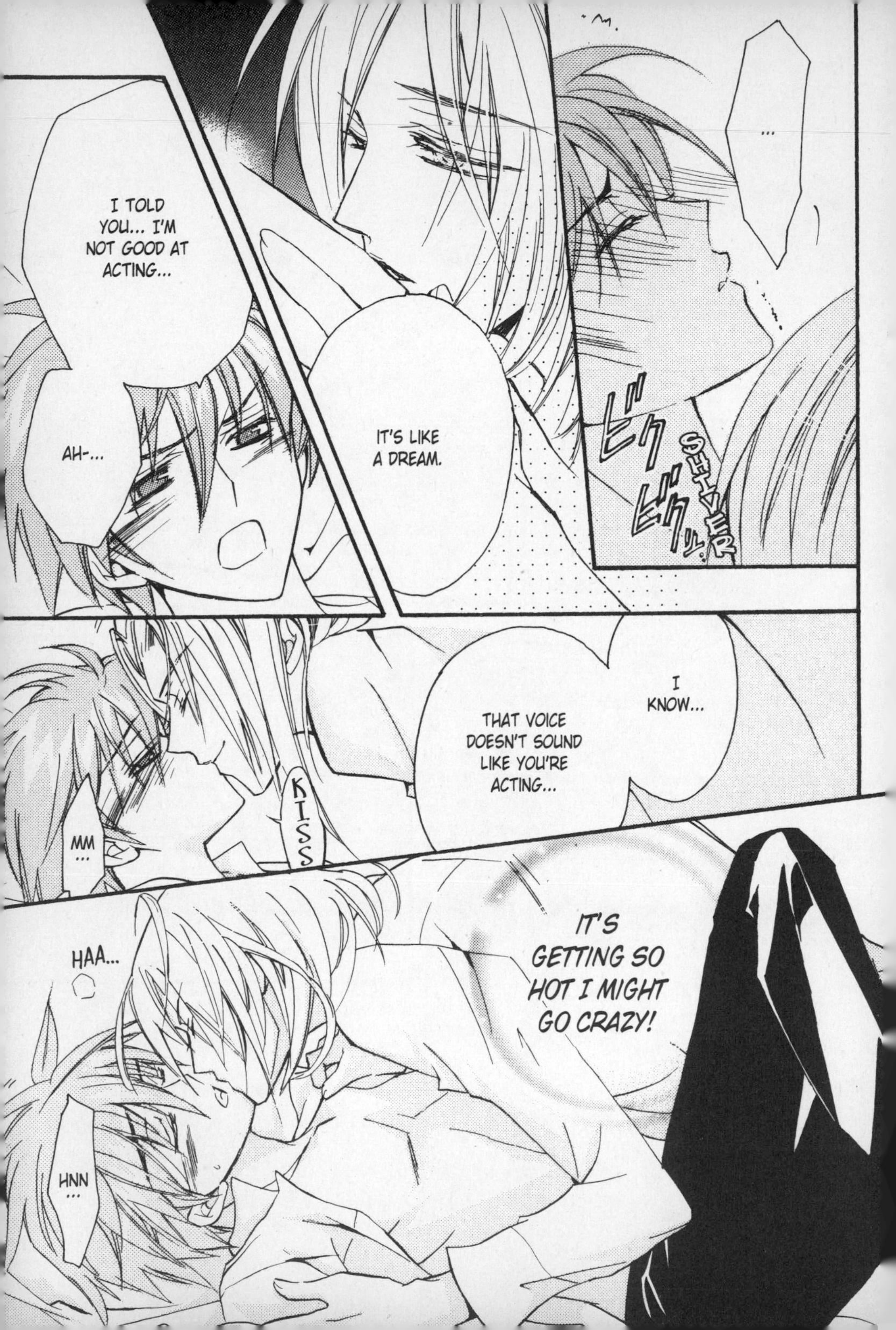
...
ビク
ビクッ
SHIVER
IT'S LIKE A DREAM.
I TOLD YOU... I'M NOT GOOD AT ACTING...
AH-...
I KNOW...
THAT VOICE DOESN'T SOUND LIKE YOU'RE ACTING...
KISS
MM ...
IT'S GETTING SO HOT I MIGHT GO CRAZY!
HAA...
HNN ...

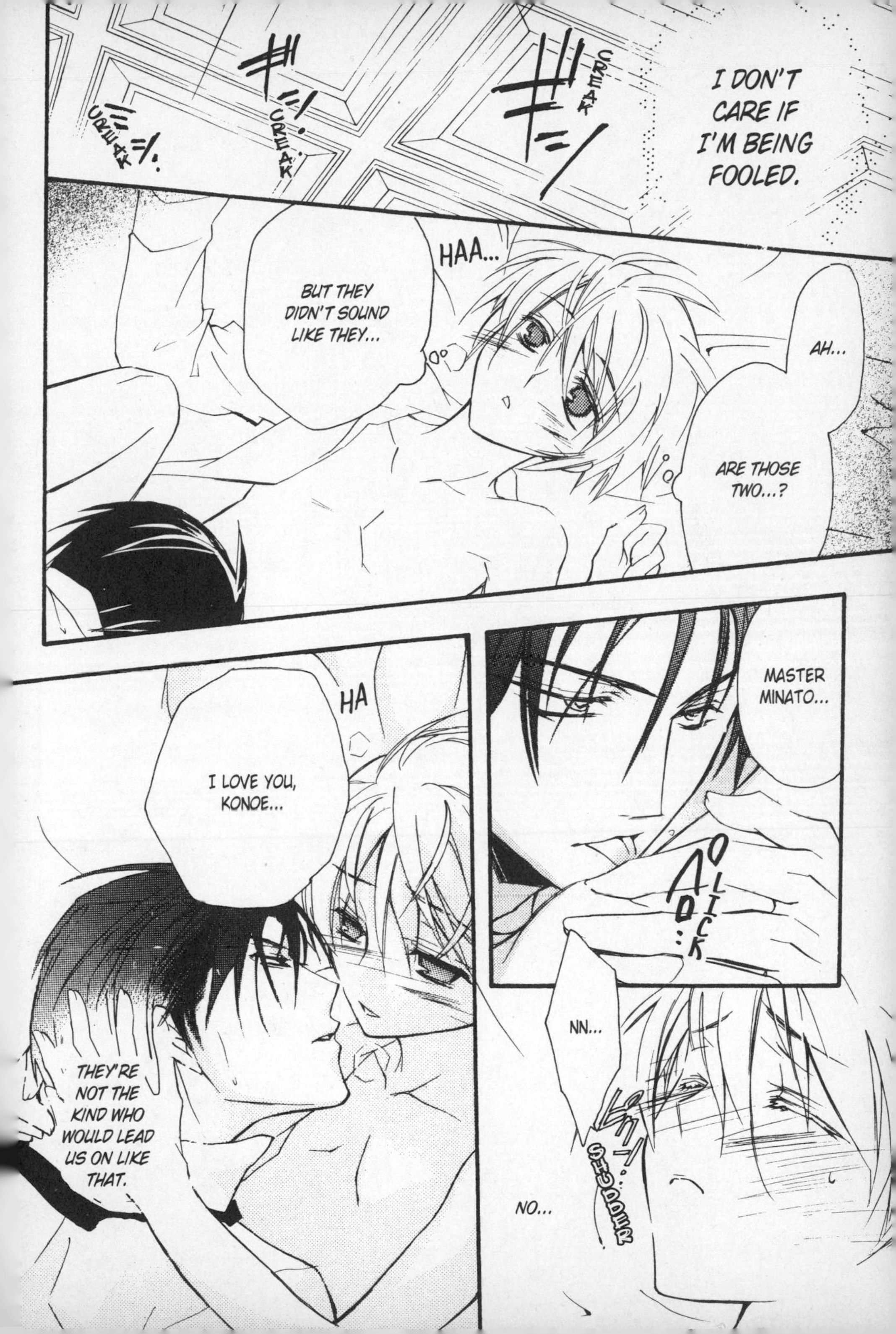
I DON'T CARE IF I'M BEING FOOLED.
CREAK
CREAK
CREAK
AH...
ARE THOSE TWO...?
HAA...
BUT THEY DIDN'T SOUND LIKE THEY...
MASTER MINATO...
LICK
NN...
SHUDDER
NO...
HA
I LOVE YOU, KONOE...
THEY'RE NOT THE KIND WHO WOULD LEAD US ON LIKE THAT.

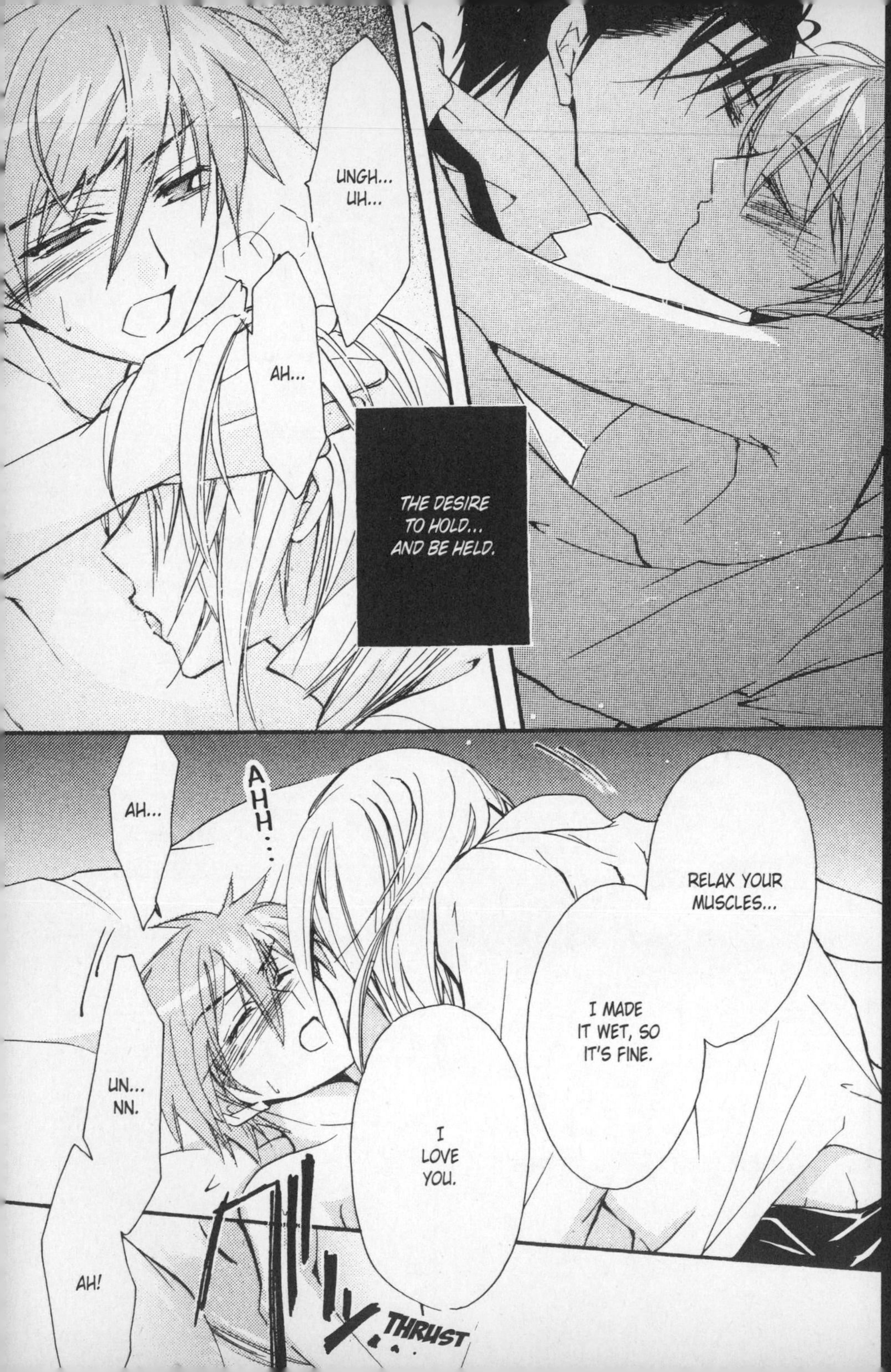
UNGH... UH...
AH...
THE DESIRE TO HOLD... AND BE HELD.
RELAX YOUR MUSCLES...
I MADE IT WET, SO IT'S FINE.
AHH...
AH...
I LOVE YOU.
UN... NN.
THRUST
AH!

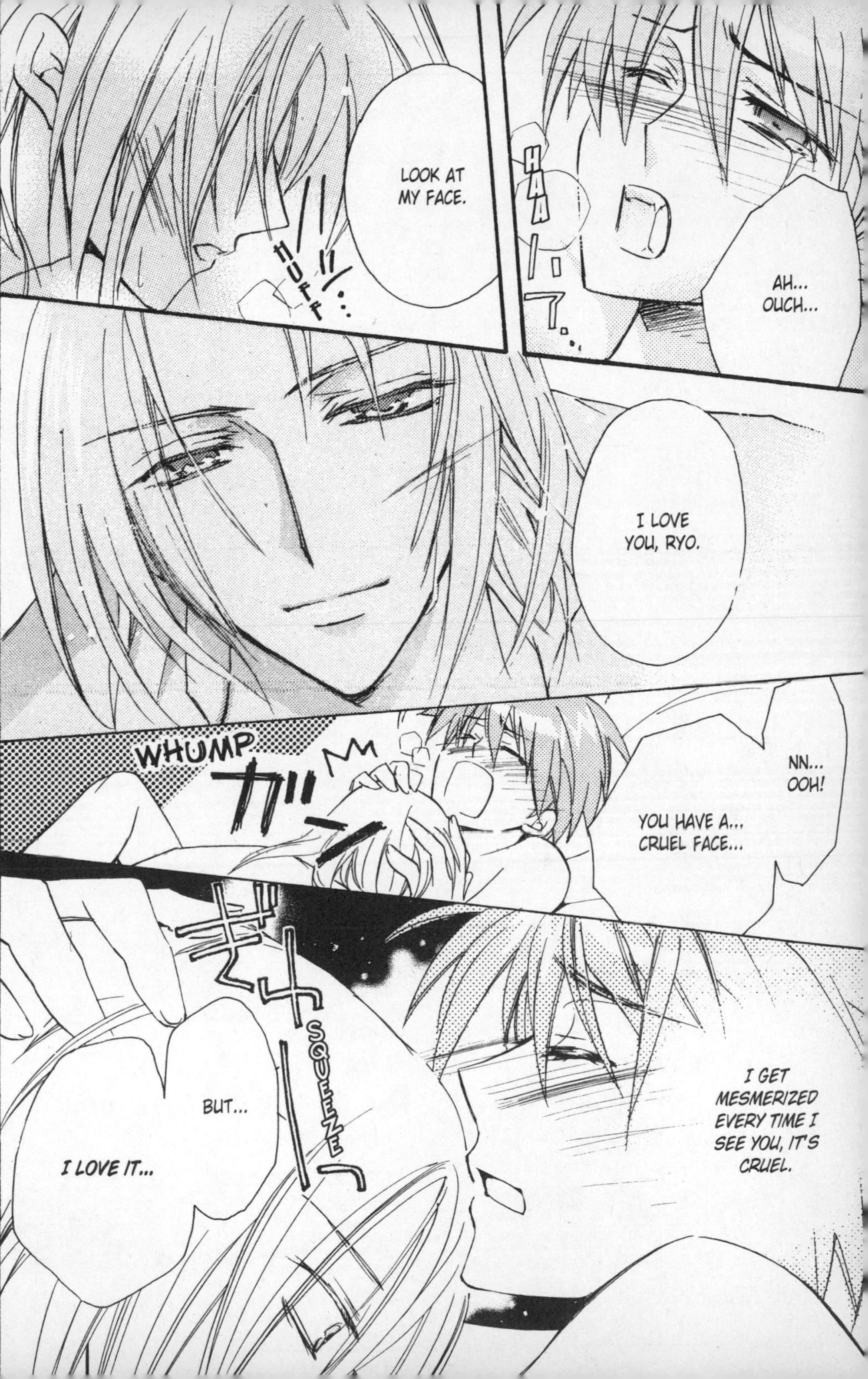
HAA...
AH... OUCH...
LOOK AT MY FACE.
HUFF...
I LOVE YOU, RYO.
NN... OOH!
YOU HAVE A... CRUEL FACE...
WHUMP
I GET MESMERIZED EVERY TIME I SEE YOU, IT'S CRUEL.
SQUEEZE
BUT...
I LOVE IT...

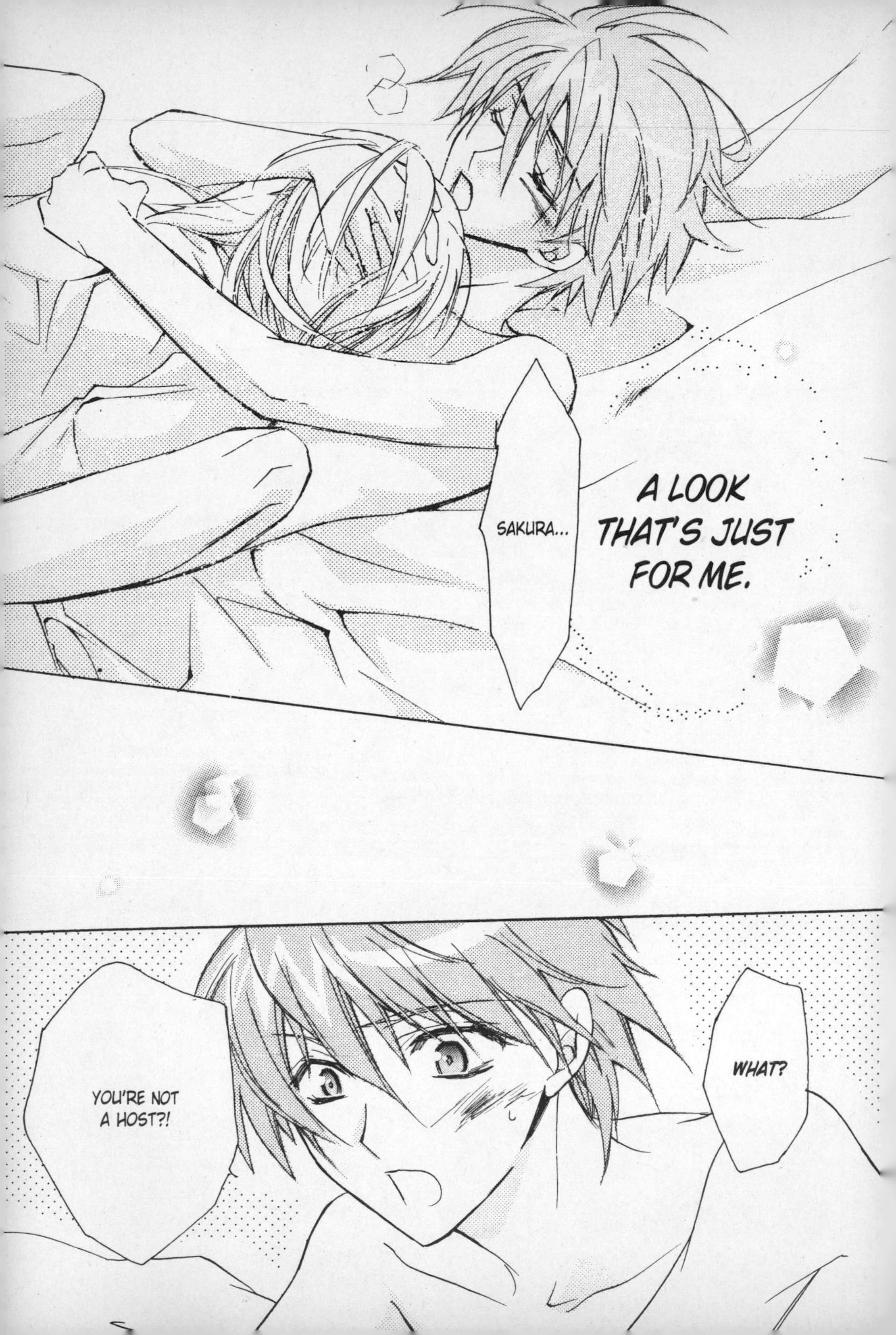
A LOOK THAT'S JUST FOR ME.
SAKURA...
WHAT?
YOU'RE NOT A HOST?!

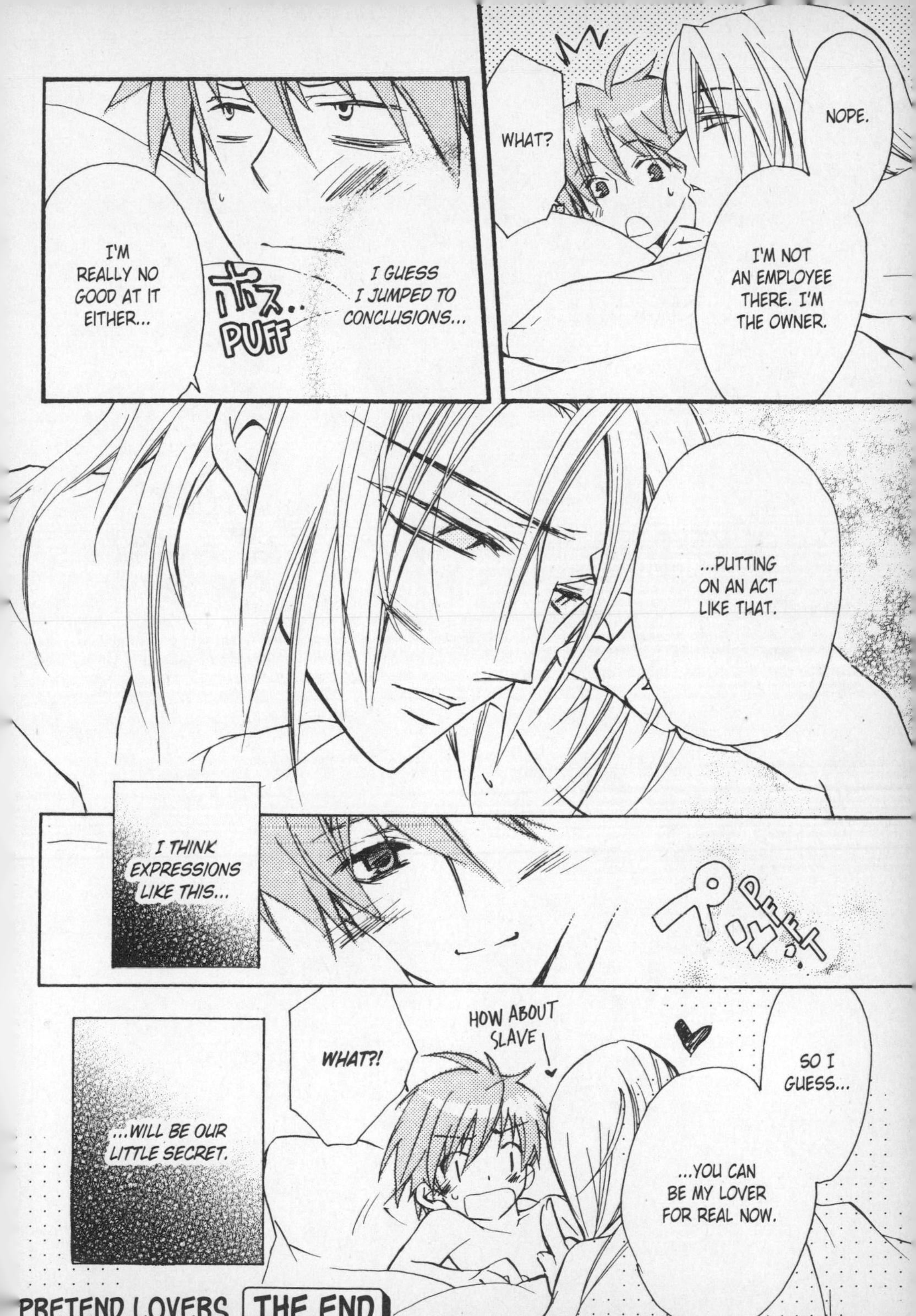
NOPE.
WHAT?
I'M NOT AN EMPLOYEE THERE. I'M THE OWNER.
I GUESS I JUMPED TO CONCLUSIONS...
ポス.. PUFF
I'M REALLY NO GOOD AT IT EITHER...
...PUTTING ON AN ACT LIKE THAT.
ペ PEEK
I THINK EXPRESSIONS LIKE THIS...
SO I GUESS...
...YOU CAN BE MY LOVER FOR REAL NOW.
HOW ABOUT SLAVE
WHAT?!
...WILL BE OUR LITTLE SECRET.

PRETEND LOVERS THE END

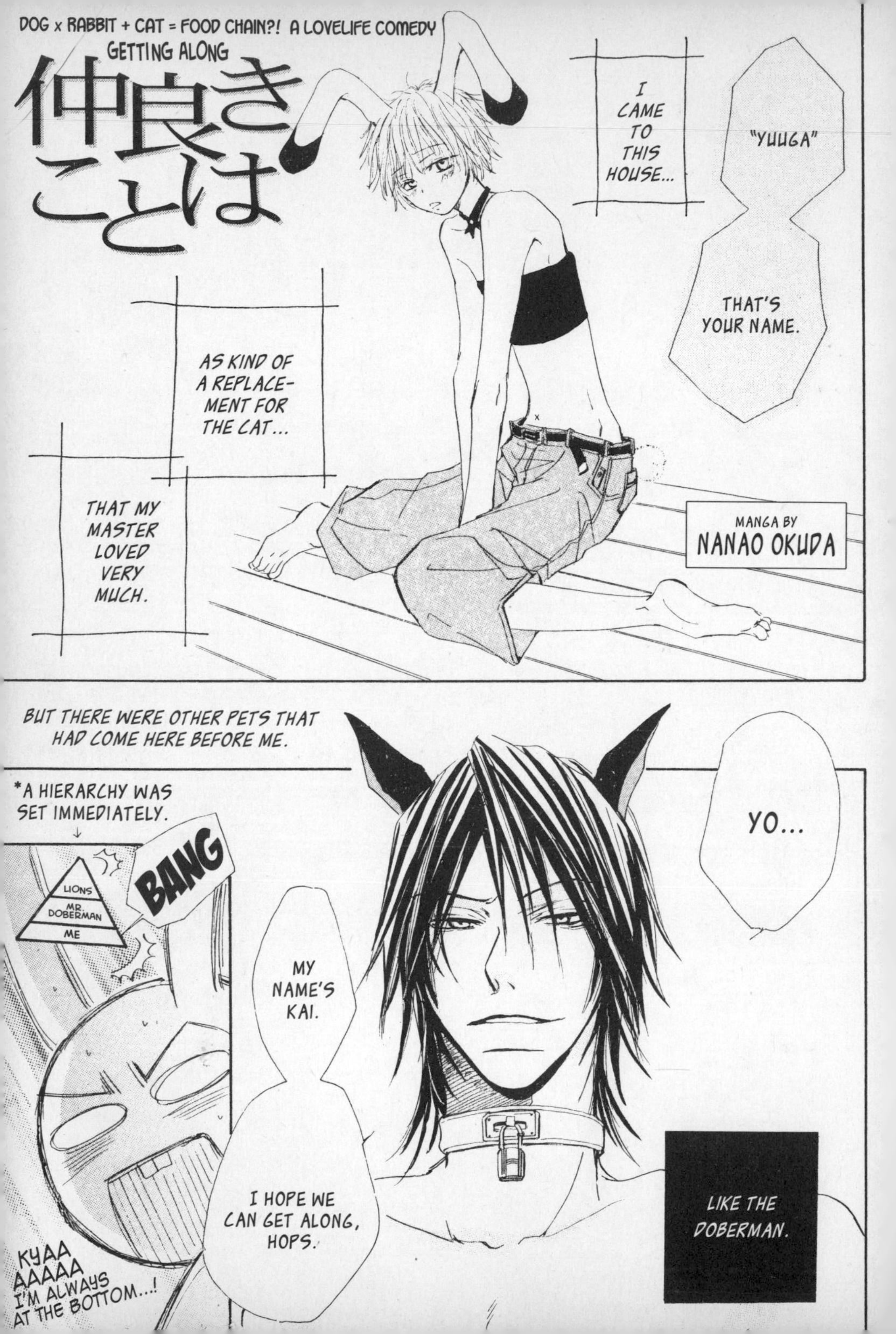
DOG x RABBIT + CAT = FOOD CHAIN?! A LOVELIFE COMEDY
GETTING ALONG
仲良きことは
"YUUGA"
THAT'S YOUR NAME.
I CAME TO THIS HOUSE...
AS KIND OF A REPLACEMENT FOR THE CAT...
THAT MY MASTER LOVED VERY MUCH.
MANGA BY NANAO OKUDA
BUT THERE WERE OTHER PETS THAT HAD COME HERE BEFORE ME.
YO...
MY NAME'S KAI.
I HOPE WE CAN GET ALONG, HOPS.
LIKE THE DOBERMAN.
*A HIERARCHY WAS SET IMMEDIATELY.
LIONS
MR. DOBERMAN
ME
BANG
KYAA AAAAA I'M ALWAYS AT THE BOTTOM...!

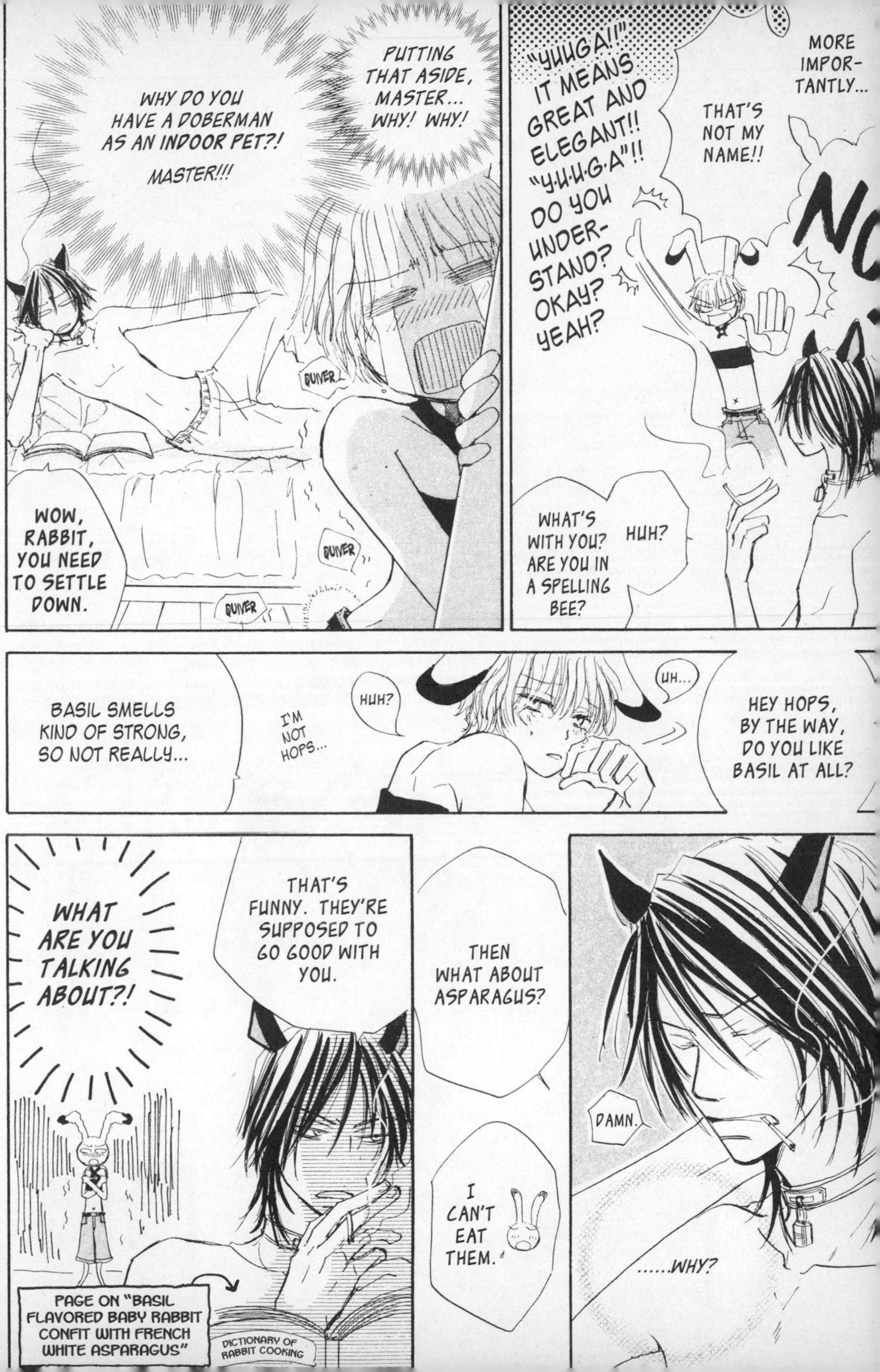
MORE IMPOR-TANTLY...
NO
THAT'S NOT MY NAME!!
"YUUGA!!" IT MEANS GREAT AND ELEGANT!! "Y·U·U·G·A"!! DO YOU UNDER-STAND? OKAY? YEAH?
HUH?
WHAT'S WITH YOU? ARE YOU IN A SPELLING BEE?
PUTTING THAT ASIDE, MASTER... WHY! WHY!
WHY DO YOU HAVE A DOBERMAN AS AN INDOOR PET?!
MASTER!!!
QUIVER
QUIVER
QUIVER
WOW, RABBIT, YOU NEED TO SETTLE DOWN.
HEY HOPS, BY THE WAY, DO YOU LIKE BASIL AT ALL?
UH...
HUH?
I'M NOT HOPS...
BASIL SMELLS KIND OF STRONG, SO NOT REALLY...
DAMN.
......WHY?
THEN WHAT ABOUT ASPARAGUS?
I CAN'T EAT THEM.
THAT'S FUNNY. THEY'RE SUPPOSED TO GO GOOD WITH YOU.
WHAT ARE YOU TALKING ABOUT?!
PAGE ON "BASIL FLAVORED BABY RABBIT CONFIT WITH FRENCH WHITE ASPARAGUS"
DICTIONARY OF RABBIT COOKING

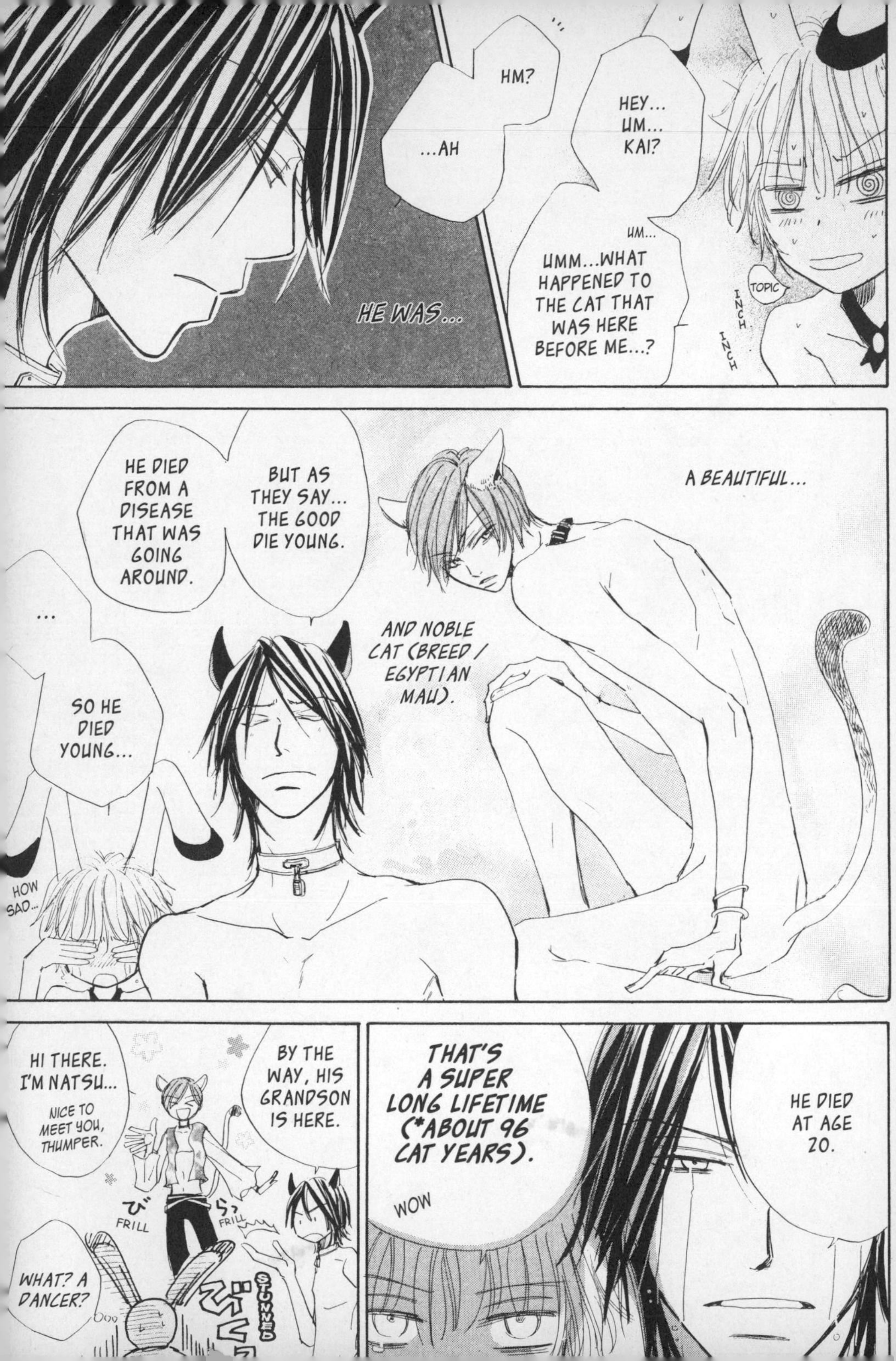
HEY... UM... KAI?
UM...
UMM...WHAT HAPPENED TO THE CAT THAT WAS HERE BEFORE ME...?
TOPIC
INCH
INCH
HM?
...AH
HE WAS...
A BEAUTIFUL...
AND NOBLE CAT (BREED / EGYPTIAN MAU).
BUT AS THEY SAY... THE GOOD DIE YOUNG.
HE DIED FROM A DISEASE THAT WAS GOING AROUND.
...
SO HE DIED YOUNG...
HOW SAD...
HE DIED AT AGE 20.
THAT'S A SUPER LONG LIFETIME (*ABOUT 96 CAT YEARS).
WOW
BY THE WAY, HIS GRANDSON IS HERE.
HI THERE. I'M NATSU...
NICE TO MEET YOU, THUMPER.
FRILL
FRILL
WHAT? A DANCER?
STUNNED

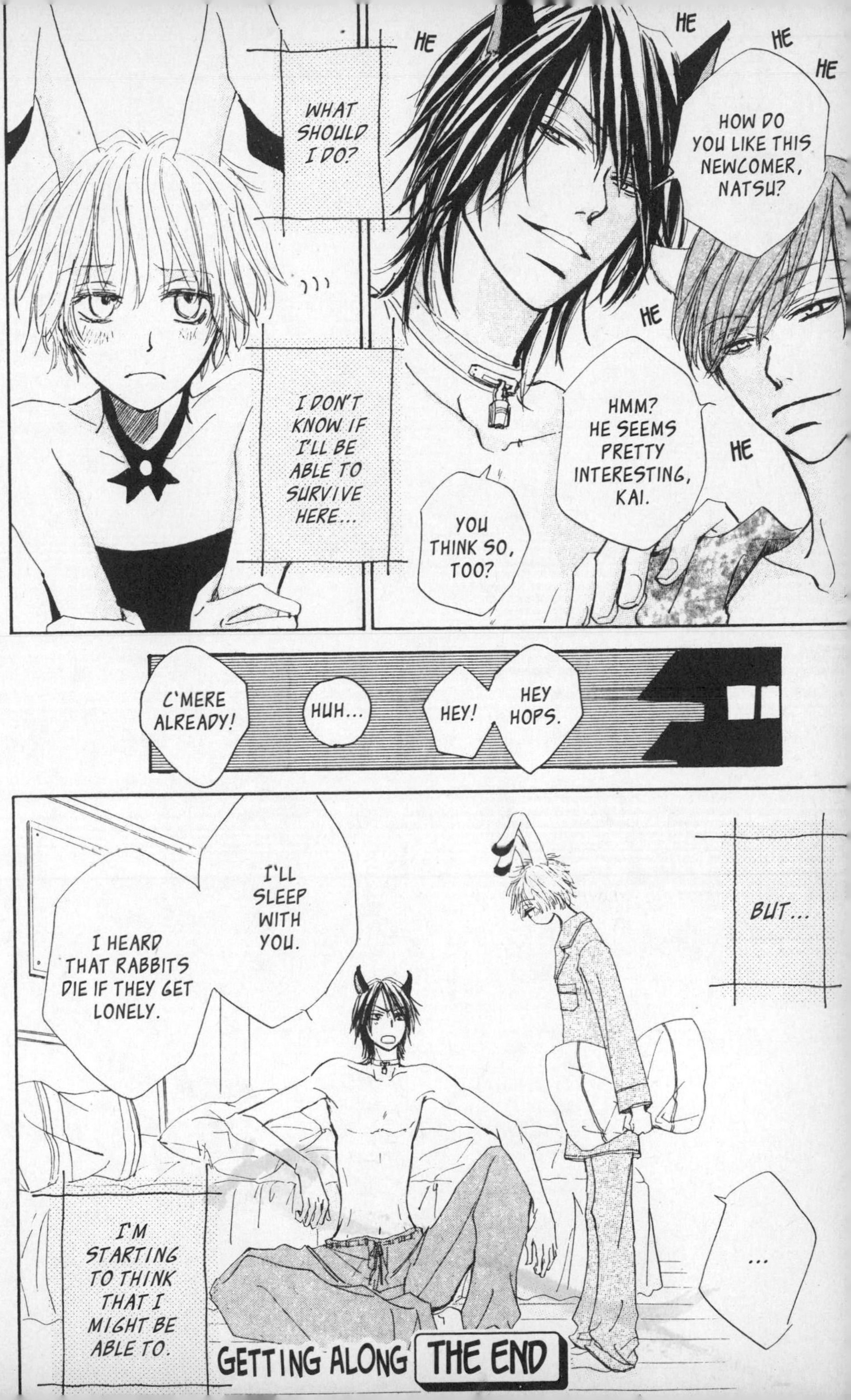
HE
HE
HE
HE
HOW DO YOU LIKE THIS NEWCOMER, NATSU?
HE
HMM? HE SEEMS PRETTY INTERESTING, KAI.
HE
YOU THINK SO, TOO?
WHAT SHOULD I DO?
I DON'T KNOW IF I'LL BE ABLE TO SURVIVE HERE...
HEY HOPS.
HEY!
HUH...
C'MERE ALREADY!
BUT...
...
I'LL SLEEP WITH YOU.
I HEARD THAT RABBITS DIE IF THEY GET LONELY.
I'M STARTING TO THINK THAT I MIGHT BE ABLE TO.
GETTING ALONG THE END

WE HAVE A HERO IN OUR HEARTS

月本てらこ

MANGA BY TERAKO TSUKIMOTO

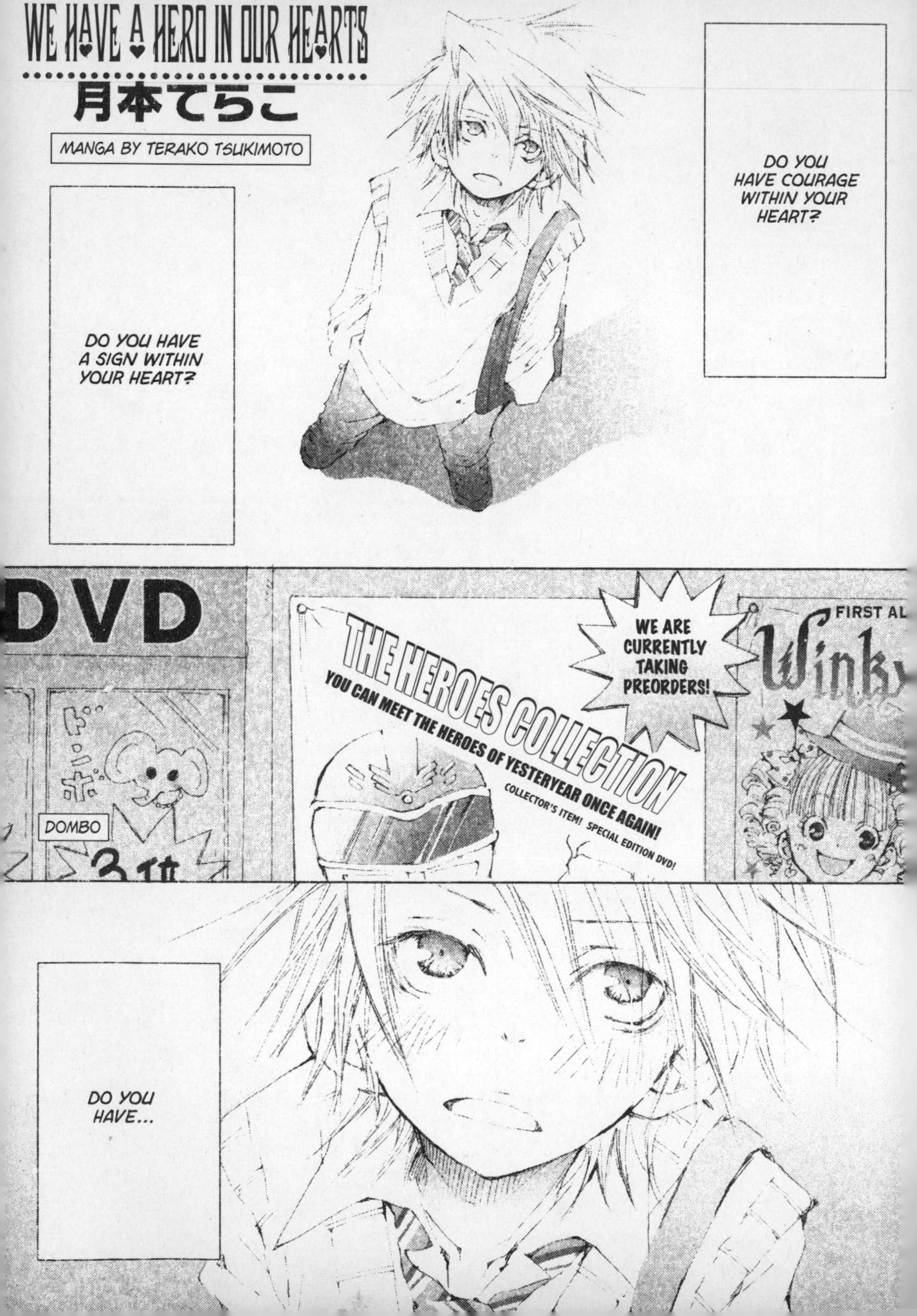
DO YOU HAVE COURAGE WITHIN YOUR HEART?
DO YOU HAVE A SIGN WITHIN YOUR HEART?
FIRST AL
Winky
WE ARE CURRENTLY TAKING PREORDERS!
THE HEROES COLLECTION
YOU CAN MEET THE HEROES OF YESTERYEAR ONCE AGAIN!
COLLECTOR'S ITEM! SPECIAL EDITION DVD!
DVD
DOMBO
DO YOU HAVE...

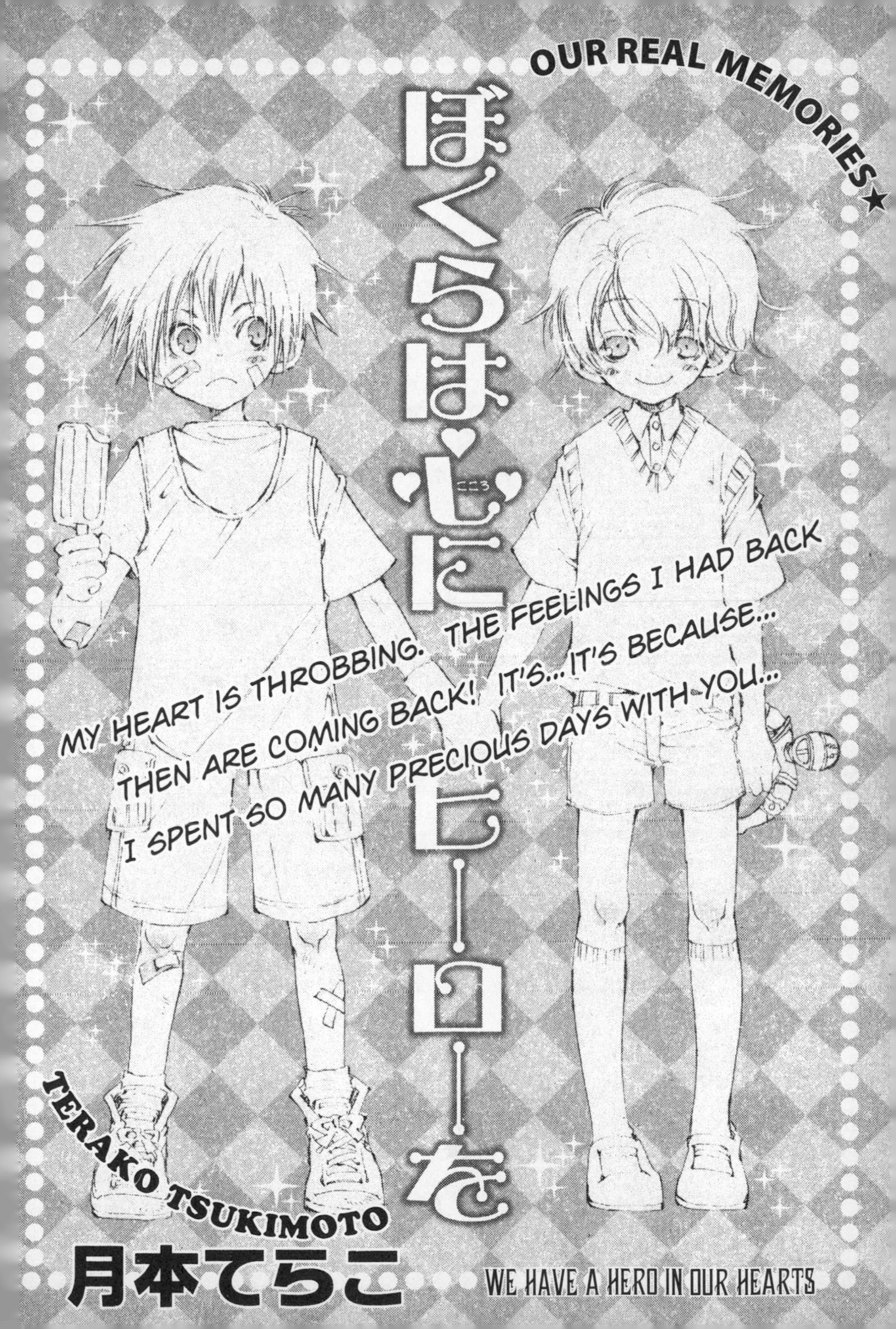
OUR REAL MEMORIES★
ぼくらは心にヒーローを
こころ
MY HEART IS THROBBING. THE FEELINGS I HAD BACK THEN ARE COMING BACK! IT'S... IT'S BECAUSE... I SPENT SO MANY PRECIOUS DAYS WITH YOU...
TERAKO TSUKIMOTO
月本てらこ
WE HAVE A HERO IN OUR HEARTS

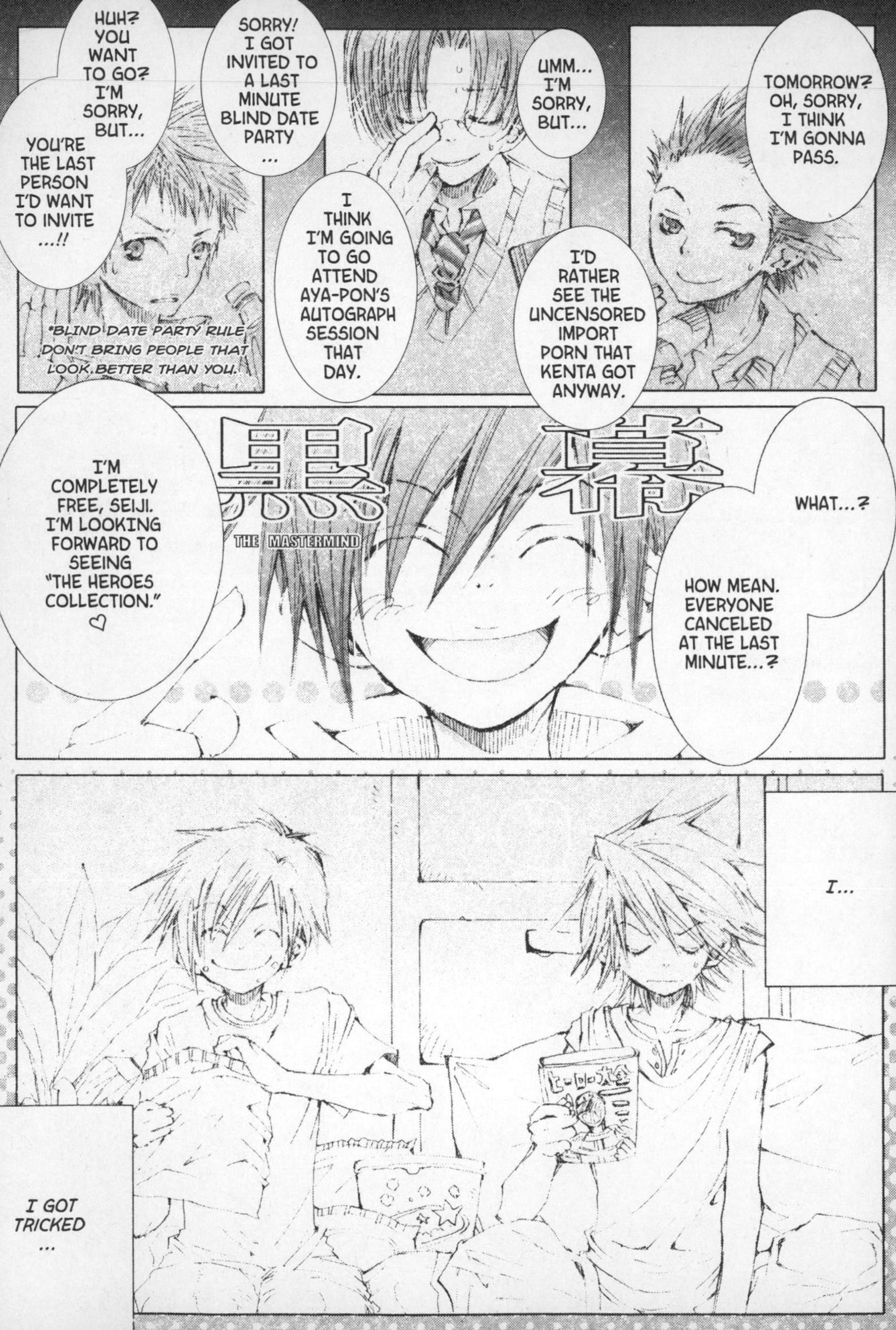
TOMORROW? OH, SORRY, I THINK I'M GONNA PASS.
I'D RATHER SEE THE UNCENSORED IMPORT PORN THAT KENTA GOT ANYWAY.
UMM... I'M SORRY, BUT...
I THINK I'M GOING TO GO ATTEND AYA-PON'S AUTOGRAPH SESSION THAT DAY.
SORRY! I GOT INVITED TO A LAST MINUTE BLIND DATE PARTY ...
HUH? YOU WANT TO GO? I'M SORRY, BUT...
YOU'RE THE LAST PERSON I'D WANT TO INVITE ...!!
*BLIND DATE PARTY RULE: DON'T BRING PEOPLE THAT LOOK BETTER THAN YOU.
WHAT...?
HOW MEAN. EVERYONE CANCELED AT THE LAST MINUTE...?
黒幕
THE MASTERMIND
I'M COMPLETELY FREE, SEIJI. I'M LOOKING FORWARD TO SEEING "THE HEROES COLLECTION." ♡
I...
I GOT TRICKED ...

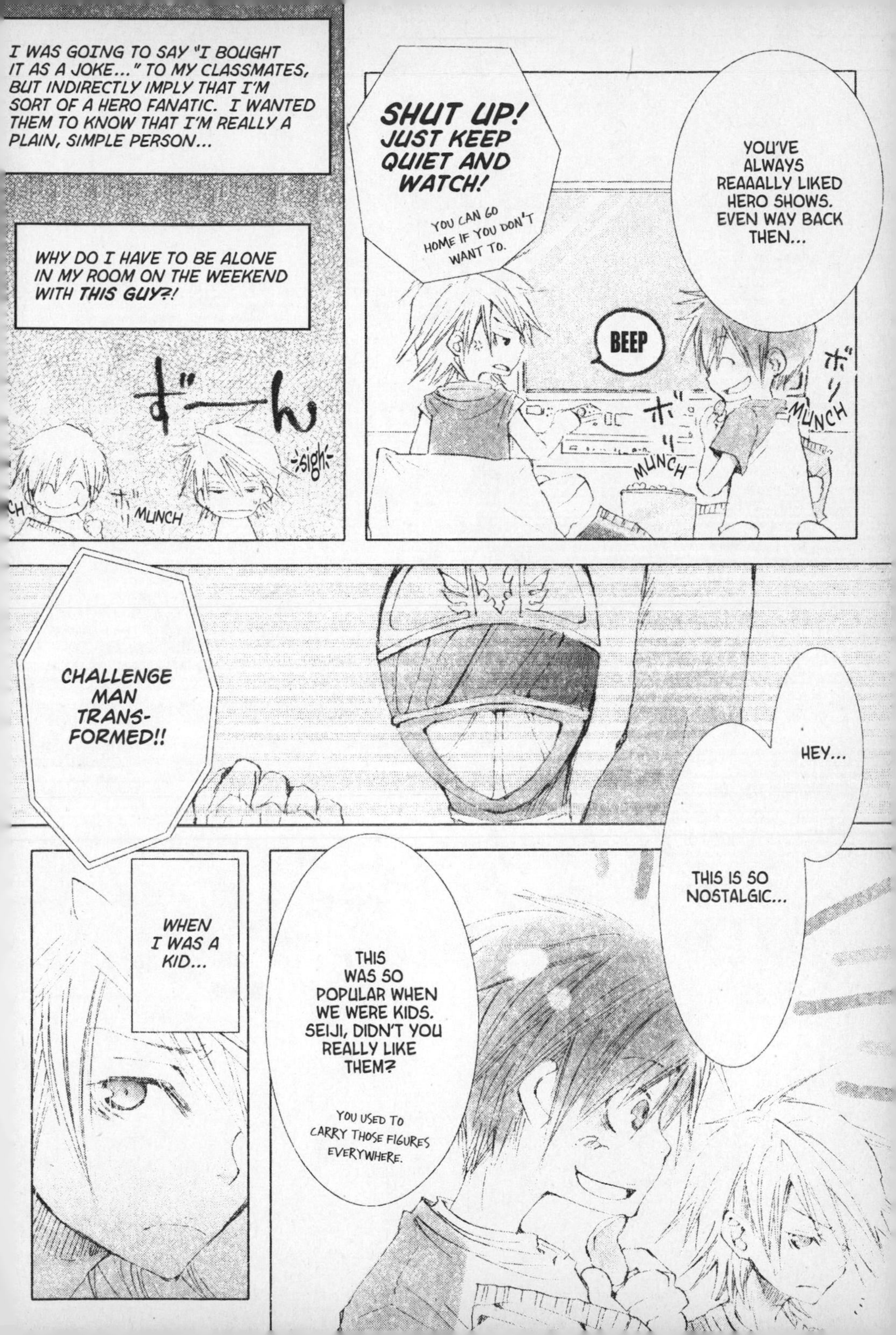

YOU'VE ALWAYS REAAALLY LIKED HERO SHOWS. EVEN WAY BACK THEN...
SHUT UP! JUST KEEP QUIET AND WATCH!
YOU CAN GO HOME IF YOU DON'T WANT TO.
BEEP
ボリ
MUNCH
ボリ
MUNCH
I WAS GOING TO SAY "I BOUGHT IT AS A JOKE..." TO MY CLASSMATES, BUT INDIRECTLY IMPLY THAT I'M SORT OF A HERO FANATIC. I WANTED THEM TO KNOW THAT I'M REALLY A PLAIN, SIMPLE PERSON...
WHY DO I HAVE TO BE ALONE IN MY ROOM ON THE WEEKEND WITH THIS GUY?!
ずーん
-sigh-
MUNCH
CHALLENGE MAN TRANS-FORMED!!
HEY...
THIS IS SO NOSTALGIC...
THIS WAS SO POPULAR WHEN WE WERE KIDS. SEIJI, DIDN'T YOU REALLY LIKE THEM?
YOU USED TO CARRY THOSE FIGURES EVERYWHERE.
WHEN I WAS A KID...

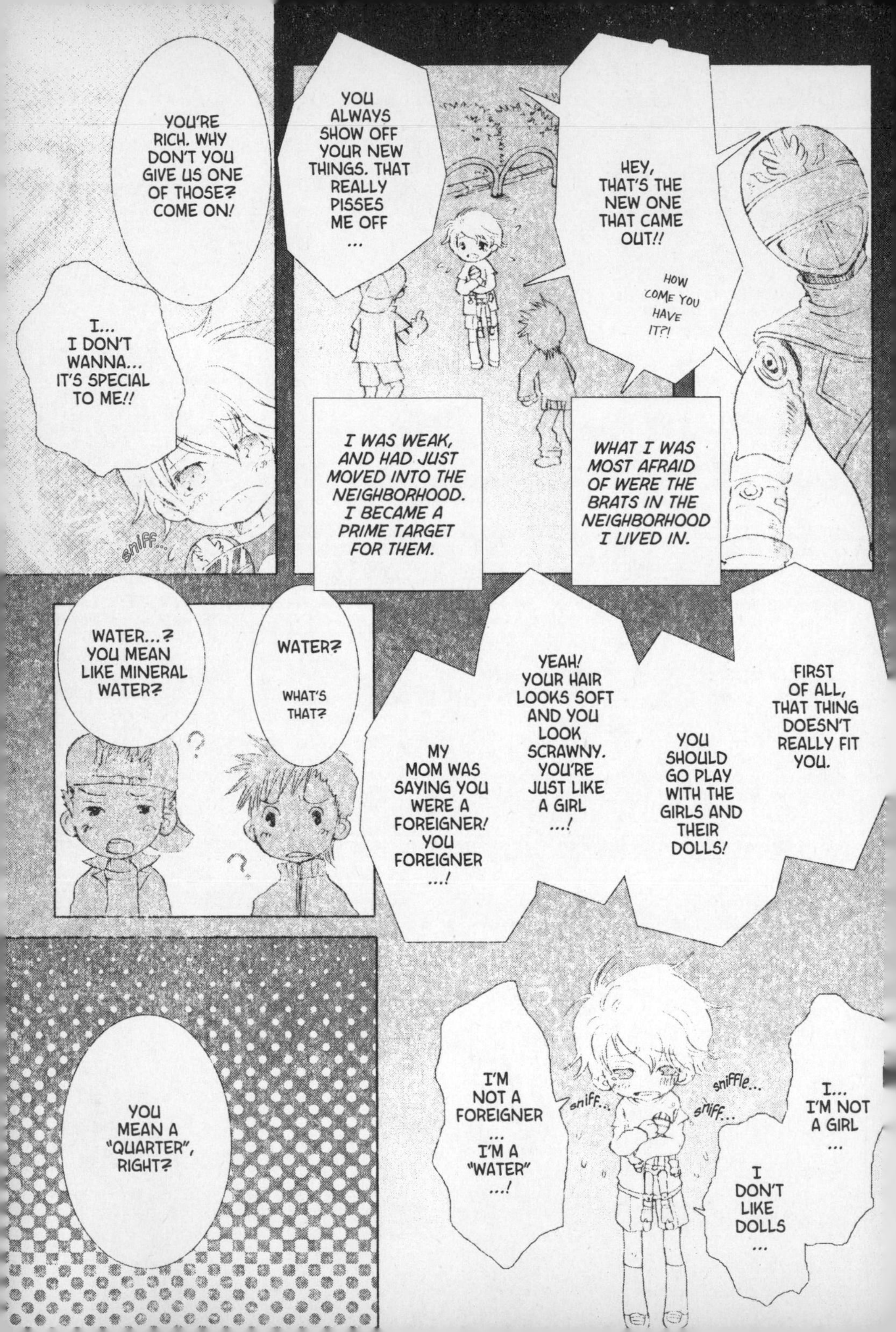
HEY, THAT'S THE NEW ONE THAT CAME OUT!!
HOW COME YOU HAVE IT?!
WHAT I WAS MOST AFRAID OF WERE THE BRATS IN THE NEIGHBORHOOD I LIVED IN.
YOU ALWAYS SHOW OFF YOUR NEW THINGS. THAT REALLY PISSES ME OFF ...
I WAS WEAK, AND HAD JUST MOVED INTO THE NEIGHBORHOOD. I BECAME A PRIME TARGET FOR THEM.
YOU'RE RICH. WHY DON'T YOU GIVE US ONE OF THOSE? COME ON!
I... I DON'T WANNA... IT'S SPECIAL TO ME!!
sniff...
FIRST OF ALL, THAT THING DOESN'T REALLY FIT YOU.
YOU SHOULD GO PLAY WITH THE GIRLS AND THEIR DOLLS!
YEAH! YOUR HAIR LOOKS SOFT AND YOU LOOK SCRAWNY. YOU'RE JUST LIKE A GIRL ...!
MY MOM WAS SAYING YOU WERE A FOREIGNER! YOU FOREIGNER ...!
WATER?
WHAT'S THAT?
WATER...? YOU MEAN LIKE MINERAL WATER?
I... I'M NOT A GIRL ...
I DON'T LIKE DOLLS ...
sniffle...
sniff...
sniff...
I'M NOT A FOREIGNER ... I'M A "WATER" ...!
YOU MEAN A "QUARTER", RIGHT?

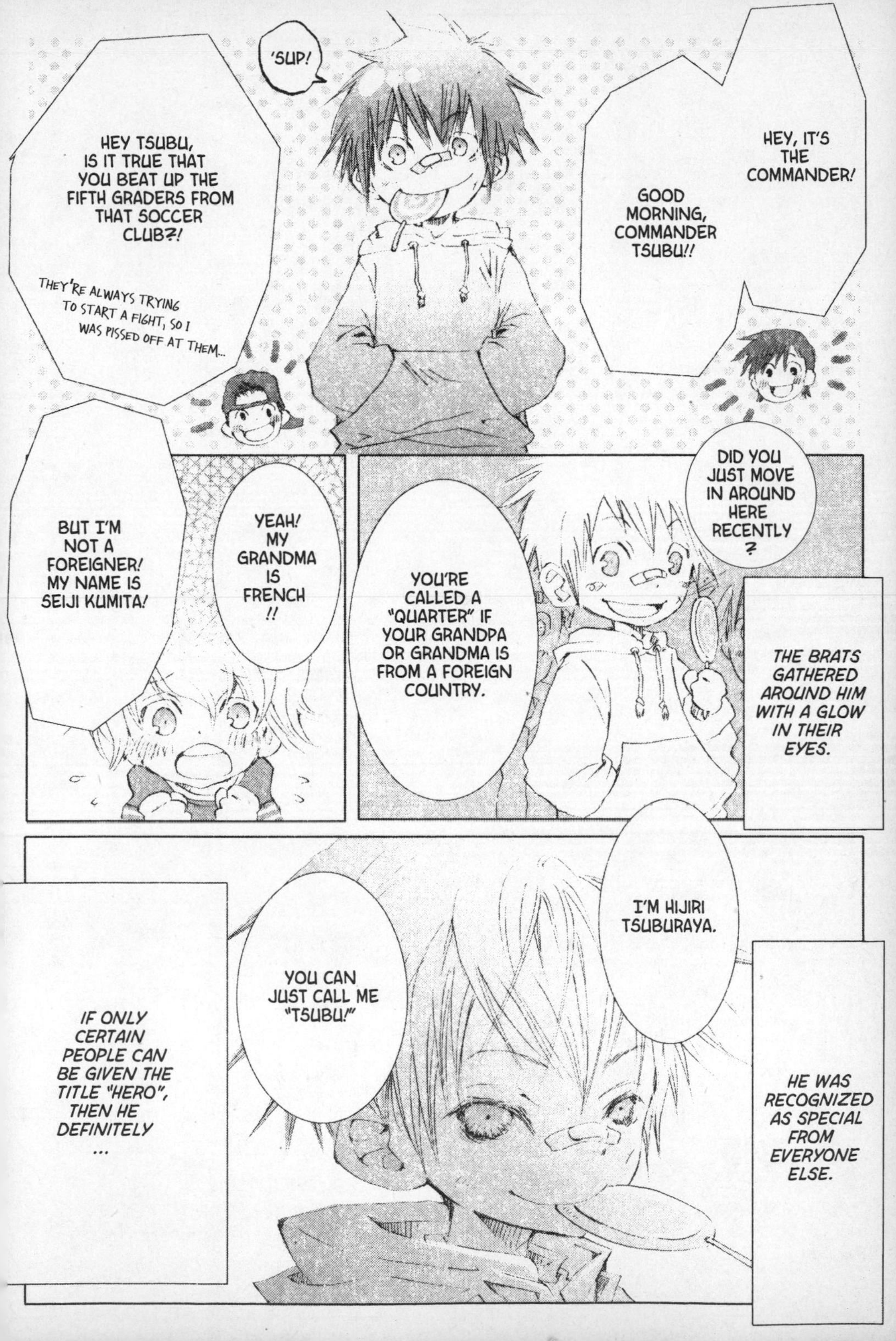
HEY, IT'S THE COMMANDER!
GOOD MORNING, COMMANDER TSUBU!!
'SUP!
HEY TSUBU, IS IT TRUE THAT YOU BEAT UP THE FIFTH GRADERS FROM THAT SOCCER CLUB?!
THEY'RE ALWAYS TRYING TO START A FIGHT, SO I WAS PISSED OFF AT THEM...
THE BRATS GATHERED AROUND HIM WITH A GLOW IN THEIR EYES.
DID YOU JUST MOVE IN AROUND HERE RECENTLY?
YOU'RE CALLED A "QUARTER" IF YOUR GRANDPA OR GRANDMA IS FROM A FOREIGN COUNTRY.
YEAH! MY GRANDMA IS FRENCH!!
BUT I'M NOT A FOREIGNER! MY NAME IS SEIJI KUMITA!
HE WAS RECOGNIZED AS SPECIAL FROM EVERYONE ELSE.
I'M HIJIRI TSUBURAYA.
YOU CAN JUST CALL ME "TSUBU!"
IF ONLY CERTAIN PEOPLE CAN BE GIVEN THE TITLE "HERO", THEN HE DEFINITELY ...

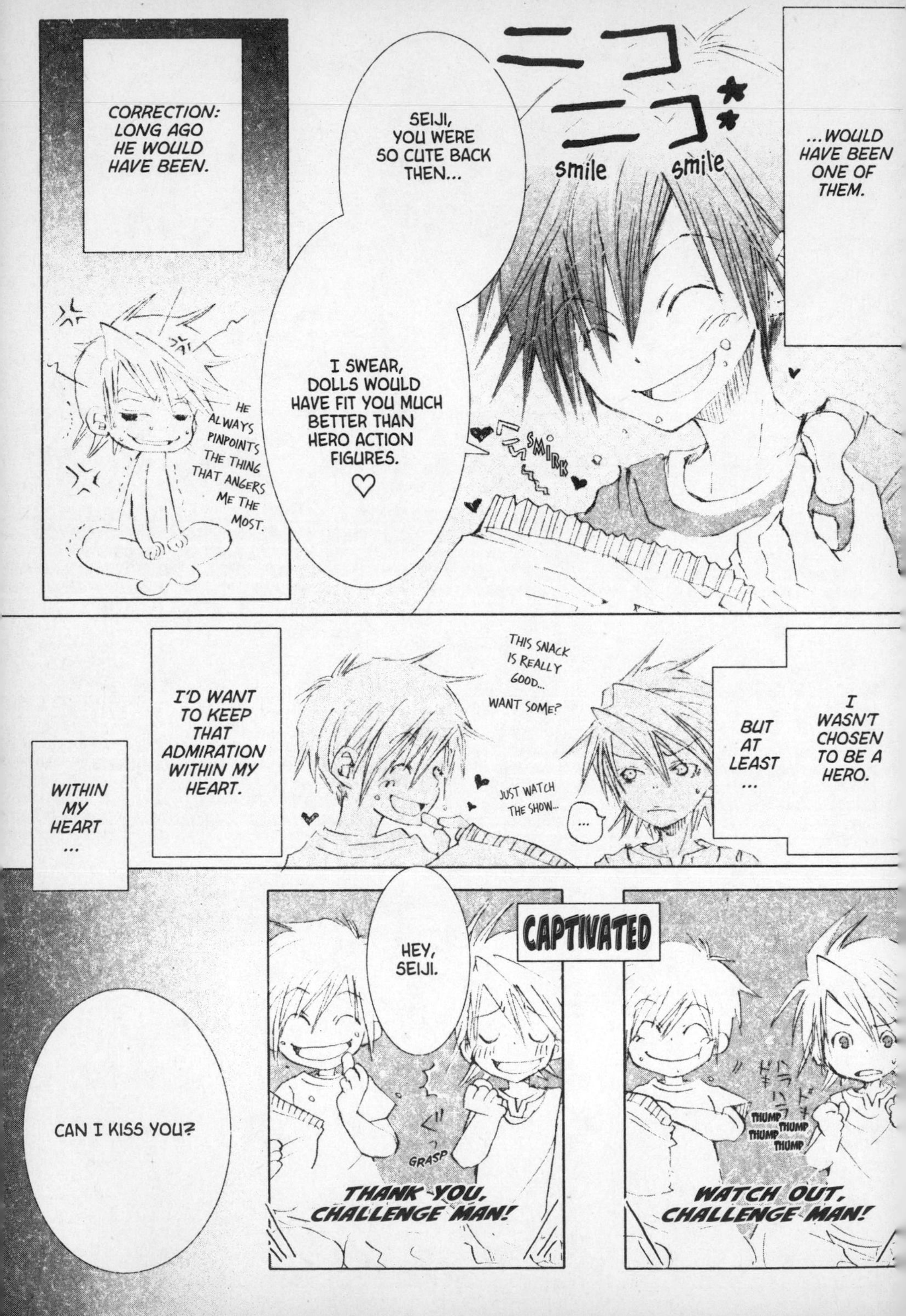
...WOULD HAVE BEEN ONE OF THEM.
smile smile
SEIJI, YOU WERE SO CUTE BACK THEN...
I SWEAR, DOLLS WOULD HAVE FIT YOU MUCH BETTER THAN HERO ACTION FIGURES. ♡
SMIRK
CORRECTION: LONG AGO HE WOULD HAVE BEEN.
HE ALWAYS PINPOINTS THE THING THAT ANGERS ME THE MOST.
I WASN'T CHOSEN TO BE A HERO.
BUT AT LEAST ...
THIS SNACK IS REALLY GOOD... WANT SOME?
...
JUST WATCH THE SHOW...
I'D WANT TO KEEP THAT ADMIRATION WITHIN MY HEART.
WITHIN MY HEART ...
CAPTIVATED
THUMP THUMP THUMP THUMP
WATCH OUT, CHALLENGE MAN!
HEY, SEIJI.
GRASP
THANK YOU, CHALLENGE MAN!
CAN I KISS YOU?

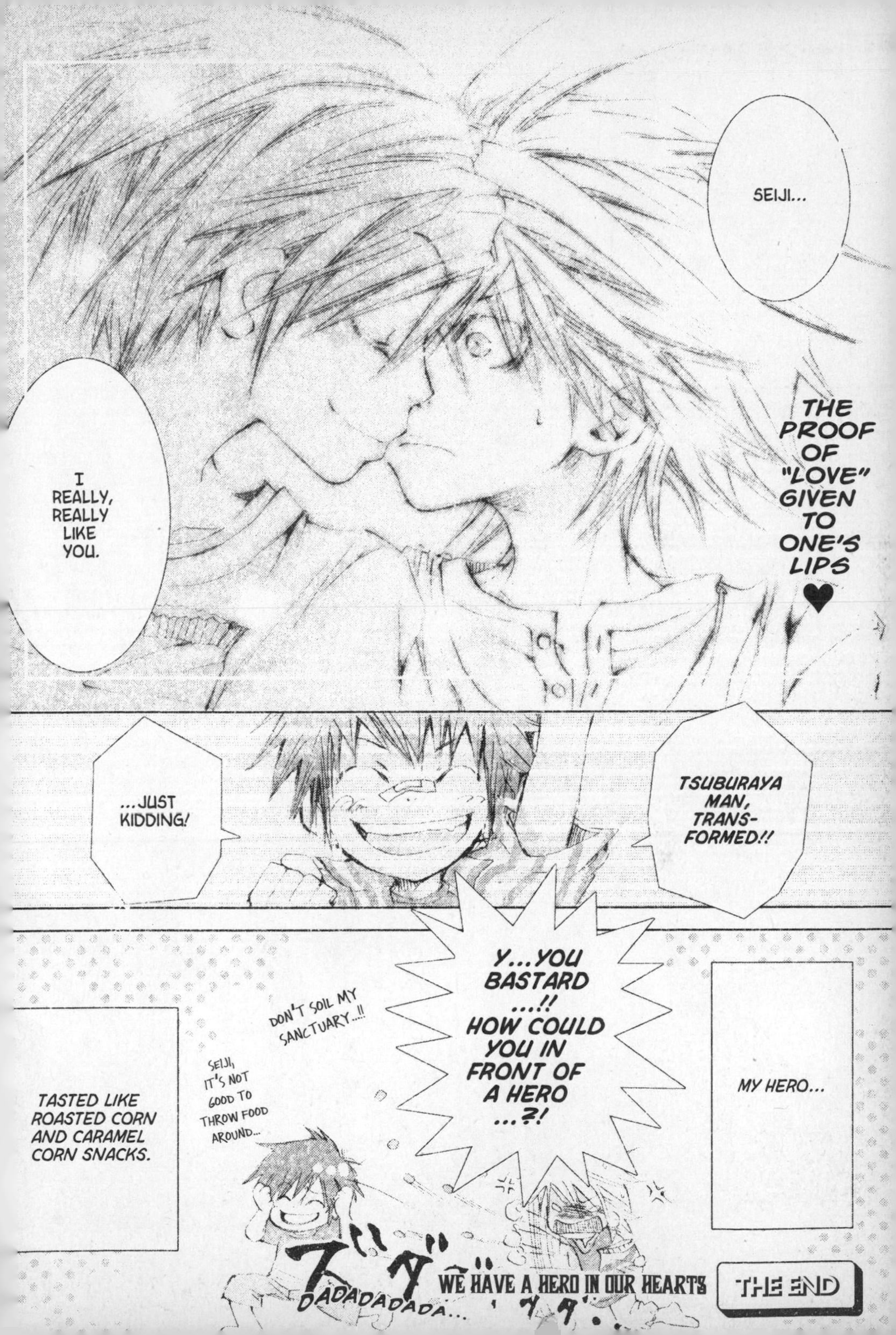
SEIJI...
THE PROOF OF "LOVE" GIVEN TO ONE'S LIPS ♥
I REALLY, REALLY LIKE YOU.
TSUBURAYA MAN, TRANS-FORMED!!
...JUST KIDDING!
MY HERO...
Y...YOU BASTARD ...!! HOW COULD YOU IN FRONT OF A HERO ...?!
DON'T SOIL MY SANCTUARY...!!
SEIJI, IT'S NOT GOOD TO THROW FOOD AROUND...
TASTED LIKE ROASTED CORN AND CARAMEL CORN SNACKS.
DADADADADADA...
WE HAVE A HERO IN OUR HEARTS
THE END

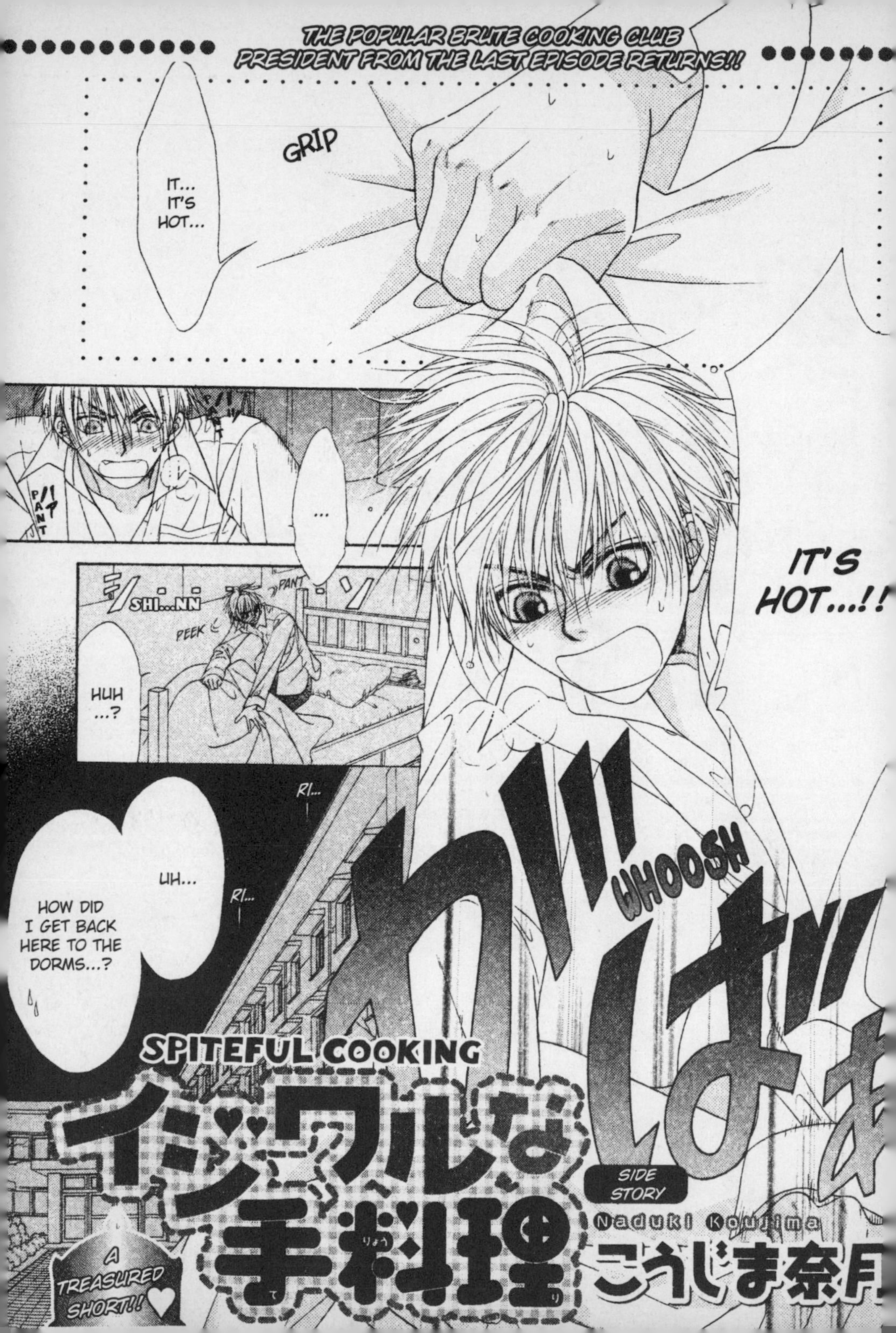

THE POPULAR BRUTE COOKING CLUB PRESIDENT FROM THE LAST EPISODE RETURNS!!
GRIP
IT... IT'S HOT...
IT'S HOT...!!
!!
PANT
...
SHI...NN
PANT
PEEK
HUH ...?
RI...
UH...
RI...
HOW DID I GET BACK HERE TO THE DORMS...?
WHOOSH
SPITEFUL COOKING
イジワルな手料理
SIDE STORY
Naduki Koujima
こうじま奈月
A TREASURED SHORT!!♥

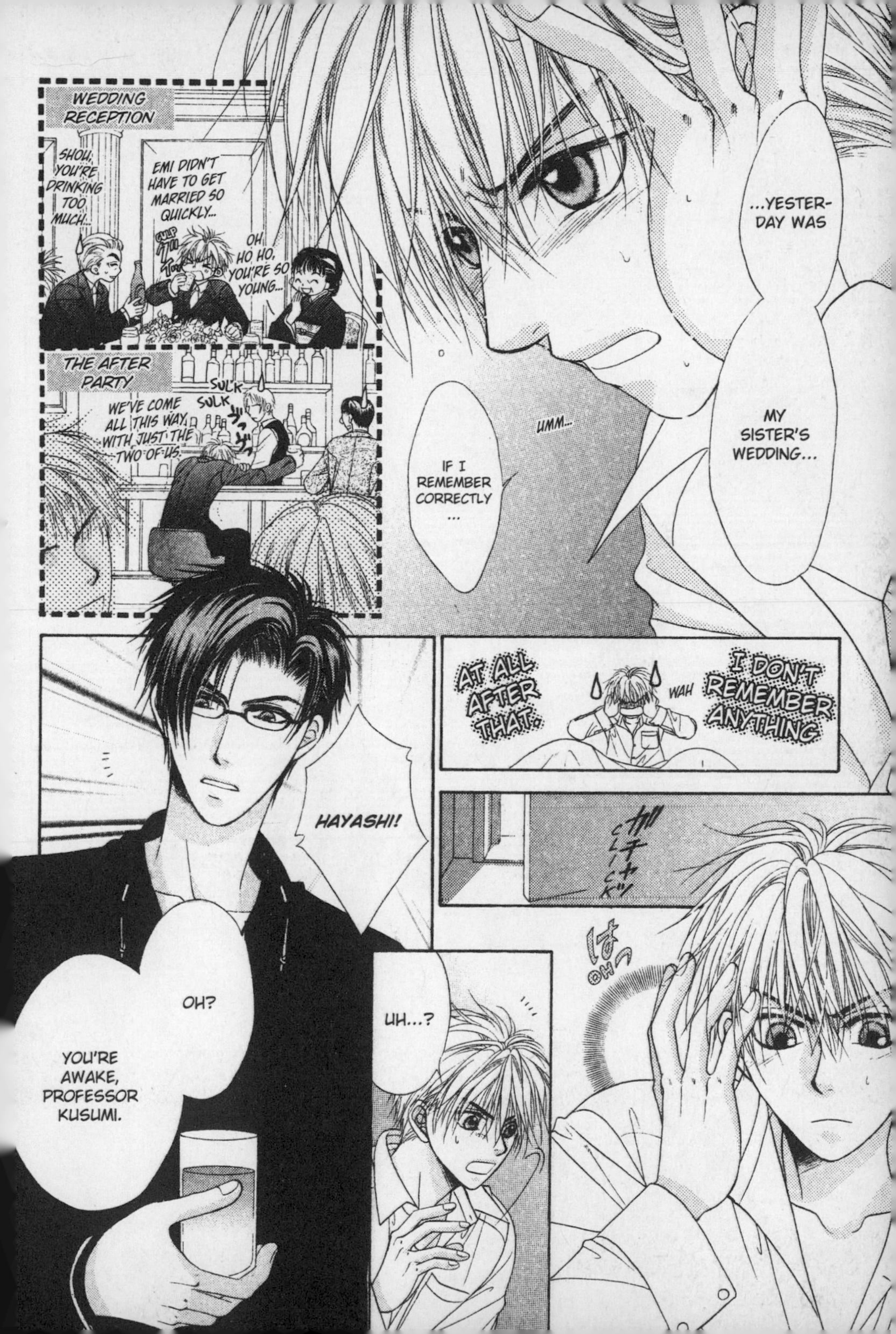

...YESTER-DAY WAS
MY SISTER'S WEDDING...
UMM...
IF I REMEMBER CORRECTLY ...
WEDDING RECEPTION
SHOU, YOU'RE DRINKING TOO MUCH...
EMI DIDN'T HAVE TO GET MARRIED SO QUICKLY...
GULP
OH HO HO, YOU'RE SO YOUNG...
THE AFTER PARTY
SULK SULK
WE'VE COME ALL THIS WAY, WITH JUST THE TWO OF US.
I DON'T REMEMBER ANYTHING
WAH
AT ALL AFTER THAT.
HAYASHI!
OH
UH...?
OH?
YOU'RE AWAKE, PROFESSOR KUSUMI.

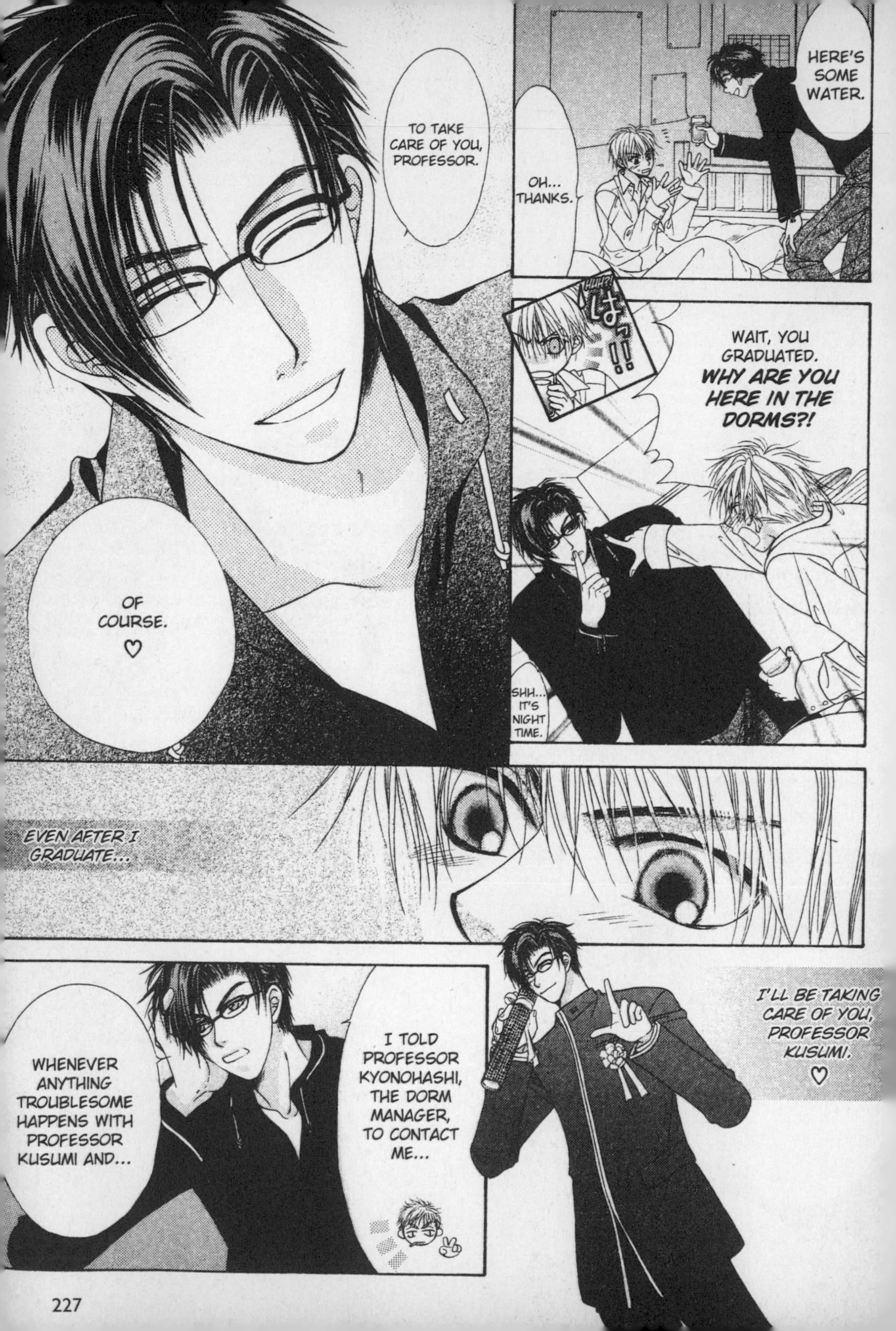

HERE'S SOME WATER.
OH... THANKS.
HUH?!
WAIT, YOU GRADUATED. **WHY ARE YOU HERE IN THE DORMS?!**
SHH... IT'S NIGHT TIME.
TO TAKE CARE OF YOU, PROFESSOR.
OF COURSE. ♡
EVEN AFTER I GRADUATE...
I'LL BE TAKING CARE OF YOU, PROFESSOR KUSUMI. ♡
I TOLD PROFESSOR KYONOHASHI, THE DORM MANAGER, TO CONTACT ME...
WHENEVER ANYTHING TROUBLESOME HAPPENS WITH PROFESSOR KUSUMI AND...

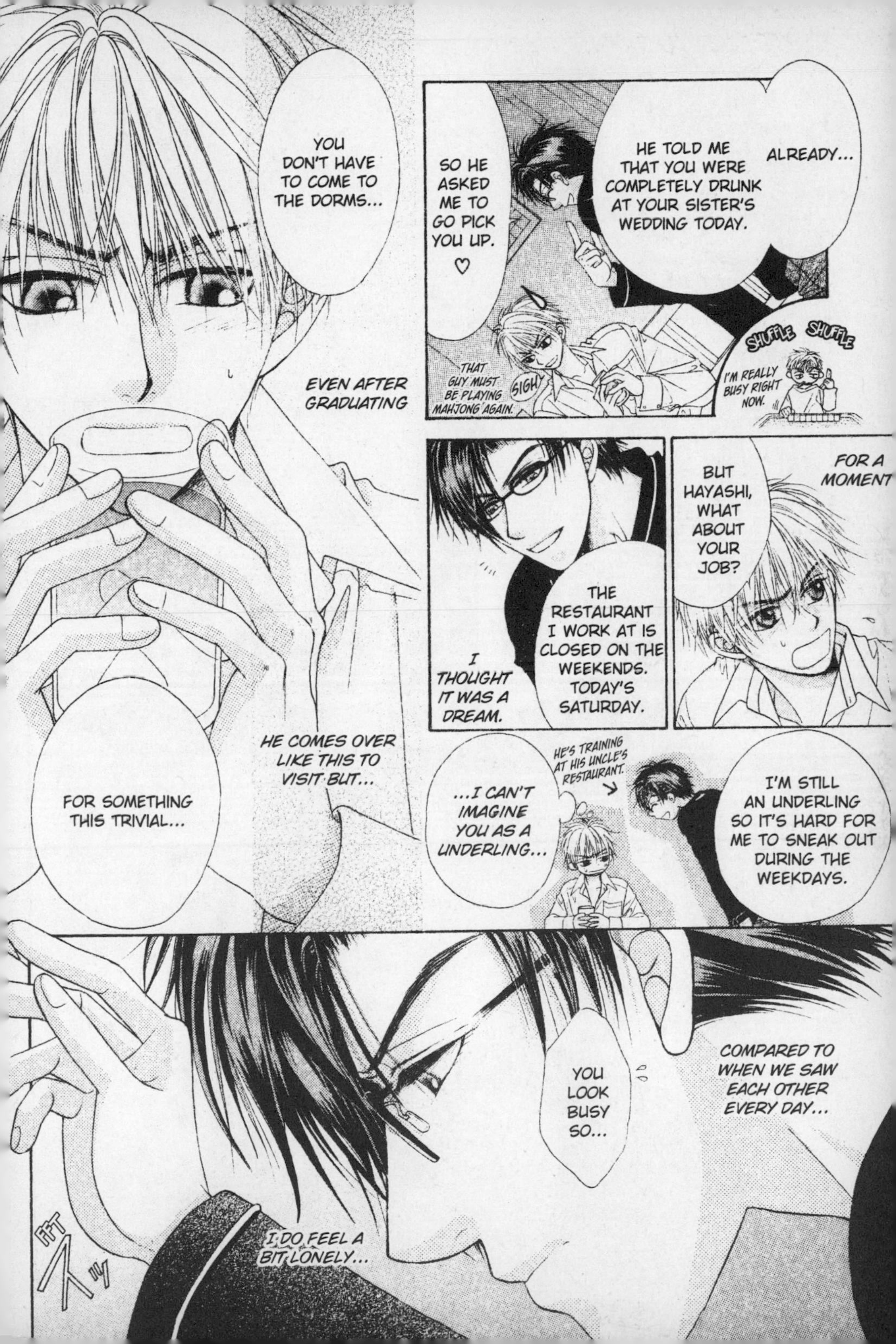
ALREADY...
HE TOLD ME THAT YOU WERE COMPLETELY DRUNK AT YOUR SISTER'S WEDDING TODAY.
SO HE ASKED ME TO GO PICK YOU UP. ♡
SHUFFLE SHUFFLE
I'M REALLY BUSY RIGHT NOW.
SIGH
THAT GUY MUST BE PLAYING MAHJONG AGAIN.
FOR A MOMENT
BUT HAYASHI, WHAT ABOUT YOUR JOB?
THE RESTAURANT I WORK AT IS CLOSED ON THE WEEKENDS. TODAY'S SATURDAY.
I THOUGHT IT WAS A DREAM.
I'M STILL AN UNDERLING SO IT'S HARD FOR ME TO SNEAK OUT DURING THE WEEKDAYS.
HE'S TRAINING AT HIS UNCLE'S RESTAURANT.
...I CAN'T IMAGINE YOU AS A UNDERLING...
YOU DON'T HAVE TO COME TO THE DORMS...
EVEN AFTER GRADUATING
HE COMES OVER LIKE THIS TO VISIT BUT...
FOR SOMETHING THIS TRIVIAL...
COMPARED TO WHEN WE SAW EACH OTHER EVERY DAY...
YOU LOOK BUSY SO...
I DO FEEL A BIT LONELY...
FFT

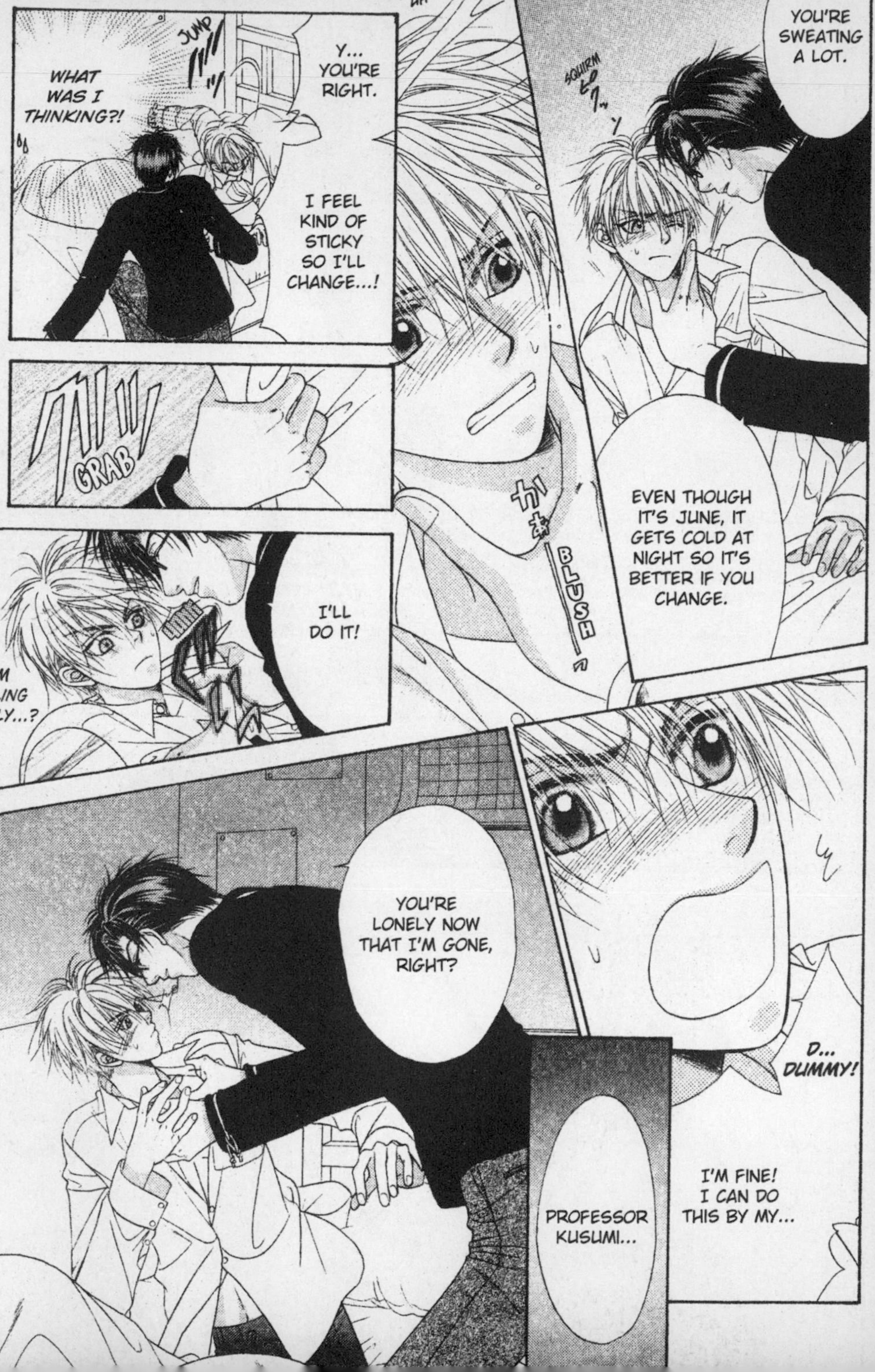
YOU'RE SWEATING A LOT.
SQUIRM
EVEN THOUGH IT'S JUNE, IT GETS COLD AT NIGHT SO IT'S BETTER IF YOU CHANGE.
UH
BLUSH
Y... YOU'RE RIGHT.
I FEEL KIND OF STICKY SO I'LL CHANGE...!
JUMP
WHAT WAS I THINKING?!
GRAB
I'LL DO IT!
I'M FEELING LONELY...?
D... DUMMY!
I'M FINE! I CAN DO THIS BY MY...
YOU'RE LONELY NOW THAT I'M GONE, RIGHT?
PROFESSOR KUSUMI...

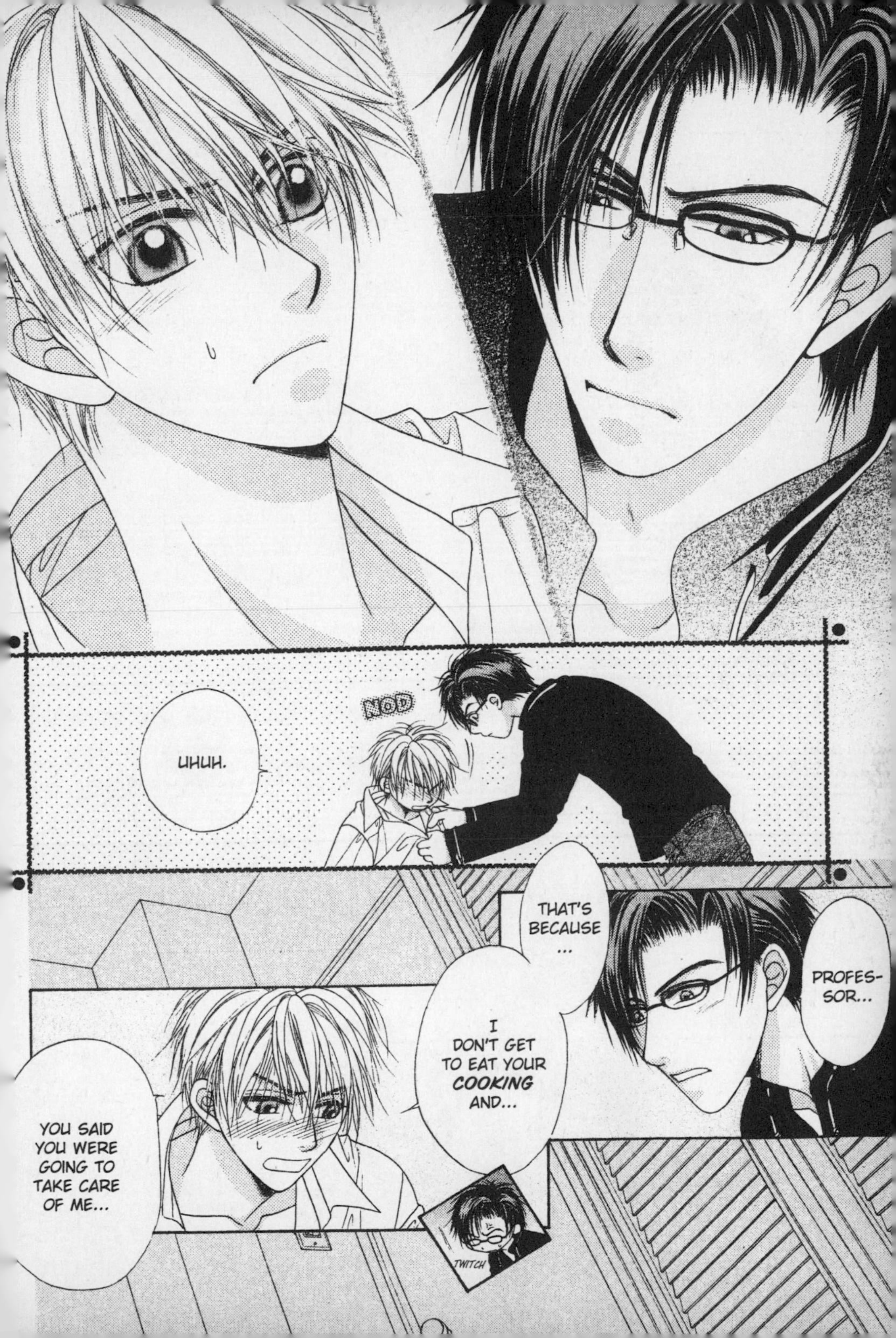
NOD
UHUH.
PROFES-SOR...
THAT'S BECAUSE ...
I DON'T GET TO EAT YOUR **COOKING** AND...
YOU SAID YOU WERE GOING TO TAKE CARE OF ME...
TWITCH

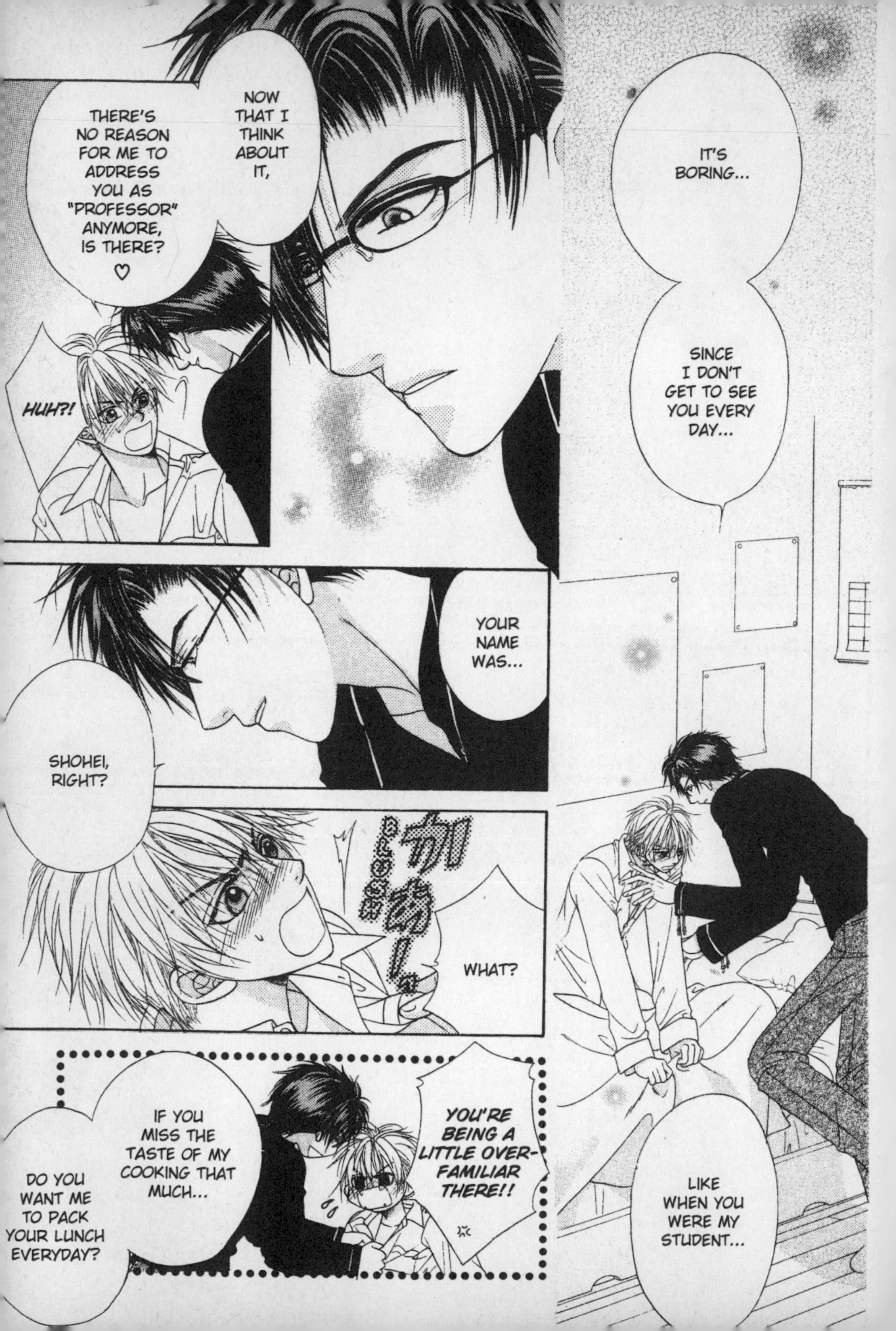
IT'S BORING...
SINCE I DON'T GET TO SEE YOU EVERY DAY...
LIKE WHEN YOU WERE MY STUDENT...
NOW THAT I THINK ABOUT IT,
THERE'S NO REASON FOR ME TO ADDRESS YOU AS "PROFESSOR" ANYMORE, IS THERE? ♡
HUH?!
YOUR NAME WAS...
SHOHEI, RIGHT?
WHAT?
YOU'RE BEING A LITTLE OVER-FAMILIAR THERE!!
IF YOU MISS THE TASTE OF MY COOKING THAT MUCH...
DO YOU WANT ME TO PACK YOUR LUNCH EVERYDAY?

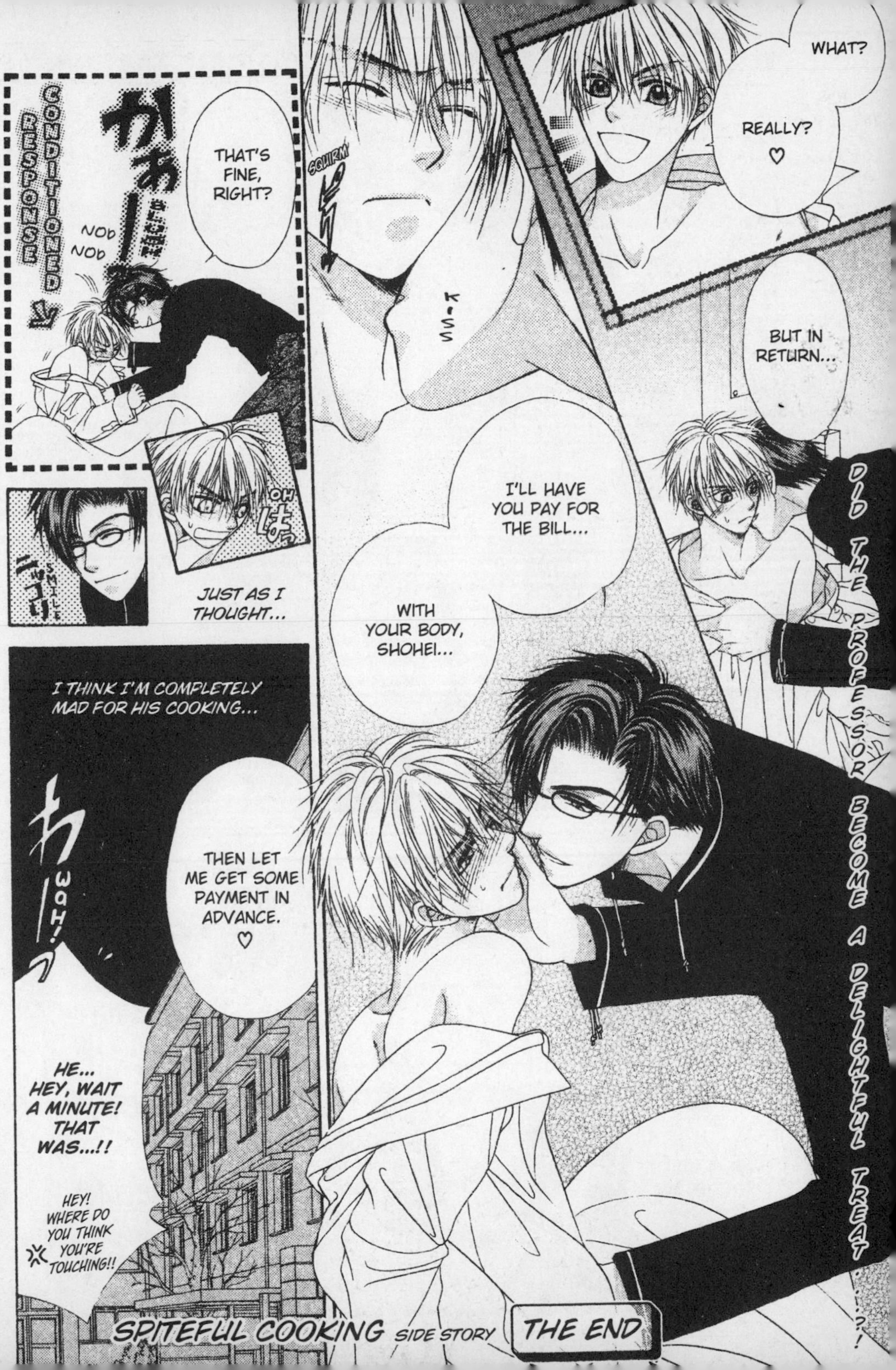
WHAT?
REALLY? ♡
SQUIRM
KISS
BUT IN RETURN...
I'LL HAVE YOU PAY FOR THE BILL...
WITH YOUR BODY, SHOHEI...
THEN LET ME GET SOME PAYMENT IN ADVANCE. ♡
DID THE PROFESSOR BECOME A DELIGHTFUL TREAT...?!
CONDITIONED RESPONSE
THAT'S FINE, RIGHT?
Nob Nob
OH
SMILE
JUST AS I THOUGHT...
I THINK I'M COMPLETELY MAD FOR HIS COOKING...
WAH!
HE... HEY, WAIT A MINUTE! THAT WAS...!!
HEY! WHERE DO YOU THINK YOU'RE TOUCHING!!
SPITEFUL COOKING SIDE STORY THE END

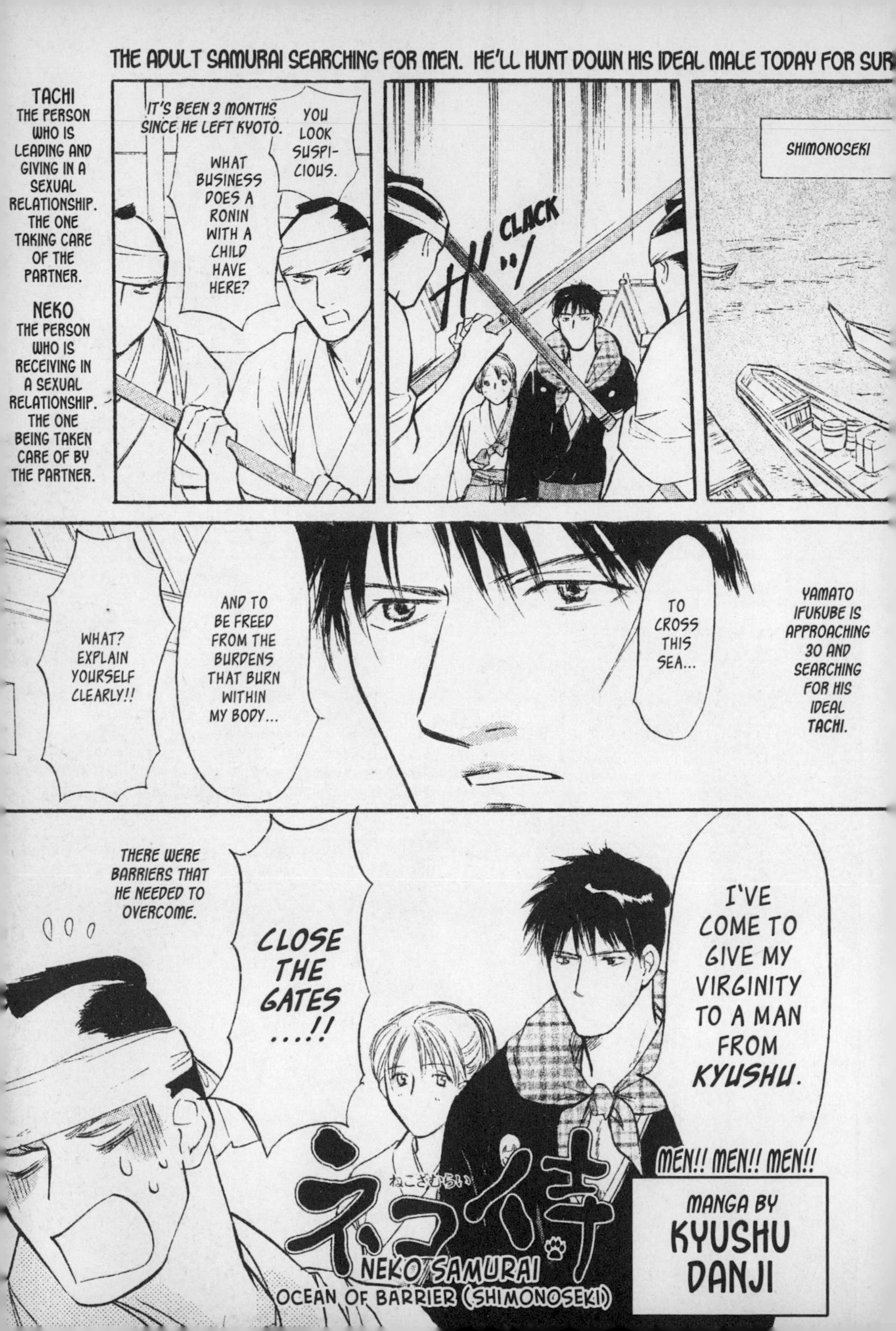
THE ADULT SAMURAI SEARCHING FOR MEN. HE'LL HUNT DOWN HIS IDEAL MALE TODAY FOR SUR
SHIMONOSEKI
CLACK
YOU LOOK SUSPICIOUS.
IT'S BEEN 3 MONTHS SINCE HE LEFT KYOTO.
WHAT BUSINESS DOES A RONIN WITH A CHILD HAVE HERE?
TACHI THE PERSON WHO IS LEADING AND GIVING IN A SEXUAL RELATIONSHIP. THE ONE TAKING CARE OF THE PARTNER.
NEKO THE PERSON WHO IS RECEIVING IN A SEXUAL RELATIONSHIP. THE ONE BEING TAKEN CARE OF BY THE PARTNER.
YAMATO IFUKUBE IS APPROACHING 30 AND SEARCHING FOR HIS IDEAL TACHI.
TO CROSS THIS SEA...
AND TO BE FREED FROM THE BURDENS THAT BURN WITHIN MY BODY...
WHAT? EXPLAIN YOURSELF CLEARLY!!
I'VE COME TO GIVE MY VIRGINITY TO A MAN FROM KYUSHU.
CLOSE THE GATES....!!
THERE WERE BARRIERS THAT HE NEEDED TO OVERCOME.
MEN!! MEN!! MEN!!
NEKO SAMURAI
OCEAN OF BARRIER (SHIMONOSEKI)
MANGA BY KYUSHU DANJI

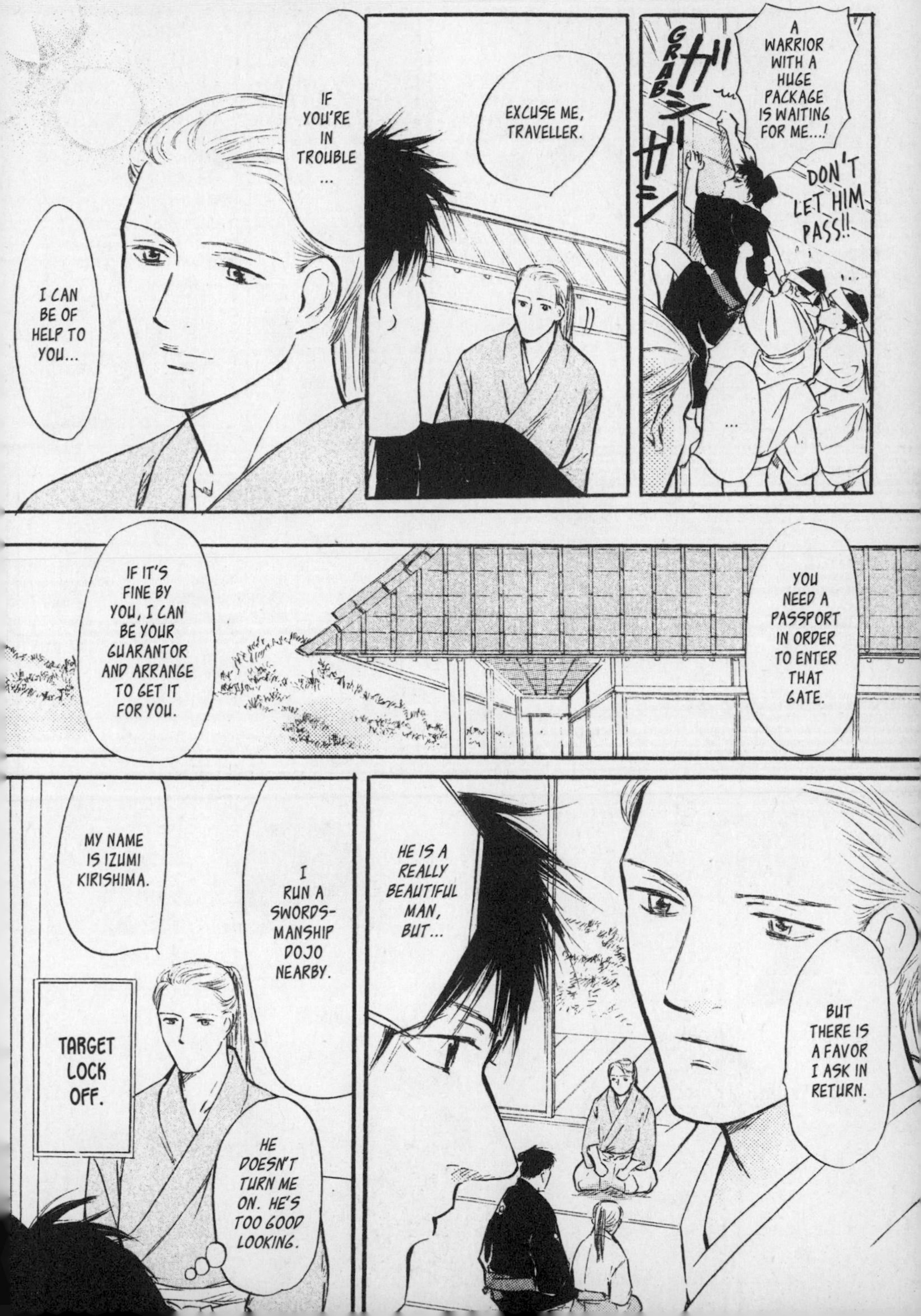

A WARRIOR WITH A HUGE PACKAGE IS WAITING FOR ME...!
GRAB
DON'T LET HIM PASS!!
...
...
EXCUSE ME, TRAVELLER.
IF YOU'RE IN TROUBLE ...
I CAN BE OF HELP TO YOU...
YOU NEED A PASSPORT IN ORDER TO ENTER THAT GATE.
IF IT'S FINE BY YOU, I CAN BE YOUR GUARANTOR AND ARRANGE TO GET IT FOR YOU.
BUT THERE IS A FAVOR I ASK IN RETURN.
HE IS A REALLY BEAUTIFUL MAN, BUT...
I RUN A SWORDSMANSHIP DOJO NEARBY.
MY NAME IS IZUMI KIRISHIMA.
TARGET LOCK OFF.
HE DOESN'T TURN ME ON. HE'S TOO GOOD LOOKING.

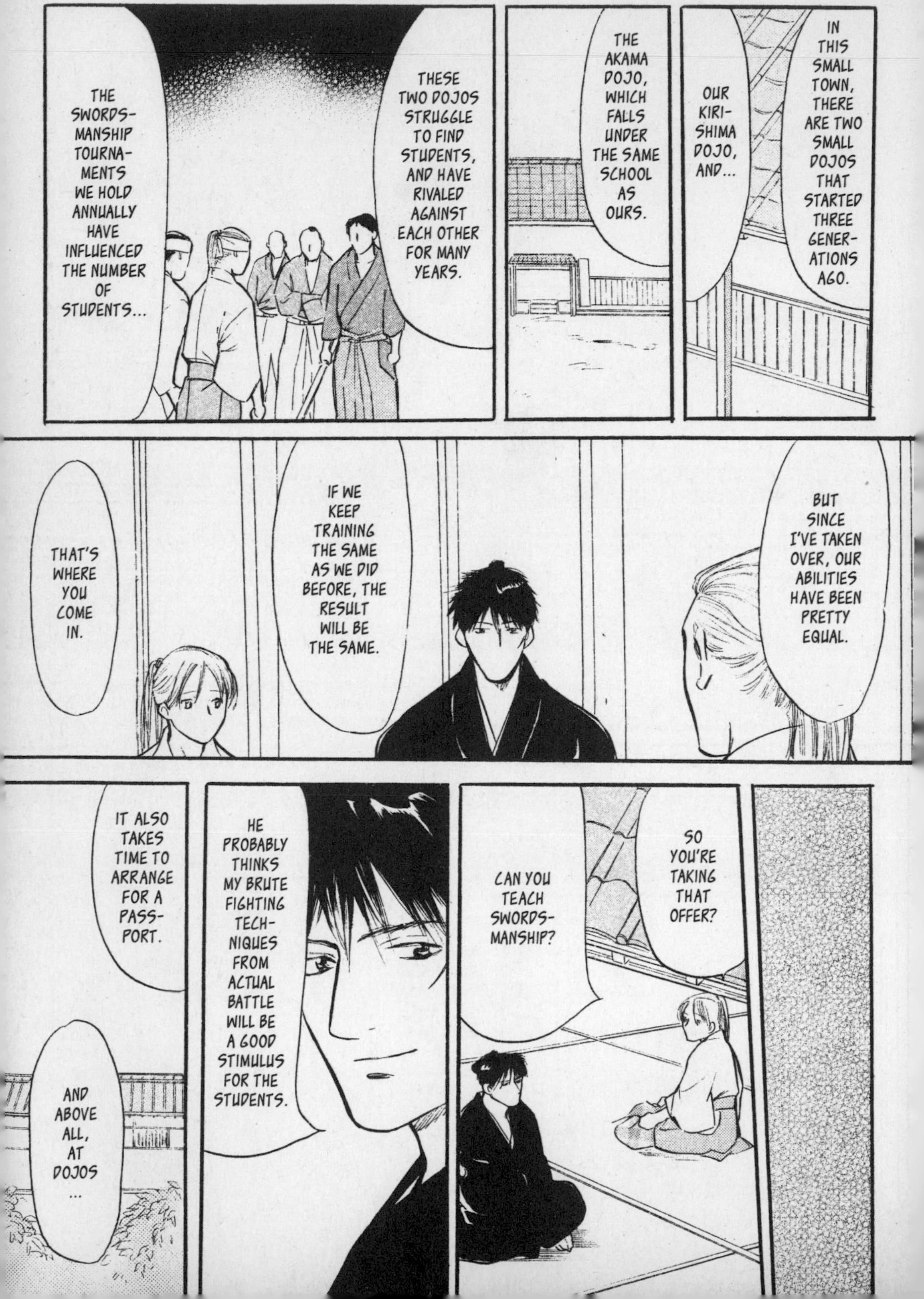
IN THIS SMALL TOWN, THERE ARE TWO SMALL DOJOS THAT STARTED THREE GENER-ATIONS AGO.
OUR KIRI-SHIMA DOJO, AND...
THE AKAMA DOJO, WHICH FALLS UNDER THE SAME SCHOOL AS OURS.
THESE TWO DOJOS STRUGGLE TO FIND STUDENTS, AND HAVE RIVALED AGAINST EACH OTHER FOR MANY YEARS.
THE SWORDS-MANSHIP TOURNA-MENTS WE HOLD ANNUALLY HAVE INFLUENCED THE NUMBER OF STUDENTS...
BUT SINCE I'VE TAKEN OVER, OUR ABILITIES HAVE BEEN PRETTY EQUAL.
IF WE KEEP TRAINING THE SAME AS WE DID BEFORE, THE RESULT WILL BE THE SAME.
THAT'S WHERE YOU COME IN.
SO YOU'RE TAKING THAT OFFER?
CAN YOU TEACH SWORDS-MANSHIP?
HE PROBABLY THINKS MY BRUTE FIGHTING TECH-NIQUES FROM ACTUAL BATTLE WILL BE A GOOD STIMULUS FOR THE STUDENTS.
IT ALSO TAKES TIME TO ARRANGE FOR A PASS-PORT.
AND ABOVE ALL, AT DOJOS ...

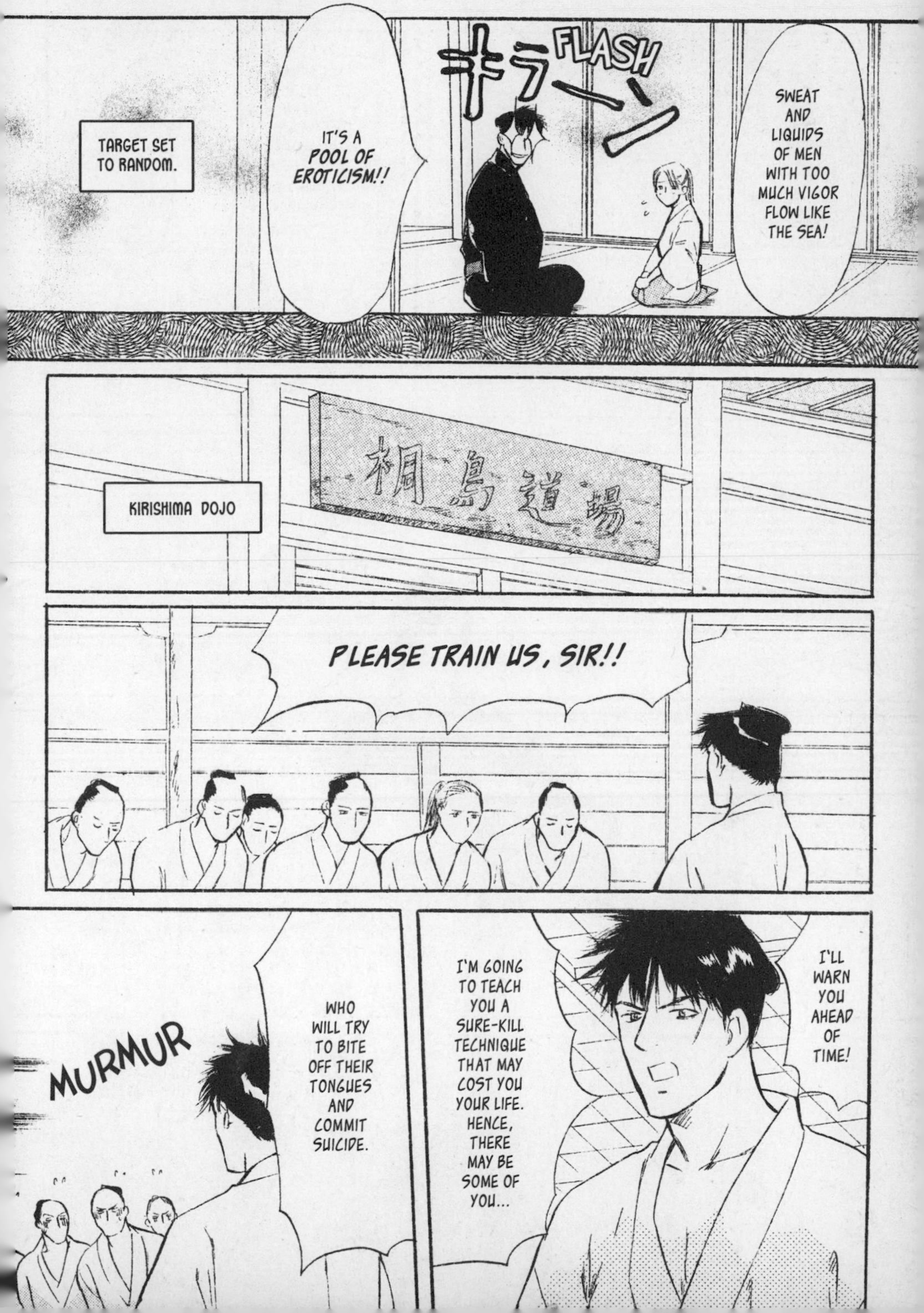
SWEAT AND LIQUIDS OF MEN WITH TOO MUCH VIGOR FLOW LIKE THE SEA!
キラーン
FLASH
IT'S A POOL OF EROTICISM!!
TARGET SET TO RANDOM.
桐島道場
KIRISHIMA DOJO
PLEASE TRAIN US, SIR!!
I'LL WARN YOU AHEAD OF TIME!
I'M GOING TO TEACH YOU A SURE-KILL TECHNIQUE THAT MAY COST YOU YOUR LIFE. HENCE, THERE MAY BE SOME OF YOU...
WHO WILL TRY TO BITE OFF THEIR TONGUES AND COMMIT SUICIDE.
MURMUR

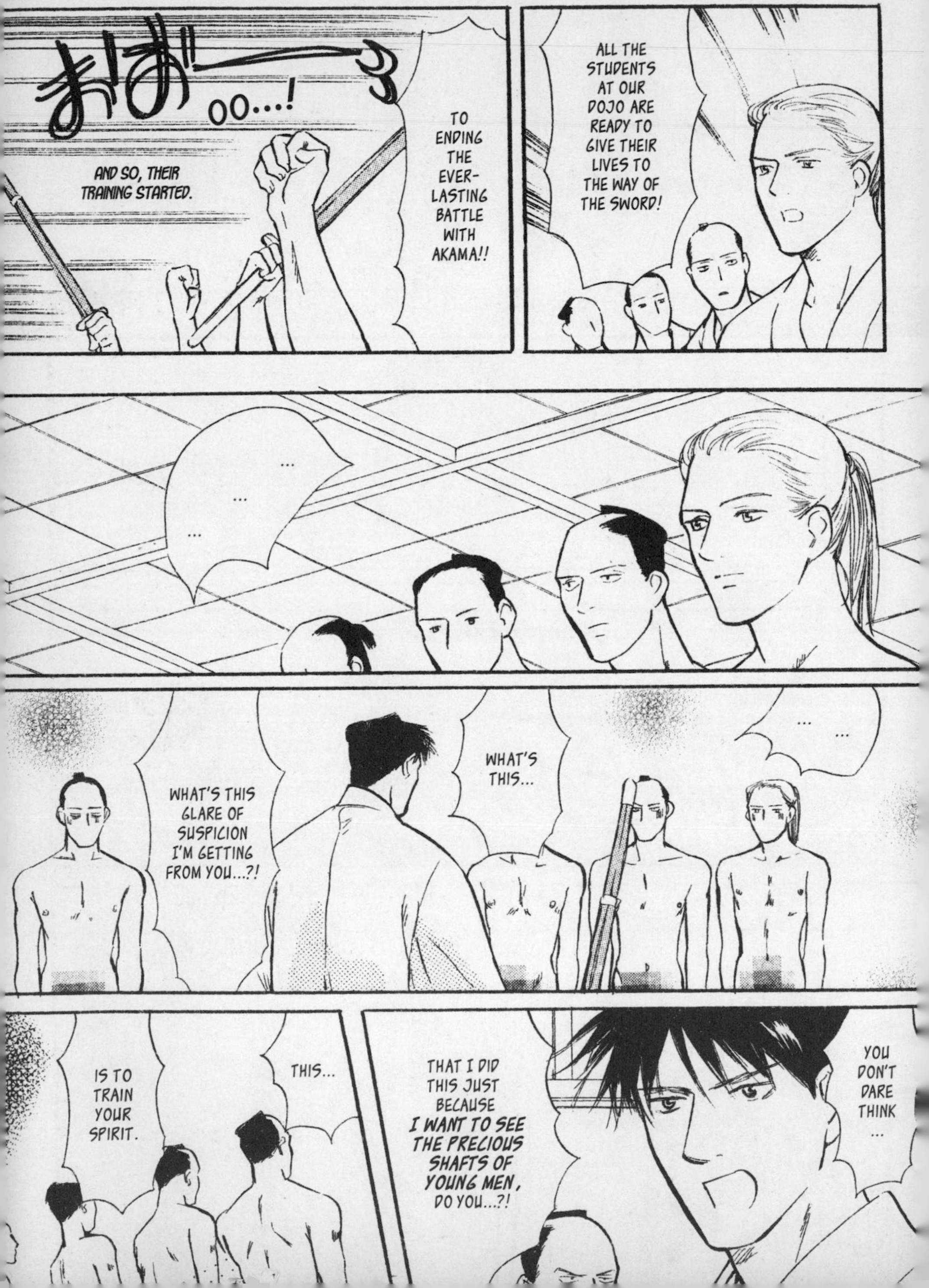
ALL THE STUDENTS AT OUR DOJO ARE READY TO GIVE THEIR LIVES TO THE WAY OF THE SWORD!
TO ENDING THE EVER-LASTING BATTLE WITH AKAMA!!
おお゛ーー
OO...!
AND SO, THEIR TRAINING STARTED.
... ...
... ...
WHAT'S THIS...
WHAT'S THIS GLARE OF SUSPICION I'M GETTING FROM YOU...?!
YOU DON'T DARE THINK ...
THAT I DID THIS JUST BECAUSE I WANT TO SEE THE PRECIOUS SHAFTS OF YOUNG MEN, DO YOU...?!
THIS...
IS TO TRAIN YOUR SPIRIT.

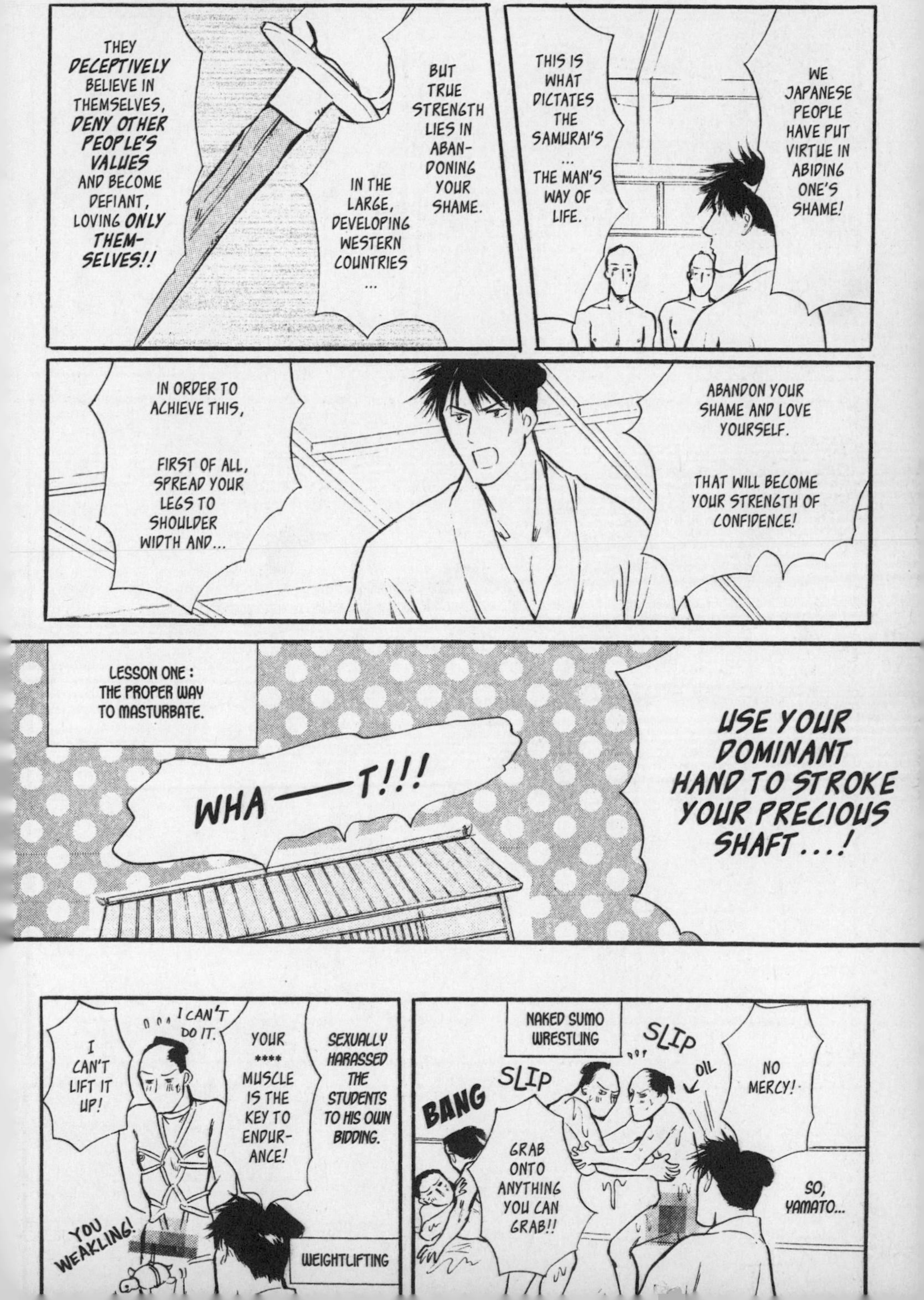
WE JAPANESE PEOPLE HAVE PUT VIRTUE IN ABIDING ONE'S SHAME!
THIS IS WHAT DICTATES THE SAMURAI'S ... THE MAN'S WAY OF LIFE.
BUT TRUE STRENGTH LIES IN ABANDONING YOUR SHAME.
IN THE LARGE, DEVELOPING WESTERN COUNTRIES ...
THEY DECEPTIVELY BELIEVE IN THEMSELVES, DENY OTHER PEOPLE'S VALUES AND BECOME DEFIANT, LOVING ONLY THEMSELVES!!
ABANDON YOUR SHAME AND LOVE YOURSELF.
THAT WILL BECOME YOUR STRENGTH OF CONFIDENCE!
IN ORDER TO ACHIEVE THIS,
FIRST OF ALL, SPREAD YOUR LEGS TO SHOULDER WIDTH AND...
USE YOUR DOMINANT HAND TO STROKE YOUR PRECIOUS SHAFT ...!
LESSON ONE : THE PROPER WAY TO MASTURBATE.
WHA——T!!!
NO MERCY!
NAKED SUMO WRESTLING
SLIP
OIL
SLIP
BANG
SO, YAMATO...
GRAB ONTO ANYTHING YOU CAN GRAB!!
SEXUALLY HARASSED THE STUDENTS TO HIS OWN BIDDING.
YOUR **** MUSCLE IS THE KEY TO ENDURANCE!
I CAN'T DO IT.
I CAN'T LIFT IT UP!
YOU WEAKLING!
WEIGHTLIFTING

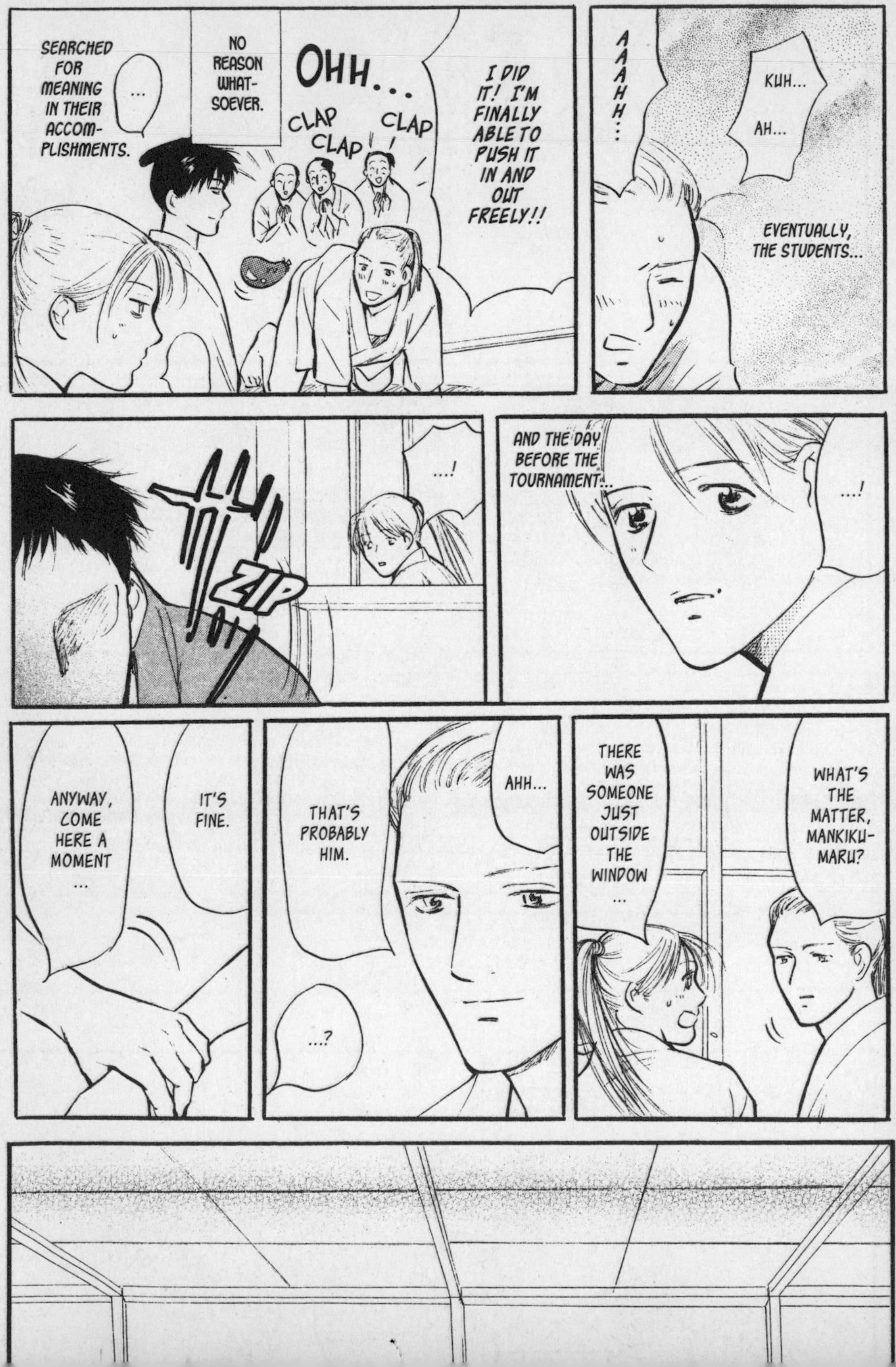
AAAAHH...
KUH...
AH...
EVENTUALLY, THE STUDENTS...
I DID IT! I'M FINALLY ABLE TO PUSH IT IN AND OUT FREELY!!
OHH...
CLAP
CLAP CLAP
NO REASON WHAT-SOEVER.
SEARCHED FOR MEANING IN THEIR ACCOM-PLISHMENTS.
...
AND THE DAY BEFORE THE TOURNAMENT...
...!
...!
ZIP
WHAT'S THE MATTER, MANKIKU-MARU?
THERE WAS SOMEONE JUST OUTSIDE THE WINDOW ...
AHH...
THAT'S PROBABLY HIM.
...?
IT'S FINE.
ANYWAY, COME HERE A MOMENT ...

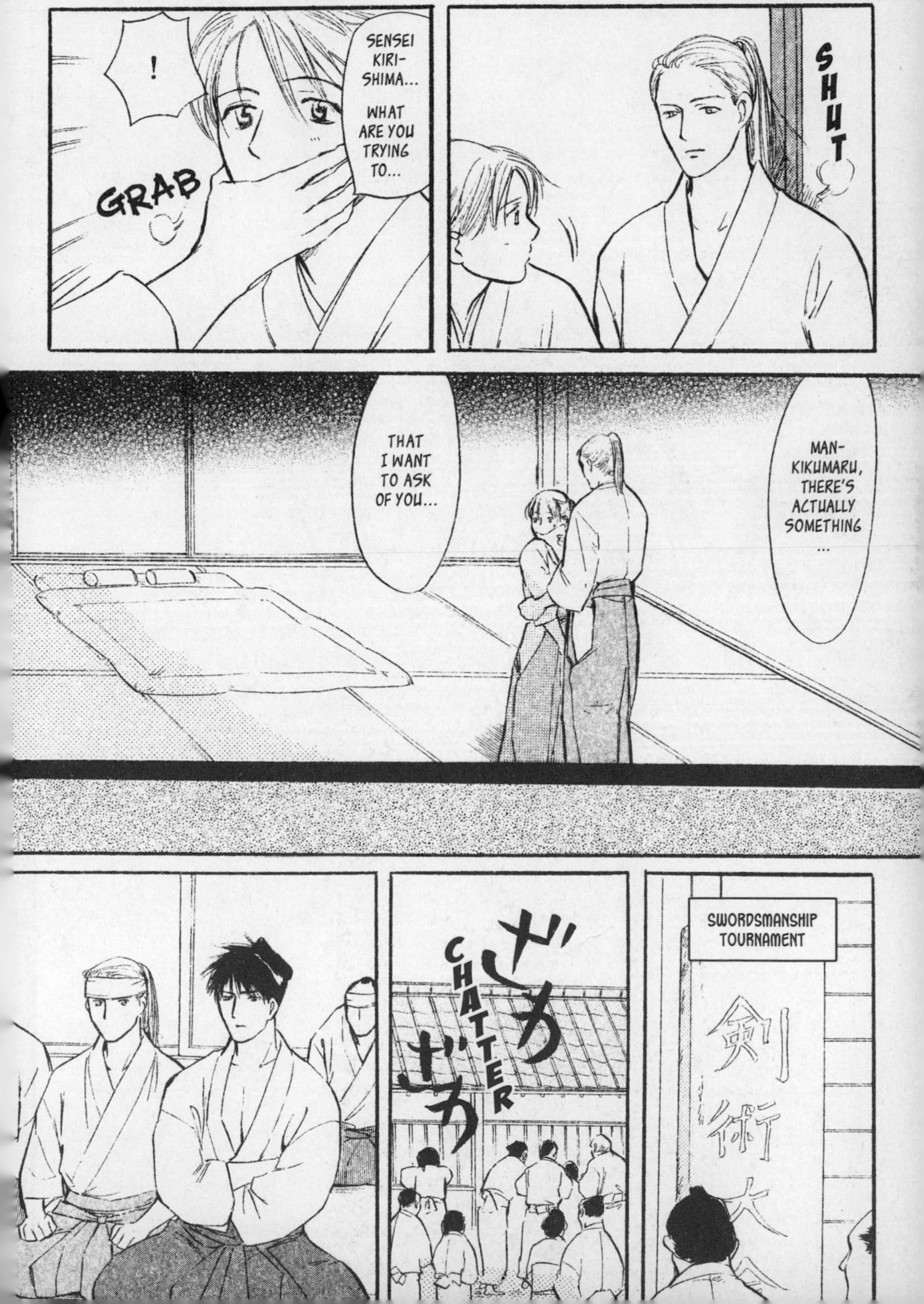
SHUT
SENSEI KIRI-SHIMA... WHAT ARE YOU TRYING TO...
!
GRAB
MAN-KIKUMARU, THERE'S ACTUALLY SOMETHING ...
THAT I WANT TO ASK OF YOU...
SWORDSMANSHIP TOURNAMENT
剣術大
ざわざわ
CHATTER

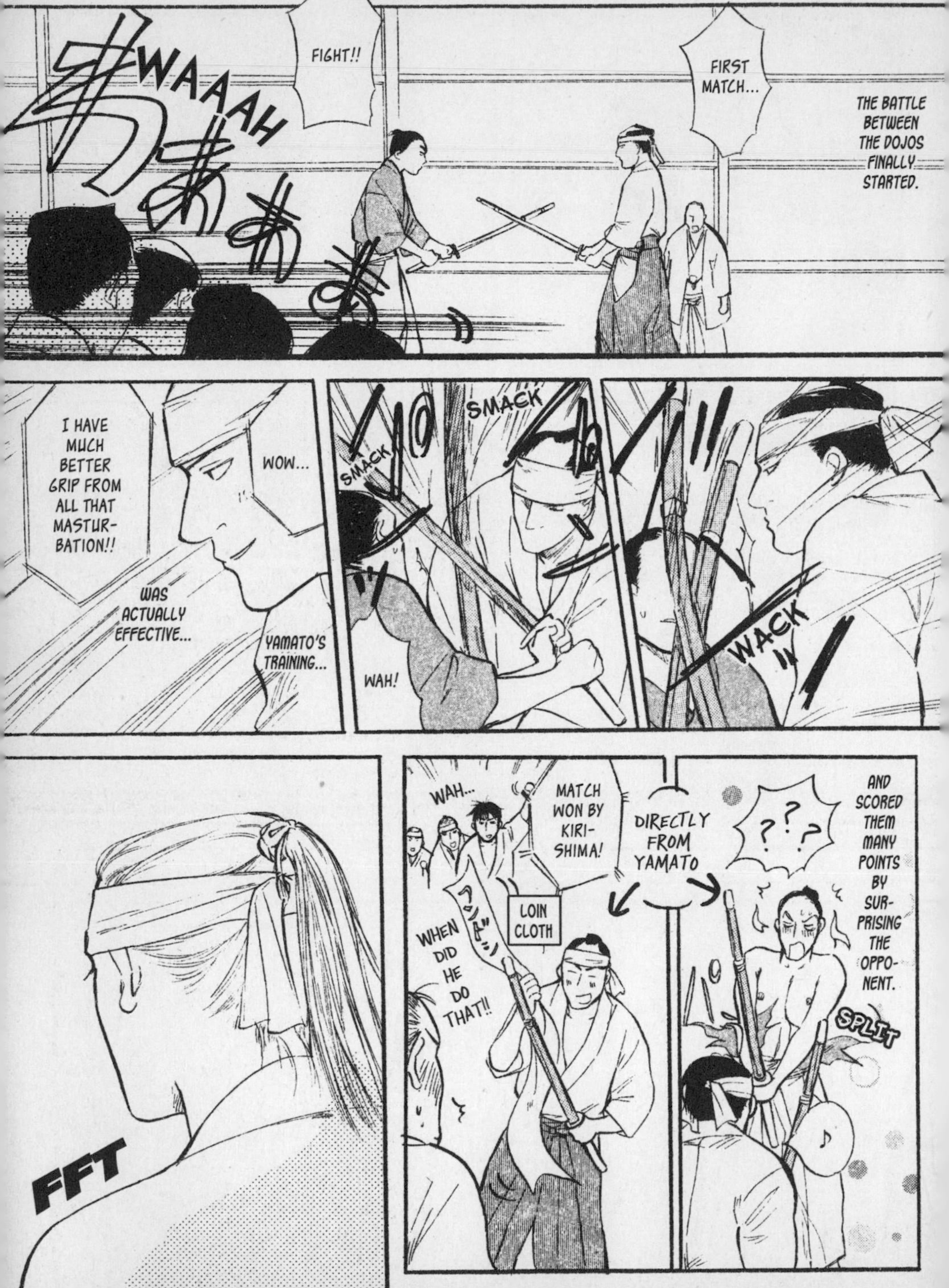
THE BATTLE BETWEEN THE DOJOS FINALLY STARTED.
FIRST MATCH...
FIGHT!!
WAAAAH
WACK
SMACK
SMACK
WAH!
WOW...
I HAVE MUCH BETTER GRIP FROM ALL THAT MASTUR-BATION!!
YAMATO'S TRAINING...
WAS ACTUALLY EFFECTIVE...
AND SCORED THEM MANY POINTS BY SUR-PRISING THE OPPO-NENT.
DIRECTLY FROM YAMATO
SPLIT
MATCH WON BY KIRI-SHIMA!
WAH...
LOIN CLOTH
WHEN DID HE DO THAT!!
FFT

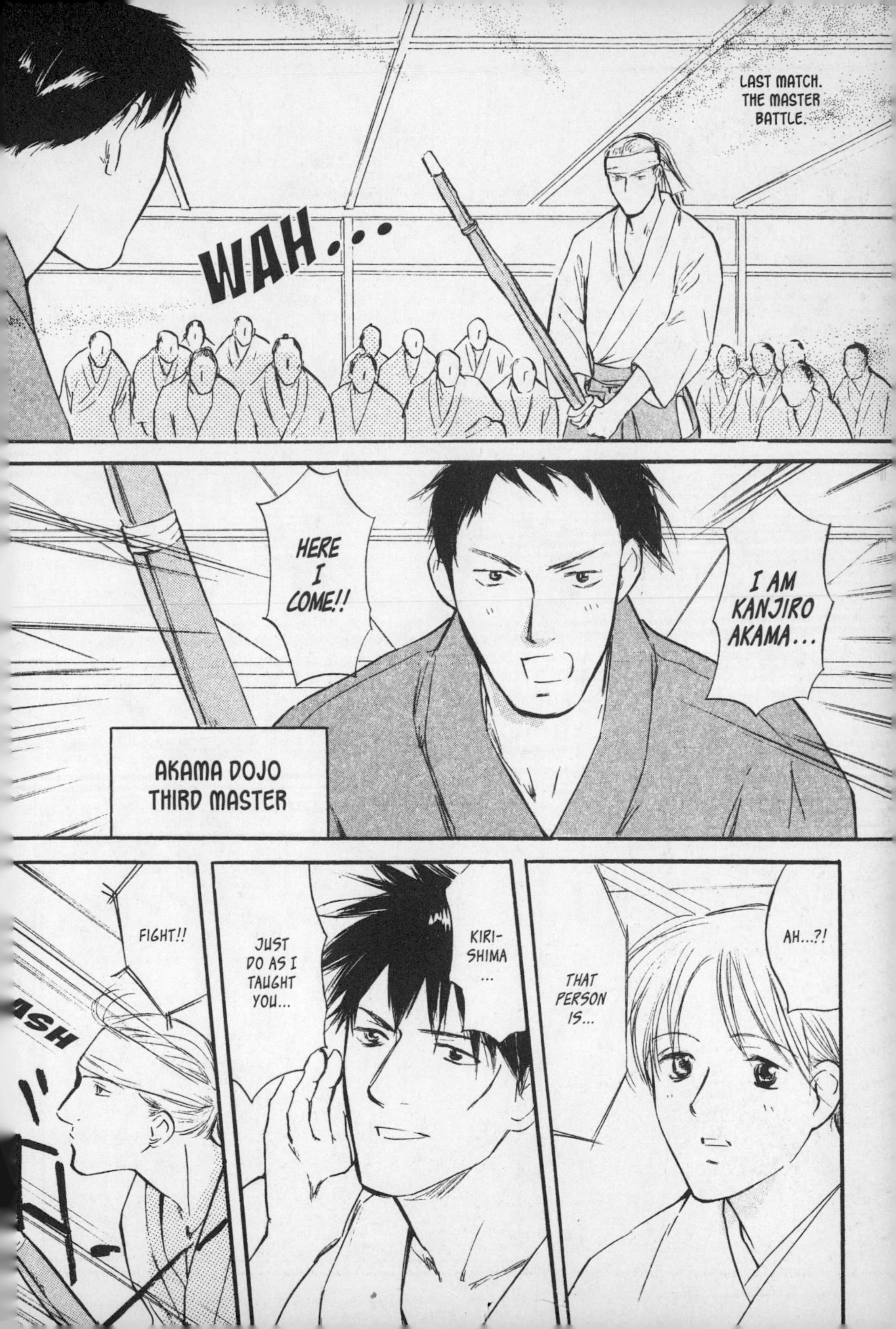
LAST MATCH. THE MASTER BATTLE.
WAH...
I AM KANJIRO AKAMA...
HERE I COME!!
AKAMA DOJO THIRD MASTER
AH...?!
THAT PERSON IS...
KIRI-SHIMA ...
JUST DO AS I TAUGHT YOU...
FIGHT!!
ASH

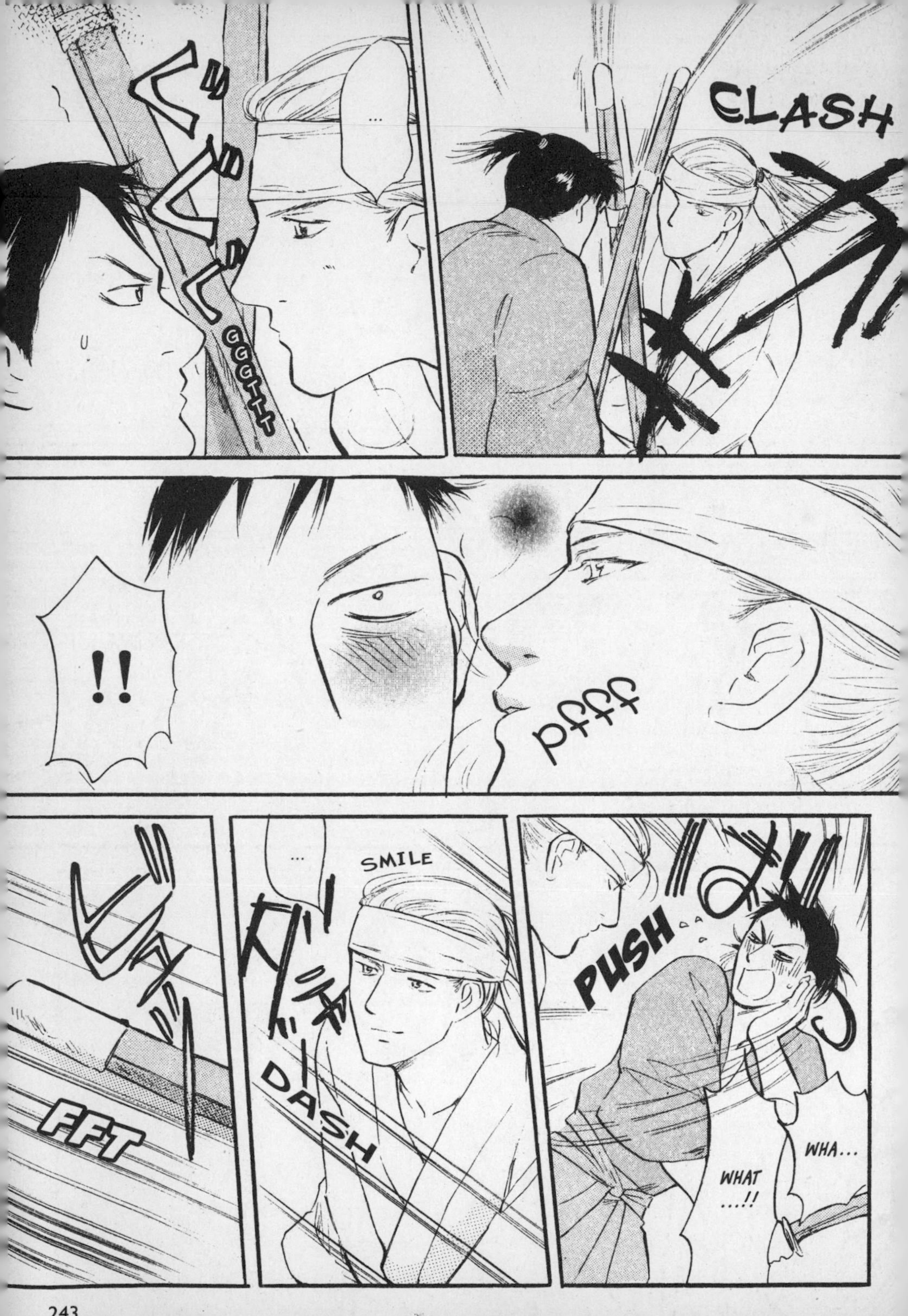
CLASH
...
GGGTTT
pfff
!!
PUSH
WHA...
WHAT
....!!
...
SMILE
DASH
FFT

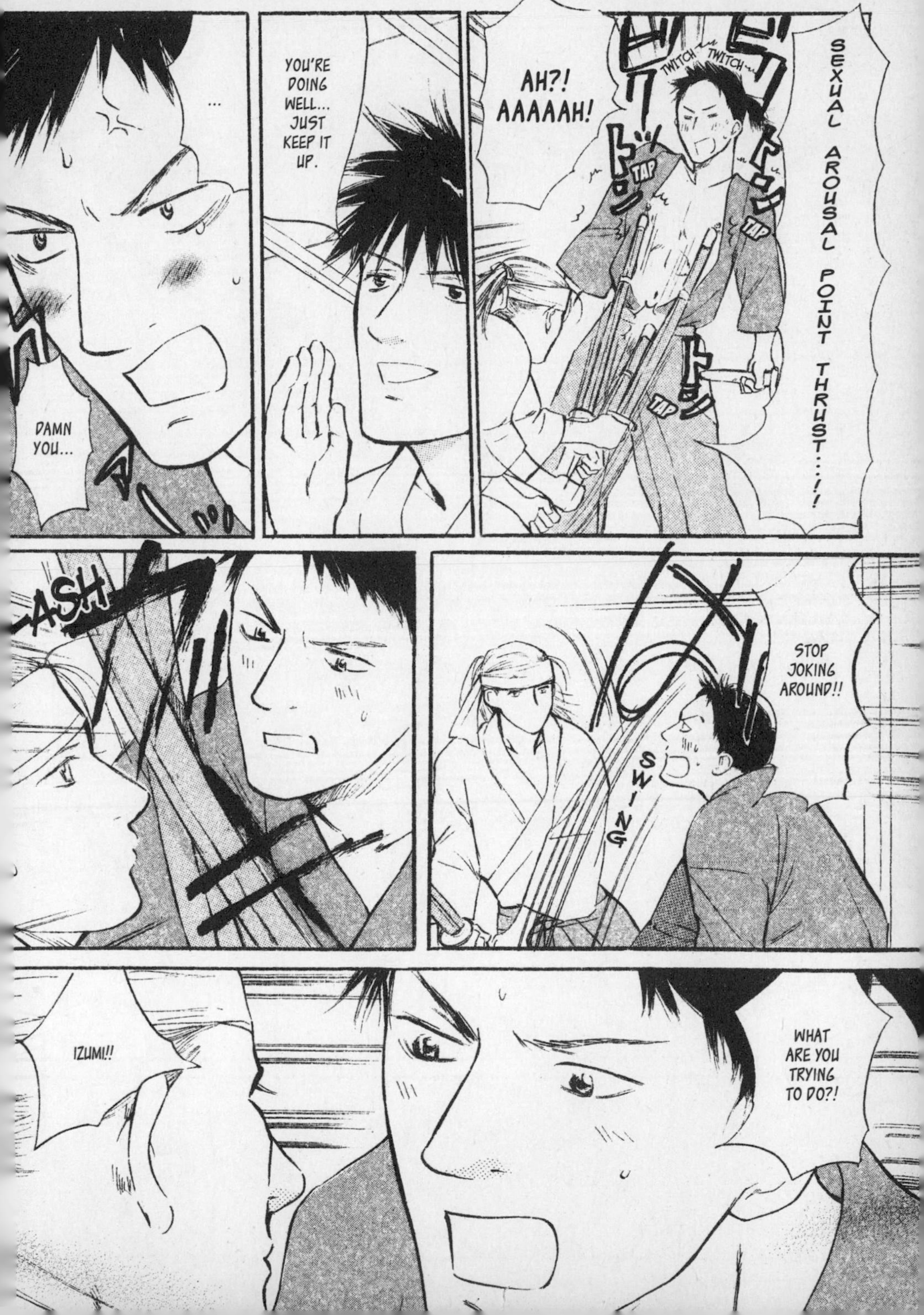
SEXUAL AROUSAL POINT THRUST...!!
AH?! AAAAAH!
TWITCH TWITCH
TAP
TAP
TAP
YOU'RE DOING WELL... JUST KEEP IT UP.
...
DAMN YOU...
STOP JOKING AROUND!!
SWING
ASH
WHAT ARE YOU TRYING TO DO?!
IZUMI!!

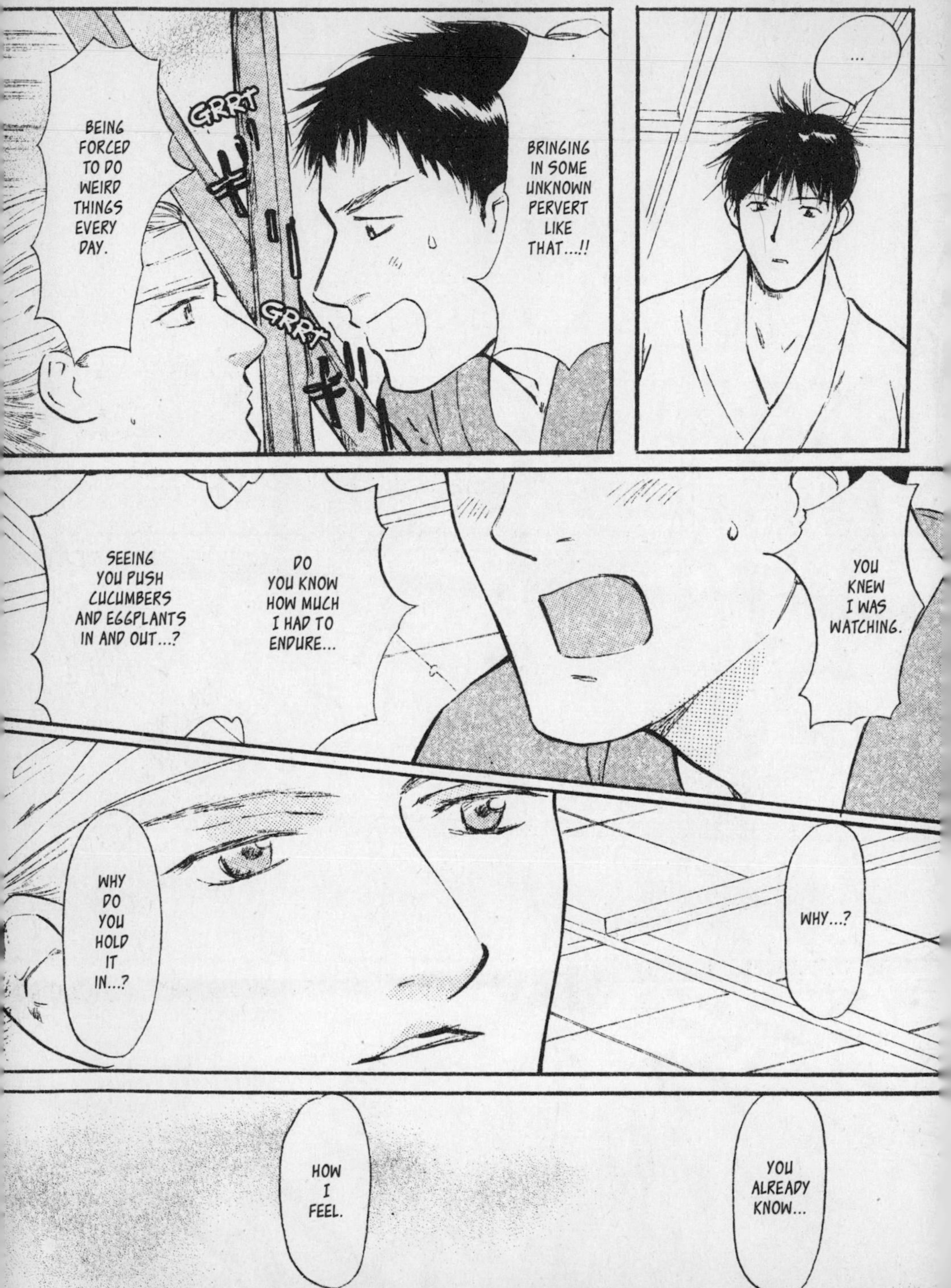
...
BRINGING IN SOME UNKNOWN PERVERT LIKE THAT...!!
GRRT
GRRT
BEING FORCED TO DO WEIRD THINGS EVERY DAY.
YOU KNEW I WAS WATCHING.
DO YOU KNOW HOW MUCH I HAD TO ENDURE...
SEEING YOU PUSH CUCUMBERS AND EGGPLANTS IN AND OUT...?
WHY...?
WHY DO YOU HOLD IT IN...?
YOU ALREADY KNOW...
HOW I FEEL.

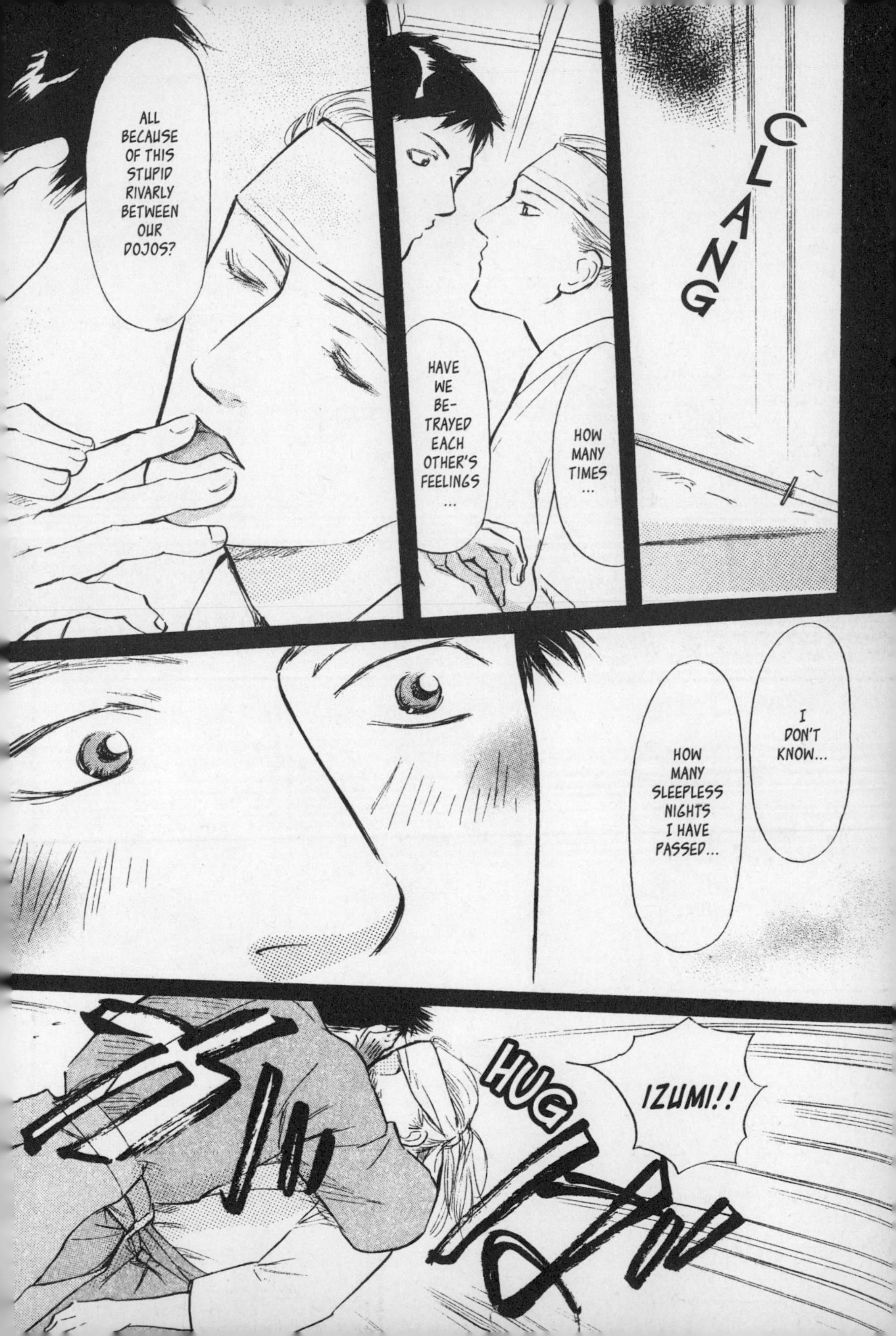
CLANG
HOW MANY TIMES...
HAVE WE BE-TRAYED EACH OTHER'S FEELINGS...
ALL BECAUSE OF THIS STUPID RIVARLY BETWEEN OUR DOJOS?
I DON'T KNOW...
HOW MANY SLEEPLESS NIGHTS I HAVE PASSED...
IZUMI!!
HUG

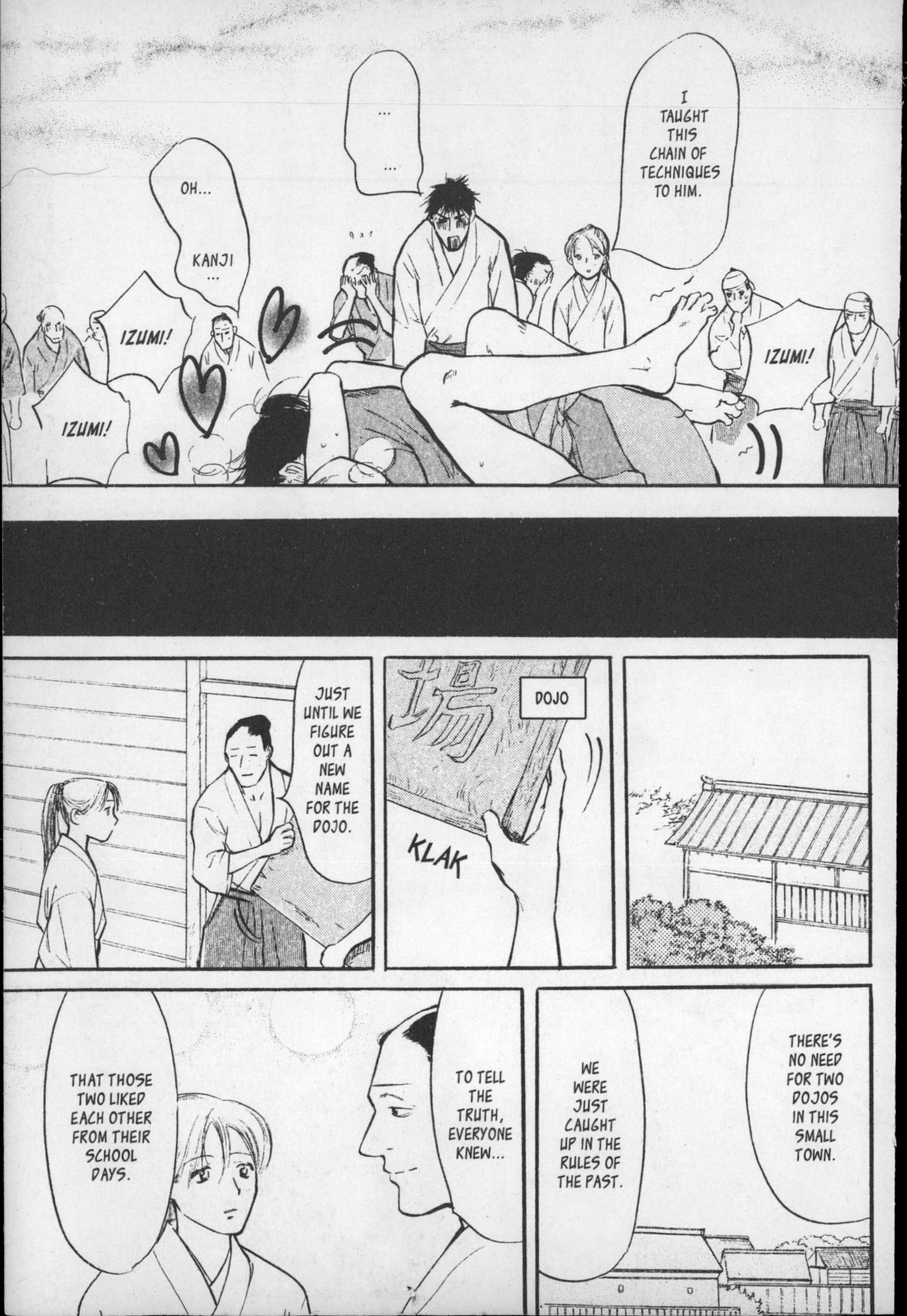
I TAUGHT THIS CHAIN OF TECHNIQUES TO HIM.
... ...
IZUMI!
OH... KANJI ...
IZUMI!
IZUMI!
DOJO
KLAK
JUST UNTIL WE FIGURE OUT A NEW NAME FOR THE DOJO.
THERE'S NO NEED FOR TWO DOJOS IN THIS SMALL TOWN.
WE WERE JUST CAUGHT UP IN THE RULES OF THE PAST.
TO TELL THE TRUTH, EVERYONE KNEW...
THAT THOSE TWO LIKED EACH OTHER FROM THEIR SCHOOL DAYS.

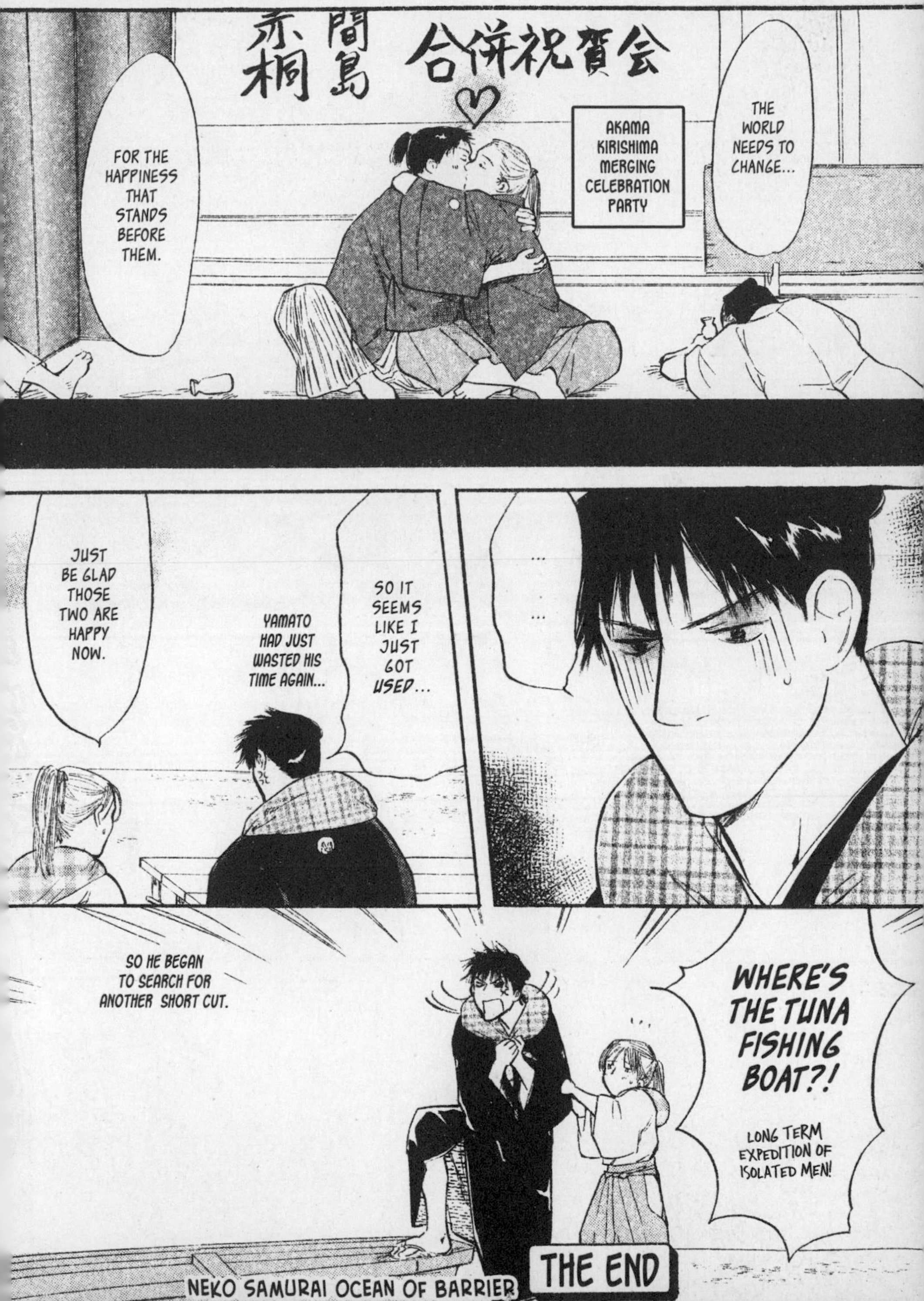
THE WORLD NEEDS TO CHANGE...
AKAMA KIRISHIMA MERGING CELEBRATION PARTY
赤間
桐島
合併祝賀会
FOR THE HAPPINESS THAT STANDS BEFORE THEM.
...
...
SO IT SEEMS LIKE I JUST GOT USED...
YAMATO HAD JUST WASTED HIS TIME AGAIN...
JUST BE GLAD THOSE TWO ARE HAPPY NOW.
WHERE'S THE TUNA FISHING BOAT?!
LONG TERM EXPEDITION OF ISOLATED MEN!
SO HE BEGAN TO SEARCH FOR ANOTHER SHORT CUT.
THE END
NEKO SAMURAI OCEAN OF BARRIER

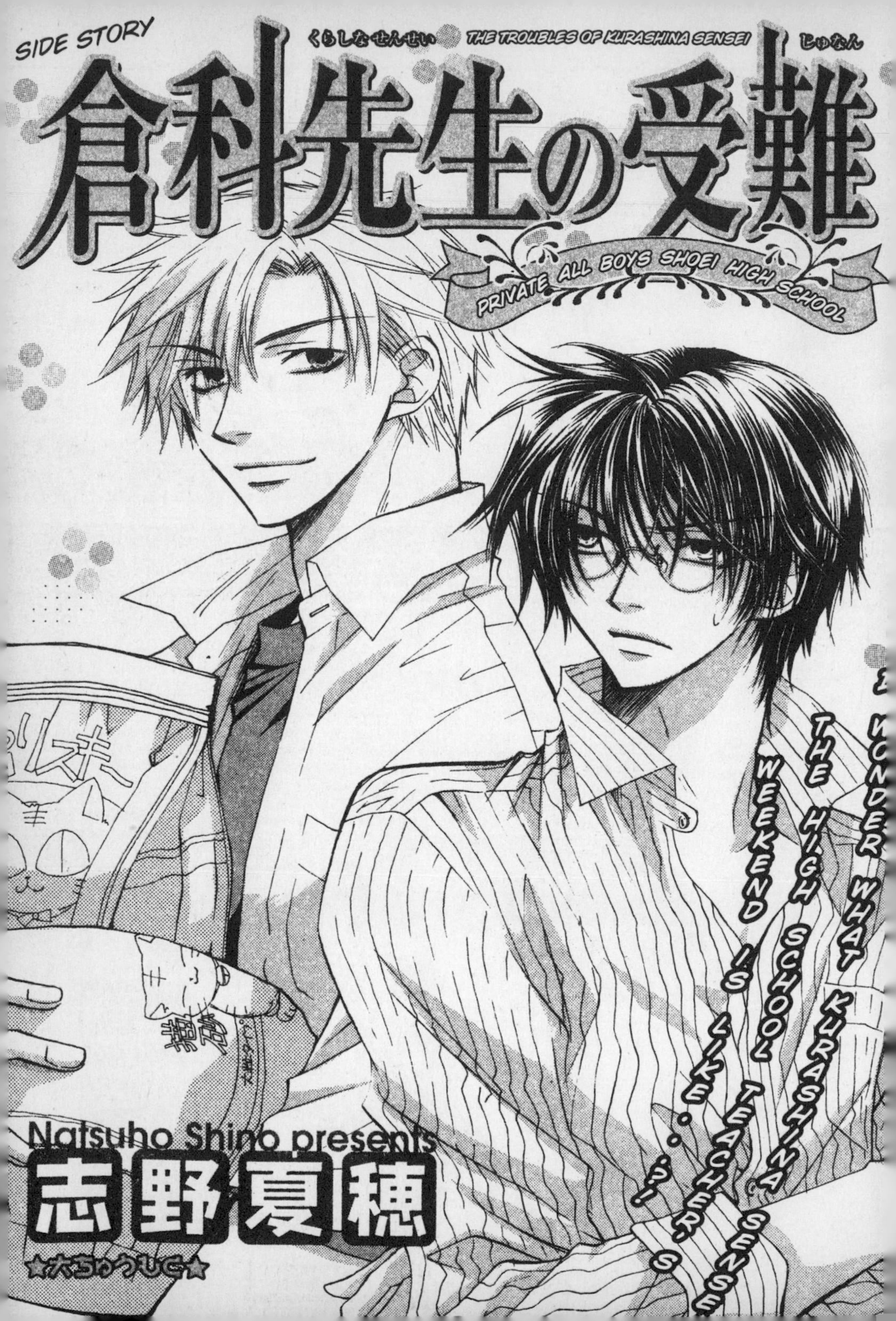
SIDE STORY
くらしなせんせい
THE TROUBLES OF KURASHINA SENSEI
じゅなん
倉科先生の受難
PRIVATE ALL BOYS SHOEI HIGH SCHOOL
I WONDER WHAT
KURASHINA SENSEI
THE HIGH SCHOOL TEACHER'S
WEEKEND IS LIKE...?!
Natsuho Shino presents
志野夏穂

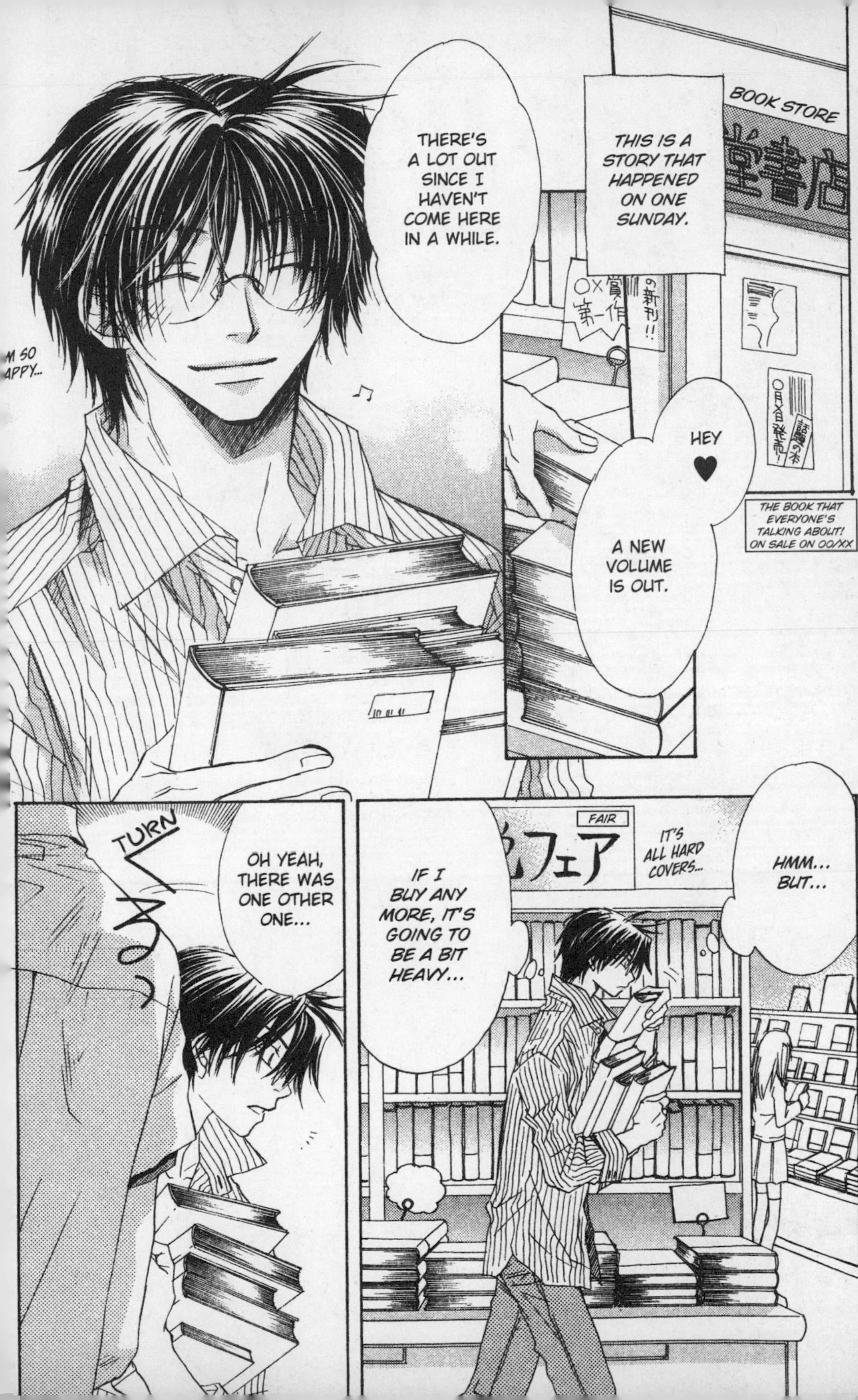
BOOK STORE
堂書店
THIS IS A STORY THAT HAPPENED ON ONE SUNDAY.
HEY ♥
A NEW VOLUME IS OUT.
THE BOOK THAT EVERYONE'S TALKING ABOUT! ON SALE ON OO/XX
THERE'S A LOT OUT SINCE I HAVEN'T COME HERE IN A WHILE.
M SO APPY...
FAIR
フェア
IT'S ALL HARD COVERS...
HMM... BUT...
IF I BUY ANY MORE, IT'S GOING TO BE A BIT HEAVY...
OH YEAH, THERE WAS ONE OTHER ONE...
TURN

MAIN CHARACTERS

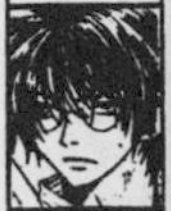

REIJI KURASHINA

A NEWLY ASSIGNED HIGH SCHOOL TEACHER TO THE PRIVATE ALL BOYS SHOEI HIGH SCHOOL. HE TEACHES JAPANESE HISTORY.

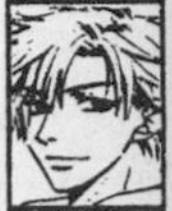

TAKASHI ASANO

SECOND YEAR HIGH SCHOOL STUDENT. HE'S THE CHAIRMAN OF THE COMPOSITE EXECUTIVE COMMITTEE. HE'S TRUSTED BY EVERYONE AT SCHOOL.

WHAT'S THE COMPOSITE EXECUTIVE COMMITTEE?

THE OFFICIAL NAME IS THE FESTIVITIES COMPOSITE EXECUTIVE COMMITTEE. THIS COMMITTEE PLANS ALL EVENTS SUCH AS THE SCHOOL ENTRANCE CEREMONY, SCHOOL FESTIVAL, AND THE SCHOOL FIELD TRIPS. MR. KURASHINA IS CURRENTLY THEIR ADVISOR.

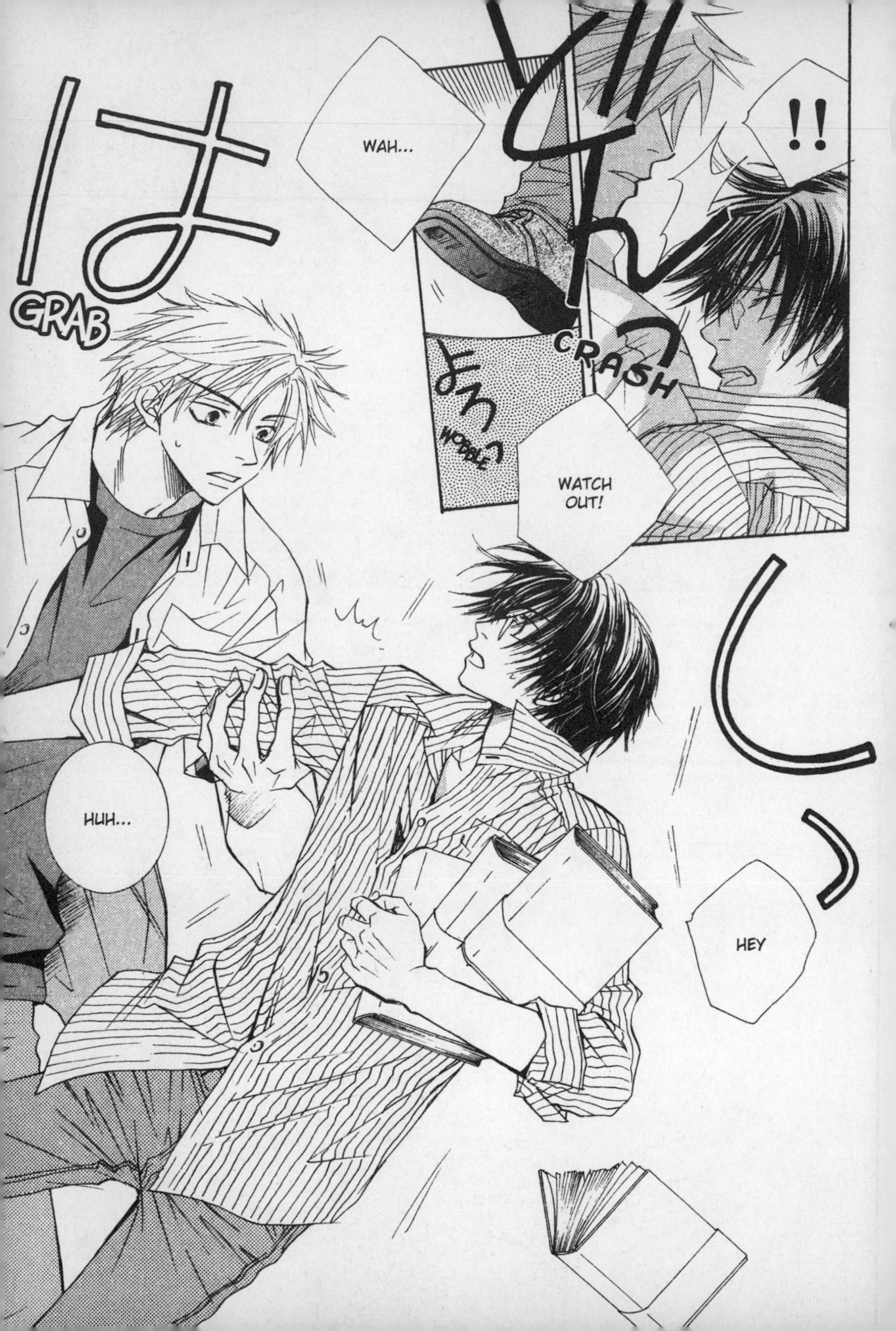
!!
WAH...
CRASH
WOBBLE
WATCH OUT!
GRAB
HEY
HUH...

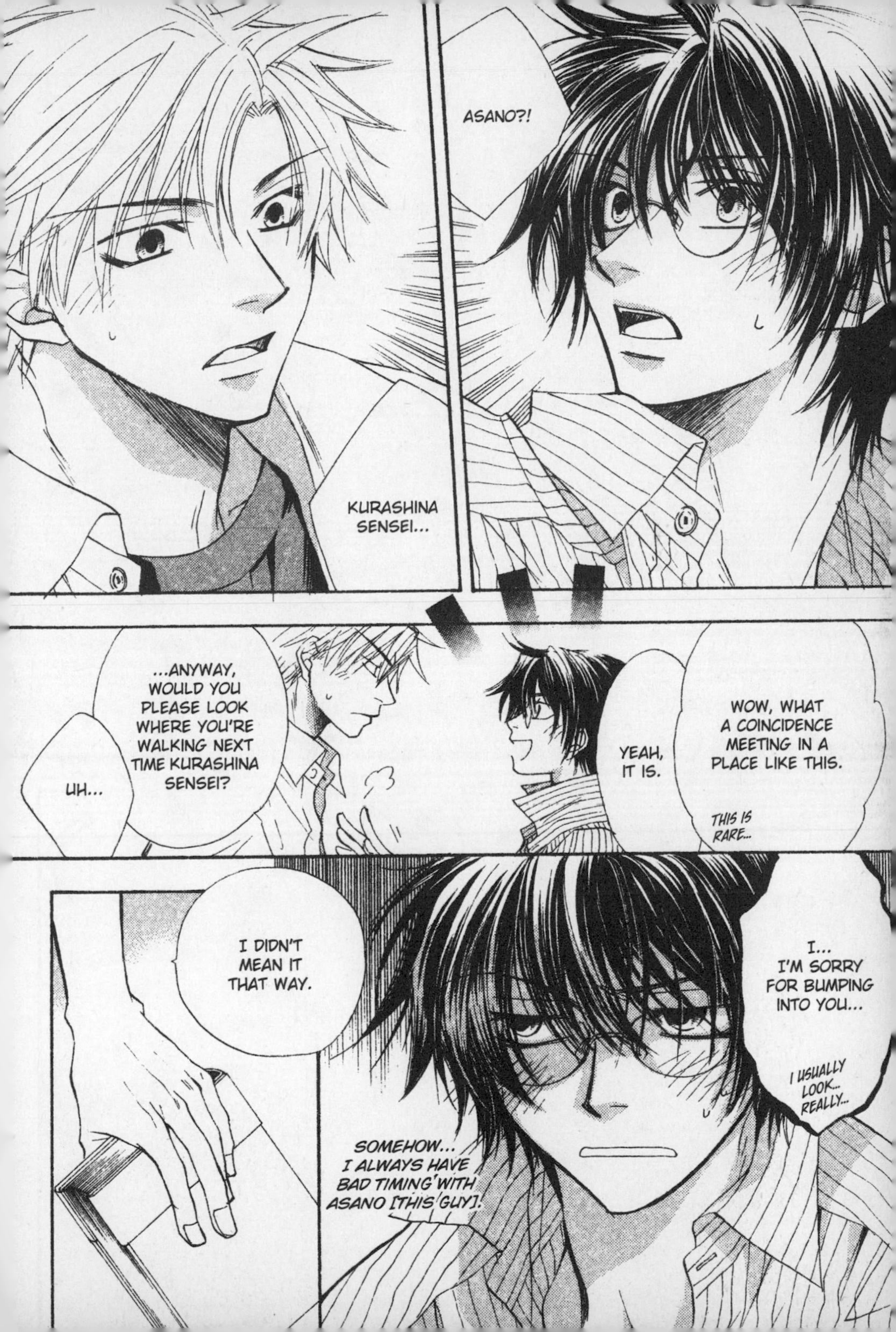
ASANO?!
KURASHINA SENSEI...
WOW, WHAT A COINCIDENCE MEETING IN A PLACE LIKE THIS.
THIS IS RARE...
YEAH, IT IS.
...ANYWAY, WOULD YOU PLEASE LOOK WHERE YOU'RE WALKING NEXT TIME KURASHINA SENSEI?
UH...
I... I'M SORRY FOR BUMPING INTO YOU...
I USUALLY LOOK... REALLY...
I DIDN'T MEAN IT THAT WAY.
SOMEHOW... I ALWAYS HAVE BAD TIMING WITH ASANO [THIS GUY].

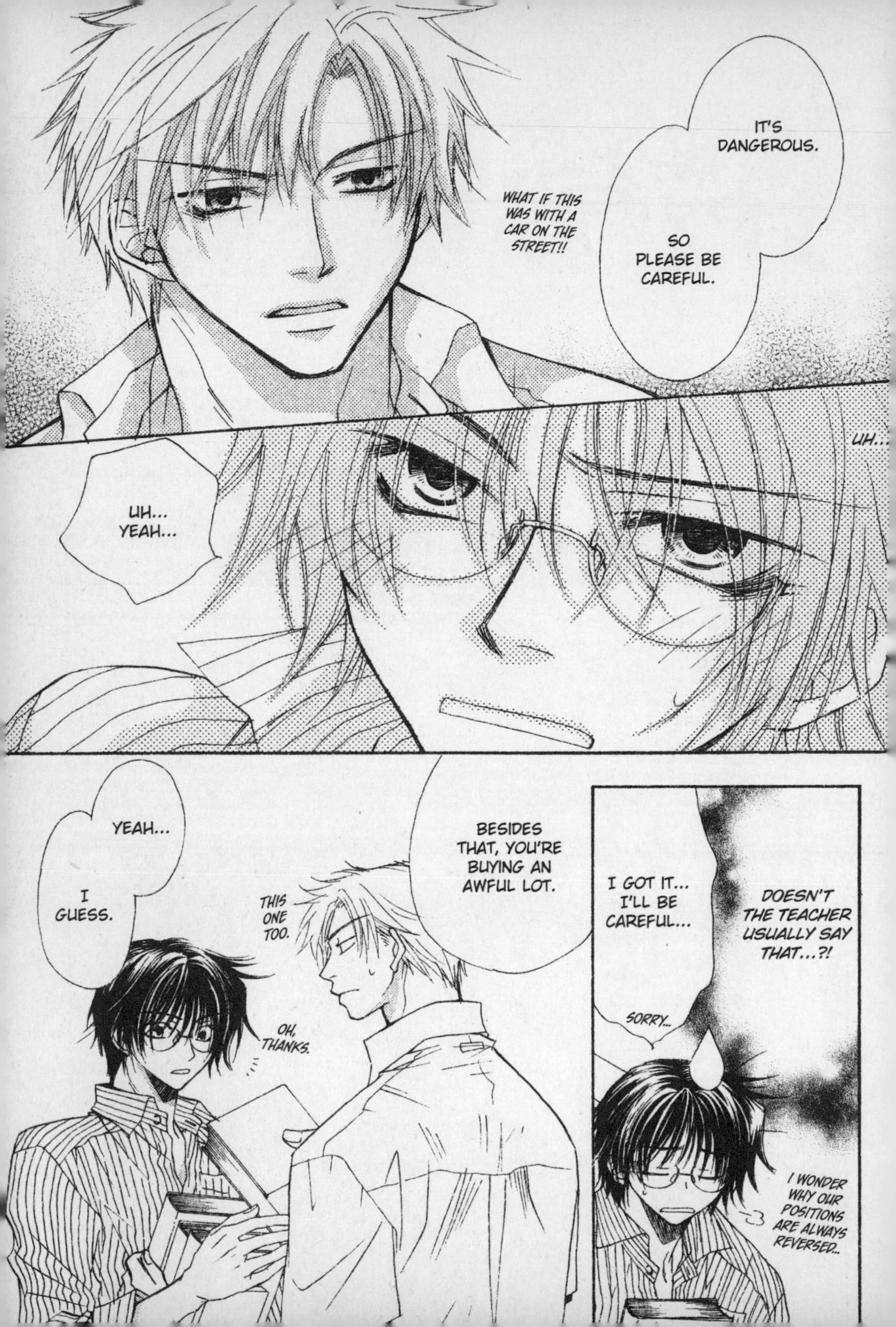
IT'S DANGEROUS.
SO PLEASE BE CAREFUL.
WHAT IF THIS WAS WITH A CAR ON THE STREET!!
UH...
UH... YEAH...
DOESN'T THE TEACHER USUALLY SAY THAT...?!
I GOT IT... I'LL BE CAREFUL...
SORRY...
I WONDER WHY OUR POSITIONS ARE ALWAYS REVERSED...
BESIDES THAT, YOU'RE BUYING AN AWFUL LOT.
THIS ONE TOO.
OH, THANKS.
YEAH...
I GUESS.

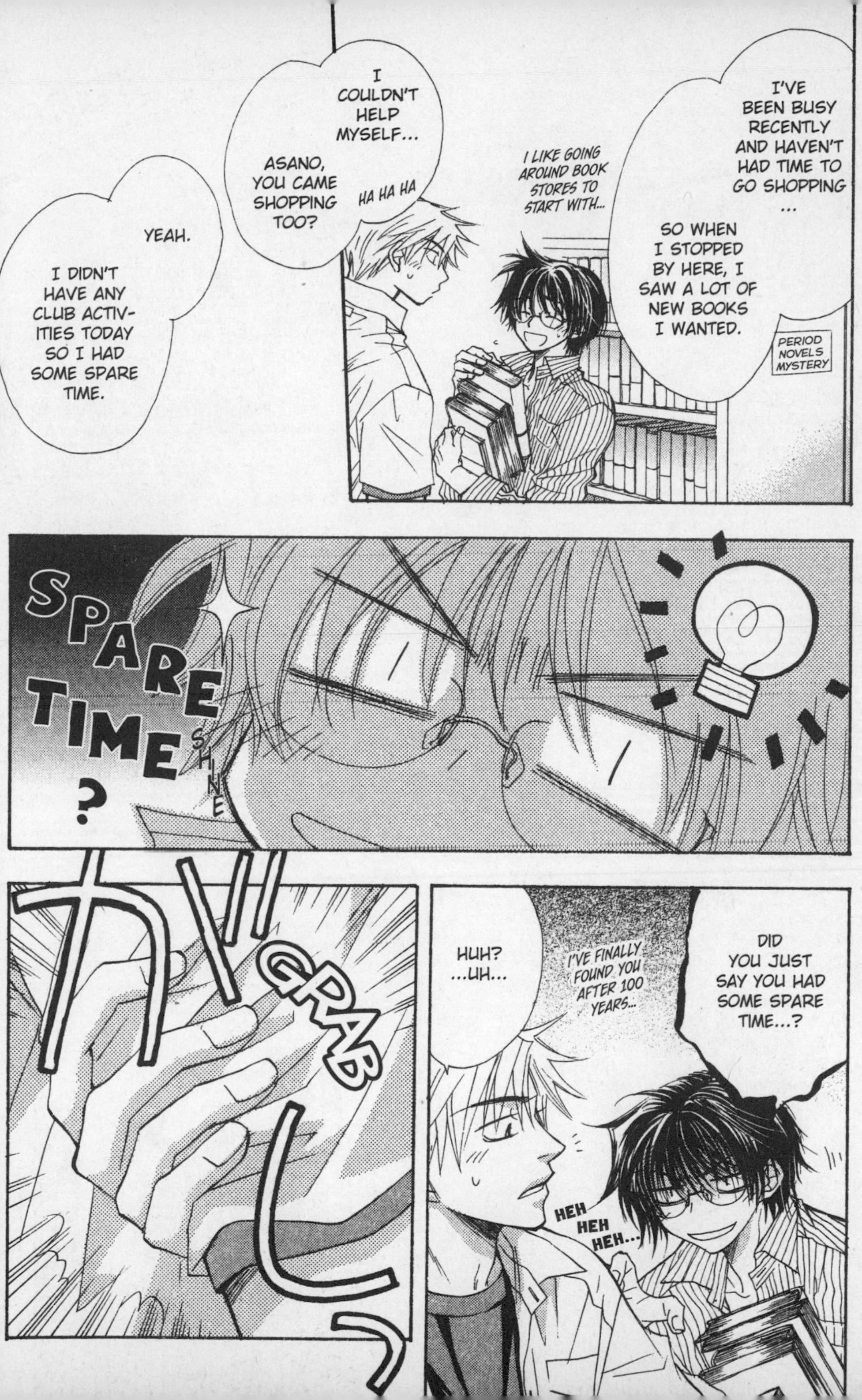
I'VE BEEN BUSY RECENTLY AND HAVEN'T HAD TIME TO GO SHOPPING ...
I LIKE GOING AROUND BOOK STORES TO START WITH...
SO WHEN I STOPPED BY HERE, I SAW A LOT OF NEW BOOKS I WANTED.
PERIOD NOVELS MYSTERY
I COULDN'T HELP MYSELF...
HA HA HA
ASANO, YOU CAME SHOPPING TOO?
YEAH.
I DIDN'T HAVE ANY CLUB ACTIVITIES TODAY SO I HAD SOME SPARE TIME.
SPARE TIME?
SHINE
DID YOU JUST SAY YOU HAD SOME SPARE TIME...?
I'VE FINALLY FOUND YOU AFTER 100 YEARS...
HUH? ...UH...
HEH HEH HEH...
GRAB

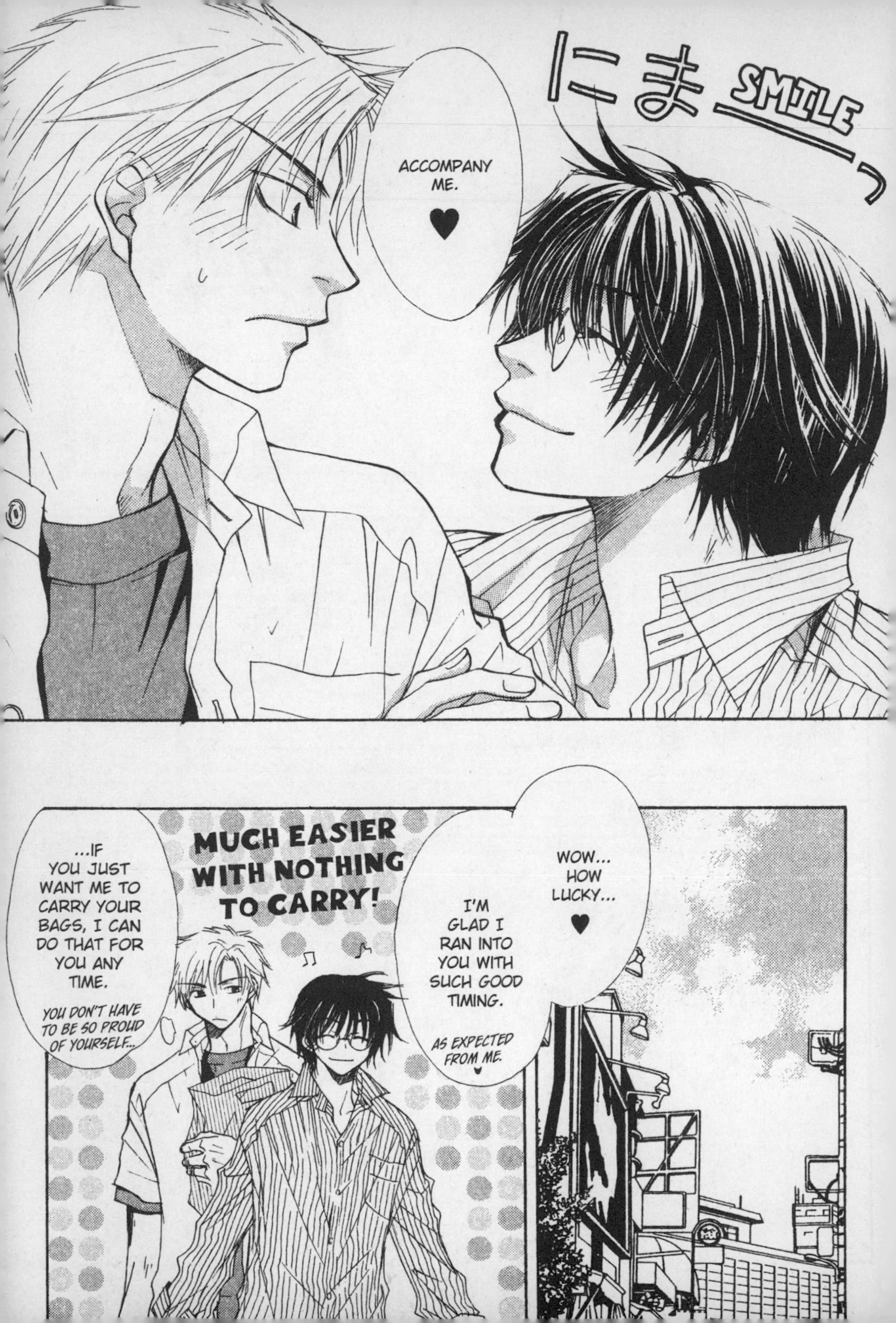
にま SMILE
ACCOMPANY ME. ♥
WOW... HOW LUCKY... ♥
I'M GLAD I RAN INTO YOU WITH SUCH GOOD TIMING.
AS EXPECTED FROM ME. ♥
MUCH EASIER WITH NOTHING TO CARRY!
...IF YOU JUST WANT ME TO CARRY YOUR BAGS, I CAN DO THAT FOR YOU ANY TIME.
YOU DON'T HAVE TO BE SO PROUD OF YOURSELF...

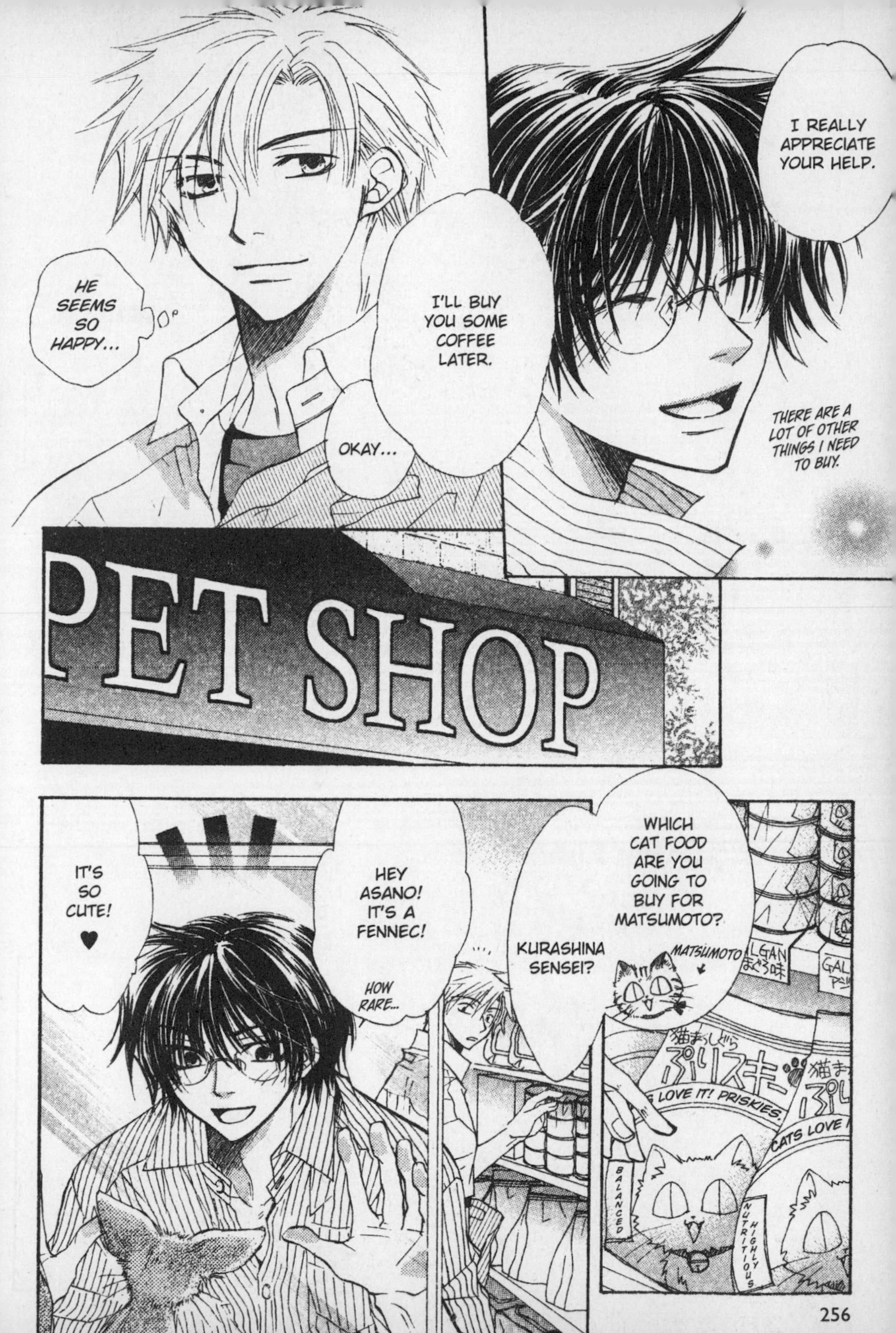
I REALLY APPRECIATE YOUR HELP.
I'LL BUY YOU SOME COFFEE LATER.
THERE ARE A LOT OF OTHER THINGS I NEED TO BUY.
HE SEEMS SO HAPPY...
OKAY...
PET SHOP
WHICH CAT FOOD ARE YOU GOING TO BUY FOR MATSUMOTO?
KURASHINA SENSEI?
MATSUMOTO
...
HEY ASANO! IT'S A FENNEC!
HOW RARE...
IT'S SO CUTE! ♥
まぐろ味
ぷりスキー
LOVE IT! PRISKIES.
BALANCED
HIGHLY NUTRITIOUS

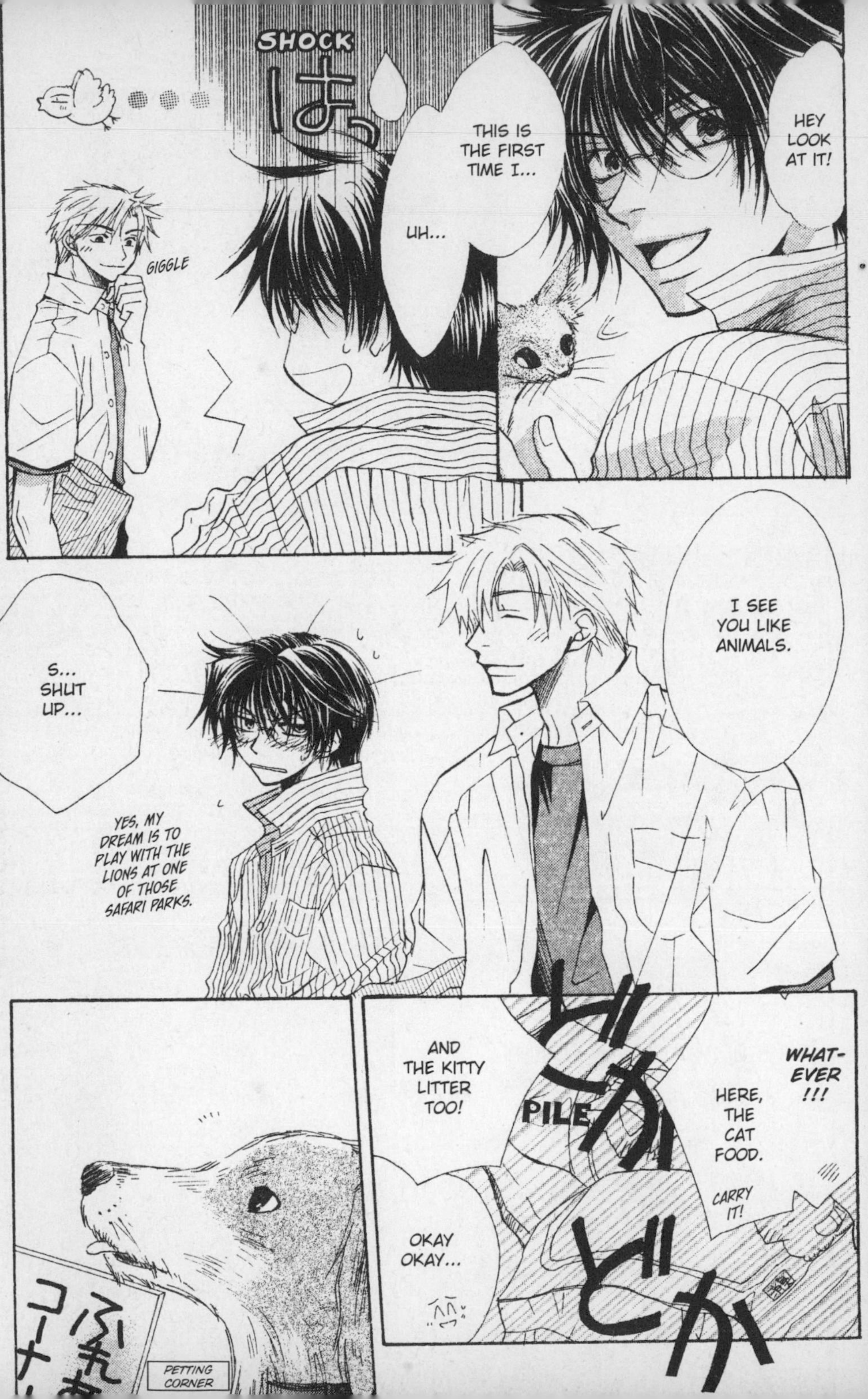
HEY LOOK AT IT!
THIS IS THE FIRST TIME I...
UH...
SHOCK
はっ
GIGGLE
I SEE YOU LIKE ANIMALS.
S... SHUT UP...
YES, MY DREAM IS TO PLAY WITH THE LIONS AT ONE OF THOSE SAFARI PARKS.
WHAT-EVER!!!
HERE, THE CAT FOOD.
CARRY IT!
PILE
AND THE KITTY LITTER TOO!
OKAY OKAY...
PETTING CORNER

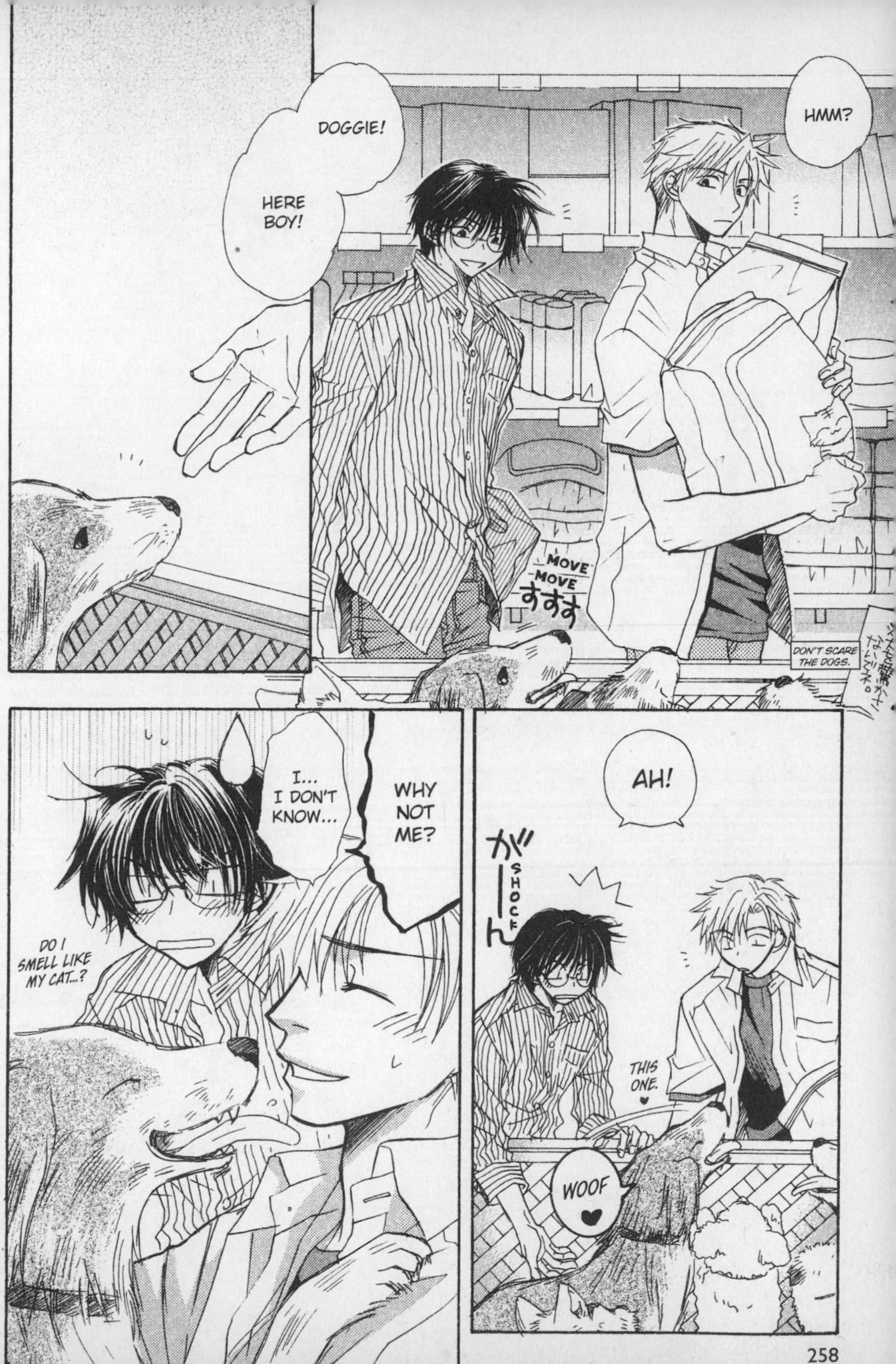
HMM?
DOGGIE!
HERE BOY!
MOVE MOVE
すすす
DON'T SCARE THE DOGS.
AH!
が ー ん
SHOCK
THIS ONE. ♥
WOOF ♥
WHY NOT ME?
I... I DON'T KNOW...
DO I SMELL LIKE MY CAT...?

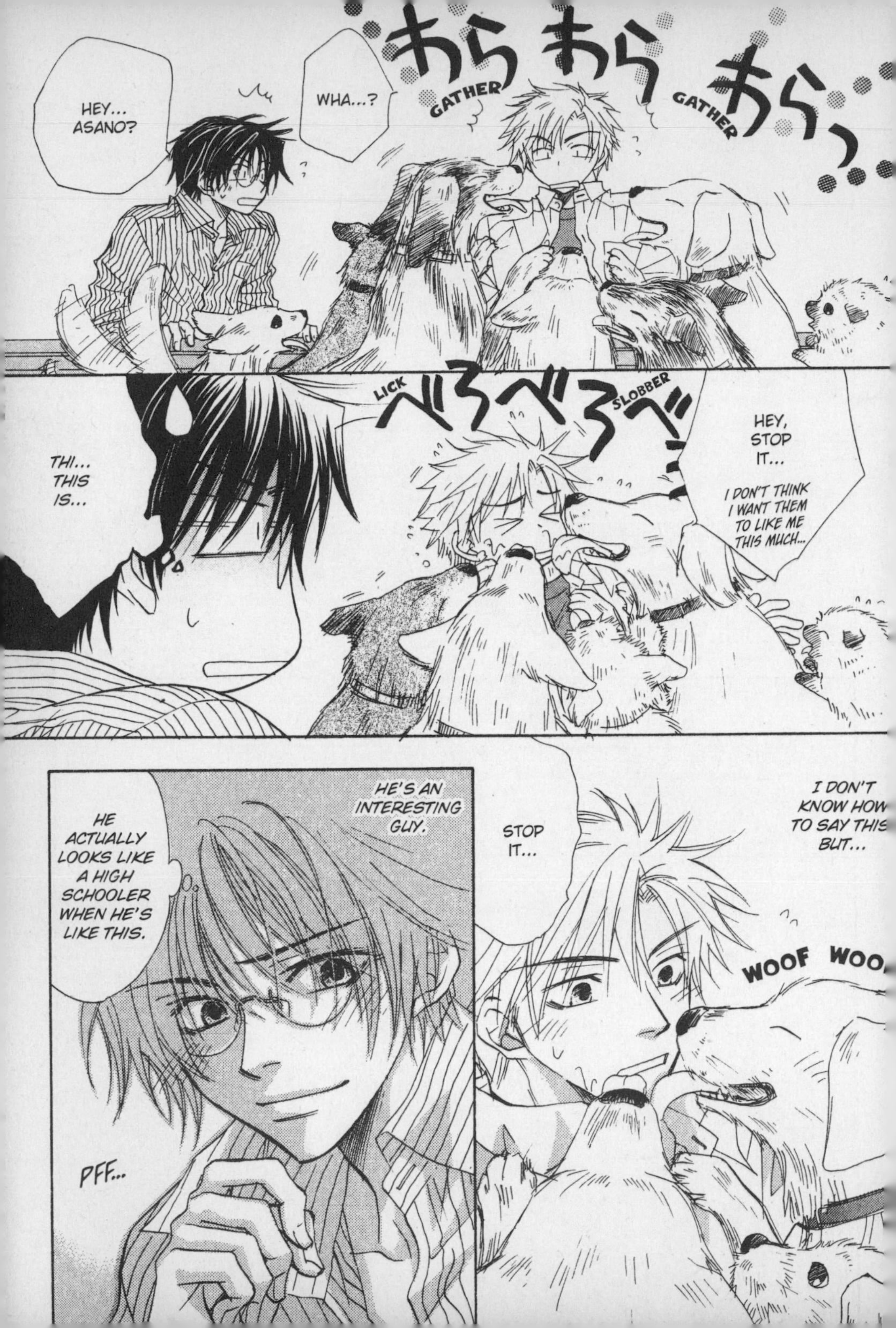

わらわらわらっ
GATHER
GATHER
WHA...?
HEY... ASANO?
HEY, STOP IT...
I DON'T THINK I WANT THEM TO LIKE ME THIS MUCH...
べろべろべ
LICK
SLOBBER
THI... THIS IS...
I DON'T KNOW HOW TO SAY THIS BUT...
STOP IT...
WOOF
HE'S AN INTERESTING GUY.
HE ACTUALLY LOOKS LIKE A HIGH SCHOOLER WHEN HE'S LIKE THIS.
PFF...

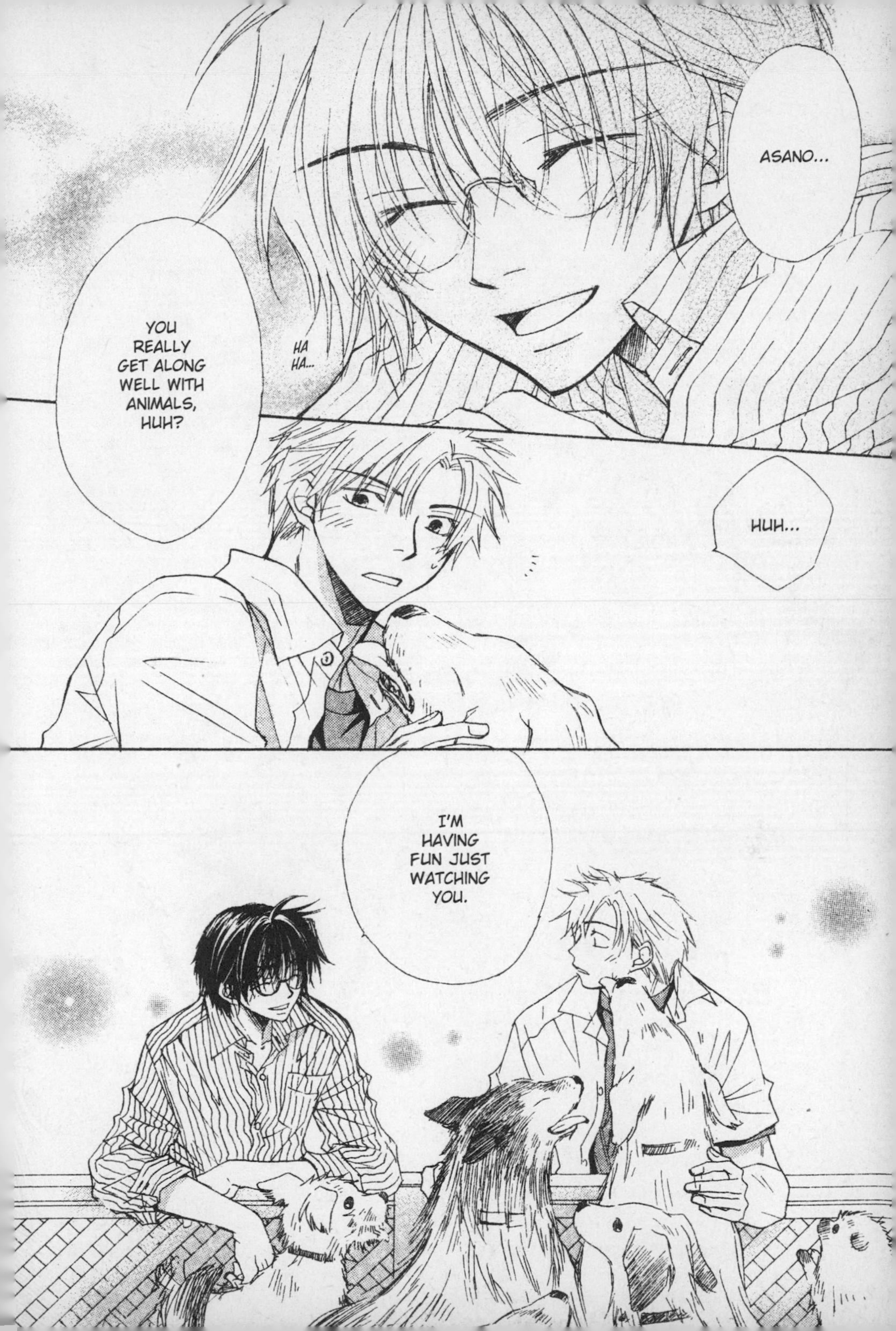
ASANO...
HA HA...
YOU REALLY GET ALONG WELL WITH ANIMALS, HUH?
HUH...
I'M HAVING FUN JUST WATCHING YOU.

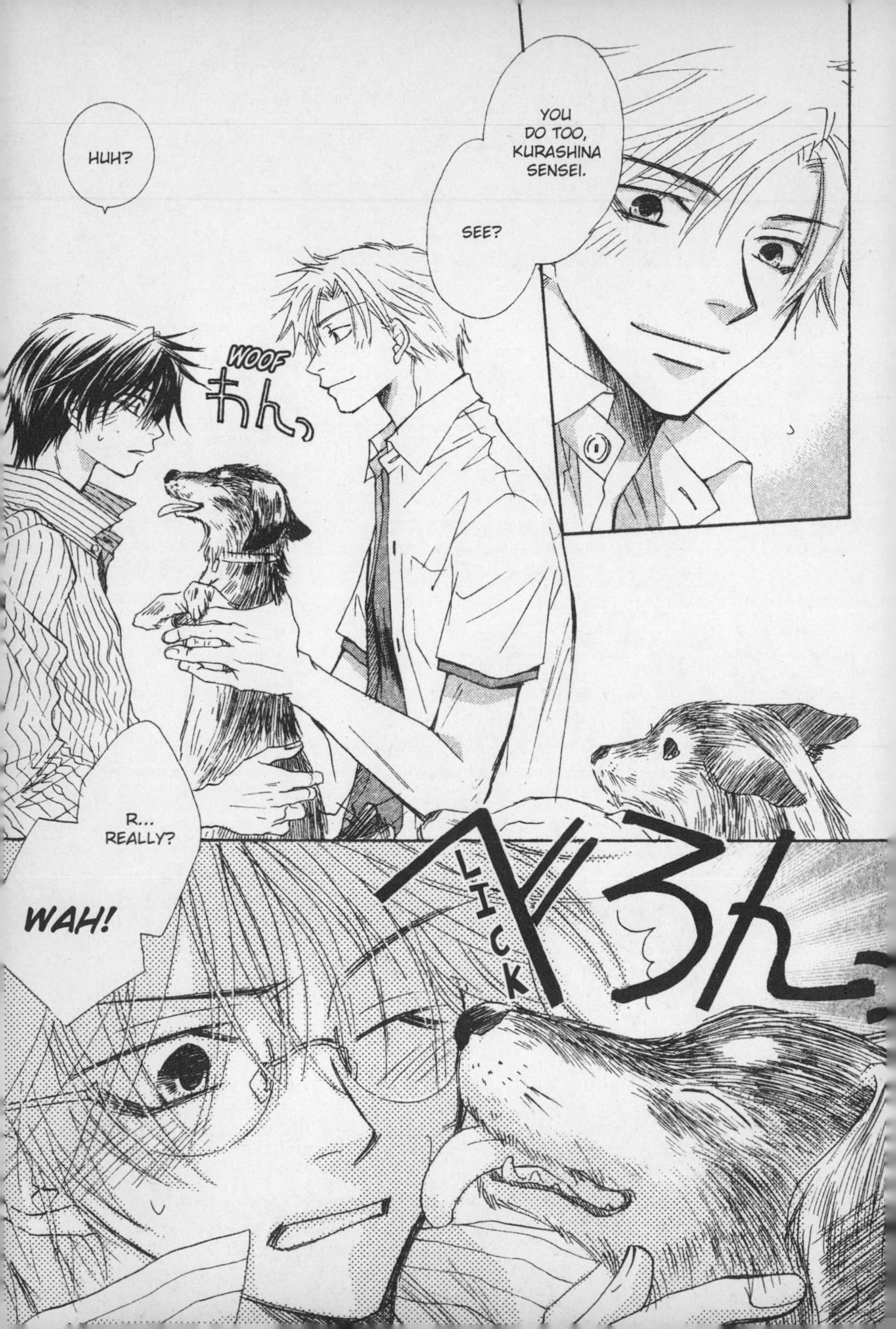
YOU DO TOO, KURASHINA SENSEI.
SEE?
HUH?
WOOF
わん
R... REALLY?
LICK
ぺろん
WAH!

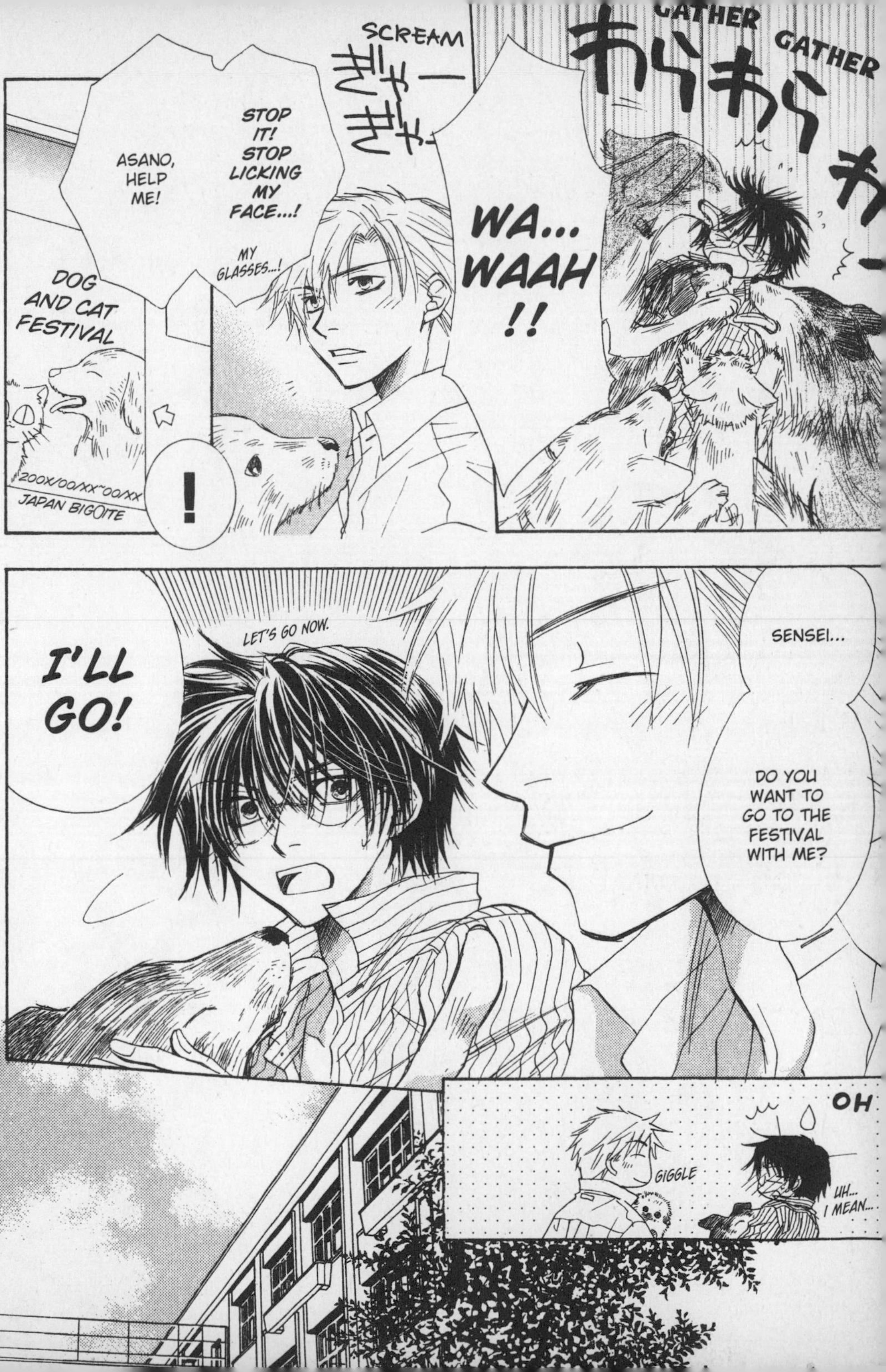
GATHER GATHER
わらわら
WA... WAAH!!
SCREAM
ぎゃーぎゃー
STOP IT! STOP LICKING MY FACE...!
ASANO, HELP ME!
MY GLASSES...!
!
DOG AND CAT FESTIVAL
200X/00/XX~00/XX
JAPAN BIGOITE
SENSEI...
DO YOU WANT TO GO TO THE FESTIVAL WITH ME?
LET'S GO NOW.
I'LL GO!
OH
UH... I MEAN...
GIGGLE

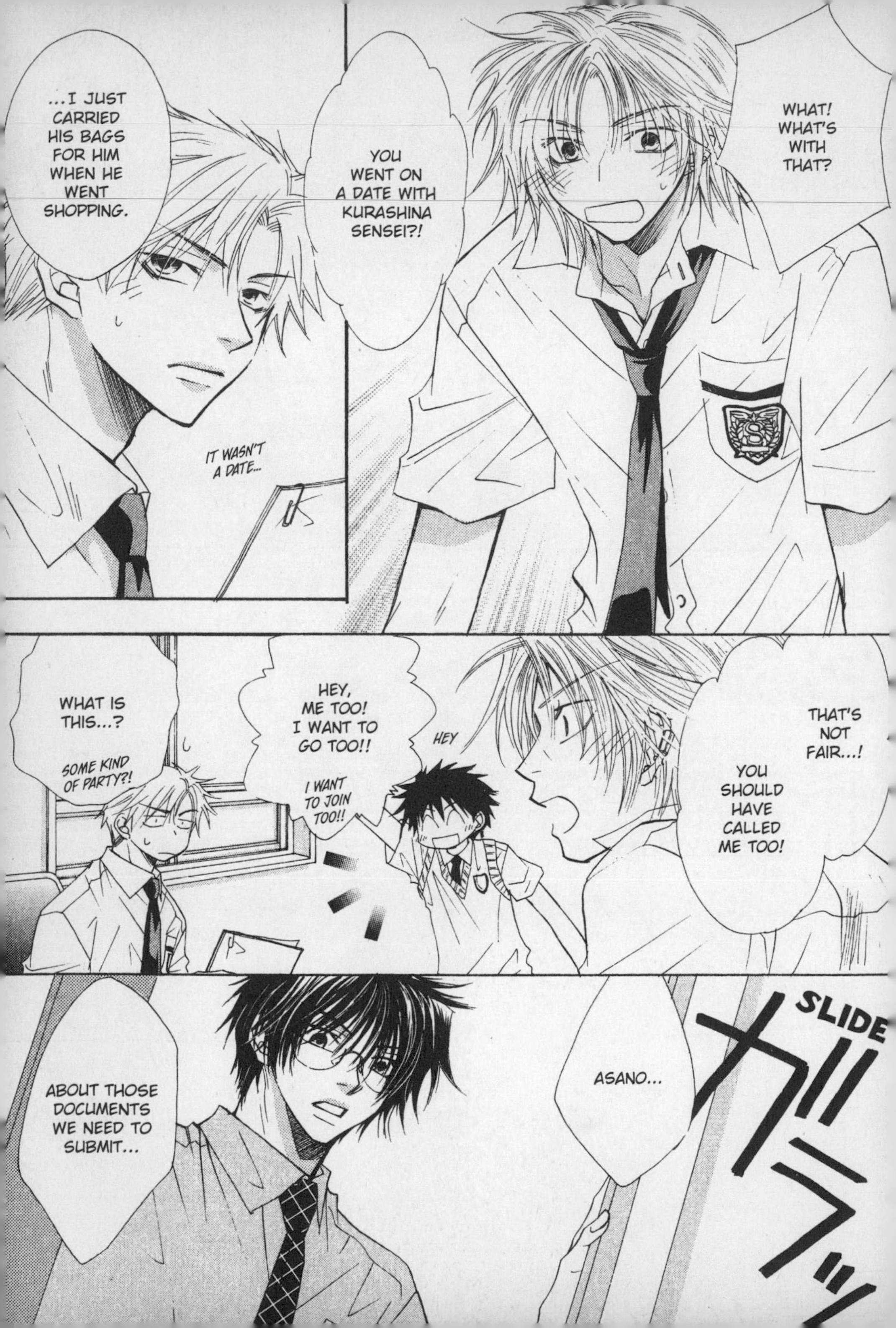
WHAT! WHAT'S WITH THAT?
YOU WENT ON A DATE WITH KURASHINA SENSEI?!
IT WASN'T A DATE...
...I JUST CARRIED HIS BAGS FOR HIM WHEN HE WENT SHOPPING.
THAT'S NOT FAIR...!
YOU SHOULD HAVE CALLED ME TOO!
HEY
HEY, ME TOO! I WANT TO GO TOO!!
I WANT TO JOIN TOO!!
WHAT IS THIS...?
SOME KIND OF PARTY?!
SLIDE
ASANO...
ABOUT THOSE DOCUMENTS WE NEED TO SUBMIT...

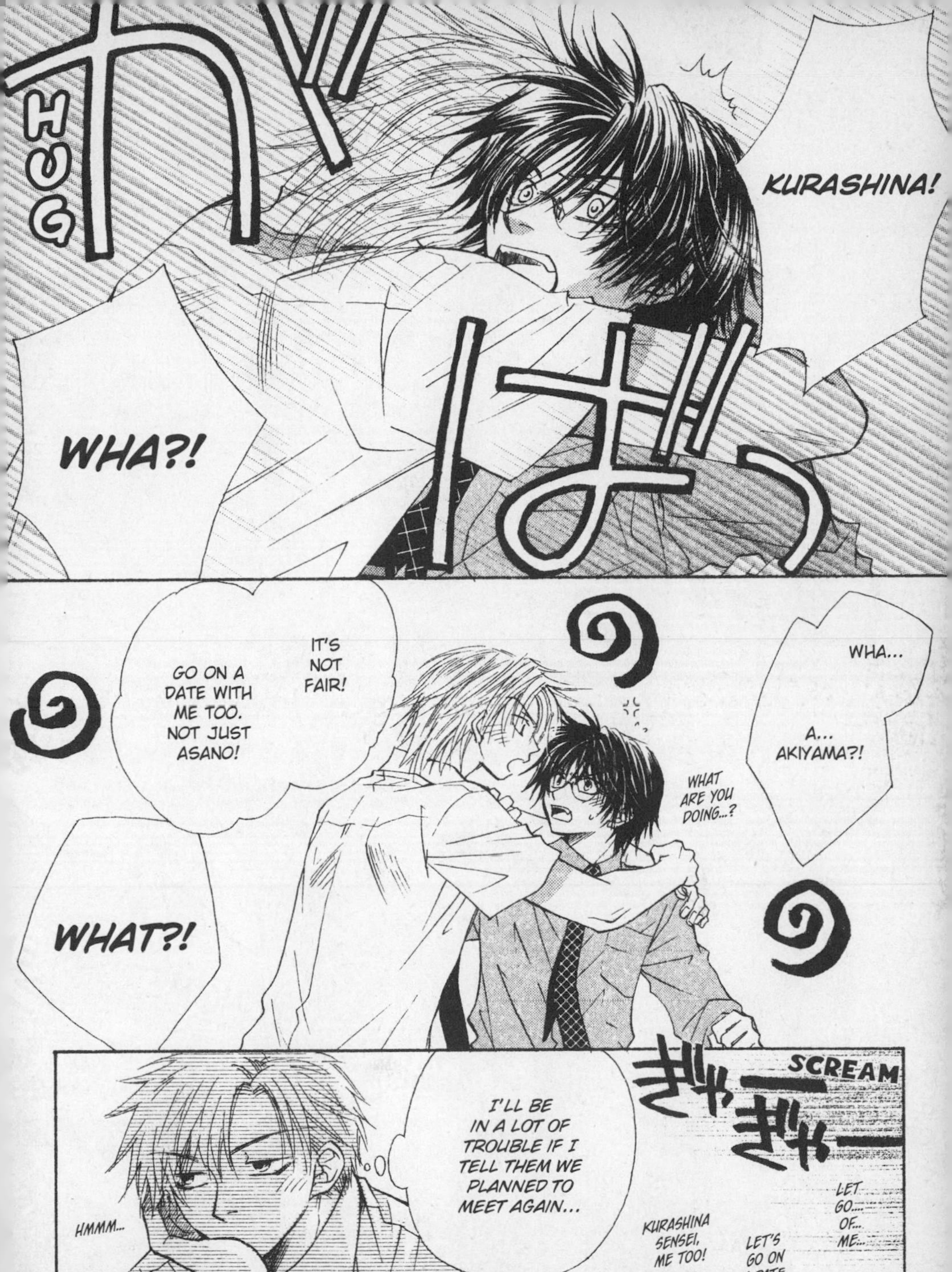
HUG
KURASHINA!
WHA?!
WHA...
A... AKIYAMA?!
WHAT ARE YOU DOING...?
IT'S NOT FAIR!
GO ON A DATE WITH ME TOO. NOT JUST ASANO!
WHAT?!
SCREAM
LET GO... OF... ME...
LET'S GO ON A DATE...
KURASHINA SENSEI, ME TOO!
I'LL BE IN A LOT OF TROUBLE IF I TELL THEM WE PLANNED TO MEET AGAIN...
HMMM...

THE TROUBLES OF KURASHINA SENSEI THE END

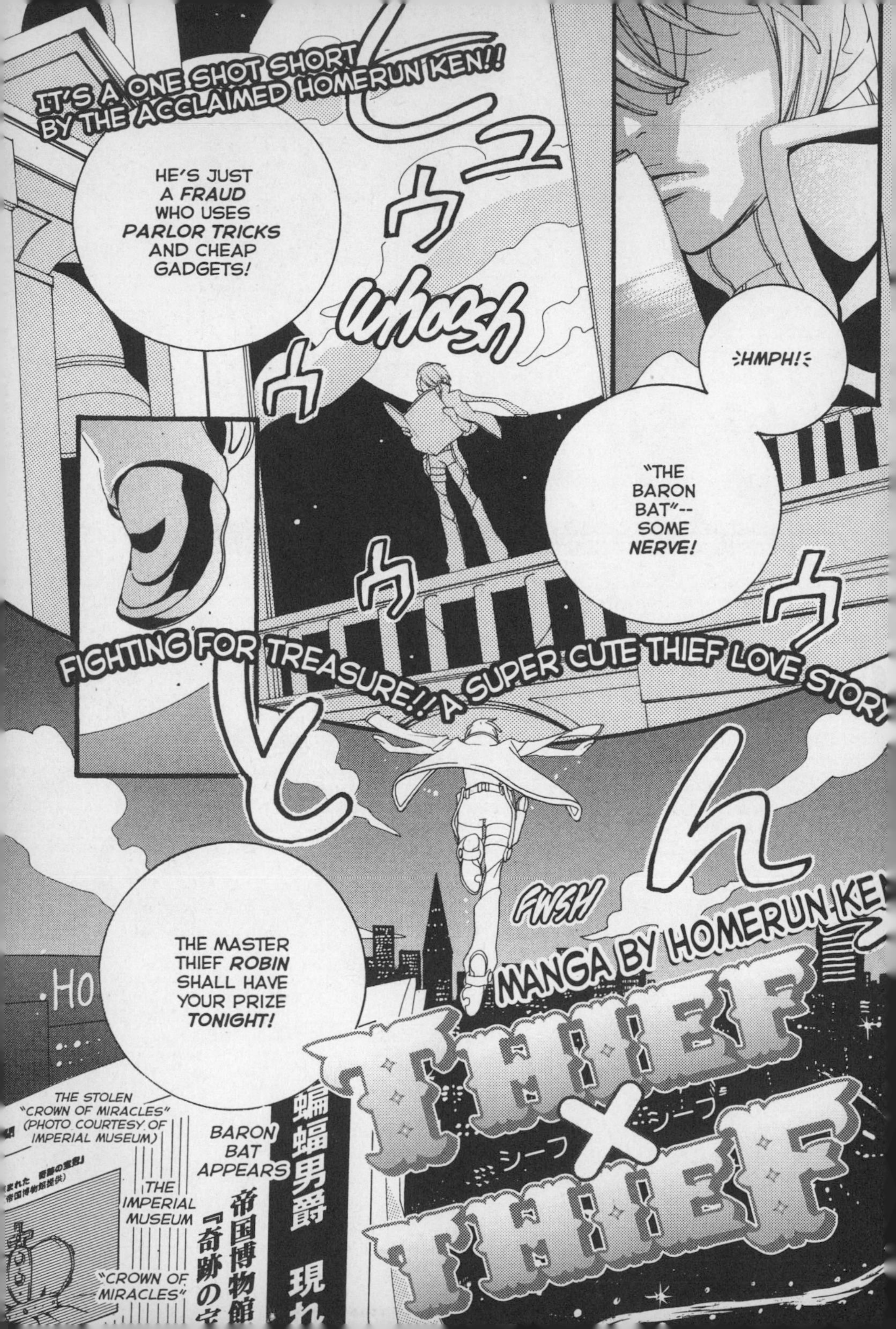

IT'S A ONE SHOT SHORT BY THE ACCLAIMED HOMERUN KEN!!
HMPH!
"THE BARON BAT"-- SOME NERVE!
HE'S JUST A FRAUD WHO USES PARLOR TRICKS AND CHEAP GADGETS!
WHOOSH
FIGHTING FOR TREASURE!! A SUPER CUTE THIEF LOVE STORY
FWSH
MANGA BY HOMERUN KEN
THIEF × THIEF
シーフ
シーフ
THE MASTER THIEF ROBIN SHALL HAVE YOUR PRIZE TONIGHT!
HO
蝙蝠男爵 現れ
BARON BAT APPEARS
帝国博物館『奇跡の宝
THE IMPERIAL MUSEUM
"CROWN OF MIRACLES"
THE STOLEN "CROWN OF MIRACLES" (PHOTO COURTESY OF IMPERIAL MUSEUM)

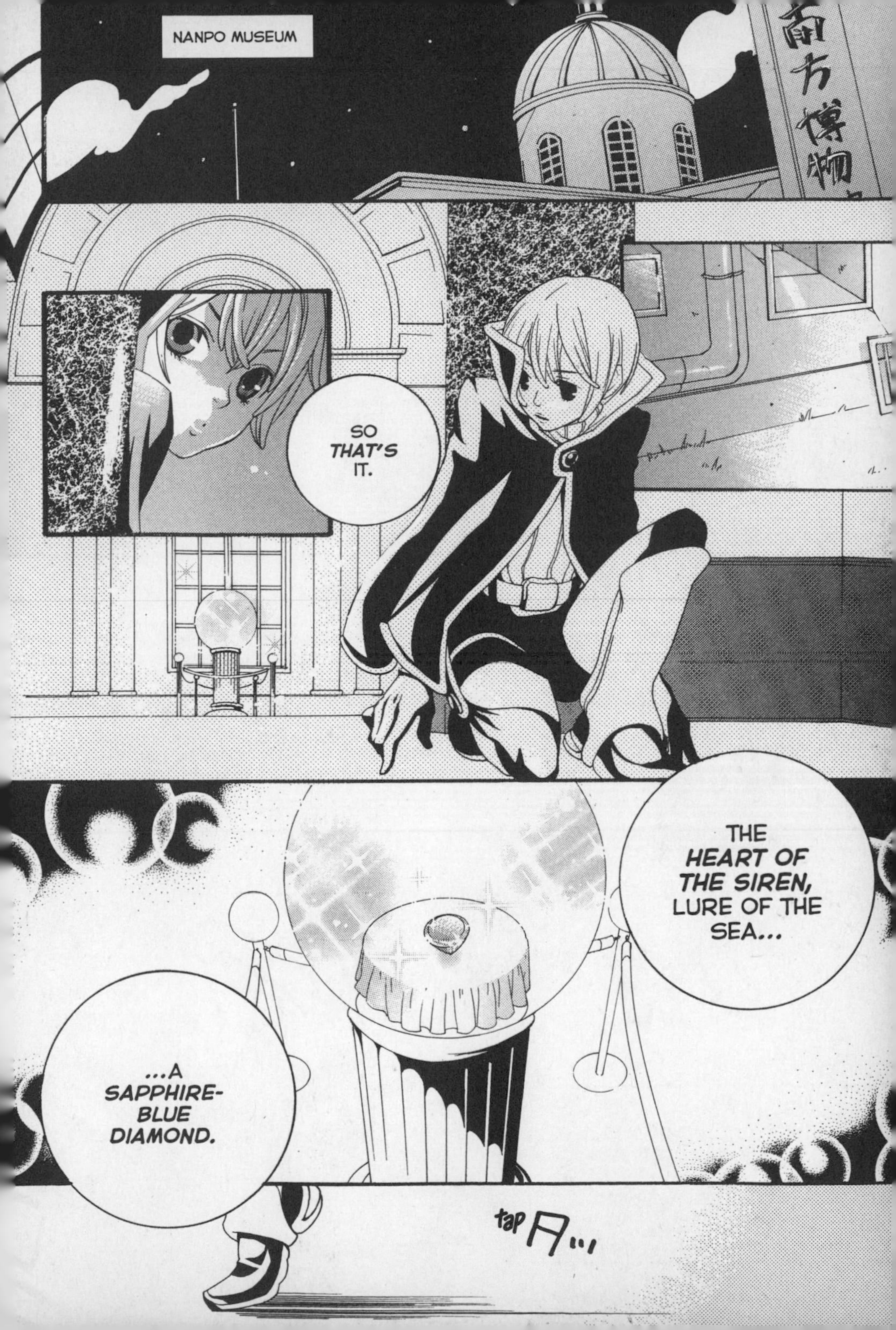
南方博物
NANPO MUSEUM
SO THAT'S IT.
THE HEART OF THE SIREN, LURE OF THE SEA...
...A SAPPHIRE-BLUE DIAMOND.
tap

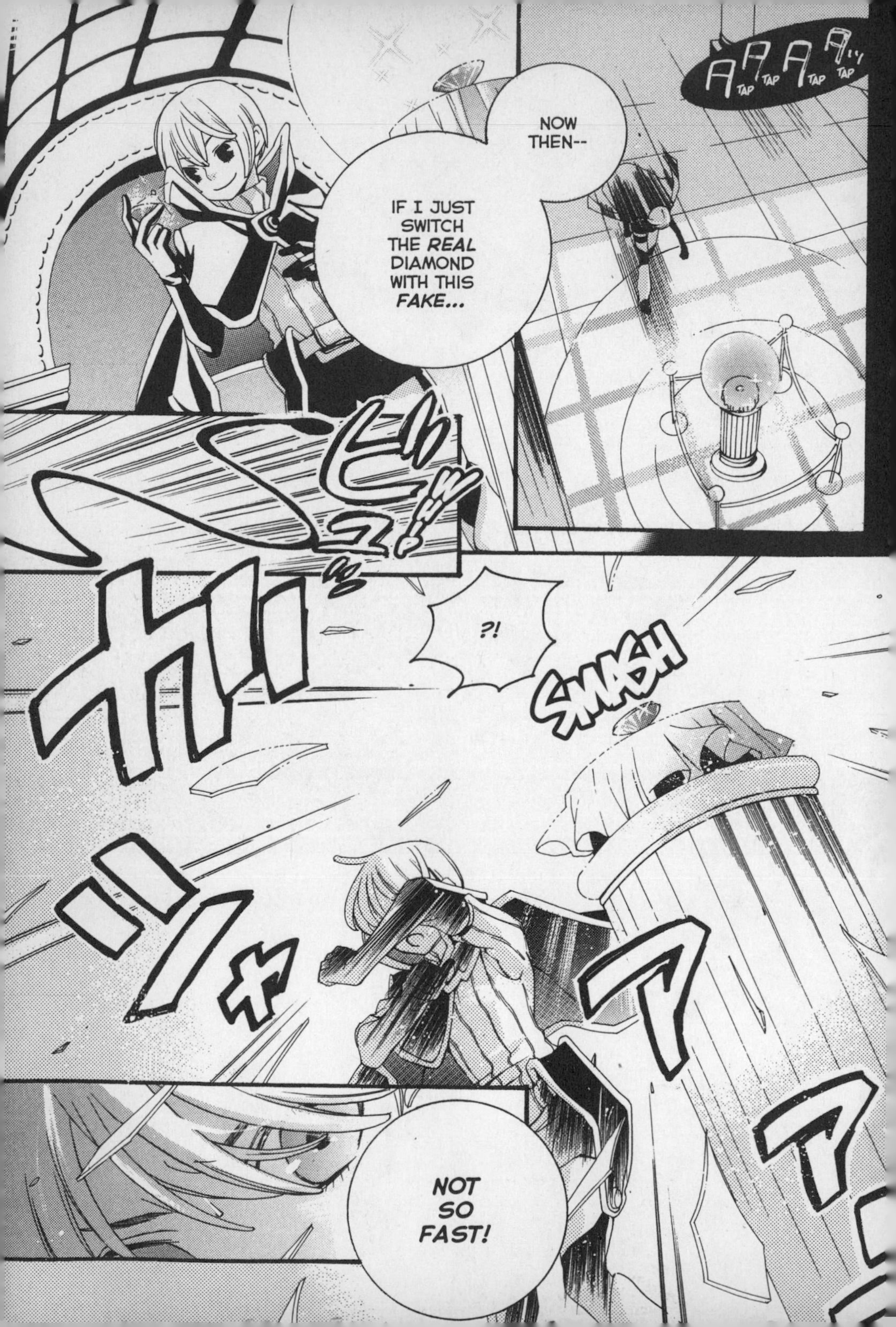
TAP TAP TAP TAP
NOW THEN--
IF I JUST SWITCH THE *REAL* DIAMOND WITH THIS *FAKE*...
?!
SMASH
NOT SO FAST!

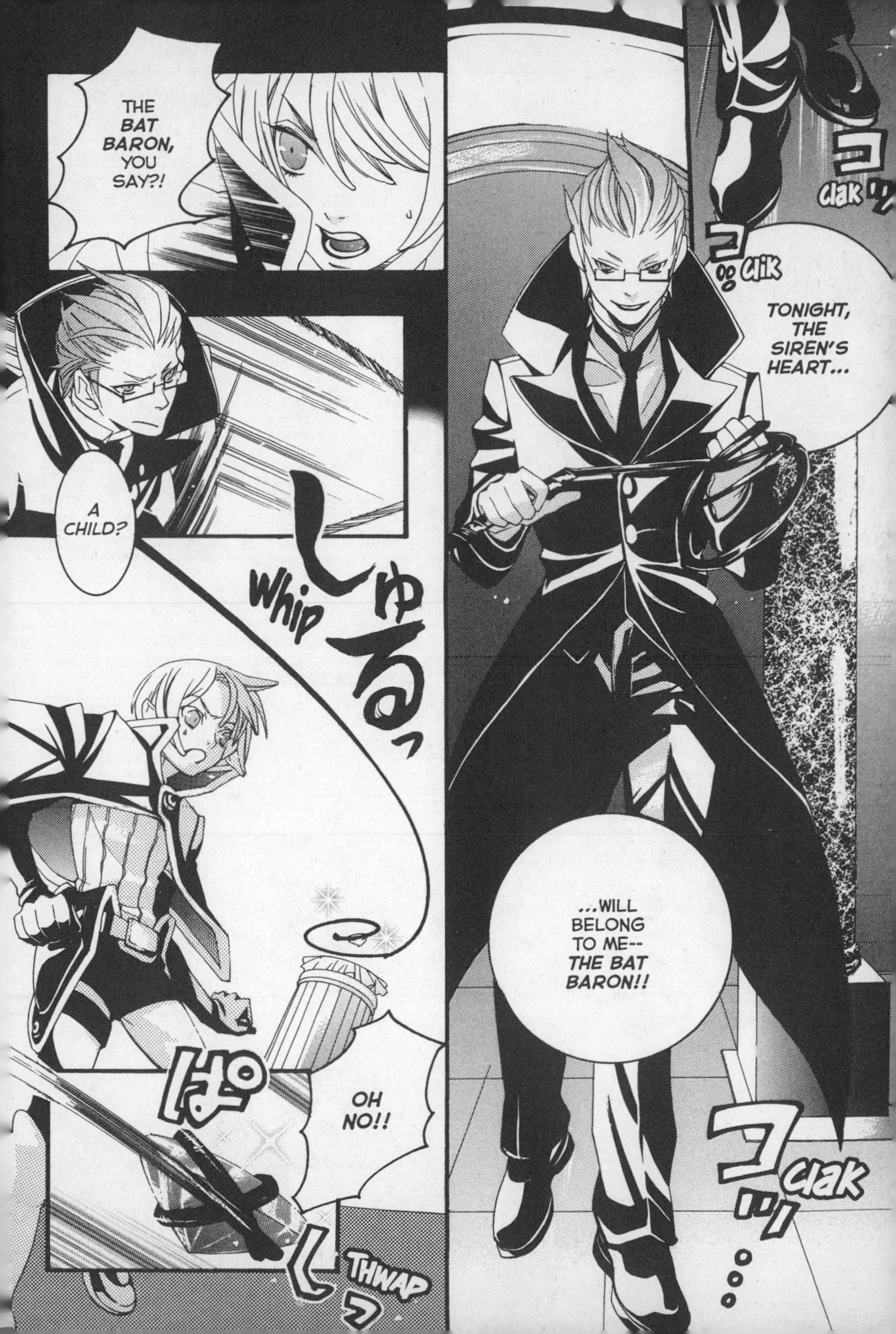

CLAK
CLIK
TONIGHT, THE SIREN'S HEART...
...WILL BELONG TO ME-- THE BAT BARON!!
CLAK
THE BAT BARON, YOU SAY?!
A CHILD?
WHIP
OH NO!!
THWAP

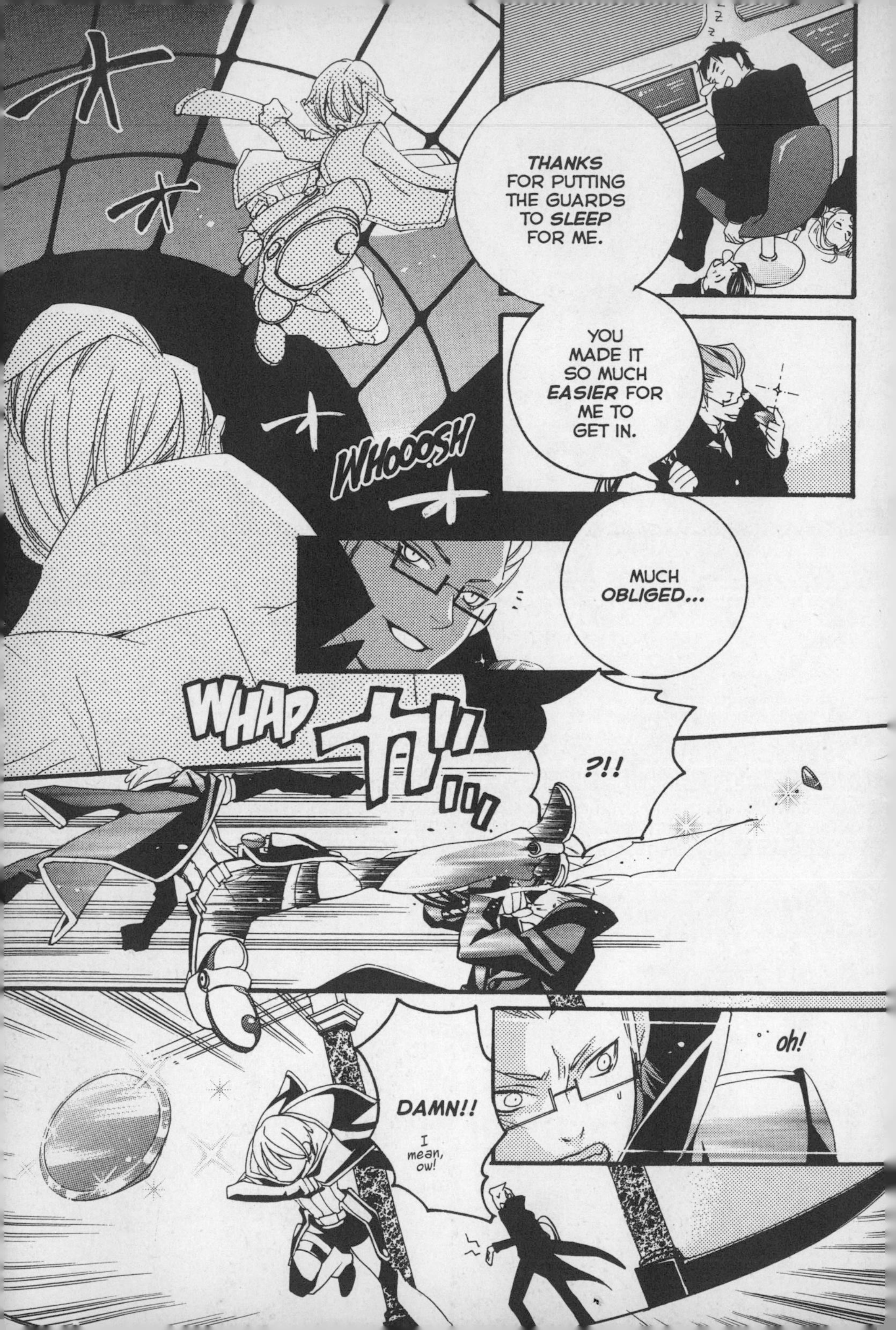

THANKS FOR PUTTING THE GUARDS TO SLEEP FOR ME.
YOU MADE IT SO MUCH EASIER FOR ME TO GET IN.
MUCH OBLIGED...
WHOOOSH
?!!
WHAP
oh!
DAMN!!
I mean, ow!

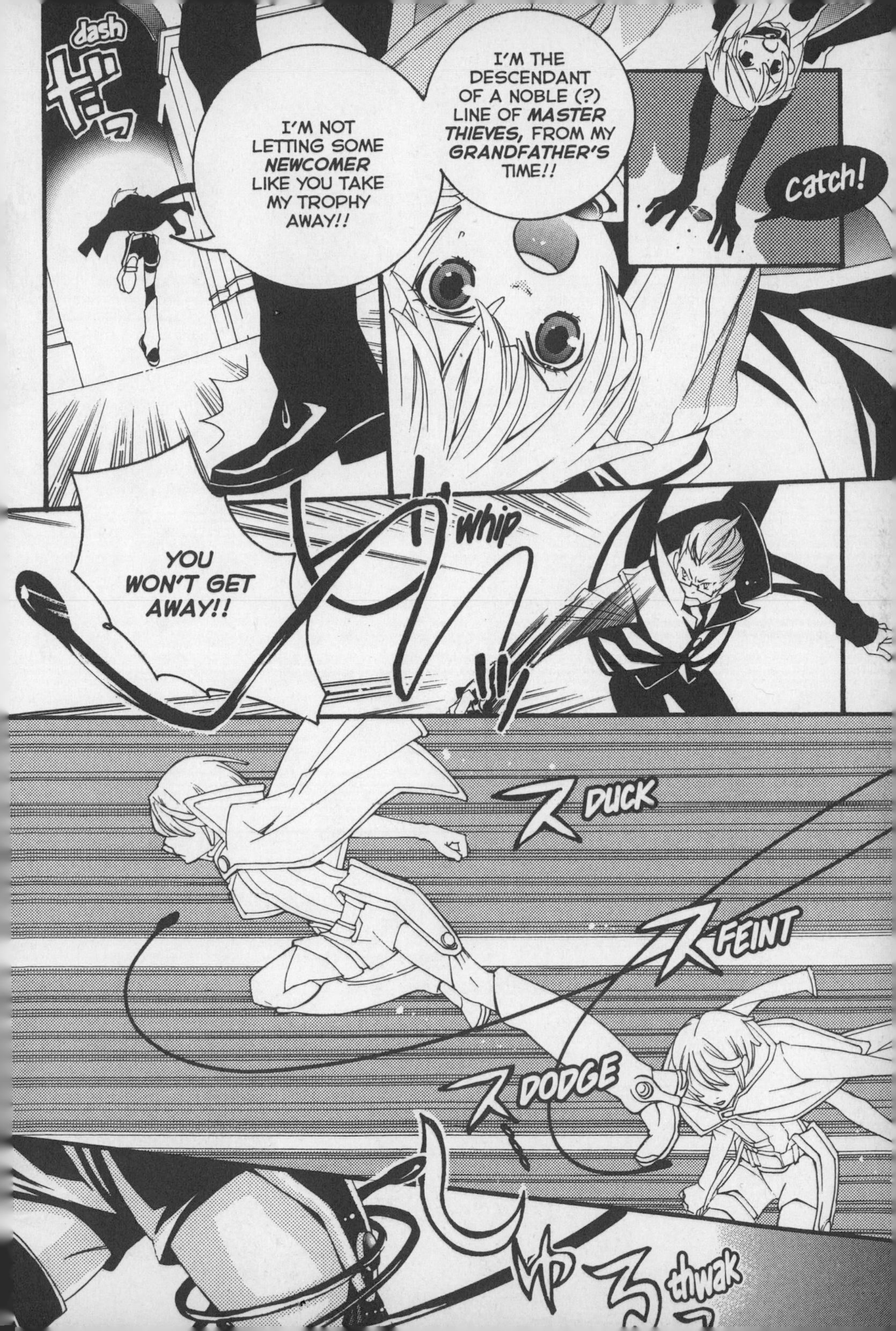
Catch!
I'M THE DESCENDANT OF A NOBLE (?) LINE OF MASTER THIEVES, FROM MY GRANDFATHER'S TIME!!
I'M NOT LETTING SOME NEWCOMER LIKE YOU TAKE MY TROPHY AWAY!!
dash
whip
YOU WON'T GET AWAY!!
DUCK
FEINT
DODGE
thwak

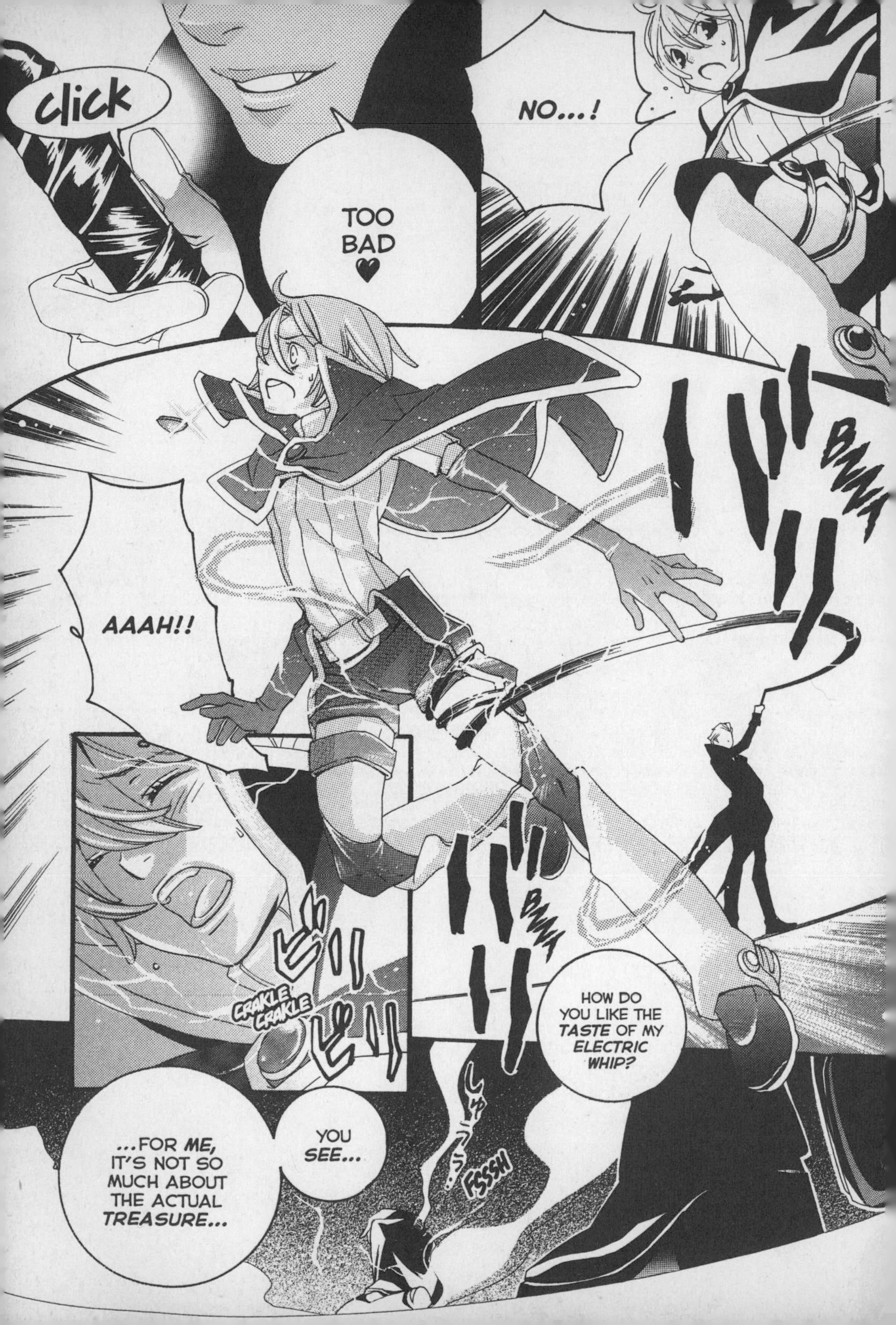
NO...!
CLICK
TOO BAD ♥
AAAH!!
CRAKLE CRAKLE
HOW DO YOU LIKE THE TASTE OF MY ELECTRIC WHIP?
FSSSH
YOU SEE...
...FOR ME, IT'S NOT SO MUCH ABOUT THE ACTUAL TREASURE...

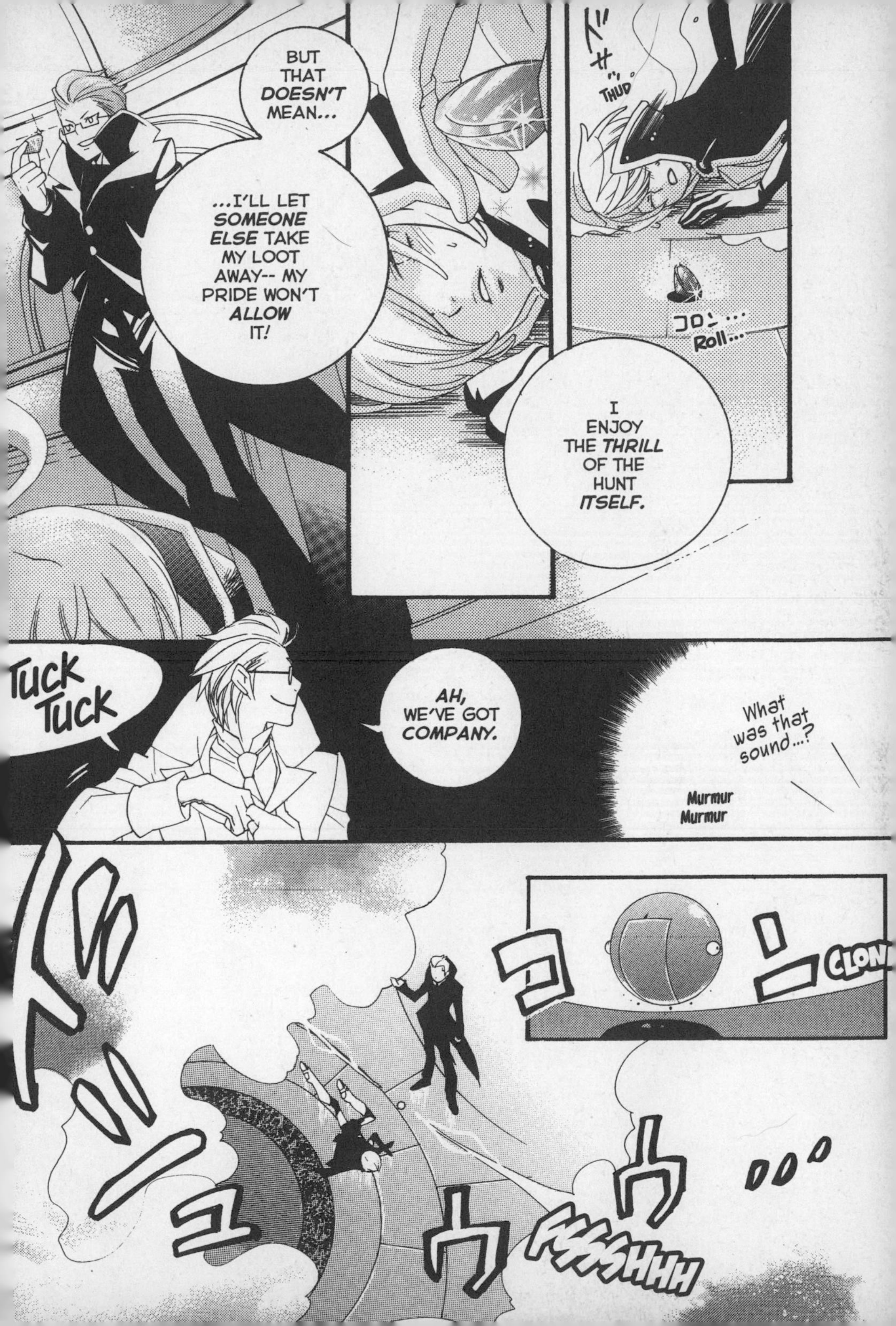
THUD
Roll...
I ENJOY THE THRILL OF THE HUNT ITSELF.
BUT THAT DOESN'T MEAN...
...I'LL LET SOMEONE ELSE TAKE MY LOOT AWAY-- MY PRIDE WON'T ALLOW IT!
What was that sound...?
Murmur Murmur
AH, WE'VE GOT COMPANY.
TUCK TUCK
CLON
FSSSHHH

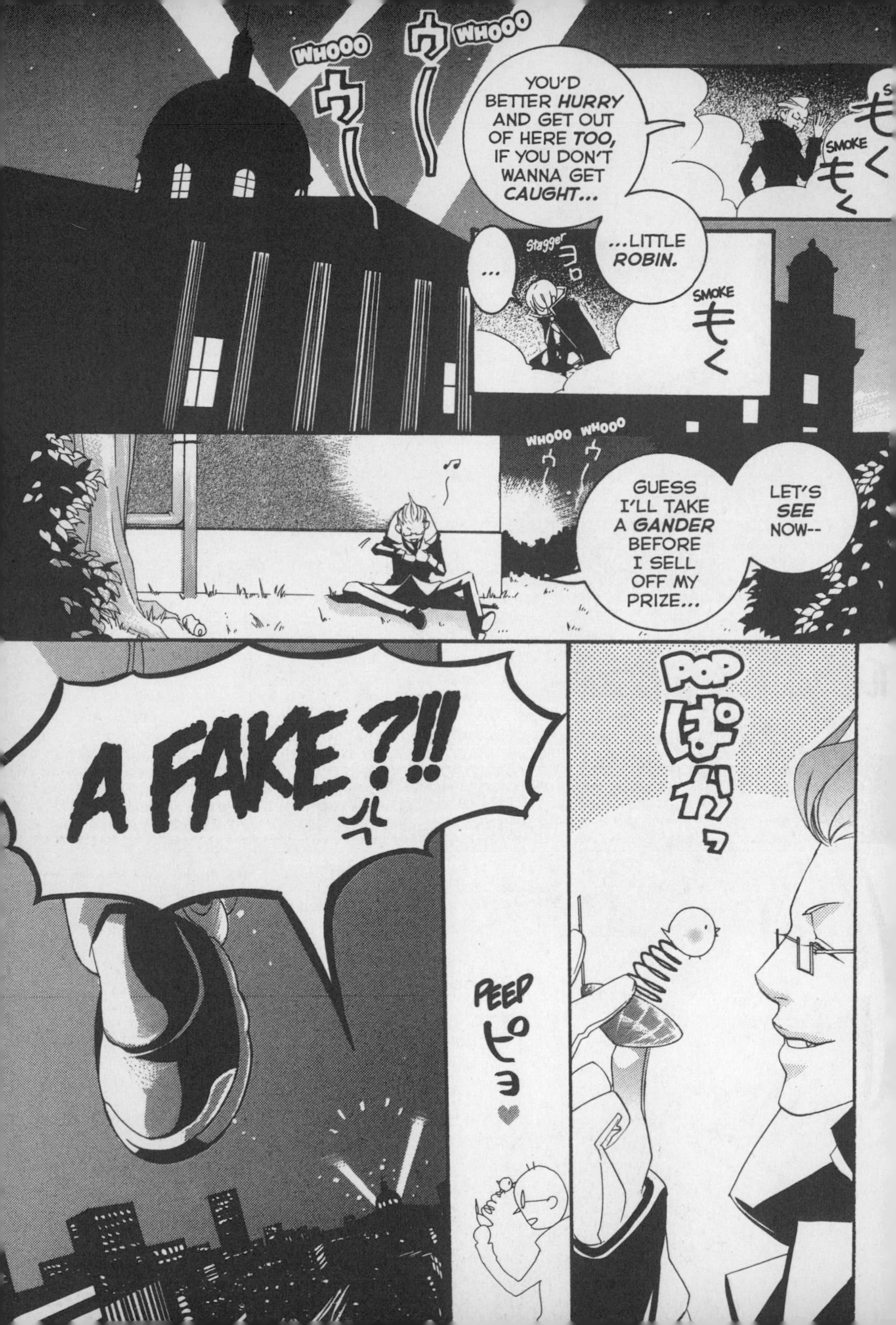

SMOKE
もくもく
YOU'D BETTER *HURRY* AND GET OUT OF HERE *TOO*, IF YOU DON'T WANNA GET *CAUGHT*...
...LITTLE *ROBIN.*
SMOKE
もく
Stagger
ヨロ
...
WHOOO
ウ~
WHOOO
ウ~
WHOOO WHOOO
ウ ウ
LET'S *SEE* NOW--
GUESS I'LL TAKE A *GANDER* BEFORE I SELL OFF MY PRIZE...
♪
POP
ぽがっ
PEEP
ピヨ
♥
A FAKE?!!

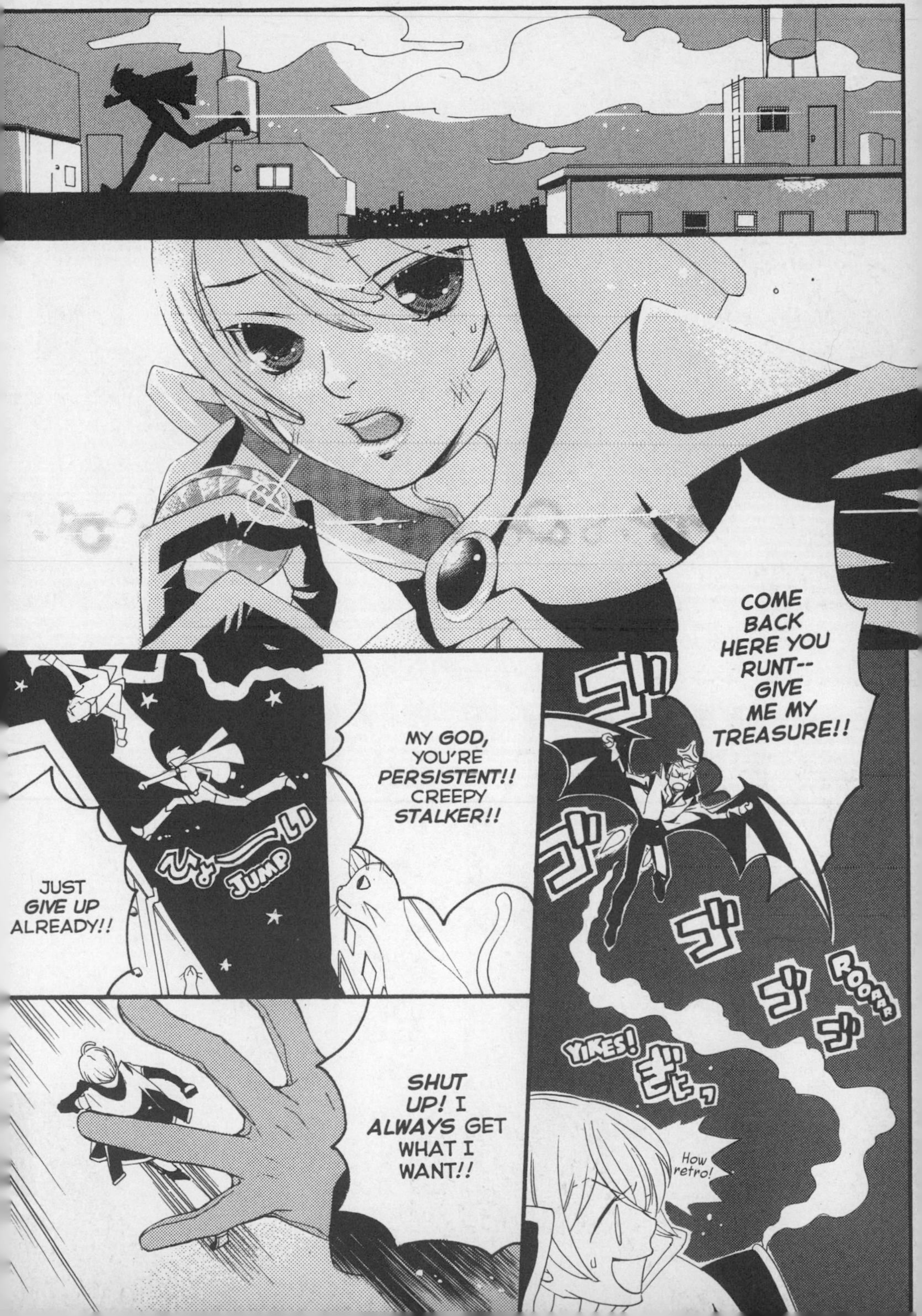
COME BACK HERE YOU RUNT-- GIVE ME MY TREASURE!!
ROOAAR
YIKES!
How retro!
MY GOD, YOU'RE PERSISTENT!! CREEPY STALKER!!
JUMP
JUST GIVE UP ALREADY!!
SHUT UP! I ALWAYS GET WHAT I WANT!!

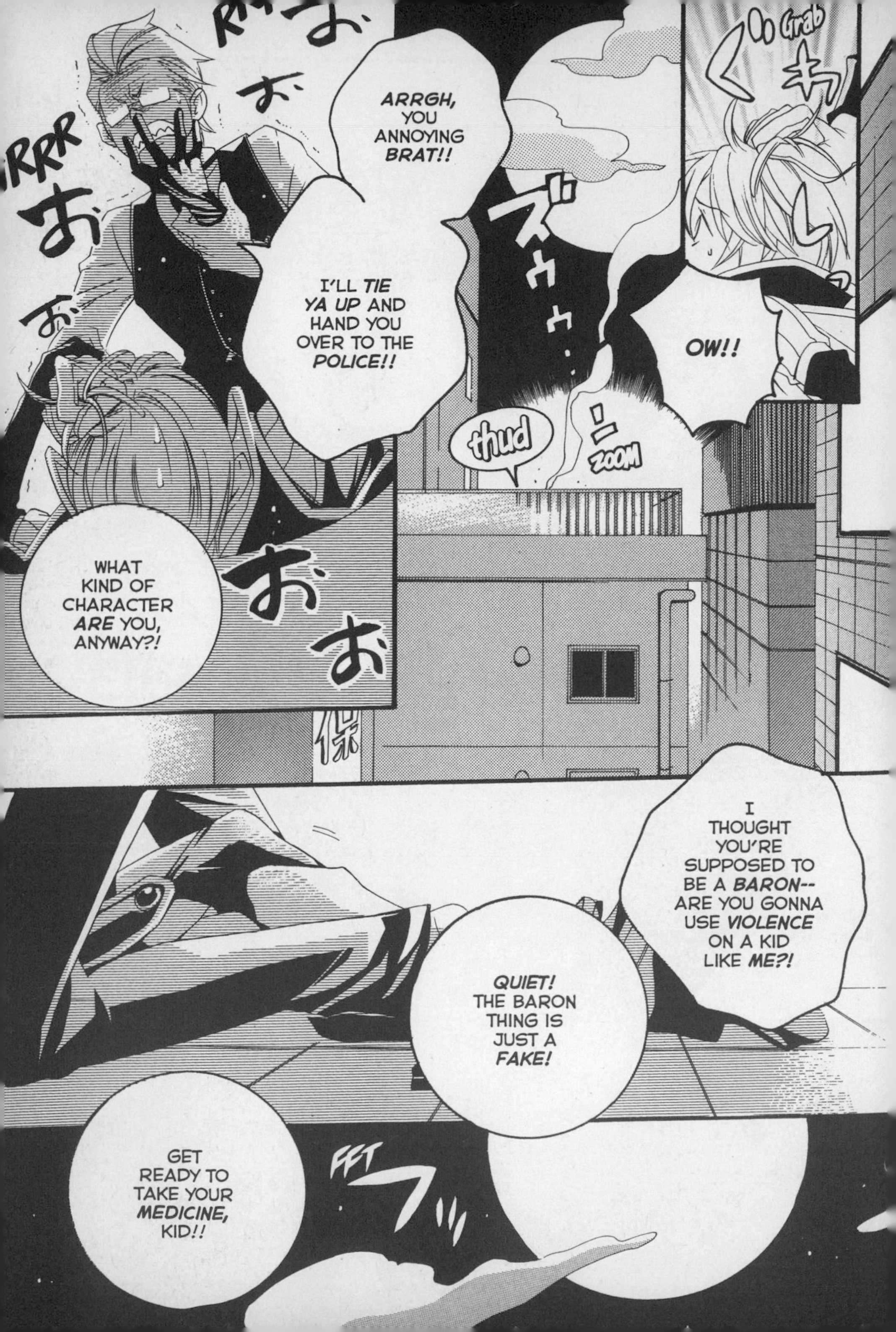
Grab
OW!!
ZOOM
thud
RRR
ARRGH, YOU ANNOYING BRAT!!
I'LL TIE YA UP AND HAND YOU OVER TO THE POLICE!!
WHAT KIND OF CHARACTER ARE YOU, ANYWAY?!
I THOUGHT YOU'RE SUPPOSED TO BE A BARON-- ARE YOU GONNA USE VIOLENCE ON A KID LIKE ME?!
QUIET! THE BARON THING IS JUST A FAKE!
FFT
GET READY TO TAKE YOUR MEDICINE, KID!!

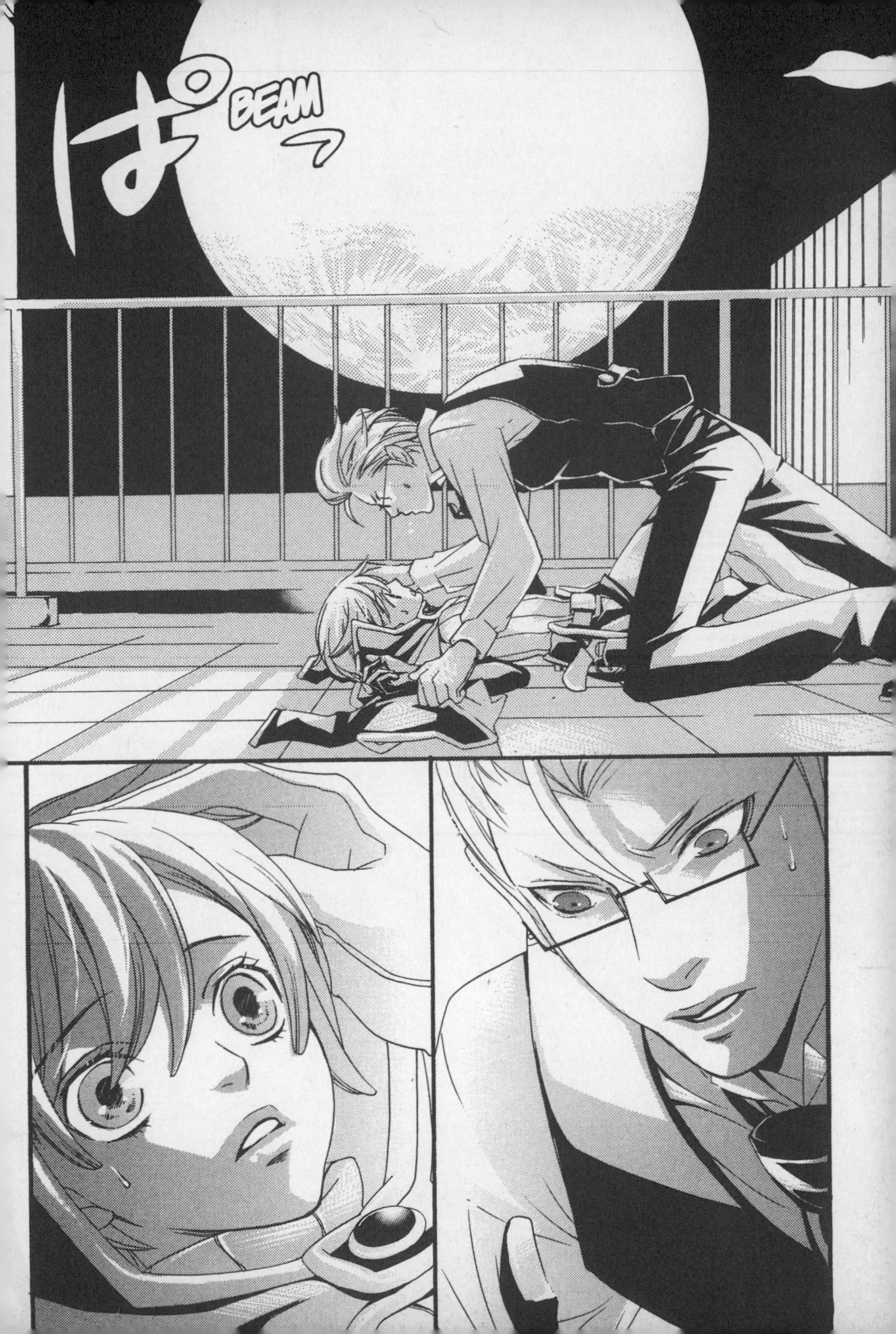
ぱ
BEAM

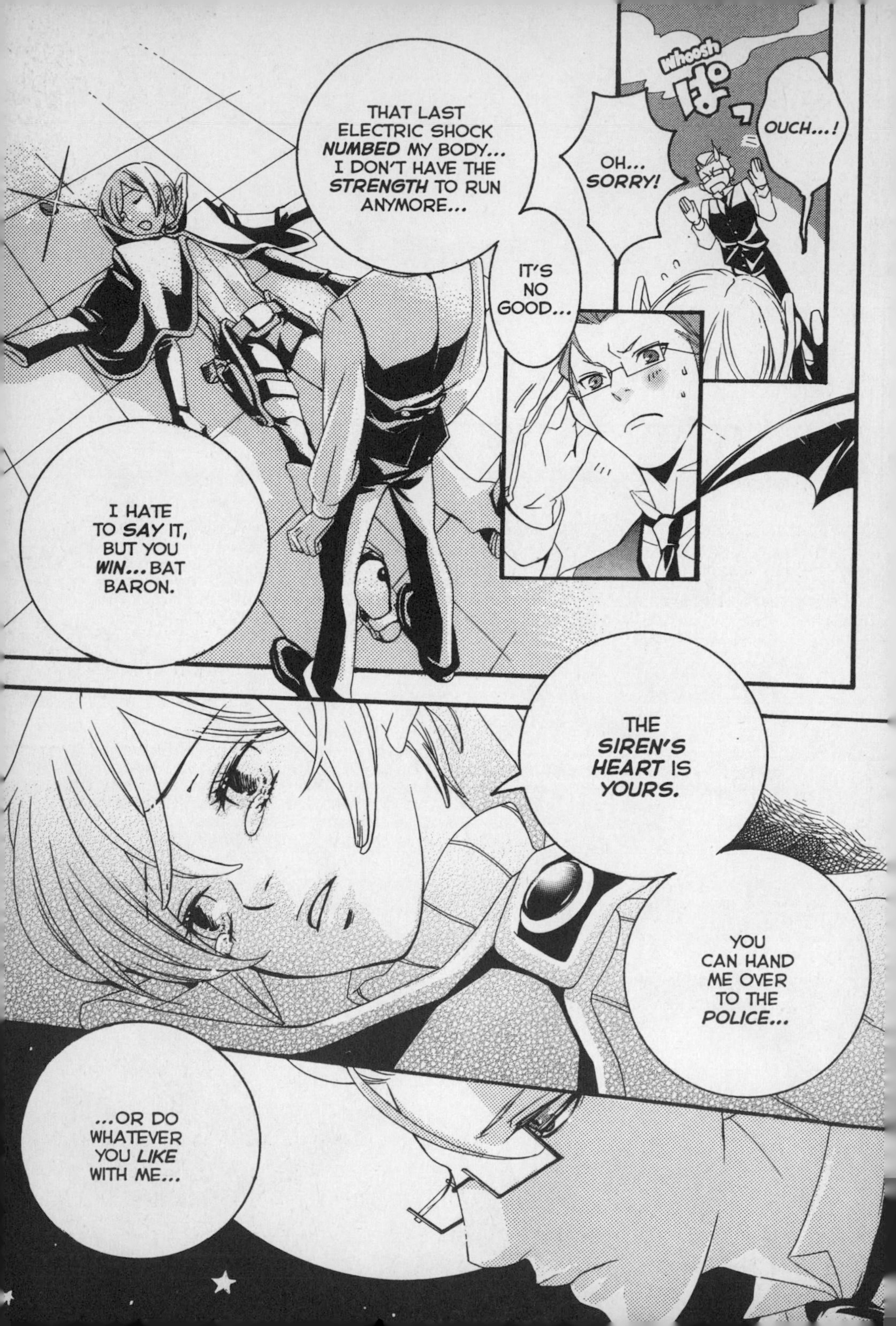
whoosh
ぱっ
OUCH...!
OH... SORRY!
IT'S NO GOOD...
THAT LAST ELECTRIC SHOCK NUMBED MY BODY... I DON'T HAVE THE STRENGTH TO RUN ANYMORE...
I HATE TO SAY IT, BUT YOU WIN... BAT BARON.
THE SIREN'S HEART IS YOURS.
YOU CAN HAND ME OVER TO THE POLICE...
...OR DO WHATEVER YOU LIKE WITH ME...

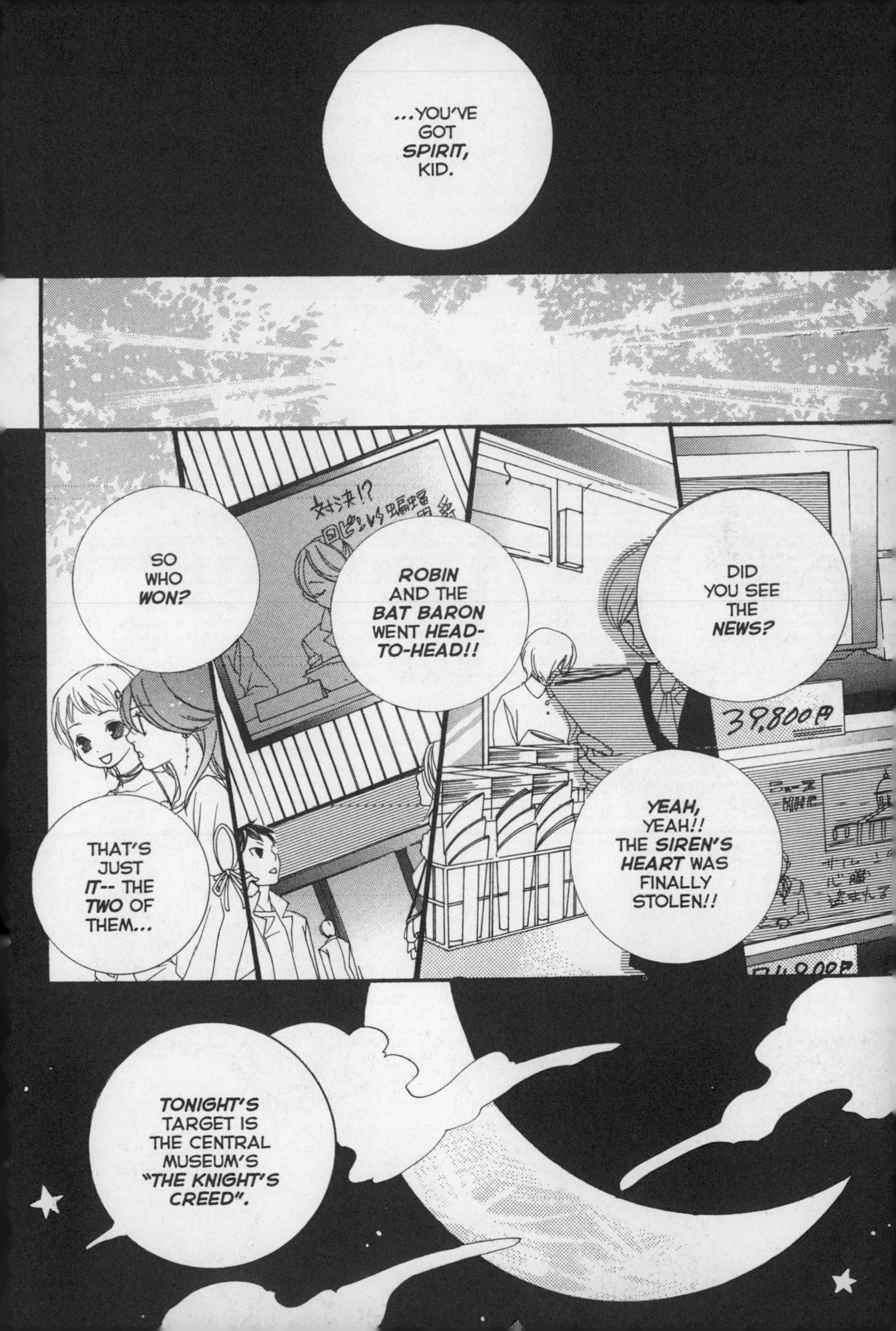
...YOU'VE GOT SPIRIT, KID.
DID YOU SEE THE NEWS?
39,800円
YEAH, YEAH!! THE SIREN'S HEART WAS FINALLY STOLEN!!
ROBIN AND THE BAT BARON WENT HEAD-TO-HEAD!!
SO WHO WON?
THAT'S JUST IT-- THE TWO OF THEM...
TONIGHT'S TARGET IS THE CENTRAL MUSEUM'S "THE KNIGHT'S CREED".

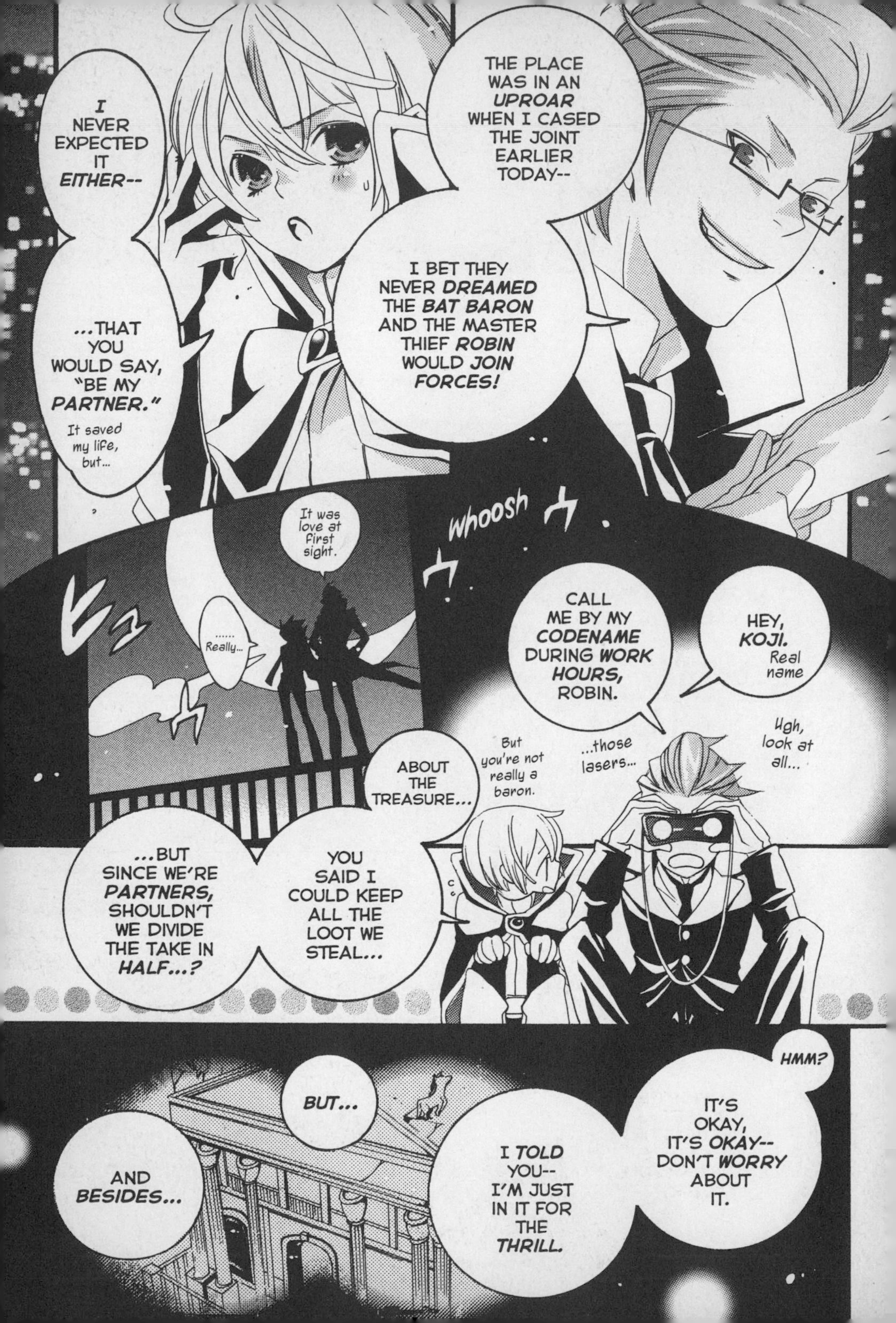
THE PLACE WAS IN AN UPROAR WHEN I CASED THE JOINT EARLIER TODAY--
I BET THEY NEVER DREAMED THE BAT BARON AND THE MASTER THIEF ROBIN WOULD JOIN FORCES!
I NEVER EXPECTED IT EITHER--
...THAT YOU WOULD SAY, "BE MY PARTNER."
It saved my life, but...
whoosh
HEY, KOJI.
Real name
CALL ME BY MY CODENAME DURING WORK HOURS, ROBIN.
It was love at first sight.
...... Really...
Ugh, look at all...
...those lasers...
But you're not really a baron.
ABOUT THE TREASURE...
YOU SAID I COULD KEEP ALL THE LOOT WE STEAL...
...BUT SINCE WE'RE PARTNERS, SHOULDN'T WE DIVIDE THE TAKE IN HALF...?
HMM?
IT'S OKAY, IT'S OKAY-- DON'T WORRY ABOUT IT.
I TOLD YOU-- I'M JUST IN IT FOR THE THRILL.
BUT...
AND BESIDES...

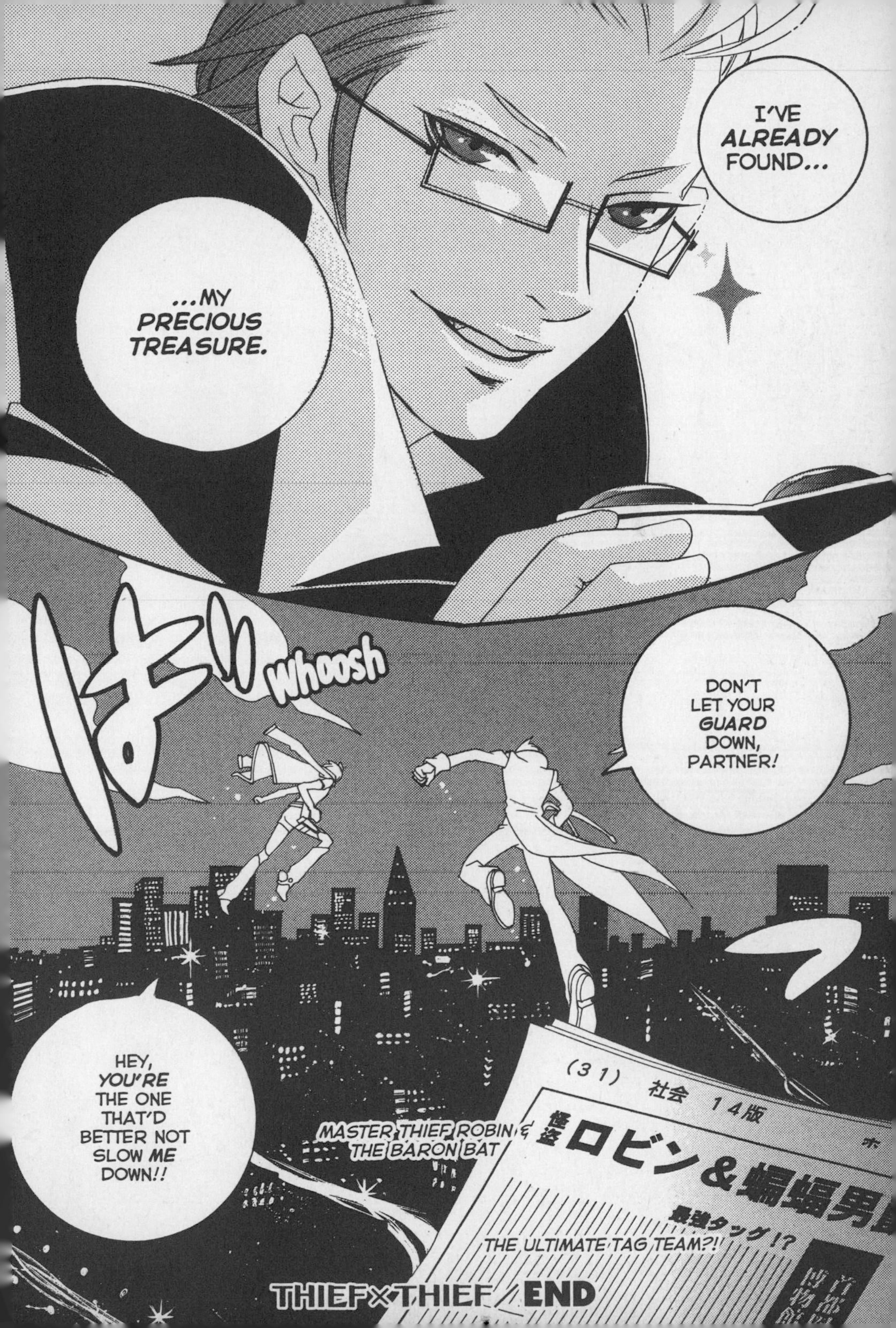
I'VE ALREADY FOUND...
...MY PRECIOUS TREASURE.
whoosh
DON'T LET YOUR GUARD DOWN, PARTNER!
HEY, YOU'RE THE ONE THAT'D BETTER NOT SLOW ME DOWN!!
(31) 社会 14版
怪盗 ロビン＆蝙蝠男
MASTER THIEF ROBIN & THE BARON BAT
最強タッグ!?
THE ULTIMATE TAG TEAM?!
THIEF×THIEF / END

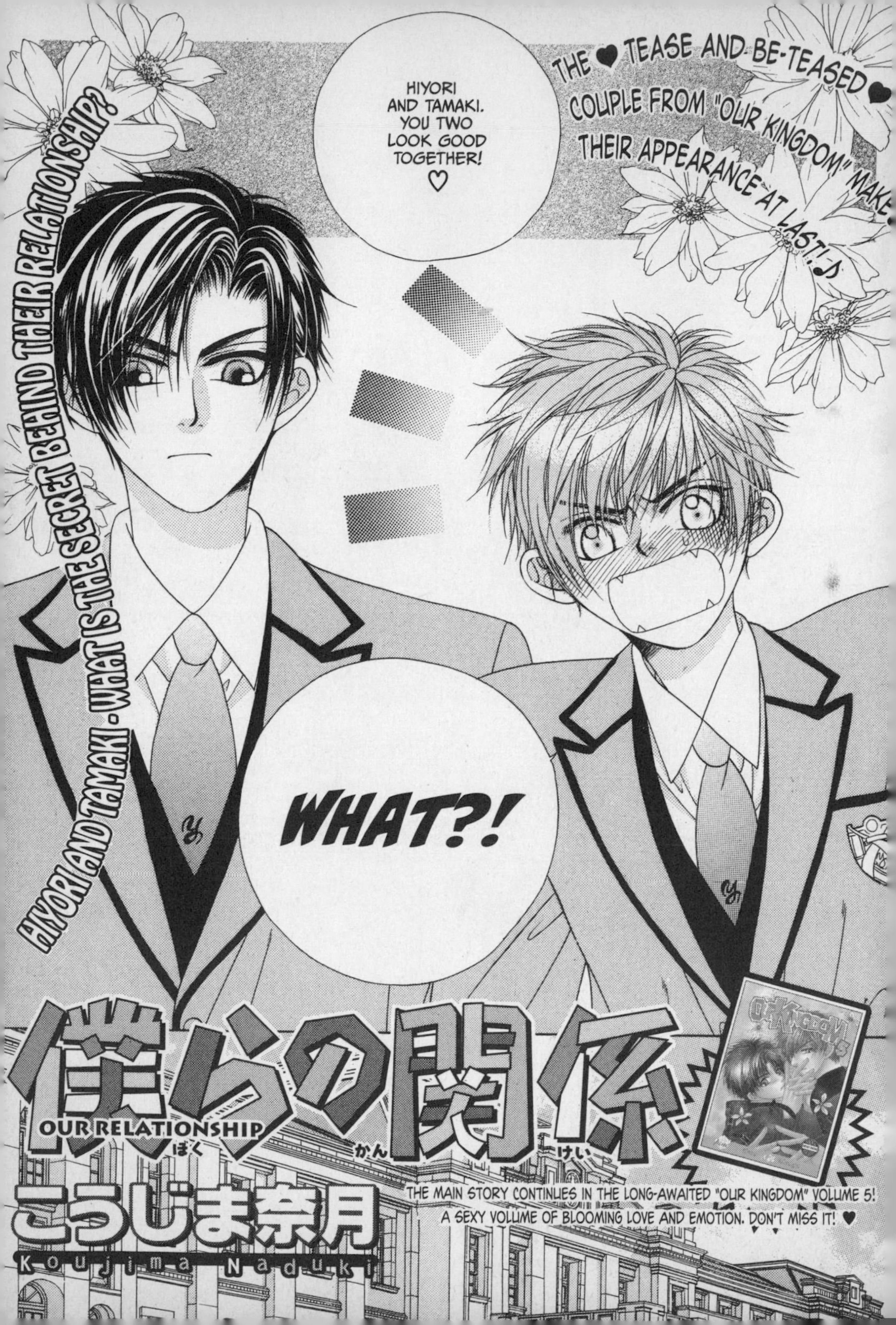
THE ♥ TEASE AND BE-TEASED ♥ COUPLE FROM "OUR KINGDOM" MAKE THEIR APPEARANCE AT LAST!♪
HIYORI AND TAMAKI. YOU TWO LOOK GOOD TOGETHER! ♡
HIYORI AND TAMAKI - WHAT IS THE SECRET BEHIND THEIR RELATIONSHIP?
WHAT?!
僕らの関係
OUR RELATIONSHIP
ぼく かん けい
こうじま奈月
Koujima Naduki
THE MAIN STORY CONTINUES IN THE LONG-AWAITED "OUR KINGDOM" VOLUME 5!
A SEXY VOLUME OF BLOOMING LOVE AND EMOTION. DON'T MISS IT! ♥

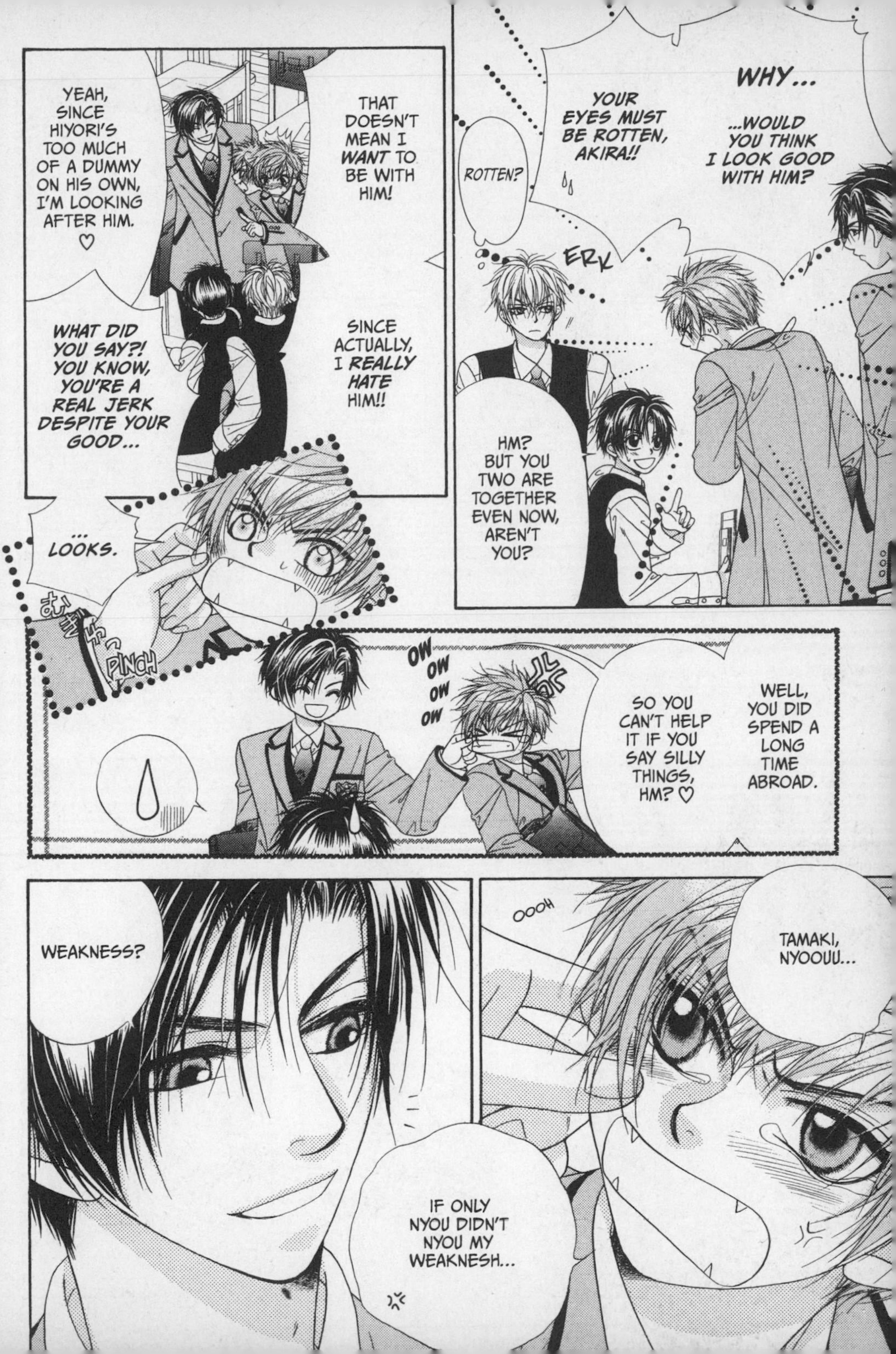
WHY...
...WOULD YOU THINK I LOOK GOOD WITH HIM?
YOUR EYES MUST BE ROTTEN, AKIRA!!
ROTTEN?
ERK
HM? BUT YOU TWO ARE TOGETHER EVEN NOW, AREN'T YOU?
THAT DOESN'T MEAN I WANT TO BE WITH HIM!
SINCE ACTUALLY, I REALLY HATE HIM!!
YEAH, SINCE HIYORI'S TOO MUCH OF A DUMMY ON HIS OWN, I'M LOOKING AFTER HIM. ♡
WHAT DID YOU SAY?! YOU KNOW, YOU'RE A REAL JERK DESPITE YOUR GOOD...
...LOOKS.
PINCH
WELL, YOU DID SPEND A LONG TIME ABROAD.
SO YOU CAN'T HELP IT IF YOU SAY SILLY THINGS, HM? ♡
OW OW OW OW
OOOH
TAMAKI, NYOOUU...
IF ONLY NYOU DIDN'T NYOU MY WEAKNESH...
WEAKNESS?

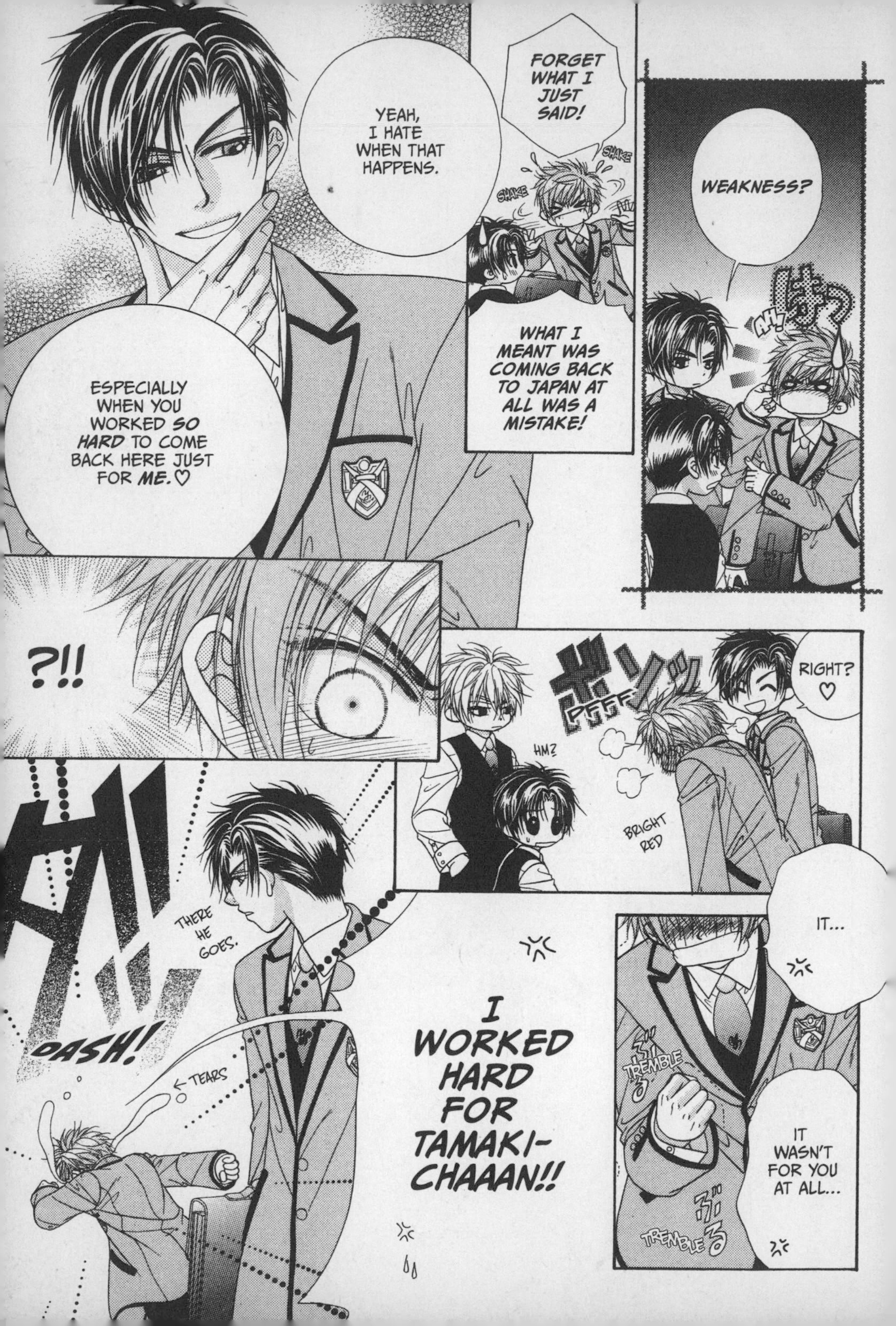
WEAKNESS?
AH!
FORGET WHAT I JUST SAID!
SHAKE
SHAKE
WHAT I MEANT WAS COMING BACK TO JAPAN AT ALL WAS A MISTAKE!
YEAH, I HATE WHEN THAT HAPPENS.
ESPECIALLY WHEN YOU WORKED *SO HARD* TO COME BACK HERE JUST FOR *ME*.♡
RIGHT? ♡
PFFF
HM?
BRIGHT RED
?!!
IT...
TREMBLE
IT WASN'T FOR YOU AT ALL...
TREMBLE
THERE HE GOES.
I WORKED HARD FOR TAMAKI-CHAAAN!!
DASH!
← TEARS

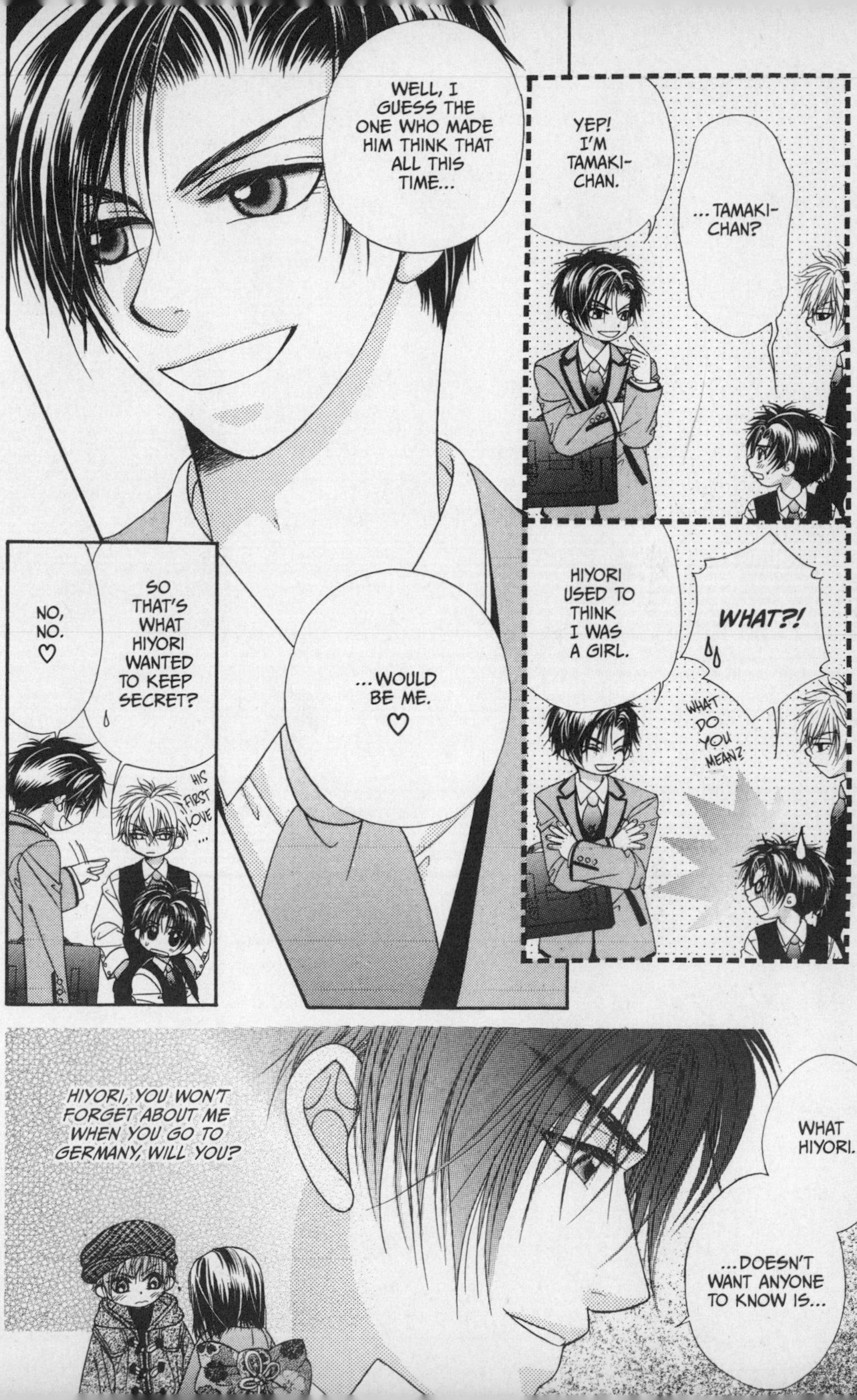
...TAMAKI-CHAN?
YEP! I'M TAMAKI-CHAN.
WHAT?!
HIYORI USED TO THINK I WAS A GIRL.
WHAT DO YOU MEAN?
WELL, I GUESS THE ONE WHO MADE HIM THINK THAT ALL THIS TIME...
...WOULD BE ME. ♡
SO THAT'S WHAT HIYORI WANTED TO KEEP SECRET?
NO, NO. ♡
HIS FIRST LOVE...
WHAT HIYORI...
...DOESN'T WANT ANYONE TO KNOW IS...
HIYORI, YOU WON'T FORGET ABOUT ME WHEN YOU GO TO GERMANY, WILL YOU?

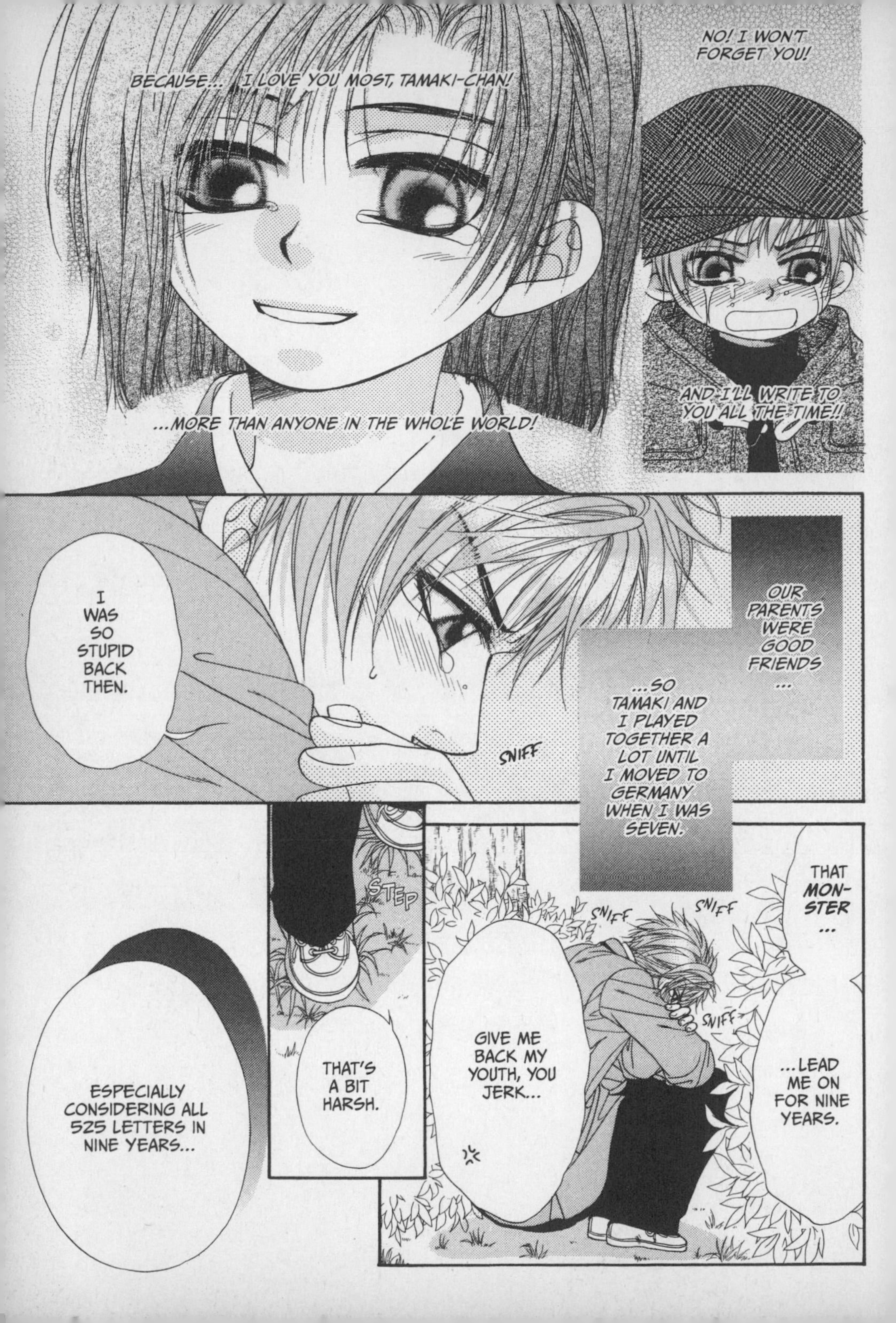
NO! I WON'T FORGET YOU!
AND I'LL WRITE TO YOU ALL THE TIME!!
BECAUSE... I LOVE YOU MOST, TAMAKI-CHAN!
...MORE THAN ANYONE IN THE WHOLE WORLD!
OUR PARENTS WERE GOOD FRIENDS...
...SO TAMAKI AND I PLAYED TOGETHER A LOT UNTIL I MOVED TO GERMANY WHEN I WAS SEVEN.
SNIFF
I WAS SO STUPID BACK THEN.
THAT MONSTER...
...LEAD ME ON FOR NINE YEARS.
SNIFF
SNIFF
GIVE ME BACK MY YOUTH, YOU JERK...
SNIFF
STEP
THAT'S A BIT HARSH.
ESPECIALLY CONSIDERING ALL 525 LETTERS IN NINE YEARS...

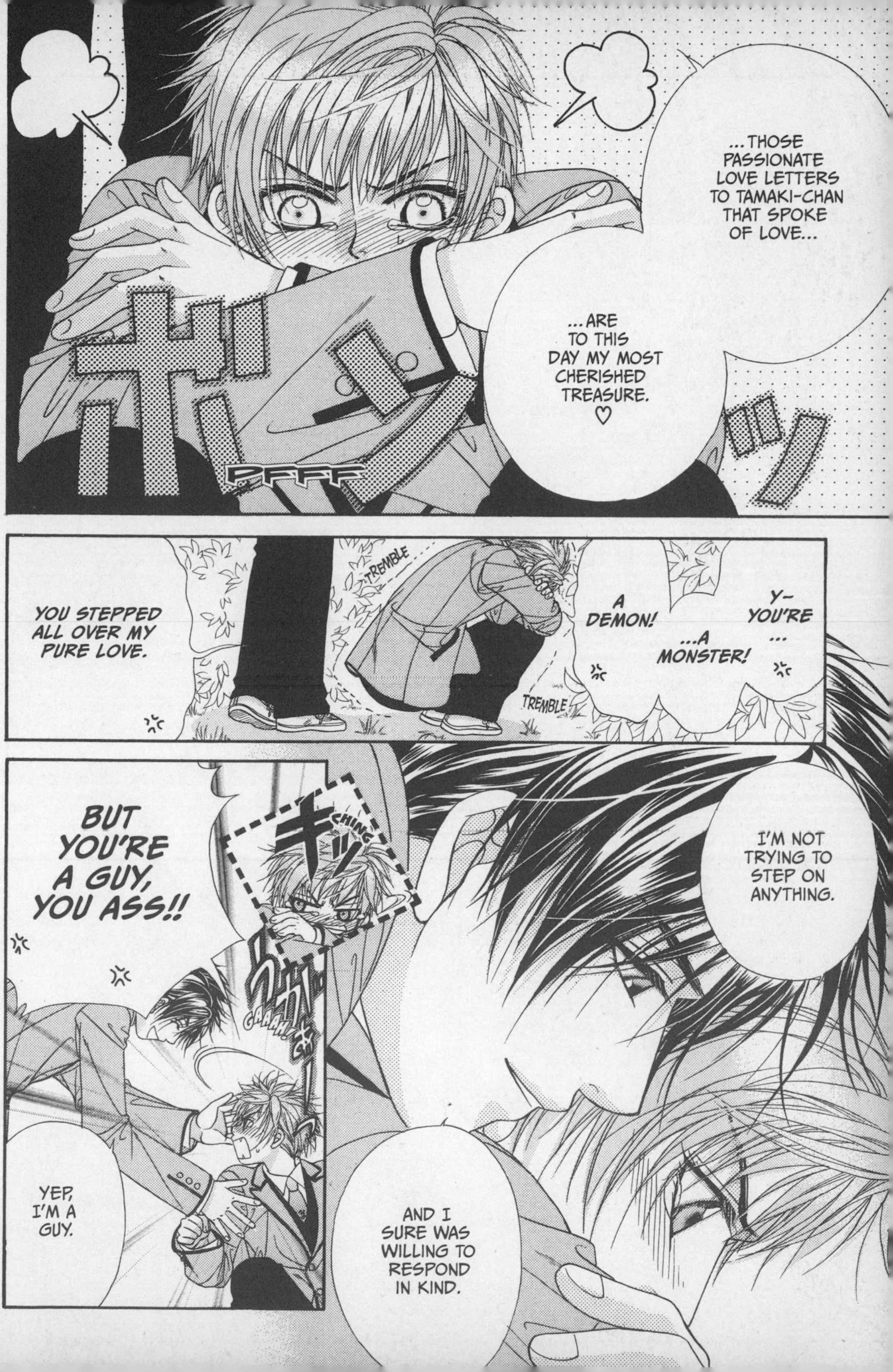
...THOSE PASSIONATE LOVE LETTERS TO TAMAKI-CHAN THAT SPOKE OF LOVE...
...ARE TO THIS DAY MY MOST CHERISHED TREASURE. ♡
PFFF
Y-YOU'RE ...
...A MONSTER!
A DEMON!
TREMBLE
TREMBLE
YOU STEPPED ALL OVER MY PURE LOVE.
I'M NOT TRYING TO STEP ON ANYTHING.
AND I SURE WAS WILLING TO RESPOND IN KIND.
BUT YOU'RE A GUY, YOU ASS!!
CHING
GAAAH!
YEP, I'M A GUY.

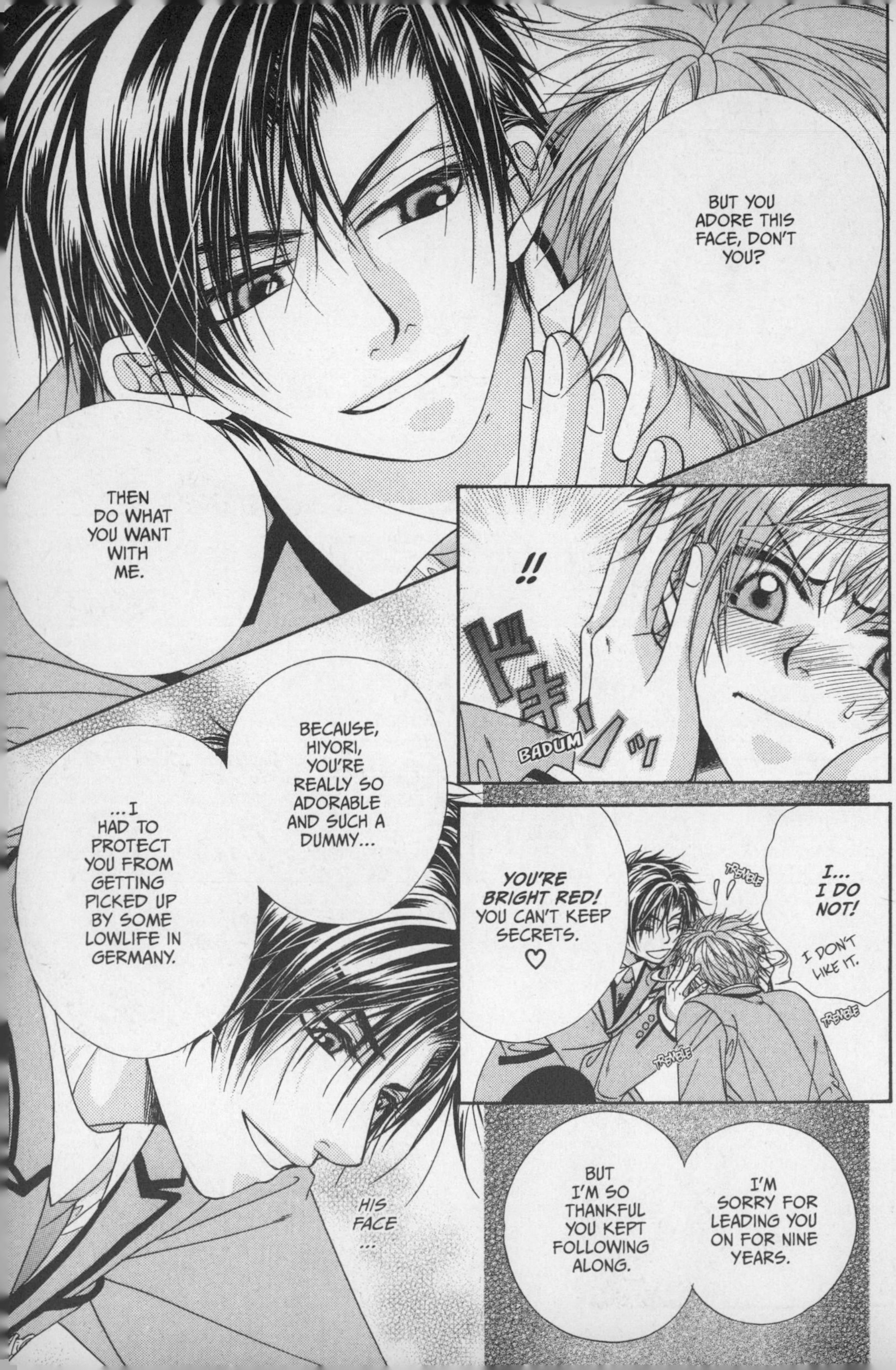
BUT YOU ADORE THIS FACE, DON'T YOU?
THEN DO WHAT YOU WANT WITH ME.
!!
ドキッ
BADUM
I... I DO NOT!
TREMBLE
I DON'T LIKE IT.
TREMBLE
TREMBLE
YOU'RE BRIGHT RED! YOU CAN'T KEEP SECRETS. ♡
I'M SORRY FOR LEADING YOU ON FOR NINE YEARS.
BUT I'M SO THANKFUL YOU KEPT FOLLOWING ALONG.
BECAUSE, HIYORI, YOU'RE REALLY SO ADORABLE AND SUCH A DUMMY...
...I HAD TO PROTECT YOU FROM GETTING PICKED UP BY SOME LOWLIFE IN GERMANY.
HIS FACE ...

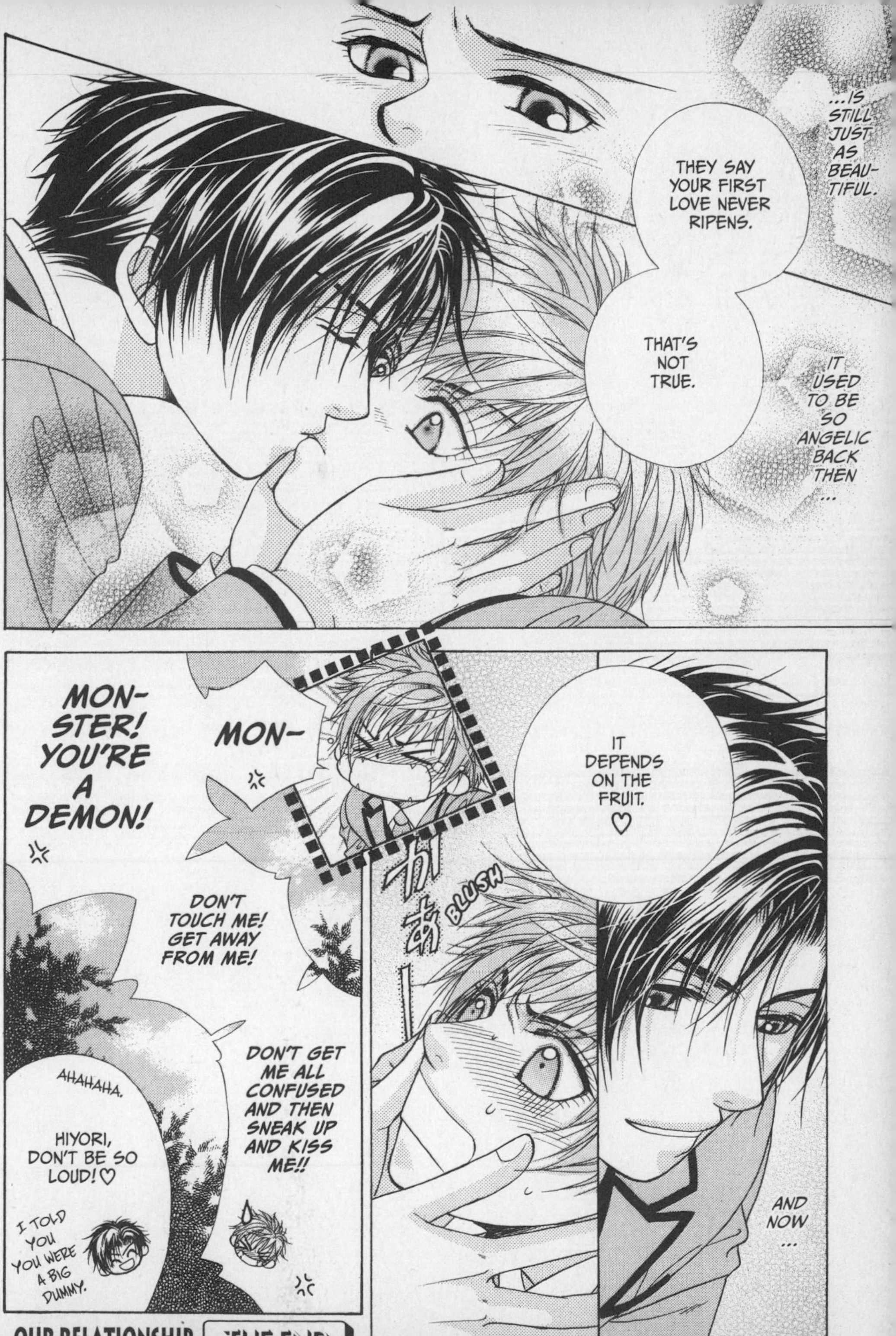

...IS STILL JUST AS BEAU-TIFUL.
THEY SAY YOUR FIRST LOVE NEVER RIPENS.
IT USED TO BE SO ANGELIC BACK THEN ...
THAT'S NOT TRUE.
IT DEPENDS ON THE FRUIT. ♡
AND NOW ...
かあ
BLUSH
MON-
MON-STER! YOU'RE A DEMON!
DON'T TOUCH ME! GET AWAY FROM ME!
DON'T GET ME ALL CONFUSED AND THEN SNEAK UP AND KISS ME!!
AHAHAHA.
HIYORI, DON'T BE SO LOUD! ♡
I TOLD YOU YOU WERE A BIG DUMMY.

OUR RELATIONSHIP **THE END**

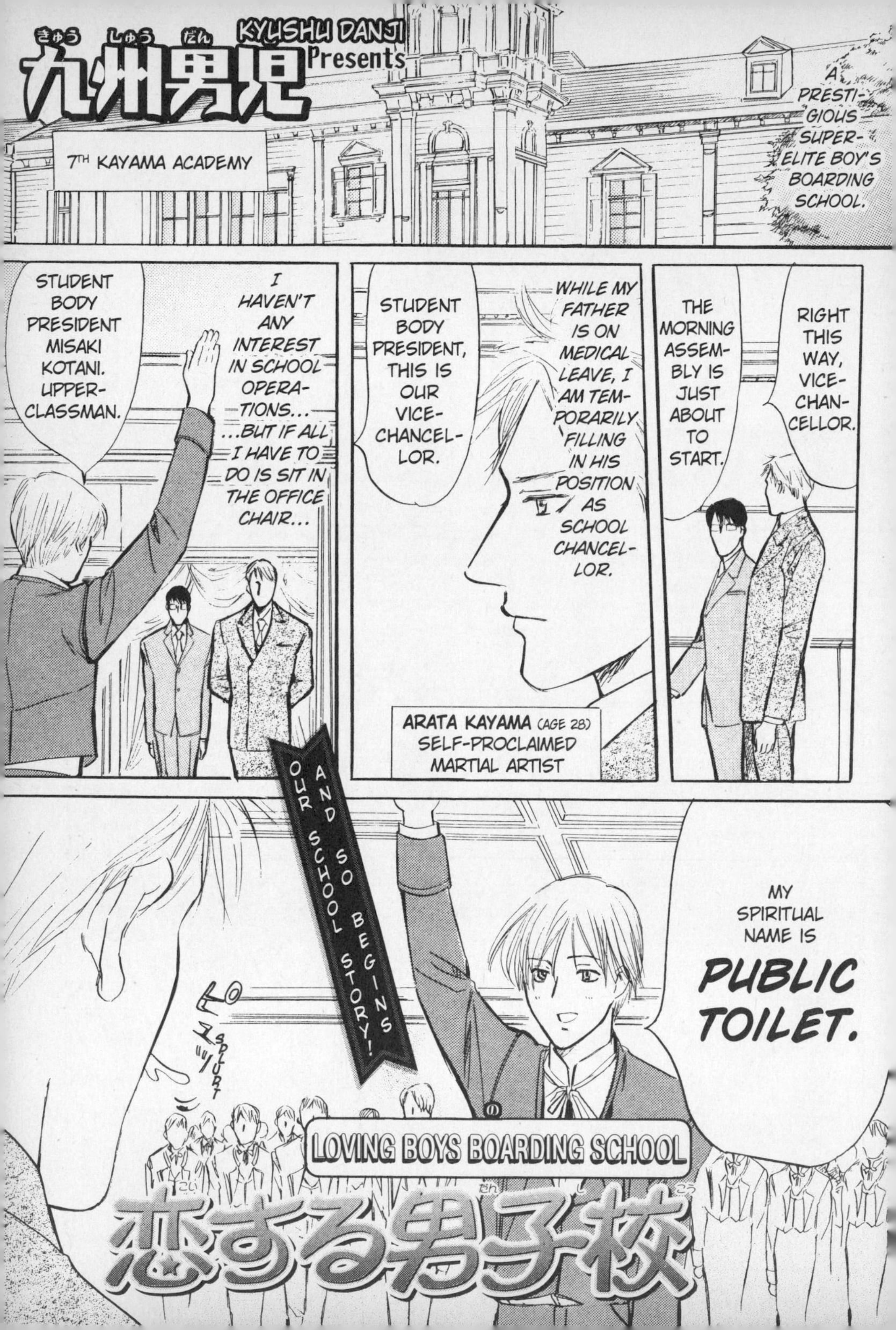

九州男児
KYUSHU DANJI
Presents
A PRESTIGIOUS SUPER-ELITE BOY'S BOARDING SCHOOL.
7TH KAYAMA ACADEMY
RIGHT THIS WAY, VICE-CHANCELLOR.
THE MORNING ASSEMBLY IS JUST ABOUT TO START.
WHILE MY FATHER IS ON MEDICAL LEAVE, I AM TEMPORARILY FILLING IN HIS POSITION AS SCHOOL CHANCELLOR.
STUDENT BODY PRESIDENT, THIS IS OUR VICE-CHANCELLOR.
ARATA KAYAMA (AGE 28) SELF-PROCLAIMED MARTIAL ARTIST
I HAVEN'T ANY INTEREST IN SCHOOL OPERATIONS... ...BUT IF ALL I HAVE TO DO IS SIT IN THE OFFICE CHAIR...
STUDENT BODY PRESIDENT MISAKI KOTANI. UPPERCLASSMAN.
MY SPIRITUAL NAME IS
PUBLIC TOILET.
AND SO BEGINS OUR SCHOOL STORY!
SPLURT
LOVING BOYS BOARDING SCHOOL
恋する男子校

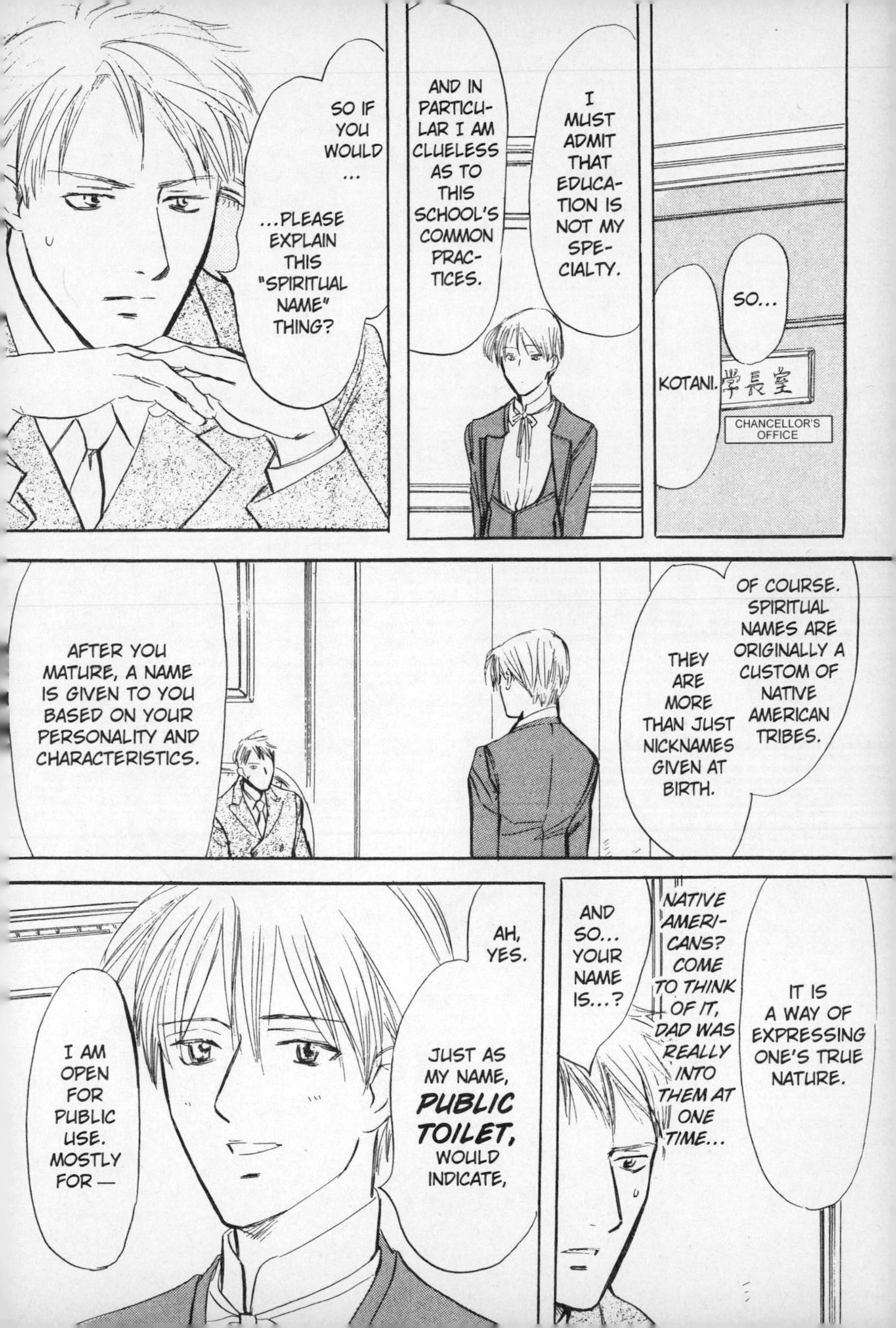
SO...
KOTANI.
学長室
CHANCELLOR'S OFFICE
I MUST ADMIT THAT EDUCATION IS NOT MY SPECIALTY.
AND IN PARTICULAR I AM CLUELESS AS TO THIS SCHOOL'S COMMON PRACTICES.
SO IF YOU WOULD ...
...PLEASE EXPLAIN THIS "SPIRITUAL NAME" THING?
OF COURSE. SPIRITUAL NAMES ARE ORIGINALLY A CUSTOM OF NATIVE AMERICAN TRIBES.
THEY ARE MORE THAN JUST NICKNAMES GIVEN AT BIRTH.
AFTER YOU MATURE, A NAME IS GIVEN TO YOU BASED ON YOUR PERSONALITY AND CHARACTERISTICS.
IT IS A WAY OF EXPRESSING ONE'S TRUE NATURE.
NATIVE AMERICANS? COME TO THINK OF IT, DAD WAS REALLY INTO THEM AT ONE TIME...
AND SO... YOUR NAME IS...?
AH, YES.
JUST AS MY NAME, ***PUBLIC TOILET***, WOULD INDICATE,
I AM OPEN FOR PUBLIC USE. MOSTLY FOR—

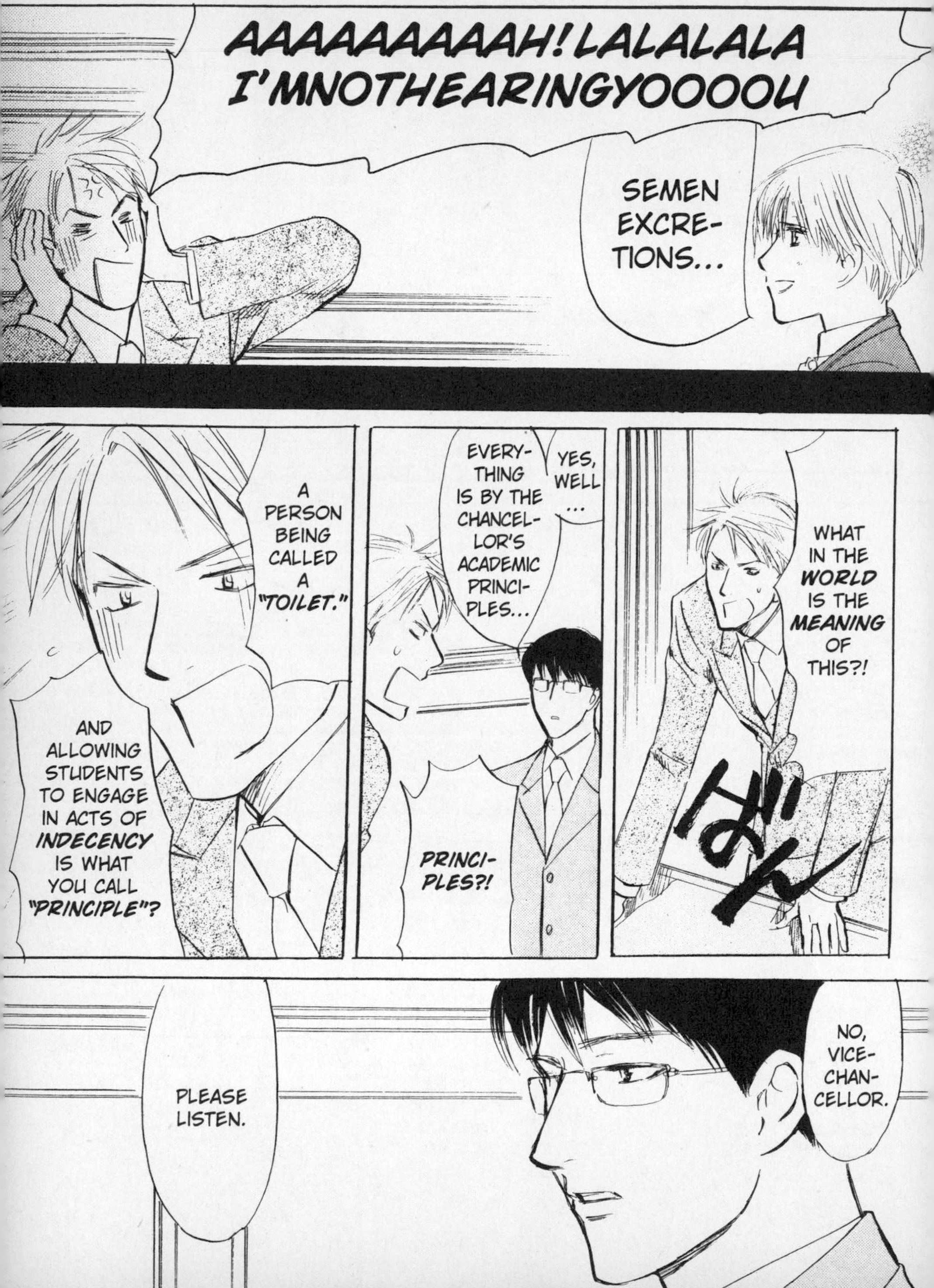

SEMEN EXCRETIONS...
AAAAAAAAAH! LALALALA I'MNOTHEARINGYOOOOU
WHAT IN THE *WORLD* IS THE *MEANING* OF THIS?!
ばん
YES, WELL ...
EVERYTHING IS BY THE CHANCELLOR'S ACADEMIC PRINCIPLES...
PRINCIPLES?!
A PERSON BEING CALLED A *"TOILET."*
AND ALLOWING STUDENTS TO ENGAGE IN ACTS OF *INDECENCY* IS WHAT YOU CALL *"PRINCIPLE"*?
NO, VICE-CHANCELLOR.
PLEASE LISTEN.

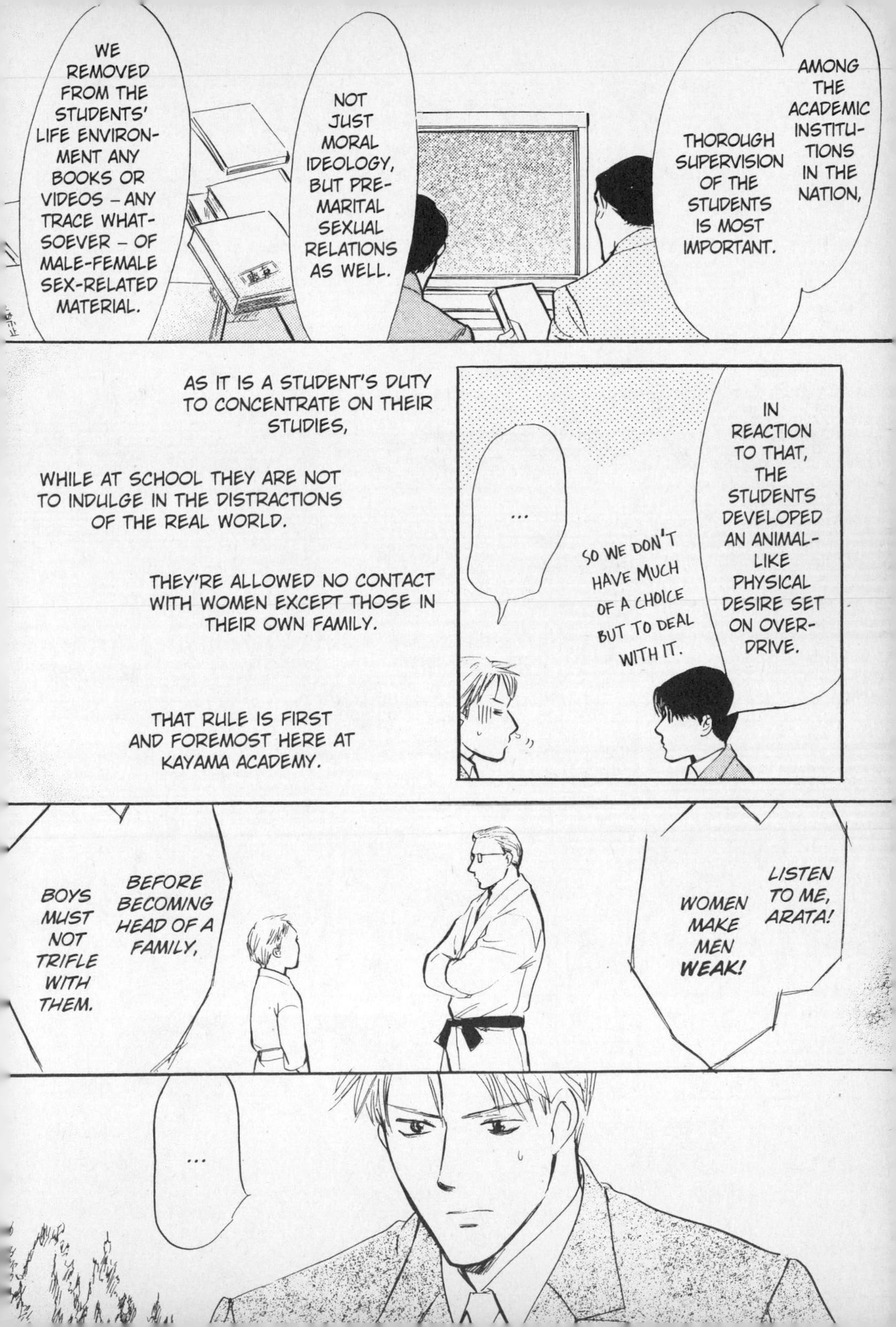
AMONG THE ACADEMIC INSTITUTIONS IN THE NATION,
THOROUGH SUPERVISION OF THE STUDENTS IS MOST IMPORTANT.
NOT JUST MORAL IDEOLOGY, BUT PRE-MARITAL SEXUAL RELATIONS AS WELL.
WE REMOVED FROM THE STUDENTS' LIFE ENVIRONMENT ANY BOOKS OR VIDEOS – ANY TRACE WHATSOEVER – OF MALE-FEMALE SEX-RELATED MATERIAL.
IN REACTION TO THAT, THE STUDENTS DEVELOPED AN ANIMAL-LIKE PHYSICAL DESIRE SET ON OVER-DRIVE.
SO WE DON'T HAVE MUCH OF A CHOICE BUT TO DEAL WITH IT.
...
AS IT IS A STUDENT'S DUTY TO CONCENTRATE ON THEIR STUDIES,
WHILE AT SCHOOL THEY ARE NOT TO INDULGE IN THE DISTRACTIONS OF THE REAL WORLD.
THEY'RE ALLOWED NO CONTACT WITH WOMEN EXCEPT THOSE IN THEIR OWN FAMILY.
THAT RULE IS FIRST AND FOREMOST HERE AT KAYAMA ACADEMY.
LISTEN TO ME, ARATA!
WOMEN MAKE MEN WEAK!
BEFORE BECOMING HEAD OF A FAMILY,
BOYS MUST NOT TRIFLE WITH THEM.
...

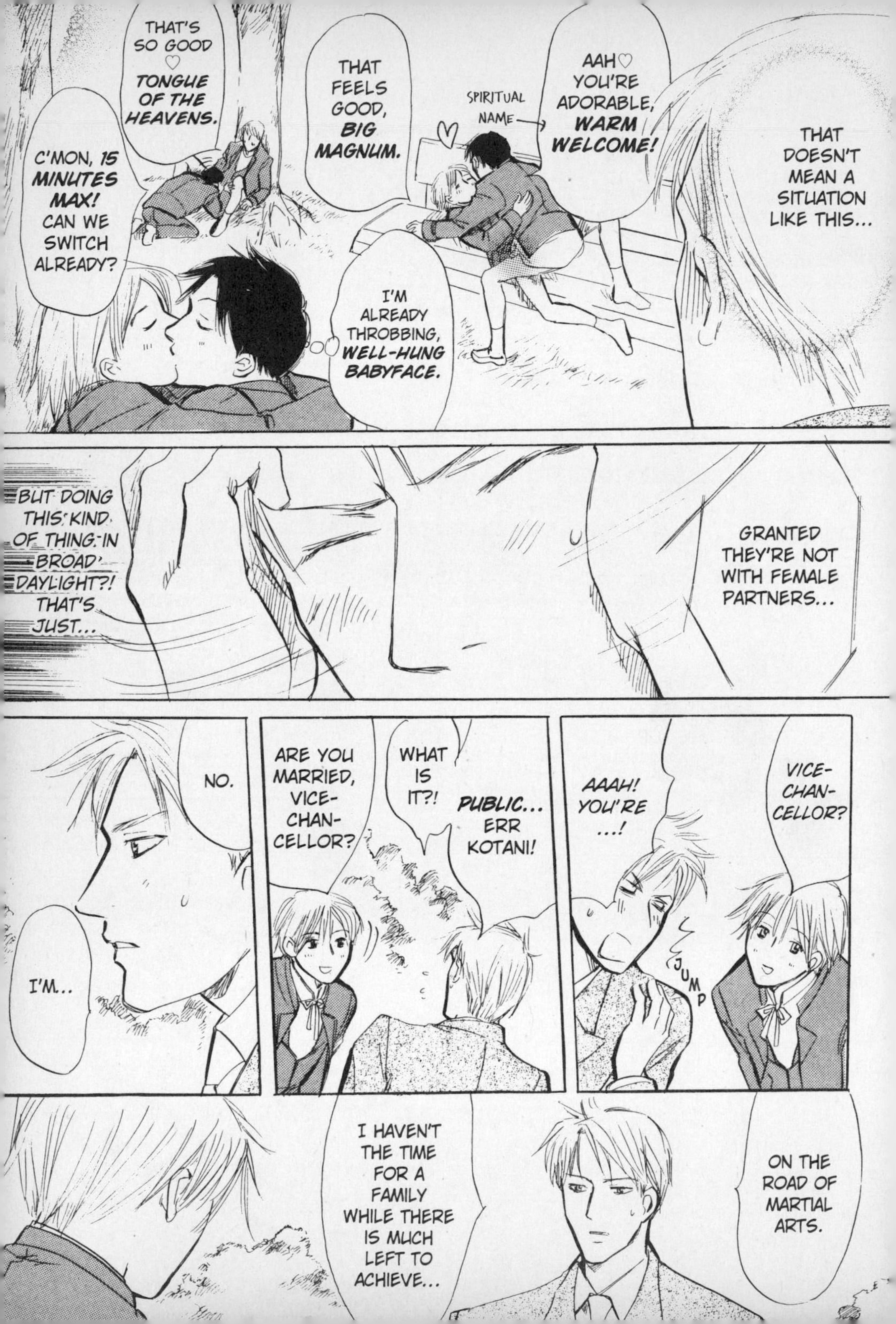
THAT DOESN'T MEAN A SITUATION LIKE THIS...
AAH♡ YOU'RE ADORABLE, WARM WELCOME!
SPIRITUAL NAME
THAT FEELS GOOD, BIG MAGNUM.
I'M ALREADY THROBBING, WELL-HUNG BABYFACE.
THAT'S SO GOOD ♡ TONGUE OF THE HEAVENS.
C'MON, 15 MINUTES MAX! CAN WE SWITCH ALREADY?
GRANTED THEY'RE NOT WITH FEMALE PARTNERS...
BUT DOING THIS KIND OF THING IN BROAD DAYLIGHT?! THAT'S JUST...
VICE-CHAN-CELLOR?
AAAH! YOU'RE ...!
JUMP
PUBLIC... ERR KOTANI!
WHAT IS IT?!
ARE YOU MARRIED, VICE-CHAN-CELLOR?
NO.
I'M...
ON THE ROAD OF MARTIAL ARTS.
I HAVEN'T THE TIME FOR A FAMILY WHILE THERE IS MUCH LEFT TO ACHIEVE...

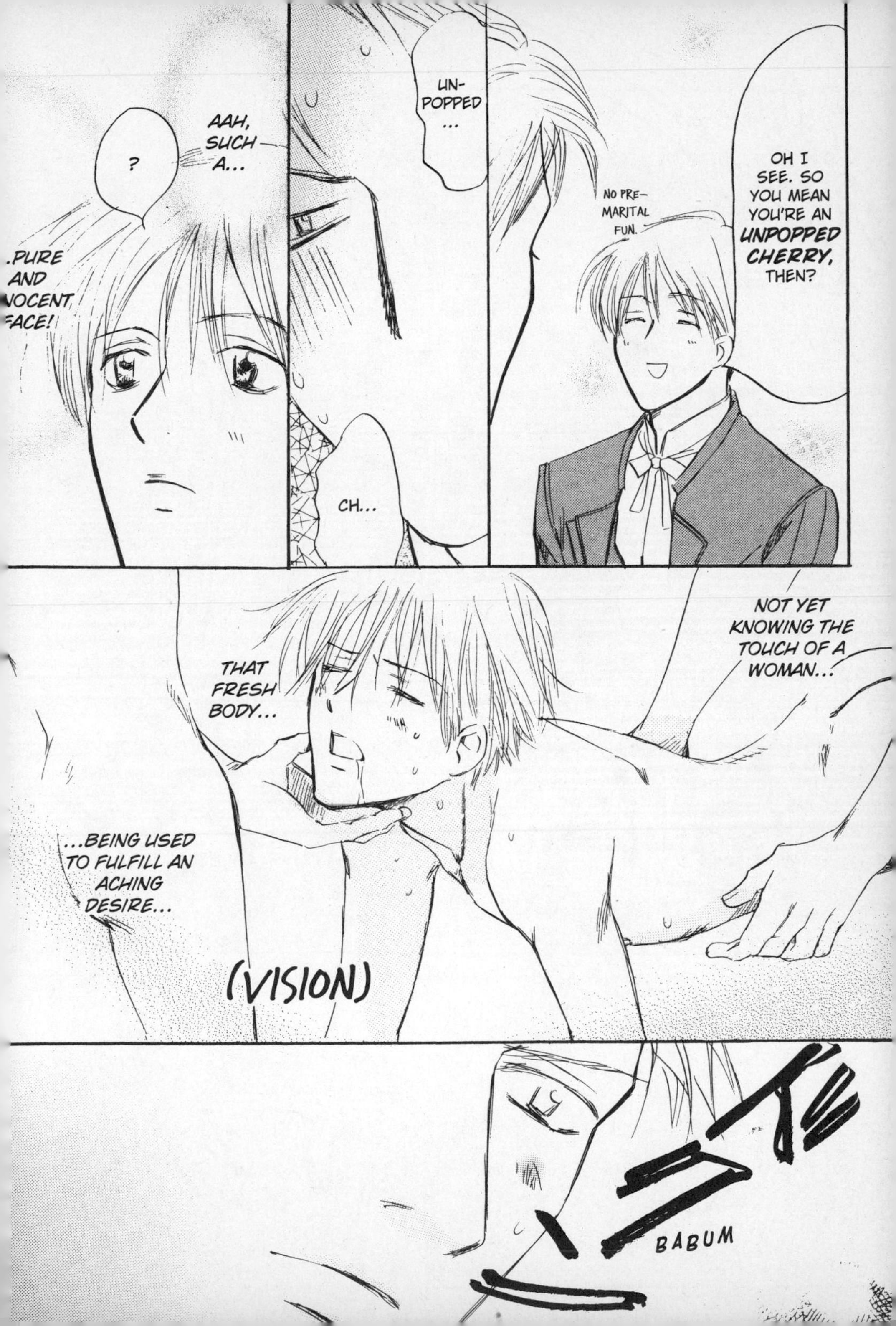
OH I SEE. SO YOU MEAN YOU'RE AN **UNPOPPED CHERRY,** THEN?
NO PRE-MARITAL FUN.
UN-POPPED ...
CH...
?
AAH, SUCH A...
.PURE AND NOCENT FACE!
NOT YET KNOWING THE TOUCH OF A WOMAN...
THAT FRESH BODY...
...BEING USED TO FULFILL AN ACHING DESIRE...
(VISION)
BABUM

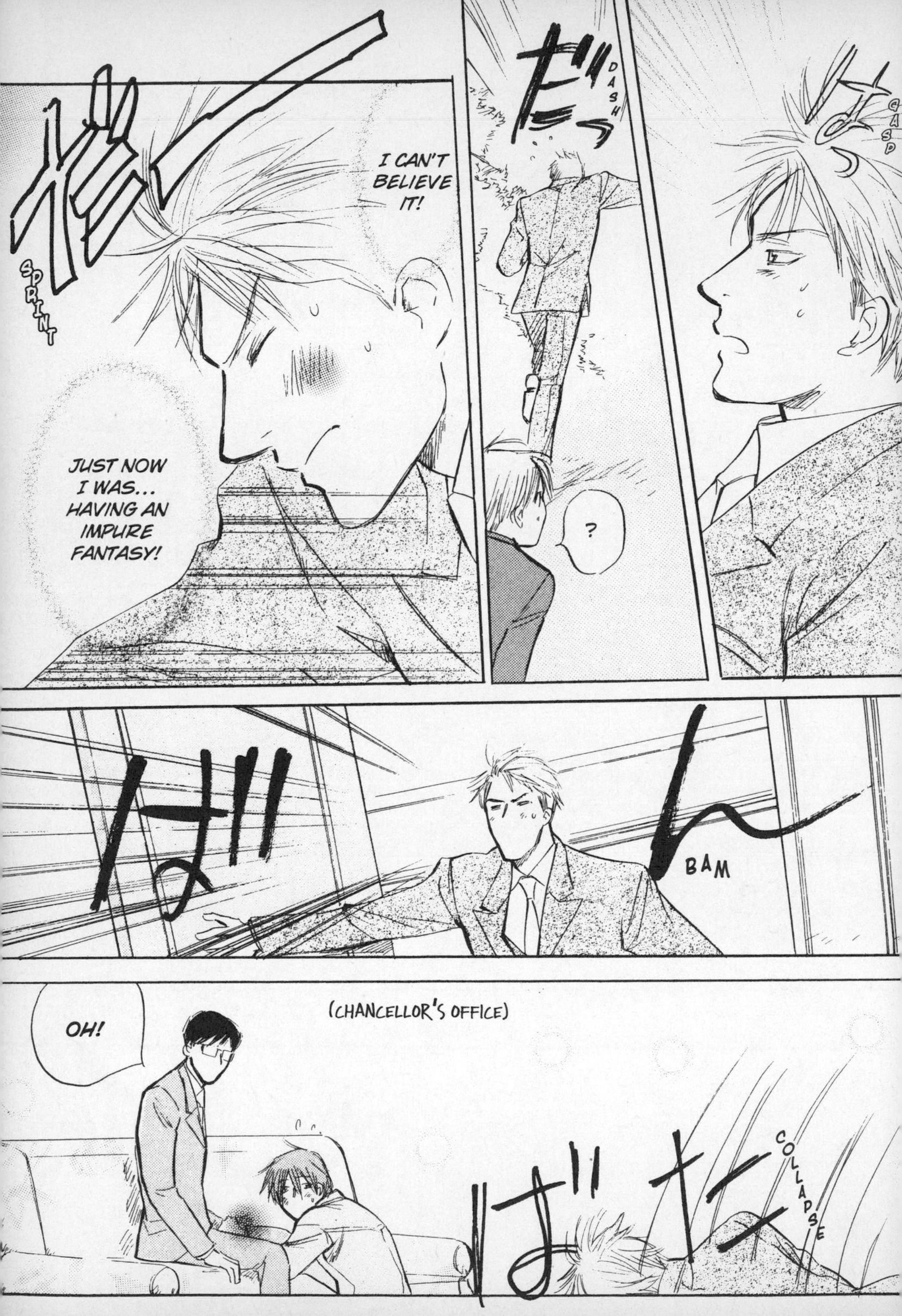
GASP
DASH
?
SPRINT
I CAN'T BELIEVE IT!
JUST NOW I WAS... HAVING AN IMPURE FANTASY!
BAM
(CHANCELLOR'S OFFICE)
COLLAPSE
OH!

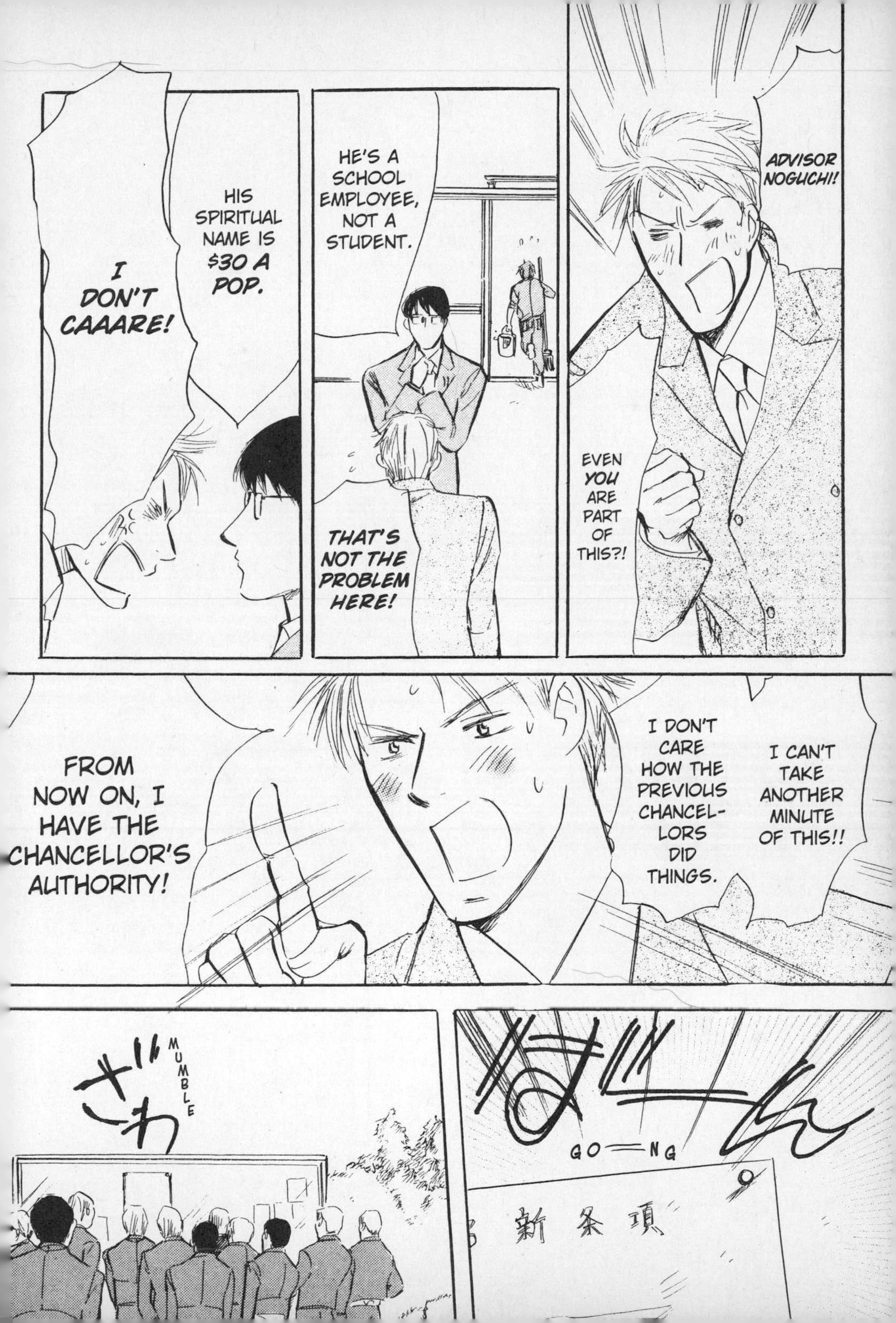
ADVISOR NOGUCHI!!
EVEN YOU ARE PART OF THIS?!
HE'S A SCHOOL EMPLOYEE, NOT A STUDENT.
THAT'S NOT THE PROBLEM HERE!
HIS SPIRITUAL NAME IS $30 A POP.
I DON'T CAAARE!
I CAN'T TAKE ANOTHER MINUTE OF THIS!!
I DON'T CARE HOW THE PREVIOUS CHANCEL-LORS DID THINGS.
FROM NOW ON, I HAVE THE CHANCELLOR'S AUTHORITY!
ばーん
GO—NG
新条項
ざわ
MUMBLE

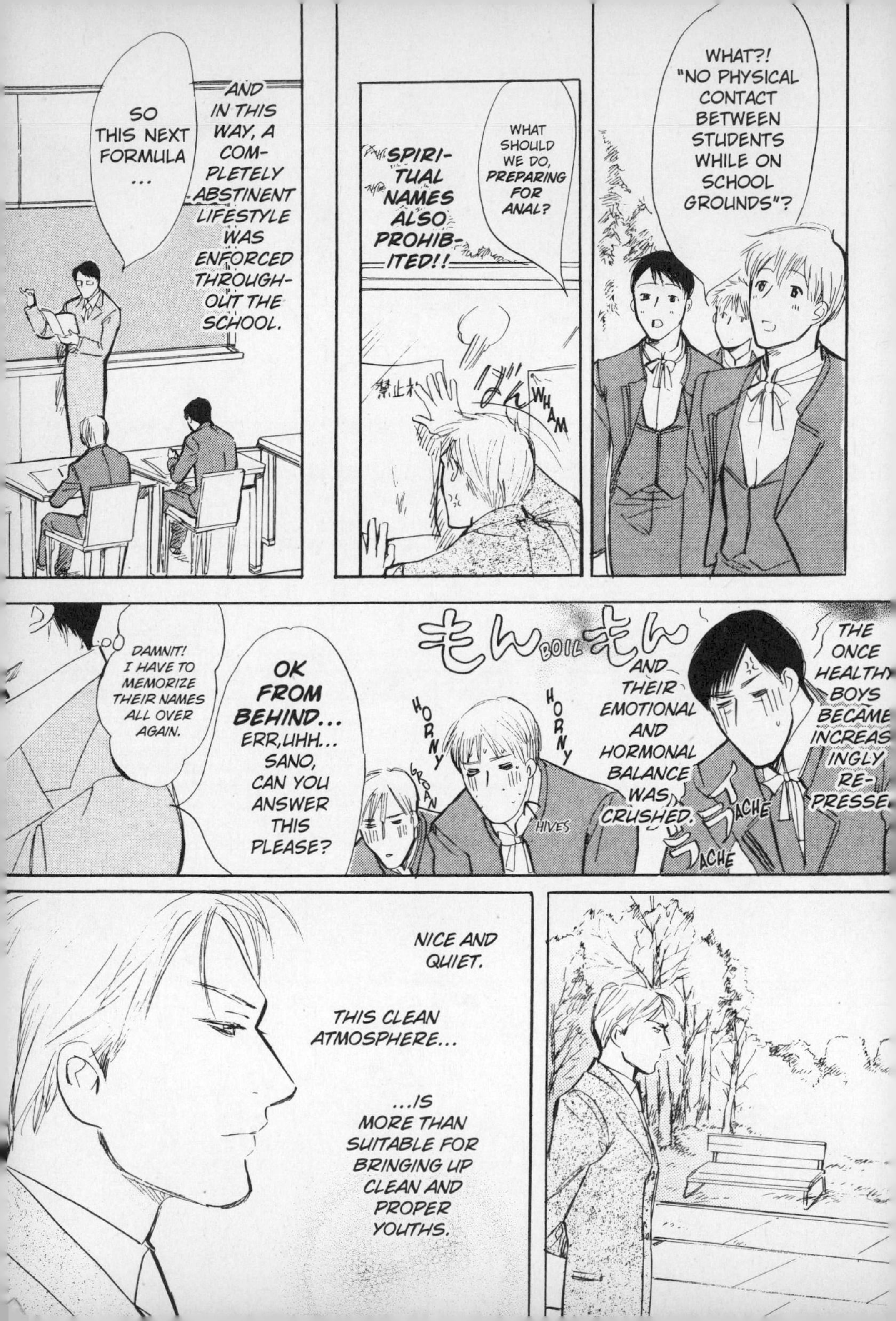
WHAT?! "NO PHYSICAL CONTACT BETWEEN STUDENTS WHILE ON SCHOOL GROUNDS"?
WHAT SHOULD WE DO, PREPARING FOR ANAL?
SPIRITUAL NAMES ALSO PROHIBITED!!
ばん WHAM
禁止札
AND IN THIS WAY, A COMPLETELY ABSTINENT LIFESTYLE WAS ENFORCED THROUGHOUT THE SCHOOL.
SO THIS NEXT FORMULA ...
THE ONCE HEALTHY BOYS BECAME INCREASINGLY REPRESSE
AND THEIR EMOTIONAL AND HORMONAL BALANCE WAS CRUSHED.
ACHE
ACHE
もん BOIL もん
HORNY
HORNY
HIVES
GROAN
OK FROM BEHIND... ERR,UHH... SANO, CAN YOU ANSWER THIS PLEASE?
DAMNIT! I HAVE TO MEMORIZE THEIR NAMES ALL OVER AGAIN.
NICE AND QUIET.
THIS CLEAN ATMOSPHERE...
...IS MORE THAN SUITABLE FOR BRINGING UP CLEAN AND PROPER YOUTHS.

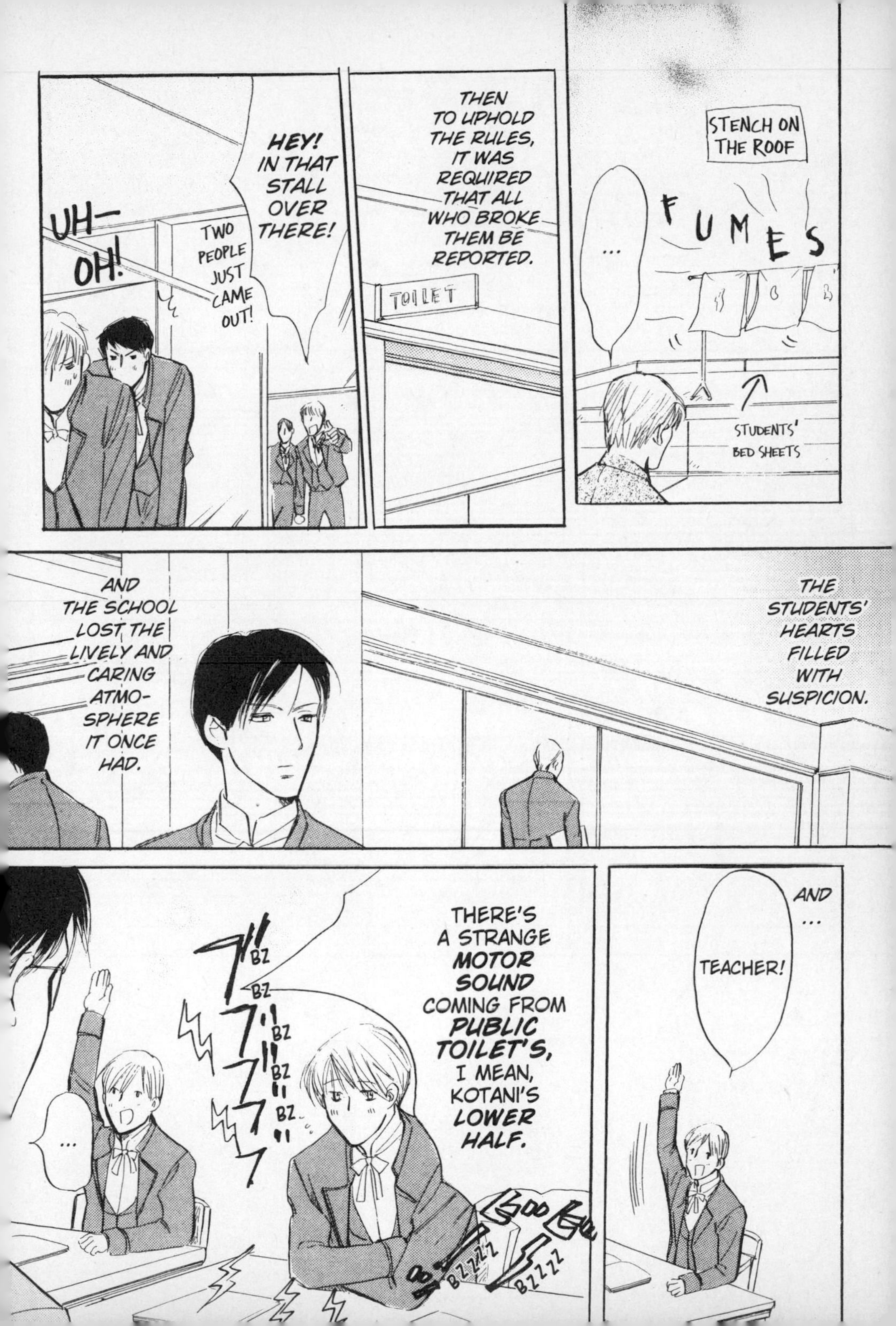
STENCH ON THE ROOF
FUMES
...
STUDENTS' BED SHEETS
THEN TO UPHOLD THE RULES, IT WAS REQUIRED THAT ALL WHO BROKE THEM BE REPORTED.
TOILET
HEY! IN THAT STALL OVER THERE!
TWO PEOPLE JUST CAME OUT!
UH—OH!
THE STUDENTS' HEARTS FILLED WITH SUSPICION.
AND THE SCHOOL LOST THE LIVELY AND CARING ATMOSPHERE IT ONCE HAD.
AND ...
TEACHER!
THERE'S A STRANGE MOTOR SOUND COMING FROM PUBLIC TOILET'S, I MEAN, KOTANI'S LOWER HALF.
BZ BZ BZ BZ BZ
...
BZZZZ
BZZZZ

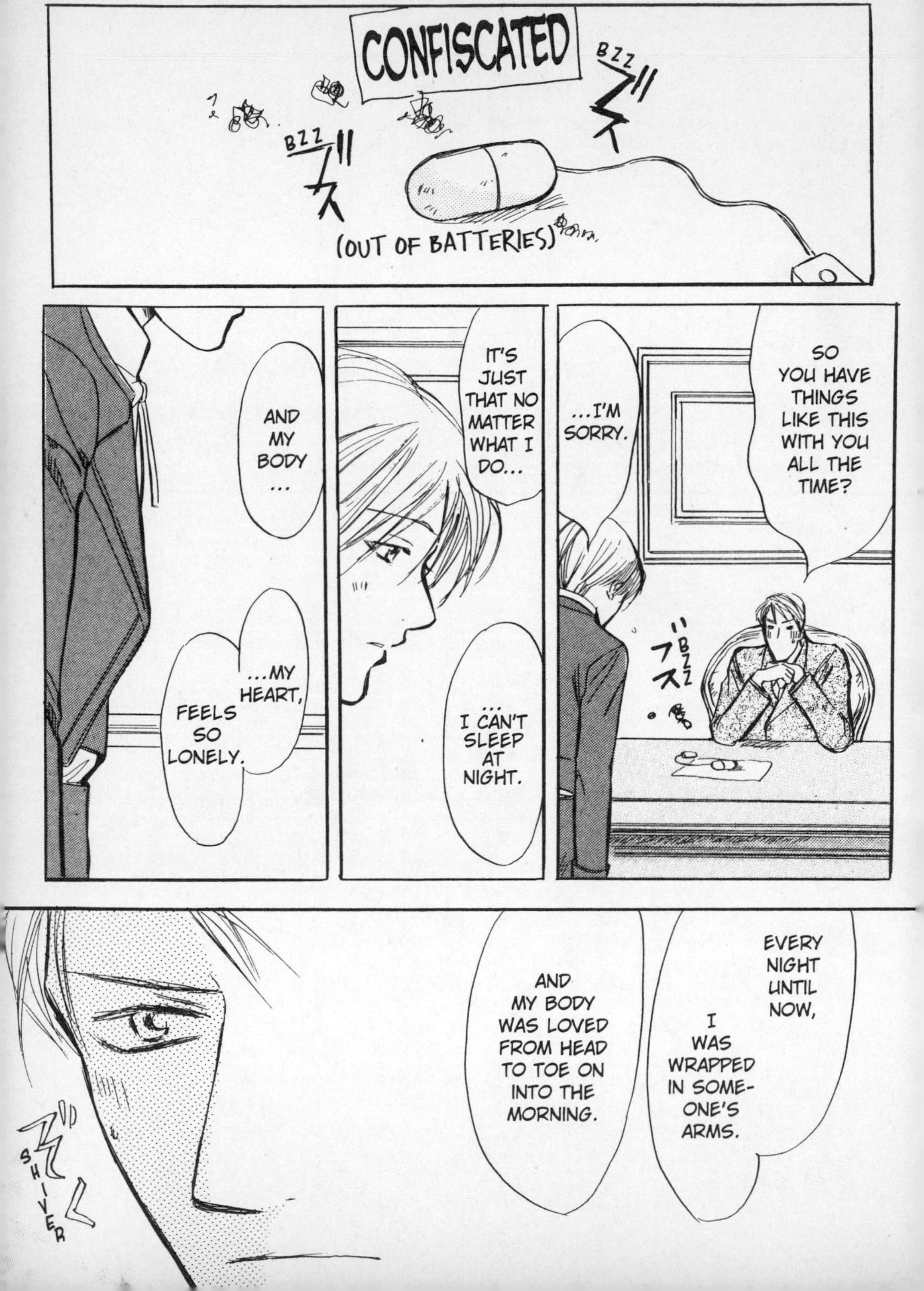
CONFISCATED
BZZ
BZZ
(OUT OF BATTERIES)
SO YOU HAVE THINGS LIKE THIS WITH YOU ALL THE TIME?
...I'M SORRY.
BZZ
IT'S JUST THAT NO MATTER WHAT I DO...
...I CAN'T SLEEP AT NIGHT.
AND MY BODY...
...MY HEART, FEELS SO LONELY.
EVERY NIGHT UNTIL NOW,
I WAS WRAPPED IN SOME-ONE'S ARMS.
AND MY BODY WAS LOVED FROM HEAD TO TOE ON INTO THE MORNING.
SHIVER

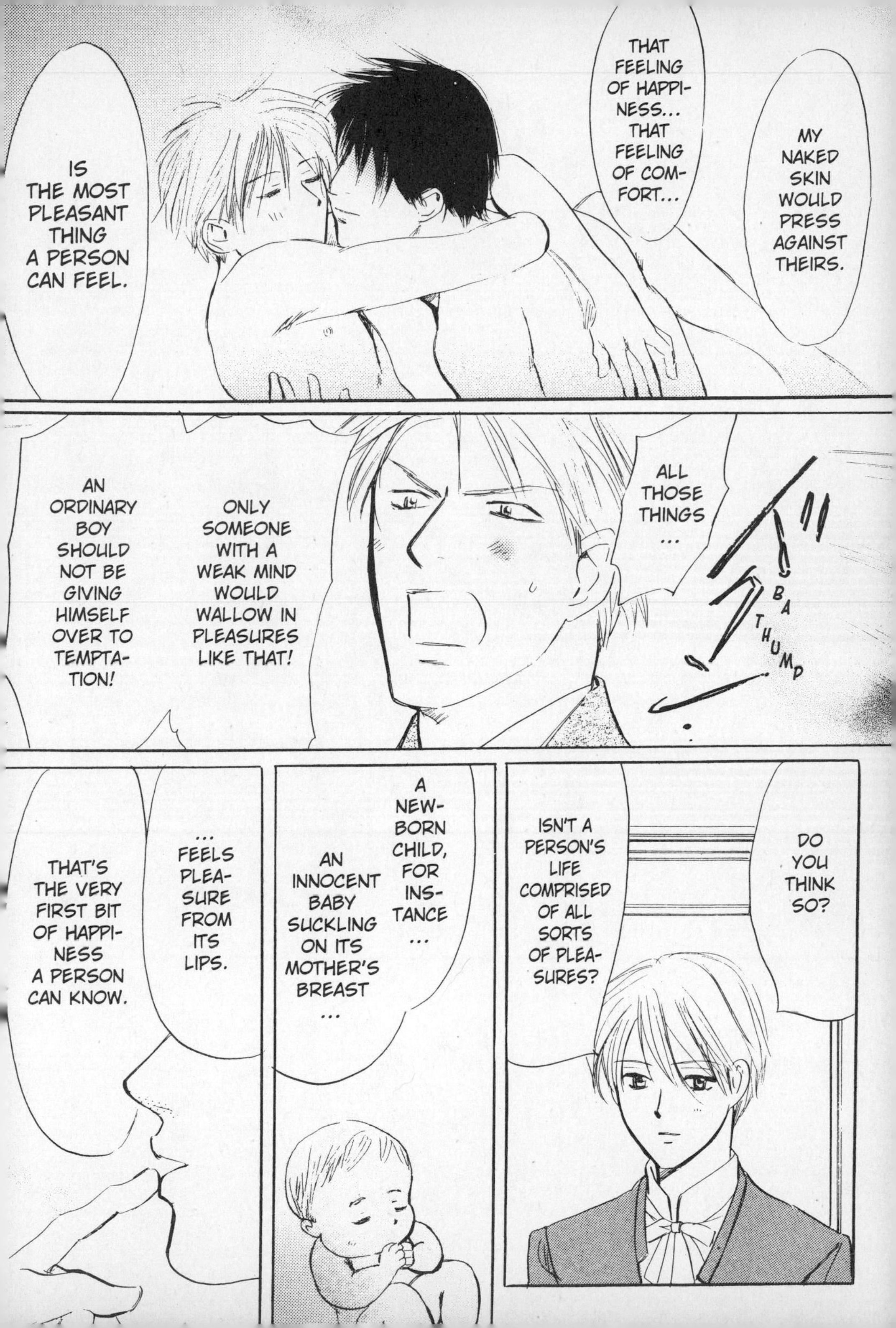
MY NAKED SKIN WOULD PRESS AGAINST THEIRS.
THAT FEELING OF HAPPINESS... THAT FEELING OF COMFORT...
IS THE MOST PLEASANT THING A PERSON CAN FEEL.
BA THUMP
ALL THOSE THINGS ...
ONLY SOMEONE WITH A WEAK MIND WOULD WALLOW IN PLEASURES LIKE THAT!
AN ORDINARY BOY SHOULD NOT BE GIVING HIMSELF OVER TO TEMPTATION!
DO YOU THINK SO?
ISN'T A PERSON'S LIFE COMPRISED OF ALL SORTS OF PLEASURES?
A NEWBORN CHILD, FOR INSTANCE ...
AN INNOCENT BABY SUCKLING ON ITS MOTHER'S BREAST ...
... FEELS PLEASURE FROM ITS LIPS.
THAT'S THE VERY FIRST BIT OF HAPPINESS A PERSON CAN KNOW.

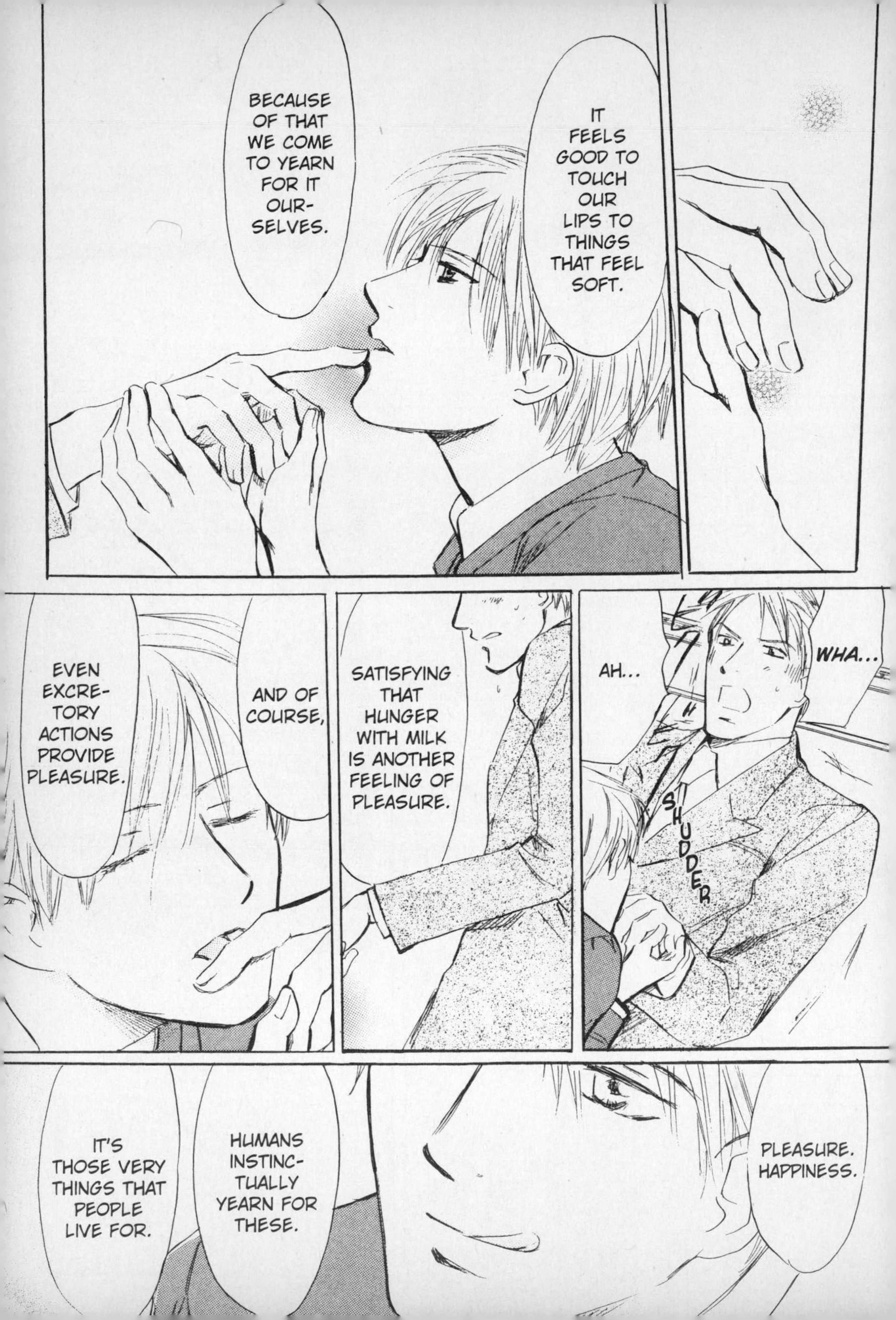
IT FEELS GOOD TO TOUCH OUR LIPS TO THINGS THAT FEEL SOFT.
BECAUSE OF THAT WE COME TO YEARN FOR IT OURSELVES.
WHA...
AH...
SHUDDER
SATISFYING THAT HUNGER WITH MILK IS ANOTHER FEELING OF PLEASURE.
AND OF COURSE,
EVEN EXCRETORY ACTIONS PROVIDE PLEASURE.
PLEASURE. HAPPINESS.
HUMANS INSTINCTUALLY YEARN FOR THESE.
IT'S THOSE VERY THINGS THAT PEOPLE LIVE FOR.

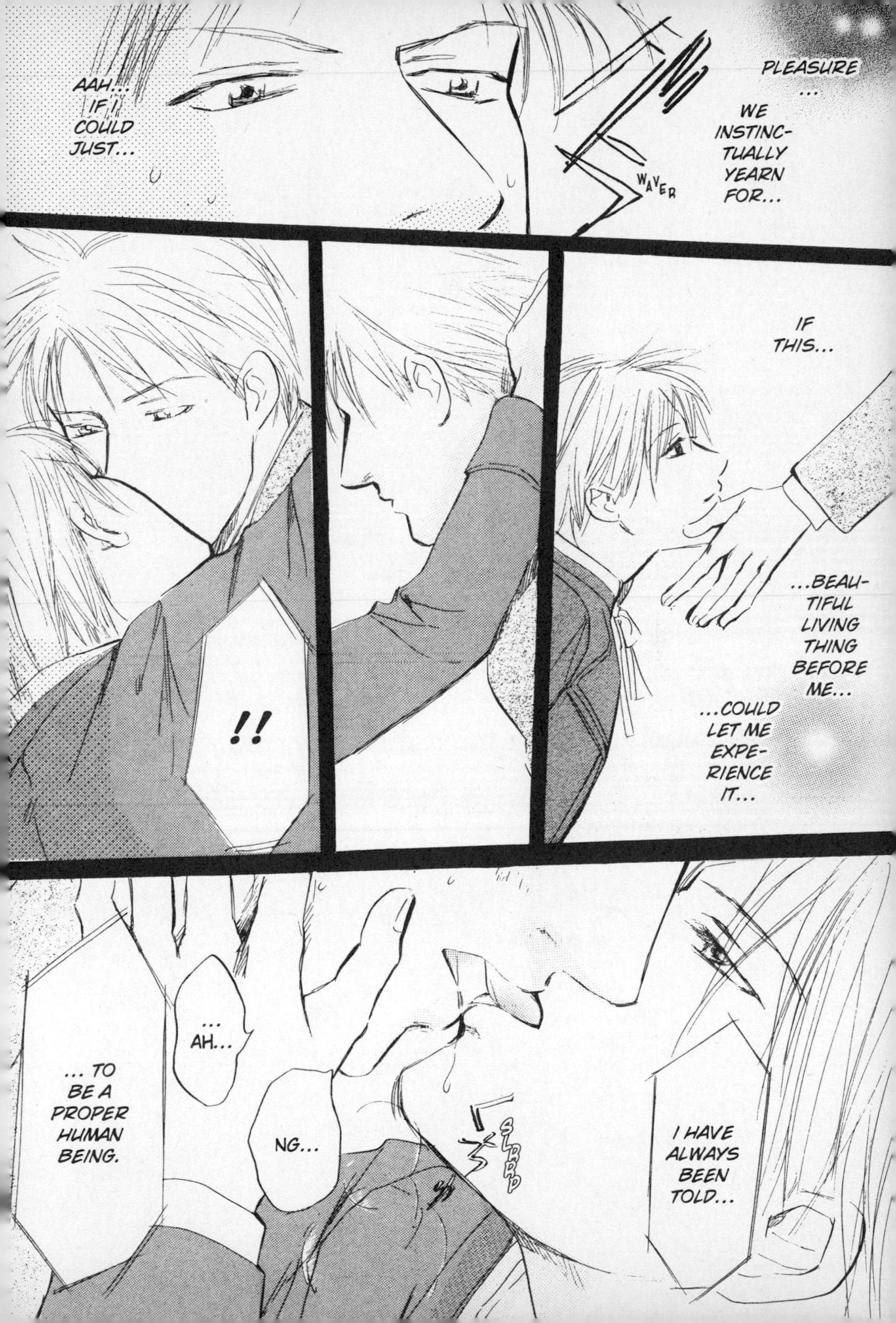
PLEASURE...
WE INSTINCTUALLY YEARN FOR...
WAVER
AAH... IF I COULD JUST...
IF THIS...
...BEAUTIFUL LIVING THING BEFORE ME...
...COULD LET ME EXPERIENCE IT...
!!
I HAVE ALWAYS BEEN TOLD...
SLRRP
NG...
...AH...
...TO BE A PROPER HUMAN BEING.

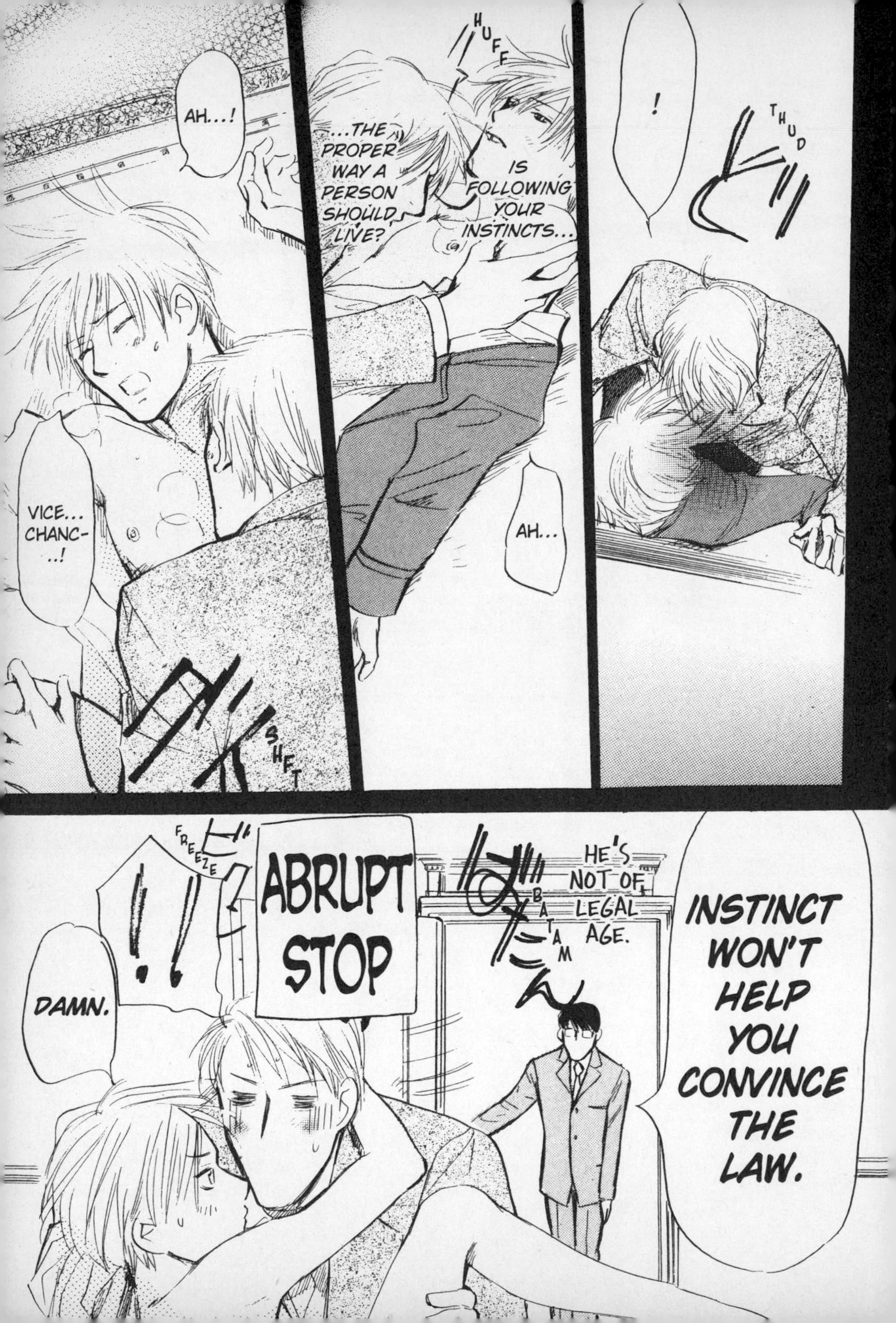
!
THUD
HUFF
IS FOLLOWING YOUR INSTINCTS...
...THE PROPER WAY A PERSON SHOULD LIVE?
AH...
AH...!
VICE... CHANC-...!
SHFT
INSTINCT WON'T HELP YOU CONVINCE THE LAW.
HE'S NOT OF LEGAL AGE.
BATAM
ABRUPT STOP
FREEZE
!!
DAMN.

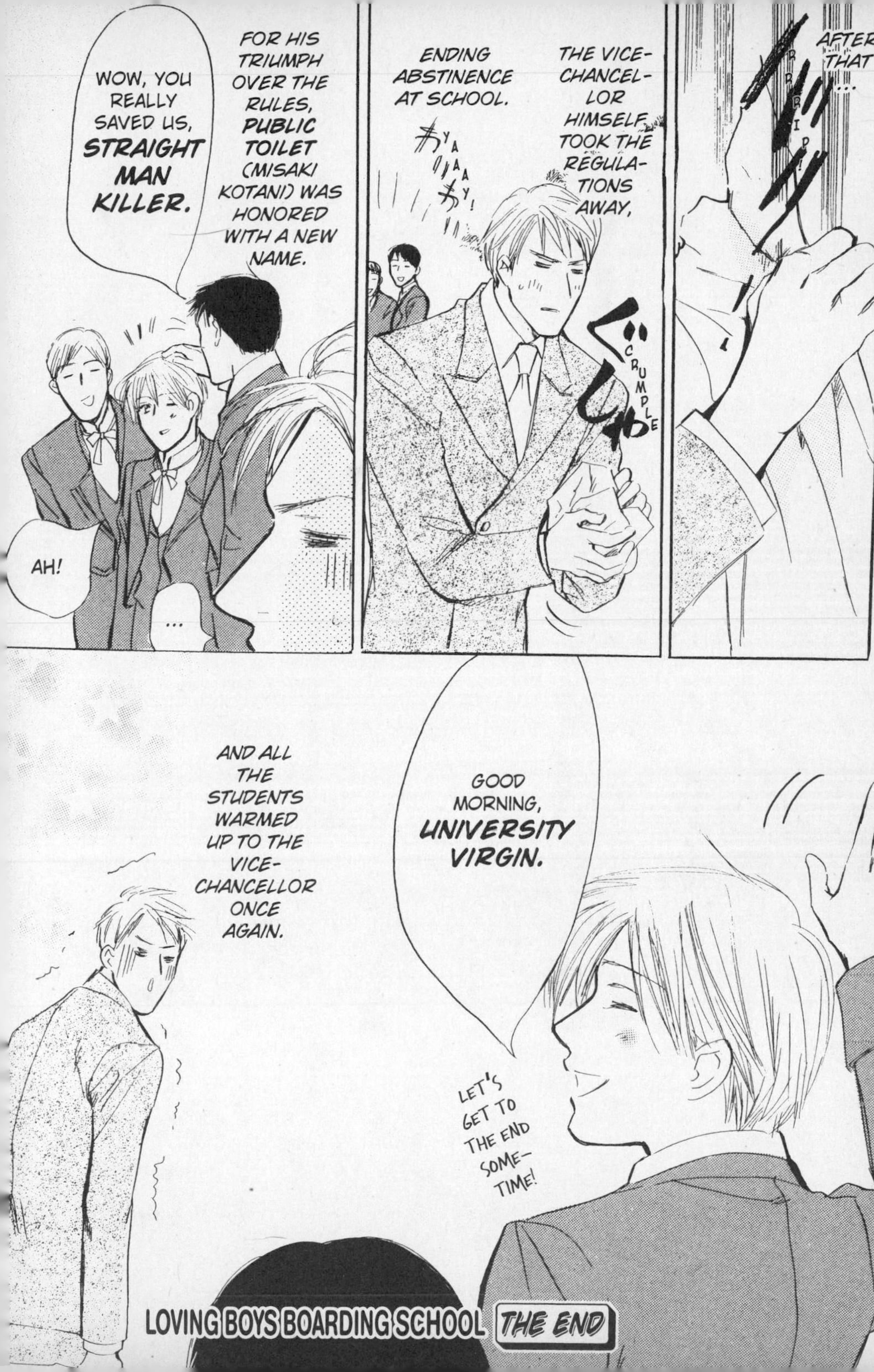
AFTER THAT...
RRRIP!
THE VICE-CHANCELLOR HIMSELF TOOK THE REGULATIONS AWAY,
ENDING ABSTINENCE AT SCHOOL.
YAAAY!
CRUMPLE
FOR HIS TRIUMPH OVER THE RULES, PUBLIC TOILET (MISAKI KOTANI) WAS HONORED WITH A NEW NAME.
WOW, YOU REALLY SAVED US, STRAIGHT MAN KILLER.
AH!
...
GOOD MORNING, UNIVERSITY VIRGIN.
AND ALL THE STUDENTS WARMED UP TO THE VICE-CHANCELLOR ONCE AGAIN.
LET'S GET TO THE END SOMETIME!
LOVING BOYS BOARDING SCHOOL THE END

HEY EVERYBODY! WHY NOT TRY GIVING YOURSELVES SPIRITUAL NAMES?

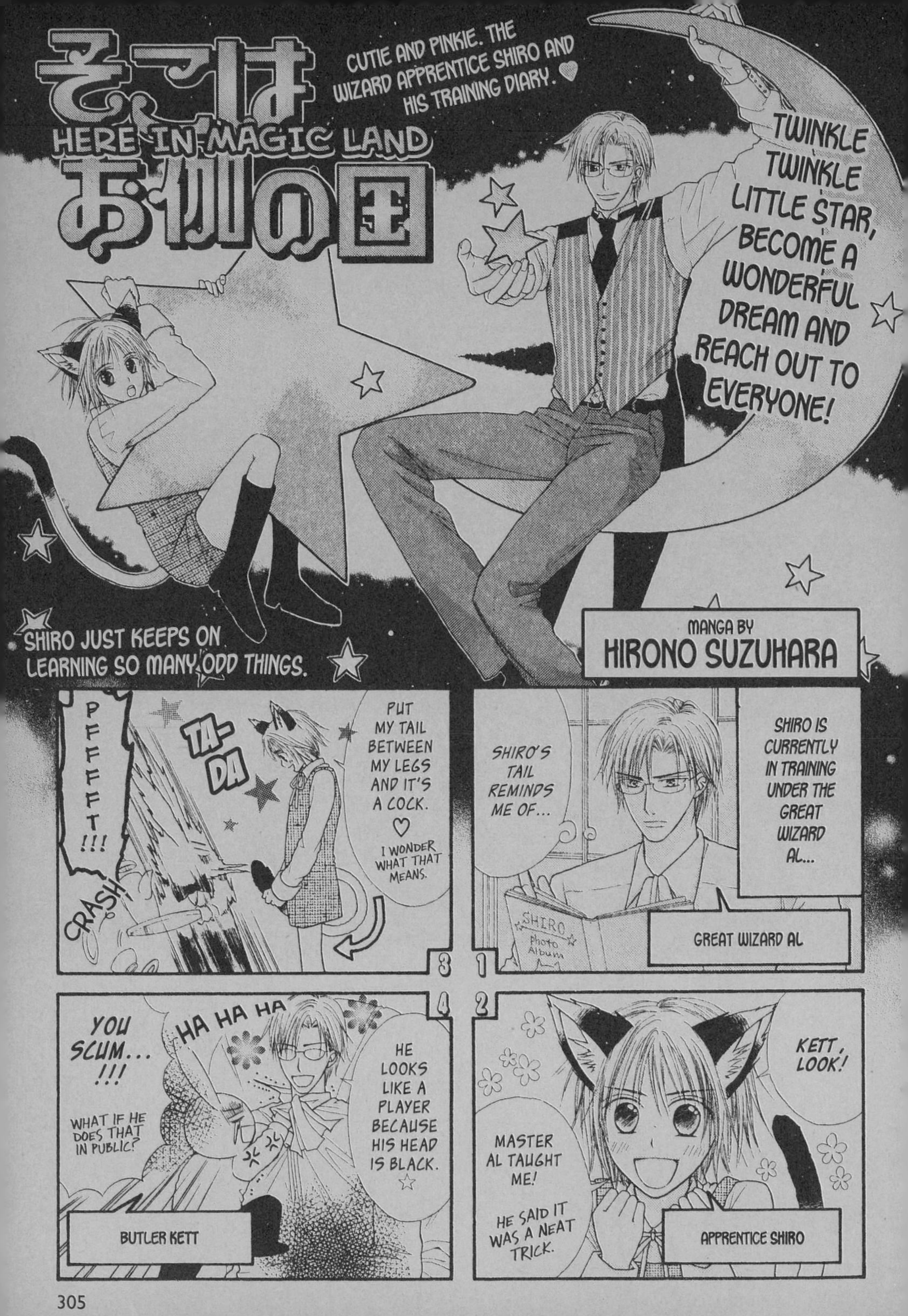

そこはお伽の国
HERE IN MAGIC LAND
CUTIE AND PINKIE. THE WIZARD APPRENTICE SHIRO AND HIS TRAINING DIARY. ♥
TWINKLE TWINKLE LITTLE STAR, BECOME A WONDERFUL DREAM AND REACH OUT TO EVERYONE!
MANGA BY HIRONO SUZUHARA
SHIRO JUST KEEPS ON LEARNING SO MANY ODD THINGS.
1
SHIRO IS CURRENTLY IN TRAINING UNDER THE GREAT WIZARD AL...
SHIRO'S TAIL REMINDS ME OF...
SHIRO Photo Album
GREAT WIZARD AL
2
KETT, LOOK!
MASTER AL TAUGHT ME!
HE SAID IT WAS A NEAT TRICK.
APPRENTICE SHIRO
3
PUT MY TAIL BETWEEN MY LEGS AND IT'S A COCK. ♡
I WONDER WHAT THAT MEANS.
TA-DA
PFFFFT!!!
CRASH
4
HE LOOKS LIKE A PLAYER BECAUSE HIS HEAD IS BLACK. ☆
HA HA HA
YOU SCUM...!!!
WHAT IF HE DOES THAT IN PUBLIC?
BUTLER KETT

MAGIC LAND FRIENDS

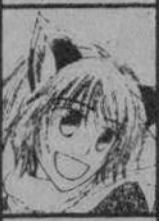

SHIRO

A BOY FROM THE CAT FAMILY. BECAME *AL'S* APPRENTICE IN HOPES OF BECOMING A WIZARD.

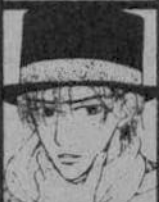

AL

A GREAT WIZARD... BUT NOT A RESPONSIBLE ADULT. ALWAYS LUSTING AFTER *SHIRO*.

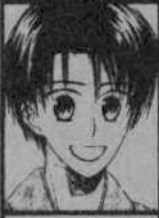

KETT

THE BUTLER AT *AL'S* ESTATE. THERE'S A PERSON UNDER THE BUNNY COSTUME.

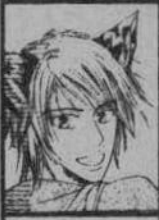

TORA

SHIRO'S OLDER BROTHER. VISITS AL'S ESTATE OFTEN OUT OF WORRY FOR SHIRO AND DESIRE TO SEE KETT.

A TALKATIVE BROOM 1

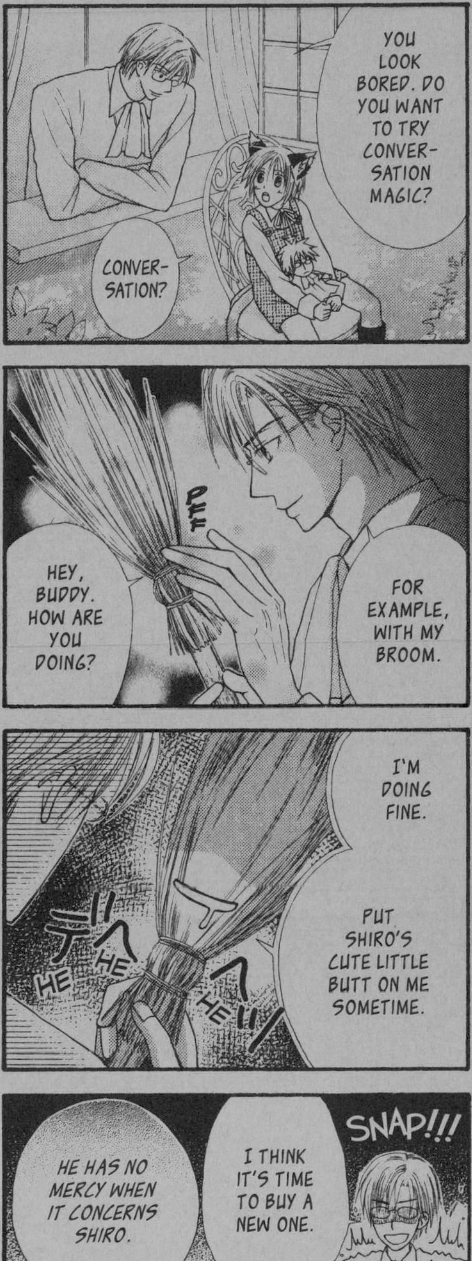
YOU LOOK BORED. DO YOU WANT TO TRY CONVERSATION MAGIC?
CONVERSATION?
FOR EXAMPLE, WITH MY BROOM.
HEY, BUDDY. HOW ARE YOU DOING?
I'M DOING FINE.
PUT SHIRO'S CUTE LITTLE BUTT ON ME SOMETIME.
HE HE HE
SNAP!!!
I THINK IT'S TIME TO BUY A NEW ONE.
HE HAS NO MERCY WHEN IT CONCERNS SHIRO.
I GUESS I'LL USE THIS AS FIREWOOD.

A TALKATIVE BROOM 2

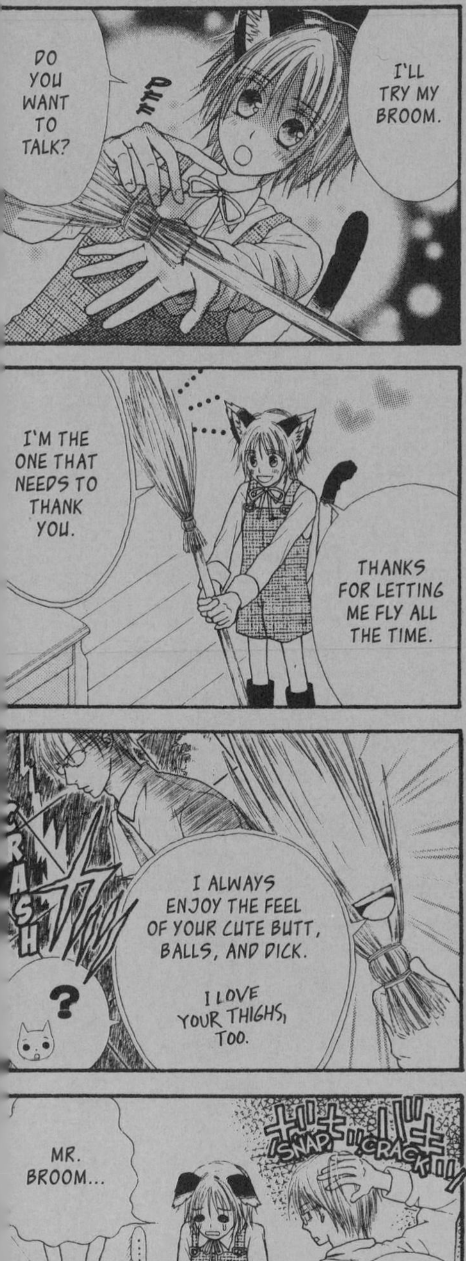
I'LL TRY MY BROOM.
DO YOU WANT TO TALK?
THANKS FOR LETTING ME FLY ALL THE TIME.
I'M THE ONE THAT NEEDS TO THANK YOU.
I ALWAYS ENJOY THE FEEL OF YOUR CUTE BUTT, BALLS, AND DICK.
I LOVE YOUR THIGHS, TOO.
CRASH
?
SNAP
CRACK
MR. BROOM...
...
I'M SORRY, MY HANDS SLIPPED.
CRUMBLE

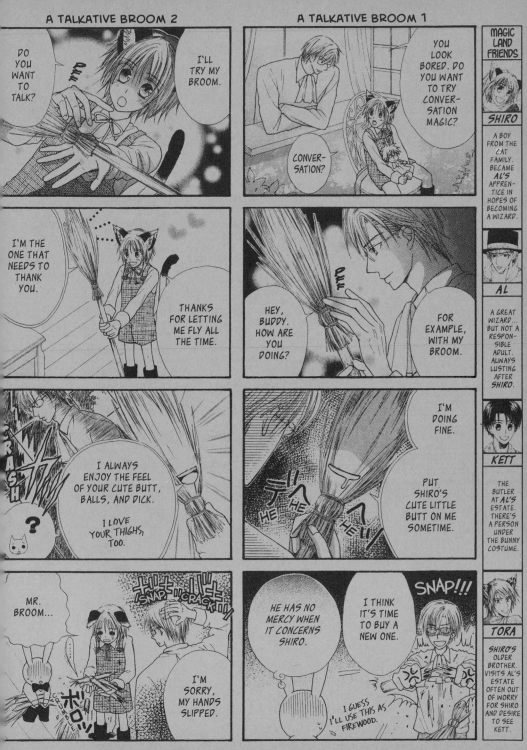

ASSEMBLY OF PETS 1

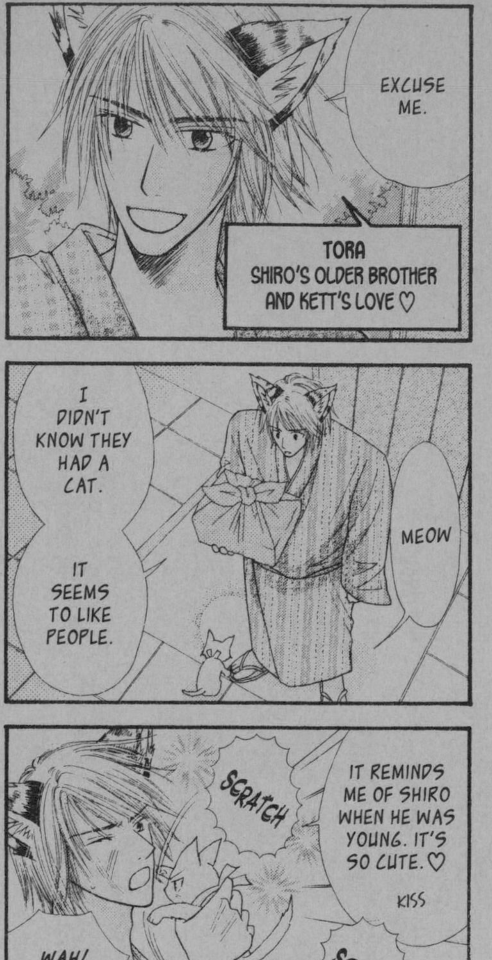
EXCUSE ME.
TORA
SHIRO'S OLDER BROTHER AND KETT'S LOVE ♡
MEOW
I DIDN'T KNOW THEY HAD A CAT.
IT SEEMS TO LIKE PEOPLE.
IT REMINDS ME OF SHIRO WHEN HE WAS YOUNG. IT'S SO CUTE. ♡
KISS
SCRATCH
SCRATCH
WAH! WHAT'S THE MATTER?
POOF!!
DON'T PICK ME UP SO CARELESSLY.
BLECH
おえー
I WAS ABOUT TO KISS YOU
WHAT ARE YOU TRYING TO DO, YOU BORED WIZARD?!

ASSEMBLY OF PETS 2

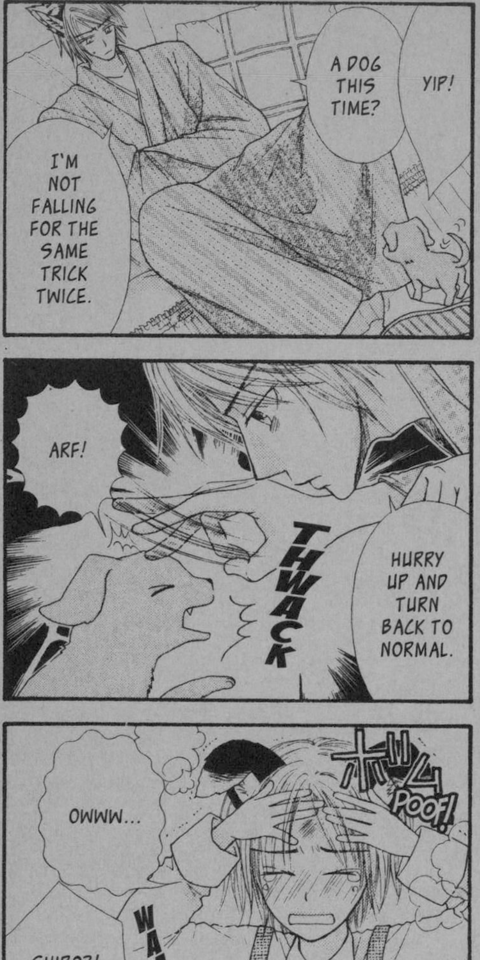
YIP!
A DOG THIS TIME?
I'M NOT FALLING FOR THE SAME TRICK TWICE.
HURRY UP AND TURN BACK TO NORMAL.
THWACK
ARF!
POOF!
WAAAH...
OWWW...
SHIRO?!
SOB SOB
I HATE YOU BIG BRO!!
I WANTED YOU TO SEE MY TRANSFORMATION MAGIC.
CLOSE CALL FOR THE GUY WITH THE BROTHER COMPLEX.

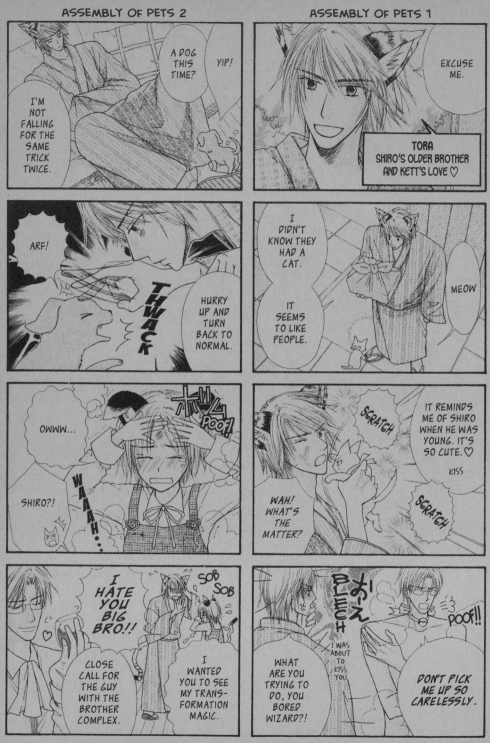

A SENSATIONAL MEMORIAL

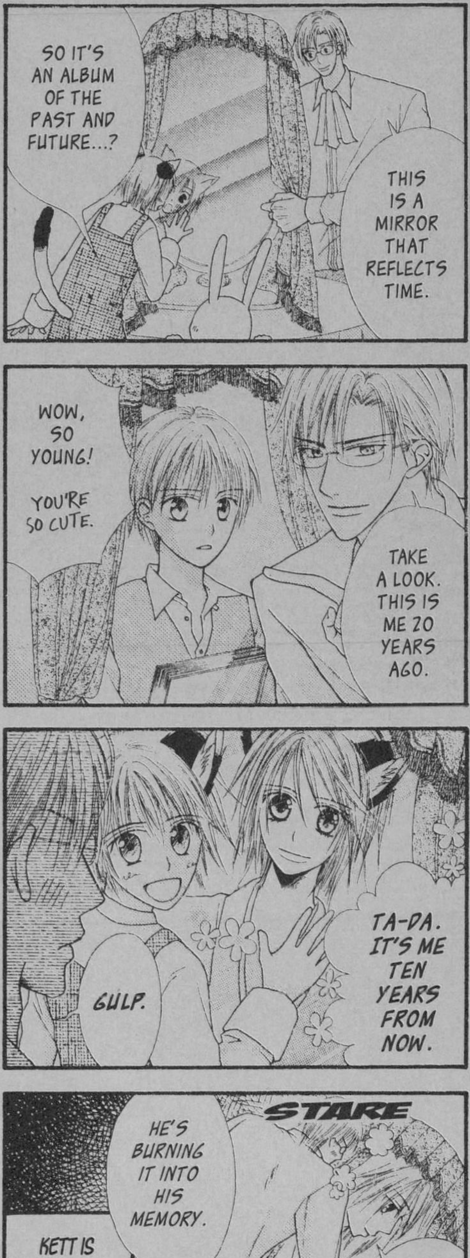
THIS IS A MIRROR THAT REFLECTS TIME.
SO IT'S AN ALBUM OF THE PAST AND FUTURE...?
TAKE A LOOK. THIS IS ME 20 YEARS AGO.
WOW, SO YOUNG!
YOU'RE SO CUTE.
TA-DA. IT'S ME TEN YEARS FROM NOW.
GULP.
STARE
I CAN USE THIS TO-NIGHT.
HE'S BURNING IT INTO HIS MEMORY.
KETT IS ADULT ENOUGH NOT TO ASK "FOR WHAT?"

A SORROW MEMORIAL

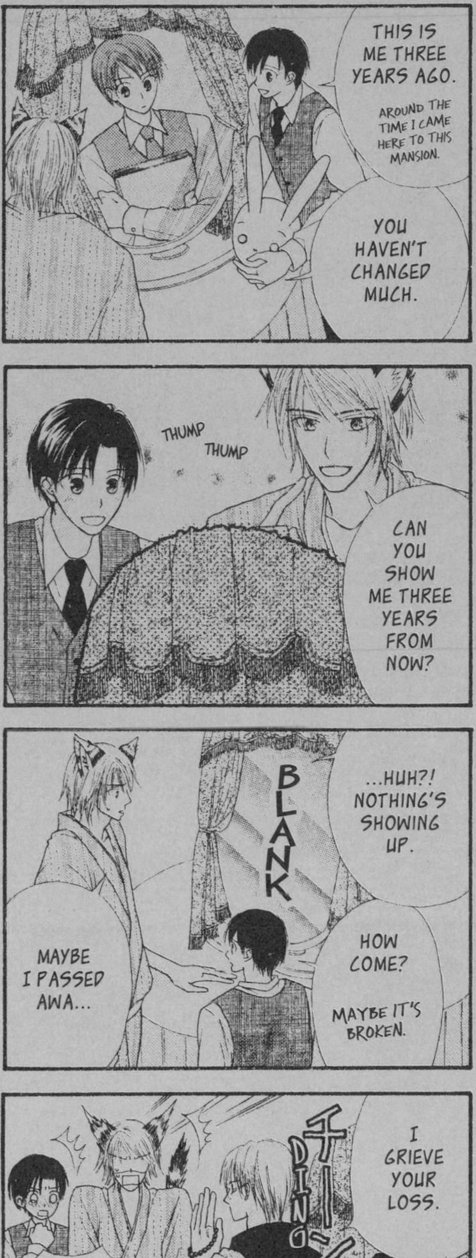
THIS IS ME THREE YEARS AGO.
AROUND THE TIME I CAME HERE TO THIS MANSION.
YOU HAVEN'T CHANGED MUCH.
CAN YOU SHOW ME THREE YEARS FROM NOW?
THUMP THUMP
...HUH?! NOTHING'S SHOWING UP.
BLANK
HOW COME?
MAYBE IT'S BROKEN.
MAYBE I PASSED AWA...
I GRIEVE YOUR LOSS.
DING-!
THREATENING HAMMER
STOP IT. IT'S A JOKE, RIGHT?!
AM I GOING TO DIE?!

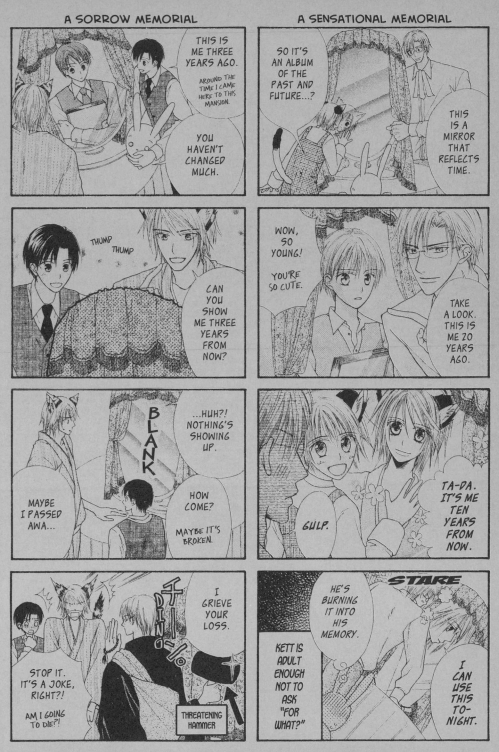

A SWEET MEMORIAL

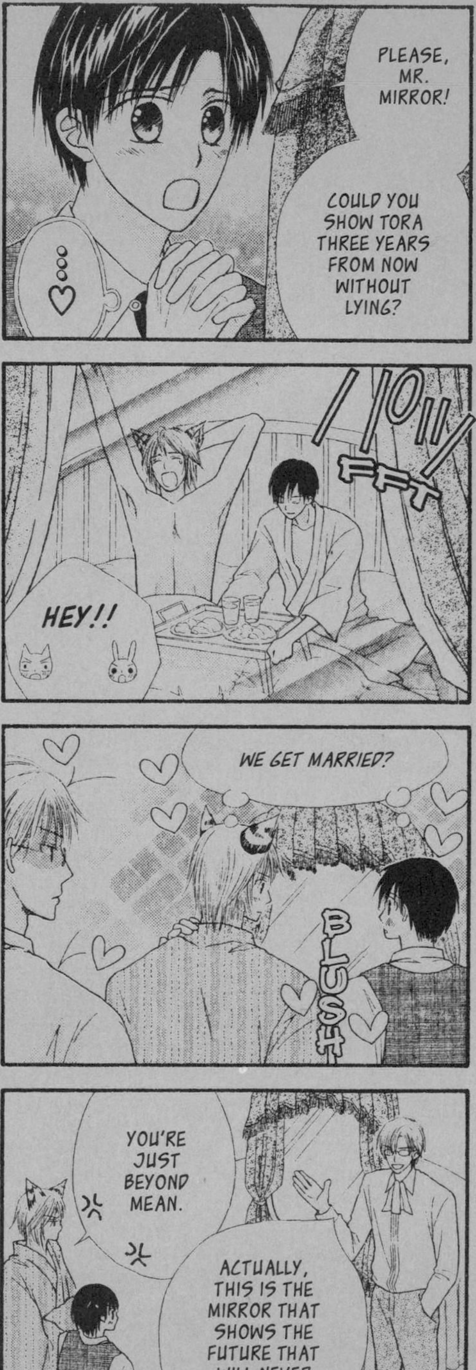
PLEASE, MR. MIRROR!
COULD YOU SHOW TORA THREE YEARS FROM NOW WITHOUT LYING?
...♡
FFT
HEY!!
WE GET MARRIED?
BLUSH
YOU'RE JUST BEYOND MEAN.
ACTUALLY, THIS IS THE MIRROR THAT SHOWS THE FUTURE THAT WILL NEVER COME TRUE.

A PRANK MEMORIAL

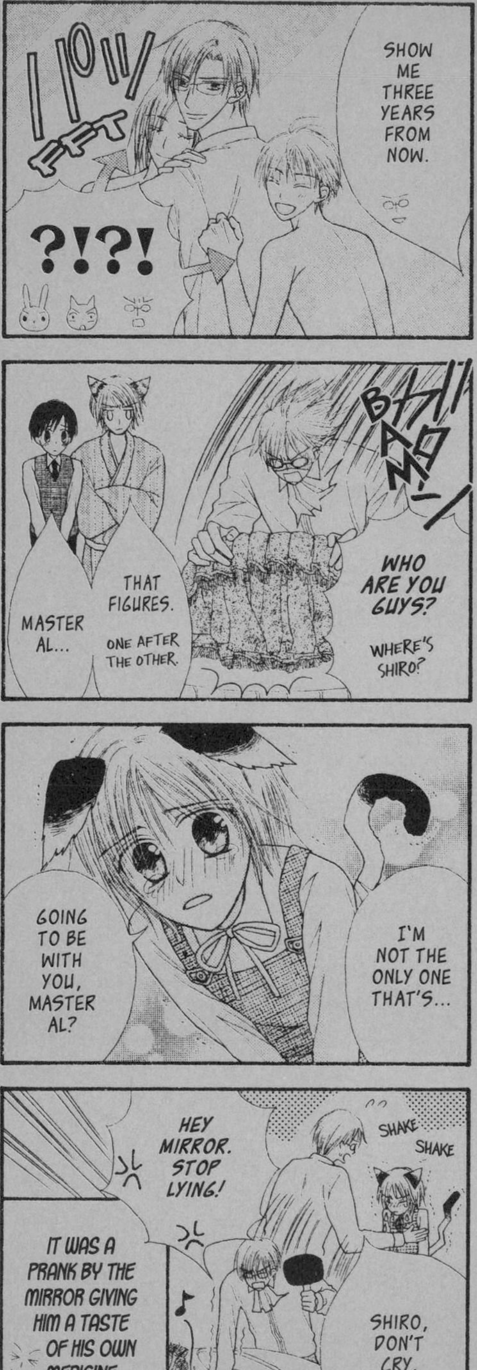
SHOW ME THREE YEARS FROM NOW.
FFT
?!?!
BAM
WHO ARE YOU GUYS?
WHERE'S SHIRO?
THAT FIGURES.
ONE AFTER THE OTHER.
MASTER AL...
I'M NOT THE ONLY ONE THAT'S...
GOING TO BE WITH YOU, MASTER AL?
HEY MIRROR. STOP LYING!
SHAKE
SHAKE
SHIRO, DON'T CRY.
IT WAS A PRANK BY THE MIRROR GIVING HIM A TASTE OF HIS OWN MEDICINE.

A RIVALRY

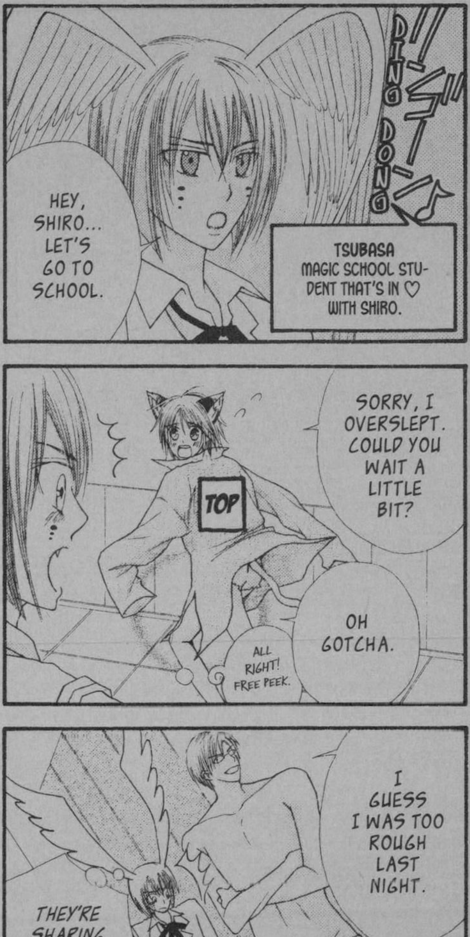
DING DONG
HEY, SHIRO... LET'S GO TO SCHOOL.
TSUBASA MAGIC SCHOOL STUDENT THAT'S IN ♡ WITH SHIRO.
SORRY, I OVERSLEPT. COULD YOU WAIT A LITTLE BIT?
TOP
OH GOTCHA.
ALL RIGHT! FREE PEEK.
I GUESS I WAS TOO ROUGH LAST NIGHT.
THEY'RE SHARING PAJAMAS!
HE'S SHOWING IT TO ME ON PURPOSE!!
BOTTOM
HAVE FUN AT SCHOOL.
BE CAREFUL OF THE BOY NEXT TO YOU.
KISS♥
HE'S TAUNTING THE BOY...
SO CHILDISH...

A DANGEROUS RELATIONSHIP ♡

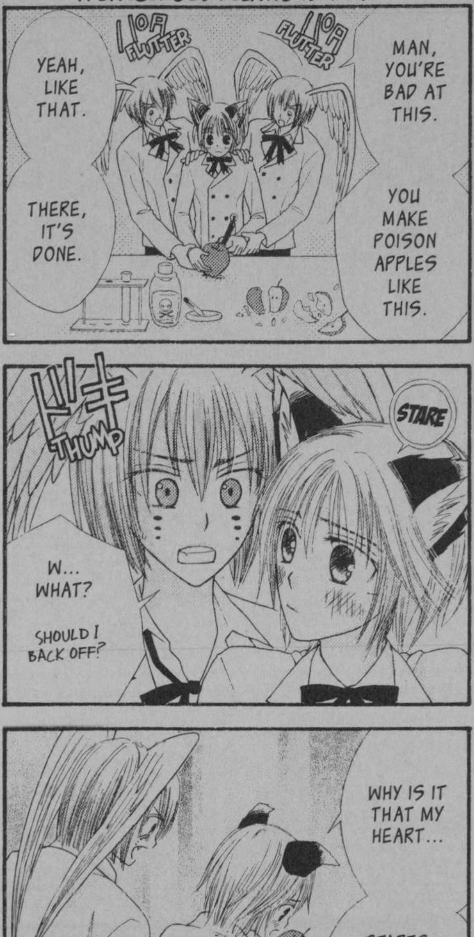
MAN, YOU'RE BAD AT THIS.
YOU MAKE POISON APPLES LIKE THIS.
FLUTTER
FLUTTER
YEAH, LIKE THAT.
THERE, IT'S DONE.
STARE
THUMP
W... WHAT?
SHOULD I BACK OFF?
WHY IS IT THAT MY HEART...
STARTS TO THROB WHEN YOU'RE CLOSE BY, TSUBASA?
WHAT? ♡
ITCH
ITCH
STOP BEING SO CUTE.
I'LL TACKLE YOU.
I START TO DROOL, TOO...
THAT'S PROBABLY INSTINCT.
FELINE
BIRD

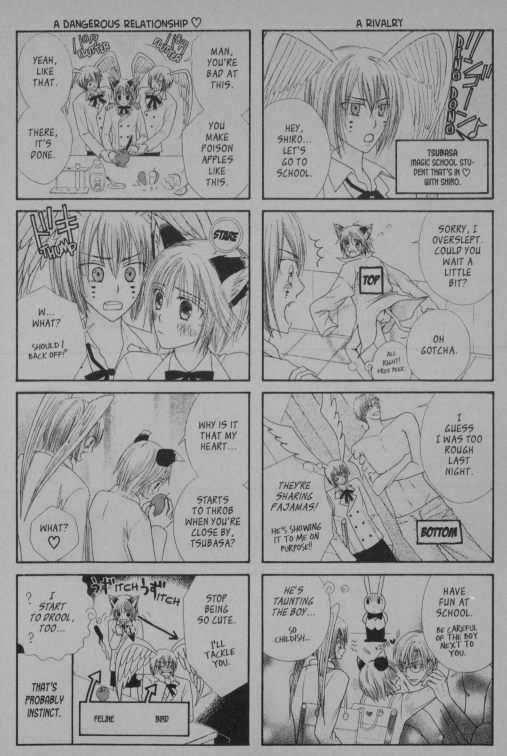

MASTER NONSTOP 1

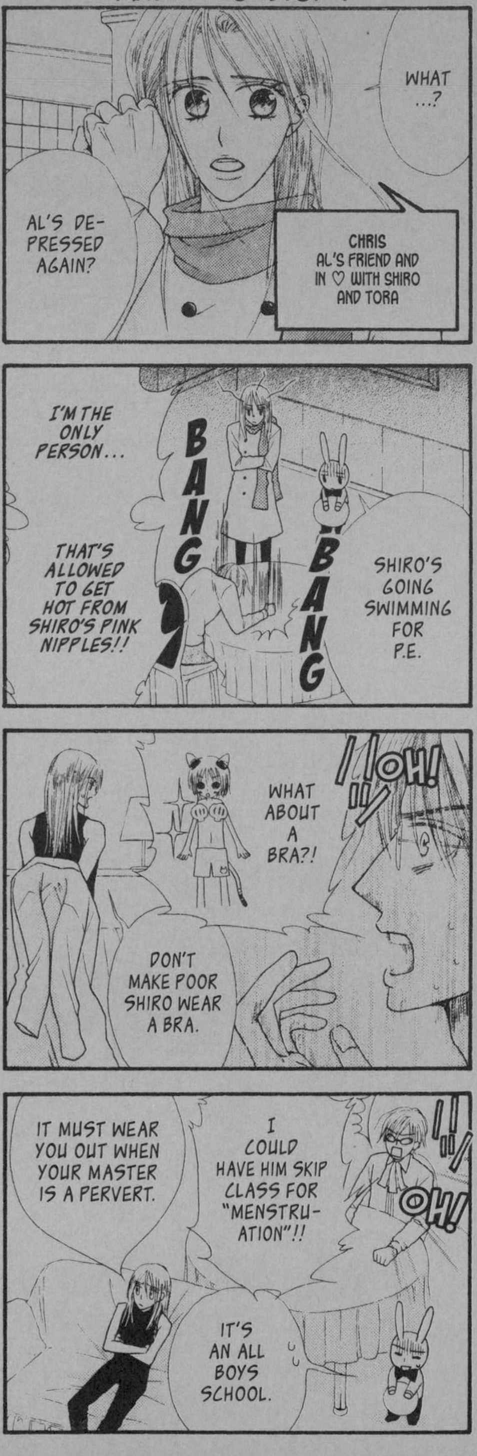
WHAT ...?
CHRIS
AL'S FRIEND AND IN ♡ WITH SHIRO AND TORA
AL'S DE-PRESSED AGAIN?
SHIRO'S GOING SWIMMING FOR P.E.
BANG
BANG
I'M THE ONLY PERSON...
THAT'S ALLOWED TO GET HOT FROM SHIRO'S PINK NIPPLES!!
!!OH!
WHAT ABOUT A BRA?!
DON'T MAKE POOR SHIRO WEAR A BRA.
!!
OH!
I COULD HAVE HIM SKIP CLASS FOR "MENSTRU-ATION"!!
IT MUST WEAR YOU OUT WHEN YOUR MASTER IS A PERVERT.
IT'S AN ALL BOYS SCHOOL.

MASTER NONSTOP 2

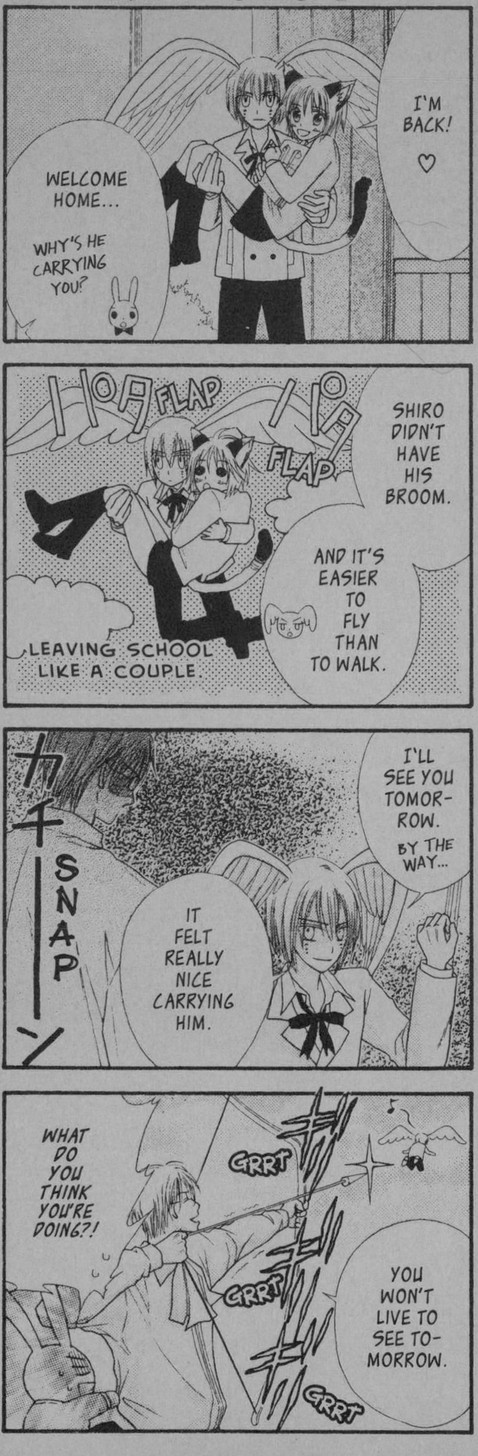
I'M BACK! ♡
WELCOME HOME...
WHY'S HE CARRYING YOU?
SHIRO DIDN'T HAVE HIS BROOM.
AND IT'S EASIER TO FLY THAN TO WALK.
FLAP
FLAP
LEAVING SCHOOL LIKE A COUPLE.
I'LL SEE YOU TOMOR-ROW.
BY THE WAY...
IT FELT REALLY NICE CARRYING HIM.
SNAP
YOU WON'T LIVE TO SEE TO-MORROW.
GRRT
WHAT DO YOU THINK YOU'RE DOING?!
GRRT
GRRT

A TENDER LOVE CALL

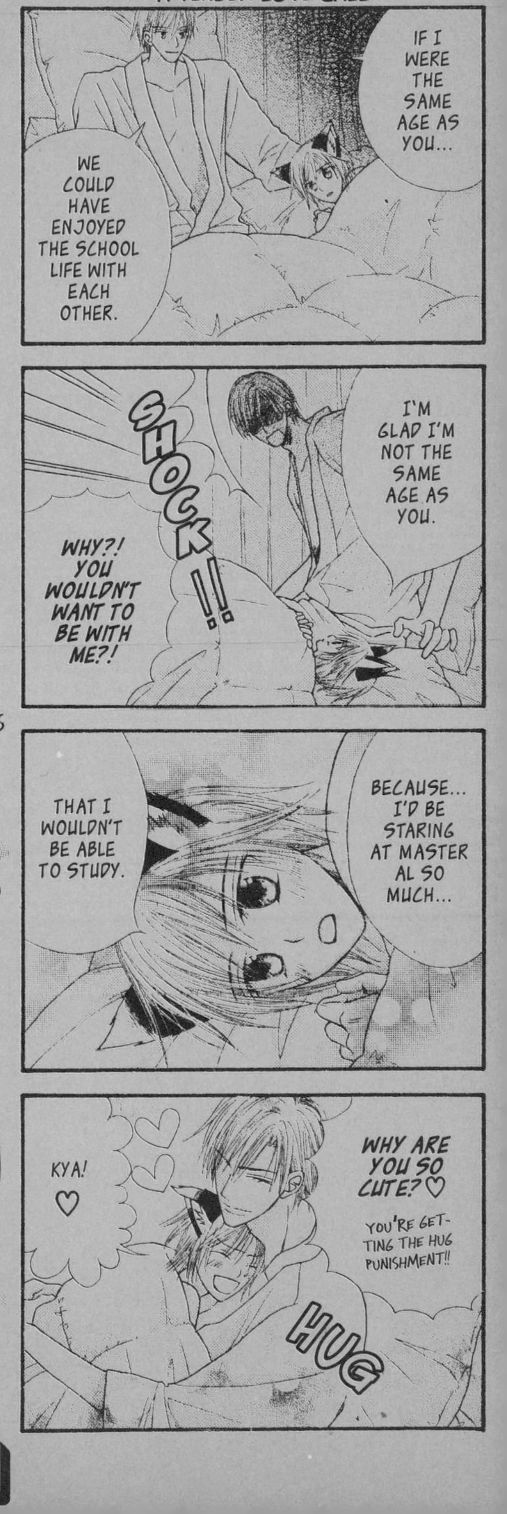
IF I WERE THE SAME AGE AS YOU...
WE COULD HAVE ENJOYED THE SCHOOL LIFE WITH EACH OTHER.
I'M GLAD I'M NOT THE SAME AGE AS YOU.
SHOCK!!
WHY?! YOU WOULDN'T WANT TO BE WITH ME?!
BECAUSE... I'D BE STARING AT MASTER AL SO MUCH...
THAT I WOULDN'T BE ABLE TO STUDY.
WHY ARE YOU SO CUTE? ♡
YOU'RE GETTING THE HUG PUNISHMENT!!
KYA! ♡
HUG

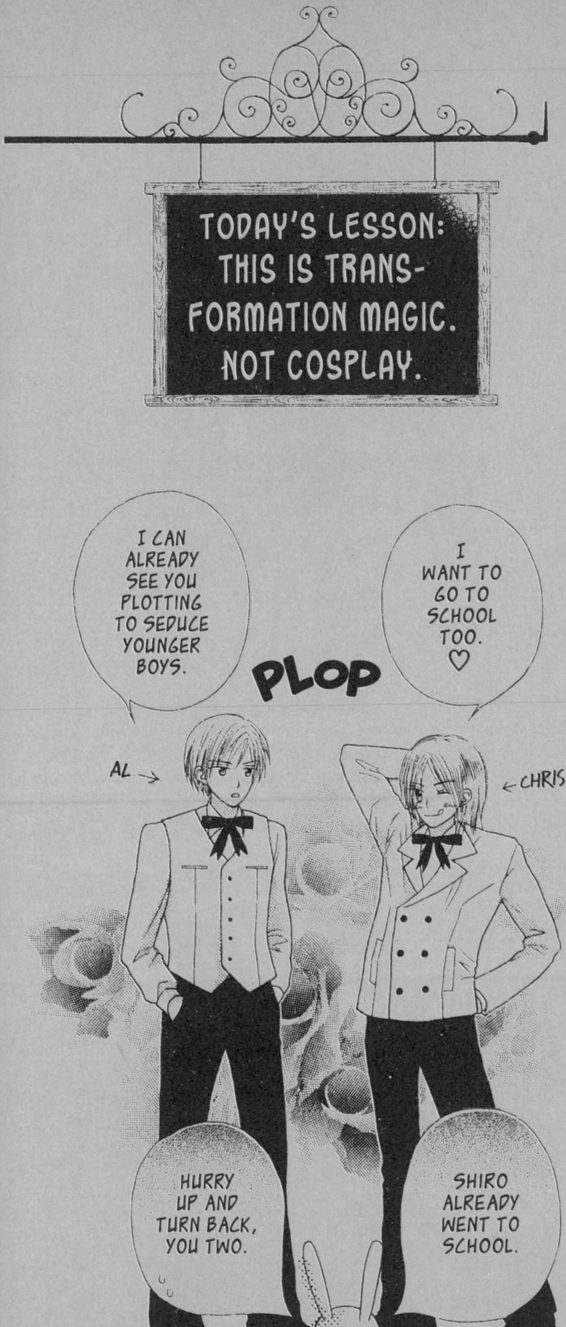
TODAY'S LESSON: THIS IS TRANS- FORMATION MAGIC. NOT COSPLAY.
I WANT TO GO TO SCHOOL TOO. ♡
I CAN ALREADY SEE YOU PLOTTING TO SEDUCE YOUNGER BOYS.
PLOP
← CHRIS
AL →
SHIRO ALREADY WENT TO SCHOOL.
HURRY UP AND TURN BACK, YOU TWO.

HERE IN MAGIC LAND THE END

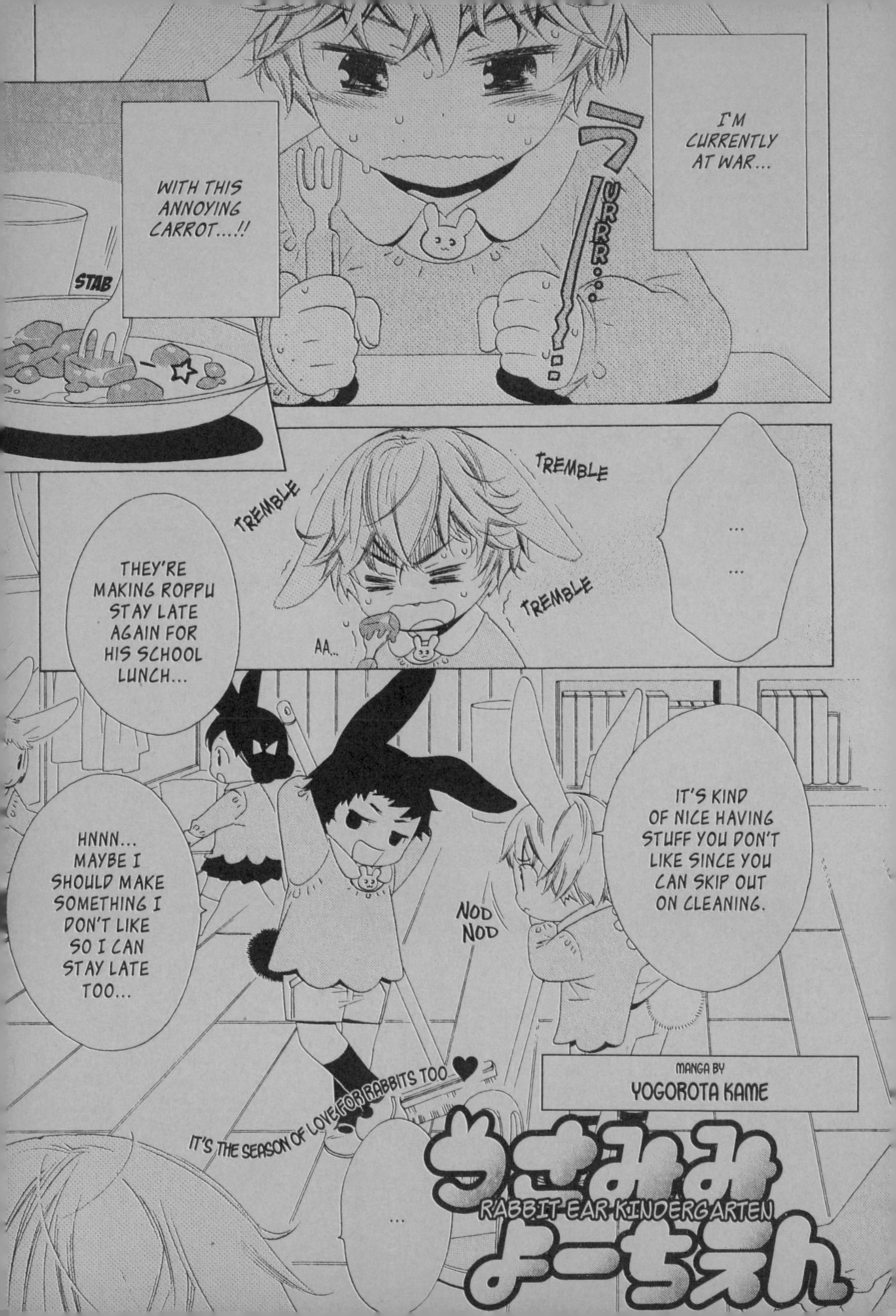

I'M CURRENTLY AT WAR...
う
URRRR...
WITH THIS ANNOYING CARROT...!!
STAB
...
...
TREMBLE
TREMBLE
TREMBLE
AA...
THEY'RE MAKING ROPPU STAY LATE AGAIN FOR HIS SCHOOL LUNCH...
IT'S KIND OF NICE HAVING STUFF YOU DON'T LIKE SINCE YOU CAN SKIP OUT ON CLEANING.
NOD NOD
HNNN... MAYBE I SHOULD MAKE SOMETHING I DON'T LIKE SO I CAN STAY LATE TOO...
MANGA BY
YOGOROTA KAME
IT'S THE SEASON OF LOVE FOR RABBITS TOO
うさみみ
RABBIT EAR KINDERGARTEN
よーちえん
...

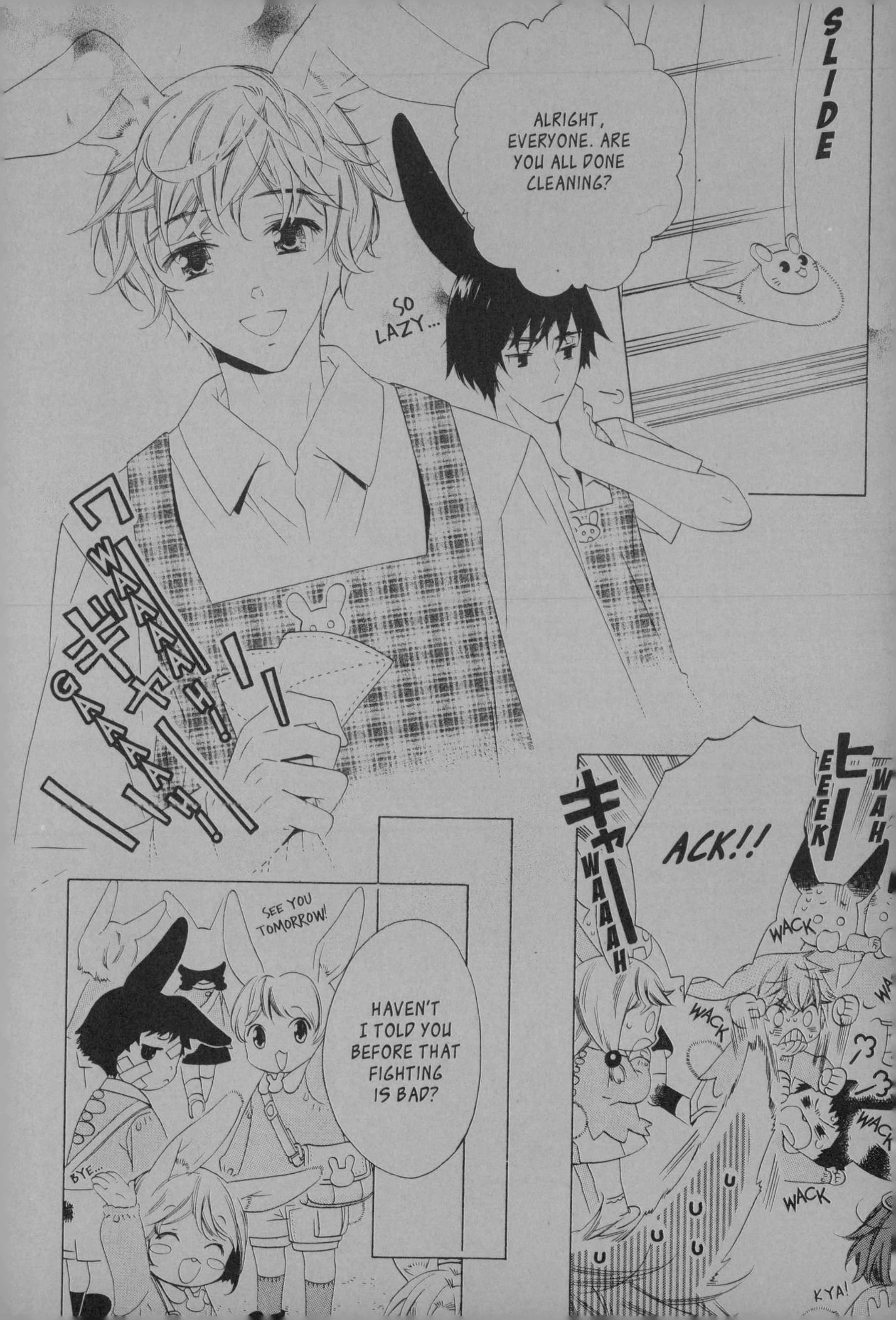
SLIDE
ALRIGHT, EVERYONE. ARE YOU ALL DONE CLEANING?
SO LAZY...
WAAAAAH!
GAAAAAH!
ヒー
EEEK
WAH
ACK!!
キャー
WAAAAH
WACK
WACK
WACK
WACK
UUUUU
KYA!
SEE YOU TOMORROW!
HAVEN'T I TOLD YOU BEFORE THAT FIGHTING IS BAD?
BYE...

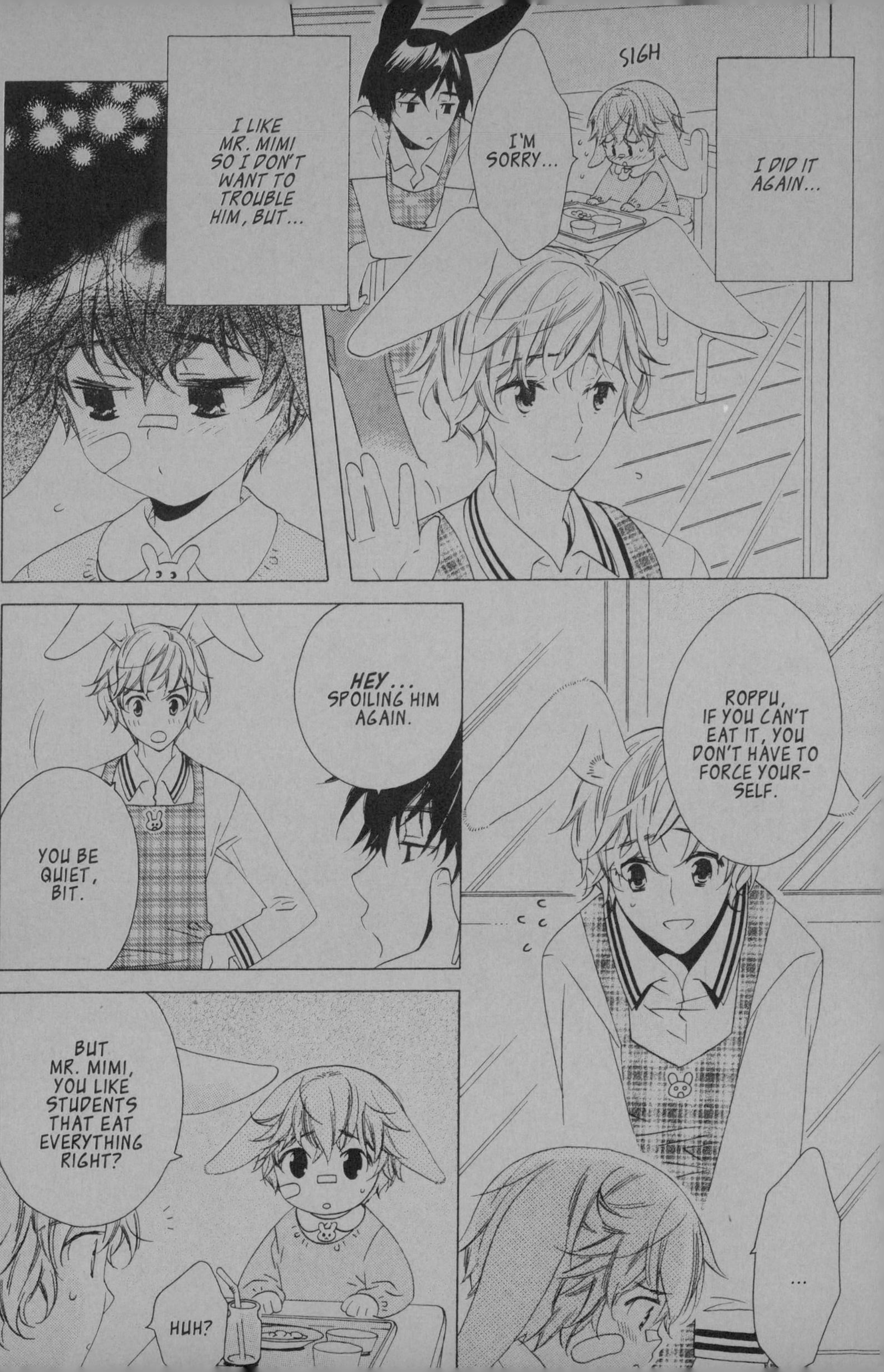
SIGH
I DID IT AGAIN...
I'M SORRY...
I LIKE MR. MIMI SO I DON'T WANT TO TROUBLE HIM, BUT...
ROPPU, IF YOU CAN'T EAT IT, YOU DON'T HAVE TO FORCE YOUR-SELF.
...
...
HEY... SPOILING HIM AGAIN.
YOU BE QUIET, BIT.
BUT MR. MIMI, YOU LIKE STUDENTS THAT EAT EVERYTHING RIGHT?
HUH?

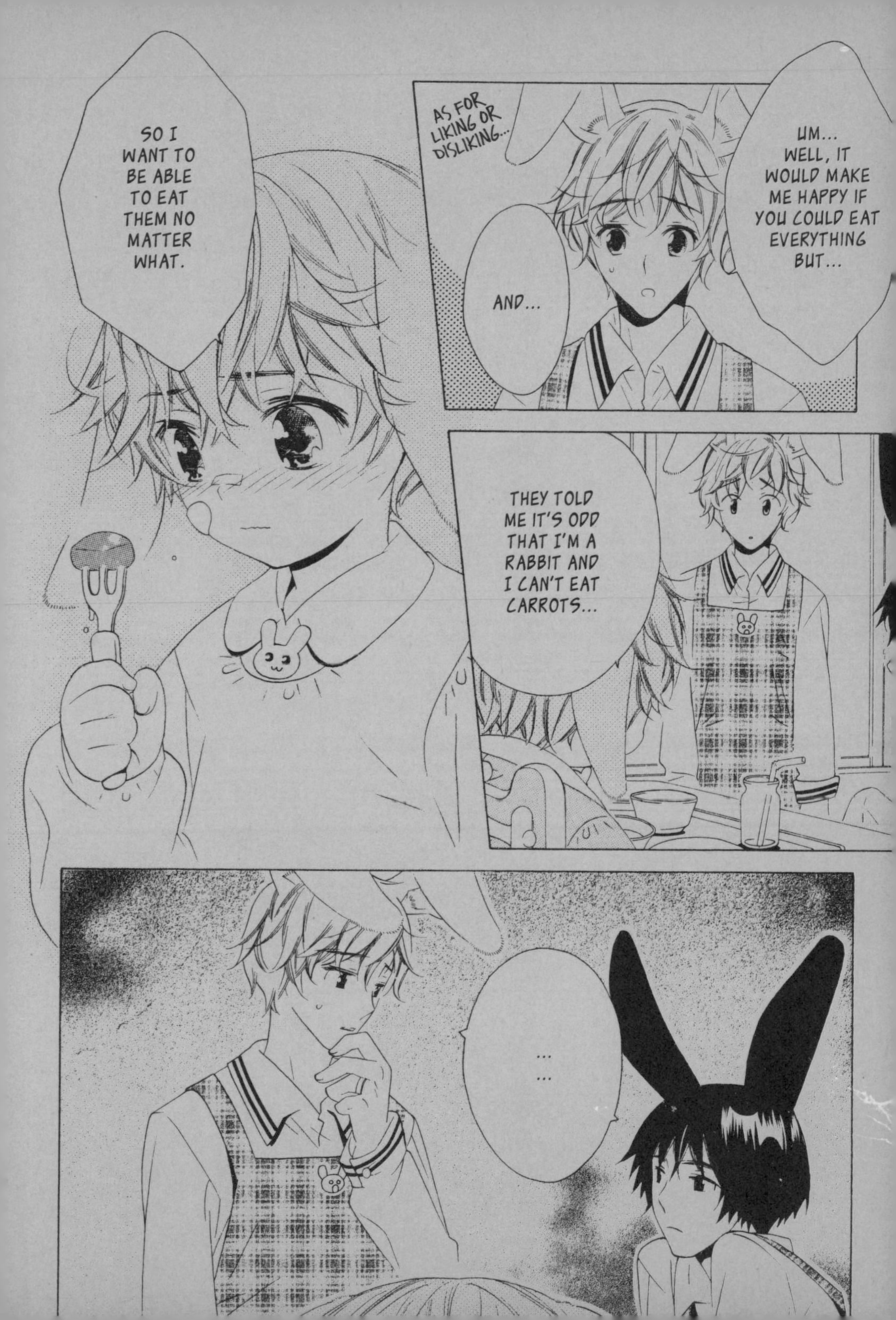
UM... WELL, IT WOULD MAKE ME HAPPY IF YOU COULD EAT EVERYTHING BUT...
AS FOR LIKING OR DISLIKING...
AND...
THEY TOLD ME IT'S ODD THAT I'M A RABBIT AND I CAN'T EAT CARROTS...
SO I WANT TO BE ABLE TO EAT THEM NO MATTER WHAT.
... ...

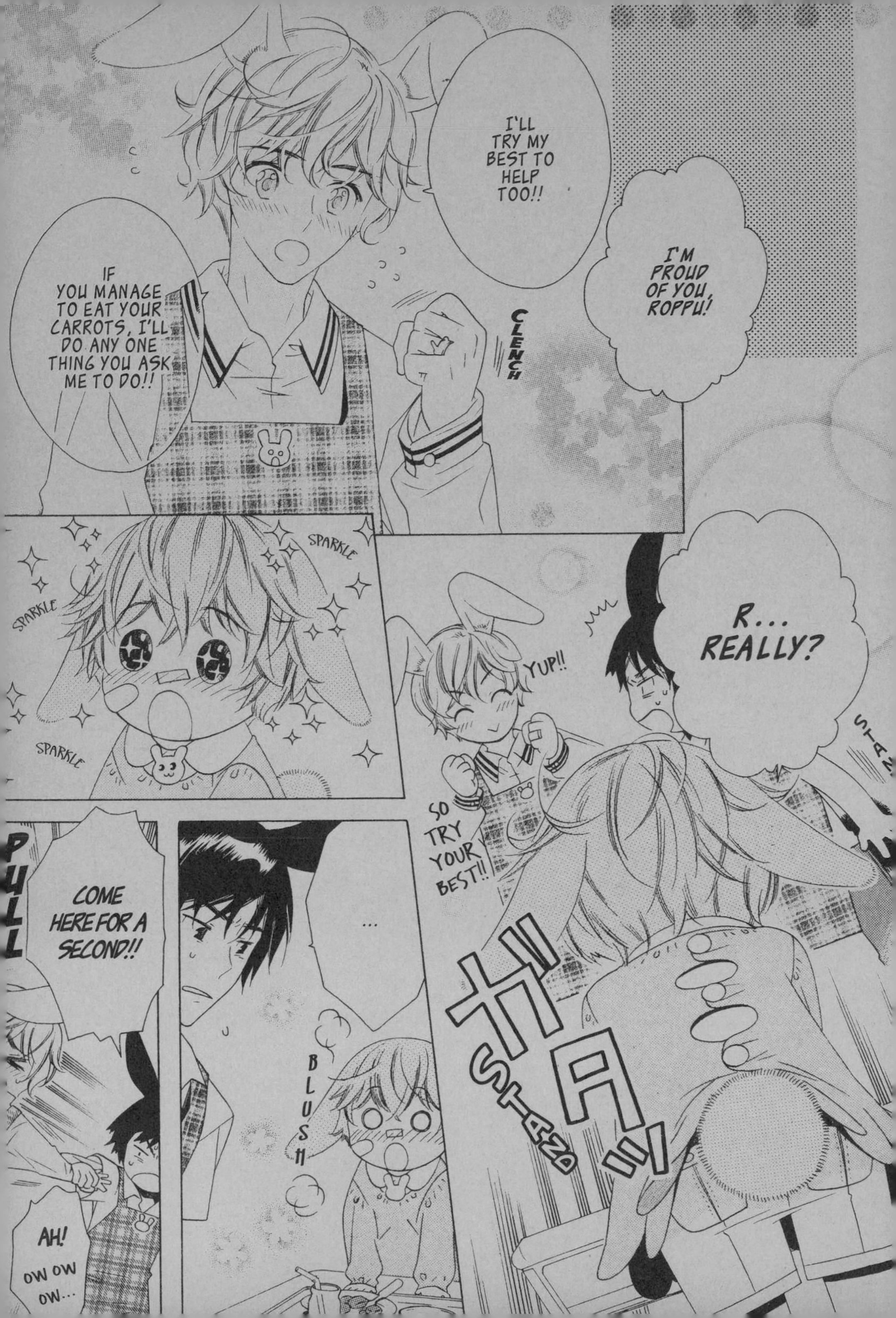
I'LL TRY MY BEST TO HELP TOO!!
I'M PROUD OF YOU, ROPPU!
CLENCH
IF YOU MANAGE TO EAT YOUR CARROTS, I'LL DO ANY ONE THING YOU ASK ME TO DO!!
R... REALLY?
YUP!!
SO TRY YOUR BEST!!
STAZA
SPARKLE
SPARKLE
SPARKLE
...
BLUSH
PULL
COME HERE FOR A SECOND!!
AH!
OW OW OW...

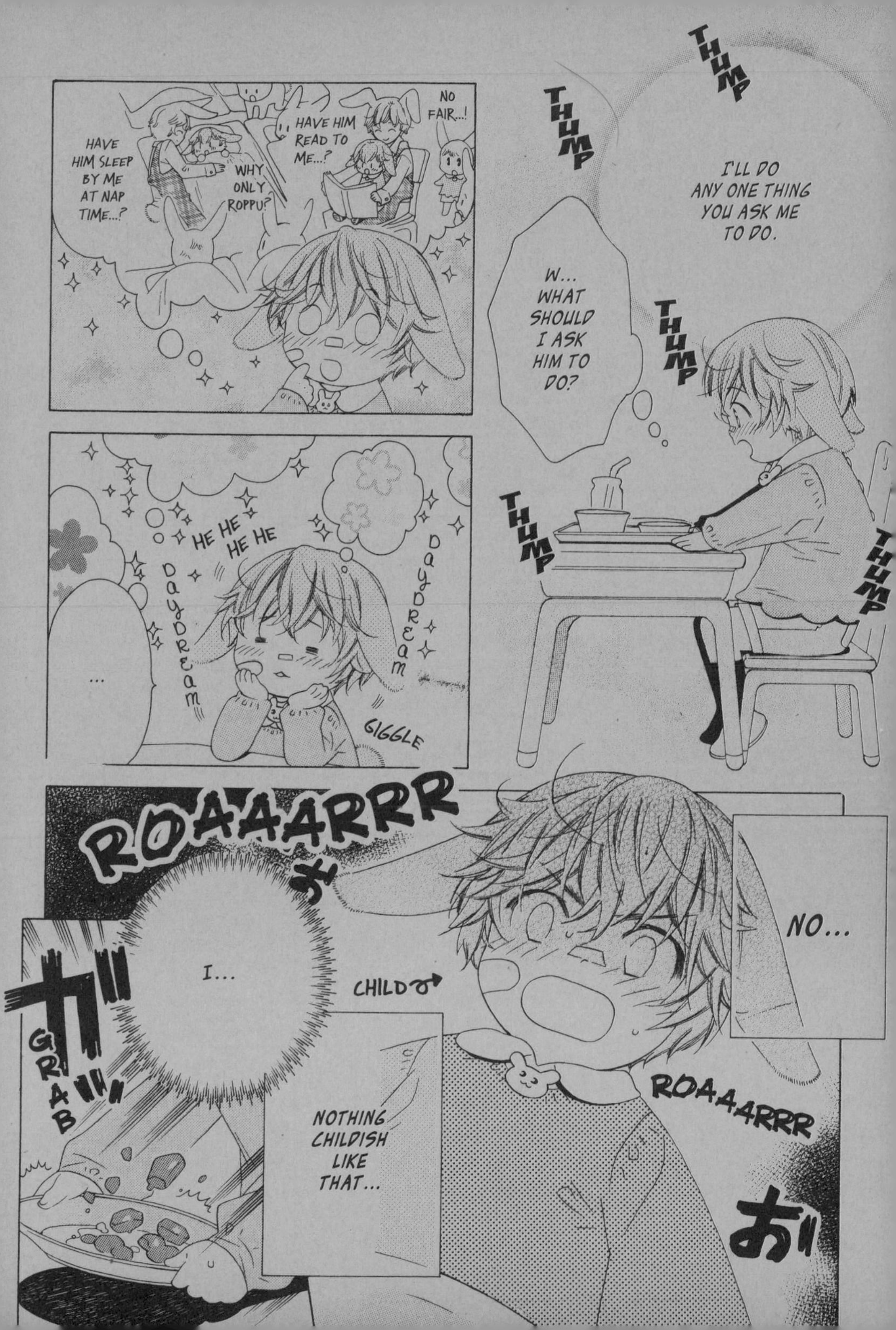
THUMP
THUMP
I'LL DO ANY ONE THING YOU ASK ME TO DO.
W... WHAT SHOULD I ASK HIM TO DO?
THUMP
THUMP
THUMP
NO FAIR...!
HAVE HIM READ TO ME...?
WHY ONLY ROPPU?
HAVE HIM SLEEP BY ME AT NAP TIME...?
DAYDREAM
HE HE HE HE
DAYDREAM
GIGGLE
...
NO...
ROAAARRR
お
I...
CHILD
NOTHING CHILDISH LIKE THAT...
ROAAARRR
お
ガ
GRAB

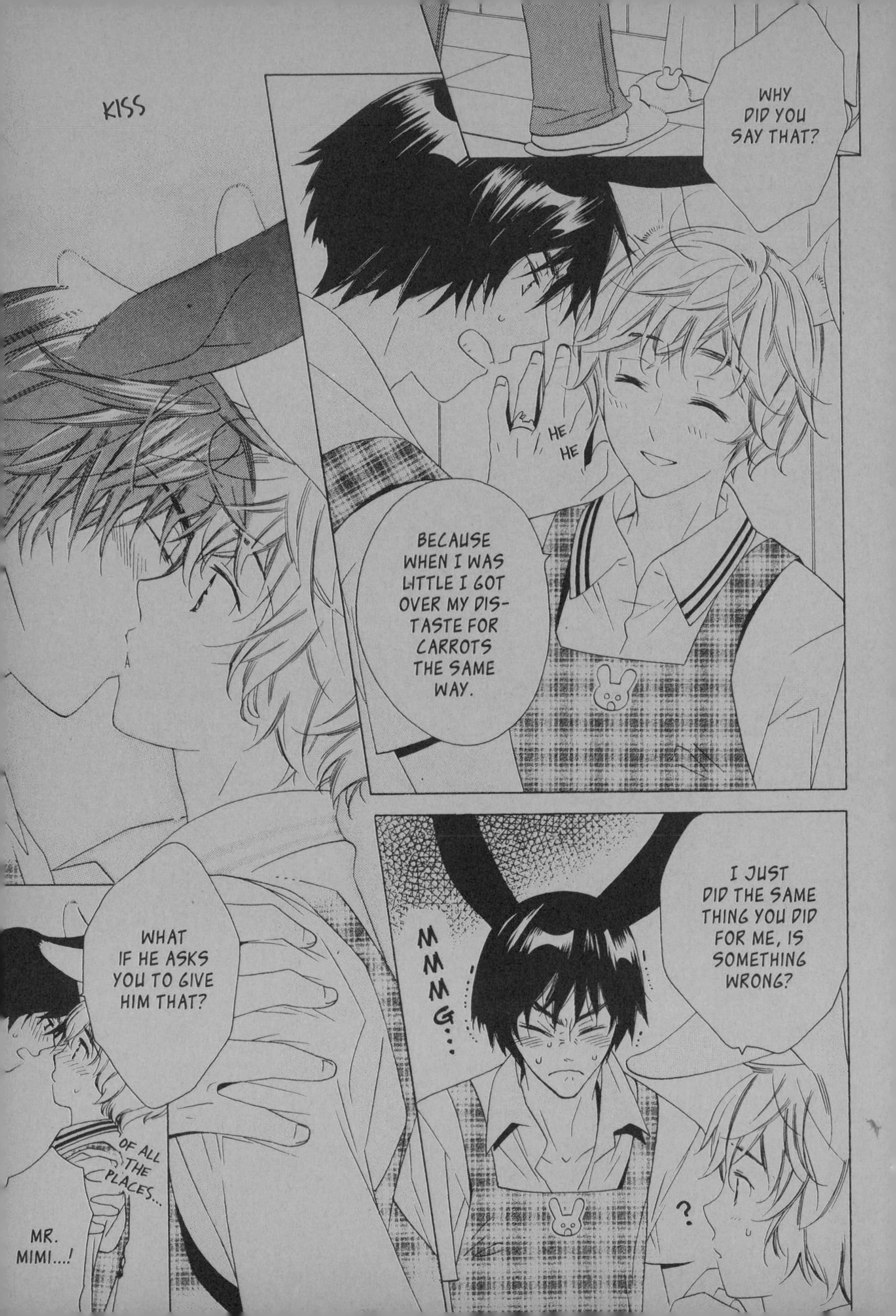
WHY DID YOU SAY THAT?
HE HE
BECAUSE WHEN I WAS LITTLE I GOT OVER MY DIS-TASTE FOR CARROTS THE SAME WAY.
KISS
I JUST DID THE SAME THING YOU DID FOR ME, IS SOMETHING WRONG?
MMMG...
?
WHAT IF HE ASKS YOU TO GIVE HIM THAT?
OF ALL THE PLACES...
MR. MIMI...!

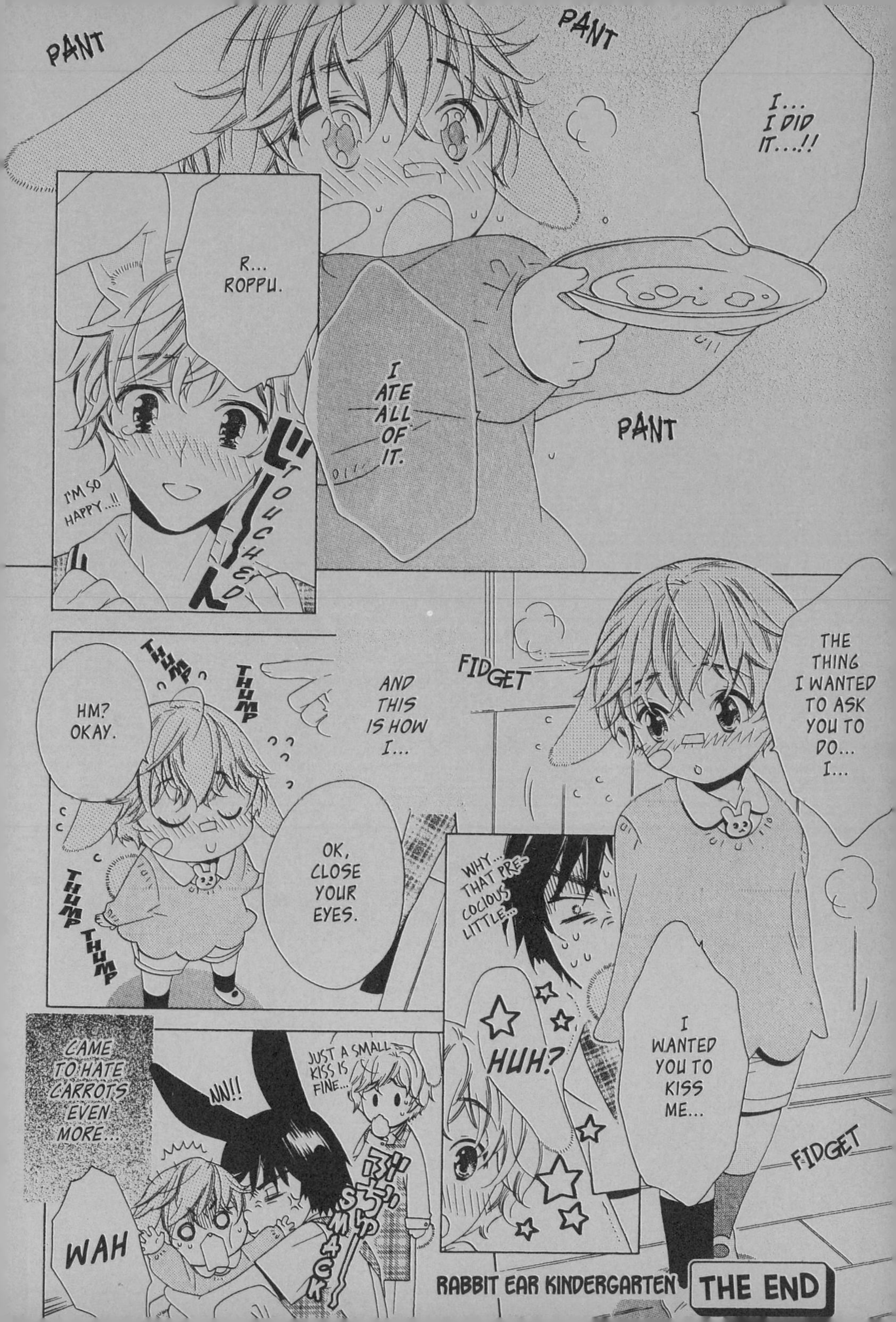
PANT
PANT
I... I DID IT...!!
I ATE ALL OF IT.
PANT
R... ROPPU.
TOUCHED
I'M SO HAPPY...!!
THE THING I WANTED TO ASK YOU TO DO... I...
FIDGET
I WANTED YOU TO KISS ME...
FIDGET
WHY... THAT PRE-COCIOUS LITTLE...
HUH?
AND THIS IS HOW I...
HM? OKAY.
THUMP
THUMP
THUMP
THUMP
THUMP
OK, CLOSE YOUR EYES.
JUST A SMALL KISS IS FINE...
NN!!
SMACK
CAME TO HATE CARROTS EVEN MORE...
WAH
RABBIT EAR KINDERGARTEN
THE END

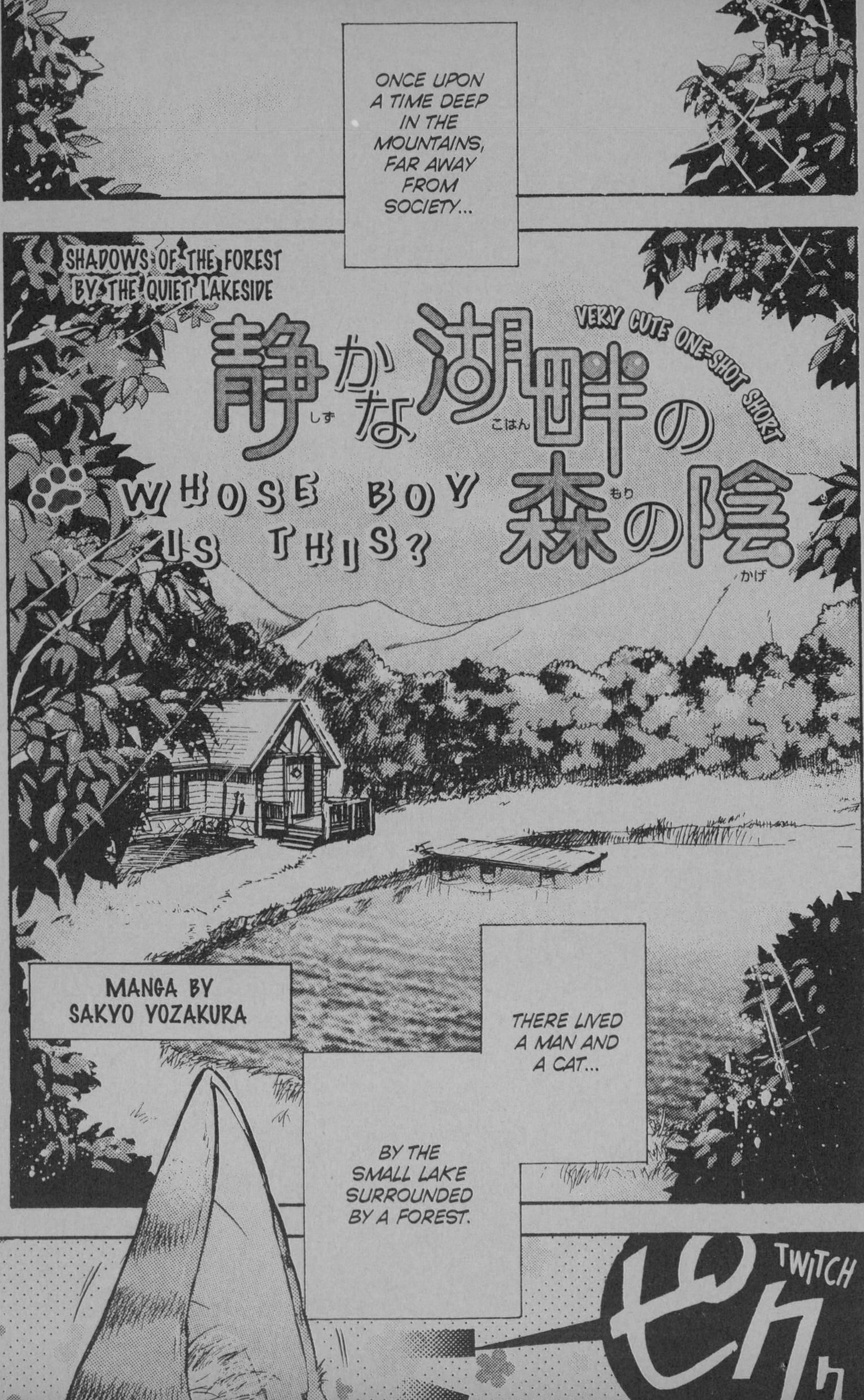
ONCE UPON A TIME DEEP IN THE MOUNTAINS, FAR AWAY FROM SOCIETY...
VERY CUTE ONE-SHOT SHORT
静かな湖畔の森の陰
SHADOWS OF THE FOREST BY THE QUIET LAKESIDE
WHOSE BOY IS THIS?
THERE LIVED A MAN AND A CAT...
BY THE SMALL LAKE SURROUNDED BY A FOREST.
MANGA BY SAKYO YOZAKURA
ピクッ
TWITCH

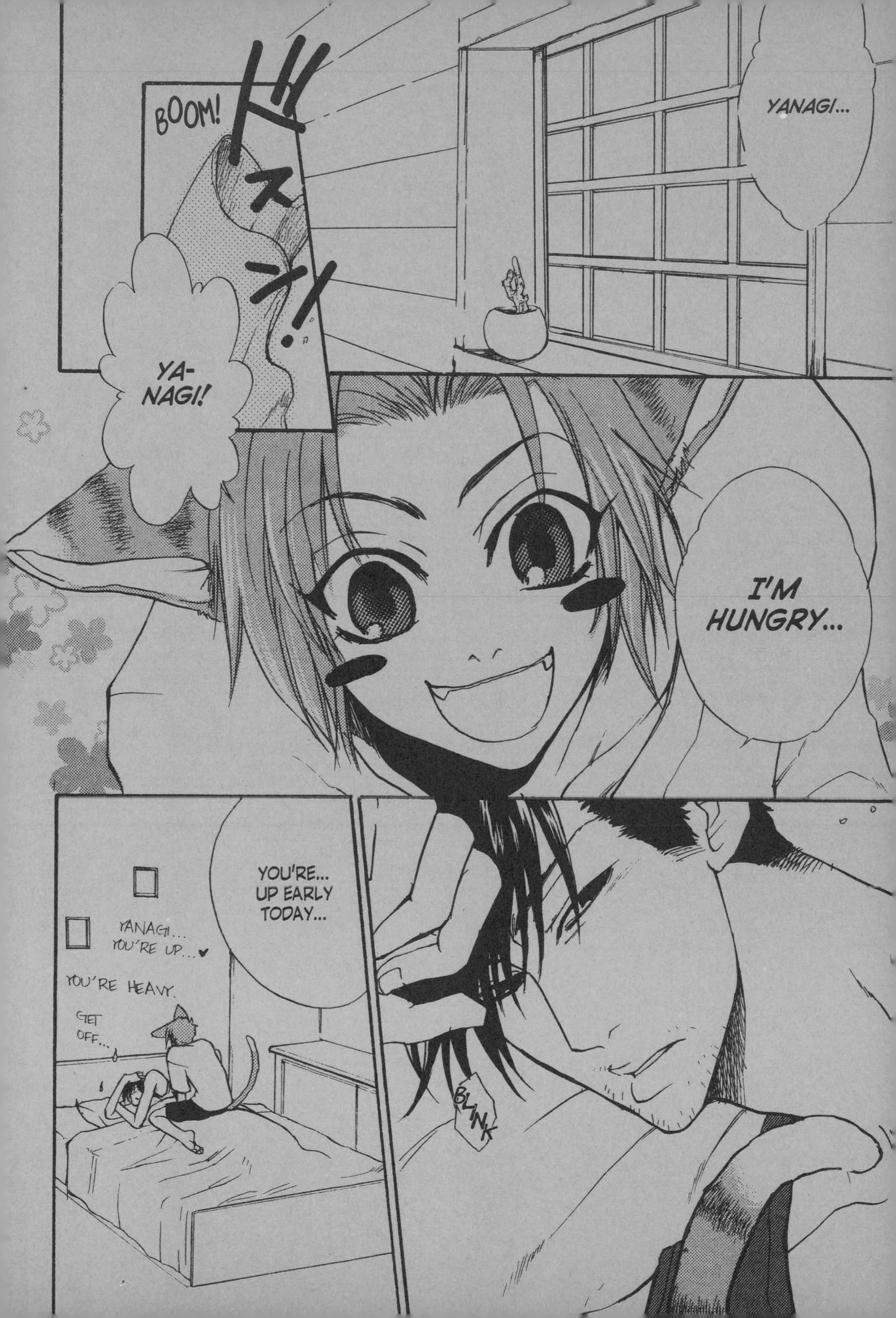
YANAGI...
BOOM!
YA-NAGI!
I'M HUNGRY...
BLINK
YOU'RE... UP EARLY TODAY...
YANAGI... YOU'RE UP...♥
YOU'RE HEAVY.
GET OFF...

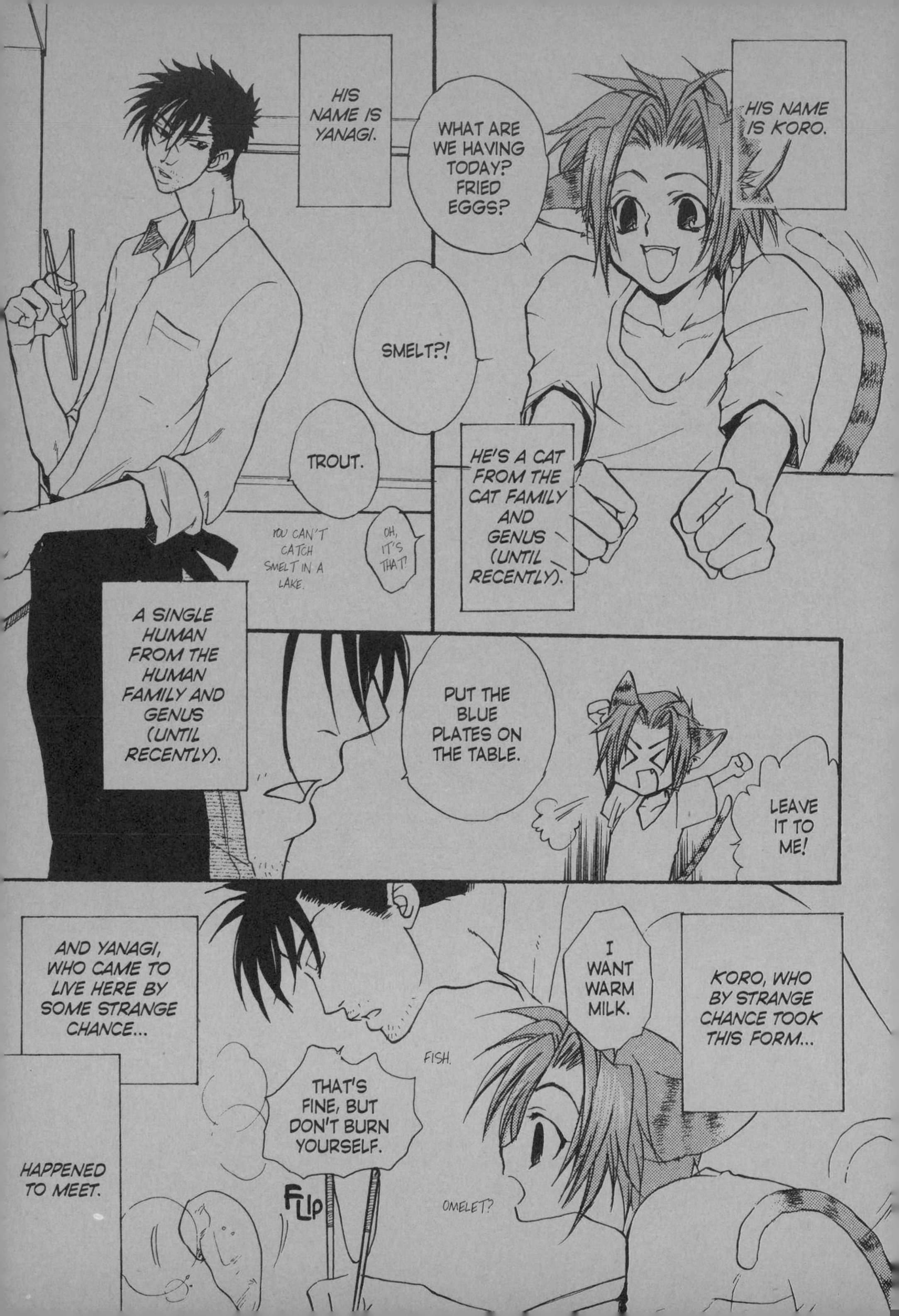
HIS NAME IS KORO.
WHAT ARE WE HAVING TODAY? FRIED EGGS?
HE'S A CAT FROM THE CAT FAMILY AND GENUS (UNTIL RECENTLY).
HIS NAME IS YANAGI.
SMELT?!
TROUT.
OH, IT'S THAT?
YOU CAN'T CATCH SMELT IN A LAKE.
A SINGLE HUMAN FROM THE HUMAN FAMILY AND GENUS (UNTIL RECENTLY).
PUT THE BLUE PLATES ON THE TABLE.
LEAVE IT TO ME!
KORO, WHO BY STRANGE CHANCE TOOK THIS FORM...
I WANT WARM MILK.
AND YANAGI, WHO CAME TO LIVE HERE BY SOME STRANGE CHANCE...
FISH.
OMELET?
THAT'S FINE, BUT DON'T BURN YOURSELF.
FLIP
HAPPENED TO MEET.

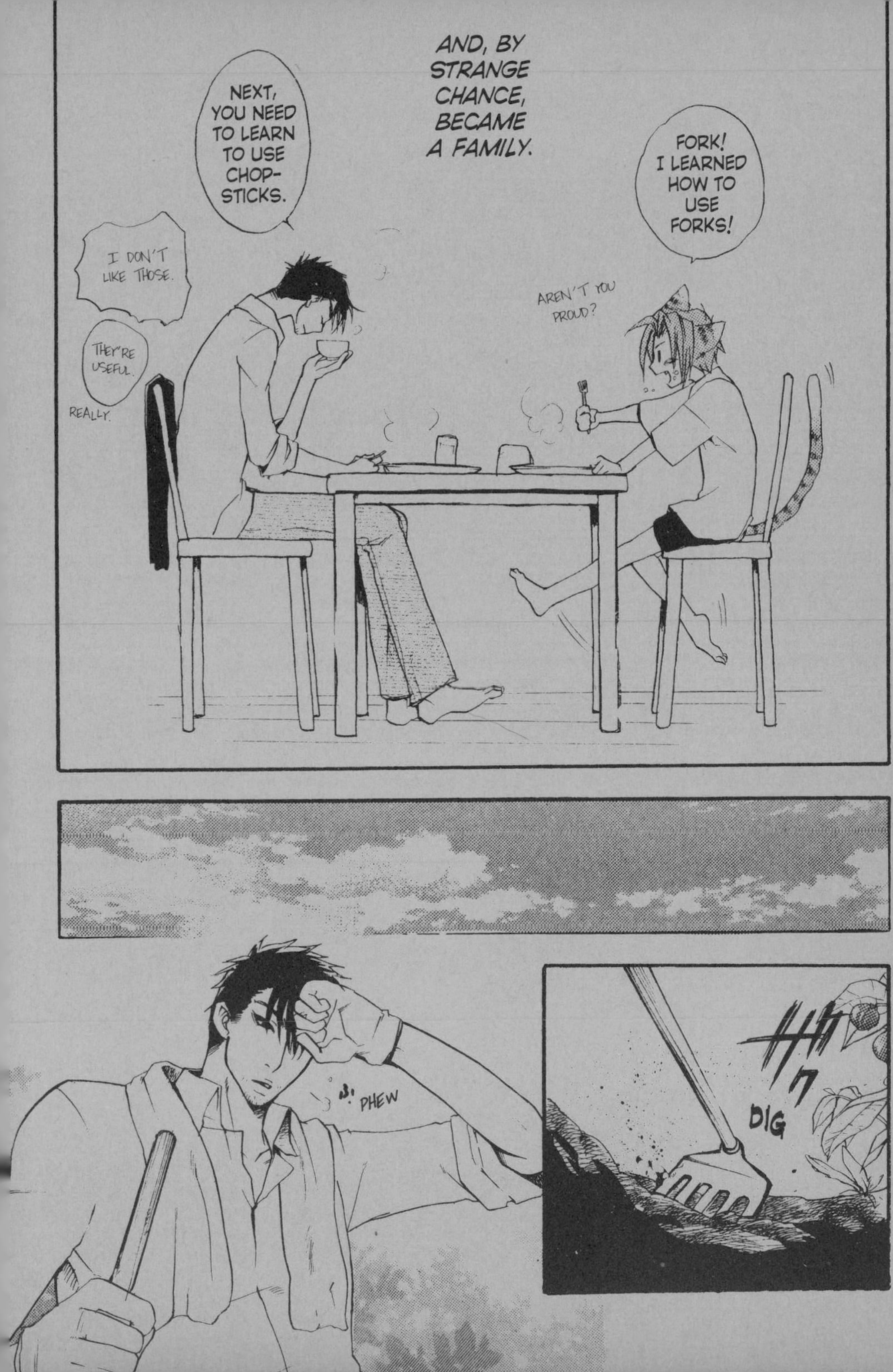
AND, BY STRANGE CHANCE, BECAME A FAMILY.
FORK! I LEARNED HOW TO USE FORKS!
AREN'T YOU PROUD?
NEXT, YOU NEED TO LEARN TO USE CHOP-STICKS.
I DON'T LIKE THOSE.
THEY'RE USEFUL.
REALLY.
DIG
PHEW

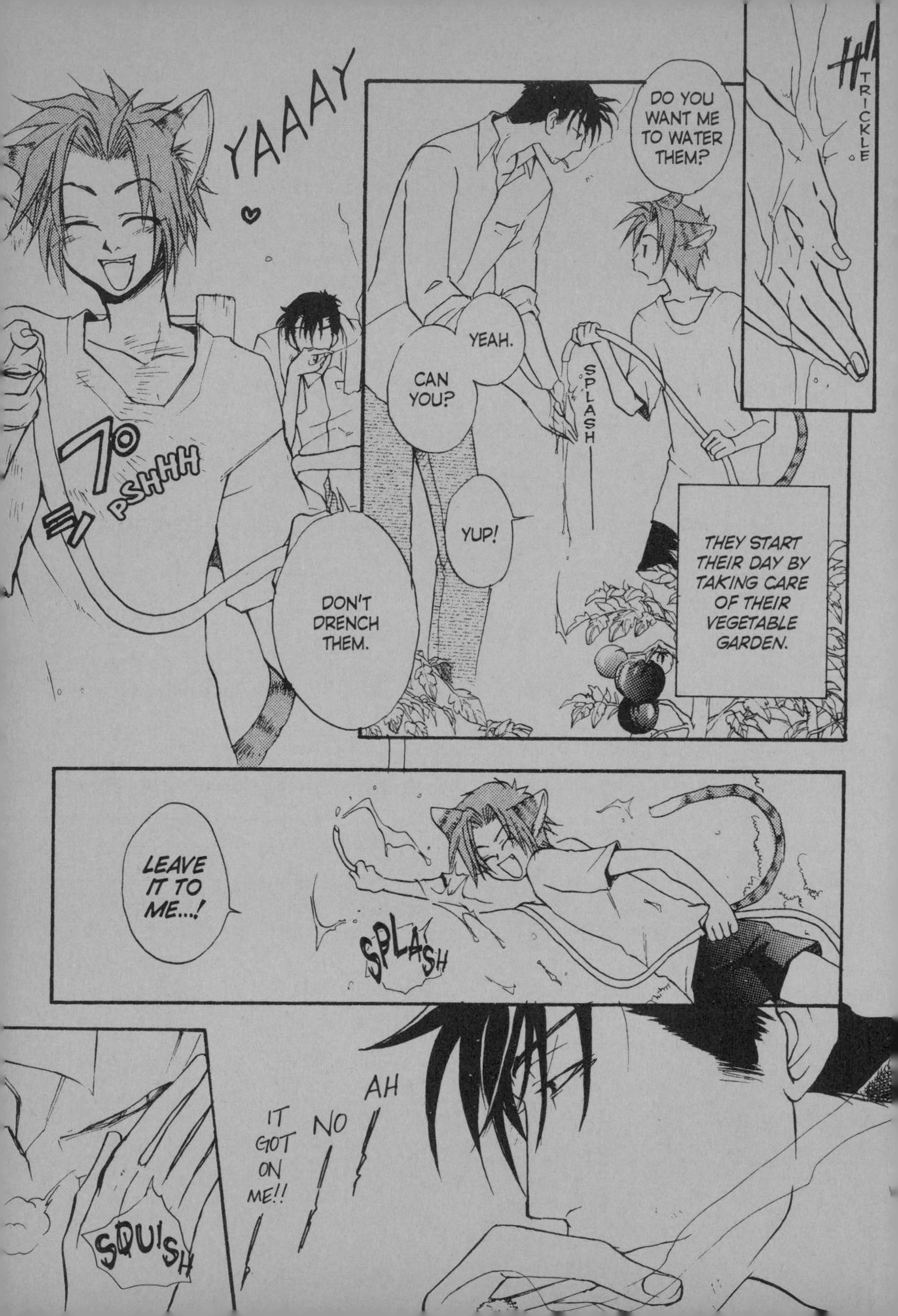
TRICKLE
DO YOU WANT ME TO WATER THEM?
YEAH.
CAN YOU?
SPLASH
YUP!
THEY START THEIR DAY BY TAKING CARE OF THEIR VEGETABLE GARDEN.
DON'T DRENCH THEM.
YAAAY
PSHHH
LEAVE IT TO ME...!
SPLASH
AH
NO
IT GOT ON ME!!
SQUISH

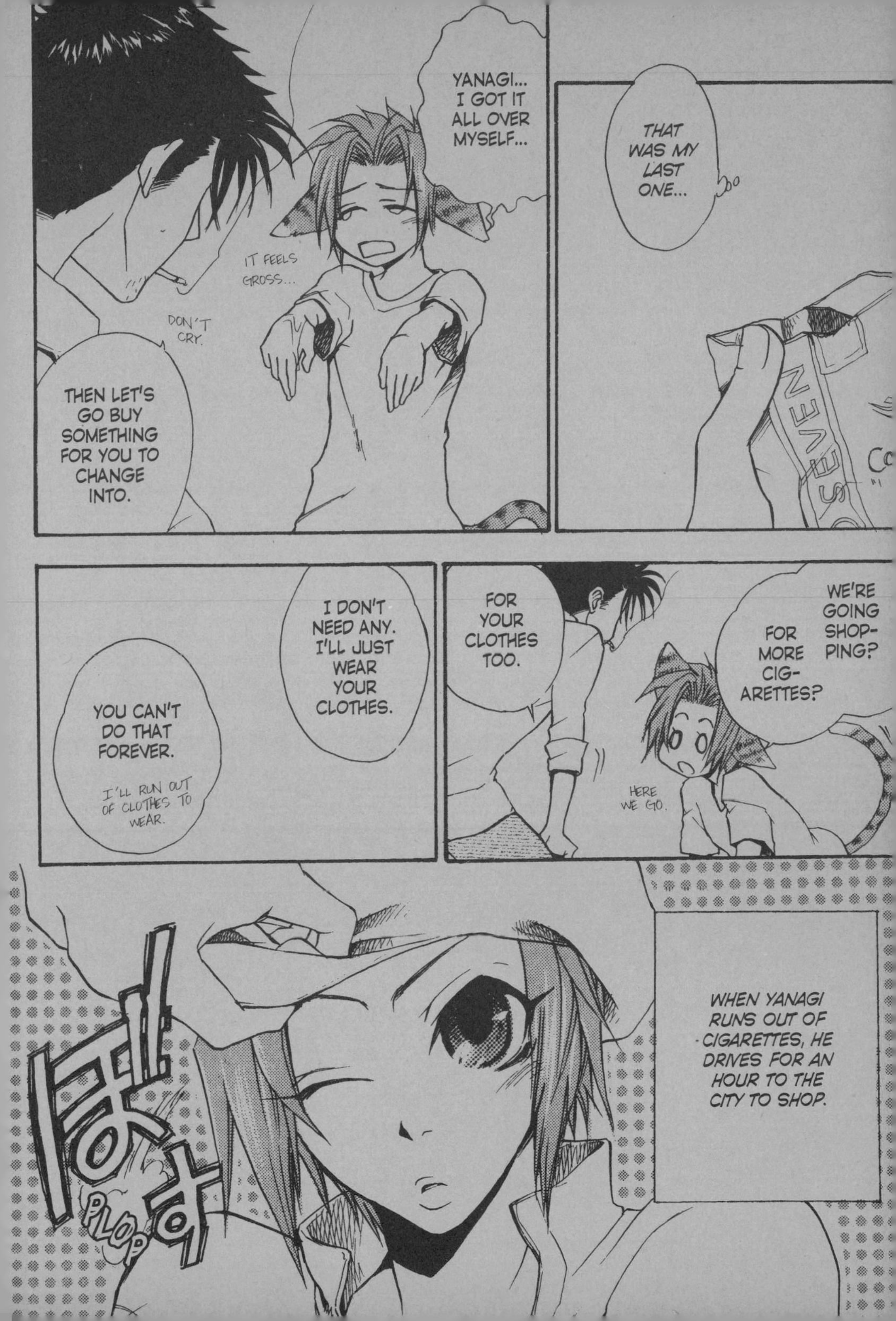
THAT WAS MY LAST ONE...
SEVEN
YANAGI... I GOT IT ALL OVER MYSELF...
IT FEELS GROSS...
DON'T CRY.
THEN LET'S GO BUY SOMETHING FOR YOU TO CHANGE INTO.
WE'RE GOING SHOP-PING?
FOR MORE CIG-ARETTES?
FOR YOUR CLOTHES TOO.
HERE WE GO.
I DON'T NEED ANY. I'LL JUST WEAR YOUR CLOTHES.
YOU CAN'T DO THAT FOREVER.
I'LL RUN OUT OF CLOTHES TO WEAR.
WHEN YANAGI RUNS OUT OF CIGARETTES, HE DRIVES FOR AN HOUR TO THE CITY TO SHOP.
PLOP

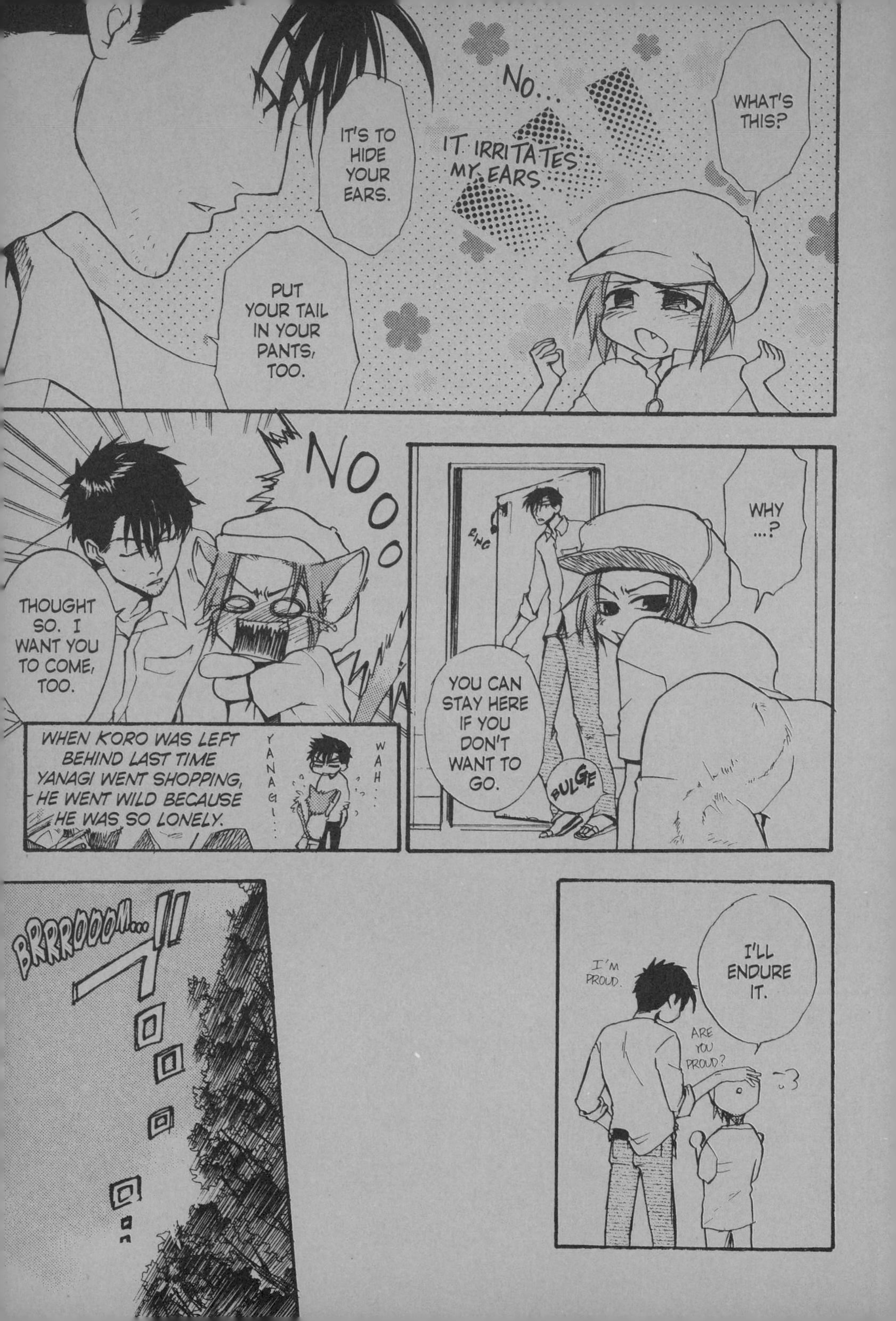
WHAT'S THIS?
NO... IT IRRITATES MY EARS
IT'S TO HIDE YOUR EARS.
PUT YOUR TAIL IN YOUR PANTS, TOO.
WHY ...?
YOU CAN STAY HERE IF YOU DON'T WANT TO GO.
BULGE
NOOO
THOUGHT SO. I WANT YOU TO COME, TOO.
WHEN KORO WAS LEFT BEHIND LAST TIME YANAGI WENT SHOPPING, HE WENT WILD BECAUSE HE WAS SO LONELY.
YANAGI...
WAH...
I'LL ENDURE IT.
I'M PROUD.
ARE YOU PROUD?
BRRROOOM...!!

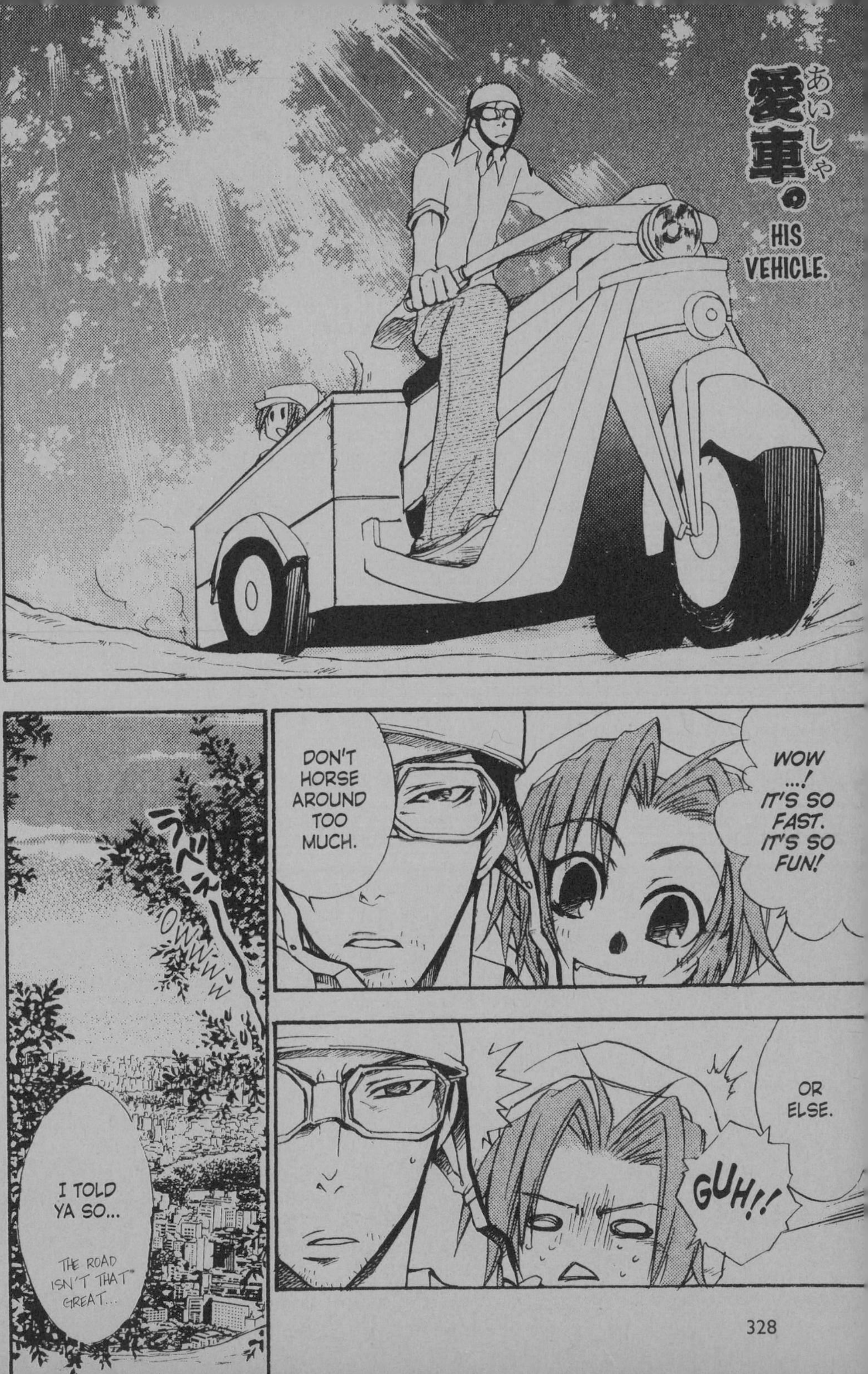
あいしゃ
愛車。
HIS VEHICLE.
WOW...! IT'S SO FAST. IT'S SO FUN!
DON'T HORSE AROUND TOO MUCH.
OR ELSE.
GUH!!
OWWWW
I TOLD YA SO...
THE ROAD ISN'T THAT GREAT...

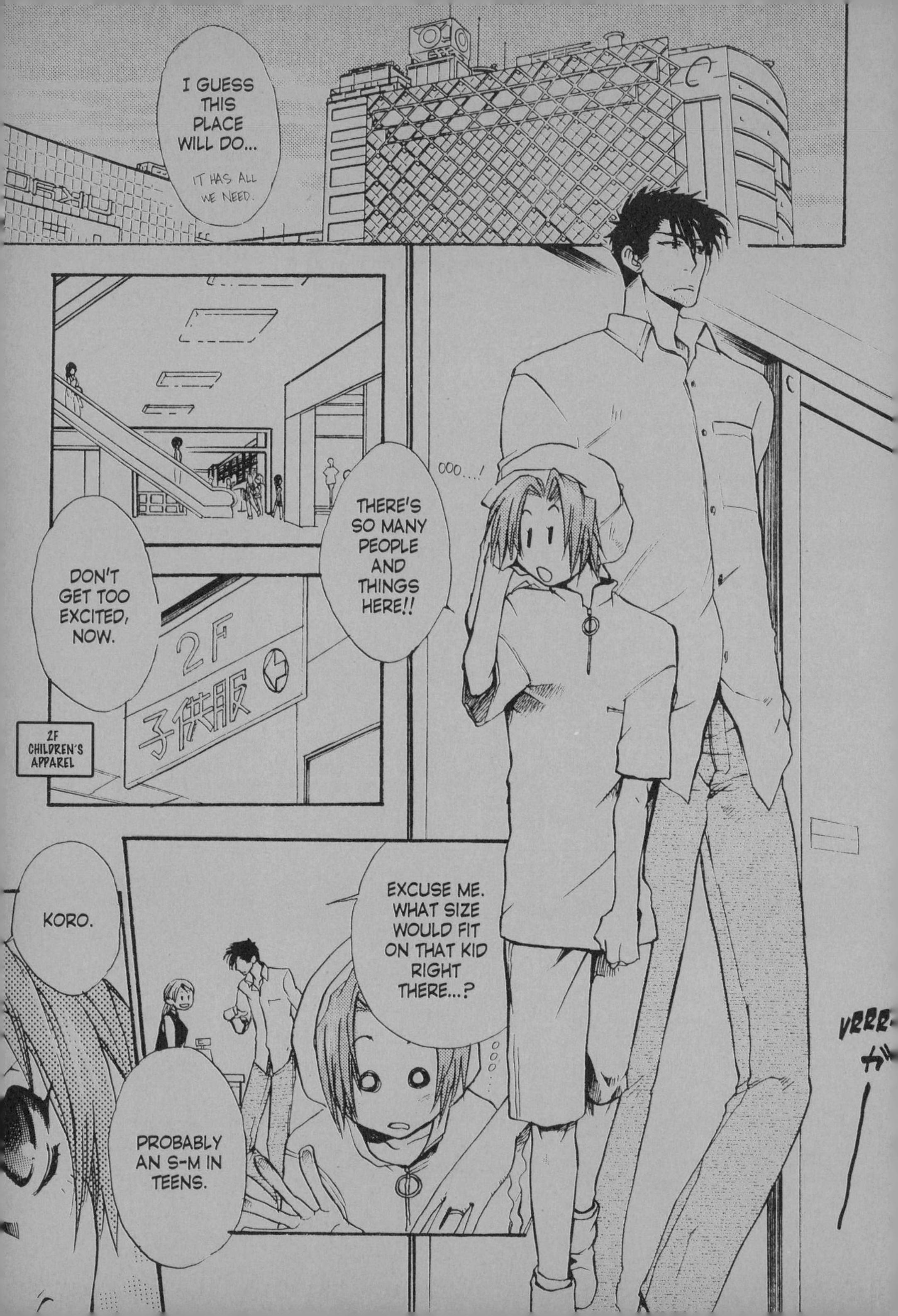
I GUESS THIS PLACE WILL DO...
IT HAS ALL WE NEED.
OOO...!
THERE'S SO MANY PEOPLE AND THINGS HERE!!
DON'T GET TOO EXCITED, NOW.
2F 子供服
2F CHILDREN'S APPAREL
EXCUSE ME. WHAT SIZE WOULD FIT ON THAT KID RIGHT THERE...?
KORO.
OOO...
PROBABLY AN S-M IN TEENS.
VRRR-
ガ

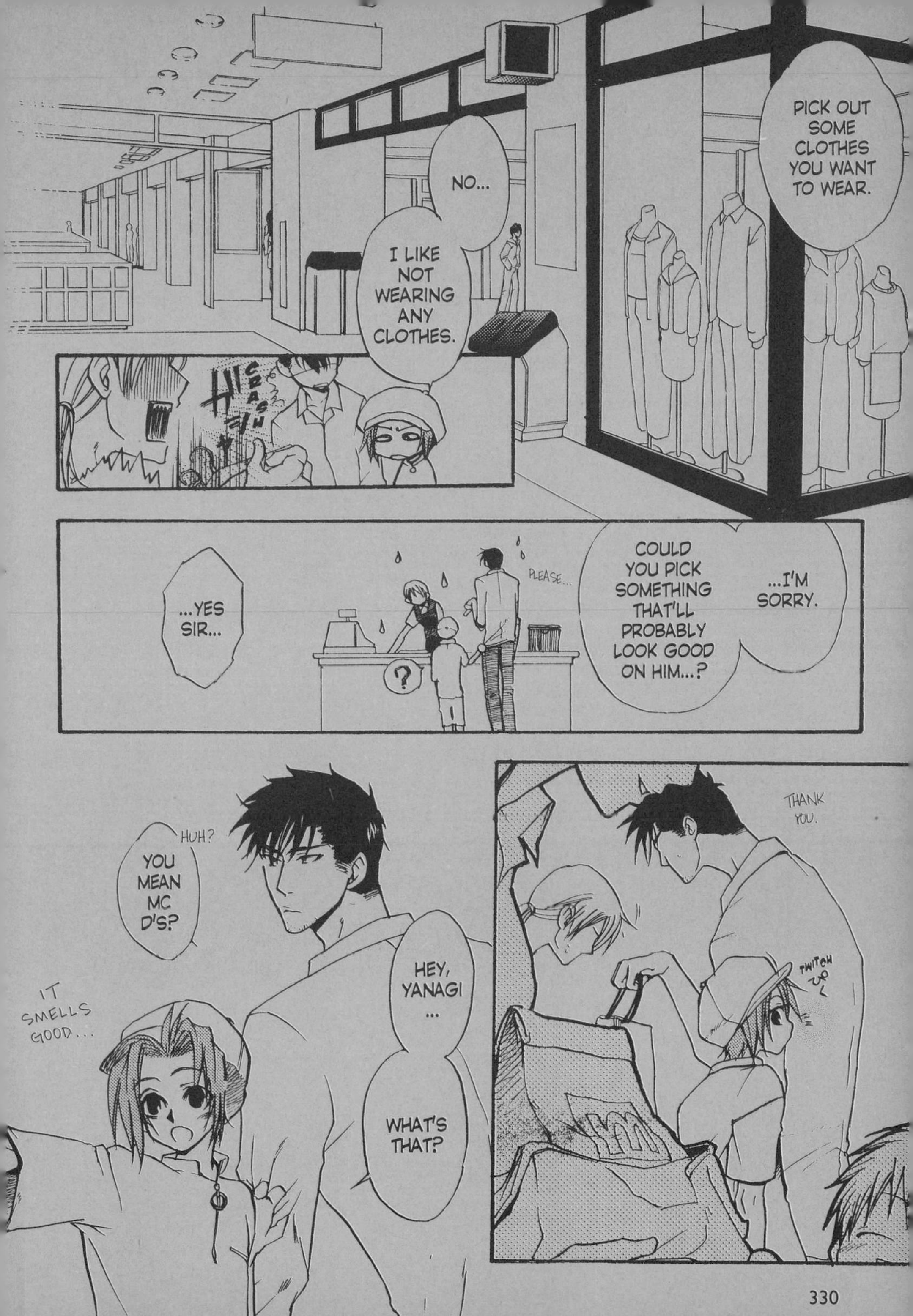
PICK OUT SOME CLOTHES YOU WANT TO WEAR.
NO...
I LIKE NOT WEARING ANY CLOTHES.
CRASH
...I'M SORRY.
COULD YOU PICK SOMETHING THAT'LL PROBABLY LOOK GOOD ON HIM...?
PLEASE...
?
...YES SIR...
THANK YOU.
TWITCH UP
HEY, YANAGI ...
WHAT'S THAT?
HUH?
YOU MEAN MC D'S?
IT SMELLS GOOD...

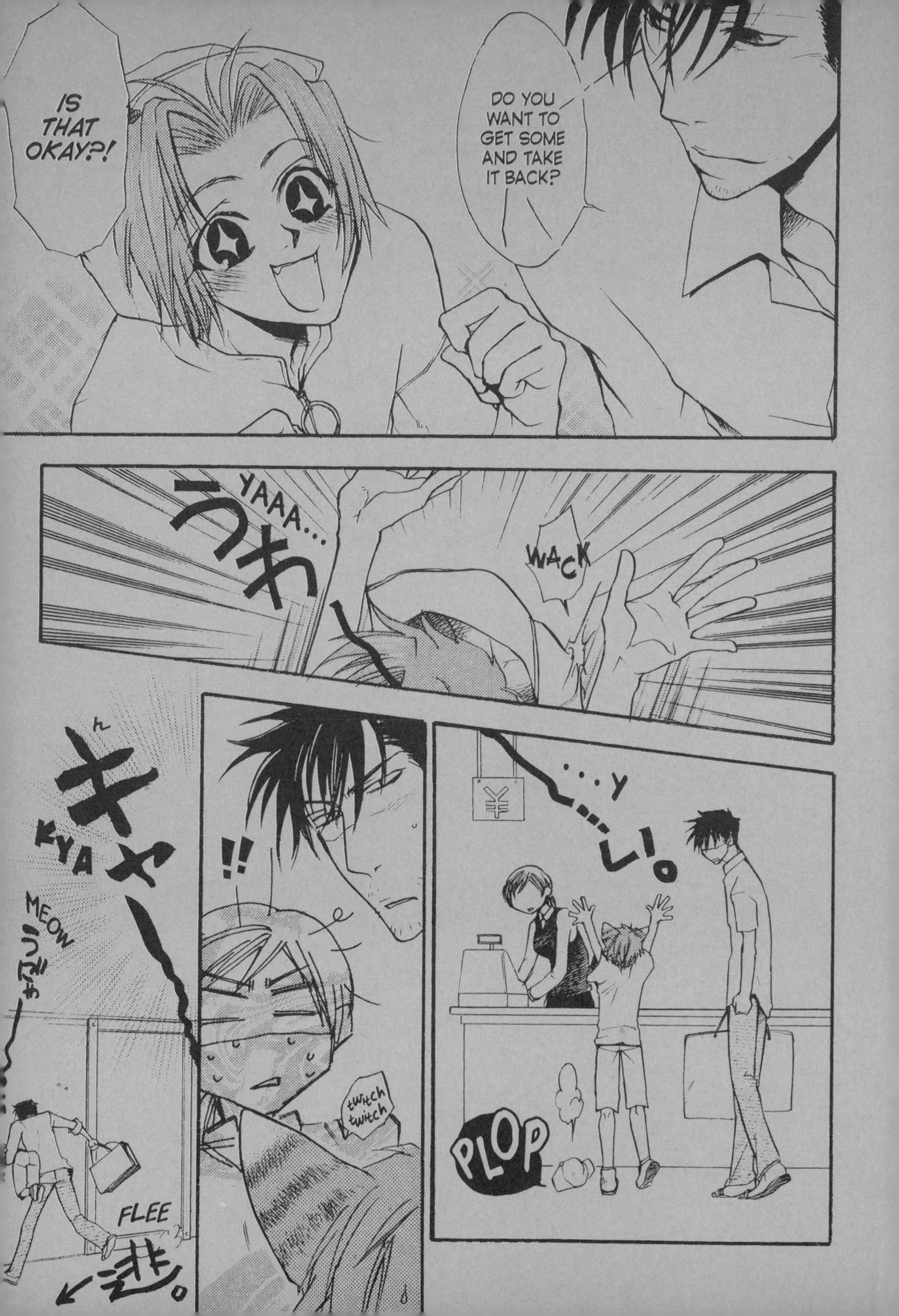
DO YOU WANT TO GET SOME AND TAKE IT BACK?
IS THAT OKAY?!
うわ
YAAA...
WACK
...y
PLOP
!!
twitch twitch
キャー
KYA
MEOW
FLEE

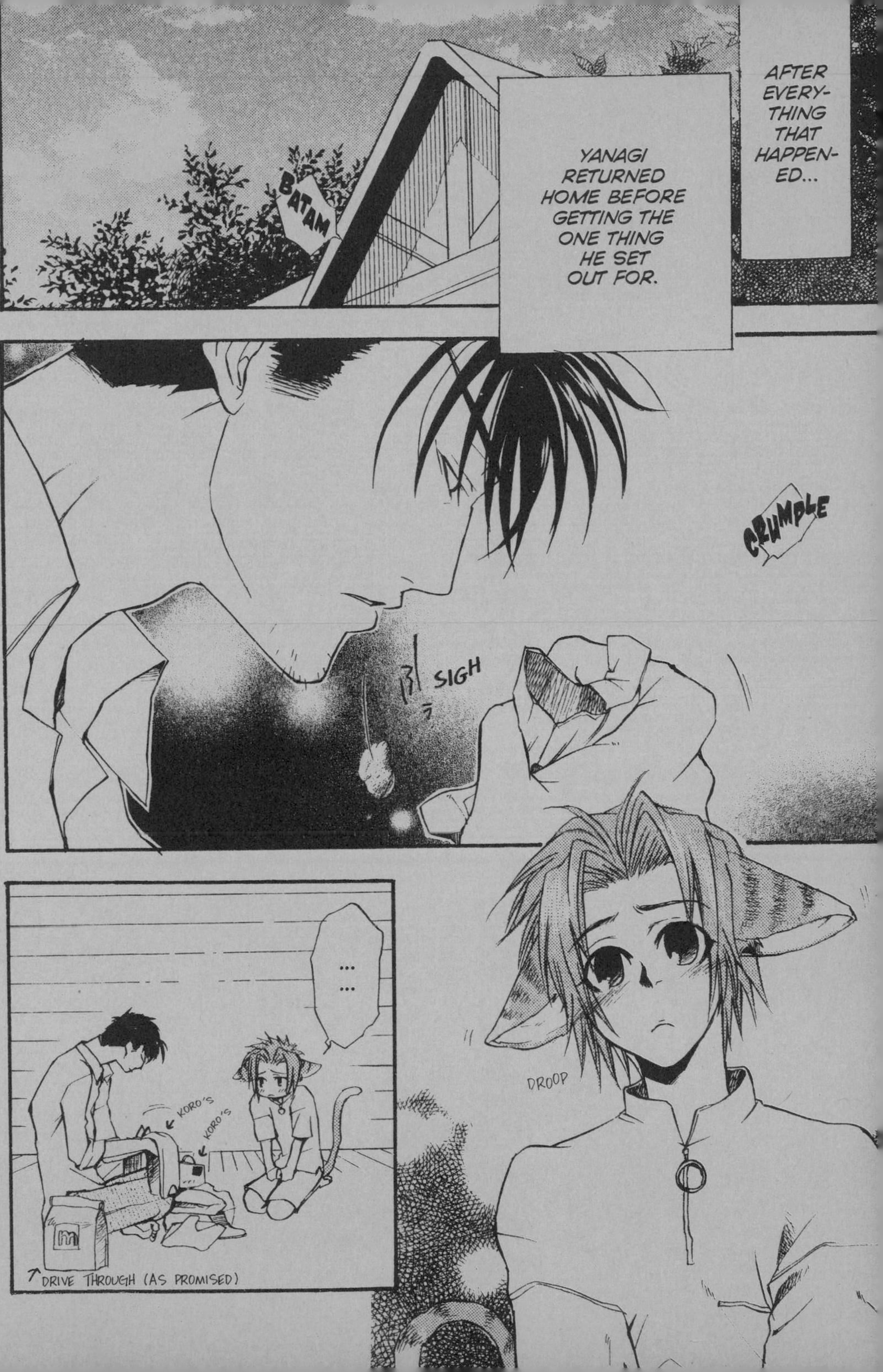
AFTER EVERY-THING THAT HAPPEN-ED...
YANAGI RETURNED HOME BEFORE GETTING THE ONE THING HE SET OUT FOR.
BATAM
CRUMPLE
SIGH
DROOP
...
...
KORO'S
KORO'S
DRIVE THROUGH (AS PROMISED)

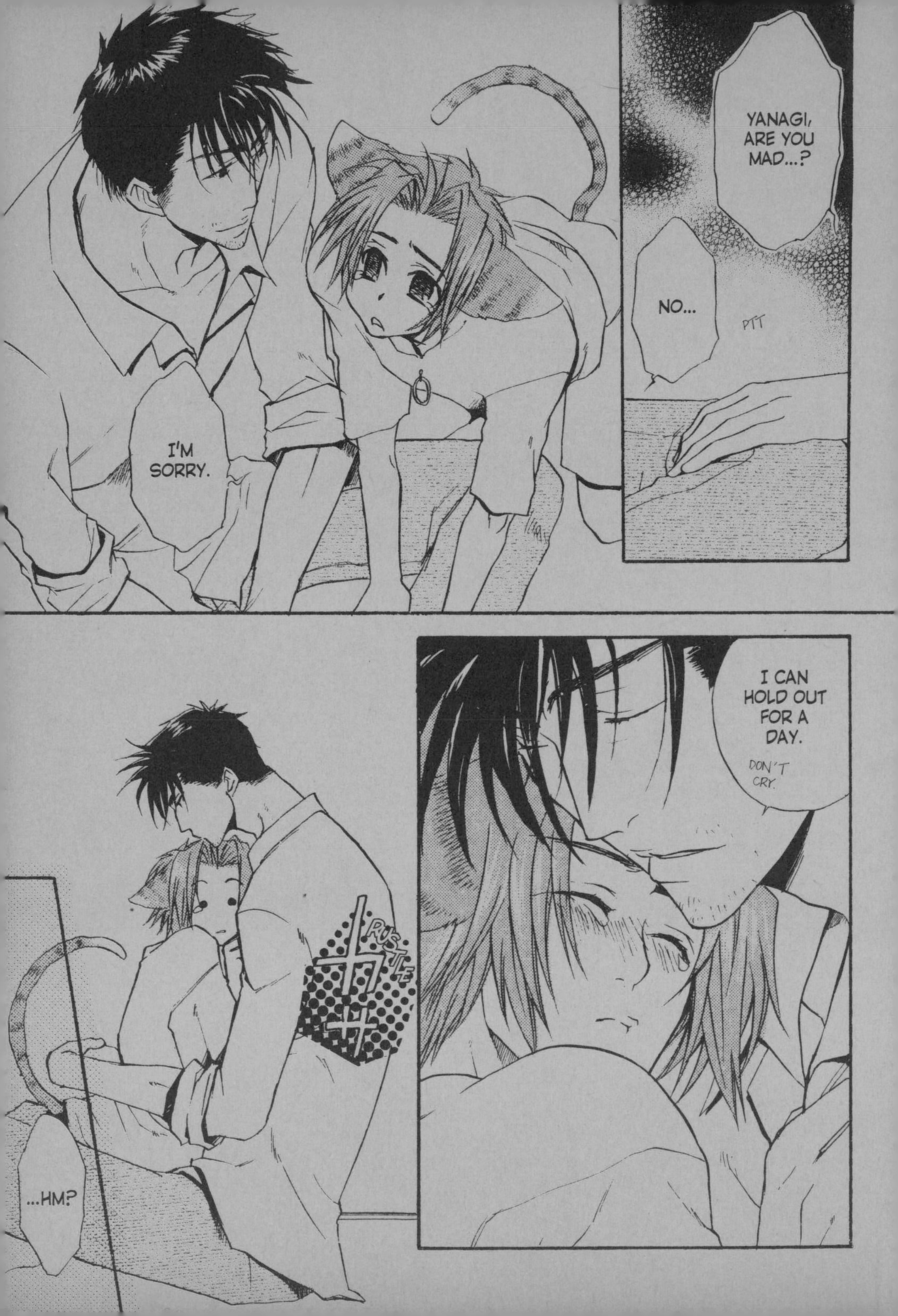
YANAGI, ARE YOU MAD...?
NO...
PTT
I'M SORRY.
I CAN HOLD OUT FOR A DAY.
DON'T CRY.
RUSTLE
...HM?

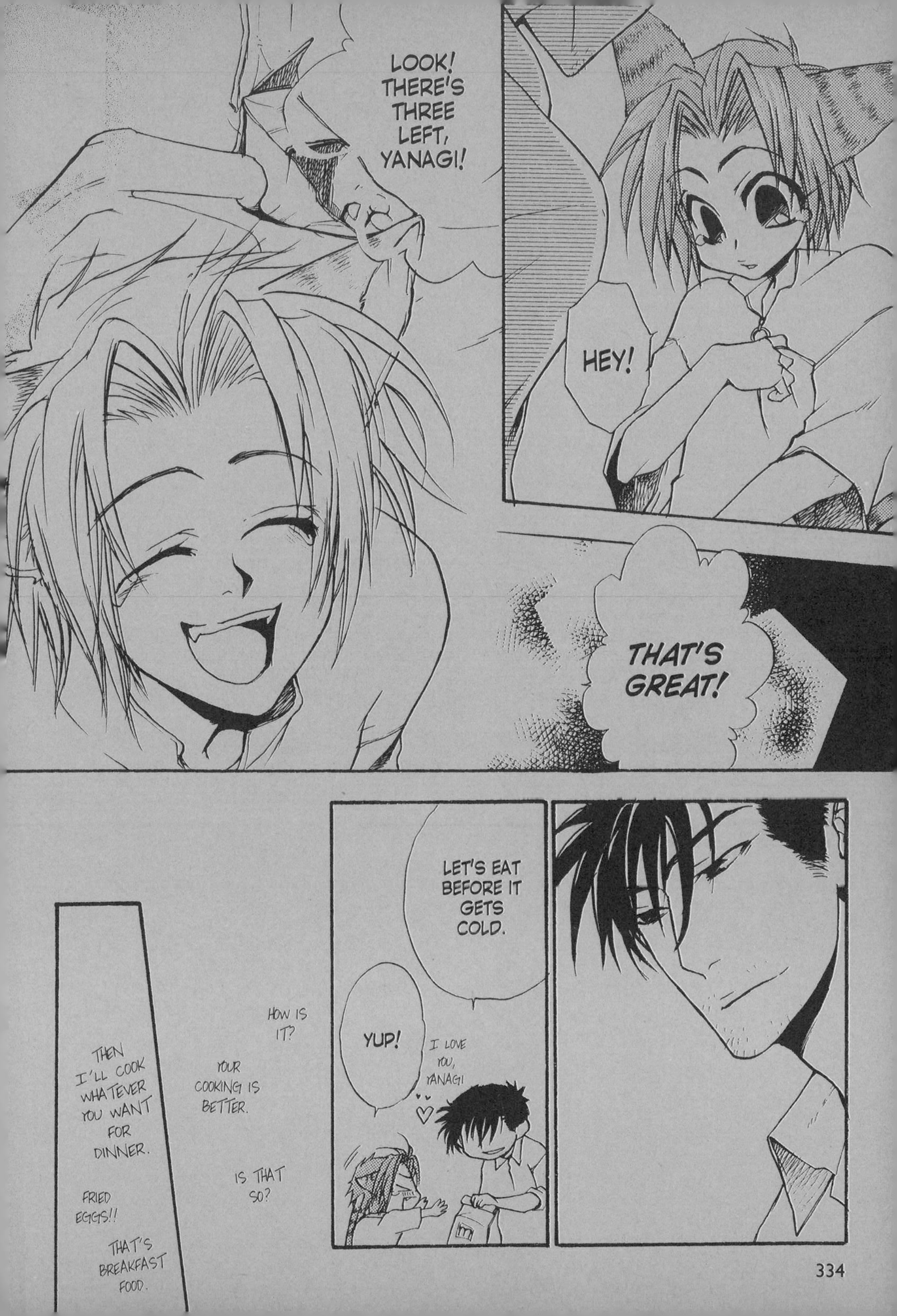
HEY!
THAT'S GREAT!
LOOK! THERE'S THREE LEFT, YANAGI!
LET'S EAT BEFORE IT GETS COLD.
YUP!
I LOVE YOU, YANAGI
HOW IS IT?
YOUR COOKING IS BETTER.
THEN I'LL COOK WHATEVER YOU WANT FOR DINNER.
IS THAT SO?
FRIED EGGS!!
THAT'S BREAKFAST FOOD.

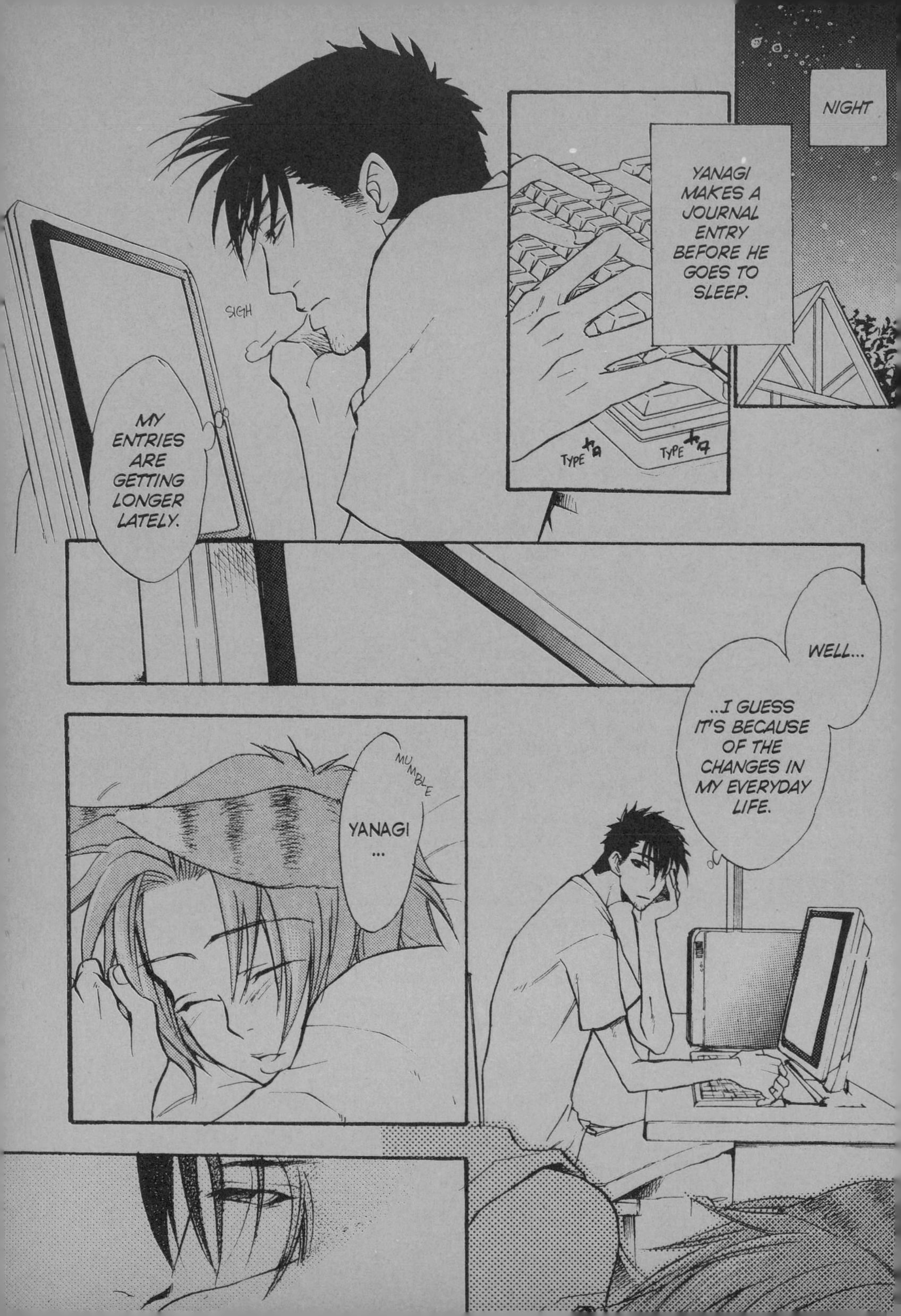
NIGHT
YANAGI MAKES A JOURNAL ENTRY BEFORE HE GOES TO SLEEP.
TYPE
TYPE
SIGH
MY ENTRIES ARE GETTING LONGER LATELY.
WELL...
...I GUESS IT'S BECAUSE OF THE CHANGES IN MY EVERYDAY LIFE.
MUMBLE
YANAGI ...

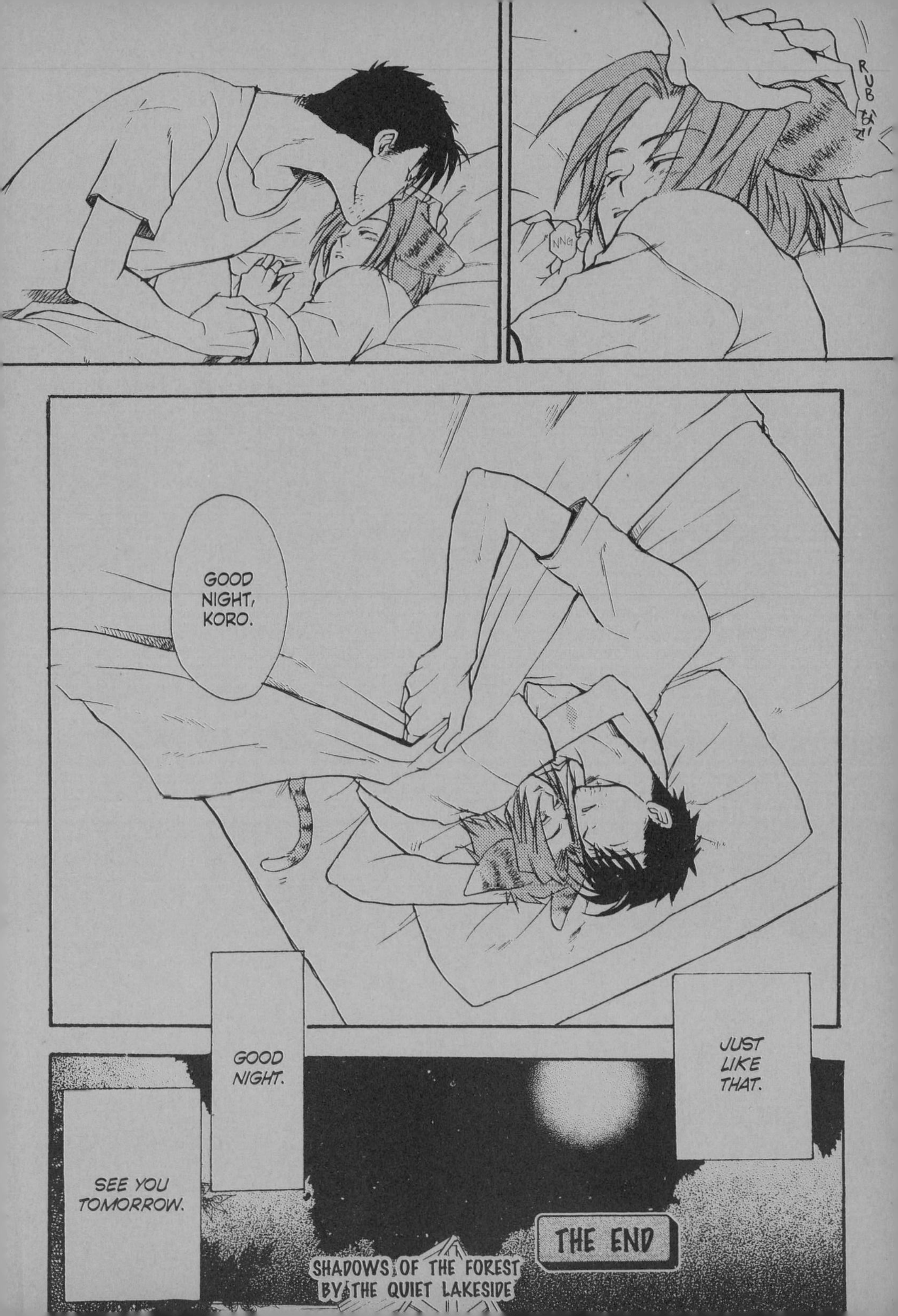
RUB
NNG
GOOD NIGHT, KORO.
JUST LIKE THAT.
GOOD NIGHT.
SEE YOU TOMORROW.
THE END
SHADOWS OF THE FOREST BY THE QUIET LAKESIDE

そこはお伽の国

HERE IN MAGIC LAND

THE EXCITING TRAINING DIARIES OF THE GREAT WIZARD AL AND HIS APPRENTICE SHIRO ♥

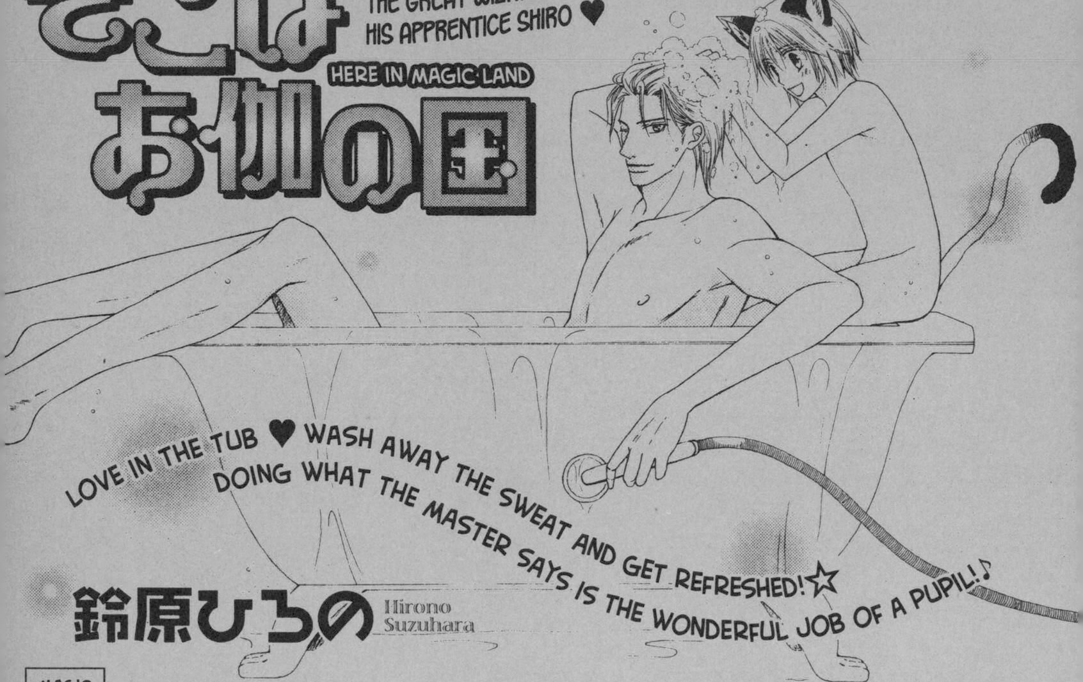

LOVE IN THE TUB ♥ WASH AWAY THE SWEAT AND GET REFRESHED!☆
DOING WHAT THE MASTER SAYS IS THE WONDERFUL JOB OF A PUPIL!♪

鈴原ひろの Hirono Suzuhara

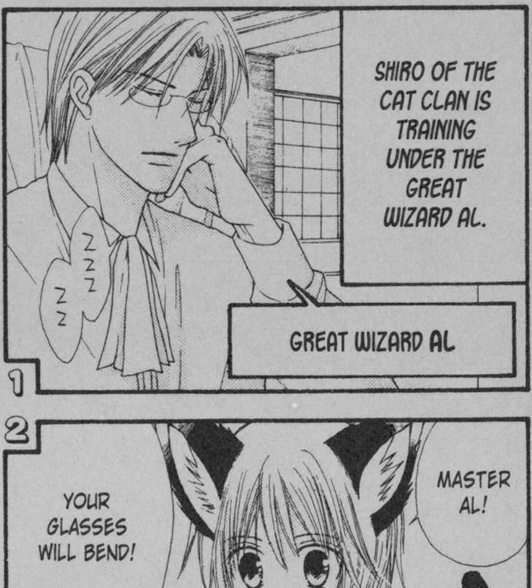

SHIRO OF THE CAT CLAN IS TRAINING UNDER THE GREAT WIZARD AL.
Z Z Z
GREAT WIZARD AL
MASTER AL!
YOUR GLASSES WILL BEND!
Z Z Z
APPRENTICE SHIRO

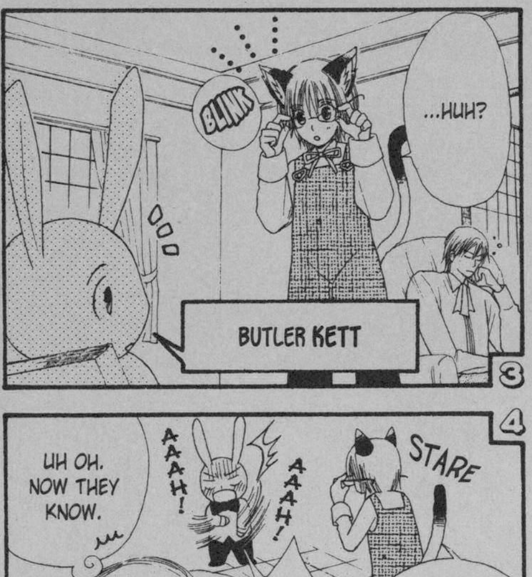

...HUH?
BLINK
BUTLER KETT
STARE
AAAH!
AAAH!
UH OH. NOW THEY KNOW.
THESE GLASSES MAKE EVERYONE NAKED!
YOUR CLOTHES ARE SEE-THROUGH!
WHAT?!

MAGIC LAND FRIENDS

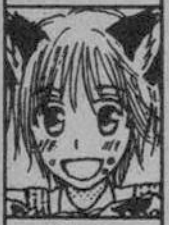

SHIRO

A BOY FROM THE CAT CLAN. BECAME AL'S APPRENTICE IN HOPES OF BECOMING A WIZARD.

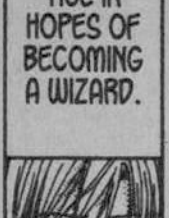

AL

GREAT WIZARD... BUT A TROUBLED SOUL: EVERY DAY HE LUSTS AFTER SHIRO!

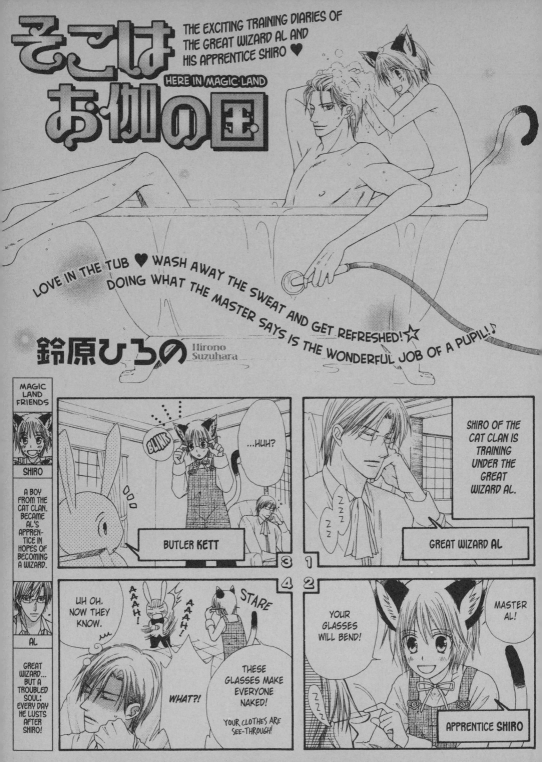

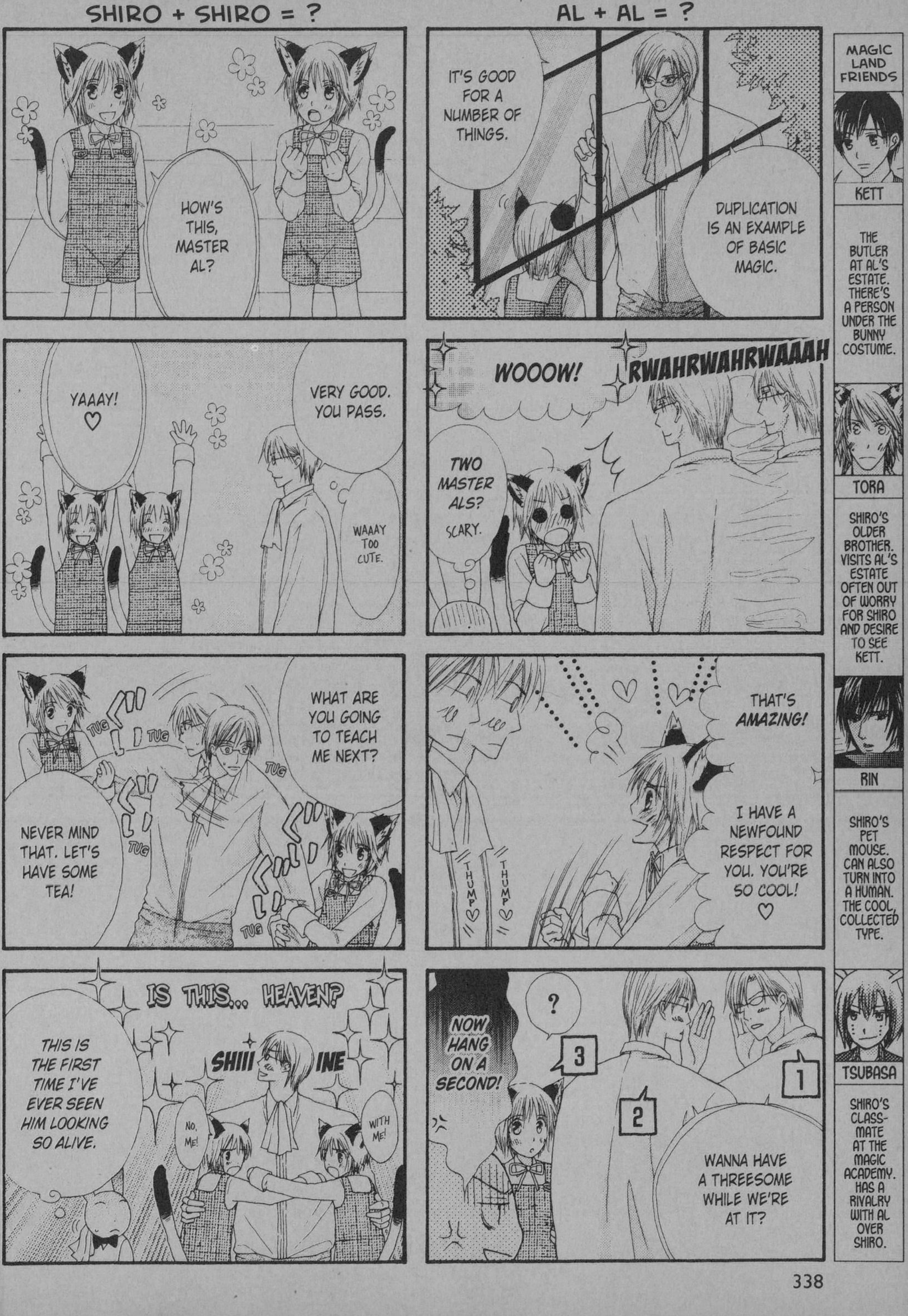
MAGIC LAND FRIENDS
KETT
THE BUTLER AT AL'S ESTATE. THERE'S A PERSON UNDER THE BUNNY COSTUME.
TORA
SHIRO'S OLDER BROTHER. VISITS AL'S ESTATE OFTEN OUT OF WORRY FOR SHIRO AND DESIRE TO SEE KETT.
RIN
SHIRO'S PET MOUSE. CAN ALSO TURN INTO A HUMAN. THE COOL, COLLECTED TYPE.
TSUBASA
SHIRO'S CLASS-MATE AT THE MAGIC ACADEMY. HAS A RIVALRY WITH AL OVER SHIRO.
AL + AL = ?
DUPLICATION IS AN EXAMPLE OF BASIC MAGIC.
IT'S GOOD FOR A NUMBER OF THINGS.
RWAHRWAHRWAAAH
WOOOW!
TWO MASTER ALS?
SCARY.
THAT'S AMAZING!
I HAVE A NEWFOUND RESPECT FOR YOU. YOU'RE SO COOL! ♡
THUMP ♡
THUMP ♡
1
2
3
WANNA HAVE A THREESOME WHILE WE'RE AT IT?
?
NOW HANG ON A SECOND!
SHIRO + SHIRO = ?
HOW'S THIS, MASTER AL?
VERY GOOD. YOU PASS.
WAAAY TOO CUTE.
YAAAY! ♡
WHAT ARE YOU GOING TO TEACH ME NEXT?
TUG
TUG
TUG
TUG
TUG
NEVER MIND THAT. LET'S HAVE SOME TEA!
IS THIS... HEAVEN?
SHIIIINE
WITH ME!
NO, ME!
THIS IS THE FIRST TIME I'VE EVER SEEN HIM LOOKING SO ALIVE.

DOKIDOKKINGU 1

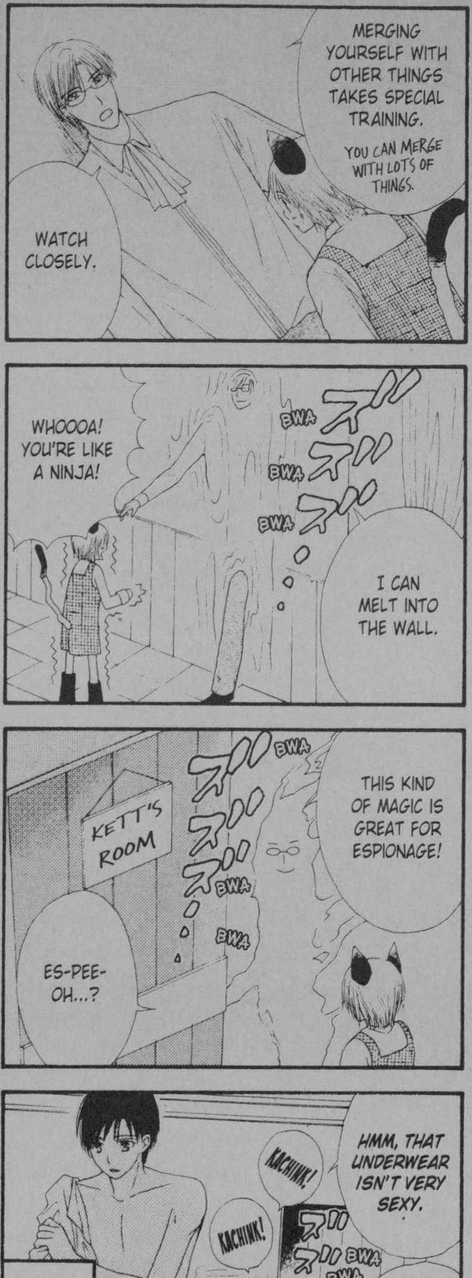
MERGING YOURSELF WITH OTHER THINGS TAKES SPECIAL TRAINING.
YOU CAN MERGE WITH LOTS OF THINGS.
WATCH CLOSELY.
BWA
BWA
BWA
I CAN MELT INTO THE WALL.
WHOOOA! YOU'RE LIKE A NINJA!
BWA
THIS KIND OF MAGIC IS GREAT FOR ESPIONAGE!
KETT'S ROOM
BWA
BWA
ES-PEE-OH...?
HMM, THAT UNDERWEAR ISN'T VERY SEXY.
KACHINK!
KACHINK!
BWA
BWA
SO THIS IS ESPIONAGE!
THIS IS ILLEGAL.

DOKIDOKKINGU 2

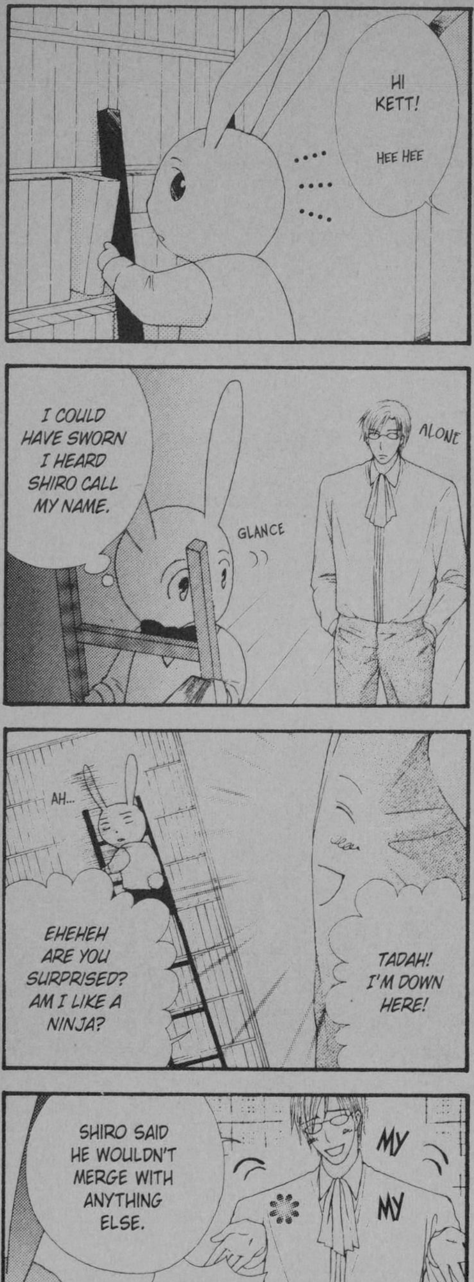
HI KETT!
HEE HEE
ALONE
GLANCE
I COULD HAVE SWORN I HEARD SHIRO CALL MY NAME.
TADAH! I'M DOWN HERE!
AH...
EHEHEH ARE YOU SURPRISED? AM I LIKE A NINJA?
MY
MY
SHIRO SAID HE WOULDN'T MERGE WITH ANYTHING ELSE.
AL'S UNDERWEAR
LIAR!
100% PURE LIE!

THE GREAT IMAGINATION WAR! 1

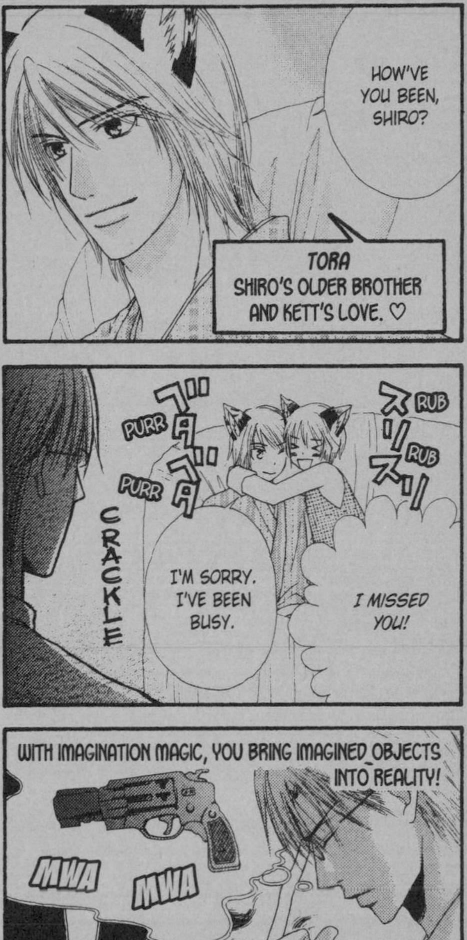
HOW'VE YOU BEEN, SHIRO?
TORA
SHIRO'S OLDER BROTHER AND KETT'S LOVE. ♡
RUB
RUB
I MISSED YOU!
PURR
PURR
I'M SORRY. I'VE BEEN BUSY.
CRACKLE
WITH IMAGINATION MAGIC, YOU BRING IMAGINED OBJECTS INTO REALITY!
MWA
MWA
?
CHK CHIK
BANG
WHOA!
WHAT KIND OF MAGIC ARE YOU USING?!

THE GREAT IMAGINATION WAR! 2

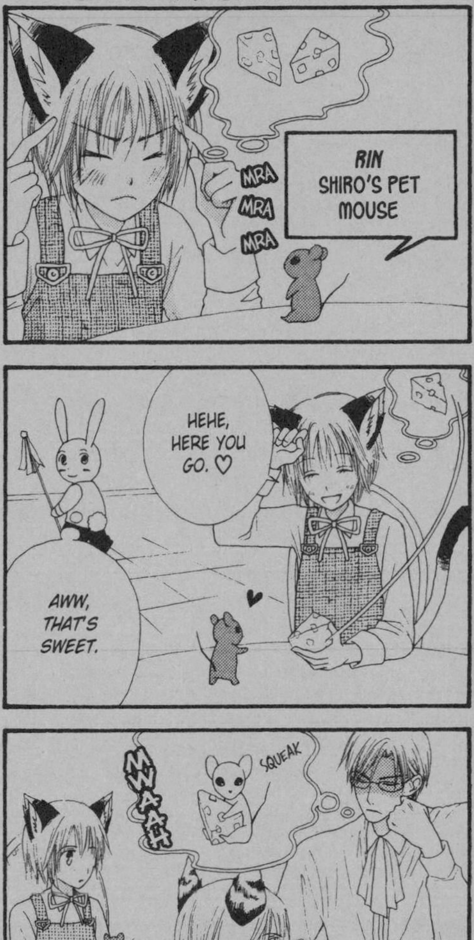
MRA
MRA
MRA
RIN
SHIRO'S PET MOUSE
HEHE, HERE YOU GO. ♡
AWW, THAT'S SWEET.
SQUEAK
MWAAAH
DIVERSION
YOINK
HERE YOU GO! ♡
CATS LOVE THESE, RIGHT?
SQUEAK
I AM *NOT* GOING TO EAT THAT.
NO POINT IMAGINING IT...

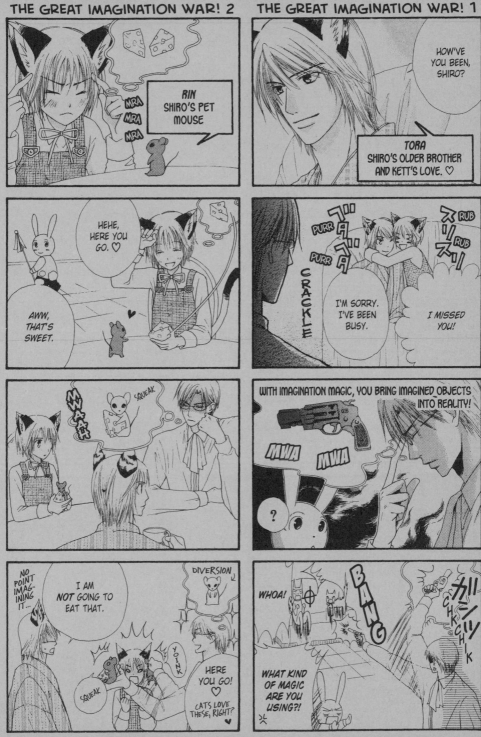

IMAGINATION BLIZZARD! 1

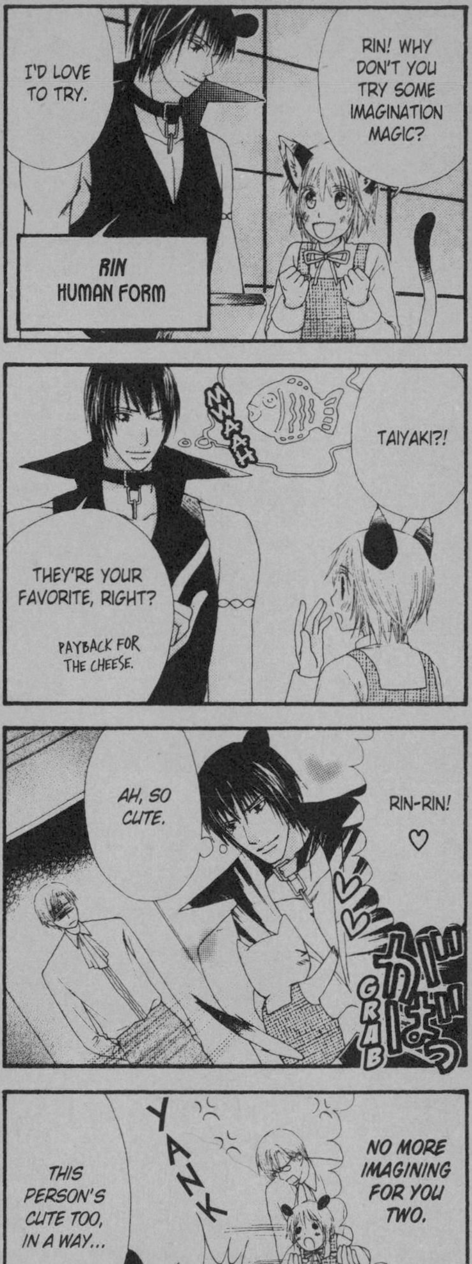
RIN! WHY DON'T YOU TRY SOME IMAGINATION MAGIC?
I'D LOVE TO TRY.
RIN HUMAN FORM
TAIYAKI?!
MWAAH
THEY'RE YOUR FAVORITE, RIGHT?
PAYBACK FOR THE CHEESE.
RIN-RIN! ♡
AH, SO CUTE.
GRAB
NO MORE IMAGINING FOR YOU TWO.
YANK
THIS PERSON'S CUTE TOO, IN A WAY...
AWW!!

IMAGINATION BLIZZARD! 1

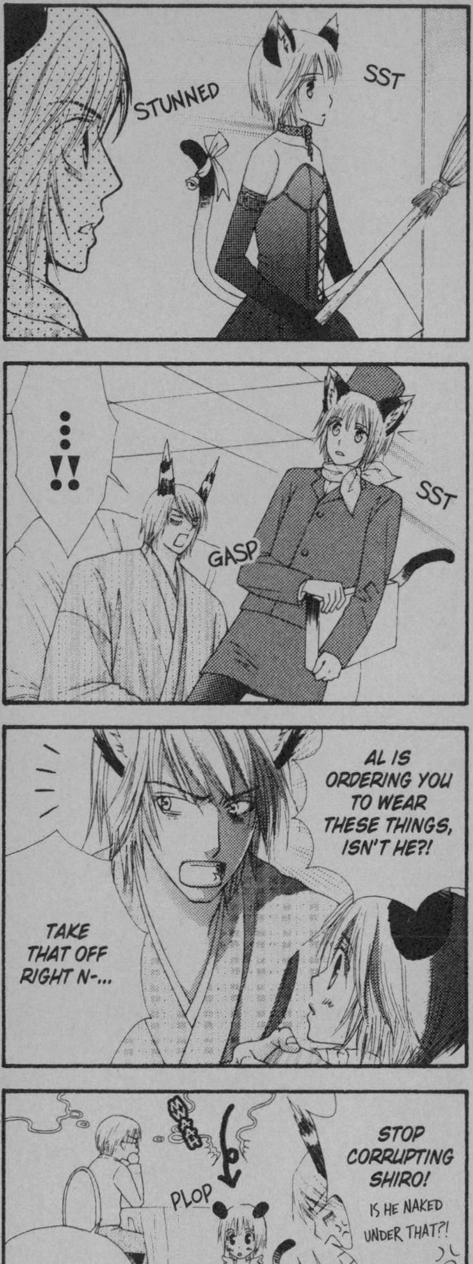
SST
STUNNED
SST
GASP
...!!
AL IS ORDERING YOU TO WEAR THESE THINGS, ISN'T HE?!
TAKE THAT OFF RIGHT N-...
STOP CORRUPTING SHIRO!
IS HE NAKED UNDER THAT?!
MWAH
PLOP
BE QUIET, I'M CONCEN-TRATING.

IMAGINATION VIRGIN 1

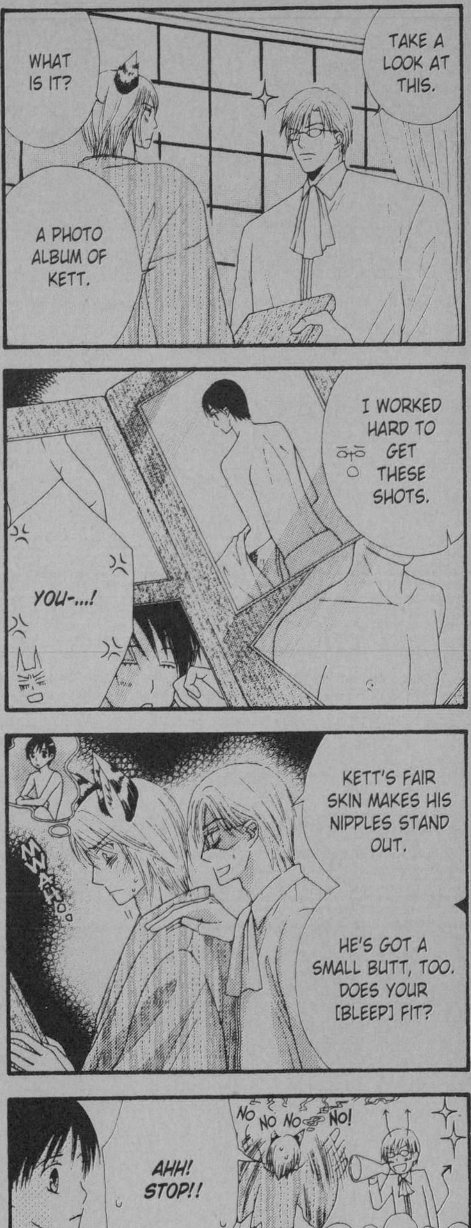
TAKE A LOOK AT THIS.
WHAT IS IT?
A PHOTO ALBUM OF KETT.
I WORKED HARD TO GET THESE SHOTS.
YOU-...!
KETT'S FAIR SKIN MAKES HIS NIPPLES STAND OUT.
HE'S GOT A SMALL BUTT, TOO. DOES YOUR [BLEEP] FIT?
NO NO NO NO!
AHH! STOP!!
ATTENTION! I'M ABOUT TO MATERIALIZE TORA'S IMAGINATION! ♡

IMAGINATION VIRGIN 2

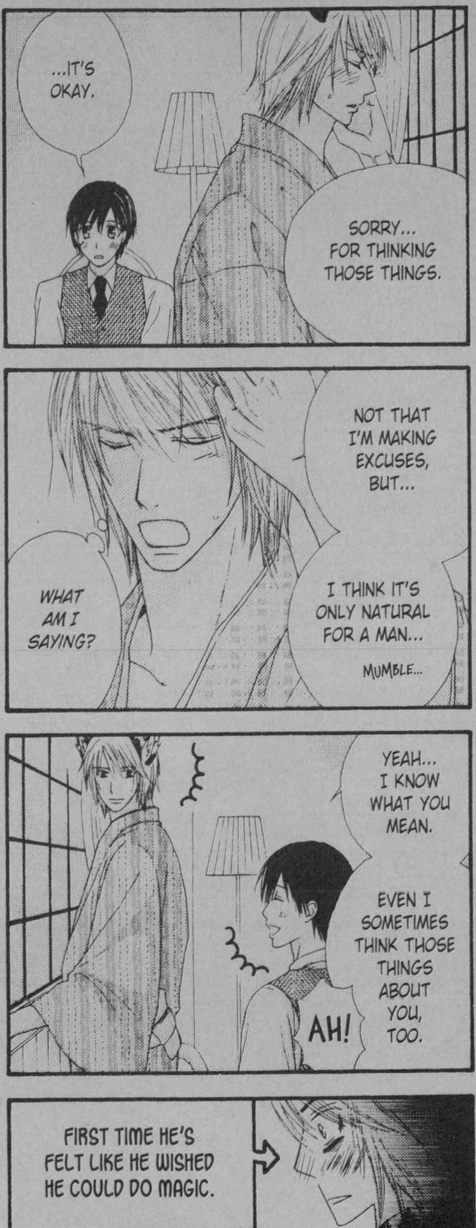
SORRY... FOR THINKING THOSE THINGS.
...IT'S OKAY.
NOT THAT I'M MAKING EXCUSES, BUT...
I THINK IT'S ONLY NATURAL FOR A MAN...
MUMBLE...
WHAT AM I SAYING?
YEAH... I KNOW WHAT YOU MEAN.
EVEN I SOMETIMES THINK THOSE THINGS ABOUT YOU, TOO.
AH!
ABOUT ME?
FIRST TIME HE'S FELT LIKE HE WISHED HE COULD DO MAGIC.
WHAT'S HE IMAGINING?!

IMAGINATION HEAVEN ☆ 1

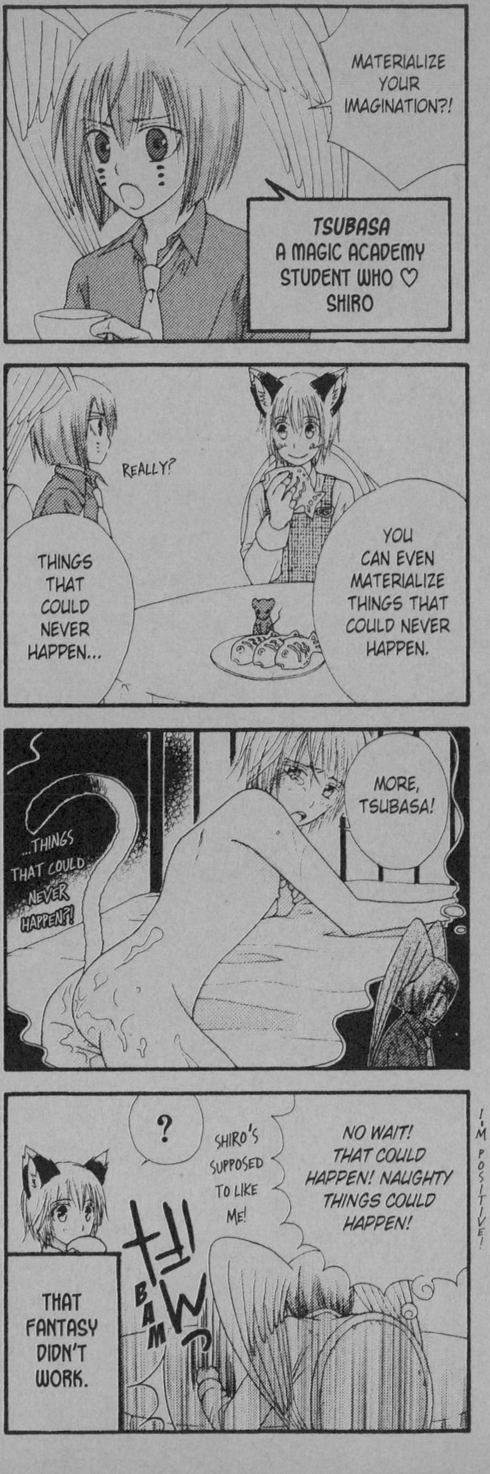
MATERIALIZE YOUR IMAGINATION?!
TSUBASA A MAGIC ACADEMY STUDENT WHO ♡ SHIRO
YOU CAN EVEN MATERIALIZE THINGS THAT COULD NEVER HAPPEN.
REALLY?
THINGS THAT COULD NEVER HAPPEN...
MORE, TSUBASA!
...THINGS THAT COULD NEVER HAPPEN?!
I'M POSITIVE!
NO WAIT! THAT COULD HAPPEN! NAUGHTY THINGS COULD HAPPEN!
SHIRO'S SUPPOSED TO LIKE ME!
?
BAM
THAT FANTASY DIDN'T WORK.

IMAGINATION HEAVEN ☆ 2

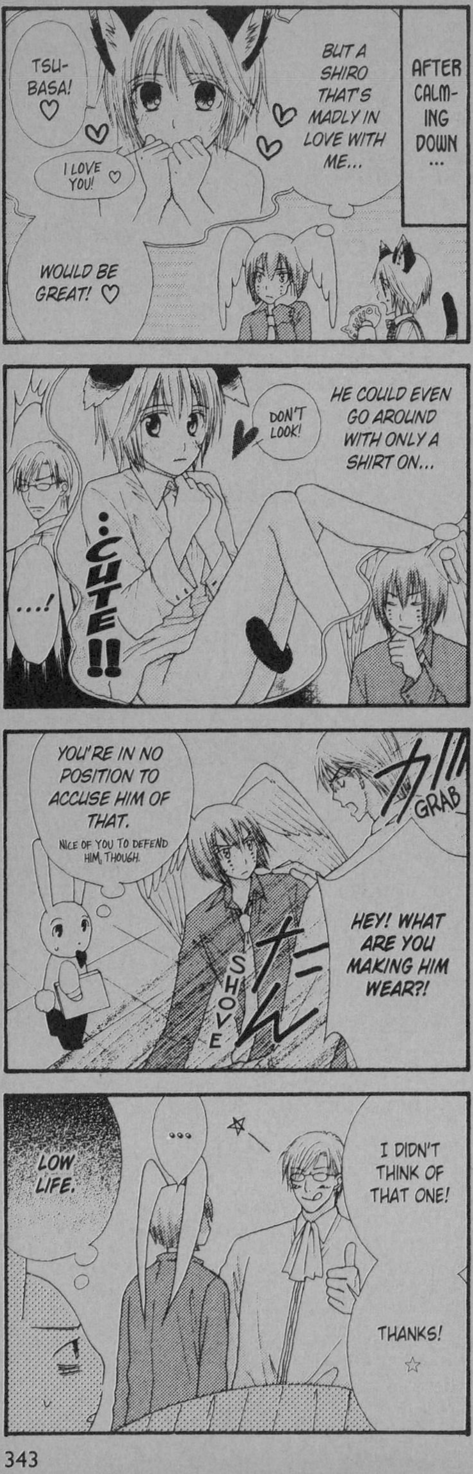
AFTER CALMING DOWN...
BUT A SHIRO THAT'S MADLY IN LOVE WITH ME...
TSU-BASA! ♡
I LOVE YOU! ♡
WOULD BE GREAT! ♡
HE COULD EVEN GO AROUND WITH ONLY A SHIRT ON...
DON'T LOOK!
...CUTE!!
...!
GRAB
HEY! WHAT ARE YOU MAKING HIM WEAR?!
SHOVE
YOU'RE IN NO POSITION TO ACCUSE HIM OF THAT.
Nice of you to defend him, though.
I DIDN'T THINK OF THAT ONE!
THANKS! ☆
...
LOW LIFE.

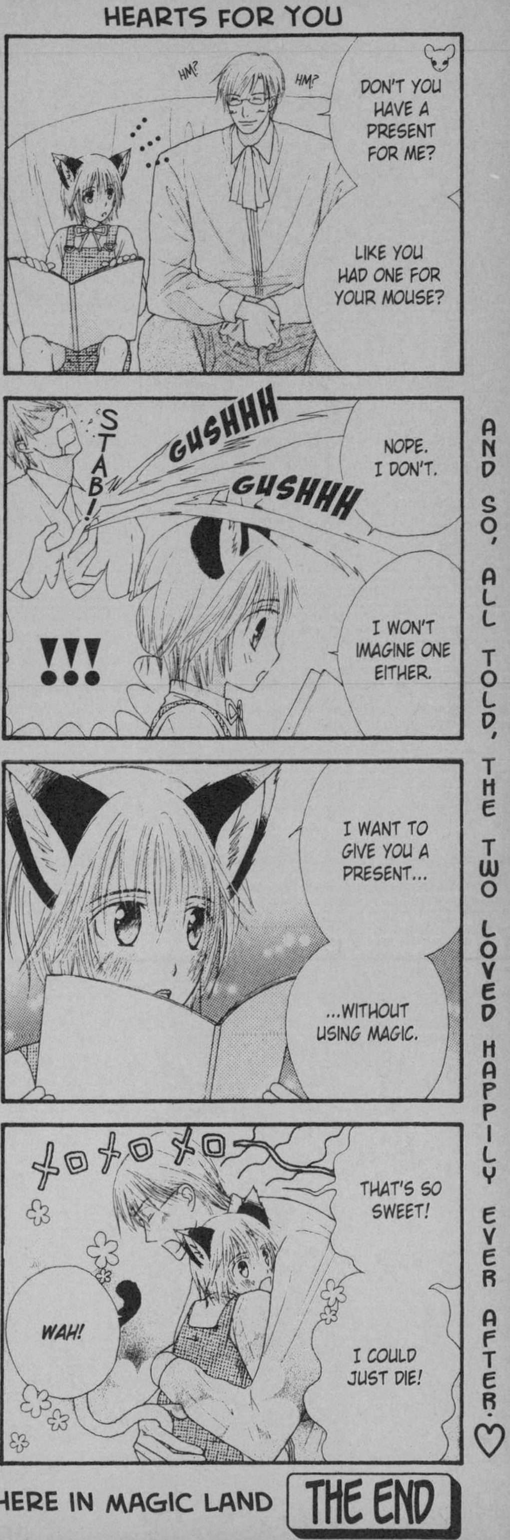
HEARTS FOR YOU
HM? HM?
DON'T YOU HAVE A PRESENT FOR ME?
LIKE YOU HAD ONE FOR YOUR MOUSE?
STAB!
GUSHHH
GUSHHH
NOPE. I DON'T.
!!!
I WON'T IMAGINE ONE EITHER.
I WANT TO GIVE YOU A PRESENT...
...WITHOUT USING MAGIC.
XOXOXO
THAT'S SO SWEET!
I COULD JUST DIE!
WAH!
AND SO, ALL TOLD, THE TWO LOVED HAPPILY EVER AFTER.♡
HERE IN MAGIC LAND
THE END

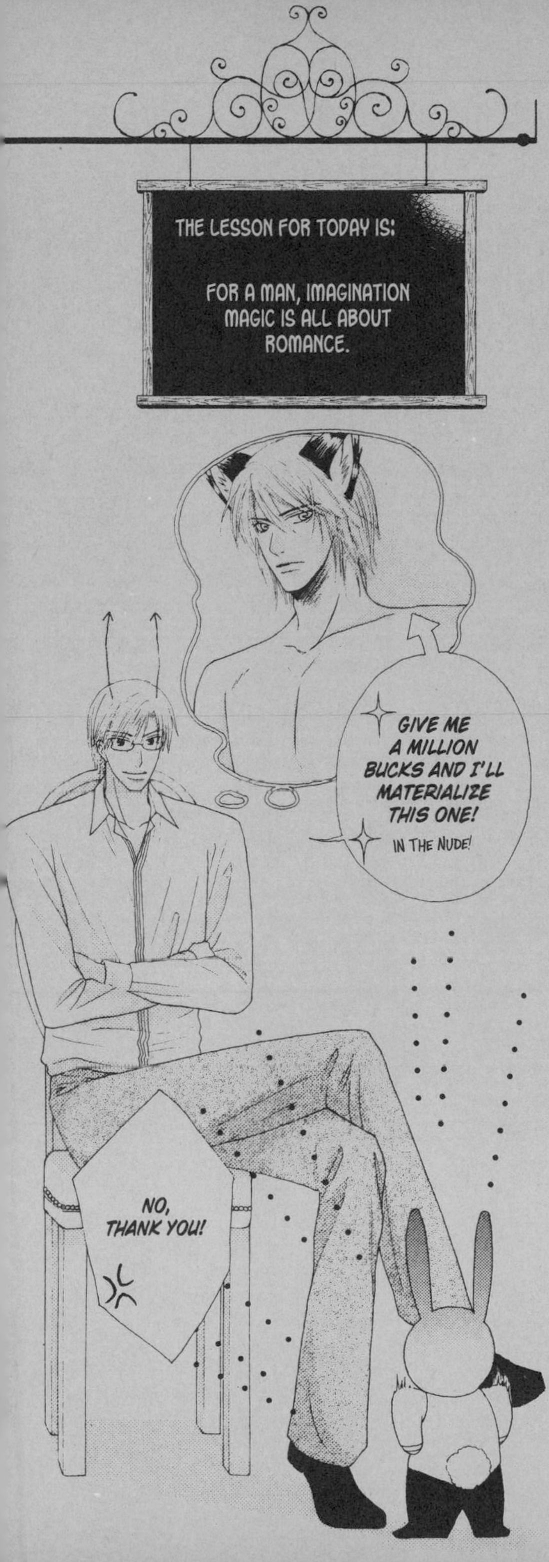
THE LESSON FOR TODAY IS:
FOR A MAN, IMAGINATION MAGIC IS ALL ABOUT ROMANCE.
GIVE ME A MILLION BUCKS AND I'LL MATERIALIZE THIS ONE!
IN THE NUDE!
NO, THANK YOU!

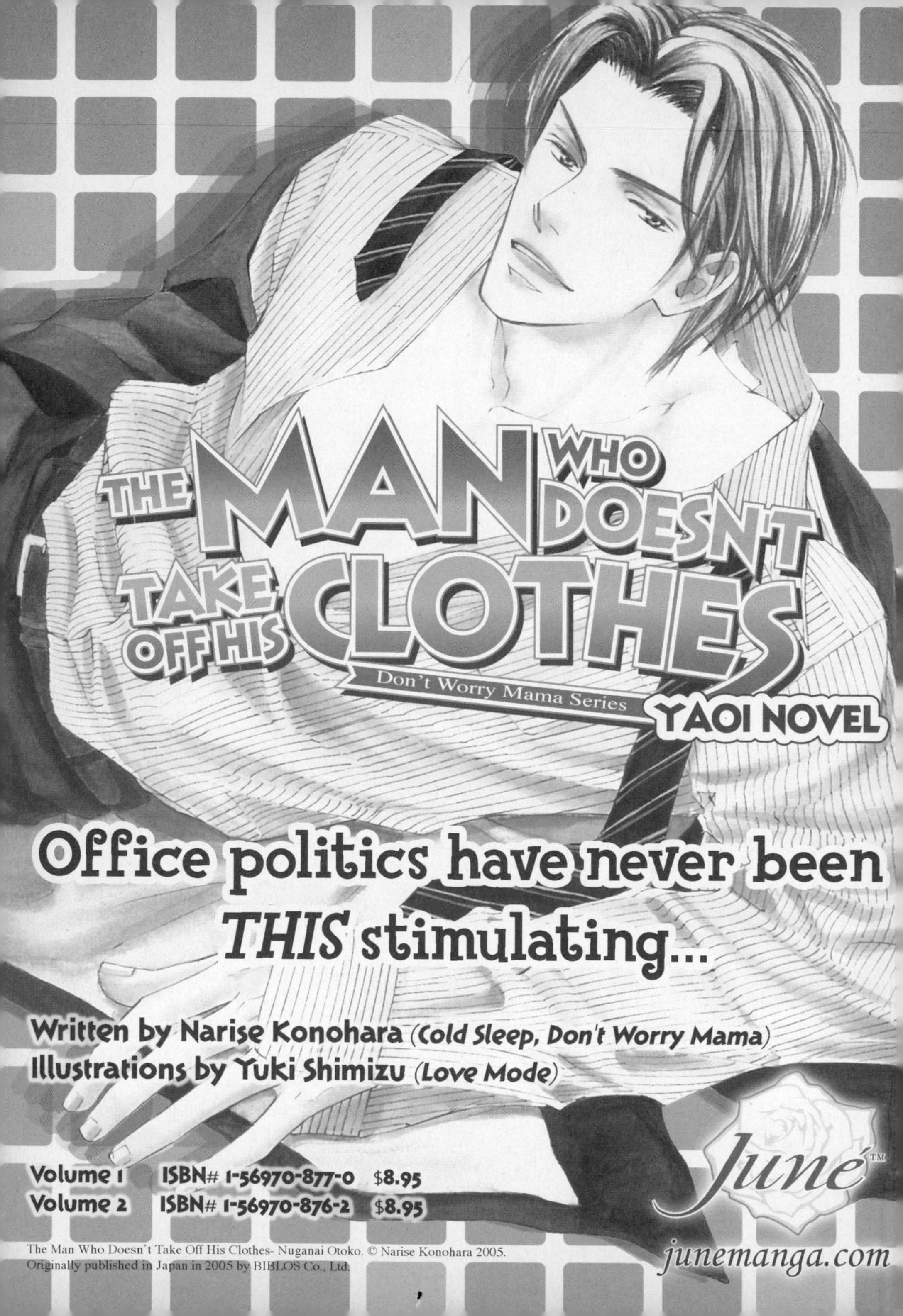
THE MAN WHO DOESN'T TAKE OFF HIS CLOTHES
Don't Worry Mama Series
YAOI NOVEL
Office politics have never been THIS stimulating...
Written by Narise Konohara (Cold Sleep, Don't Worry Mama)
Illustrations by Yuki Shimizu (Love Mode)
Volume 1 ISBN# 1-56970-877-0 $8.95
Volume 2 ISBN# 1-56970-876-2 $8.95
Juné™
junemanga.com
The Man Who Doesn't Take Off His Clothes- Nuganai Otoko. © Narise Konohara 2005.
Originally published in Japan in 2005 by BIBLOS Co., Ltd.

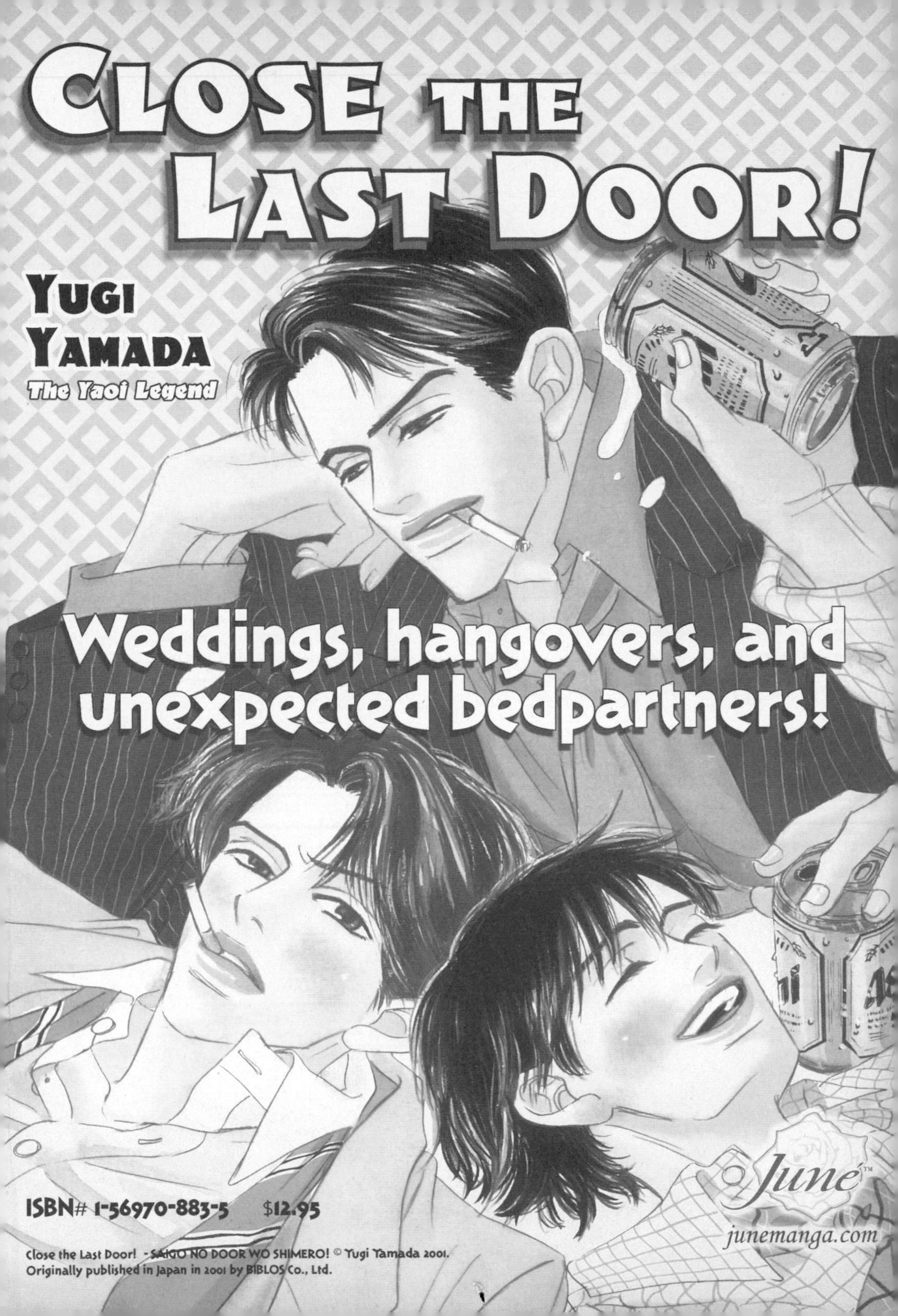
CLOSE THE LAST DOOR!
YUGI YAMADA
The Yaoi Legend
Weddings, hangovers, and unexpected bedpartners!
June™
ISBN# 1-56970-883-5 $12.95
junemanga.com
Close the Last Door! - SAIGO NO DOOR WO SHIMERO! © Yugi Yamada 2001.
Originally published in Japan in 2001 by BIBLOS Co., Ltd.

Princess · Princess

By MIKIYO TSUDA

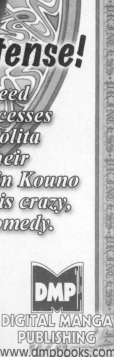

Peer pressure...
has never been this intense!

When students need a boost, the Princesses arrive in gothic lolita outfits to show their school spirit! Join Kouno and friends in this crazy, cross-dressing comedy.

VOLUME 1 - ISBN# 978-1-56970-856-9 $12.95
VOLUME 2 - ISBN# 978-1-56970-855-2 $12.95
VOLUME 3 - ISBN# 978-1-56970-852-1 $12.95
VOLUME 4 - ISBN# 978-1-56970-851-4 $12.95
VOLUME 5 - ISBN# 978-1-56970-850-7 $12.95

DMP

**DIGITAL MANGA
PUBLISHING**

www.dmpbooks.com

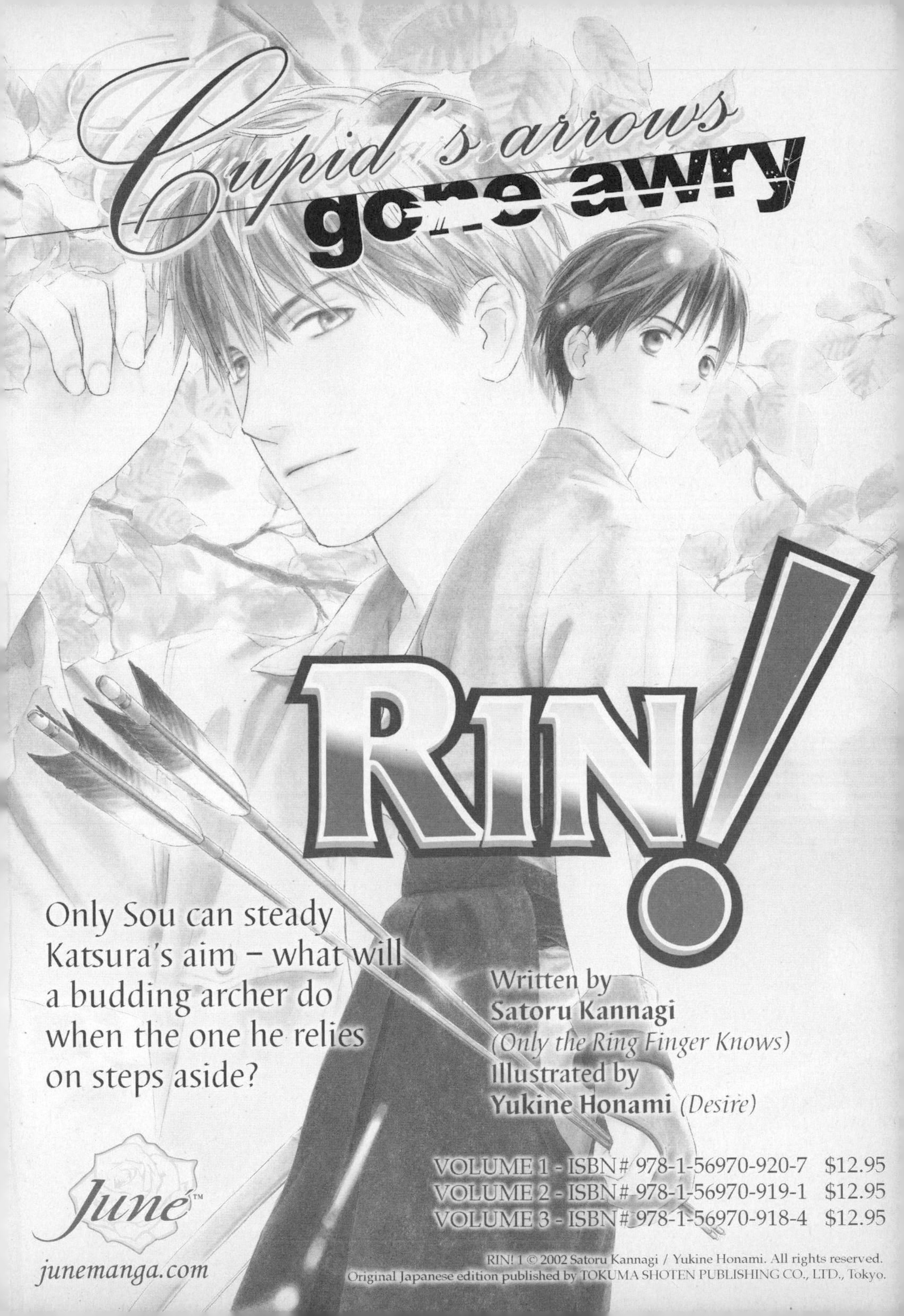

Cupid's arrows gone awry

RIN!

Only Sou can steady
Katsura's aim – what will
a budding archer do
when the one he relies
on steps aside?

Written by
Satoru Kannagi
(*Only the Ring Finger Knows*)
Illustrated by
Yukine Honami (*Desire*)

June™

VOLUME 1 - ISBN# 978-1-56970-920-7 $12.95
VOLUME 2 - ISBN# 978-1-56970-919-1 $12.95
VOLUME 3 - ISBN# 978-1-56970-918-4 $12.95

junemanga.com

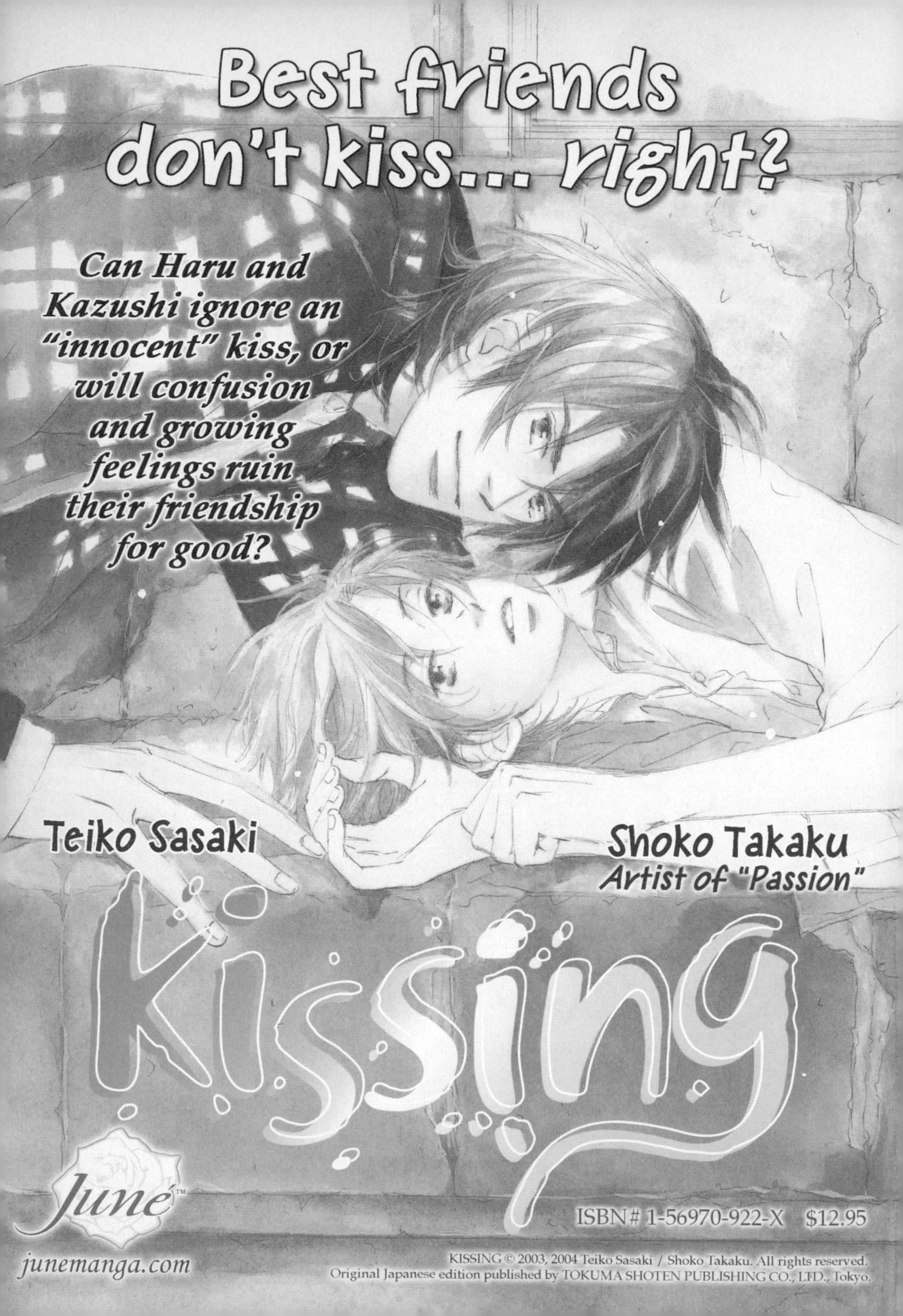
Best friends don't kiss... right?
Can Haru and Kazushi ignore an "innocent" kiss, or will confusion and growing feelings ruin their friendship for good?
Teiko Sasaki
Shoko Takaku
Artist of "Passion"
Kissing
June™
junemanga.com
ISBN# 1-56970-922-X $12.95
KISSING © 2003, 2004 Teiko Sasaki / Shoko Takaku. All rights reserved.
Original Japanese edition published by TOKUMA SHOTEN PUBLISHING CO., LTD., Tokyo.

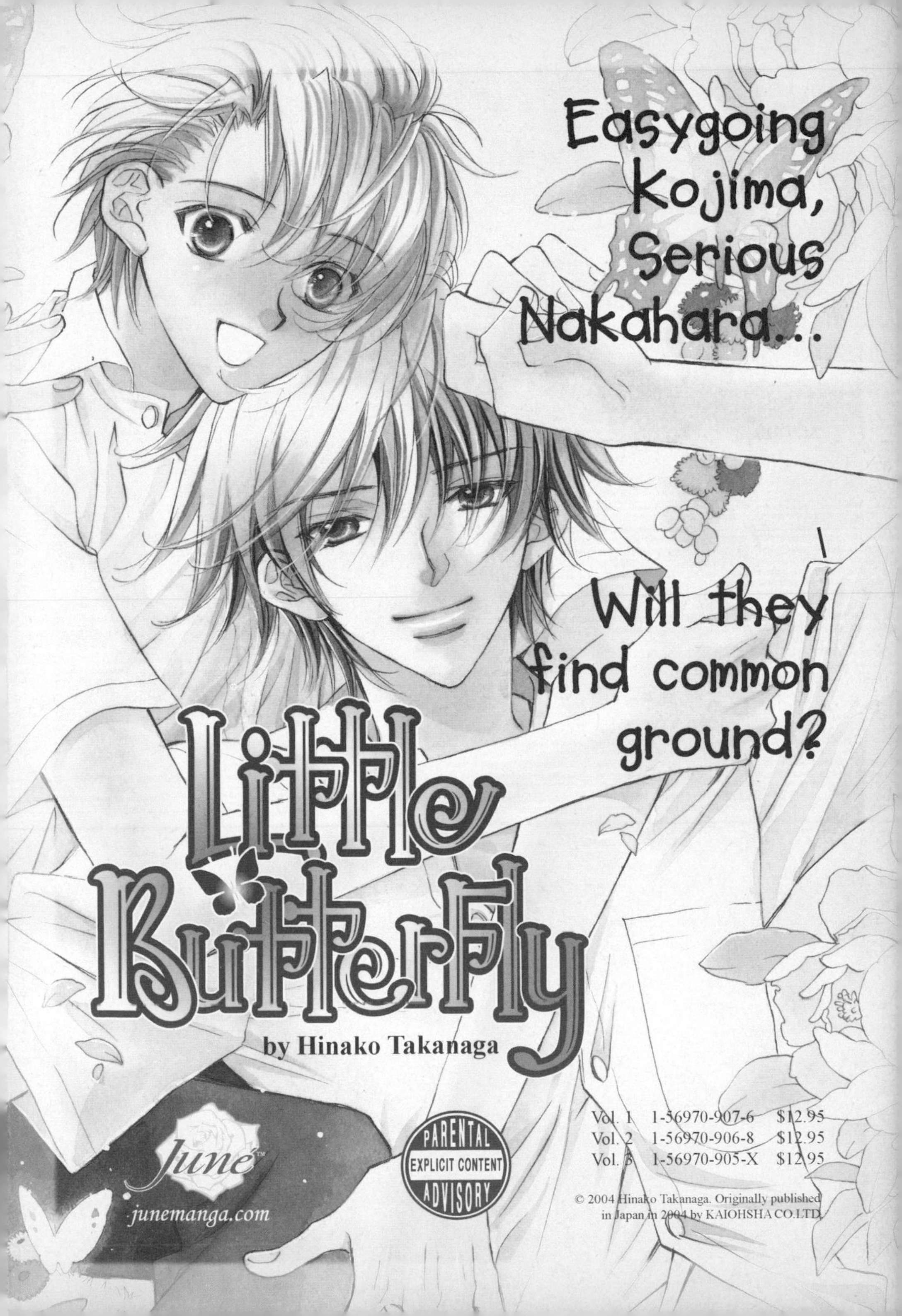
Easygoing Kojima, Serious Nakahara...
Will they find common ground?
Little Butterfly
by Hinako Takanaga
Vol. 1 1-56970-907-6 $12.95
Vol. 2 1-56970-906-8 $12.95
Vol. 3 1-56970-905-X $12.95
PARENTAL EXPLICIT CONTENT ADVISORY
June™
junemanga.com
© 2004 Hinako Takanaga. Originally published in Japan in 2004 by KAIOHSHA CO.LTD.

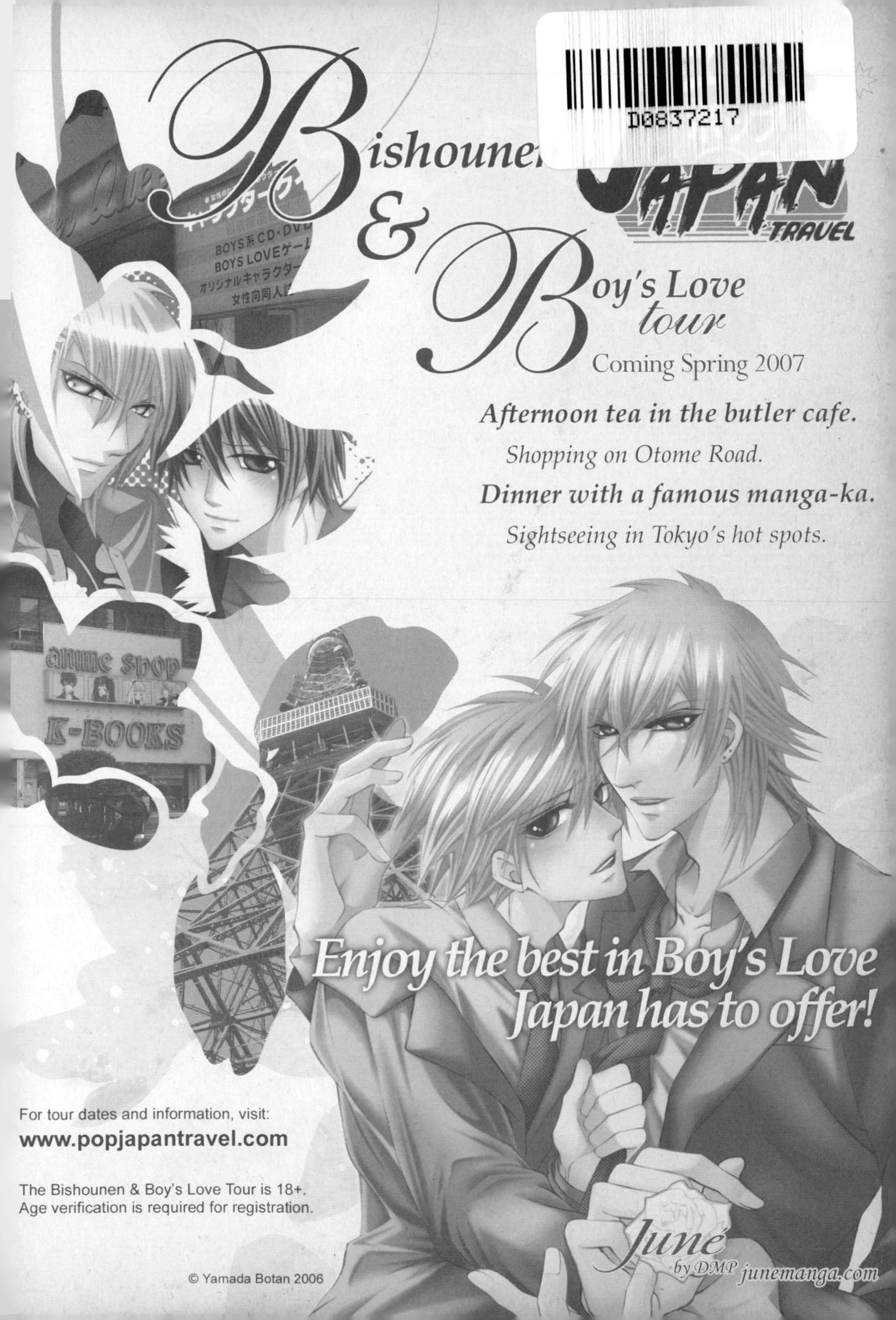

D0837217
Bishoune
& Boy's Love tour
JAPAN
TRAVEL
Coming Spring 2007
Afternoon tea in the butler cafe.
Shopping on Otome Road.
Dinner with a famous manga-ka.
Sightseeing in Tokyo's hot spots.
BOYS系CD・DVD
BOYS LOVEゲー
anime shop
K-BOOKS
Enjoy the best in Boy's Love Japan has to offer!
For tour dates and information, visit:
www.popjapantravel.com
The Bishounen & Boy's Love Tour is 18+.
Age verification is required for registration.
© Yamada Botan 2006
June
by DMP junemanga.com